ALL AMERICA'S
REAL ESTATE BOOK

ALL AMERICA'S REAL ESTATE BOOK

Everyone's Guide to Buying, Selling, Renting, and Investing

CAROLYN JANIK
AND
RUTH REJNIS

VIKING

VIKING
Viking Penguin Inc., 40 West 23rd Street,
New York, New York 10010, U.S.A.
Penguin Books Ltd, Harmondsworth,
Middlesex, England
Penguin Books Australia Ltd, Ringwood,
Victoria, Australia
Penguin Books Canada Limited, 2801 John Street,
Markham, Ontario, Canada L3R 1B4
Penguin Books (N.Z.) Ltd, 182–190 Wairau Road,
Auckland 10, New Zealand

First published in 1985 by Viking Penguin Inc.
Published simultaneously in Canada

Library of Congress Catalog Card Number: 84-48832 (CIP data available)
ISBN 0-670-80510-6

Printed in the United States of America
by The Maple-Vail Book Manufacturing Group, York, Pennsylvania
Set in Caledonia

Second printing January 1986

To Our Readers . . .

Real estate affects your life. It doesn't matter if you are rich or poor, young or old, ambitious or complacent, you are certainly living in, working in, and playing in or upon pieces of real estate (yours or someone else's). And no matter where you are in your life or where you are going, you will, sooner or later, almost certainly enter the real estate marketplace to rent, to buy, to sell, or to invest. How successful will you be? It depends.

With more than its fair share of blind alleys, treacherous curves, and confusing detours, the real estate marketplace is rarely easy to navigate. Usually those who are most successful have been there before, or they have been able to obtain some inside advice and acquire some special know-how. They got hold of a roadmap to the marketplace, as it were. That is what this book should be for you—a roadmap to the real estate marketplace. The most comprehensive, most informative, and, we hope, most entertaining roadmap you'll ever hold in your hands. With it we wish you *Good Fortune!*

Carolyn Janik

Ruth Rejnis

Contents

PART I

How to Be a Winning Tenant

1

Who's Renting... and Why

Nadine is a public relations representative for a major New York City bank; her husband is a corporate lawyer. They have one child, a nine-room country house in Westport, Connecticut, and no money problems. Yet from Sunday night to Friday afternoon of every working week they live in a two-bedroom rented apartment in Greenwich Village.

"Why?" you ask. "Certainly they could afford to buy a co-op or condominium if they want a place in the city!"

Absolutely true—but they would be foolish to do so. Nadine found and rented the apartment ten years ago when she was single and just getting started. She stayed on as a number of roommates came and went, as her income climbed, and after her marriage. At first, the neighborhood was convenient to her work place; over the years it has become highly desirable. The apartment is large, well maintained, and cheap.

Rent control in New York City has made apartment living the mode of choice for anyone who can hold on to a good place. Why should Nadine invest her money in a co-op or condo and tie up as much as 50 percent of the purchase price as a required downpayment? She can put that money elsewhere for a better return on her investment, better tax advantages, or, at the very least, more liquidity (access to her cash).

Buying a co-op apartment would also mean taking on a share of the building's maintenance expenses. What if heating costs skyrocket, or the roof caves in, or poor management loses so much money that maintenance fees increase at a rate ten times the national cost-of-living index? Nadine and her husband would then have to make higher and higher monthly payments. In their rent-controlled apartment, all those risks are assumed by the landlord. And since they have a comfortable home (and a secure hedge against inflation) in their house in Westport, their savings on the low-rent apartment far outweigh any benefit they might realize by purchasing even the most luxurious and desirable penthouse high above Park Avenue.

"So why is anyone buying co-ops or condominiums in New York City?" you might ask.

There are many excellent reasons for buying apartments there and almost everywhere. In New York City, for example, good rental units are almost as scarce as flowers blooming in the subway. A person buying an apartment can lay claim to good location. But we'll get to buying in Part II. Right now, let's consider the reasons for renting.

For the vast majority of Americans, renting is a means to shelter during at least some part of their lives. For many, buying and owning a home is neither possible nor even desirable. Let's meet some of these renters. You may be surprised to catch glimpses of yourself or your friends in this group.

Warren and Peggy

We'll begin with the most widely publicized type, the typical American renting couple. Married fourteen months and both working, they're living on Peggy's income alone. Warren's paycheck goes directly into the bank. Their thriftiness has nothing to do with Warren's Scottish heritage, it's just the best way (or at present the only way) to move toward what they want most: a place of their own. Warren and Peggy are saving for a downpayment, and they are renting the smallest and cheapest acceptable apartment they could find.

Their story, however, is not quite so simple as "a year of hard work and no fun equals the necessary 5 percent down for an FHA mortgage." Warren and Peggy need more than a downpayment, they need a large enough downpayment to make their monthly mortgage payments affordable. And to complicate the process, rising house prices in their area effectively cancel out part of their savings each year.

Warren and Peggy will rent until they have saved that downpayment, until their incomes increase enough to allow them to carry the higher payments on a mortgage, and until they have a large enough cash cushion to pay closing costs and some maintenance expenses. It's no wonder demographers have "discovered" that Americans are having children later in life!

Sylvia

Sylvia is divorced. All of her children have graduated from college and are out on their own. Last June the couple's big suburban house was sold and the profits were split. She has a high-paying job, but she doesn't like it much. And she's just getting used to the idea that she can do what she wants and go where she wants with no strings attached. She's renting a luxury studio apartment.

For tax and investment purposes, Sylvia would probably be wise to buy a condominium: all the advantages of homeownership and no maintenance responsibilities. But she chooses not to buy. At this time in her life, she wants total flexibility, which is what she gets with her month-to-month lease.

Jack and Jill

They live in the same building, but not in the same apartment. Both are young, single, college-educated, and upwardly mobile. Both want all the comforts of home, with no responsibilities for maintenance or long-term ties to the property. To them, renting offers total freedom. If a new job takes them across the country or a love interest takes them across the street, they want to be able to pack up and leave. They might indeed have to argue over a broken lease, but leases are broken more frequently than are legs at Aspen. Usually, the most the tenant loses is the security deposit.

Arnold

Arnold is not so young anymore. He's divorced and he rents a two-bedroom apartment in the same town where he and his ex-wife still own a house together. (He is kicking in half of the mortgage payment.) When the kids are grown, he and his ex-wife will sell the house and Arnold will get half. Until then he simply doesn't have the cash to buy a place for himself.

Bertha

Her husband died a year ago. They had always rented and they'd been in this apartment for eleven years. It's a little harder now to pay the rent, but Bertha doesn't want to move. She gets by on his Social Security benefits, insurance money, and the company's surviving spouse pension plan. In two years, she'll be eligible for low-cost senior-citizen housing, and she's already got her name on the waiting list.

Sylvia, Jack, Jill, Arnold, and Bertha are all part of a growing group of renters. United States Census Bureau statistics and independent demographic studies across the nation show that the number of *single-person households* is increasing at all age levels. This trend has been a factor in the growing demand for rental housing in many areas. Some experts say that it will also be a factor in driving rents higher over the next two decades.

Loretta

Loretta cleans houses, but not legally. On official records, she is listed as unemployed, and receives funds from her state's Aid to Dependent Children program since the father of her two sons deserted for parts unknown. The money she makes for cleaning is always paid in cash, and she never mentions it to anyone at the welfare agency. It helps to pay the rent and to buy occasional movie tickets.

Katherine

Also a single parent, but far from poor, Katherine chooses to rent. After her divorce, her husband continued to make support payments for their two daughters. Thus, Katherine could have used her half of the equity and profit from the sale of their house to buy another house or a condominium. By adding her modest inheritance from her parents, she could have kept mortgage payments on a small house well within her qualification limits. But her concern was with income and with cash reserves, and her thinking ran to ideas seldom explored by the proponents of homeownership.

If she put all or most of her cash into a downpayment, she thought, she would be at the mercy of tax increases and the demands of maintenance. Her reserve fund, which represented her security, would be tied up in an investment that might be growing in value but was certainly not generating any usable income. In fact, her homeownership would generate *more* expense, adding to the strain on her income.

So Katherine rented a condominium apartment that was owned by an investor. The decision allowed her to live in a community as prestigious as that in which she had lived before her divorce. She invested her cash in tax-free municipal bonds, savings certificates, and some blue chip stocks. Thus she generated income for extras and maintained a source of ready cash if she should need it.

Katherine has prospered and has been promoted in her job since she made her decision to rent. "You can afford more house now," a real estate agent recently told her. But again she has chosen a path less traveled. Rather than buy a house, she will stay in her condominium apartment "home" and buy property solely for investment.

There is a two-family house for sale in an area of her town where she would not choose to live but that commands respectable rents. Rental income from the property would cover its mortgage payments, taxes, insurance, and most maintenance costs. The tax benefits would be greater than those she would reap from homeownership. She will probably buy it and become a landlord but not a homeowner!

Dick and Jane

Yes, they have three kids and a dog and they're renting a house in the Milwaukee suburbs. However, they own a house in Los Angeles that they decided to hold on to when Dick's corporation transferred him. The transfer was for three to five years, with the promise of return to his old location. The couple just couldn't bring themselves to give up their 8½ percent mortgage when they knew they'd be returning. So they are now renting that property to another family with three kids and a dog.

Meanwhile, the rent they pay in Milwaukee is lower than the mortgage payment they were making in Los Angeles, so their budget looks better. The rent they receive on their Los Angeles house is higher than the monthly mortgage payment, also bringing in extra income. In addition, depreciation allowances and maintenance cost deductions will bring Dick and Jane a juicy tax refund in the spring. It all looks very rosy, except that the family will need some good tax advice when and if they do reclaim their California home. Switching a property from a residence to an income property and then back to a residence causes lights and beeps in the IRS computers.

Paul and Alice

Paul has a new job, and Alice is busy with a new baby. They have enough cash for the downpayment on a house, and they had planned to buy this year. Now they are having some second thoughts.

Paul is getting great training with his company, but he's still not certain that he wants to make the job his career. If he and Alice buy a house now, they worry, they may run into trouble two years down the road. What if Paul takes a job with another company in another state? They'd have to sell their home then, and there would probably be no help from the new company. How long would it take to sell the house? What if the economy were bad and they couldn't sell it?

Paul and Alice are also calculating costs: closing costs, moving costs, broker's commissions, and points. Points are the real pain. If they pay 4 points (4 percent of the face amount of their mortgage) to get the loan, and then only keep it for two years. . . . The thought of paying all that money and then having to pay again for another mortgage tips their thinking. They decide that it would be better to invest their downpayment money and continue to rent until Paul is more certain of his job.

John and Sandra

John and Sandra also have the downpayment and income to buy a small starter house, yet they too have chosen to continue renting. Their reason, however, is just the opposite of Paul and Alice's. John works in his father's company, which he will eventually inherit. The business is sound and the future looks bright, but the location is suburban Detroit.

Because of the depressed housing market in the area, John and Sandra do not want to buy a starter house. Modest houses are plentiful and cheap right now, but they are appreciating slowly, if at all, and they are very difficult to resell. In some areas, home values have actually gone down over the past five years. As an investment, therefore, buying a small interim house would probably be a mistake.

John and Sandra have decided not to buy a starter home and then step up to a more expensive house. They will rent, and save, and invest their savings in liquid investments until they can buy a larger house—a house they will want to keep for many, many years.

Richard and Raymond

They share the rent, but they hardly ever see each other. Both men travel for a living. Richard is a musician and Raymond an international gem salesman. The apartment they keep is a mailing address, a place to store personal belongings, a place to go to rest, a place to call "home." Richard, in fact, is living with a woman in the same town. But he wants his own apartment as a measure of his independence—just in case.

Arthur

Arthur has a wife, two kids, a dog, three cats, and a house in Denver. Why is he renting an apartment in Jersey City? Because it beats living in a hotel and eating every meal in restaurants.

Arthur is on a special assignment for his company. The assignment will probably last nine months to a year, too short a time to uproot his family and move them east only to move them back again at the end of the job. So he rents . . . and the company pays for an every-other-weekend flight home.

Al and Judy
Recently retired, Al and Judy sold their house in Shaker Heights, a Cleveland suburb. They took the one-time, $125,000 tax exemption people over 55 are allowed when they sell their homes. They considered buying a condominium just outside Phoenix but decided to rent instead. They are still feeling young, and would like to try living in several areas of the country before settling down. By investing the equity and profit from the house they sold, they have generated an income that almost pays their rent. They use their pension and Social Security money to have a little fun in their lives.

Cynthia and Gerry
Cynthia and Gerry are city people and career people. They are married, but do not intend to have children. Nor do they like to garden or wallpaper. Weekends are important to them as recreation and relaxation time. If you ask them about homeownership, they'll say, "It's okay in theory, but we never want to be slaves to a house." Therefore, their shelter choices are rental or the ownership of a condominium or co-op apartment.

They've thought about a condo, but in the end they decided to continue renting.

"It's a matter of choices," says Gerry. "In this city, the widest selection of apartments and the best locations are rentals. *Where* we live is important to us—more important than owning something."

Tom, Dick, and Harry / Sue, Jean, and Penny
People. Ordinary middle-class Americans. Experts, economists, and crystal-ball gazers are predicting that more and more of them will be tenants throughout their lives.

In major European cities and in the Far East, people are paying up to 50 percent of their income for *rented* shelter, and never even think about homeownership. Such a situation may just cross the seas. There will then no longer be so much talk about buying real estate. Housing success will be finding a good rental unit.

Back to today, however. Whether people choose to rent or rent from necessity, they can name very specifically their reasons for renting. Those who must rent cite finances as their chief reason:

renting is cheaper than owning, or they cannot save enough money for a large enough downpayment. If they were pressed, however, many of these people would also admit that they have no desire to take on the maintenance and costs that homeownership demands.

Of those who rent by choice, mobility and financial freedom (freedom to invest their money in liquid investments) are the top-ranking answers. Most will also include freedom from maintenance as a reason for renting, but the growth and proliferation of condominiums is punching holes in that reason.

Just to get an overview of why people rent, let's look at the motivations of the tenants we've met in this chapter.

Why Rent?	Cheaper or Better Shelter	Mobility	Financial Freedom	Inability to Qualify for a Mortgage	Maintenance Time & Cost Not Required
Nadine	✔		✔		✔
Warren and Peggy	✔			✔	
Sylvia		✔			✔
Jack and Jill		✔	✔		✔
Arnold	✔			✔	✔
Bertha	✔			✔	✔
Loretta	✔			✔	✔
Katherine				✔	✔
Dick and Jane	✔	✔	✔		
Paul and Alice	✔	✔	✔		
John and Sandra			✔		
Richard and Raymond	✔	✔			✔
Arthur		✔			
Al and Judy		✔	✔		✔
Cynthia and Gerry	✔	✔	✔		✔
Tom, Dick, and Harry Sue, Jean, and Penny				✔	

For More Information

"Wise Rental Practices," available from Department of Housing and Urban Development (HUD) regional offices across the country and government bookstores.

You can get advice from a computer on your particular buy/rent dilemma using *your* pertinent numbers. Write: Buy-Rent Analysis, Consumer Economics and Housing Department, Cornell University, Ithaca, N.Y. 14853

2

Apartment Hunting
Without Tears

It's time to look for an apartment. Or another apartment—a larger one, a less expensive one, or one closer to your job. Perhaps you're getting married or divorced, or you're setting out on your own after college. Whatever your life situation, the hunt is on. If you are looking in a city with an apartment vacancy rate of about 2 percent, you may dread the whole awful business. If there are dozens of attractive rental buildings and complexes where you are—congratulations! Apartment hunting for you need not be traumatic.

Whether apartments are abundant or scarce, all would-be renters share the same concerns. Unlike homebuyers, there is no need for renters to worry about chimney cracks, puddles in the basement, or the ominous-sounding "dry rot." Nor will they be burdened with $50,000 or $100,000 mortgages for the better part of their lives.

But if the responsibility of ownership is missing, tenants can still find plenty to stew over. They may, as mentioned, be frustrated by hunting in an apartment-scarce area. There is the worry about a potential condominium or cooperative conversion. They may run into discriminatory rent practices. Rents increase steadily. And the apartment chosen had better be in good condition because it is often difficult to get repairs made by a surly landlord. Or superintendent. Or handyman.

All of these concerns—from how to look for an apartment to making life comfortable for yourself once you are settled in—are considered in the next few chapters. However, the apartment situation and the subject of landlord-tenant rights and responsibilities vary widely from one state to another, and even from one community to the next. If, for example, you live where vacancy rates are low, you

12

may not be able to hold out for many of the features you want in an apartment. On the other hand, if you are shopping where apartments are plentiful, you will be able to make a decision based on market comparisons. So these chapters are necessarily broad in advice. For more information to use during your apartment search and in your time as a tenant, contact your local or state tenant organization, or the state agency that handles landlord-tenant matters. Get whatever printed material these offices have on landlord-tenant rights and responsibilities and suggestions for handling any problems. Along with such aids, the following pages will help you become a savvy renter.

The tenant condition is not a perfect one, any more than the homeowner's lot is. But, as mentioned in Chapter 1, renting does have its pleasures. Here's how to start taking advantage of them.

Taking Stock

It seems an obvious point, but we'll mention it anyway. The very first concern of any would-be tenant should be how much rent he or she can afford to pay. Ah, but there's more here than a quick "about $475 a month." You will find as you go apartment shopping that some landlords will not consider tenants whose gross income is not at least four to four and a half times the rent figure. Others will not inquire at all about your ability to pay. They will check your references to be sure you are employed where you say you are, but will not ask about your salary, assuming that if you are looking at that particular apartment, you can obviously afford it. So you will be left on your own here, and it will be up to you to set a figure that will be the top rent you can afford to pay. In a tight rental market, many tenants wind up spending more for housing than they should—and making concessions in other areas of their lives. If you want a flossy apartment and are willing to forgo a car, that annual ski vacation, and a few other niceties, so be it. Just be sure, if you are spending more than a quarter of your income for rent, that you know you will have to cut back somewhere in your spending. Depending on your landlord and his sympathy quotient (never very high), you could well find yourself evicted for nonpayment of rent when the first money squeeze comes along.

If you are required to tell a prospective landlord your income, you should report your gross salary, and also include regular payments from child support, stocks, and any other investments. Overtime pay is usually not considered a stable source of income.

Questions to Ask Your Local or State
Tenant Organization and/or Your Local Rent Office
Before You Go Apartment Hunting

It's wise to make these phone calls before you start inspecting apartments. A prospective landlord or rental agent, or even a homeowner renting a basement apartment, may not have the time or the inclination to explain local rent laws to you. More important, asking too many questions may work against you. The unscrupulous property owner will know that you are not aware of your rights, and may take advantage of you. Asking too many detailed questions may give other landlords the impression that you are too concerned with your rights, and are a potential troublemaker.

It's better to acquaint yourself with community rules in advance. A question or two to the landlord is fine, but get more information from the offices that work for your protection. Perhaps they will have a free booklet they can mail to you. If time is a factor, they will answer your questions on the phone. Here's what to ask:

Does this community have a rent control law? (It may go under another term where you are, such as *rent leveling* or *rent stabilization*.) If there is such a law, how often can rents be raised, and by what percentage?

Is there some sort of vacancy decontrol law that governs the amount a landlord can increase rents when apartments become vacant? Am I entitled to know the present tenant's rent? Where do I go if I think I am being charged an illegal rent?

What about the state's security deposit law? How much can the landlord ask? Must the landlord deposit that amount in an interest-bearing account in my name? (Laws vary here, not just among states, but according to the size of the rental dwelling. For example, owner-occupied homes with three units or less may be exempt from interest payments.)

Are there any signs or rumors of the building I have in mind being converted to a condo or co-op? If the talk seems legitimate, how should I proceed as a would-be tenant?

What is the reputation of the building's landlord?

Am I entitled to the name and twenty-four-hour phone number of someone representing the building whom I can call for emergency repairs?

Are smoke detectors required by law in apartment buildings of a certain size in the community?

Is there a law requiring landlords of certain buildings to supply window guards for small children? (In some areas landlords must make that installation for children ten years old or younger. You may have to pay the installation fee and perhaps a small charge each month thereafter.)

When calculating, bear in mind that in taking a new apartment you will have to pay a month's security deposit in advance (sometimes more), perhaps a real estate agent's fee (maybe another month's rent), moving expenses, the cost of hooking up utilities, and the usual odds and ends that go along with setting up a new household. One rather new development in apartment rentals is establishment of separate heat meters for each tenant. So be sure that you will not have to spend another $100 a month above the $475 rent for your own heat. (Paying your own electricity and cooking gas bill is common practice.)

You should bear in mind, too, that Big Brother may be following you as you make your way from Seattle to St. Augustine. Larger property owners sometimes subscribe to the growing number of credit-check companies geared specifically to landlords wanting fast computer checks on prospective tenants. These records will show your full tenant history, including arrears reports. The information can also include data on any participation in a rent strike, in organizing tenants, or other activities. These companies are not illegal. To protect tenants' rights against this form of what tenants call blacklisting, legislation is pending in several states—laws making landlords show just cause for rejection of a tenant, for example. If you have had any trouble at all with previous landlords, a wise move is to contact your regional or state tenant organization or legal aid clinic to see if such computer checks are in operation in your area, and how you can protect yourself.

Whereas some building owners may use services geared specifically to a prospective tenant's earlier tenant history, others are plugged into general credit-checking companies. Here, too, it makes sense to secure a copy of your credit history from the regional agency serving your part of the country, and to add an explanation, if you have one, to any material that appears detrimental to you. You can do this with some of the tenant-checking services as well. For example, if your previous landlord sued you in small claims court, be sure that the fact you won the suit is on file. The record may merely state that the landlord took you to court. The landlord may not have bothered to add the information that you won.

Location and Lifestyle

Commuting to your job should also be considered when evaluating a move, if that applies to you. If your new apartment is six train stops away from work instead of the one stop you now travel, can you swing the additional commutation fare? Is the new apartment close to work but awkwardly situated so that it is not on a bus or subway line? If you are moving to the suburbs from the city, will you have to purchase an automobile to get around? Can you afford one? Conversely, will you have to sell your car if you are moving from suburbia to a center-city apartment and can't afford the garage rent each month?

Must you be close to schools, houses of worship, stores? Does the apartment complex you are considering offer bus service to the business section of town, or to shopping malls?

It is important to note the type of renter certain buildings attract. For example, there are the so-called singles complexes. Lots of baby carriages in the hallways and children's toys on the ground are pretty sure signs of a complex filled with young families. A group of elderly men chatting on lawn chairs of a small garden apartment complex may be a sign that that community has many retired persons. The question to ask yourself is whether you would fit in to those buildings or would be happier living elsewhere.

Prepare yourself to be realistic throughout your search. There is probably no perfect place to live, no matter how much rent you can afford. A $1000 apartment may bring cockroaches along with its more agreeable amenities. A $1500 apartment may have no parking space. Whatever the rent, it may be more than you can afford. The floors may be in bad shape, the view may be of Mrs. O'Leary's wash line, or the place may be too far out of town. You can live with any of these gripes (although try for an apartment that doesn't carry all of them!), but it is important to like *something* about the place you finally take. Even two years is too long a time to spend in an apartment you hate. So if a vanishing apartment supply is leaving you with few choices of where to live, try to enjoy the fact that while the apartment might not be much, at least you are able to live in an elevator building, or you can walk to work.

Coping with Discrimination

Discrimination is against the law, isn't it? Well, sometimes it is and sometimes it isn't. Laws protecting renters against many forms of discrimination are constantly changing and being strengthened, but discrimination still exists.

According to federal law, you cannot be denied rental housing because of your color, religion, national origin, or sex. Some areas have added state and/or regional laws that prohibit discrimination because of marital status, the presence of children in a family, sexual orientation, age, handicaps, and even political affiliation. But other states have no such protections, and even where laws exist, they can be difficult to enforce. For example, California and New York are two of a handful of states that have state rulings prohibiting discrimination against children in rental housing. Yet both states have their share of would-be tenants claiming they are turned down for apartments because of their kids.

Part of the problem here is that property owners do have choices in accepting applicants. While all are forbidden bias because of color, religion, national origin, and sex, there is leeway in other areas. Some landlords, such as those who live in their small buildings, are exempt from certain provisions.

Proving discrimination can be difficult. Landlords can offer any number of reasons for denying you an apartment—it's been taken; the person who handles renting is out; you'll have to put your name on a waiting list—and it's up to you to decide whether that is indeed bias and whether you want to go to court to fight the landlord.

If you know before you start looking for an apartment that you could face discrimination, it's wise to call your local fair housing council, open housing center, human rights commission, or whatever office oversees the matter in your locale to see how you should handle yourself when apartment hunting. They can advise you if bias against you is indeed against the law where you are. They can also tell you how to (1) be sure you have every chance to secure the apartment you are entitled to and (2) understand how to file a complaint if necessary. You will be told, for example, that you should keep a notebook of your apartment inspections, jotting down the date and time of the appointment, the address of the building, and the name of person to whom you spoke. Keep any printed material about the building or complex you are handed or pick up. Write down as accurate a transcription as you can of what the landlord/ agent/broker told you. Bear in mind before you charge discrimination, though, that you must qualify for the apartment in other respects. Your income must be adequate for the rent, references from previous landlords must be good, and you must not be trying to fit too many people into too small a unit. Negatives in these areas are legitimate reasons for a turndown.

When you call back the fair housing office with your report, they will probably send out another applicant for that apartment who will match your qualifications exactly, with one exception. He or she will be white if you are black, or will be of a different religion, or will have no children, or whatever makes him or her more "acceptable" to the landlord than you were. If that applicant is awarded the apartment you were denied, you will probably have a justifiable case of discrimination. You would then be advised how to proceed. Sometimes one phone call from a fair housing office to the landlord is enough to win you the apartment. If you want to take the case as far as court, you may be awarded an apartment (probably the next vacancy to come up), plus court costs, legal fees, and perhaps compensation for emotional stress.

You can also call the U.S. Department of Housing and Urban Development's (HUD) Fair Housing and Equal Opportunity Department's toll-free number—(800) 424-8590—to seek guidance before and during an apartment hunt.

Finally, there's the issue of cohabitation, or as it is more commonly known, "living together." Unmarried couples presenting themselves as such when they go apartment hunting will probably have little trouble these days, at least in larger buildings and complexes. An apartment in someone's home may be another story. Remember, too, that some states still have laws against cohabitation.

You may also, with or without a boyfriend or girlfriend, be denied rental (1) because zoning laws in your community mandate that several unmarried and unrelated persons not share the same house, or (2) you are crowding too many tenants in a space the landlord (or your local housing code) does not consider large enough. Here, too, it's wise to consult your local fair housing office and/or tenant rights group for an update on the living-together or zoning picture in your locale.

Discrimination may not go away after the apartment is rented. It can also occur in subletting an apartment, in rent increases and harassment, and with tenants being denied use of certain facilities. Before taking your own action against a landlord, however, call the appropriate agency in your region that can help you proceed properly.

How to Hunt in an Impossibly Tight Market

Most of the following applies to apartment hunting in a rental market with few vacancies, where special tactics are called for. But it can be useful to those living in areas with choices, too, since the good apartments are the ones that are quickly snapped up.

September and October may be difficult months in which to search for an apartment because students are settling down for the college year (sometimes in apartments) and many people wait until after the summer to change jobs and move. So there's competition there, but there's also activity, or turnover, which can work to your advantage. A fair number of leases expire in September, too, which has always made October a traditional month for moves in rental housing. But aside from early fall, no one season is better than another. It is best to avoid weekends if you can, when everyone else is canvassing. Try to hunt during weekday business hours. The best time to look is the last ten days of the month. That seems to be when vacancies are posted by landlords and building managers. Just after the first of the month, when everyone is presumably settled in, is the worst time.

If you are normally close-mouthed about your life and what's going on with you, this is one time to chatter away to everyone whose path crosses yours. Tell your neighbors and friends and co-workers, your local merchants, and nearby relatives that you are looking for an apartment. Any of them could pass along a tip that will send you to just the right place, so don't be shy. Being referred by someone the landlord knows may, in fact, help you. More apartments are rented from word of mouth in the community than from outside advertising.

You might also consider putting an advertisement in your company's newsletter and even posting notices on bulletin boards around the building. Running an "apartment wanted" advertisement in your local paper is futile in a tight market. No landlord needs to read such ads to rent units. That is far too passive a strategy, if it can even be called a strategy.

Take a walk through the sections of town you find appealing—and you can afford to live in. Talk to doormen. Yes, you will have to pay those individuals to let you know about vacancies if you want any results. How much depends on how bad the apartment situation is in the community and the amount your competing apartment hunters are spending. Some will offer a doorman or building superintendent $10 or $25 for just a tip about a vacancy; others promise those individuals a month's rent if they eventually get the place. Remember that doormen or superintendents are not renting agents and cannot award you an apartment. But they can tell you who's moving and where to go, *fast*, to apply for that apartment.

If you are looking in a residential neighborhood, talk to the residents there, too—the folks sweeping their sidewalks, walking their dogs, or carrying home a bag of groceries. Postal carriers are another source of good leads. They know who is moving. Reward them every week or two for passing on information to you. Another frequently successful ploy is ringing the doorbell of a house with bare windows on one floor. Often that merely announces window washing or drapery cleaning, but more than one apartment hunter's boldness has been rewarded by finding a vacant apartment.

Cute flyers announcing your search and distributed in buildings and put up on local bulletin boards usually do not work in a tight rental market. Again, the strategy is too passive.

If you expect the hunt to be long, you might also join some groups in the area that interest you—book clubs, political organizations, environmental groups, and the like. The object here is to talk to as many people as you can to catch the openings as they occur, before they are advertised or listed with a real estate agent.

Real Estate Agents

You should, of course, register with as many offices as you can in an area that interests you. Apartment listings do not work like house listings, which are generally circulated as part of a Multiple Listing Service from which, in the main, any real estate office can sell you the house that interests you. Each real estate office usually keeps its own apartment listings, and in a tight market an attractive unit can be gone fifteen minutes after it is listed in an office. Here again it is action that wins the apartment. Registering with real estate agents does not mean sitting and waiting for the phone to ring. You must call them frequently, without making a nuisance of yourself, to keep your name in their minds and at the top of what could be lengthy waiting lists. Agents' fees are due only after you find an apartment, and can be based on any standard set by the broker—a month's rent, a percent-

---

Questions to Ask Tenants Living in
Any Building You Are Considering

Only the people living in an apartment house *really* know how life is there. Talk to one or two tenants, or get their names from mailboxes and call them. If you have access to a reverse telephone directory (available at some public libraries), you can look up the address of the building and find the tenants' names there. Most should be willing to talk to you, especially if there are problems. Ask them:

Have there been any rumors of the building going condo or co-op?

How is maintenance in the building? Are repairs made reasonably promptly? Who handles those chores—a super? The management company?

Is there enough heat in the winter?

Have there been any security problems? A rash of robberies of individual apartments, say, or muggings in the lobby?

---

age of annual rent, etc. In rare instances the landlord pays the fee; more often it is the tenant. Some realty offices accept credit cards for payment, and others allow a staggered payment schedule.

Never rely entirely on a real estate agent, or even a dozen agents, in a community with a low vacancy rate. You have to get out there and do your own digging.

Newspaper Classified Advertisements

The papers in your locale will be a great help to you in apartment hunting. While most carry "apartments for rent" classified ads daily, they usually have a special Saturday or Sunday issue that is particularly heavy with real estate listings. If you can get an early edition of that day's paper, you will have a few hours' head start on your competition. Call the paper's circulation department and ask where early copies are delivered so you can pick yours up literally hot off the presses.

Translating the classified advertisements is only sometimes difficult. Reading "2BR," for example, will (almost) clearly tell you the apartment for rent has two bedrooms. Similarly, "incl utils" translates into "including utilities"—the gas and electric bills will be included in the rent. But other abbreviations can be a puzzle, and since they are used by building owners to save money in advertising, they can make a tightly packed two-line advertisement virtually incomprehensible to the novice. It's important that you understand those hieroglyphics. Would you want to drive twelve miles to see an apartment you've read has a "pull k" to find that the term means a small kitchen when you have two children and are looking for a kitchen large enough to accommodate tables and chairs?

To help you through this alphabet jumble, here are some common abbreviations you will come across under "Apts. Unfurn.":

AC or A/C	*Room air conditioner(s)*. You'll probably pay the electricity bill for their use.
CAC or cen A/C	*Central air conditioning*. Usually provided at no extra charge, unless each tenant has a separate utilities meter.
Cons	*Concessions*. Offered by the landlord to stimulate renting. These can be a month's free rent, free membership in the swim club, or any other attraction.
Conv Trans	*Convenient to transportation*. You might also see reference to "1 fare zone" or "2 fare zone," meaning you may or may not have to transfer from one bus or subway to another to get from the apartment to the downtown business center.
DR	*Dining room*.
Drm	*Doorman*.
Dup	*Duplex*. An apartment on two floors of a building.
Eff	*Efficiency*, or studio, apartment. This means one room with a separate bath; the kitchen can be either a part of the main room or be in a small, separate space.
EIK	*Eat-in kitchen*.
Exp Brick	*Exposed brick*. The plaster has been removed from an interior wall (or several walls) to expose the underlying brick wall. This is considered a desirable design feature these days, and one that may bring the landlord more rent money than plain plaster or sheetrock walls.
Flr thru	*Floor through*. An apartment taking up the length of a building, from the front to the back. Usually means the structure is an entire floor in what was once a private home.
Frplc	*Fireplace*. But sometimes it's just there for adornment. To be sure it works, look for "Wbfp"—woodburning fireplace—or "working frplc."
Full K	*Full kitchen*. Here you will find a full-size sink, stove, and refrigerator, but not necessarily a space large enough for tables and chairs.

G/E	*Gas and electricity.*
GAR	*Garage.*
Georgetown area, Society Hill area	The key word here is "area." An advertising come-on that can mean the apartment offered is *on the fringe of the desirable area but not in it.* Sometimes realty agents run three or four ads under the heading "_____ Area." Some may be within the desirable area's boundaries, some not.
H/HW	*Heat, hot water.*
Kitchenette	*A very small kitchen area.* Not large enough for table and chairs.
L or L-shaped	Usually, *a living room in the shape of an L.* The bottom of the L is often used for a dining area, or perhaps for a sleeping alcove.
Lanai	A Hawaiian word for *balcony.*
MBR suite	*Master bedroom suite.* Usually, but not always, includes a separate bath.
Mod appl	*Modern appliances.*
Newly ren	*Newly renovated.*
Penthouse	*Apartment on the top floor of a building.* It almost always includes a terrace.
Pull K	*Pullman kitchen.* The stove, sink, and refrigerator are lined up along one wall, but sometimes not enclosed in a separate room.
Refs	*References* are required.
Sec	*Security.* The meaning of the term depends on the advertiser's interpretation. It could mean the building has adequate protection devices; otherwise, it means that a security deposit is required.
Sl alcove	*Sleeping alcove.* This is an area large enough to accommodate a bed, but usually not another piece of furniture.
Sl loft	*Sleeping loft.* A platform at least six feet above the floor, containing a bed. A ladder leads up to the loft. These are found in small apartments where every effort is made to utilize space cleverly.
So exp	*Southern exposure,* meaning the apartment faces the south and receives good sunlight.
W/D	*Washer and dryer.*
W/W	*Wall-to-wall carpeting.*

How the advertisement is signed can give you a clue to the type of apartment offered. If the signature says "Owner/Mgmt" (owner management), that could be a small apartment building or a private home where the owner does the renting. Naturally, you pay no fee here. If the ad reads "Mgmt co." or "agent," a company or individual is representing the landlord in handling tenant selection and leasing. The building or complex is probably a large one, but there is no fee here either. Ads specifying "bkr" ("broker") refer to a real estate agent. You will have to pay a fee if you take that apartment. Ads followed simply by a telephone number can be by the owner or by a realty agent. Who signs the advertisement has no relation to the apartment's value or to the landlord's reputation. The only difference to you is that with a real estate agent you will almost certainly have to pay a fee for the apartment. By all means ask when you call about an ad whether there is a fee involved, so that you know before you go out to inspect the apartment.

Can you believe all you read in classified ads? Naturally not. They are rarely subjected to a newspaper's acceptability or standards department for close scrutiny, since there are simply too many of them. Thus, an apartment may boast an "ocean view" when you must stand on your toes in the shower stall to see a brief glimpse of the surf—at high tide. "Cozy" almost always means "small"; "prewar beauty" may describe a unit with high ceilings and marble mantles, but the building may not have been painted or repaired since the war—and they are referring to World War I. So it's important when responding to any classified ad to pump as much information as you can from the answering party to save yourself the time, expense, and aggravation of chasing around to inspect totally unacceptable apartments.

For example, how landlords judge what constitutes a "room" is a subject that has supplied comedians with gags for years. There's the one about the rental agent showing 2 × 4 pantries and walk-in closets as second bedrooms, for example. Opinions vary here, but generally bathrooms, foyers, alcoves, dinettes, kitchenettes, and terraces are not considered full rooms. A space must usually have at least one window and a minimum floor area of 50 square feet to be called a room.

Identifying Apartment Styles

An apartment is a self-contained unit usually featuring a kitchen, a bathroom, and any number of other rooms, located in a larger building generally consisting of similar residential units. But that "apartment" building can be a former hat factory, a sleek high rise on a commercial downtown thoroughfare, or a sprawling garden complex five miles from the nearest neighbor. The following is a directory of the most common apartment styles you will come across in your hunt. (Private homes for rent are not mentioned here. They are considered separately in Chapter 7.)

Ultra-luxury buildings. The highest rent will be commanded by these. You probably know instantly of one or more of these in your locale. They are either very old, possibly historic structures, or very new buildings with the latest features. Old or new, however, they are expensive. There is usually a full service staff, perhaps a health club, a pool, and other amenities. Living here will mean additional expenses above rent for the use of those facilities, tipping, etc.

Modern high rises. Just a notch, price-wise, under ultra-luxury are the modern high rises. These can be handsome, but are more often nondescript buildings of ten or twenty or more stories with thin walls in the apartments and plastic plants and perhaps a doorman in the lobby. Construction is new here. Rents are high, but not quite at the level of the great buildings in town. These buildings frequently attract the young, single set, so you can expect a frequent turnover and sometimes a high noise level.

Townhouses. If you are reading about a building described as a townhouse, that could mean a haughty mansion such as those off Fifth Avenue in Manhattan, or any other very expensive, formerly one-family home in an excellent part of the city. It can be free-standing or attached. Rents depend on the condition of the building and the desirability of the neighborhood, but generally if the owner calls it a townhouse, that translates into high rent. A townhouse can also be an attached home in a development that operates under the condominium form of ownership.

Garden apartments. These might be different in your mind from what the landlord is offering. A garden apartment can be the ground floor in a house or apartment building, where the tenant has the use of the yard. More often, though, the term refers to multi-unit complexes in suburban or country areas with grass, trees, and perhaps a pool and other extras. Rents here can vary widely.

Brownstones. Then there are housing styles peculiar to urban areas. "Brownstone," for example, is a term that now has become more or less generic, used to describe any row house at least 60 years old and faced with stone. Literally, brownstone is a reddish-brown sandstone. A brownstone will be priced considerably lower than a townhouse. Brownstone owners may call their homes townhouses, but townhouse owners would never refer to their homes as brownstones.

Renovated buildings. These are usually plain structures of any construction, with no particular architectural style, and usually up to six stories to avoid the need for an elevator. Sometimes this style is called a *walkup.* It's hard to tell from the word "renovated" just where the renovations took place, but often these are clean build-

Apartments in great old city houses provide an excellent alternative to high-rise living for those who prefer life on a smaller scale.

ings in decent neighborhoods, and rents can be lower than for brownstones and high rises in the same part of town. You're just not getting any glamour for your money. It's wise to ask, though, if you see a renovated building listed in an advertisement, just what floor it is on and whether there is any elevator service.

Railroad apartment. Another urban rental style is the old railroad apartment, which is usually found in row houses (sometimes called *tenements*) but occasionally upgraded to renovated buildings. These units are laid out so that one room leads to the next, railroad-car style. To get to room C in the back, for instance, you have to walk through rooms A and B.

Lofts. These are an increasingly popular apartment style in many cities these days. Just about any sizable chunk of space can be called a loft, whether it is an empty floor above the neighborhood flower shop or several thousand square feet in a refurbished industrial plant. Most loft apartments are found in buildings that were once used for manufacturing, and what you are renting in many instances is raw space—no room dividers and, more important, sometimes no running water, heat, or electricity. Renting a loft apartment may mean having to make a sizable financial investment yourself, or you may be lucky enough—and wealthy enough—to rent a loft unit that has already been converted to residential use. One important point to bear in mind if you do want a loft apartment: Be sure the area where you are hunting is zoned for loft living before you make any important financial investment in redoing the unit. Since loft living became fashionable in the late 1960s, thousands of former factory and industrial buildings have been transformed into apartment units, frequently illegally since the neighborhoods where they are located are zoned for commercial uses only. While that illegality may not bother you if you are renting an apartment with all the necessary appurtenances, it is folly to start major rehabilitation work on an illegal loft unit—unless you want to spend your idle hours engaged in battling local officials for zoning variances. It should be pointed out, however, that many devotees of loft living indeed do just that in the interest of seeing more of those structures turned over to living spaces.

Public housing. Finally, there is public housing, which can be subsidized wholly or in part by the government—federal, state, or local, or a combination of several governmental agencies. Apartments in these buildings are rarely advertised, frequently have waiting lists, and always have income limitations. There's more about public housing in Chapter 8.

Building Management Companies

Another means of saving yourself some shoe leather is to make or acquire a list of management companies in your area. These are firms that handle the day-to-day operations, including renting, for the building owners. Some oversee several thousand units in one locale, perhaps most of the major apartment houses in that area. Once in a building, you would contact these companies about rent hikes, painting, subletting, and any other tenant concern. You can get their names from the classified advertisements (the ad will be signed "XYZ Mgmt Co." or the like) or from your local real estate board. Or, if you have a few favorite buildings, you can copy the names and addresses from the plaques outside the buildings or inside, near the mailboxes. Call those concerns and tell them where you'd like to live and what your rent ceiling is. If they have no vacancies at the moment, thank them and call back in a week or two. Sometimes the companies maintain a waiting list; more often they do not. But a cheerful, not pestering, phone call periodically should help your cause along. As mentioned previously, these offices do not charge a fee for renting.

Other Aids

If you are moving to a new town, you might want to write for a directory of apartments in that community. Apartment Directories and Guides, Inc., 7200 France Ave. So., Suite 238, Minneapolis, Minn. 55435, publishes a free list of directories for various urban areas around the country, written especially for newcomers. You can order the specific city apartment guide you want from the directory. Each book (there is a charge for the books) provides maps, a listing of apartment buildings, and information about rents, amenities, parking facilities, and so on. This is not a guide to vacancies, just to the buildings.

No matter how desperate you are in your search for a suitable apartment, it's wise to avoid apartment referral services. These offices may charge $50 or $100 to provide you with a list of supposedly available apartments in your area. But often those listings are merely copied from local classified ads and are long outdated. Sometimes the addresses are fictitious. Law enforcement agencies in many areas have run some of these outfits out of business, but they still crop up from time to time. Never pay *any* money up front for an apartment. If you do find yourself involved with one of these outfits and wish to lodge a complaint, contact your state's Department of State.

It's also useless to buy magazines and booklets purporting to offer available apartment listings. Any publication printed weekly or monthly contains outdated material, if indeed the listings are legitimate at all. This is a waste of your dollars.

One term you may come across as you hunt for an apartment is *key money*. This is a flat sum, usually charged by the existing tenant but occasionally by the building owner, to allow you to take over the apartment as a legal tenant. To get around calling it "key money," it may be called a "furnishings fee." Key money may be outlawed in your area, but sadly it is still sometimes the only way to get the apartment you want. Whether you pay or not is up to you to decide. The amount of money asked can vary from a few hundred to a brazen several thousand dollars.

One variation of this is the so-called "fixture fee," which is a charge usually made to loft tenants by the original tenant who paid thousands of dollars to get that apartment into shape. If you do decide to pay any of these monies, just be sure you are legally entitled to that apartment and have been accepted as a tenant before handing over a dime.

Roommate Placement Agencies

Want to share your apartment? Must you share? Roommate placement agencies are an excellent screening device for finding someone to split the rent. Complaints received against these services by state offices are minimal. You can deal with a roommate agency whether you are looking for both an apartment and a sharer or you already have the place and just want a roommate. Working with an agency is far easier and safer than handling phone calls from strangers and interviewing on your own in response to your own advertising. Let the agency do that work for you. Fees are low—around $25 to $50— and you are usually allowed another roommate for free if the original match doesn't take in a specified period of time. Some agencies match only male/male and female/female sharers, but others will bring together coed roommates. A growing number are specializing in matching single parents, a sizable growth market. Although most agencies operate well within the law, it's still wise to check with your state Department of State and/or your local consumer affairs agency to see if any complaints have been registered against the concern you are considering signing up with.

A word of caution here. Apartments are rented to the holder of the lease and, usually, any members of that person's immediate family who may later choose to live there with the tenant. If the tenant allows any other individual to move in *without the landlord's knowledge and consent,* he or she is violating the lease and can lose the apartment. This would apply to a young woman inviting two or three other women to move into her apartment to split expenses, as well as to heterosexual and homosexual couples sharing quarters. So be very careful when getting a roommate that the person not move in until the green light is given by the landlord. Landlords' dislike for those "living together" stems less from moral convictions than from concern about overcrowding, a strain on the building's services, and the inability in some areas to raise rents until a unit becomes vacant. A continual stream of roommates keeps the vacancy rate low.

When You Find the Apartment You Want

Maybe it's (nearly) perfect, or perhaps it's all that is available in your area, but whatever your feeling about the apartment, you have decided you want this particular one. In some buildings you will be asked for an "application fee" to show your interest, an amount of money that can vary. This can also be called a *good faith deposit*. It's

---

Checklist for Inspecting Apartments

When is rent due? It usually must be paid by the first of the month, but if your pay schedule makes the fifteenth more comfortable for you, perhaps the landlord would acquiesce. Ask.

Is heat and/or electricity supplied by the landlord, or are there separate meters for each tenant so that you pay your own bills? This is important to learn, for paying your own heat, gas, and electricity can add substantially to your monthly rent expense.

Will the landlord paint? Some are required to do so by law; others are not.

Is there parking space for you on the premises? Is there a separate charge for use of the lot or garage? If you are left to find your own parking, how safe and accessible is on-street parking?

Are pets allowed? If the landlord says okay but the printed lease says "no pets," be sure to have the landlord initial his permission on the lease form.

Is there a laundry on the premises? Down the block? Nowhere for miles? Would the landlord allow you to install a washer and dryer?

Is the building wired for cable television? Will the landlord allow it to be installed?

What fixtures come with the apartment you are considering—the refrigerator? The room air conditioner(s)?

Are the electrical outlets adequate? Running extension cords around rooms is not particularly attractive and can be a fire hazard, too.

Will you be paying a separate fee each time you use the pool or tennis courts, or are those amenities included in the rent?

What about security in the building? Is there a doorman? A closed-circuit television monitor? At the very least a locked front door? Are service entrances and fire escape doors kept locked against outsiders? If in the apartment you are considering there are bars on windows that lead out to the fire escape, how do you get out in the event of a fire?

Are you paying extra money for a high floor or a view when you'd be just as happy taking another apartment in the building that costs less?

not always money that is refunded, unless state laws mandate that the landlord return checks to applicants who did not win the apartment. Be sure you know whether you will get back that deposit if you do not get the apartment.

Just because you are the first applicant does not mean you will be awarded the apartment. The landlord may take applications from several prospects and make a selection after checking their applications and references (avoiding discriminatory practices, however). So it may take a day or so to learn if you have come out the winner.

In a soft market you may certainly dicker over the rent charged. Here, too, a landlord may look more kindly at your Siamese cat and change the "no pets" clause to read "small pets only." In an area with plenty of apartments for rent, try to win as many concessions as you can. The landlord *needs* you. In a tight apartment market, unfortunately, you will have little room to bargain.

When you and the landlord agree upon the rent, take a look at the apartment to see what repairs or improvements need to be made, and ask if that work can be done before you move in. If the landlord agrees, be sure that a clause to that effect is put into the lease. And add the phrase "before the tenant moves in" or "within sixty days after the tenant moves in," or the work may be done eighteen months after you have settled in. If the apartment is in poor shape but the landlord promises nothing, make a list of what's wrong and have him sign the paper and attach it to the lease, so it is on record that you did not cause that damage. Taking pictures of the apartment as it is when you move in is another good tactic to protect yourself from blame.

In some communities, or with certain types of housing, such as units in private homes, you will not be offered a lease—indeed, anything in writing is unheard of. Your tenant organization can apprise you of the usual procedure where you live. If you have a choice, take the lease. Oral promises hold little weight in court, if it should come to that. It's best to have everything in writing. (There is more about what to expect from a lease in the next chapter.)

For More Information

"Wise Rental Practices" is a 40-page booklet available from the federal government. It offers tips on apartment hunting, solutions to problems you may encounter as a tenant, and a brief description of your rights and responsibilities. There is no charge for the booklet. Write to Consumer Information Center, Dept. 599, Pueblo, Colo. 81009.

The Rights of Tenants by Richard E. Blumberg and James R. Grow, Avon Books. Price: $1.95. This paperback has a question-and-answer format and is published in cooperation with the American Civil Liberties Union.

"Landlords & Tenants: Your Guide to the Law" is an excellent 48-page booklet available from the American Bar Association, Circulation Dept., 1155 E. 60th St., Chicago, Ill. 60637. Price: $2. It presents an overview of the basic rights and responsibilities of both landlord and tenant.

Finally, your state office that handles landlord-tenant concerns should offer any number of free pamphlets on landlord-tenant law in your locale. So should your city or state tenant organization.

3

Your Rights as a Tenant, Lease-Wise and Otherwise

Oh boy, oh boy. Reading the standard lease, with its page after page of convoluted legalese. Could there be anything more boring?

Sure could. Plowing through instructions and warranties that come with new appliances is a tad on the dull side, too. And 204-page condominium offering plans aren't page turners, either. The world is full of uninteresting, mysterious, laborious documents that we ought to read, but often don't.

If you're one of those prospective tenants who freezes at the sight of a lease (or any other legal form), then there's good news for you. For one thing, many form leases across the country have been revised over the last few years and are now written in plain English. And, even more delightful to know, perhaps you don't have to read the lease, or at least not all of it. (More about this later.)

There are many different lease forms in existence around the country. There are thousands of landlords, each with his or her own rules and regulations. And there are hundreds of cities, towns, suburbs, and villages. Some have tight protection for renters; others offer nothing in the way of legislation or even advice.

These pages cannot address every question and potential problem that could arise from every lease. Therefore, to be a truly sharp apartment hunter, and perhaps save yourself a chunk of money and certainly a good deal of aggravation, your first step before signing a lease should be to seek advice from the pros in your locale about rents that can be charged, the rights and responsibilities of landlords, and any other question that applies to you in particular. (Can

I operate an office in my home? Can I have a roommate?) But whom should you call?

• You can check with the rent office in the community in which you are looking.

• You can call your state's Department of Community Affairs, Landlord-Tenant Bureau. Besides answering your questions, they will almost certainly have free booklets they can send you on the rights and responsibilities of both landlord and tenant.

• You can call your regional HUD office (addresses in Appendix A).

• You can contact your local or state tenant association.

• If you live in one of the few cities or states that have tenant handbooks, you can purchase one of these guides at a bookstore. A list of these handbooks appears on page 52.

It's important to be armed with all this information before you start hunting for apartments. A rental agent may not have the time or the inclination to explain the intricacies of rent control to you. A tenant organization will. The agent's eyes will glaze over as questions about security deposits become more complex. The folks at the state house will gladly explain what rules are in effect in your town.

So be prepared. A little knowledge makes the lease's appearance just a little less frightening.

A Lease or No Lease?

As mentioned before, not every tenant is offered a lease when he or she agrees to rent an apartment. In a building of five or fewer units, for instance, you may not be presented with a lease. On the other hand, if you are heading for the 300-unit Plush Towers, you will unquestionably be handed such a document.

For other buildings, it all depends on the owner's wishes and what the law says. The lease may be oral or may be in writing. It may be a little less formal than the printed lease, merely a "written agreement." You should know, however, that if you have no lease, the terms of your occupancy of the apartment can change with thirty days' notice, and sometimes less. A rental agreement running longer than one year may have to be in writing to be valid. Check your municipality.

Is it better to have a written lease? All things considered, yes. Oral promises are difficult to prove in court, if a suit is filed. Although tenants with no written leases for rental agreements of under one year generally have some protection by law, it's better to have

M915-Apartment lease, long form, plain language, 4-84

© 1984 by Arthur S. Horn, a New Jersey Attorney
Julius Blumberg, Inc., Publisher, NYC 10013

THIS IS A LEGALLY BINDING LEASE THAT WILL BECOME FINAL WITHIN THREE BUSINESS
DAYS. DURING THIS PERIOD YOU MAY CHOOSE TO CONSULT AN ATTORNEY WHO CAN
REVIEW AND CANCEL THE LEASE. SEE SECTION ON ATTORNEY REVIEW FOR DETAILS.*

APARTMENT LEASE

**The Landlord and the Tenant agree to lease the Apartment for the Term and at the Rent stated, as
follows:** The words Landlord and Tenant include all landlords and all tenants under this Lease.

Landlord ....
Print or type

Tenant ....
Print or type names of all adult Tenants who will live in the Apartment. Each must sign this Lease

....
Address in county for receipt of notices

....
Zip

Apartment .... in the **Building** at ....

Date of lease............................19.......

Rent for the Term is $ ....
The Rent is payable in advance on the first day of each month,
as follows:..

Term ....

Beginning....................19.......

Ending....................19.......

Security $................... deposited at....................

Name and address of bank or savings and loan association

*Reprinted with permission of © 1984 Arthur S. Horn, a New Jersey attorney, Julius
Blumberg, Inc., Publisher, NYC 10013.*

that written document. And most renters feel more secure with a
written lease, unless they are just passing through town and being
given the heave-ho after 90 days will not bother them.

To give you a better idea of how lease-signing works, let's follow
Kevin, a 32-year-old engineer, through the procedure. Kevin lives
in a large eastern metropolitan area, but has just accepted a new job
in a smaller city one hundred miles away. Kevin is quite pleased
about the new assignment. He likes where he will be living, the
new job brings a nice raise, and he hopes he can find a more-than-
decent 3½ room apartment. (But not too expensive, of course.)

After a good deal of legwork on weekends and days taken from his
job, Kevin does find what he wants. It's an attractive, older building
of some 90 units called Marlborough Towers. Nice name, too, Kevin
thinks. The rent is a little more than he wants to pay (but then that's
usually the case these days), and the lease runs for one year. Kevin
decides to take the place. He files an application, and within a week
his references have been checked and he is invited either to sign the
lease by mail or return to the Towers' rental office to sign. Kevin
wouldn't mind another look at the place, so he elects to sign in
person.

Translating Legalese

Your lease may be written in today's more contemporary style, but there still may be terms that puzzle you. Or you may come upon a word or phrase unfamiliar to you when talking to the landlord or a fellow tenant. Here are some definitions:

Arrears. Money that is not paid when due, such as overdue rent.

Assignment. Giving up all rights to your apartment before the lease has expired.

Ejectment. A polite word for eviction.

Goods and chattels. Your personal property—furniture, clothing, etc.

Harassment. Conduct engaged in by the building owner to force you to vacate your apartment.

Lessee. You, the tenant.

Lessor. The landlord.

Rent control. Legislation passed in some communities that holds annual rent increases in certain buildings to a certain percentage. May also be known as *rent stabilization* or *rent leveling*.

Warranty of Habitability Law. A ruling in effect in several states that gives basic protection for tenants by demanding landlords provide a standard of habitability for apartments. This includes adequate plumbing, hot water, working appliances, heat (unless each unit has its own meter) and janitorial services, plus no faulty wiring or insects.

During his apartment hunt in the town, Kevin made a few phone calls and found out what sort of rents and rent increases he could expect in that community. The rental agent had told him he would have to pay 1½ months' security money. That seemed a little steep, but Kevin learned, through another phone call, that there were no restrictions in that state on the amount of security deposit a landlord could request.

So armed with all that knowledge, Kevin returns to the rental office. The agent greets him with a wide smile and gives him a four-page, legal-size printed document with the heading "Apartment Lease." It is divided into small sections with headings like "Sublet" and "Access to Apartment," etc., which are in no particular order. The young engineer takes it over to a corner of the office, sits down and prepares to dig in.

No matter what its length, a lease is basically the confirmation of an exchange between two individuals. "In return for your paying me (a certain amount) a month," it says, "I will provide you with a habitable apartment and what is known as 'quiet enjoyment of the premises.' " Simple enough. Four to six pages that can be boiled down to one sentence.

All leases, from the most intimidating to the simplest slip of paper, should contain at the very least the name of the renter and the landlord; address of the building; description of the property; length of the lease; rent; and the landlord's regulations and responsibilities for maintenance.

All of that basic exchange between landlord and tenant is familiar to Kevin from previous apartments he has rented. He now has two choices about the lease from Marlborough Towers:

1. He can read every word of the document, to be absolutely sure he knows what is expected of him and the landlord.

2. He can read only the parts that have been typed in—special considerations between Kevin and the landlord.

If Kevin can apply himself to this chore, it is always better to read any document completely before signing. Still, he knows that this is a form lease. Every tenant is presented with the same form in that building, and there isn't much one can do about its stipulations. It's a lease that is, like many others, printed by the millions and sold at stationery stores across the country. As long as Kevin bears in mind that leases are created by landlords and/or their attorneys, looks carefully at any clauses that he thinks might cause him trouble later on, and reads any word, phrase, or clause that has been typed in, he is doing fine.

Kevin elects to read only the typed-in words and clauses. He checks, for example, to be sure the landlord has noted that he will replace the kitchen stove, which has not been working properly. The sentence is there. Kevin recalls during his inspection of the apartment back in May that the landlord assured him the hole in the living room wall would soon be filled with an air conditioner. Kevin had smiled politely, and then asked the landlord to add a sentence to the lease saying an air conditioner would be installed in just that space by June 1. That sentence is not there. He mentions it to the rental manager. Oh yes, just an oversight, no problem. The manager smiles and hands the lease to his secretary to type in the appropriate sentence.

Marlborough Towers is an attractive building, and with the wave of conversions to condo and co-op ownership still proceeding in most communities, Kevin gives a passing thought to what should happen to him if this building makes that switch. Leases usually do not protect tenants and prospective tenants against a landlord's plans to convert, unless there is a special rider to that effect put into the document. Kevin decides to skip that issue. He reasons that first, the conversion may not happen, and second, he may well want to buy his unit if it does. Like Scarlett O'Hara, he decides to think about that tomorrow.

He does look for the heading "Sublet," however. Since he is young and has been fairly mobile in his profession, he wants to be sure that if he should be transferred, or is offered another job elsewhere, he will have no trouble with the lease. There is a clause that says he is entitled to sublet the apartment if a suitable tenant can be found. Now Kevin feels he is covered, no matter what changes enter his life. The lease allows him a certain mobility without penalty.

Kevin takes a deep breath. Okay, that's it. He signs the two copies of the lease. The landlord or his representative may have already signed, so Kevin is likely to be given his copy of the lease right there. He may also be given the keys to the apartment if it is vacant, or perhaps he will not have the keys until he returns to move in. In any event, Kevin is now the newest tenant at Marlborough Towers, and the procedure didn't hurt a bit.

Here are some other points in the lease that Kevin glanced over. You may find them either more or less important to you than they were to him. Perhaps one word or one phrase will lead you to make a few follow-up calls to offices and organizations in your community and state that will help clarify the issue.

Rent

If there are no rent control laws governing your building, then rents can be set at any amount the landlord chooses.

Rent is almost always due the first day of the month. In a small building you can probably get by with being a few days late, but in larger complexes management companies sometimes fire off eviction notices by the third day of the month. It is important to see how your lease treats these payments. Some call for late charges of so many dollars per day that the tenant is delinquent, others for a flat 5 or 6 percent interest charge for late payments.

If payday for you falls once a month around the fifteenth, management might agree that your rent can be paid on that day (or the twentieth, or whatever date the two of you agree on) instead of the first. This dispensation should, of course, be added to the lease and initialed and dated by the landlord.

Who Should Sign the Lease?

The name of every adult who will be living in the apartment should be listed on the lease. Keeping secrets from the landlord on this issue can get you evicted. By law, landlords have the right to know how many people will be living in each unit.

This can be a gray area, however, and one best explained to you by your regional tenant association. Some landlords will let you have a couple of roommates (of any gender) and allow them and their successors to proceed in and out of the apartment without ever questioning the parade of new faces. Others will attempt to evict the leaseholding tenant and his or her roommates because the whole crowd of them were not named on the lease. This is increasingly done by some landlords trying to get rid of illegal tenants in order to raise the rent substantially on a unit that has not been "freed" for perhaps a decade, thanks to a constant procession of roommates. Property owners may attempt that strategy if they are planning a condo or co-op conversion. So whereas you can sometimes get away with a lot of comings and goings, in other instances you will be made to pay for keeping the landlord in the dark about who is living in your unit. And any "guest" who stays longer than two weeks is usually considered a permanent roommate.

The type of eviction in this case can also take place against what is sometimes called *POSSLQs*—"people of opposite sex sharing living quarters." Since cohabitation is still against the law in some states, the landlord can use that as grounds for eviction, although the strongest point will still be the additional people not named on the lease.

There is one "out" here. If the landlord accepts a rent check from an illegal roommate, he or she usually forfeits the right to oust that individual and the leaseholder. The landlord is in effect accepting the arrangement.

And there are two exceptions to this issue: (1) a spouse is always allowed to move in, even though his or her name is not added to the lease and even though the lease specifies that the unit is to be occupied by one person, and (2) a member of the immediate family moving in is usually exempt from the above strictures, too.

Finally, if you notify the landlord of a new roommate or two, and there is no objection, you may still be hit with a small rent increase.

The Security Deposit

A new tenant is almost always required to pay an additional sum of money besides the first month's rent as security against possible damage, breakage, or outright destruction of the apartment, or against the tenant taking off in the middle of the lease. The money is supposed to be returned no later than 15 days after the tenant has moved out, if the apartment is left in a satisfactory condition. This is a fair requirement, for property owners have a right to protect their investments.

But as sound as it is in theory, the security deposit in practice is the cause of more confusion, anger, and court cases than any other aspect of the landlord-tenant relationship.

It's wise to be sure before you sign the lease just how your landlord interprets the word *security*. Does it include a "cleaning fee," a $50-or-more charge that is nonrefundable? Is it a month's "advance rent," money that is also not to be refunded? Or is it a straight "security deposit"—one, one and a half, or two months' rent, in addition to the rent you will pay for the month when you move in? If your state has no laws to the contrary, the building owner can charge any amount of security deposit, although one month's rent is the most common amount.

More and more communities are mandating that landlords set aside tenants' security deposits in interest-bearing accounts in local lending institutions. They must notify the tenant of which bank holds the money, and even send the tenant an annual statement. That law usually does not apply to buildings containing five or six units or less, including private homes that contain apartments.

Alterations

One of the restrictions in a lease that is most interesting to tenants is about decorating: Can I put nails into the wall? Can I use wallpaper instead of paint? If I am ambitious, what about laying tile, sanding floors, and the like?

You are supposed to ask the landlord's permission before going ahead with any change to the apartment that will permanently alter its appearance. But if you do go ahead without authority—and how many of us have asked permission to hang a few pictures?—you may be able to get away with the alterations. Take the nails question. In some leases it seems that hammering into the wall is technically grounds for termination of the lease. But if it comes to court, it is a rare judge who will side with the landlord. In fact, in one ruling on the subject the judge said he regarded "the lease prohibition against the driving of picture or other nails in the walls or woodwork as unreasonable and unenforceable. The apartment . . . was leased for residential living purposes and not as a monastic cell."

However, the unusually large holes and chips left when a massive wall-length shelf system is removed is an example of structural damage that will probably be repaired at your expense by way of a deduction from your security deposit.

A way to get around some decorating restrictions that should not offend the landlord is to save what you're replacing. For example, if you install a new ceiling lighting fixture, set the original one away carefully and then put it back into place when you are leaving.

Most leases quite clearly prohibit tenants from making any alterations without checking with the landlord first. So better make that call before wallpapering, exposing a brick wall, putting up paneling, and the like. If you do work against the landlord's wishes, or without notifying him or her, and you are sued, it's a gamble whether the judge will rule that the "improvement" you made adds to the value of the apartment. It will probably be up to the judge's taste and your skill in doing the job.

There's no question that some improvements can get you into all kinds of trouble. You certainly wouldn't start tearing down interior walls without permission—one of the walls may be holding up the house. If you try to install a partition to make two rooms out of one open space, the building code in your community may say no. Each "room" must have a window, and maybe your new creation doesn't. You're getting the landlord in trouble with the building inspector. It's always smarter to ask first. You may be saving yourself a huge bill for putting the place back to its original condition when you leave. And the bottom line here is that in most cases that come to court, the landlord wins. It *is* his or her property, after all, no matter how talented and clever you are.

Make too many improvements in your dingy studio walkup and in an open market with no rent control, and the landlord may slap you with a rent increase. If you are moving into an apartment that does need plenty of work, try to make an arrangement with the landlord that you will do specific jobs (1) in exchange for a lower rent for a specified period of time, (2) if he or she purchases supplies, c (3) if he or she will agree to a rent freeze for a specified time. Naturally, you should put those agreed-upon stipulations into the lease.

Pets

This is a continually changing arena where much is left unsaid, so it pays to know just where you stand before you move in with your furry companion. By not investigating properly, you may have to move out again rather quickly, or part with your pet.

If the lease says "no pets," then that's that, unless you can get the landlord, for some reason, to make an exception in your case. If an exception is made, be sure that there is a rider to that effect in the lease when you sign it.

If the lease says nothing about pets, don't open your mouth. It is generally conceded that the tenant can then bring in good old Fido.

One point to be aware of. If the lease says "no pets," but on your inspection of the building and grounds you see someone walking a dog, don't automatically assume that the clause is no longer in effect. Perhaps that individual is the landlord's Aunt Rose, who has been living in the building since 1967 and seems exempt from the pet ban. She may have a clause in her lease that once her 16-year-old pooch heads for the last roundup she will not get another. Indeed, the landlord may well have put the pet ban into effect only recently, allowing those who had animals to keep them, but not replace them. So you'll have to do some asking around before assuming that the "no pets" clause is a dead issue around that building.

If you are found to have a pet that is truly there illegally, you will probably be given ten days to get rid of the animal. If you don't, you will face eviction.

But remember that this is a changing arena, full of gray areas here and there. So sometimes you will find if you keep your pet openly for several months—and certainly for several years—the landlord cannot then come up to you and complain about the animal. He or she is considered to have given tacit approval to its being there. (Naturally, when we talk of pets and evictions here, we are *not* talking about animals that have become a nuisance and are causing problems within the entire building or complex.)

Also, some landlords are threatening these days to evict tenants for pets simply because they want vacant apartments. But in a growing number of instances the courts are finding, especially when it comes to elderly tenants, that threatening eviction under those conditions is unconscionable.

You can send for the free booklet, "A Tenant's Guide: Pets Are

Wonderful Urban Dwellers", available from the Pets Are Wonderful Council, 500 North Michigan Avenue, Suite 200, Chicago, Illinois 60611.

Finally, apartment hunters who are blind should know that most states do allow dog guides in apartment buildings, even if there is a "no pets" ban. The tenant is, of course, liable for any damage caused by the dog. Some states allow a landlord to charge the tenant an extra deposit because of the dog, but others forbid that practice.

Responsibility for Maintenance and Repairs

The law is extremely complicated in the area of a landlord's responsibility versus the tenant's for repairs. Generally, landlords must fix anything they promise in leases or written or oral agreements to furnish and maintain. They must also keep public areas, such as hallways, in repair. In many states there is a "warranty of habitability" law, which means that landlords must at the very least provide (among other basic services) hot and cold water, heat (unless there is a separate meter for each apartment), ceilings that do not fall down, and apartments that are not mice or rat infested.

Tenants are responsible for keeping things shipshape in their apartments, and for repairing any damage to the units or the appliances caused by their own negligence or carelessness.

If you somehow manage to break the kitchen stove, you fix it. If the stove's thermostat is just plain worn out, it could be up to the landlord to make repairs or buy a new one—unless there is no mention of the stove in your lease, in which case the new purchase is open to interpretation and some haggling.

Whether the landlord must paint your apartment should also be specified in the lease. Some will, every three years, following local health code regulations. Others, the smaller landlords in particular, are not required to do so, although sometimes they will supply the paint if you will do the work. So barter over this issue if you aren't entitled to an outright free paint job. Any concessions you win should be written into the lease.

Sadly, the difference between what landlords are supposed to do and what they actually come forward and fix can be like the difference between day and night. To get proper repairs made may be far more difficult than merely pointing to your lease and telling the landlord you're entitled. You may find yourself calling your tenant organization or city agency for guidance. (More about that in the next chapter.) For now, at lease-signing, be sure you have as many protections as possible in writing.

You should bear in mind that there's an area of repairs in which no one is quite sure who is responsible: repairing the damage caused by natural disasters such as floods, fires, or hurricanes. Unless the lease says otherwise, neither the landlord nor yourself can be held accountable.

When the Landlord Can Enter Your Apartment

You may not be too crazy about the idea, but the landlord has a so-called right of access to your apartment for safety's sake.

There may be no state law in effect where you are that mandates tenants must give the landlord keys to their apartments, but if your lease contains a provision obligating you to furnish a key, you will probably have the choice of doing it or petitioning a local court to let you out of the clause. If there is no law either way, and if there is no mention in the lease of a key to be given, then the landlord cannot evict you for withholding the key. However, in owner-occupied dwellings of three units or less, the key must usually be given to the homeowner. If it is not, then the landlord can order the tenant to vacate the apartment within thirty days. If the tenant doesn't comply, eviction proceedings can begin.

Of course, even if you do not have to furnish your landlord with a key, he or she must have access to your unit to make repairs and inspections, with twenty-four hours notice to you. In emergencies, immediate access must be given, an entry you will no doubt be

---

Who is Your Landlord, Anyway?

The answer to this question is easy if you live upstairs in Ben and Helen Flanagan's house. But when you get into multi-family dwellings, from three to five units on up, it may not be such a simple question. Many landlords prefer anonymity. No 3 A.M. phone calls for them, thank you. No riotous tenant association to deal with.

"My landlord is the XYZ Corporation," you say. But what exactly is that group? Where are they located? Who are the principals? If you wanted to reach them, how would you go about it? Is all you know of them the recording you get when you call the number you have been given: "This is the XYZ Corporation. At the sound of the tone please leave your name and message and someone will get back to you"?

You may live in your apartment for one year or thirty-two years and never have any quarrel with management or any desire to know or contact your real landlord. But then again, a situation may arise where you will have to be able to identify that individual or group in order to take them to court. Phantom "front" companies cannot be sued. And you can't sue the superintendent or the rental agent if you are really filing a case against the building's owners.

The first step is to check with your local tenant association and/or your state Department of Community Affairs, Landlord-Tenant Bureau. A growing number of states are passing laws that force landlords to identify themselves to tenants, either with a notice stating name and address in the building lobby, or with full disclosure in the lease, or through some other approved method. Even if your state does not have that protection, a savvy tenant association may be able to give you information at the snap of a finger.

Perhaps they will direct you to city hall or the county seat to do some detective work, visiting the assessor's office and plowing through block and lot numbers and real estate transactions on file there. If you come up with only a corporation name as owner of your building, you can check with your Secretary of State's office for the corporate officials' names. They are the ones you need. Take any assistance you can get along the way to those magic names, because they are frequently tough to dig out. The process could be time-consuming, tedious, and annoying, but if your landlord is a true villian, you will have to have accurate information about him or her before seeing that justice is done.

delighted to offer your landlord if the upstairs tenant's bathroom is flooding over into your unit.

Who's Making All That Noise?

As has been mentioned, you are entitled to "quiet enjoyment of the premises." So how come that dog is barking all weekend long in the apartment next to yours? How come Freddy upstairs is allowed to practice—what *is* that instrument he plays, anyhow?—into the early morning hours? Does living in fairly close proximity to your neighbors mean you have to overhear every quarrel, every vacuum cleaner, every hammer?

If you have noise complaints about sounds outside your building or complex, you will have to contact the local police department or the Department of Environmental Protection. Both offices, however, must hear the noise before they can issue a summons. All attempts at mediation will be made, however, before that summons is delivered.

But check your lease. That "quiet enjoyment of the premises" mention can be interpreted to mean no *undue* noise. Occasional late-night parties, vacuum cleaners, even piano practicing well into the evening hours—all are considered normal hubbub that goes with apartment living. With today's so-so construction, you can almost expect to be able to hear the leaves drop from your neighbor's ficus tree. The only way around that noise is to muffle your apartment with ingenious decorating solutions. But if you're in 3D and 3E has loud parties *every night*, or the dog in 3C howls all day every day, then you have a legitimate complaint.

First, talk to the building management, citing your right to a reasonably quiet environment. They can approach the tenant and deal with any possible abuse. If nothing happens, then you can try talking nicely to those folks, something along the line of "You may not have noticed this but. . . . " Still no response? Then you can call the official agencies, and perhaps consult an attorney. No matter how many steps you take, put *everything* in writing. And follow up personal visits and phone calls with memos to yourself or notes to the people with whom you spoke ("Following our telephone conversation this morning . . .").

Harassment

Harassment is a particularly nasty form of attack by the landlord and is usually made to get you to move out. If you're not a good tenant, then it is obvious what is motivating the harassment (although it may still be illegal). Tenants who are harassed for holding out for more relocation money are another story, too.

More often, however, harassment is carried out by building owners who want otherwise good tenants to throw up their hands and say, "Okay, you win. We'll move out." The departures will free the apartments for conversion; or will get out "troublemaker" tenants who are organizing the building (or the city); or will remove tenants in rent-controlled apartments where the landlord is looking for higher income; or any number of other reasons.

Sometimes the entire building is subject to the harassment. The intimidation, whether against an individual or a group of tenants, can take several forms. The landlord can cut off, or drastically reduce, heat and hot water. Elevator service can be discontinued. Locks on doors can be changed without notice, and tenants can be threatened and engaged in all forms of verbal abuse, including late-night phone calls. A landlord can enter a tenant's apartment while no one is at home and mess up the place so that it looks as if a burglary has taken place.

If any of this happens to you, run to your nearest tenant office, lawyer, or legal aid office. The landlord can be fined, and can even land in jail for a brief spell. You do need special advice here on how to proceed, though, because harassment can be hard to prove. Trying to handle a severe harassment case on your own just won't work with a determined landlord.

Your lease may say nothing about harassment—after all, it was drawn up by and for the landlord—but its absence does not mean you have no protection against this attack.

Breaking a Lease

Technically tenants must move at the expiration of their leases and after they give the landlord the required thirty-day notice. But changes in people's lives do not always coincide with lease renewals. Divorces, job transfers, and just plain itchy feet make many tenants want to move before the expiration of their leases.

If you live in an apartment-scarce area, the building owner might not mind a mid-lease vacancy, since there will be no trouble finding another tenant. In fact, the landlord may offer hosannahs that you are leaving—now the apartment can get a higher rent! Similarly, if there is a sublet clause in your lease, you may be able to get out of your commitment that way. A growing number of landlords will accept a compromise solution. For example, if you find a new tenant of whom the landlord approves, you will be released.

Always bear in mind that the lease is a legal document, and if the landlord is not willing to let you off the hook, you are responsible for all its tenets until it expires. Take off in the night to avoid the obligation and you can be slapped with a lawsuit if you're found.

Subletting

Not all leases have clauses allowing the tenant to sublet. When they do have them, the wording is still not totally permissive. It usually reads something like this: "The tenant agrees not to sublet this lease without the landlord's consent, which consent will not be unreasonably withheld."

Subletting really places the tenant in an awful, Janus-like position. He becomes both landlord and tenant trying to keep his own landlord happy as a tenant, while playing landlord to the subtenant. For if a subtenant wrecks the apartment, the leaseholder is responsible. If the subtenant skips with no notice, the leaseholder has full responsibility for picking up those rent payments.

Still, there are times when it becomes necessary to sublet, and if you decide that it is the best solution to your predicament, there's one important point to note that most tenants are not aware of: Be sure you understand the difference between the "assignment" and the "sublet" of a lease. In the former you release all your rights to the apartment, and of course move out all your furniture. That is one solution for getting out of a lease, but it is not as common as the plain old sublet, where the original tenant is still very much responsible to the landlord.

Some leases will forbid subletting, but even if yours has a clause that allows it, you should still approach the landlord when a long-term sublet is planned. What about renting your place for just the summer? That's one of those gray areas. The tendency is often to go ahead and find a subtenant, conveniently forgetting to notify the landlord. A tip will ensure the doorman's cooperation. Co-op owners frequently adopt this ploy, since boards of directors usually frown on short-term rentals.

Can you get away with not notifying management of a long-term sublet, and just continue to send rent checks as usual in your name? This is a gamble where you'll have to figure the odds in your situation. If you live in a building where the landlord is just itching to get rid of all of the tenants, he or she may be delighted to catch you in a lease violation in order to pitch you out.

In some regions of the country it is against the law to make a profit from a subtenant; you must charge him or her the same rent that you are paying. Other times and other places allow the leaseholding tenant to make a 5–10 percent profit on the deal. However, "key money," or the practice of charging a subtenant an upfront fee of several hundred or several thousand dollars for the privilege of taking the apartment, is illegal in many areas. It's considered rent gouging.

There is a procedure to be followed if you desire to sublet. Usually you must send a registered letter to the property owner asking permission; telling about the proposed subtenant; giving that individual's name, address, and telephone number; and offering details about the sublease and the temporary address where you can be reached during the term of the sublet. The landlord then has about ten days to ask for additional information from you, then another thirty days to make a decision. If you haven't heard from the landlord by then, that's considered an okay. Generally you can be refused only if the landlord does not agree to the tenant you have found for some legitimate reason, or if you are moving to a new primary address and don't intend to return.

Renewal

Your lease may have a clause saying you will be allowed to renew automatically, assuming you have been a satisfactory tenant. In owner-occupied dwellings, however, the landlord may have the option of not renewing and not offering any explanation.

Some lease renewals mean an automatic rent increase. In others, the landlord can raise the rent or not—there's no mention of increases in most leases. Sometimes your lease will be renewed automatically from one year to the next without your having to sign a new form—and if you don't plan to renew you'd better be pretty quick to notify management before you're automatically tied up for another year—legally.

Depending on rent laws in your community, you may become a "statutory tenant" when your original lease expires, meaning that you are still protected by the original lease's provisions. In other buildings and locales, staying on after an expired lease makes you a "holdover tenant." In this case, the law in some states says that the lease remains in effect for another identical term; other states call for the lease to be in effect from month to month. In still other situations you can remain in the apartment only as long as the landlord allows you. See how uniform all this is?

Best bet: Check with your local tenant association, or your city or town hall, to see what protections you have vis-à-vis renewal *before* you go apartment hunting so that you can judge buildings and landlords according to, among other points, how they will treat you when lease time is up.

Don't expect to be offered much more than a one-year lease these days, or two years in a sluggish market area. Three-year leases are almost unheard of anymore.

Remember that the advantage of a long-running lease is not that you won't have to pay rent increases. Your rent may well rise at the end of each year. But if you plan to stay awhile in that building or complex, the longer lease at least gives you some protection in writing against the landlord's whims or other mishaps that could befall you.

Eviction

Probably your worst housing nightmare—certainly far more awful than being a few dollars short of a month's rent payment—is coming home one evening to find all your possessions out on the sidewalk. You have been evicted!

Don't worry. How often have you seen that scenario? Not even once, right? More likely, your nightmare might be that you come home to find a padlock on your door and a notice of some type taped to the door. Of course, that's not a sweet dream either.

Full-fledged evictions are rarer than you think, especially in these days of tenants' rights. Almost always the evicted one truly deserves to be given the boot. Otherwise, judges are loath to resort to that drastic solution to a landlord's complaint. Sometimes, though, impatient landlords won't wait for a court decision and will try to force a tenant out by changing the door locks and not giving the tenant a key, by asking for enormous rent increases, or by padlocking the door.

Legitimate grounds for eviction differ from one state to the next, but broadly speaking they fall into two categories: (1) failure to pay rent and (2) everything else. For the former, all the landlord really wants is your rent money and not a vacant apartment (unless there is some scheme for the building, like a conversion or massive rehabilitation).

In the other instances, the landlord *does* want you out, but these are not that common and the tenant often has some recourse. Tenants with a written lease have more protection than those without, and those who are under some form of rent control have more protection than those who are not. Everyone, however, is entitled to have the landlord request them to leave before resorting to a formal eviction procedure.

Some other grounds for eviction, besides nonpayment of rent, could be the following:

• Violating the lease and not correcting the violation after being warned (not getting rid of the illegal pet, for instance, or having illegal roommates whose names are not on the lease).

• Causing damage to the apartment or interfering with the comfort or safety of the landlord and/or the other tenants (persistent noisy parties, keeping a few snakes, refusing to get rid of a water bed in a building that cannot take the weight).

• The landlord "in good faith" needs the apartment for his or her own purposes, usually for use by himself or a member of the family.

• In some subsidized housing, arrest (but not necessarily conviction) of any member of the family in residence.

• Eminent domain. Say some local authority wants the building or the land for public use (usually tenants in those instances are offered a cash settlement and perhaps another apartment).

• The landlord plans extensive renovations that would radically alter the appearance of the building; for example, switching it from an apartment-hotel to a cooperative.

• The tenant has been charged with or convicted of using the apartment for illegal purposes—drugs, prostitution, arms storage, and the like. You should know that one pot bust will not necessarily lose you your apartment, but storing hard drugs could.

"Immorality" can be declared by the landlord under a "morals" or "moral turpitude" clause if there is such a paragraph in your lease, but judges do not often uphold them. It's getting pretty hard to define morality these days. It is a rare tenant who will be evicted for having a lover sleep over, or for having regular, high-stakes poker parties. And rarely is an unwed mother evicted from her building. As for prostitution, often payoffs are made to the building staff, and frequently no one bothers the professionals doing their jobs, even though tenants may complain. Bear in mind that if you are living in a two-family home, however, the landlord usually has more latitude in keeping you out or putting you out. It's the anonymity of larger buildings that offers the most protection.

Eviction is a court procedure, and there are prescribed steps a landlord must follow in securing one. It can be a lengthy process, too, sometimes taking nearly a year (which is why some building owners resort to the padlock instead of waiting for a legal go-ahead). Don't panic if your landlord is threatening to evict you for a cause other than nonpayment of rent. Usually vocal threats take the place of eviction. But you still might want to check with your local rent or housing office or tenant association to see just what your rights are. Perhaps the oral threat is a prelude to a formal eviction request, and you may want to engage an attorney to represent you. In any event, don't waste time on your own trying to "make nice" with the landlord. Perhaps in the end you will have to move, but with appropriate counsel you may be able to win some concessions from the landlord—help in finding a new apartment; a larger relocation settlement; a few more months in which to look for a new place.

Finally, a word about one of the meanest eviction attempts: the retaliatory eviction. This is where the landlord seeks to terminate a tenancy because the resident has complained about the building's state of disrepair to local officials, or has organized a tenant association, or is lobbying for rent control or engaging in some other practice of which the landlord does not approve. Leases offer some protection against this attempt, not in wording but by the fact that the tenant does possess one. And judges are increasingly ruling in favor of the tenant when these cases come to court, basing their decision on the precept that the First Amendment to the Constitution guarantees the right of free speech and assembly. In a housing context that means tenants may complain about the landlord and can organize for protest, too. Simple, isn't it? And hurray for the First Amendment!

For More Information

"Wise Rental Practices" is 39-page booklet published by HUD. No charge for single copies. Write to Publications Service Center, HUD, Rm. B258, Washington, D.C. 20410.

"The Rights of Tenants." Write to the American Civil Liberties Union, Literature Dept., 132 W. 43rd St., New York, N.Y. 10036. Price: $2.50, plus $1 for postage and handling.

"The American Lawyer: How to Choose and Use One" is published by the American Bar Association. Price: $1. Write to ABA, 1155 E. 60th St., Chicago, Ill. 60637.

The following books have been published covering individual cities or states to assist those residents with rental housing: *California Tenants Handbook*, by Myron Moskovitz et al, Nolo Press, P.O. Box 2147, Berkeley, Calif. 94702 ($7.95); *The Eviction Book for California*, by Leigh Robinson, Express Publishing Co. ($10); *Delaware Landlord-Tenant Handbook*, by Doris E. Harris, Michie-Bobbs ($12.50); *SuperTenant: New York City Tenant Handbook*, by John M. Striker and Andrew O. Shapiro, Holt, Rinehart & Winston ($4.95); *Tenants' Rights: A Guide for Washington State*, by Barbara A. Isenhour et al., University of Washington Press ($6.95).

4

How to Be the Safest, Most Secure, Best-Insured Tenant Possible

Your home is your castle. But the castle these days, especially if it is an apartment, has been taking on the appearance of a fort. There are bars now on the Roman-shaded windows and expensive electronic alarms at key entry points. The front door has a brace of impenetrable (one hopes) locks.

Unfortunately, such elaborate defenses seem necessary. Burglary rates continue rising, and apartment dwellers are particularly vulnerable. In fact, insurance actuaries report that far more renters than homeowners suffer from thieves.

It isn't difficult to see why apartment dwellers are so vulnerable. Tenants are often away during the day, leaving the way clear for criminals. There are many units that can be pilfered under one roof, and often several entrances to—and speedy exits from—the building. Tenants often do not know one another, so a burglar can pass among them freely. High rise buildings invite crime more than smaller buildings. There are stairways, corridors, and elevators in high rises that offer thieves and muggers any number of opportunities and escape routes.

So what can be done? Does "tenant" automatically translate into "victim"? Must you as a renter expect to come home periodically to see that your apartment has been hit? More and more tenants are saying no, and are being as strenuous in fighting crimes against their property as the criminals are in perpetrating them.

The most important point to remember in defending your home

53

is that burglars look for the easiest hit—the apartment with the fewest defenses, the lock that is the least trouble to pick. They literally haven't time to waste. Therefore, by taking even the most elementary precautions you are setting up barriers that should keep thieves away. They won't spend the five minutes needed to get into your place when one down the hall promises a quick ten-second access.

Here's how to protect yourself.

The Landlord's Responsibility

When it comes to apartment burglaries, courts have traditionally held that landlords have no responsibility for crimes committed against their tenants. But that has changed in the last several years as increasing consumerism has brought more tenants to court fighting what they claim is inadequate security that led to muggings, burglaries, or even rapes.

For example, if the landlord fires the night doorman who had been employed when you signed your lease, and you are robbed in the lobby one midnight, have you grounds for a lawsuit? Courts are now hearing that type of complaint. If the landlord hasn't fixed a broken exterior lock, and a burglar gets inside and hits a few apartments, can those tenants win a suit? They almost certainly can. Laws vary greatly from one state to another, and new cases are being brought to the docket all the time. One generalization that can be made, however, is that whereas landlords are not insurers of tenants' safety, these days they are not disinterested bystanders, either.

The "warranty of habitability" clause in your lease guarantees you a habitable apartment, and that includes a few basic security protections: adequate (but not necessarily the best) locks on the door(s) to your unit; probably locked exterior doors, if not the main front door, certainly side doors and service entrances; well-lighted hallways and other public areas such as garages and parking lots. If there is a laundry room, tenants and the landlord can probably arrange to keep that door locked, with keys distributed to tenants. If there is a doorman, he is expected to be at his post, not running errands for tenants or resting somewhere out of view of the lobby. There ought to be a peephole in each apartment door; this may be mandated by your state's laws.

It's worth a phone call to your state office handling landlord-tenant relations, or to your local tenant rights group, to acquaint yourself with security measures guaranteed by law in your area.

Naturally, if you're entitled to a few devices you don't now have, you will ask for those protections.

Perhaps your building has a tenant organization. That group may have been formed following a rash of thefts in your building, or because of an unsafe lobby or some other lack that was contributing to crime. If that was the case, your fellow tenants have probably done a splendid job of plugging up what you may call security leaks. They may even have invited a representative from the police department to address a tenants' meeting on safety measures to be taken in the building, in the apartments, and even on the streets outside. That service is provided by many police departments around the country with no charge to the tenant group. A strong tenant association naturally has more power than a lone renter when it comes to fighting a recalcitrant landlord, so if conditions in your building are truly deplorable, band together and take joint action.

The Tenant's Responsibility

No matter how many security devices and safety practices you can win from a landlord, most of the work of protecting yourself will fall on you.

Locks and Doors

These are grouped together because security depends not only on the locks, but also on the doors to which they are affixed. Can you imagine the effectiveness of a $100 lock on an all-glass French door?

Ideally your apartment should have a metal or a solid hardwood door. It must fit tightly into the frame, so a burglar has no room to insert a crowbar or even a plastic card. Hollow doors and those with glass panels aren't good. The average hollow door—usually found inside an apartment or house, between rooms—can be kicked in by a twelve-year-old child. Also bad are doors with the hinge pins on the outside: a burglar can hit the hinges a few times and take the door right off.

Once you've determined the kind of door you have, you can go find the best lock. Whole books have been written about locks, but the best advice is that no lock is truly burglar-proof—not in a home, not in a bank, nowhere. Police concede this, tenants agree, and burglars boast of the fact. Still, what you are looking for is a deterrent.

Two factors are always in a thief's mind while "at work": noise and time. If you make it more complicated for a burglar to get into your home, he or she will move on. So while you ought to invest in the

Safety in Your Building

Don't be smug because you feel you live in a building no enterprising burglar would touch. Today even visibly run-down apartment houses contain television sets, stereos, and other items that can be stolen and fenced.

Never leave a note taped to your mailbox or doorbell announcing that you've "just gone around the corner. Back in a minute." You're announcing that your apartment is ripe for plucking.

Too much greenery around ground floor windows is excellent camouflage for thieves. If you have any say in landscaping, you'll be safer with a flower bed than with high hedges or, worse, trees. There should be adequate lighting around those windows, too.

Arrange to have the mail taken in while you are away on vacation or business so that it doesn't clog the mailbox, another giveaway that no one's home. If the building staff won't take in your mail, perhaps a fellow tenant will. Some tenants are wary of notifying the post office of their absence, and it's true that the fewer people who know you're away, the better. So no social notes to the local paper about your vacation in Bali until you're back home.

If you are a woman, you should not put your full name on the mailbox. "J. Jones" is better than "Jennifer Jones," but just plain "Jones" is best of all. Then no one can tell if the occupant lives alone. One woman whose two roommates moved out years ago still has the three names on her mailbox for protection.

Never admit people into your lobby or vestibule just because they are coming in behind you. That's how many burglars gain an effortless entrance. Yes, you may be snubbing fellow tenants, but they should appreciate your caution. In one twenty-unit building a rash of pre-Christmas robberies was traced to someone holding the door open for a thief disguised as a pizza deliveryman!

Stepping into an unmanned elevator with a stranger can be nerve-wracking, so don't do it. If you're concerned about appearances, snap your fingers as if you've forgotten something and then step out of the car. If the two of you are waiting for the lift in the lobby, fiddle around for something in your briefcase or purse or check your watch as if waiting for someone and let the stranger enter the car alone. If it's too late and the door has closed on both of you, you're more or less trapped. But do stay near the control panel, and if you are accosted, push the emergency button or as many floor buttons as you can.

Equally frightening can be a solo trip to the laundry room. Keeping the door to that room locked can help, but that still leaves the walk down to the basement through potentially dangerous corridors and stairs. Best bet is to arrange to do the laundry with a fellow tenant, even if you advertise for a specialized buddy on the bulletin board and the two of you never do anything else together *but* the laundry.

Get your keys out while you are walking toward your building so you can make a fast entry without fiddling around out front. One woman who was mugged in the vestibule of her building no longer stops even to pick up the mail when she is late getting home. She waits until the next morning.

Security patrols staffed by neighborhood residents are becoming more prevalent in crime-ridden areas. They're effective, too. If you have an active tenant association in your building, or a concerned block association, check into the possibility of starting one of these patrols in affiliation with that group. Your local law enforcement agency will be pleased to assist all of you.

---

best lock you can afford, the *appearance* of a good defense can also help keep you safe.

Installing a new lock—including cylinder, bolt, and all attachments—is a job best left to professionals, since calculations even a fraction off in the installation can mean less effective protection. Replacing a cylinder, however, is a job you may be able to do yourself.

Buying a new cylinder for your exterior doors is the first step any tenant ought to take, even before unpacking. You don't know how many keys to your apartment are floating around, unless it's a brand new building, and changing the cylinder is a premier defense. Stop in at a local locksmith and get advice. Not only will you discover the most effective locks for the type of door you have, you'll also learn the latest news about the types of burglaries in your area, which can help. Ask for a system with a key impossible to duplicate without your permission.

Basically, the best locks are those with the word *dead* in them—as in *deadbolt* or *deadlock*. This type (costing $40–over $100) requires you to use a key when locking the door from the outside. It's best to avoid what are known as *double-sided bolts*, which require a key to open and lock from the inside as well. These are dangerous in case of fire, and are against the law in some areas.

The deadbolt is far superior to the so-called *spring lock*, which locks automatically when you close the door and is opened by using a key. These can be picked or pushed in effortlessly.

If you have a weak door, there are special locks you can buy to reinforce the one you now have. If there are glass panels in your door, you might consider covering them with wood, heavy plastic, or even chicken wire—anything to make a burglar think your place is going to be too much trouble. At the very least, have the lock some distance away from the glass so a thief can't break the glass and simply reach in to unlock the door.

Police locks, also known as *brace locks*, can also reinforce a weak door. Here a long bolt acts as a brace between the door and floor for inward-opening doors, and bracing against the walls for doors that open outward. The principle is that a burglar will be pushing against the floor or wall and not the door. Professional installation is not needed.

If you have glass patio doors, a cut-off broomstick in the bottom track, and a screw in the overhead one, can prevent the door from being lifted off its tracks. You can also buy specially designed locks for this style door.

Chain guards are a total waste of money and offer an alarmingly false sense of security. You can break one of these by just pushing your weight against it. If you want to see who's outside, make the inexpensive investment of a peephole that allows a 180-degree sweep of the hallway. Peepholes, as mentioned earlier, may be required by law in your community.

Another good (and inexpensive) investment: a *cylinder plate* that covers your lock, leaving only the keyhole open. These gadgets, which you can put on yourself, are installed with bolts from the inside, so a burglar can't pick at or kick in the lock. Cost: under $3. If you don't already have one of the more expensive locks that hide everything but the keyhole, this plate is a wise investment. Shop around, though. Some can be chiseled or drilled through.

Another good buy, if you live in a building where the door does not perfectly fit the frame, or if you have a weak door, is a steel-edged guard plate that's attached to the door frame adjacent to the lock, leaving no room for the insertion of a crowbar.

Your locksmith can guide you on all these purchases. You'll be surprised at the number of security devices available these days and at the low cost of some of them. (The lowest, of course, being a five-penny nail fitted into a window. More about that later.) Most can be installed without professional help, even by usually all-thumbs tenants.

Alarm Systems

These can range from a simple door alarm at the entrance to an apartment to a complicated system hooked up to a private security agency or the police department. Neither is inexpensive. How much you invest in this type of protection will depend on how valuable you consider your possessions and how worried you are about a break-in. Generally, alarm systems are more popular in private homes, where there are several means of access and perhaps an isolated location.

It's important to decide at the outset whether you expect an alarm (1) to scare off thieves or (2) to bring aid from neighbors or others who hear the siren. Maybe you're looking for both results.

As far as scaring off burglars, you can expect that most *will* flee at the sound of an alarm, and most will also not bother entering a home if they see a decal posted on a window announcing a protection system. But some will not let alarms deter them. They'll try to disconnect the system, or they'll bank on getting in and out before aid arrives.

You'll also have to bear in mind that when an alarm sounds, there aren't going to be many folks eager to help you, whether you're home or your apartment is vacant. Some systems periodically set off false alarms for one reason or another. Several police departments have advised homeowners that after responding to three false alarms, they won't come around anymore. One man in a fourth-floor walkup accidentally set off a simple and inexpensive alarm at the door to his apartment one Saturday at noontime as he was moving in some furniture. Not one tenant opened a door to see what was happening. Understandable, you say? Who would want a confrontation with a thief? But no one called the police, or even called the tenant to see if all was well. In this case the young man, whether he knew it or not, was depending on the alarm to scare away a thief, without a hope of it bringing aid from neighbors. Moral: Be sure you know who will answer if your system is set off, and don't be surprised if it's no one.

If you can't afford an alarm system, or if you don't want to make that kind of investment, consider purchasing just a cleverly worded decal to be pasted on the likeliest means of entrance. The trick here is to make the decal a little more than the usual "These premises are protected by ABC Alarm System." Try for the exotic, like "These premises are protected by a silent alarm system. It will automatically photograph any intruders." Most burglars are not likely to pause to wonder about the alarm system. The decal is just confusing enough—and different enough—to make them scoot.

Protected Windows

Accessible windows—those on the ground floor level or facing fire escapes—ought to be protected even more carefully than those on other levels. At the minimum, take care that swivel locks are always in place when the windows are closed. A practically free device that will afford added protection is drilling a hole through both upper and lower sashes where they meet in the middle when closed. Slip a nail into the hole and it's locked. Slide the nail back out whenever you want to open the window. This is certainly a simple gimmick that can even be operated by a small child, an important aspect of protecting any window that may be needed for emergency exit. And police say this is one of the most effective means of combating thievery. You can also purchase (under $5) and install a stop lock, which limits window openings to ventilation spaces too small to permit entry.

To combat the possibility of a thief breaking a window, you might consider replacing glass windows in potentially dangerous locations with panes of tough plastic. This substance looks like an ordinary window but is practically unbreakable. It can go over your own window or be installed instead of a regular pane of glass. It's expensive, though. Better check your local building code before purchasing some, especially for use on fire escapes or other exits from your unit.

Storm windows are good additional protection; screens less so, since they can be cut. Iron bars and steel gates also offer good protection, although they are expensive and can be unattractive. Here, too, better check with your building department or fire department before going ahead and spending money on these devices. Just about every community has rules on window protection, and some styles are strictly forbidden. There are models of gates that can be opened from inside without a key. These are the styles more likely to get a green light.

Health code regulations in your area may require landlords of buildings with three or more families to supply and install window guards where children ten years of age or younger live. You might check this one out with the health department in your community. If the regulation *is* in effect, by all means ask for the guards (you may have to ask; they probably will not be offered automatically). The heavy-duty plastic already mentioned is additional window safety for children. Far too many tragedies occur from tots playing around open windows. Provide some protection at windows, even if you have to pay for it yourself.

Fire Safety

Fire in a private home is frightening. The thought seems especially nightmarish in a high rise apartment building. Still, apartment dwellers may not be as bad off as they think. For one thing, more and more owners of multifamily residences are being required to install fire and smoke detection devices. Also, in terms of construction, most modern high rises (defined as any building more than eight to ten stories tall) are safer during a fire than single-family homes. The floors in the multi-story building are built of concrete and usually have a four-hour fire resistance rating; the walls, more than two hours. Many apartment fires can be confined to one unit or a single floor. In the average single-family house, the floors are wood and there is always the danger of cave-in.

The major difficulty with apartment house fires, however, is that the flames must be fought from within. Aerial equipment cannot be used on tall buildings.

In the case of many, if not most, fires, fire officials say it isn't the flames that cause fatalities. The inhalation of toxic fumes and suffocation from smoke can be even more dangerous. The most important point to remember if fire breaks out in your building and you must leave your unit is to immediately wet a large damp cloth and keep it with you until all is clear. You may need it to breathe clearly.

If fire does break out in your apartment, or if you smell smoke somewhere in the building, call the fire department immediately, and then alert your neighbors. If the fire is somewhere else in the building, don't leave your apartment without first testing your door before opening it. If it feels warm to the touch—the knob is a more accurate indicator—don't open it, since the corridor will probably be impassable. Stuff wet blankets or other pieces of wet cloth under the door.

If you cannot get out, immediately seal the doors with wet sheets and towels and throw open the windows. Seal off the bathroom, too, since smoke can rise through the plumbing shafts. Sit tight (that will be tough) and wait for rescue.

If you are able to leave the apartment, don't forget to lock the door behind you and take your keys. You don't want to have your apartment robbed while you're all standing around watching a small laundry room blaze. And of course, when you leave take along that damp cloth.

As tragic deaths in skyscrapers have proved, it is foolish to use elevators for exit, for too often they become coffins. Many elevators have heat-activated buttons that will cause the car to stop and open on the floor where the fire is. Talk about delivering you to disaster! Or there may be a power failure and the car will become stuck in the shaft. Use the outside fire escape or fire-resistant stairways instead. Of course, nothing should be cluttering outdoor fire escapes that would prevent tenants' hasty exit—no barbecue gear, no victory garden, nothing. It's against the law.

Smoke Detectors

This is a relatively new development that has contributed greatly to apartment safety. Your community may require your landlord to have these devices installed, not only in hallways but also in individual apartment units. It's smart to check with local agencies to see whether this regulation is indeed in effect. If it is and the landlord hasn't made the installation (not too likely, as fire departments do make inspections), get after him or her.

If you're without such a ruling, by all means consider installing the devices (or having the job done for you) and paying for it yourself. The landlord should not object, and indeed, if you make the right approach he may offer to pick up the bill or at least a portion of it. The cheapest are certainly cheap enough—around $15. But note that if the landlord installs an alarm that starts to drive you crazy by going off when you turn on the tea kettle, you cannot permanently disconnect or remove that alarm if it is required by law in your community.

Smoke detectors emit a loud, piercing wail (once you've heard the sound, you won't forget it) guaranteed to wake everyone within hearing distance and, ostensibly, allow them to get out of the area before the fire escalates.

There are two styles: photoelectric and ionization. There are points favoring each style, so it's pretty much a matter of your own preference. Do some shopping around to acquaint yourself with the devices before you decide.

The *ionization* alarm detects smoke in the room. It also emits a minute amount of radiation. According to the U.S. Nuclear Regulatory Commission, if you were to hold an ionization smoke detector close to you for eight hours a day for a whole year, you would receive only a tenth as much radiation as you'd get on one round-trip airline flight across the country. Still, there are those who say that any amount of radiation is too much.

The *photoelectric* alarm detects particles in the air—from a burning chair, say, or curtains. This style won't go off from simple cigarette smoke and has no radiation. It's also more costly.

If the landlord is required to pay for smoke detectors he will likely opt for the less costly ionization model.

Complaints abound about smoke alarms being set off by the dropping of a leaf or a waft of cigarette smoke. Not much can be done about this until manufacturers make changes in the products, but you might want to check around with neighbors and friends to see what their experiences have been with false alarms.

If the system you select is operated by batteries rather than regular household current, you'll have to be sure that those batteries are always functioning, which means regular checkups. Battery-operated detectors are easier to install, of course. This job you can do yourself, while the house-current models are best left to licensed electricians. The house-current alarm will, of course, be useless in case of a power failure (unless it has backup batteries).

When shopping for any style of smoke detector—and there are dozens of manufacturers—it's a good idea to check several brands and study the instructions and guarantees on the packaging. Look for indication that the brand has been tested and certified by a recognized testing organization—Underwriters Laboratories, for instance. If you don't see such verification, or if the name of the testing laboratory is not familiar, then think twice about buying that brand. Perhaps it doesn't meet minimum performance standards. There's nothing wrong with shopping for an inexpensive model. Just be sure it's one that will work. Good protection, you will probably find, is worth a few extra dollars.

Fire Extinguishers

Fire extinguishers in the hallways of multi-family dwellings may be required by your local fire ordinances. It's smart to keep a small extinguisher (or two) in your own unit as well. You can purchase a multipurpose ABC fire extinguisher (that's not the brand name; it's the classes of fire the model can fight), which puts out fires from

Safety in Your Apartment

Don't go to the incinerator room, or visit across the hall, and leave your door open. Not even for a minute.

It is folly to admit automatically into your building everyone who buzzes your doorbell. That is how many thieves are allowed inside.

The average burglar picks victims at random and only hits the apartment that appears easiest to enter. Therefore, at least the illusion of occupancy is important. If you are going out for a while, leave a television or radio playing, or even the air conditioner on and humming. Taking these steps during the day is important, too, to discourage the growing number of daylight burglaries. (Be sure curtains are closed so that a burglar can't see inside and *know* there's no one home.) The burglar may suspect all that noise is a ruse, but may decide not to take the chance.

Consider that burglars who work during the daytime presumably want to avoid a confrontation with tenants. Those who work at night *know* the tenant is there asleep, and this breed is likely to be prepared for any confrontation. These are the guys to worry about. If a burglar breaks in during the night, your best defense is to feign sleep. Your life could be on the line.

Dogs are good protection, if only for their bark, but do give thought to the size and temperament of the one you adopt. Is it fair to keep a German Shepherd, no matter how fearsome, confined in a two-room apartment alone for twelve or fourteen hours a day?

If you are in a ground-floor apartment or in a private home, use timing devices to turn lights on and off when you are away at night. They're inexpensive, and you should get several. You will perhaps want one in the living room that shuts off those lights at 11 P.M., another in the bedroom that runs lights from 11 to 11:30 P.M., and so on, repeating your usual living pattern. Light timers can turn radios on and off, and that can be useful in high rises and other places where a burglar inside the building would not see any interior lights.

Consider using a safety deposit box for valuables instead of keeping them in your apartment. Be sure you know all about insurance coverage for any possessions you leave in a bank or with any other boxholder. You may not always be insured for all possessions in the event of, say, a bank robbery.

Turn your phone down while you are away, so its loud ringing doesn't give away the fact that no one's home.

If you have a telephone answering machine, word the message so that no one can tell you are away for a lengthy stretch of time.

If you don't recognize them, don't allow repair people, salespeople or landlord's representatives into your apartment without first checking their credentials. That could mean calling the company where they are employed. (This is one safeguard tenants must be employing in great numbers, because many door-to-door soliciting organizations concede they have trouble operating, particularly in urban areas, because no one who is home will open a door to them.)

If you are going away for any length of time, consider having someone apartment-sit for you. Besides guaranteeing occupancy of your apartment, the sitter can also care for your pets and plants, take in the mail, and answer the phone. You can advertise for a sitter on neighborhood and office bulletin boards and in regional magazines. Naturally, references should be carefully checked.

If you return home to find your door unlocked, don't assume you forgot to lock it and confidently step inside. Locking the door as you leave is a pretty automatic reflex, so it's more likely that you have been burglarized. Instead of going in—the thief may still be there—head for the super or a nearby apartment. One tenant glanced inside his unlocked apartment, spotted the refrigerator door open (thieves find many people hide money and drugs in the refrigerator), immediately shut his front door and left. *Report the crime to the police* even if you haven't a hope of seeing your belongings again. For one thing, your insurance company will ask if you have done so.

After a burglary, have the cylinder for your door lock replaced immediately.

wood, paper, cloth, flammable liquids, and electricity. These are about a foot and a half high and cost around $10. If you buy only one, keep it near the kitchen door, away from the stove.

Renter's Insurance

Before you file an insurance claim, you'll have to prove that the stereo that was swiped was indeed yours and did cost you $900 when new. Law enforcement and insurance officials have long suggested that tenants record the serial numbers or some other identification of typewriters, television sets, and other items of value to facilitate reclaiming them if they are stolen. As examples:

• If a television set is recovered from a thief, how can you prove that it is yours?

• If a police officer is standing at the bottom of a fire escape as a thief lands carrying your fur coat, can you prove that it's your coat?

• How can you prove that anything, once it leaves your premises, belongs to you?

Identifying your belongings in the event they are lost or stolen is the answer. It's a chore best left to a rainy Sunday afternoon, but it won't take long and you'll certainly feel virtuous and safer when it's done. It's a two-part job: identifying property and taking inventory.

Identifying Property

Something resembling an electric pencil can now be purchased for just under $15 that will etch your name and address (or a design you select) on any surface such as metal, wood, or plastic. A burglar can't file off the markings without leaving damage that could lessen the value (to him) of the item, and there are methods, too, of restoring the engravings.

A number of police departments across the country offer these engraving tools as part of "Operation Identification" programs. You can borrow the gadget for three to five days at no cost. Late returns usually mean a small fee. As the items are marked, they are listed on a special form which is then filed with the police department when the engraving pencil is returned. You will keep a copy of that form. You will probably also be given decals to put in your windows alerting thieves to this form of protection.

You can identify property outside your home, too. Law enforcement officials suggest, for instance, that you engrave the hub caps of your car.

Inventory

This is an excellent means of recording your possessions in the event of theft or loss. A listing of your valuables is important, since you can hardly engrave furs, fine china, and the like. A proper inventory will detail all your valuable possessions (even the ones you have marked with the electric pencil), listing their brand names, serial numbers if any, date and place of purchase, and sale price. Sales and repair receipts and appraisal forms can also be kept with the inventory. Having this information makes dealing with police departments and insurance companies at a stressful time easier.

It's also a good idea to have photographs of art, jewelry, furs, and antiques. In fact, take pictures of your entire apartment, with all your possessions in place. You can use an instant camera so you won't have to send the film out to a stranger to be processed.

An inventory can be scribbled on any sheet of paper, of course, but many insurance companies and stores that sell smoke alarms provide forms you can take home and fill out. They'll usually have a pouch for bills, receipts, etc., so everything's kept in a neat package. It's a good idea to have separate inventories for your summer home, office, college dormitory room, boat, or camper.

You can store the inventory folder in a fire-retardant strong box, in your office (under lock and key), or with a relative or friend.

Tenant Insurance

Do you need it? You may think not as you look around your place. What's to steal anyway? But think again. If your apartment were badly damaged by fire and most or all of your possessions were destroyed, how much would you have to spend for replacements? That's all your furniture and appliances and clothes. Most tenants can come up with at least $5000 worth of belongings, usually quite a bit more, and that's a sizable chunk to have to fork over for new things if you are not insured. Remember, too, that the landlord carries insurance only for the building, not any of your belongings, and no liability coverage for any accidents you incur.

A basic tenant's insurance "package" provides the following coverage:

1. Damage to or loss of your possessions in the event of fire or theft and such accidents as frozen plumbing and other domestic malfunctions.

2. Losses that take place outside your home (if your luggage is stolen from your car, for example).

3. Payment of your living expenses if your apartment becomes uninhabitable because of fire or flood or some other disaster.

4. Liability insurance, so that if someone slips on an area rug in your place the insurance company will pay his medical bills. Liability also covers any damage or injury caused by your pet. And it includes legal costs of your defense if you are sued.

Certain special possessions or expensive art, antiques, or other collections will probably need supplemental coverage.

Shop around to see the kinds of coverage various insurance companies have to offer and don't overlook discount insurers. An insurance "agent," represents and sells coverage for just one company; a "broker" represents many different companies.

As you look around you will see that a renter's policy usually requires a *deductible*. That's the amount you must pay before the insurance company picks up the rest of your loss. So if your $700 stereo is stolen and your policy calls for a $100 deductible, the insurance company will pay you $600. The higher your deductible, the lower your premium payment. You may want to consider, however, a policy with *full* replacement coverage, which should cost you 20 to 40 percent more.

The cost of your policy will also vary according to the amount of protection you buy and the community where you live. In general, a three-room apartment should carry $20,000–25,000 in renter's insurance. That's payment of up to $25,000 in losses, and liability coverage of up to $100,000. That would cost you around $100 a year with a $250 deductible. One week's net pay is considered a good deductible. That makes your annual payments lower, and you may hesitate filing small claims for fear of cancellation, so why pay high premiums when you don't plan to collect?

Special Plans

Tenants in high-risk crime areas may find themselves unable to get insurance from the major private companies. They have to look elsewhere for coverage.

If you fall into this category, your agent may refer you to the *FAIR* plan—Fair Access to Insurance Requirements. This special high-risk property insurance was instituted in 1968 and is in effect in twenty-eight states. It consists of state-sponsored insurance "pools" composed of various member insurance companies who share any losses incurred. The plan works differently in just about every state, and while it costs approximately what you would pay for a private policy, coverage may not be as extensive. Your insurance agent or broker can tell you more about FAIR.

Then there's *Federal Crime Insurance*. Available since 1971, this plan is offered for both residential (homeowner and tenant) and commerical properties in high-risk neighborhoods. Renter's insurance will protect you against losses of up to $10,000 resulting from robbery or burglary. As the name of the program implies, protection is only for crime, not for fire or floods. If you take out a $10,000 policy (the highest amount offered), you will pay an annual premium of $120. The deductible is $100 or 5% of the gross amount of the loss, whichever is greater.

There are also a number of limits to and requirements for this program. For example, your home or apartment must have protective devices specified by the insurance agency. These include deadbolt locks on outside doors and locks on windows and sliding doors. There will be an inspection of your property before the policy is written.

You can learn more about Federal Crime Insurance from your local agent or broker, or you can call (800) 638–8780 to ask questions or request printed material. You can also write to Federal Crime Insurance, P.O. Box 41033, Bethesda, Md. 20814. The program is in effect in twenty-eight states, the District of Columbia, and the Virgin Islands.

One of the principal advantages of both FAIR and Federal Crime Insurance is that your policy cannot be canceled if you file a claim. (If your private policy is canceled, you can always appeal to your state insurance department.)

If You Are Hit

If your apartment is burglarized and you are uninsured, check with your regional IRS office about a tax deduction. If you do indeed have an unreimbursed (tax talk for uninsured) loss, you can deduct at this writing only that portion of the loss that exceeds 10 percent of your adjusted gross income, plus $100. This limit applies to all your losses for the year, not just for one incident. For more about these claims, contact your regional IRS office for Publication 584, "Disaster and Casualty Loss Workbook."

How do you prove your loss? The first step is to be sure you report the burglary to the police so it's on the record somewhere. Then look to your property inventory. You should have receipts there for whatever was stolen, and perhaps photos as well. If not, jot down everything you know about the piece. If it was jewelry, write a description of the object, when you bought it, what you paid, etc. Then show the figures to a jeweler and ask for an estimate of the present value of the piece. This can be a range, not necessarily a specific figure. The jeweler, although never having seen the item, can say, "Based on the information furnished to us, we would estimate . . ." Keep that piece of paper in a safe place in the event the IRS questions you about the deduction. They probably will.

If you *are* insured and the stolen item is recovered, you will have to do some negotiating with the insurance company. They may have paid you the full value for the piece, in which case they would now own the object. Or they may have made a partial payment to you, making them own only a portion of it. You may be allowed to buy it back, or, in the event of partial interest by the insurance company, you can allow them to sell the object, take out their share, and pay you the rest. This is the usual procedure if you have already replaced the item—if, for example, it was a television set that was stolen. The IRS will also require you to report regained property as income if you have already taken a casualty loss on it.

Burglaries do happen. But each step you take to protect yourself from a thief makes it less and less likely that your apartment will be one of the unlucky ones. There isn't necessarily a large cash outlay required, just small purchases here and there and a large measure of common sense. Then your home can once again become your very well fortified, practically impenetrable castle.

For More Information

"How to Crimeproof Your Home," an 18-page U.S. government booklet, is directed at both homeowners and tenants. Price: $2.75. Write to Consumer Information Center, Dept. K, Pueblo, Colo. 81009.

"Seniors Against Crime" is another U.S. government-produced booklet, this one covering safety strategies on the street and in one's home, and directed at those over 65; also, it describes how to avoid common swindles and community programs to make one's neighborhood safer. Price: $2.50. Write to Consumer Information Center, Dept. K, Pueblo, Colo. 81009.

"Tenants Insurance Basics," "Home Security Basics," and "Taking Inventory" are three of the free pamphlets offered by the Publications Service Center, Insurance Information Institute, 110 William St., New York, N.Y. 10038. Send a self-addressed, stamped, legal-size envelope. You can also call the institute at (800) 221–4954. Ask for their publications list to see what else they offer that would be of interest to you.

"Smoke Detectors" is an eight-page U.S. government booklet discussing the differences between ionization and photoelectric detectors; battery-powered and electronic detectors; where and how to install; and maintenance of the devices. Price: $2.25. Write to Consumer Information Center, Dept. K, Pueblo, Colo. 81009.

The National Sheriffs' Association, 1250 Connecticut Ave. N.W., Washington, D.C. 20036, offers free printed material on the National Neighborhood Watch Program. A manual describes the program and how residents can organize one in their locale. Also available are brochures on home and neighborhood security, and sample decals.

5

Coping with Tenant Life

There's more to life as a renter than the black and white of a lease form or a tenant's insurance policy. Naturally you want the best possible life for yourself in your building or complex, and that includes a good working relationship with the landlord, the service staff, and your neighbors. What follows are suggestions for achieving that pleasant state.

S. Zimmerman

Where to Complain

First comes, in a manner of speaking, the condition of the roof over your head. Some forty states and the District of Columbia now have in force "warranty of habitability" laws, whereby your landlord must provide a certain standard of service, such as proper heat, hot water, repairs made when needed, and, in some buildings, elevator service, air conditioning, and electronic security systems. Failure to provide and maintain these services violates the warranty. You don't have to have a written lease to be protected by its provisions. Even in states with no such law, you are guaranteed an apartment fit for habitation.

This is not for nitpicking, though. A sloppy paint job does not qualify as a violation of the warranty. No heat in January, and no repair person in sight to fix the broken system, certainly does.

Before taking any complaint to outside agencies, it is vital that you first discuss your grievance with your landlord, preferably in writing so that you have a record of contacting him or her and of the response, if any. Don't go directly to City Hall or to other offices; that's bad form and will only antagonize the landlord. If after repeated pleas repairs are still not made, *then* you can take matters further.

You might first call your local or state tenant organization. They can advise you of complaint procedures and offer the names and telephone numbers of appropriate agencies in your area. One woman wandered into a tenant headquarters storefront in her neighborhood—an organization she had not known existed—and found that they represented her apartment house. They took her case to their arbitration panel, and it was settled to her satisfaction, at no cost to her. Many tenant groups retain legal counsel or are partially staffed by volunteer lawyers who are willing and even delighted to fight for tenants' rights, especially in areas of conflict they consider particularly interesting or of landmark status. You can call your state Department of Community Affairs or Department of Consumer Protection to see if there is any such group in your area.

Unfortunately, many tenants take the first step against a landlord on their own, and that is to withhold rent until repairs are made, or to make the repairs themselves and deduct the cost from their next month's rent check. Withholding all or part of your rent is grounds for eviction and is an action that should be undertaken only after consultation with an attorney who knows the proper procedure. At the very least, contact your state office governing landlord-tenant law, or seek out a knowledgeable tenant advocacy group in your area that can explain the steps to take. Do not take this drastic action without proper guidance.

If there is no tenant organization in your area, the offices listed below can be of assistance in answering landlord-tenant queries. Their exact names and areas of responsibility may vary and overlap from one community to another. Complaining about your landlord, it should be pointed out, does not mean he or she can evict you to rid himself of a problem tenant. So-called "retaliatory evictions" are usually against the law, although it would work better for you if you were a model tenant otherwise so that the landlord has no legitimate grounds for evicting you when you start griping to outsiders.

City Agencies

Health Department. Call here if there are mice, rats, and/or cockroaches in your building or complex. The owner may be required to provide extermination at no cost to tenants. This office also handles complaints about lack of or insufficient heat or hot water, out-of-order plumbing, insufficient garbage cans, rubbish on the premises, and any other unsanitary living condition. It will also deal with questions about lead poisoning and lead-based paint.

Fire Department. Register complaints here about unsafe gas heaters or appliances, an inadequate fire escape system, and lack of fire extinguishers. Ask about smoke alarms required in multifamily buildings in your area and whether iron bars on windows violate any fire law.

Public Utility. If there is immediate danger from leaks in gas lines or stoves or electricity problems, call the utility that provides the service. They usually have numbers you can dial around the clock.

Building Inspection Department/Buildings Department/Office of Code Enforcement. Most communities have housing codes that place specific responsibilities on building owners. This agency (not to be confused with the local Housing Authority, which oversees public housing complexes) acts principally on maintaining building standards. Register complaints here about structural or electrical defects, overcrowding, inadequate lighting in hallways, peeling paint and plaster, leaking roofs, substandard plumbing facilities, out-of-service elevators, broken windows, inadequate security, and insufficient janitorial services. You can also ask about inspection reports on your building, but a lawyer representing you or your tenant organization may have more luck obtaining these papers than a single tenant would.

Bear in mind that in reporting complaints against your building you may win the battle but lose the war, since the building may be declared unfit for human habitation. Also, if the landlord owns a number of marginal slum dwellings, he or she usually knows very well how to skirt code violations. Maybe a few minor repairs will be made to keep the department quiet, and forget the rest. Or the inspectors may be paid off. Corruption flourishes in this area, so you may be letting yourself in for weeks and months of aggravation. If you have a lengthy list of legitimate code violations in your building, you would do well to organize with your fellow tenants and then tackle the landlord and the local governing agencies, rather than trying to right everything on your own.

Rent Office. If there is one in your community, this department handles the setting of rents, lease provisions, rent increases and rent controls. Call here to check if your landlord can legally "pass along" to you any extra charges for fuel bills, property taxes, or any other expense.

Consumer Affairs Department. Register with this office complaints about unfair practices by real estate brokers or managing agents, apartment finding services, and roommate placement agencies. (Your Secretary of State's office should be notified as well.) In many communities, this office's enforcement powers are slight or nonexistent, but they can effectively lobby for legislation in problem areas and they do manage to attract media attention to shady deals. There may be a similar bureau operating on the state level.

Housing Court. Where it exists, Housing Court has been set up as a separate branch of the Civil Court system, designed specifically to settle landlord-tenant disputes. Tenants do not need a lawyer, but larger landlords are frequently represented by counsel. The courts hear primarily cases involving nonpayment of rent, eviction, and code violation, although they can dip into other areas. The effectiveness of Housing Court is always being disputed, but whether it is accused of being pro-tenant this week and pro-landlord the next, it is a means of having your day in court with the landlord.

Conciliation Board. This office, where it exists, mediates landlord-tenant disputes outside a courtroom setting.

State Agencies

Office of the Secretary of State, Division of Licenses. You can bring complaints here against a variety of business people, including real estate brokers and salespersons. (You might also direct any complaints against these persons to the state Real Estate Commission).

Attorney General's Office. In states with well-formulated laws, this office deals with complaints about condominium and cooperative conversions and new condo and co-op offering plans. You can, for example, take your gripes about harassment here. The office also handles grievances about misuse of security deposit monies.

Outside Agencies

If the aforementioned offices cannot help you, you can take your case to outside agencies. Some that may help are listed below:

Small Claims Court. Besides Housing Court, this is another means of allowing landlord and tenant to meet in court. Suits by those two parties account for about 30 percent of all small claims cases brought by consumers. Most by tenants are about security deposit refunds, but renters also bring suit for other grievances: against landlords for a faultily installed shelf that toppled and broke an expensive set of dishes, or a neglected ceiling leak that ruined a good carpet, or against subtenants who skipped without paying rent. No eviction cases are handled here; they go to another court.

Going through Small Claims Court is an informal procedure in that you do not need a lawyer, although it should be pointed out that once the party you are suing is notified of your action, he or she may settle immediately and your court date will be canceled. All cases brought to Small Claims Court, though, must be for a monetary award, and not on the grounds of harassment, trespassing, and the like. The maximum amount either side can be awarded is around $1500, varying from one state to another.

An invaluable aid to winning your case is written documentation of your correspondence with the landlord or agent (or with whomever you are suing). Bring receipts and bills, too. All of that shows you tried to settle things amicably out of court. The tenant with the broken dishes should sweep them into a cardboard box and bring them along. The one with the ruined rug should bring at least a sizable portion of the rug.

You may be allowed the choice of an arbitrator or a judge, and you and your opponent will have to agree on which to use. If you think you have only an outside chance of winning, take the arbitrator. Otherwise, and especially if you feel you are 100 percent in the right, go with the judge. An arbitrator's decision cannot be appealed, although appealing a judge's verdict is expensive and rarely successful. Also, the arbitrator is usually a lawyer and may unconsciously side with your opponent, who may be a fellow lawyer representing the landlord. A judge would be more likely to side unconsciously with the underdog on the legal knowledge scale—you. Studies have found arbitrators more likely than judges to make compromise decisions. You will get something, that is, but probably not as much as you want.

So you win. Can you collect? If the landlord is still in town and still operating his business(es), you may have little trouble. If the landlord or a tenant you are suing has left town or gone bankrupt, your chances of collecting worsen. Hold on to the court decision, though—you can collect for the next ten years, and if the individual resurfaces you may still be able to get your money. A court clerk can advise you about collection procedures.

If *you* are being sued, read the complaint closely. If it is accurate, pay up and save yourself the time spent in court, where you would lose anyway. If you think the charge is unjust, collect your material and arrange for witnesses if they can help. If you need more time, try to have the trial date postponed.

Small Claims Courts are listed under city, state, or federal government offices. In some areas of the country they have other names: justice of the peace courts, conciliation courts, magistrate's courts. States with especially well-constructed courts—California, Connecticut, Massachusetts, New Jersey, and New York, to name a few—offer residents free "How to Sue" booklets that include maps showing you how to get to court. If you can't locate a court near you, check with your state Attorney General's office.

Arbitration. Another out-of-court means of settling landlord-tenant disputes is binding arbitration, which means that the arbitrator's decision is final and must be accepted by both parties. Check your lease to see if it contains an arbitration clause in the event of grievances. If it does not, you will have to get your landlord to agree to the process, since both sides must want the procedure. There is an administrative fee charged for hearing each case, which depends upon the amount being claimed in the charge. The American Arbitration Association offers free printed material on the efficacy of arbitration in problem solving. The group has offices in Atlanta; Boston; Charlotte, N.C.; Chicago; Cincinnati; Cleveland; Dallas; Denver; Detroit; Garden City, L.I.; Hartford, Conn.; Los Angeles; Miami; Minneapolis; New York City; Philadelphia; Phoenix; Pittsburgh; San Diego; San Francisco; Seattle; Somerset, N.J.; Syracuse, N.Y.; and Washington, D.C.

The media. Radio, television, and print news editors are always on the lookout for good feature stories. They're not going to be interested in one tenant's hassles with a landlord over a wheezing refrigerator (unless one party shoots the other), but what will get you, or your tenant association, some attention is an interesting case and what is known in the trade as "good visuals"—something about your story that will look good on television or make a nifty picture for the newspapers. An example: Tenants in one apartment house conducting a rent strike hung from windows a huge sheet with the enormous handpainted message, "This building is a lemon." They even drew a huge lemon on the banner. The press loved it. The landlord was interviewed. He promised repairs, and an editorial eye was kept on the story to see if the work would be done. Surely you and/or your tenant group can come up with an equally engaging gimmick.

The beauty of this approach is that in the interest of hearing both sides your landlord will be interviewed. If he refuses to talk, that looks bad. If you're obviously in the right and the landlord makes a weak explanation, its weakness will be apparent. The landlord will know it, and no one wants to appear foolish or unethical in front of the entire community or to endure being hounded by reporters. He or she would be wise to fix things and get out of the news fast.

Another approach for you as an individual is calling your local radio, television, or newspaper "Action Line," "Help," or "What's Your Problem?" person. Free advice can be obtained from those persons whose beat is finding satisfaction for consumer complaints.

Do you need a lawyer? There are instances when none of the suggestions mentioned here will work and you will have to retain a lawyer. One consultation might help, and for that you can expect to pay anywhere from $20 to over $100. If your landlord is suing you for a good deal of money, or if you are suing him for many thousands of dollars, you need counsel. Of course, if you are thinking of withholding rent, see a lawyer before keeping back a penny. If you have an untreated rat infestation in your building and you want to move out, you can see a lawyer to help you break your lease and get money damages, including moving expenses, from the landlord. All of these are individual cases where the only recourse is legal counsel.

Your local tenant association or consumer group can refer you to an attorney. But try to engage one who is familiar with landlord-tenant law. This is a complex, constantly changing area, and your brother-in-law, whose specialty is admiralty law, will probably be of far less value to you in this arena than a housing specialist. Lower-income tenants can seek the assistance of Legal Aid clinics.

Organizing Tenants

One renter complaining about building conditions and services is certainly not as effective as a hundred tenants uniting, calling themselves the Willow Arms Tenants Association, and then making a joint complaint to the building owner. You may have reached that conclusion after reading the last several pages.

The banding together of tenants to form building, neighborhood, city, and even state associations began in the late 1960s and early 1970s when various segments of society discovered the power of organization and a wave of consumerism swept the country.

If you think your building could stand a little unity, you will first have to find a purpose for bringing everybody together. You could use a serious matter like unconscionable rent increases, a condo

---

The First Tenant Association Meeting

---

1. Circulate a flyer before the meeting listing not only the date and time but also the subject to be discussed and any pertinent facts that will help prepare tenants for the meeting.

2. Restrict the discussion to one subject or issue.

3. Have a strong tenant leading the session, one who will keep bringing the discussion back to the original topic when it begins to wander.

4. Allow everyone to speak. First meetings, especially when the subject is a volatile one, are usually full of complaints, anger, and shrill rhetoric (another reason for having a good leader). All of that should disappear in future sessions.

5. Keep the meeting as brief as possible. The audience is probably tired after a day's work, and a meeting that drags on usually accomplishes no more than a reasonable one- or two-hour meeting would.

6. Curiosity brings out the crowds initially, but expect attendance to drop at future meetings. Understand that this does not necessarily mean less interest in the union. If you're good, tenant support will be there when you need it.

7. Send around another flyer a few days later reporting on the meeting.

---

conversion you've all heard rumors about, or perhaps a lack of proper security in the building that resulted in one tenant being mugged and seriously injured in the lobby.

The issue doesn't have to be a serious one, of course. You can call a meeting to plan a whale of a garage/lobby/sidewalk sale, or a rooftop party one summer weekend. No doubt at that meeting someone will suggest that the group become a permanent one.

That initial meeting need not be formal, but it is important that everyone who wants to speak be allowed to speak. No need to make an empire-building production of organizing, either. Some unions are put together rather loosely, headed only by a steering committee. Others are formal, with officers, a constitution, and minutes of every meeting. If you do decide on elections, you will need a president, a vice president, a secretary, and a treasurer (you will want to have annual dues to bring in some money). You will also need individuals or committees to handle publicity, finances, and correspondence, as well as an in-house contact (someone to announce meeting dates and to send around flyers).

The type of people you elect can make or break your organization. Your cause may be justified, but don't let your venom make you shrill, hysterical, or careless about all the facts and figures, especially the long-range picture, when dealing with management, local officials, and the press. You could be turning off the very people you need.

Before the first meeting you should collect any printed material on the subject you plan to discuss from your local government and your local or regional tenant association. Perhaps someone from those offices can be invited to join the group for the meeting. You won't need a lawyer right away, unless you are planning to withhold rent. Otherwise, assistance from a savvy tenant association in your area can see you through most of your battles.

To repeat a point made earlier: Never lodge a formal complaint against your landlord outside the building without first giving him a chance to respond to your grievances. The time that can elapse before receiving a reasonable response from the landlord varies according to the problem. But if you receive no quick response to emergency calls, you will have to contact outside agencies for help.

In Peace and War

After what brought you all together has been accomplished, from a rent strike to a Fourth of July cookout, you can stay united to enjoy a variety of recreational activities, and to remain a positive, united force before management. You can organize a baby-sitting cooperative in the building, and with the help of management, perhaps turn some unused space into a playroom for the kids. You may be able to win expanded parking or laundry facilities. Management may allow those of you who are interested to start a vegetable garden somewhere on the land. Remember that tenant unions can function in peace as well as war, and it is important that you remain a viable group during quiet times so that you can spring into effective action when anything drastic occurs.

Some other peacetime activities for a tenant association:

• You can start a buying club in your building, through which bulk orders of vegetables, fruit, health foods, and certain nonprescription drug items may be purchased at considerable savings. For suggestions on organizing, contact the Cooperative League of the U.S.A., 1828 L St. N.W., Washington, D.C. 20036.

• If your building has more than two hundred tenants, you may be able to secure your own credit union charter, which means possibly lower interest rates on loans and other benefits. Contact the National Credit Union Administration, 1776 G St. N.W., Washington, D.C. 20456.

• You can publish a newsletter, an excellent way of fostering good-will among tenants and of getting out important news about the building. The paper can be a typed two-sided sheet that is photocopied and slipped under each door. It can be several mimeographed sheets, perhaps with cover art volunteered by one of the tenants. Or it can be a sleek offset job. A local printer can aquaint you with choices according to the size of your building and the state of your budget.

The paper can be printed monthly, or just a few times a year, but there should be a regular publication schedule. You will all have to decide at the outset the approach the newsletter will take. Some are kept light, while others concentrate on the serious business of tenant life: reports on landlord-tenant legislation, other tenant group meetings, and the like. If you live in a building where there is much work and reform needed, you may have to look for someone in the building who can truly be a "crusading editor."

Your newsletter might include reports on your building's tenant meetings, messages from management, clarification of new rent laws and other local ordinances that affect all of you, letters to the editor, a classified advertising column, poetry by residents, or back-fence news—birthdays, wedding anniversaries, vacations, etc. The paper can carry advertising or not. Obviously the ads you sell will help to pay for production costs, but will make putting together the newsletter more troublesome and time-consuming.

Newsletters are usually distributed free to tenants, with copies also going to management personnel, to neighborhood services and businesses, and sometimes to local politicians and media persons.

Tenant association dues and fund-raising events should pay for newsletter production. Management may be willing to chip in toward expenses, but bear in mind that if you take a few dollars from them they are hardly going to stand for your criticism of them in the newsletter. In the interest of editorial independence you may choose to go it alone.

Some buildings and complexes publish newsletters and even full-blown newspapers that are entirely underwritten by building management, and perhaps written by them as well. These publications are frequently used as sales tools for the building. Naturally, you will never see a serious gripe in the ones used for advertising and promotion. You might contact one or two of the editors, though, for some overall tips on newsletters.

Roaches and Other Rabble

Following a murder and a spate of other crimes in his building, a high-rise tenant was interviewed by a newspaper reporter. The tenant remarked, "It's a lousy thing to say, but you get insensitive to it. I'm more worried about the cockroaches."

By every count the cockroach must be the most detested pest on earth. They are *the* apartment nuisance, whether the unit rents for $300 or $3000 a month. Moving to a brand-new building doesn't help either. Cockroaches feed on the remains of workmen's lunches at construction sites, so when the building is opened they have already been long in residence and are waiting to greet new tenants.

Cockroaches have been around for some three hundred million years and are as difficult to get rid of individually as they are as a species. The insect's speed and elusiveness are two of its more unlovely features. Step on it and, like a turtle, it will retreat under a hard outer shell. Pick up your foot and it's off. Even getting it under your foot counts for points.

Disgusting as they are, though, there are still debates about their hazard to human health.

Roaches eat just about anything and are particularly fond of starch, food, glue (from magazines and books), and even soiled clothing. Extermination is relatively simple in single-family homes, but when it comes to apartment houses, it is difficult, if not impossible. Still, there are ways of at least keeping roaches out of sight, and most tenants will settle for that.

Your Own Devices

Roaches are most commonly found in a building's basement or sewer lines, and from there they travel through the walls or pipes to exit at any location in an apartment. They can also be brought in from the outside in laundry bags, soda cartons, briefcases, and shopping parcels, so it's important to give bags a quick shake before bringing them into the apartment.

Maintaining good housekeeping habits helps keep the population down. That means taking out the garbage frequently and not leaving food, especially sticky bottles and cans, around. Take bundles of newspapers and magazines out regularly. Mop up spills quickly and try not to leave dirty dishes or clothing soaking in the sink for long periods of time, especially in unlighted rooms. It's the combination of warmth, moisture, and darkness that brings out roaches.

Scrubbing wood floors and baseboards unfortunately contributes more to the problem than to the solution. The water that seeps in between the floorboards will either bring roaches out of hiding right there or scatter them so that they surface in other places. Do check floors, baseboards, and walls for cracks or holes, though. Pay special attention to gaps around water and steam pipes and around window screens and storm windows. A caulking compound can seal them up, and so can plain steel wool.

To Spray or Not to Spray

Since roaches represent such nice steady business, dozens of products for killing them are available on supermarket shelves. Most don't help much. Either the roaches ignore them from the outset or they eventually build up an immunity to their ingredients, which was what happened with DDT. The problem with spraying is that you may kill one or two roaches, but the fumes that reach their nests will stir things up there and scatter the pests to other spots, but will not be strong enough to kill them.

If you are determined to spray, however, don't purchase sprays from your exterminator, which will be stronger than what you can find on store shelves and should be used only by a pro.

Spraying doesn't mean delicately misting a few areas of a room. This is a down-on-your-knees job. Spray—or better for your lungs, use a paint brush dipped in the liquid—behind the sink, stove, and refrigerator, in wall cracks (sealing them up is preferable), around the garbage pail, window frames, pipes or conduits, and the undersides of tables and chairs. Roaches love the warmth of running motors, too, so don't forget fans, air conditioners, behind electric wall clocks, and kick panels of refrigerators. Stay clear of cooking and food preparation areas, and storage spaces for food. And it's always best to keep toddlers and pets away from the solution until it dries, lest they inadvertently lap up some. The solutions, especially the popular brand-name ones, are quite safe to use, but if you have any doubt about the spray you're considering, you can call your state Department of Environmental Protection for advice.

Extermination Services

You might also consider a professional extermination service. They will do a better job and are not that expensive. Extermination certainly makes sense in a multi-unit dwelling where residents are pretty much at the mercy of communal walls and pipes and their neighbors' housekeeping habits, and where, if left untended, the problem could become uncontrollable.

Rates depend on several factors: the size and overall condition of the apartment house, the degree of infestation, whether your building is near a food store or above a restaurant, etc. Generally, you can expect to pay from $35 to $90 for an initial "clean out" of your unit, with follow-up calls every month or two costing around $10– $20. Attempt to have the landlord pay for that service; if he is not obliged to do so according to local ordinances, then try to get your fellow tenants to chip in for extermination.

No matter who pays, it is important that every apartment be accessible for the cleanout, since the purpose of that treatment is to get the problem down to a level where it can be routinely handled by follow-up calls. Perhaps a system can be worked out where keys are left with a tenant who expects to be at home that day.

Exterminators' trucks are usually unmarked, specifically to protect customers' sensibilities. The workers leave no traces behind them either.

Boric Acid

One sign of hope in the cockroach war is the use of boric acid powder. It appears to work, but it is slow-acting, so don't expect an immediate roach-free apartment. After walking through the powder, cockroaches ingest it by licking their feet to clean themselves. In two weeks' time, you should see a snow-covered corpse or two. After three weeks, nothing. This works better than traps, since the traps can't be placed on every square inch in a problem area, while the powder can. And the roaches must traipse through the dust, while they can avoid the trap.

Here too it is important to reach the pests' hideouts. Use a plastic squeeze bottle or bulb duster to cover the same areas you would with a spray. Be lavish with the stuff. It can be purchased at drugstores in pure form or at chemical supply houses or hardware stores where it may be mixed with an additive to prevent it from caking. One or two pounds should be enough for the average-size apartment.

Boric acid is not toxic to adults, and you would have to ingest pounds of it to become ill. Still, ordinary precautions should be taken to keep it away from small children and pets, and while you are applying it, away from your eyes or from any open cuts.

Conversation Piece Cures

Some last-ditch methods of control that should also provide lively dinner party conversation are:

• A *tarantula*—a method of roach killing quite popular in some areas of the world and a few parts of this country, too. Contrary to belief, tarantulas are quite harmless to humans. The spider's venom can only kill something nearer its own size—say, of cockroach proportions.

• A *gecko lizard*—a reptile ranging from five inches to a foot long that comes out only at night, same as the roaches. The lizard can be tied to a bathtub or kitchen sink or, for the more adventurous, allowed to roam the apartment. They are relatively clean, carrying no more germs than humans, and they come in decorator colors.

• The *purple pitcher plant* (*Sarracenia purpura*)—which thrives on cockroaches. A carnivorous green plant only a couple of inches high, it has bell-shaped pitchers that secrete a sweet substance which attracts roaches. After munching their way a short distance into the pitcher, the insects quietly and aesthetically dissolve. No messy bodies to sweep up.

Rats and Mice

Cockroach stories can be bandied about with a touch of black humor, but mice, and especially rats, bring no such smiles.

Mice can be found occasionally in even the cleanest buildings. Sometimes a few head inside in the fall, looking for a warm spot for the winter. Occasionally they come in following a nearby demolition. Hardware store suggestions such as mouse traps and poisons should work nicely, and so should sealing up holes or other openings in your unit. If you have a serious problem all year round, however, ask your landlord to bring in an exterminator. If you get no satisfaction, contact your local rent office and/or board of health.

Rats are more serious. Typically rat infestation has been associated with the poorest buildings, but they can be found in and around other types of housing, too. Again, tearing down a nearby building may bring them out of hiding, and so might sewer and street excavation. Areas around docks are particularly susceptible. Rats can come in through cracks in a building's foundation, holes around pipes or electrical inlets that enter the foundation, or through holes in the floor around piping. Floor drains offer another exit from the underground. Outside, rats can be found rummaging through trash piles and open garbage cans.

If there is a rat problem in or around your building, the landlord is definitely responsible for getting rid of them. Rat infestation is usually a housing code violation. Although do-it-yourself poisons and traps are available, a rat problem is serious enough to get professional help.

If you decide to use poisons as a follow-up to an extermination, or as a preventive measure, be careful which one you choose. Some are dangerous indoors and are best suited for use around wood piles and outside garbage cans.

If for some reason you are paying for extermination yourself, you should know that the cleanout process for rats is less expensive than for roaches. That's because the cockroach job involves treating individual apartment units, whereas rodent treatment is confined to the exterior and basement of the building.

Tipping the Building Service Staff

What gifts to purchase and other Christmas decisions pale beside the apartment dweller's really serious holiday quandary: what to tip the building service staff.

This is a tough one, and a question no one is particularly eager to help you with either. Many building managements clam up and offer no guidance. One's neighbors have their own budgets to stay within and frequently different obligations to the maintenance people. And asking the gifted ones themselves is out of the question. With a cleverness born of necessity, an employee may lament to one set of tenants how sad it is that he is unappreciated and not remembered. That will make the tenant dig deeper for a large tip. To another group he will cheerfully boast how kind the residents have been to remember him this year, and so generously, too. The outcome here is the same: The tenant digs deeper for a large bill, this time to outtip the Joneses.

There are ways, however, of getting through the holiday season without making tipping bloopers. Your first move should be to see if there is any established pattern of tipping in your building or complex. Perhaps there is a "pool gift," where everyone chips in a specific amount, or maybe just what they care to contribute, and the total is then meted out to employees in their order of importance. Or you may all be left to your own devices. If it's the latter, you might want to call building management to see if they have any suggestions. Although many do not want to become involved in this ticklish area, others will offer a printed list of employees and may even suggest a range of suitable tips. It's worth a phone call.

If you are left totally on your own, a general guideline is to tip 10 to 15 percent of your monthly rent at Christmas. That figure depends, naturally, on the size of your building staff. If it's just three or four people, you will probably give less. A larger and very posh complex might call for a larger amount.

If you are on a tight budget, you should bear in mind that the most important person in any apartment house is the superintendent. Never omit a holiday tip to that individual, and he or she should also receive the largest amount of any of your tips, no matter how good or bad that person's performance during the year. It doesn't pay to be on the super's bad side. If your building has a deskman, he ranks just below the super. If there isn't one where you live, then the handyman comes next. This is a person you may have tipped during the year for various jobs, but this is also a person you want to keep in your corner. Spend as much as you can. Next come elevator operators, porters, and garage attendants. Doormen sometime receive small holiday gifts because they are usually tipped throughout the year as well. Don't forget the behind-the-scenes staff. Building management or your own tenant association can tell you who they are.

Some ballpark tipping figures are given here, varying according to your own community and building practices. Tenants in luxury buildings should lean toward the upper end of the scale, those in more modest complexes, the lower: superintendent, $15 to $100; handymen, doormen, elevator operators, and garage attendants, $10 to $50; porters, $5 to $20. If your budget is so tight that extra cash is just about nonexistent, then it is certainly proper to give the staff home-baked goodies, handmade items, and any bottle of bubbly you receive at the office. If you are not hard-pressed, though, remember that what building employees *truly* want in an otherwise warm-hearted season is cold cash.

For More Information

Many state offices that regulate landlord-tenant relations offer free booklets under such titles as "Guide to the Rights and Responsibilities of Residential Tenants and Landlords" or "Truth in Renting." You can contact your state department of Community Affairs or your state attorney general's office.

Everybody's Guide to Small Claims Court, by Ralph Warner, Addison Wesley. Price: $11.95. A California lawyer's guide to that court system.

The Grassroots Fund Raising Book, by Joan Flanagan, Contemporary Books, 1982. Price: $8.75. Included are techniques your building association (and larger groups) can adopt to bring in funds. A 24-page bibliography contains the latest fund-raising publications. If you can't find this book in your bookstore, write to The Youth Project, 1555 Connecticut Ave. N.W., Washington, D.C. 20036. Please make your check payable to The Youth Project.

"Cockroaches: How to Control Them" is a government booklet available from the Superintendent of Documents, Washington, D.C. 20402. Ask for booklet #001-000-04226-2. Price: $2.25. "Controlling Household Pests" is a 31-page government booklet also available from the Superintendent of Documents. This one offers advice for combating roaches as well as other household nuisances such as clothes moths, ants, silverfish, spiders, and termites. Ask for booklet #001-000-03927-0. Price: $3.50.

6

Conversion: Does It Spell Opportunity or Eviction?

Newington is a small suburban town near the geographic center of Connecticut. Apartment buildings there are far outnumbered by single-family houses, and Surrey Drive Apartments is one of the largest complexes in town. Its seven two-story buildings contain twelve units each. The street is residential.

"This is our last home. It has everything we want." The Dabtukas had repeated those words to virtually every guest that was proudly shown through their newly leased Surrey Drive apartment. Retired, in their mid-sixties, with Ellen suffering from emphysema, their hunt for a ground floor, affordable, quiet place to live had been long, but they were now happy with their choice.

Before that first year's lease had run its course, however, the Dabtukas received a notice that Surrey Drive Apartments was to be

converted to condominium ownership. For ninety days they were offered the exclusive right to purchase their apartment at the same price that it was to be offered to the general public. That price was too high for their pension and social security income.

There was no attempt among the tenants in the complex to organize in an effort to negotiate lower prices, and little hope of success if they had. In late 1978, the Connecticut real estate market was excellent, and outsiders were quite literally filling waiting lists to buy converted units. And nothing in Connecticut's conversion legislation gave the tenants any power to stop the conversion.

Once the ninety-day, exclusive-right-to-purchase period expired, the Dabtukas were interrupted several times a week by prospective buyers being shown through their home. Within the month, they were notified that it had been sold; they would be required to vacate within three months.

But William Dabtuka was not about to settle for that without a fight. He called the mayor's office. No one there knew anything about the conversion and eviction laws. He wrote a letter to the Connecticut Secretary of State explaining his situation, and received in return seven typed pages outlining the state's condominium statutes.

The sponsor of the conversion was required to inform the tenants of comparable housing available in the area. For low-income families, he was also required to pay one month's rent (up to $500) in moving expenses. Nothing more. Since his wife was seriously ill and they needed time to find a suitable apartment, Dabtuka went to housing court and was granted a six-month extension. Ellen's condition worsened, and they were granted another extension. Finally, under pressure, the couple moved in January 1981. Ellen died three weeks later.

A two-hour drive from Newington, New York City must be the apartment dwellers' capital of the nation. It also currently has the nation's highest conversion rate and most stringent housing legislation. There, in January 1981, another family was moving.

Richard and Fran Baker had heard a rumor that a building uptown would probably soon be converted to cooperative ownership. They signed a lease there in hopes that they would be able to get a good "insider's" price, and within three months, they found a "red herring" at their door. (*Red herring* is a New York City nickname for the proposed prospectus of a conversion plan that has been submitted for approval to the state attorney general's office.)

Excitement ran high in the building, and that very night there was a meeting of all the tenants. An association was formed; Dick Baker was named its president. The group hired a conversion specialist lawyer to represent them in negotiations with the sponsor of the conversion and an engineering firm to inspect and report on the condition of the building. The tenants were in a position of power. The real estate market was now sluggish because of high interest rates, and city ordinances at the time required that 35 percent of the tenants in the building must sign subscription agreements to buy their apartments in order to convert the building and evict the other tenants. (This law now requires 51 percent of tenants to agree to purchase.) By standing together as a group and refusing to buy, the tenants could stop the conversion, or they could use their power to negotiate prices on their apartments far below fair market value.

The process took well over a year, but when it was over the Bakers bought their apartment (actually, they bought shares of stock in the corporation that owned the building and the right to occupy the apartment attached to those shares) at a price that was almost 60 percent below the appraised market value of the unit. They had negotiated financing for five years at 3 full points below the prevailing interest rate, and extensive repairs and renovations to the building had been completed before the date of conversion. Dick and Fran Baker and their three-month-old son owned their apartment at a price they could easily afford.

These two stories are true, both in their specifics and as prototypes. There is only one answer to the question "Will an apartment house conversion mean hardship or good fortune to the tenants?" That answer is "It depends." It depends, for example, on:

1. *The price of the unit.* Is it at or below market value?
2. *The condition of the building.* Will future maintenance costs drive up the cost of ownership?
3. *Location.* Will the value of apartments in the building appreciate?
4. *The available financing.* Is the interest rate low enough and are the financing terms secure enough to offer tenants minimal risk?
5. *The mood of the local real estate market.* Are there other less expensive places to live? Are people anxious to buy apartments?
6. *The income of the individual tenant.* Can he, she, or they afford to own after considering both tax breaks and maintenance costs?
7. *State and local conversion laws.* Do tenants have legislated support that gives them bargaining power?

Variables! These are but the most common possibilities and questions pertinent to virtually every conversion. Throw them up into the air, mix them together, and you'll come out with an absolutely unique situation for each unit in every building in the country. If you are a tenant in a building subject to conversion, therefore, it is you who must determine whether or not conversion is an opportunity. There are, however, secure steps you can take in making that evaluation, and people who can help you.

Why Conversions?

The first step is to understand how and why the conversion is occurring. There is nothing altruistic in a conversion. The owner of the building, or *sponsor*, is motivated by profit (or lack of it). In areas with rent controls, the rate of return on an investment apartment building is often less than optimum. By converting to condominium or cooperative ownership, the sponsor can liquidate the investment, realize a sizable profit, and go on to other things. And even where there are no rent control laws, tax laws as of this writing make long-term ownership less profitable than frequent turnovers. Rather than seek a buyer for the whole building, many a building owner finds it easier and much more profitable to sell the property as individual units.

All of this, however, is predicated upon the law of supply and demand. No apartment building owner would go through the process of converting a building if there were no buyers for the individual units. But the fact is that there are buyers. The condominium and cooperative, as forms of home ownership, have been accepted by the general public virtually everywhere. In most areas, conversions represent least-cost housing; they are a way into home ownership. Also, condos and co-ops are especially appealing to two-career couples, single persons, single-parent families, and the elderly, all growing groups in our population. And to intensify the situation, new housing starts of rental units and single-family houses fell far short of filling housing needs during the early part of the 1980s. Demand for housing and affordable ownership is therefore high, and conversion is a response to that demand.

How Will It Happen?

Like the Dabtukas, you may open your mail one day to discover that your apartment will soon be for sale as part of a condominium. In Connecticut today, you would have a minimum of 180 days' notice before eviction, even if your lease expired at the end of the

---

Apartment Buildings at Risk for Conversion

Buildings in rent-controlled areas.

Moderate- to high-priced buildings in areas where single-family houses are priced out of the reach of most first-time home-buyers.

Buildings in major metropolitan areas where the demand for housing is strong and single-family houses are virtually non-existent.

Buildings in popular vacation areas.

Any building anywhere during a time of high housing demand and inadequate supply.

---

month. In Pennsylvania, you would have a year; in New Jersey, three years. If you lived in Alabama, Hawaii, Kansas, Texas, or any of several other states, however, you would have no legislated protection whatsoever. At the opposite extreme, in New York, tenants can stop a conversion when 50 percent of them refuse to buy when what is called an *eviction plan* is presented.

In some areas, city and county laws supplement state legislation. Thus, Delaware has no conversion legislation, but Wilmington prohibits eviction for 180 days after notice of conversion and protects senior citizens and the handicapped against eviction for eighteen months. In California, state legislation is supplemented in Los Angeles, Los Angeles County, Marin County, Oakland, Palo Alto, San Diego, and San Francisco, with other local governments currently considering the issue. In 1979, in response to this diversity of conversion legislation, the federal government got into the act with a HUD-drafted bill that would have put condominium sales under federal legislation, but the bill was never passed into law. Inconsistency, therefore, remains the status quo, with changes occurring or imminent in many areas of the country.

Given such diversity, we cannot tell you exactly what rights you have in your impending conversion. Getting that information is going to take a little work on your part. We can tell you, however, where to get it and, even more important, what to ask about or look for in the printed material you receive.

First, write to your state attorney general's office and request information on condominium and cooperative legislation (sometimes called Horizontal Property Acts). Specify that you want to know the rights of tenants in a conversion. Then call the county clerk's office and ask if there are any county regulations governing condominium or cooperative conversion. Do likewise at the city level; small towns are unlikely to have specific legislation, but larger cities will usually have a housing commission or other housing agency listed in the phone book. Finally, check to see if your area has a Community Housing Resource Board. Called "cherubs" (CHRBs) after the angels, these nongovernment, nonprofit groups are organized to protect the housing rights of consumers. Often they can provide up-to-the-minute information and also explain the legal jargon in the existing laws. Ask the following questions or look for this information in the printed material that you receive:

1. *Is there a minimum time period between notice of conversion and possible eviction?* In areas where protective legislation exists, 120 to 180 days is most common, but the range is from no time at all to three years.

2. *Is there a designated time period during which the tenant has the exclusive right to purchase the unit or the right of first refusal?* The exclusive right to purchase is self-explanatory. A right of first refusal allows the tenant to match the accepted offer of an outside party and purchase the apartment.

3. *Is there legislation that prohibits the unit being offered to the general public at a price lower than that at which it is offered to tenants?* Currently, California and Oregon have this protective legislation. Florida reserves the right of a tenant to match a negotiated lower price even after the initial right-of-first-refusal period has expired. Such tenant protection laws may be forthcoming in other areas, especially if the housing market becomes pressured and sponsors of conversions are tempted by the opportunity to squeeze a few more dollars out of the tenant who has nowhere else to go or who wishes to save the expense and trouble of a move.

4. *Is there legislation that allows continued tenancy during the term of the existing lease and, after the expiration of the lease, during relocation efforts?* In some areas additional time, beyond that required for notification of conversion, is allowed for relocation efforts.

5. *Can tenants cancel an existing lease after being notified of a conversion?* Where such legislation is in effect, tenants can usually cancel a lease and move out with only thirty days' notice.

Hints of an Imminent Conversion

"Warehousing"—the holding of vacant apartments even though housing demand in the area is high.

Repeated inspections—visits to the building by the owner, the owner's lawyer, real estate appraisers, engineering firms, etc. (there is a realistic limit as to how many "insurance inspectors" the owner can ask you to allow through your apartment!).

Unrequested renovation and improvement—especially if it is essentially cosmetic.

Photographers taking pictures—usually done in preparation for sales brochures.

---

6. *Is there legislation that guarantees the right to quiet enjoyment of the leased unit?* What happens if you decide not to buy and the law says you can stay six months or a year or longer? What protection is there against harassment by the sponsor? Florida law specifies that tenants who do not choose to buy may not be denied the rights, privileges, or services they enjoyed before conversion. Other states are not so specific, but many have laws against construction or renovation activities and the intrusions of prospective buyers.

7. *Is the sponsor of the conversion required to provide relocation benefits?* There is a wide variety of such laws across the country, ranging from the requirement to provide a list of comparable rental housing in the area to the requirement for payment of moving expenses up to specified amounts or the equivalent of one or two months' rent.

8. *Are there special provisions for elderly, handicapped, or low-income tenants?* The range of legislation here is also wide and subject to change. Appeals to housing court can be made in special situations.

What You Can Do

There is something imposing about a notice of condominium conversion. The landlord (a wealthy individual, a powerful group, or perhaps a corporation) has started a complicated process. The tenants, usually with limited cash reserves and no experience in real estate ownership, are intimidated. Often as not, they shrug their shoulders and say, "What can you do?" If they can afford the price and like the apartments, they will buy. If not, they will start to look for other places to live.

Such an attitude will rarely earn you golden years in the sun. Actually there is much you, the tenant, can do. Your most important action is to make a rational evaluation of the apartment offering rather than a mere response to the pressure of a conversion. Is the sponsor's offer "a good deal"? Do you want to buy? Can you afford the price and terms? Can you do better elsewhere? As an investment, will your apartment appreciate?

Only slightly less important is immediately organizing the tenants into a group that will effectively balance the power of the sponsor. Group work will certainly answer some of your "Is this a good deal?" questions; it will probably negotiate a better price and terms for every tenant who wants to buy than anyone thought possible on the day that the conversion notice arrived.

Naturally some group and individual activities will overlap. Let's start with the steps every individual should take, with or without a group. Then we'll go on to what the group can do.

Start by Learning

Statistics indicate that almost all tenants in a conversion are potential first-time buyers. Their lack of real estate experience is a significant handicap in their dealings with the investor/owner and the sales agents. The handicap, however, can be compensated for, if not entirely eliminated. Nothing equals firsthand involvement; but a knowledge of basic principles helps one to sort out what is happening and then to make rational decisions. The basic principles of real estate are timeless and universal and can be learned without too great a commitment of time and effort. Reading is the easiest way.

Much of the material on home ownership in Part II of this book applies to condominiums and cooperatives. Where special situations apply to apartments rather than single-family houses, we discuss them. Pamphlets further explaining condominium and cooperative ownership principles are available from the federal government and private sector groups. (Some are listed at the end of this chapter.) Send for them, or check with your local library: many have extensive pamphlet files. After you have read several pieces of material, try to get other tenants in the building to read them. Or better yet, encourage them to search out and read other materials. Compare notes with those who do; explain what you have learned to those who don't. You'll find that you will clarify your own knowledge by trying to explain it to others.

Finally, like the professional investor (the sponsor of your building's conversion), use the knowledge and advice of expert specialists. We'll tell you how to do this as a tenant organization.

Go into the Marketplace

No one ever got rich sitting and reading in an armchair. If you really want to evaluate the worth of your apartment, you must compare it to other apartments being sold in your area. Go out with an agent, listen to what he or she has to say, ask questions, inspect other apartments, and finally compare those apartments and their asking prices and terms with what you are being offered on your apartment. Also, ask real estate agents to tell you the actual selling prices of the apartments near you that have sold during the past year. How do those figures compare with the price you are being offered? This kind of market research is a primary tool of the residential appraiser. Using it will help you to put the offering plan of your building into perspective.

While you are in the marketplace, it is also imperative that you become aware of the mood there. Is it a buyer's market, where properties are selling slowly and only after much negotiation over price? Or is it a seller's market, where buyers are scrambling to see new properties as soon as they come on the market, sales are quick, and there is little room for negotiation? The state of the real estate market in your area will have a significant effect upon your negotiating power. If the market is slow, the tenants as a group will be able to negotiate long and hard. If the market is quick, you may have to do your negotiating under the pressure of waiting buyers.

Evaluate Your Personal Financial Status

What does "afford to buy" really mean? First, you will need cash for the down payment, anywhere from 5 to 20 percent of the purchase price for a condominium, sometimes as much as 33 percent or even 50 percent for a cooperative apartment. Second, you will need income adequate to make monthly mortgage, tax, and insurance payments. And third, don't forget the monthly maintenance fee. The total of the second and third factors should not exceed 30 percent of your gross income, given normal debt and spending patterns.

In a conversion, however, it's a good idea to be a little conservative in your estimates of how much you can afford, since the actual operating expenses may be higher than the sponsor projects, which in turn would mean substantially higher maintenance fees after the first year. A 5–7 percent increase per year is pretty much normal, but could you manage a $50 a month increase?

To better understand maintenance fees, go out with an agent and look at some comparably priced apartments in well-established, operating condominiums or co-ops in other parts of your town. How much are maintenance fees there? Have they increased no more than 5–7 percent a year over the past few years? What caused especially large jumps? How do these monthly fees compare to the projected fees for your building?

The Tenants' Association

The strongest card tenants have is unity. They can educate and support one another, and they can pool financial resources to hire the advisers necessary to meet and negotiate on equal terms with the conversion sponsor. David Goldstick, who is a senior partner in one of New York City's largest conversion law firms, maintains that "Tenants must stand together to be effective. They will all lose if they let the sponsor pick them off one by one."

If your building does not already have a tenants' association, the best time to form one is immediately after the notice of impending conversion. Feelings are running high, and attendance will be excellent. Elect a steering committee of twelve to fifteen persons with a designated chairperson. Then establish a working fund. An assessment of $50–$100 per tenant is usually sufficient at the outset. Open a checking account with two signatories required.

The most important functions of the tenants' association will be investigating the offering plan for its market value and negotiating for a better deal. Among the professionals whom the steering committee should consider hiring are an engineering firm to evaluate the physical condition and useful life of the property and its working systems; a real estate appraiser to provide a written evaluation of fair market value; an accountant to evaluate the sponsor's projected operating expenses; and an attorney to check the legal conversion documents and to negotiate on behalf of the tenants.

Why such a big deal? Because state legislation regarding condominium and cooperative offering plans and buyer protection varies even more widely than conversion legislation protecting tenancy. Again, some states have no legislation whatsoever; others have extensive and complex procedures and statutes. At either end of the spectrum and everywhere in between, you will need a lawyer to assure that your rights are being protected both in your consideration to buy and in your actual purchase.

Your steering committee should start by interviewing several attorneys and choosing one who has extensive local experience in your type of conversion. The attorney should be able to recommend engineering firms, appraisers, and accountants that he or she has worked with and who have a proven track record.

The Engineering Firm

Many states and some municipalities require that all condominium or co-op offerings include a property report based upon professional inspection of the building. The range of this legislation runs from listing the building code violations to a detailed report on the condition and useful life expectancy of all the structural elements and work systems.

You may therefore receive an engineer's report with the sponsor's offering plan. Life being what it is, however, such reports tend to lean in favor of the people who paid to have them done. Without much effort, you can probably think of several other things wrong with the building that don't appear in the report, the two guys next door can probably think of others, and the elderly lady on the first floor who likes to sit out on the steps in the summer can probably list twenty.

So hire your own inspection firm. Supply them with a list of tenant complaints, then let them do their work. The written report you receive may sound as though it evaluates a different building from the one described in the sponsor's report. You now have a major bargaining tool for fix-up costs, a *reserve fund* to be established by the sponsor as insurance against future maintenance expenses, and price reductions.

The Real Estate Appraiser

Understand that the price the sponsor puts on the apartments is not necessarily an accurate statement of their market value. The only real test of market value is the willingness of a buyer to buy at a given price. In a conversion where the tenants are offered an exclusive right to purchase for a given period of time before the marketing of the property, *there are no other buyers*. Therefore, there can be no real testing of the market.

The sponsor of the conversion naturally wants to make as great a profit as possible on the sale of the apartments and is aware that the threat of eviction is an incentive to buy. But tenants should *not* overpay because of this threat. The question of value comes down to the word of the seller versus the word of the buyer.

The sponsor's offering plan may include a professional appraisal of the value of each apartment, but like the sponsor's engineer's report, that appraisal should be tested. Some tenant associations prefer to do their own market comparisons. A number of tenants inspect comparable apartments on the market and report to the group on price, terms, location, condition, and maintenance costs. Actual selling prices of units recently sold can be gathered from public real estate records or from Realtors' data kept on file in the offices of member firms. A composite list is drawn up listing all pertinent data, and value comparisons are made from the list. The system works if the tenants are willing to put in the time necessary to inspect and compare area offerings. Sometimes a specialized and experienced conversion lawyer will also advise tenants on the value of their apartments.

If your group feels uncertain about the question of fair market value, however, or if you think the sponsor's asking price is very high and you want more clout in the negotiations over that price, hire the services of a professional appraiser. And be sure he or she receives a copy of *your* engineer's inspection report.

The Accountant

The federal government requires full disclosure of loan and closing costs in the sale and purchase of real estate. It doesn't, however, oversee or regulate in any way the calculation of projected maintenance fees in apartment house conversions. Some states require disclosure of the building's previous operating expenses. (Among them are New Jersey, for the five years previous to conversion; Connecticut, the District of Columbia, Georgia, and New Hampshire, for the three years previous to conversion; and Illinois, for the two years previous to conversion.) In other areas, access to account books for the tenants' organization or prospective buyers must be negotiated.

Unless you have unusual faith in the honesty of your conversion's sponsor, hire an accountant to review the projected operating costs of the building; if possible, compare them to the expense records of the past several years. Sometimes your conversion lawyer will also assist in this process. Listen carefully to these evaluations, for they are essential to the question of buying or not. You do not want to start homeownership thinking your maintenance fee will be $120 a month only to discover six months after closing that it will have to be raised to $230 a month!

The Lawyer

Among the obvious duties of a tenants' attorney will be checking the condominium or cooperative documents for accuracy and supervising closing procedures to assure the buyers' clear title to their condominium units or uncontested ownership of stock in the co-op corporation. But we've already mentioned several other roles that he or she could play in the conversion process; in fact, the job often becomes quite extensive. A good attorney will, among other things:

• Explain condominium or cooperative ownership principles to the tenants and answer their questions.

• Review warranties on the roof, appliances, plumbing, heating, elevators, wiring, etc., both expressed and implied. (Statutes vary greatly from one state to another.)

• Check management contracts.

• Negotiate the use and amount of any commercial lease space (ground floor space is most common) to be held by the sponsor or controlled by the owners' association.

• Assure compliance with state or local legislation to protect the elderly or the handicapped.

• Negotiate price and terms on behalf of the tenants.

Before your steering committee hires an attorney to represent your association, ask your prospective choices what services each of them usually performs and what the fee will be. Attorneys' fees vary widely. Be sure that you are going to get the services you want and that your group can afford and is willing to pay for them.

The No-Buy Pledge

Many successful tenant groups have used *no-buy pledges* to strengthen their negotiating power. This pledge, drawn up by their attorneys, assures that all those tenants who sign it will not buy until a stated percentage of them agree that the best price and terms have been reached. Failure to sign such a pledge does *not* obligate anyone to buy. The pledge prevents special deals on the side by which the sponsor's sales agents pick off the most vulnerable buyers one by one. In New York, where it is most often used, the pledge has been upheld as legally binding in court hearings.

The Beat of a Different Drummer

There is another way to deal with the imminent conversion of the building in which you live or, for that matter, with its abandonment

---

What to Negotiate

Purchase price. In areas without governmental rent controls, 10 to 20 percent off market value is a good reduction. Where rent controls make conversion dependent upon a given percentage of sales to tenants, the sky's the limit: 40–60 percent off market value is common.

Financing for tenants. Seller buy-downs, special plans reducing interest rates by 2 to 3 points, represent real cash savings. In some areas, conversion sponsors can be persuaded to take back purchase money notes at significantly reduced interest rates.

Increase in cash reserve fund. Ask that the sponsor provide additional working capital for building repairs, refurbishing, or improvements.

Repairs or refurbishing. This is of apartment interiors, and also appliance repairs or replacement.

Right of tenants to assign their purchase contracts or subscription agreements to another party prior to closing.

Amendments to by-laws. When does the owners' association take control from the sponsor? Who chooses the management company? Is ownership limited to a certain age group? Anything that bothers a majority of the tenant/prospective owners should be discussed.

Building code violations. These should all be remedied before closing.

---

by the owners to city tax auction: *doing your own conversion*. But this way is not for everyone. If you have a nucleus of tenants that includes people who are knowledgeable in business principles, persevering, determined, fair and open-minded, optimistic, willing to work hard and long, tactful, and willing to take a financial risk, you might explore the option of forming a partnership or corporation, purchasing your apartment building, doing your own conversion, and then selling (profitably) the apartments of those tenants who do not wish to buy into your cooperative or condominium.

You will need professional help; a conversion specialist lawyer is indispensable. And you will need time; a year or more is about average. City ordinances, rehab plans and expenses, conversion legislation, and people problems will be among your concerns (and headaches). But when accomplished, do-it-yourself conversions usually benefit the tenants who become owners, and are also very profitable.

You will need some cash from the nucleus group. Then, with proof of your seriousness, business sense, and creditworthiness, you should be able to find a lender who will support your conversion efforts by allowing you enough money to buy the building and cover conversion expenses. Sometimes the building's sellers will accept delayed payment while your conversion is in process, for a share of future profits.

Choosing No

Suppose that after joining a tenants' association, paying your assessments for costs, and seeing negotiations through to the best offer the sponsor is willing to make, you decide that buying at this time or in this particular building is not for you. Have you failed or wasted your time and money? Absolutely not!

You've participated in a very valuable learning experience. Even though this deal is not right for you, you've learned concepts and techniques that will stay with you and be applicable to future real estate dealings. They are priceless and not easily attained.

"What Ifs?" for Tenants in a Conversion

What if your apartment is priced at $60,000 but your tenant association negotiates an insider's price of $51,000? You sign a contract to purchase with a closing in ninety days. One month later you are offered an excellent job in another state. What can you do?

If your purchase contract or subscription agreement contains a clause giving you the right to assign your contract, you can actually sell at a profit without ever closing on your unit. For a fee, say $2000 to $3000, you can sell someone who is *not* a tenant the right to buy your $60,000 apartment for $51,000. Everyone wins. If your contract does not contain the right to assign, you may have to close on the deal and then put the unit up for sale. You can, however, sell below the $60,000 asking price of the other apartments.

What if you, a single woman, buy your apartment in a conversion knowing that the by-laws stipulate no children under age 14 as permanent residents? Two years later you marry and your husband moves in. A year after that you have a baby. Can you keep your apartment?

As of right now, probably not, except in California. Such cases have been taken to court in New York, Florida, and several other states, and the rulings have been that a condominium or cooperative has the right to set age limits for owner/inhabitants. In California, however, children can *not* be prohibited from a condominium community. But this law is being contested, and there is much similar legal activity in other states. The eventual outcome will undoubtedly be decided state by state, but no one can predict what it will be.

What if the elevator in your building breaks down beyond repair two weeks after closing? Who will pay for replacement?

It depends upon the terms of the condominium conversion plan. How long does the sponsor have control? How long is he or she responsible for maintenance? It also depends upon your state's condominium legislation. Some states mandate expressed or implied warranties of one or even two years on the buildings' working systems. Check with your attorney.

What if the sponsor offers you a two-year buy-down at 9 percent interest, followed by a twenty-eight-year adjustable rate mortgage, but you know of a lender who will write a thirty-year fixed rate loan at 10¾ percent? What should you do?

Go to your lending institution and ask them to calculate how much it is costing your conversion sponsor to buy down the loan to 9 percent for two years. For the sake of this discussion, let's assume the cost is $5000. Offer the sponsor an all-cash deal (that is, you get your own financing) of $6000 less than the purchase price with the buy-down terms. You may have to come up $1000 in your offering price, but you will have both the security of long-term fixed-rate financing and the discount, too.

What if your apartment is assigned a greater percentage of the undivided interest in the common elements (or a greater number of shares in the co-op) than an identical apartment on the floor below and you object to paying a higher percentage of the building's maintenance costs than your neighbor for the same amount of living area? What can you do?

If your conversion is still in the proposed offering stage, your attorney can negotiate to have the share allotment adjusted. If, however, the building has already been converted to a condominium or co-op and the sponsor is simply selling the units, a change in undivided interest ownership of the common elements or shares of stock assigned to your apartment can be made only by unanimous vote of the unit- or share-owners. If the unit below yours has been sold, its owner can vote to keep the lower share of the maintenance payments exactly as it is, and that one vote will prevent any change.

For More Information

Books:

Bullock, Paul, *How To Profit From Condominium Conversions*, Enterprise Publishing, 1981.

Clurman, David, *Condominiums and Cooperatives*, John Wiley & Sons, 1983. $46.95

Goldstick, David T., and Janik, Carolyn, *The Complete Guide to Co-ops and Condominiums*, New American Library, 1983. $7.95

Pamphlets:

"Condominium Buyers Guide," published by the National Association of Home Builders, 15th and M Sts. N.W., Washington, D.C. 20005

"The Condominium Home—a Prospective Owner's Guide," published by the National Association of Realtors, 430 N. Michigan Ave., Chicago, Ill. 60611. $1.00

"Questions About Condominiums—What to Ask Before You Buy," published by U.S. Dept. of Housing and Urban Development, Washington, D.C. 20410

Annotated Bibliography:

"The Conversion of Rental Housing to Condominiums and Cooperatives," U.S. Dept. of Housing and Urban Development, Office of

Policy Development and Research, Washington, D.C. 20410. Contains a list of books, pamphlets, and magazine articles on national and local aspects of condominium or cooperative conversion. Also addresses and prices.

7

Single-Family Houses and Not-Quite-Ordinary Rentals

City dwellers usually envision high-rise towers when they think of rentals. Suburbanites and people in small towns think of garden apartment complexes, duplexes, two- or three-story low-rise developments, or perhaps units in multi-family houses. All of these rental units are apartments, and taken together, apartments represent the rental housing of the majority of American tenants, but by no means *all* American tenants.

There are thousands of people who rent single-family houses. And there are people who pay "landlords" for the use of houseboats, off-season vacation trailers, or even out-of-use lighthouses. In truth, you can rent practically any kind of shelter if you look hard and long enough for it. And you can be pretty sure that somewhere else in the country, someone else has had the same idea, the same problems, and the same advantages.

Since offbeat rental possibilities are limited primarily by human ability to reach an agreement over how much money a certain amount and kind of space is worth (and sometimes by zoning laws), we will mention only the most common of these. If you were to pursue any one rental form, however, you would probably find a good many unexplored "opportunities." Let's start with the most common nonapartment rental: the single-family house.

Single-Family Houses

George Eliot and Yeats caused rental problems for the Johnson family, Yeats being an Irish wolfhound and George Eliot a domesticated alley cat. High rise, low rise, garden—the variety didn't matter; no rental agent or landlord would have them.

The situation was getting desperate when the Johnsons turned to the houses-for-rent section of their newspaper. On their third call they chanced upon a dog-lover who was being assigned to Saudi Arabia for two years. There was even a fenced dog run on the property. Owners and prospective tenants, human and otherwise, liked each other at first sight, and it was handshakes and hugs all around when the Johnsons agreed to care for Heide, a German Shepherd, during the time in Saudi Arabia.

If pets are a part of your family, your chances for finding a rental are better in the single-family house market than in multi-unit buildings. Homeowner landlords are more likely to have had pets themselves. Also, the pet problems that often occur in shared spaces such as hallways, elevators, parking lots, and playgrounds are not a factor in the rental.

Children are also more readily accepted, especially in suburban neighborhoods where "three kids and a dog" are a way of life. Landlords, after all, are human, and subconsciously at least, they want to like their tenants. "Liking" often equates to "being like us" and, sometimes, to fitting into the neighborhood.

If you have neither children nor pets, however, why would you choose to rent a house rather than an apartment? Most people wouldn't, and they have good reasons for choosing more conventional rental housing. Most common among the *disadvantages* of single-family house rental are:

• *Time and work*. Day-to-day maintenance work such as mowing, raking, and snow shoveling is usually expected of the tenants in a single-family house. In a sense they must "act like homeowners" although they don't share in the tax benefits or property appreciation of homeowning.

• *Added costs*. It costs more to heat a single-family house than it does to heat an apartment, since the entire outside perimeter of the living space is usually exposed to outside temperatures. Most house tenants must also pay for water and, in many towns, for refuse collection. Hot water is rarely included in the rent of a single-family house, and heating that water can add many dollars to the electric bill or keep an oil furnace running all summer.

• *Transportation*. Especially in suburbia, most single-family houses have little or no access to public transportation. Renting a house can make one and possibly two cars necessary, or the stay-at-home spouse may be imprisoned during working hours. Monthly gasoline costs also go up when picking up a quart of milk means driving two miles, or Cub Scouts require a three-person carpool.

• *A distant landlord.* When a pipe freezes and bursts in your rental house in Fargo, North Dakota, at 11 P.M., and your landlord lives in Miami Beach, what do you do? The lack of a resident super or maintenance staff of any kind is sometimes a problem for the house tenant who often must make and pay for emergency repairs. Costs are settled with the landlord later. Sometimes it works out all right and sometimes it doesn't.

• *A limited market.* There simply are not many houses for rent in any given area at any given time, so choices for the tenant are limited. Finding a house to rent takes perseverance and a lot of work. You'll have to keep in touch with real estate agents, fee-charging rental referral companies, newspaper ads, and anyone else who might have a lead on "special" real estate situations.

Despite these disadvantages, however, there are people of all types, with and without children and pets, who do rent single-family houses. Why? Because there are advantages as well:

> • *Privacy.* Like the homeowner, the house tenant can put some amount of space between himself or herself and the neighbors. The yard which must be mowed is also a place to sunbathe, to play ball with the dogs, or to hold a family get-together. Indoors, there are no shared walls to be pounded upon if a party gets a little noisy at 1 A.M. or an argument gets a little out of hand.
>
> • *Spaciousness.* It is generally acknowledged that you will get more living space for your dollar in a single-family house than you will in an apartment. This fact may not hold true when the extra costs of house rental are added in, but many tenants prefer space to service and convenience.
>
> • *The land, the basement, and the garage.* For the gardener, the woodworker, or the antique car restorer who must rent, there may be no other option but a house. Houses provide space and facilities for hobbies. Even wallpapering and redecorating are often allowed.

Unlike apartment buildings, single-family houses are not built with the express intention of renting. Any builder will tell you that would not be profitable. So rental somehow "happens" in the history of a house. Because of this chance availability, there is no clustering of rental houses; you'll find them in every price range and scattered in every part of town.

Rental house owners generally fall into one of two categories: homeowners who are forced to rent, and investors. The nature of your landlord will affect the character of your tenancy.

Investor-Owned Houses

Most people think of the single-family house investor-landlord as an individual who had some extra cash, saw a good deal, bought a house, and is now renting the property for a period of time before putting it up for sale. These investors do exist in great numbers. They often advertise and show their own properties and collect the rent. It's not unusual to find them doing or supervising repair or maintenance work.

But recent high interest rates have somewhat diminished the number of such private investor landlords, especially in areas where tight money has prompted lenders to limit mortgage loans to owner-occupied dwellings. At the same time the economic bad times increased the number of other types of investor-owners. Financial institutions sometimes rent houses acquired through foreclosure. Builders sometimes rent their model homes or other houses that they built on speculation, often with an option to buy or right of first refusal included in the deal. Relocation companies, acting on behalf of corporate clients, sometimes rent the houses sold to the company by transferred executives. And in recent years, several new and growing investment firms have chosen to specialize in limited partnership investment in single-family residences. They buy the houses, rent them for a time, and then sell at a profit.

If the owner of your rental house is a private individual "trying to make a buck" in real estate, there are almost unlimited possibilities to the rental arrangements you can negotiate. You may or may not have a written lease. Your rental term may be short, long, or unspecified. And work that you do, such as interior or exterior painting or landscape planting, may be exchanged for a lower rent.

If your investor landlord is a real estate professional or a corporation, however, you will probably be required to conform with "usual and customary" rental practices. Among these are:

• *The written lease.* Many tenants don't bother to read theirs before signing; *you* should. Check for deductibles on repairs. Do you pay the first $50 if the dishwasher breaks down? Check also for an option to buy or right of first refusal clause. And check to see if a continued month-to-month tenancy is allowed at the end of the lease if the house is put up for sale.

Two Inside Tracks to Homebuying for Tenants

The Option

An option could be your ticket to a housing bargain. There are only a few agreements in the real estate world that benefit one party in a transaction without providing some benefit in return to the other party, and the option is one of them. All the pluses fall on the side of the buyer. But to reap the benefits you must understand how an option works and why it is valuable.

A tenant's option on a single-family rental house or condominium guarantees you the right to buy the home at an agreed-upon price during an agreed-upon period of time. At no time, however, and under no circumstances are you ever obligated to buy the property unless you exercise the option and sign a contract to purchase. The owner, on the other hand, cannot sell the property to anyone else before the expiration date of your option. And the option price cannot be changed.

Since the property's price tag is agreed upon when the option is signed, time can be very profitable to you. If the house appreciates quickly while you live in it, you can exercise the option and buy it at what has become a bargain figure. Yet you are completely protected from the risk of losing money in a sour economy or a sluggish local real estate market. If the house does not appreciate well during your option period, or if you find serious faults in its structure or working systems, or if you simply don't like living there, you can walk away without exercising the option.

In commercial real estate, options are investments and cost money. The right to buy or lease a property at a given price during a given period of time is sold for an agreed-upon dollar figure. In residential real estate, however, an option to buy is most often written as a clause in a lease. There is rarely a *consideration* (charge) beyond the monthly rent. If, however, an option fee does come up in your discussion of a residential property, don't turn away too quickly. If you think you might buy the house you are about to rent, consider whether or not the potential bargain would be worth the fee. If you are willing to pay now for the possibility of savings six months, a year, or two years in the future, ask that the option clause be written as a *full credit option*. Under this type of agreement, the price paid for the option is fully credited toward the purchase price, if the option is exercised.

Some homeowner/sellers who are forced to rent their homes include an option in their leases as an inducement to a quick rental. A few even go so far as to agree to credit a portion of the rent toward the purchase price if the option is exercised. If such an offer is mentioned to you on a property that you like, be sure that it is clearly written into the lease agreement. It's an opportunity you don't want to lose.

The Right of First Refusal

A right of first refusal may keep you from being evicted from a house or condominium that you are renting, and it may get you a bargain price, too, but there are no guarantees. Tenants holding a right of first refusal have the first opportunity to buy the house in which they are living when it is offered for sale. The best agreements allow tenants to purchase the property by matching any bona fide written offer that is acceptable to the seller.

Landlords prefer the right of first refusal to the option since it does not set a price or a time for the property's sale. In fact it does not even guarantee that the property will be offered for sale. It simply states that if it is offered for sale, the tenant will get a chance to buy it. Thus the landlord retains the advantage of deciding when and if to sell and collects any potential appreciation in value during the time that you occupy the property.

For tenants, the right of first refusal is less advantageous than the option. Within a certain time after the house is first offered for sale, or whenever an offer acceptable to the seller is made by a third party, you must decide to buy or not to buy. You have no control over the price. Exercising a right of first refusal is really a response to the actions of another party.

Let's assume, for example, that the househunting Pinkmans fall in love with the house in which you are living. Blinded by infatuation, they offer your landlord $5000 *more* than what you had decided was a fair price for the house. In order to exercise your right of first refusal, you would need to match their price. If you were unwilling to do so, the property would be sold to the Pinkmans, and you, in all likelihood, would be evicted.

On the other hand, let's assume that the Greenbacks, savvy buyers especially skilled at negotiating, convinced your landlord to sell them the house at a price $3000 below what you had secretly been willing to pay for it. You could then exercise your right of first refusal and buy the property at the bargain price. The Greenbacks would get nothing for their negotiating efforts.

So you can see that waiting to exercise a right of first refusal is a chancy thing. It may work for you, and it may work against you. If you have a choice, always choose the option. If there is no choice, a right of first refusal is better than no protection at all.

• *A twelve-month lease.* Leases of less than a year are rare for professionally owned single-family rentals. When the lease runs more than two years, most landlords include a rent escalation clause, but even with such a clause, a long-term rental commitment is hard to come by.

• *A required security deposit.* Plan on putting down a month's rent at least, sometimes a good deal more. To protect your money, be prepared to do an inspection of the property with the rental agent just prior to your occupancy. Note the contents of every room and the condition of the structure and all working systems. Date your inspection sheet, sign it, have the rental agent sign it, keep one copy for yourself, and give one to the agent. (See the sample inspection form on pages 116–119.) There will be another inspection when you vacate, and you should be there with the agent when it is done. The same form should be used and you and the agent should discuss (and agree upon) what damage has occurred, if any, that is beyond normal wear and tear.

• *Professional property management.* Expect that an agent will show the property, draft the lease, collect the rent, and authorize necessary repairs. Such professional management often involves more red tape than dealing directly with the owner, but on the other hand, you know that you won't be stuck with a flooded basement while the owner is touring African game preserves.

Homeowners Forced to Rent

Few homeowners who must move from their homes can afford to let them stand empty for very long. Most homes are mortgaged, and mortgage payments, to say nothing of taxes, insurance, and maintenance costs, on unoccupied property are a huge cash drain. So the houses are rented.

Homeowner-Landlords Who Plan to Reoccupy

Interest rates in double digits have prompted many corporate executives to ponder the wisdom of accepting a transfer. Increasingly, these people are negotiating temporary transfers, a "tour of duty" in another area lasting two to five years with written guarantees that they will be brought back to their present location. When such an arrangement is made, these business people often rent their houses in order to keep their low-interest-rate mortgages.

Such homeowners-turned-landlords usually seek a very particular kind of tenant, as much like themselves as possible. In fact, another temporarily transferred family is ideal. Stability is a primary consideration, and a family willing to make a commitment to remain in the house the entire time that the owner is away and then move out whenever the owner returns might be able to negotiate a lower rent.

Such long-term house rentals usually do not include furnishings, except in cases where the transfer is to a foreign country. Then the homeowner-landlord sometimes prefers to leave belongings in the house for the use of the tenants, rather than in storage.

There is rarely any professional management of the property in situations where the homeowner plans to reoccupy. Rents are mailed directly to the owner, and the tenants are usually responsible for day-to-day maintenance. When there is property management, it is usually a local real estate agency performing the function for a fee, or a friend or relative who lives nearby.

In shorter rentals involving a sabbatical leave of six months to a year or an extended vacation of several months, houses are usually rented furnished. (The cost of moving the furniture out, storing it, and moving it back in is too great to be economically feasible over a short period.) Often there is no written lease, high expectations for care and maintenance, relatively low rent, and a respectable reliance on the goodwill of both parties.

If you do rent a house for a short-term occupancy, try to get the name of a local friend or relative of the homeowner-landlord who is willing to take the responsibility for decisions in the event of an emergency. Who will do the repair work if lightning strikes a nearby tree and it crashes through the roof? Should you contract to have it patched, or get a new roof? What color? What kind of roofing? These questions are impossible for a tenant to answer, especially if the landlord is away studying the reproduction habits of insects on the Canadian plains.

Homeowner-Landlords Who Must Sell

When homeowners must sell their homes and can't find a buyer, they soon find themselves scraping the bottom of their financial barrel. Renting then becomes a means of cash income, a way to keep solvent until things "get better."

Some such homeowners are willing to remove their property from the market for a year or more in the hope that times will be better later. You, the tenant, can usually negotiate a lease of a year or more with the possibility of month-to-month extensions when the house is put back on the market. Try also for an option to buy at the market value when you take occupancy (you and the homeowner-landlord must agree upon and name the dollar figure). The option should run to the expiration date of your lease. You might even try to have part of your rent money credited toward the purchase price if you do exercise your option to buy.

In times of high interest rates and tight money, there are always some homeowner-sellers who want to rent their homes for the cash income but also want to keep the property on the market. They invariably choose to rent on a month-to-month basis. Month-to-month is acceptable if you only want a short-term rental, but be sure you and the homeowner agree to two months' notice before eviction. (This is not an unreasonable request, since closing procedures prior to a house sale routinely take four to six weeks.) Also be sure, before you move in, that you'll be able to tolerate the intrusions of househunters and real estate agents.

An option to buy is not possible in this kind of situation since the owners want to sell as quickly as possible and an option would prevent any sale except to you. You can, however, have the right of first refusal written into your rental agreement, and you should try for it if you are even remotely interested in owning the property. It will cost you nothing and might buy you a bargain. Imagine, for example, that you rent month-to-month for nine months before someone makes the homeowner-seller an offer $20,000 below market value. The price is negotiated up $5000, but the weary homeowner finally succumbs and accepts the offer. At that time, if you choose, you can step in and buy the house for $15,000 less than you think it's worth.

Be aware, however, that some homeowner-sellers refuse to give tenants the right of first refusal because they know that real estate agents are less enthusiastic about selling such properties. In other

Move In/Move Out Inspection Checklist

Inspections of the property should be done simultaneously by the owner or the owner's agent and the tenant. Evaluations and inventories made on this sheet should be agreed to by both parties, or differences of opinion noted. Both the owner or agent and the tenant should sign and keep a copy.

Address _____

	Move In	Move Out
Present at inspection:		
Tenant		
Owner or agent		
Date		

EXTERIOR

	Move In	Move Out
Windows		
If broken or cracked or storms missing, name room		
Siding		
Note broken shingles, dented aluminum, chipped stucco, any defacement		
Gutters and downspouts		
Note condition, missing pieces, etc.		
Mailbox		
Note style, location		
Outdoor lighting		
Name fixtures, note condition		
Fences		
Note broken boards, holes, etc.		
Swimming pool		
Note condition		
Lawn, shrubs, and driveway		
Note cracked or broken blacktop; pits or ruts		

	Move In	Move Out

Lawn, shrubs, and driveway (cont.)
in lawn; broken branches
caused by accident;
and list lawn
and garden furniture

Garage or outbuildings
Note general condition;
condition of doors and
windows; cracked slabs;
and whether garage door
opener works

INTERIOR

Basement and Working Systems

Heat
Note condition of ducts,
registers; and whether
system is functioning

Plumbing
Working sump pump?
Condition of pipes?
Leaky faucets? Check
under cabinets for
leaky pipes

Electricity
Check for frayed
wires, broken fixtures,
switches that do not
work

Room Inventories

Kitchen
List appliances, check
for working condition;
note floor covering,
condition of walls,
moldings, doors,
ceilings

Living Room
Note type and condition
of floor covering, wall
covering, ceiling,
doors and moldings;
also light fixtures,

	Move In	Move Out
Living Room (**cont.**) fireplace fixtures: list draperies, shades, window hardware, and note condition		
Dining Room Note type and condition of floor covering, wall covering, ceiling, doors and moldings, light fixtures, built-in furniture; list draperies, shades, window hardware, and note condition.		
Family Room Note type and condition of floor covering, wall covering, ceiling, doors and moldings, fireplace fixtures; list draperies, shades, window hardware, and note condition		
Bathroom 1 (Color:) Note condition of tile. and fixtures, light fixtures, floor covering		
Bathroom 2 (Color:) Note condition of tile and fixtures, light fixtures, floor covering		
Bathroom 3 (Color:) Note condition of tile and fixtures, light fixtures, floor covering		
Bedroom 1 (Color:) Note floor covering, condition of ceiling, light fixtures, doors and moldings, window hardware, and draperies or shades		

	Move In	Move Out
Bedroom 2 (Color:)		
Note floor covering,		
wall covering,		
condition of ceiling,		
light fixtures, doors		
and moldings, window		
hardware, and draperies		
or shades		
Bedroom 3 (Color:)		
Note floor covering,		
wall covering,		
condition of ceiling,		
light fixtures, doors		
and moldings, window		
hardware, and draperies		
or shades		
Bedroom 4 (Color:)		
Note floor covering,		
wall covering,		
condition of ceiling,		
light fixtures, doors		
and moldings, window		
hardware, and draperies		
or shades		
Other Rooms		
Inventory, condition,		
comments		
Notes:		

Tenant_____ Owner or agent_____
       Signature   Signature

words, the right of first refusal is a bonus if you get it, but not a necessity for a mutually beneficial rental.

Selecting the Single-Family Rental

More often than not, there are few properties to choose among, perhaps a half-dozen houses in your price range and acceptable geographic area. But when you do have choices, you should use the same criteria in selecting a rental house that you would use in selecting a home purchase. Read the chapters on location and features to watch for and watch out for in Part II of this book. Inspect the property and its working systems before you sign a lease, since you want as few maintenance problems as possible. And compare cost to housing value.

Research conducted by Epic Realty Services Inc., the nation's largest single-family house and condominium property management firm, indicates that lower-priced houses rent at a greater percentage of their value than higher-priced houses. Which means that, if you can afford it, you might be able to get a lot more house for $100 more a month rent.

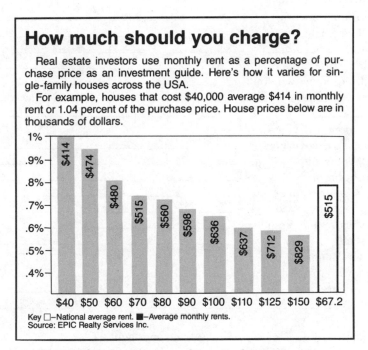

How much should you charge?

Real estate investors use monthly rent as a percentage of purchase price as an investment guide. Here's how it varies for single-family houses across the USA.

For example, houses that cost $40,000 average $414 in monthly rent or 1.04 percent of the purchase price. House prices below are in thousands of dollars.

Key □—National average rent. ■—Average monthly rents.
Source: EPIC Realty Services Inc.

Reprinted with permission of Epic Realty Services, Inc.

Condominiums, Co-ops, and Sublets

Condominiums, co-ops, and sublets are usually apartments, not single-family houses, and they're not exactly offbeat rentals either. We've included them here, however, because you can rent one from its owner or current tenant, and that situation causes other special situations.

In a condominium or co-op community, you must abide by the bylaws or move out. If the bylaws say "no children," your 12-year-old daughter cannot live with you three months of the year even if she's pretty as a picture and a joy to be with. And if the bylaws state that you are allowed to keep a pet only if it can be carried in elevators, on stairs, and through shared space areas, you will have to carry your German Shepherd. If you put him down at the top of the stairs, you can be evicted, even if the owner of your condo apartment loves dogs and was completely agreeable to your keeping one.

Bylaws extend even further into the lives of co-op apartment owners, because the owner of the apartment doesn't really own it. He or she owns stock in the corporation that owns the building. With the stock goes a proprietary lease for the apartment. Your rental of someone else's co-op apartment therefore is really a sublet.

Usually the board of directors of a co-op building has the right to approve or deny a shareholder's right to sublet, *and* the right to approve or deny any prospective tenant for that sublet. An interview between the prospective tenant and the board is often required. If you are called to such a meeting, be honest and be yourself—you don't want to live where you're not wanted. If you are refused tenancy, you have little recourse. Courts have upheld boards' rights to refuse occupancy for any reason or no reason (except, of course, those reasons prohibited by fair housing laws).

In rental buildings, sublets of apartments are common in areas where good rental housing is hard to come by, particularly in major cities and in areas where rent control keeps a lid on rent escalation. A tenant who plans to be away for several months or even a year or more will often try to sublet the apartment, planning to reoccupy on return under the terms of the old lease and with rent control still in effect. If you consider renting such an apartment, you will pay your rent to the tenant, who will pay his or her rent to the landlord. Before moving in, however, be certain that the sublet is allowed under the terms of the original lease. If it isn't, you may find yourself out on the street.

In-Law Apartments

It's not uncommon for the zoning board in a moderately large city to hear petitions for variances to allow the remodeling of a house in a single-family housing zone so that aging relatives may be given a place to live. Additions are built, separate entries are cut into walls, and kitchens and baths are added to these houses in order to allow the relative privacy, self-sufficiency, and the nearness and support of family members. Few such requests are denied by zoning boards.

It's somewhat more difficult to get approval for an addition for a newly married son or daughter, however. Given current cohabitation practices, "single-family" has been loosely interpreted over the past decade, but many towns maintain that a house in a single-family zone should have only *one* kitchen. Yet a separate kitchen is essential to providing privacy and autonomy to young marrieds or other relatives living on the same land as the house's owner. So the impasse over "single-family" zoning is really a question of how many kitchens. Some zoning boards insist on proof of economic need or hardship, and the variance can be tied up in paperwork for months.

Quietly, however, in cities, towns, and rural areas across the nation, people have responded to the recent housing crunch by doubling up. In-law apartments (more properly called *accessory apartments* since they aren't always for in-laws) have been added to many homes without the consent or knowledge of the local zoning board. And often when the board does know about the conversion or addition, it overlooks the fact. Only if and when someone formally complains are orders issued to stop construction work. And once an apartment is complete and people have moved in, it takes court procedures to evict them.

So houses with two kitchens and two "families" living in them exist in single-family-zoned neighborhoods, both legally and illegally. If you are renting one of the illegal apartments, you could be evicted if a neighbor is somehow prompted to file a complaint. But what if you thought you were renting a legal apartment? For example, you may be in an apartment that had originally been built with zoning board approval for an elderly relative who had died within a year of moving in. Your apartment may or may not be legal.

In some instances the variance for two-family occupancy in a one-family zone reverts to the original zoning upon the death of the relative. Such houses are often seen advertised in newspapers with captions like "mother/daughter dream house," and they often sit long upon the market waiting for the "right" buyer.

But much more often, the original owners of the house find a tenant for the apartment and life goes quietly on. If this is done without zoning board consent (which in practice it usually is), there is always the possibility that someone will complain and the matter will be brought before the board. If it is, lawyers and owners usually argue that the precedent for occupancy of the apartment had been set by "prior use." Another common plea used to justify the rental is economic hardship. Something like: "We spent all this money for our relative's apartment and he died three months after he moved in. We can't afford to carry the payments on the construction loan without financial help. We must therefore rent the unit." Unless there is a vociferous complaint from several neighbors, most boards will allow the rental.

If you choose this kind of rental, however, be aware that there is the possibility, though slight, that you may be forced to move or at least have to wait out several months of zoning board hearings. You may decide that this risk is a small price to pay for the opportunity to live in a neighborhood that you could not otherwise afford.

Few of these single-family-zone accessory apartments are ever advertised in newspapers. They are rented through word of mouth, friends, associates, and what seems to be an underground grapevine. Often tenancy is without a written lease, everything being cemented by a handshake.

Mobile Homes

"Oh no!" you think to yourself, "You'll never get me to live in one of those oversized tin shoeboxes, even as a rental!"

But look again before you voice those thoughts. Mobile homes are now officially called "manufactured homes," and they've changed. There are only a few crowded, highway-side, dusty "trailer parks" left. Newer parks have paved roads, landscaping, recreation areas, and often spacious but relatively inexpensive rental units.

These mobile homes usually become rental units when their owners move out and decide *not* to have their home moved. Often the owner of the park (or the sponsor in the case of a mobile home park condominium conversion) will purchase selected homes at bargain prices. Sometimes these models are put back on the market for sale, and sometimes they are rented.

Tenants pay for their own utilities and heating, but their homes are usually completely furnished. For the most part these rentals are good deals; their primary drawback, however, is usually poor location. Many parks are still situated in out-of-the-way places where public transportation is not always available. A car may be a necessity, and monthly gasoline costs might well be higher than those for apartment tenants. On the other hand, parking is usually free and at your doorstep.

Carriage Houses and Guest Houses

Have you ever dreamed of living on a 20-acre estate with space for your dog to run free and a barn for your children to play in on rainy days? You say you don't see it in your future on the $400 a month you can afford to pay for housing? You might be wrong, especially if you live near an area where estates and "gentlemen farmers" are not uncommon.

Most large estates have outbuildings on their land: carriage houses, guest cottages, barns, pool houses, etc. In today's economy, even the wealthy are discovering that unused buildings are an unnecessary drain on income. Many of these buildings have been remodeled partially or totally into rental units.

Rents on such cottages and apartments are surprisingly low, especially when privacy and the beauty of the surrounding land is considered. But the housing is not always easy to find. Many tenants are referred to the owners by friends or acquaintances, and the others are carefully screened. You will undoubtedly need references to qualify for an estate rental, and you may also need some skills and/or spare time.

Would you be willing, for example, to spend six hours a week on a riding mower to rent a five-room converted carriage house for $325 a month? Other common rent-reducing arrangements include animal care (horses, dogs), security protection (especially when the owners are out of town), and child care.

Unused Commercial Space

Perhaps you would be willing to live behind a store. How about a funeral parlor?

Eric, a college junior in New Haven, Connecticut, found a two-room apartment with a private bath for $85 a month on the second floor of a funeral home. He was not allowed to do any cooking in the apartment (the smell of onions browning at 6:30 P.M. would hardly be appropriate or respectful to mourners), but he was allowed to keep a small refrigerator.

Besides "no cooking," Eric also had to agree to no guests and no music during the hours that the building was open to the public. But at $85 a month, he felt he could hardly complain, and the enforced quiet and privacy was conducive to studying. Even the work he agreed to do to keep the rent low was a good late-evening break. Just when his eyes would be feeling sandy, Eric would make himself a cup of coffee and vacuum all the carpeting in the house. By the time he finished his job, his pulse would be beating a little more quickly and he'd be ready for another hour or two of study.

Everywhere creative people, especially the young, are fighting the housing crunch by making arrangements for living space. In a small town in West Virginia, Clyde and Nancy found both a home and a permanent job in a local movie theater. Clyde was working there as a projectionist when he discovered three unused rooms behind the projection booth. He approached the owner of the theater: Could he live there without charge if he remodeled the rooms himself, cleaned the theater each night, and did some work renovating the building? Without paperwork of any kind, the two men worked out an agreement. Six weeks later, Clyde moved in with Nancy. Today the couple are married and have a baby boy. They still live rent-free, and the theater has increased its business by 21 percent.

And have you considered a riding stable? You could muck out the stalls in exchange for the small apartment upstairs. A veterinary hospital? Many have apartments and are seeking someone to live on-site in case of emergency when the hospital is closed during the night or on weekends. And of course there's the motel room or apartment in exchange for cleaning services. Use your imagination! Housing doesn't have to be conventional to fill your needs. Barter is often a factor in a good deal. Think about what you need and what you can do, and approach the owners of potential properties. Rarely are there written leases in such creative arrangements; few people consult zoning laws; and life goes on profitably for tenants and landlords alike.

Off-Season Vacation Houses

You'll see the ads in the newspapers late in August: *Furnished house, lakefront, available September 15 to June 1.* Invariably these are vacation homes rented for the off-season and usually at rather low rates. The catch, of course, is that you must move out when the season approaches again.

Renting nine months a year may be ideal for you if you have a limited-year job, such as teaching, and have somewhere to go for the summer, but consider these points before you leave a deposit or sign a lease:

1. *Heat.* What is the heating mode for your cottage? Is it adequate? How expensive is it? Poor insulation could drive your heat and your heating bill through the ceiling.

2. *Water.* Some vacation communities supply water during the season only. If this is your situation, you will need to depend upon a well. How many gallons a minute are pumped? Has the water been tested for purity?

3. *Refuse removal.* Does the town collect refuse in the vacation community? If not, where is the local dump?

4. *Snow removal*. Is the town responsible or will you and other year-round residents have to hire someone to plow access roads?

5. *Isolation*. Will you mind being one of the five families occupying houses in the 438-house vacation community? How will the children get to school? Will there be any playmates for them? How will you feel about noises in the night? Some people find the emotional adjustment to isolation a difficult one.

Other Possibilities

In areas where a high number of corporate specialists are brought in on short term (three- to nine-month) task force assignments, real estate agents sometimes arrange "creative" house rentals, especially if clients (sellers who have given the agent a listing to sell their house) are unable to sell in a slow real estate market. A four-bedroom colonial, for example, might be rented to four different people. Each has a bedroom of his or her own, and they all share the living room, family room, and kitchen. They also divvy up parking space.

Of course there have always been single rooms to rent in private houses, with or without board or kitchen privileges and with or without the knowledge and permission of the local authorities. More recently, group rentals of two- or three-bedroom apartments have also become commonplace, especially near college campuses.

And what else? Well, would you live upstairs in a gas station? What if the rent were so cheap you'd hardly miss the money? How about a kids' summer camp in the woods? Would you consider being the winter caretaker? As we said, the possibilities for living space are almost limitless.

For More Information

"Wise Rental Practices," HUD470-NVACP(2), is available from the U.S. Dept. of Housing and Urban Development, Washington, D.C. 20410.

Your Best Source for Single Family, Townhouse, & Condominium Rentals is available from EPIC Realty Services, 5205 Leesburg Pike, Suite 400, Falls Church, Va. 22041.

8

When the Government Helps with the Rent

Carrie is a single mother of three. The two oldest children are 6 and 4, and the baby is just a year old. Carrie is newly divorced and has not been able to look for a job while the baby is so small, so she is almost totally dependent on public assistance. Alimony and child support from her former husband have virtually stopped. Carrie lives in a two-family house which the owner has just sold. The buyer wants her apartment for personal use. Looking for another apartment is not going to be easy for Carrie. What landlord is going to take a welfare mother with three children?

Ralph is 67 years old. His wife recently died, and now the small apartment where the two had lived is about to be taken from him. A developer has purchased the twelve-unit building and plans to convert it to condominiums. Unfortunately for Ralph, his state has no law protecting senior citizens caught in a conversion process, and Ralph cannot afford to purchase his unit, so he must move. His savings were drained by his wife's illness, and Ralph's income is now almost entirely from Social Security, with a few thousand dollars extra each year from working occasionally with an old friend who is a bricklayer. Where can Ralph find an affordable apartment?

Dan is 23 years old and is confined to a wheelchair. He's in a work-training program with a social services agency and also holds a part-time job with that office. Soon he will qualify for a permanent, full-time position at an open-market salary, but for now his income, even with government assistance, is not high enough to afford an apartment in the large metropolitan area where he lives. He'll need an apartment that's wheelchair-accessible, too, another complication. Dan would like to live independently—but where?

Lori is an artist. Her watercolors have been well received by local critics, and she sold three of her paintings at the state museum's recent exhibition of new artists. Still, a 26-year-old usually can't make a living painting. Most of Lori's income is from the tour-guide job she holds at a nearby cultural center. Must Lori be penalized in housing because her career choice is an ill-paying one, at least for now?

What Carrie, Ralph, Dan, and Lori have in common is a serious financial problem running alongside an equally serious nationwide rental situation. Where can anyone on a limited income—and one that they can do little to improve—look for an apartment in a tight, competitive, high-rent market? Where can these people find a decent place to live for $150 to $200 a month, which is roughly what they can afford to pay (based on no more than a quarter of one's income spent for shelter)?

There is help available. Dismayed would-be tenants often turn to the country's largest landlord—local, state, and national government. Frequently the solution is what is known as "public housing," sometimes also called "assisted" or "subsidized" housing. The units can be run by federal, state, or local governments.

The federal government, through the Department of Housing and Urban Development (HUD), sponsors dozens of programs, usually in conjunction with local governments, to assist those who want to rent, buy, build, or rehabilitate homes or land—just about anyone about to put down money in some sort of real estate transaction. Occasionally there are income limits and other restrictions, but sometimes there are no strings at all.

When we come to public housing on the consumer level, there are two general programs under which most Americans living on limited financial means are likely to find apartments.

First, *public housing* is run by some two thousand public housing authorities nationwide. Here tenants must live in buildings owned by the local housing authority—the New York City Housing Authority, for instance, or the San Francisco Housing Authority. The buildings are state or locally run, usually with federal financial assistance. There are income restrictions, of course. Criteria for admission vary, but generally a family will have an income of only 50–80 percent of the median income for that community. So if the average family of four in your town is found to earn $21,500, then a family of four seeking a home in public housing there can be admitted with an income as high as $17,000.

Tenants pay as rent the higher of 30 percent of adjusted income, 10 percent of gross income, or the portion of welfare assistance designated to meet housing costs.

Second, there is what is known as *Section 8 housing*, which was enacted in 1974. It receives its name from Section 8 of the Federal Housing Act of 1937, which set up public housing nationwide.

The new-construction phase of Section 8 was discontinued in 1982. What remains are existing buildings operating under the program, and a sort of voucher system. To explain how vouchers work, let's use Carrie as an example. Perhaps she would be able to move into a Section 8 apartment building in her town. Instead, she is given a voucher, called a *Certificate of Family Certification*, by the local housing authority. The voucher would enable her to seek an apartment from a private landlord anywhere within the jurisdiction of the housing authority, because it means that the housing authority will make up the difference between what Carrie can pay and the fair-market rent of the apartment. The unit chosen must adhere to certain HUD standards, and the landlord must be willing to accept a Section 8 tenant. If agreement is reached, both parties sign a lease. The owner of the building and the housing authority then sign a contract. If the apartment could be rented at $600 a month, and Carrie can only pay $200, then HUD will pay the landlord the extra $400 each month.

Section 8 was enormously popular during the 1970s. It has been considered an imaginative approach to luring private developers into constructing or rehabilitating buildings for low- and moderate-income families. Although there is no more new construction, the government remains committed to existing Section 8 buildings and to the voucher program.

One of the factors that more or less did in Section 8 was that it attracted developers who abused the program. Charges of bribery and influence-peddling within the program were rampant. There were claims of developers taking advantage by running up extra costs in their buildings for "luxuries," bringing them higher rents, and causing middle-income tenants to complain that *they* couldn't afford to live in those fancy government buildings. Section 8 certainly *was* a very good deal for developers. Besides being assured a full rent roll in their buildings, builders were lent construction money by HUD and provided with a few other financial goodies. It didn't take long for a rush to build or rehabilitate Section 8 apartments to develop, by just about anyone who could read of its advantages. Where there is money involved and profit to be made, corruption cannot be far behind, right? Yet there was general acclaim for the program, since it lessened the federal government's role in housing subsidies.

Whereas many of the Section 8 apartments are far better than those found in public housing, the program is not perfect. Waiting lists are almost always lengthy. If Carrie uses the voucher system, she may also find it difficult to secure an apartment. The neighborhoods where participating private landlords have their buildings may not be the nicest (although downright slums are avoided). Landlords of any persuasion seem to discriminate against single mothers and their children, and since only a few states have laws prohibiting that form of bias, Carrie may well have a time-consuming and frustrating apartment hunt ahead of her. Still, Section 8 is a program that has answered a need, and there may yet be an infusion of new funds to get new construction going again.

Generally speaking, in any public housing program only families, single persons over 62 years old or handicapped people may apply. (There is more information about housing for the handicapped in Chapter 34.) Artists' housing is still just a tiny speck on the assisted-housing landscape. A young, single artist such as Lori might live in a building devoted to artists' housing, or perhaps in a section of a complex set aside for artists among predominately low-income residents. In that case, she is far luckier than 99.9 percent of the nation's artists. "Artist," by the way, is very broadly defined. Qualified painters, sculptors, actors, craftspersons, writers, graphic artists, and the like are invited to apply for artists' housing. They are judged only on the seriousness of their approach to their work, with no value judgment made on their "talent." Of course, there are income guidelines, too.

At this writing there are rental complexes specifically for single custodial parents living on reduced incomes (they offer adjacent or nearby day-care facilities for the children) in California, Colorado, and Rhode Island.

Other requirements for admission to subsidized housing vary, usually according to whether federal monies are involved. There may be a residency requirement, for instance, or there may not. Generally, families with an eviction history are not admitted, and neither are those in which one member has an arrest record. Apartment sizes vary widely, too, running from one- to four-bedroom units.

Working people do live in public housing. Only about 25 percent of all public housing tenants are living wholly or in part on public assistance.

Problems

Got a few hours? Depending on the community in which you are searching for public housing, you may be in for quite a headache. The building you're inquiring about is likely to have more than a few problems, too.

Public housing, while without question serving a need in thousands of communities, has been bogged down with inefficiency, red ink, tumbling-down buildings, and unfair tenant selection processes for years. This does not refer to all buildings in all locations. But it is not uncommon to hear Uncle Sam referred to as . . . well, not the nation's finest landlord. Buildings run specifically for senior citizens appear to be more attractive and better run—and the residents happier—than those for all ages, but age and lack of money for upkeep and replacements can take their toll on those complexes, too.

Public housing began during the Great Depression, when a ravaged national economy forced some Americans out into the streets. In 1934 New York's mayor, Fiorello H. LaGuardia, filed a notice with that state to found the New York City Housing Authority. The city planned to take a row of tenements, rehabilitate them, and offer them to needy New Yorkers. That "project" became known as First Houses, and Eleanor Roosevelt officiated at its dedication in 1935. It is still in operation today in lower Manhattan.

The Federal Housing Act of 1937 brought public housing to the rest of the nation. The federal government would build the units, and local housing authorities would pay for their operation and upkeep, using tenants' rents. The apartments in those days were meant to be a way station for the new poor during the Depression days, a stop to provide them with at least a roof over their heads until they (and the rest of the country) were able to get back on stable financial footing. In those first days in New York City there were 270 tenants living in 123 units. By 1983, with federal assistance in the picture, there were 171,229 subsidized units in that city, with a population of more than 490,000.

So public housing has grown huge, and in the process has strayed far from its modest intention of the 1930s. Today, the homes are often not seen as way stations but rather as permanent housing for some tenants into the second and third generations. The government—federal, state, local—cannot keep up with the demand for more units and often has no funds to make needed repairs on existing complexes. So there are broken elevators; dark, crime-ridden hallways; graffiti-defaced interiors and exteriors; broken heating plants during the harshest winter days; and a host of other neglects. Again, it should be stressed, not every building in every town has these problems. But a study released in 1983 showed that nearly 25 percent of the nation's 134 major public housing authorities are foundering financially. The condition of the complexes is not entirely the fault of the government. Some tenants living in assisted housing freely point out that their neighbors contribute to the bad state of repair in some buildings. Most projects have their share of undesirables and troublemakers.

All of this is a dreary picture, to be sure. It is presented here to show you just what you should think about when applying to public housing, and what you are likely to find if you are able to secure an apartment for yourself or a relative or friend.

There is one way to prepare yourself to win a spot in the building you want. It will take some preparation and foresight.

Apartments are usually apportioned according to need—with six income levels set—rather than on a first-come, first-served basis. But there will always be a few housing authorities that dole them out to whomever they wish and let regulations be hanged. There are waiting lists for even the grimmest projects, and they can be up to ten years long. It's polite, of course, to wait your turn, even if you're number 124,000 on the list. But if the situation is desperate, it would help to use whatever measures you think can help. Contact your local politicians for assistance in getting you into a subsidized housing complex. Is there anyone at your local social services agency who can help? Any member of the clergy? Planning ahead can help most of all. In Carrie's case that would not have been possible, but Dan can start his apartment hunt early, looking for a wheelchair-accessible unit a year or more before he is ready to move.

Senior citizens such as Ralph can do some crystal-ball gazing, too. If you're in your own home and think you might like to sell in the future and move into that new senior citizen complex, better make application now (if you're at least 62 years of age). You can legally apply to as many complexes as you like. Actually, retirees have a few options when it comes to subsidized housing. More and more communities are allowing them to convert their single-family homes into two-family houses, renting the other unit to a senior citizen under the Section 8 program. So whether you have an apartment to offer or are looking for a place to live, if you are 62 years of age or older this program can work well for you. We can expect to see more of these conversions as suburban governments relax zoning codes to enable their retired residents to stay in their communities after they have no need for large houses or cannot afford to maintain them. Looking ahead a few years to see what your needs might be and how your financial situation could affect your present home may well take at least the interminable wait out of public housing.

For More Information

For additional information about any type of subsidized housing you can contact your local housing authority (listed in the telephone book under municipal offices), or your regional HUD office (addresses can be found in Appendix A).

PART II

Successful Homebuying and Selling

9

Homebuying as the "American Dream"

Ellen and Bob lived for fourteen years in the second floor apartment of a two-family house in a lovely section of town. Their children had become teenagers there, and have now left home for college. The couple had no intention of moving. Their life was settled, happy, regular. Until the day the owner walked up the back stairs from the first floor apartment.

"Bob, Ellen . . . I hate to tell you this," he began. "You've been good neighbors and great tenants all these years, but. . . . Well, you see, my daughter is getting married in May. What I'm trying to say is, well, your lease expires April 1 and I'm afraid we have to ask you to leave then."

There was an awkward silence. No one knew what to say.

"We understand," volunteered Ellen, trying to smile. Bob was already holding the door open for the man. "Yeah, we understand," he added. "Glad you could give us the three months' notice."

Bob and Ellen had never aspired to owning a house or getting rich. They saw themselves as working people, people who just wanted to be left free to lead their lives peacefully. But family came before friendship for their landlord, and now their life was being turned upside-down with an eviction. Like a rejected lover on the rebound, they "retaliated." They would have security in their lives. This would never happen again. They bought a condominium.

Security, the knowledge that virtually no one can say "It's time to move on," is, and always has been, a prime reason for owning property. And once ownership has been established, people cherish their piece of the earth. Wars have been fought over who has the right to occupy a

137

certain piece of land. Besides possession, however, there are financial, physical, and emotional considerations involved in homeownership. In this country those considerations have made owning one's residence a big part of the promise that is America. Although homeownership is neither right nor possible for everyone, it is one of the most often and persistently pursued life-goals in our society.

One of the most important steps to successful homeownership is a recognition and evaluation of your own motivations to buy. A clear perception of why you are househunting will help you decide what to buy. Let's look carefully therefore at the question "Why buy?"

Who's Buying

Truly there is something for sale in the housing marketplace for almost everyone. But are there "typical" homebuyers? Many fall into more than one category.

The Rich

Despite publicized reports of houses becoming smaller, sales of large and elegant houses are only slightly affected by housing slumps. Financing is not so great a problem when you're in the top 1 percent of national income statistics. It seems the rich will continue to buy comfort.

The Not-So-Rich

There are still government programs around to help home-buyers, and there are plenty of private lenders and insurers willing to take small risks on "good people" with minimal down-payments. People may be buying less than their dream home, but they are still buying, even when they must use a large portion of their income to do so.

The Young

They still have their dreams, and a home of their own is still one of them. They may start smaller and not move up so quickly or so far, but they *are* in the housing market. Condominiums have much appeal for them.

The Old

Seniors are another group contributing to the popularity of condominium ownership. They are seeking the security of ownership without the maintenance headaches (and backaches).

Singles

Many singles are attracted to condominium ownership also, but some try their hands at detached housing. Multi-family buildings are especially popular, and some handyperson types like to buy, fix up, and move on.

Single Parents

A growing group in our population, many single parents still number among their primary goals a home of their own for themselves and their children.

The "Typical" American Family

Husband, wife, kids—and pets—are still the largest group of househunters in the nation.

Financial Considerations

Investment Appreciation

For the last thirty years, most Americans have thought of their houses as both homes and investments. The 1950s saw modest appreciation in the value of American residential real estate, but the 1960s and 1970s saw skyrocketing prices that far outpaced the rate of inflation. People seemed to be climbing over one another to buy a house. Homeownership was a ticket to wealth, and you needed a "starter house" to get into the game. "Step-ups" fired the real estate boom. Many, many people routinely sold every three or four years to move to bigger and better quarters.

A number of "experts" are now predicting that the housing price-spiral will slow in the coming decade. But these predictions are just that, predictions, guesses more or less educated. In the future into which these experts gaze, there is a huge pent-up demand from people in their twenties and thirties who have been locked out of the housing market by painfully high interest rates. Will the public response to interest rates be similar to its response to gasoline prices? Once the shock of paying more than a dollar a gallon had passed, people adapted and continued to drive. In fact, *bigger* cars are back in demand! Will potential homebuyers also save a little longer or work two jobs in order to buy a place of their own? It seems likely. The lure of ownership is a force that is not easily evaluated by economic criteria. And if the demand for housing remains high, prices (and investment value) will continue to go up.

But whether the national average cost of housing outpaces inflation or lags behind it, there will always be areas where housing is an excellent investment because of potential growth and high demand, and areas where housing as an investment will be a poor bet because of soft economic conditions or overbuilding. And within each of these areas, some individual houses will be good investments, and some poor investments.

If investment appreciation is an important factor in your choice of a home, you must learn to evaluate what makes for good resale potential. Even if you are a homebuyer seeking only good shelter and not riches, it's nice to know that the monthly payment you would normally make for housing might also be a good investment for the future.

One of the greatest benefits of housing as an investment in this country is not completely understood by most of the people who use it. Real estate professionals, however, understand it very well. It's called *leverage*. In essence, leverage means investing as little as possible of your own money to make as large as possible a purchase. Thus, you use borrowed money (the mortgage loan) as a means to purchase your home investment. As a result, a small percentage of appreciation in home value can mean a fabulous return on the cash you actually put into the purchase. Let's look at an example.

David and Eva want to buy a $100,000 house. Because the couple has high potential income growth, the bank is willing to stretch its qualification limits a bit and agrees to accept 10 percent down on a privately insured mortgage loan.

Houses are appreciating at a very conservative rate of 5 percent per year in David and Eva's area. At the end of year one, therefore, the house is worth $105,000, at the end of year two, $110,250, and at the end of year three, $115,760. At that time, David and Eva are ready to sell and step up to a grander house. Because of especially fine decorating, their house sells for $119,000. After expenses they net $111,000. After paying off the mortgage, which still has a balance of nearly $89,000, they have slightly more than $21,000 cash-in-hand. Their $10,000 investment therefore more than doubled in three years, all thanks to leverage. And these numbers are very conservative. Some leveraged investments in homes bring their owners 300–400 percent returns on their investment dollars in three years or less.

Tax Benefits

Owners of newly purchased homes often take spring vacations. That's when their tax refunds arrive.

Interest paid on a mortgage is deductible from your gross income on federal tax returns. So are real estate taxes. The two together usually comprise all but a few dollars of the monthly payment made to the mortgage holder in the early years of homeownership. Thus, for the homeowner, housing becomes, in effect, a deductible expense. There are no such benefits for tenants.

Our government so strongly supports private homeownership that it also allows a tax deferment on all the profits from the sale of a personal residence if another residence of equal or greater value is purchased to replace it. (The purchase must take place within two years before or after the sale.) Tenants must pay on the gains from taxes most of the money they invest.

The homeowner's tax deferment may be carried forward as long as the homeowner chooses to buy more expensive homes. But there comes a point when the government encourages a sale and a step down in housing size. The "encouragement" is in the form of a gift, almost.

When a homeowner, or either owner in a married couple, reaches the age of 55, he, she, or they can sell their home and keep up to $125,000 in profit without paying a tax. Each person can do this only once in his or her life, and if one person in a married couple has already claimed the exemption, the couple cannot claim it again even if divorce and remarriage has cut one of the partners off from the exemption.

To claim this senior citizen's tax exemption, you must be selling your principal residence and you must have lived in it for three of the preceding five years. When you qualify and collect your tax-exempt profit, you'll have a nice little nest egg to start retirement. Not an insignificant part of the American Dream, right?

Equity Growth

Some people just can't save any money! Everything left over after the bills are paid, they spend. For many of these people (and many more of us are in that number than we'd like to admit), owning a house is a way to save. Although the payments on the mortgage in the first years are almost all interest, as time goes by, you do begin to pay off the loan. Combine the gradual principal reduction with appreciation and protection against inflation and you have growing *equity* (the cash amount difference between what you owe on the mortgage and what the house is worth). It really *is* a savings plan!

Payment Stability

Despite the flowering of adjustable-rate financing plans since the turn of the decade, the fixed-rate, long-term mortgage is still a popular form of home financing. Why? The *contract* (mortgage agreement) assures the homeowner of a constant base payment for housing for twenty or thirty years. Inflation or an increase in housing demand and its resulting increase in housing costs will not

---

Comparison Worksheet—Renting vs. Buying

Pertinent facts and estimates:

Annual income	_____
Tax bracket after deductions not related to homeownership	_____
Purchase price of the house	_____
Probable rate of appreciation annually	_____
Downpayment (cash investment)	_____
Mortgage term (years)	_____
Mortgage interest rate	_____
Annual property taxes	_____
Annual insurance costs	_____
Estimate of monthly maintenance and utility costs	Rent _____
	Buy _____
Closing costs upon purchase	_____
Assumed rate of return on savings invested while renting	_____

Real cost of housing for first year after buying:

	Rent	Buy
Total annual payment for rent or mortgage payments		
Real estate taxes ADD		
Insurance ADD		
Utilities (twelve-month total) ADD		
Income tax savings resulting from deduction of interest and property taxes SUBTRACT		

	Rent	Buy
Earnings on renter's investment of downpayment plus closing costs at above assumed rate of return SUBTRACT		
Tax on the investment earnings of the renter ADD		
AFTER-TAX COSTS TO RENT OR BUY		
Appreciation on home SUBTRACT		
FIRST YEAR'S REAL COST OF HOUSING		

change the payment. Real estate taxes and maintenance costs might increase, but the greater part of the payment is fixed. Even most of today's adjustable rate mortgages include caps on possible increases in monthly payments.

Economy

There are those who take the position that a house is a constant drain upon time and money, and sometimes it is. But ownership can also be a most economical way to live.

You've probably heard of "sweat equity," the value that homeowners add to their properties by making improvements through do-it-yourself projects. Add to that "sweat maintenance," the value of do-it-yourself snow shoveling, mowing, and leaf raking, and ownership of a detached single-family house can begin to look pretty good even to penny pinchers. For the tenant, improvements in living quarters or increased maintenance costs usually mean increased rent.

For real economy, however, homeownership demands more than do-it-yourself, day-to-day maintenance work. Can you replace a water heater? Paint the peak of a two-story house? Rid the basement of mice? Install a sump pump? The handyperson is a natural candidate for homeownership. And many people who never thought of themselves as handypersons become very handy after they buy their first home.

Besides saving on fix-up costs, homeowners can often save money on living costs as well. Since heat is not included in the "rent," homeowners more readily remember to turn the thermostat down when they go out for the day. And it seems that more homeowners than tenants are willing to wear sweaters in winter.

Another moneysaver, believe it or not, is food. Many homeowners use their lots to grow vegetables during the summer which they then freeze or preserve for the winter. Others get into storage or food co-ops, or into stockpiling the lead sale items in the grocery store each week. Some homeowners use their homes to make money. Some rent out a room or half the house, and some offer bed and breakfast. A few raise purebred dogs or create products in the basement that are marketed by local businesses. A basement or spare room can also be the storage area for a mail-order business. The possibilities for using a home to make money are somewhat limited by local zoning laws, but creative individuals seem to think of new ones again and again.

Lifestyles and Creature Comforts

Indoor Space

Generally you get more living space for your monthly housing dollar in a house than you do in an apartment. And if your family is large, you may find homeownership your only viable housing option. Four-bedroom apartments are hard to find.

But it's more than a matter of bedrooms. Homeownership usually buys you storage space in the attic, basement, or garage, all of which may also double as hobby or working space. And where else can 10-year-old children build "forts" out of card tables, old furniture, and blankets on winter days? Also, kitchens are generally larger and closets more plentiful in houses.

Outdoor Space

Many people choose homeownership for the land. Their lot lines separate them from their neighbors; their back yards are a place to run the dogs, or raise rabbits, or put in a sandbox, climber, and swings for the kids. For many, owning the land is synonymous with having the right to garden. For some it is an opportunity for self-expression through landscaping. Even tiny city lots are often "farmed" into beauty. Owning a separate piece of outdoor space, however, is one ownership consideration that is not usually available to condominium or co-op apartment owners.

Privacy and Autonomy

The amount of land that surrounds your house is pretty directly correlated with the amount of privacy you feel in your community. But even on the smallest lot, you don't have to overhear your neighbors' domestic arguments through the wallboard, or allow them to hear yours.

To a great degree your home is also your kingdom. You can own a Great Dane or three, and/or as many cats as you can afford to feed. You can paint your house red, white, and blue for the nation's bicentennial if you wish. (One man in Chester, New Jersey, did exactly that!) Your 7-year-old can raise turtles in the bathtub, and your teenager's rock band can rehearse in the basement.

But homeownership is not a free license to any lifestyle you can dream up. You, the owner of the land, must still conform to community laws. You certainly won't be able to rent your lawn to nude sunbathers, you most likely will need a building permit to add a screened-in porch to your house, and you probably won't be able to keep a horse on your quarter-acre lot.

Because homeownership of a condominium or co-op apartment does not usually include ownership of your own piece of land, some of the advantages of privacy and autonomy are lost. In regard to these considerations, shared-space ownership is more like renting.

Stability

Whereas one of the chief benefits of renting is mobility, one of the chief attractions of ownership is stability. Usually people who buy are ready to settle down. They are seeking something constant, a place to watch their children grow up, a place where decorating dollars are an investment, not a passing fancy. Many are also seeking neighborhoods or communities that are unlikely to change in the near future.

Security

Security means many things besides the right to live in a particular place as long as you may wish. To some homeowners, it also means safety. They buy to escape areas where the crime rate is high, and they usually buy in neighborhoods where they feel the people are "like themselves." Often, these same buyers interpret security to mean the ability of their children to play safely in the neighborhood without supervision and to go to a school where they are unthreatened by their contemporaries.

To some homebuyers, security means the protection of their investment dollars. "My money is safe here," they think, "because my home will surely appreciate in value." These people want neighborhoods that are stable and protected by strict zoning laws.

Recreation

Yes, some homebuyers buy for recreation. Not for the fun of buying, but for the fun of owning a place on a lake or in the mountains. Many whose residence is in the city during the work week own alternative residences in the surrounding countryside for weekends and vacation times.

A Matter of Pride

Status

To some people, homeownership is a status symbol that outweighs all others, except perhaps the automobile. Pride in their home is extremely important to these buyers. Often they see their homes as extensions of themselves, reflections of their unique personalities.

But pride in ownership is not restricted to the homeowner. Our society as a whole regards owning property as a very positive status symbol. As a homeowner, it's easier to get credit or a loan. And the "right address" can still open doors, as it has done for centuries.

Creativity

A home is a hobby for some buyers. Michael, an unmarried executive with a major corporation, moved out of a luxury condominium to buy a hundred-year-old, 28-foot-wide, three-story stone house on the banks of the Delaware River. To live there, he must drive fifty minutes each way to work, every working day. Ah, but on days off, he has his house. He's both restoring and modernizing it, peeling off paneling to allow the stone walls to show in the living room, adding skylights in the bedrooms.

He shops at antique shops, flea markets, and garage sales for just the right furnishings. He's bought a canoe and built a boathouse. And he has planted seventeen white pine seedlings. Homeownership is, most of all, a satisfying experience for Michael, an outlet for his creativity.

Why Are You Buying?

	Not a Factor			A Most Important Factor
	0	1	2	3
Investment appreciation				
Tax benefits				
Equity growth				
Payment stability				
Economy				
Indoor space				
Outdoor space				
Privacy and autonomy				
Stability				
Security				
Recreation				
Status				
Creativity				

Is It Worth the Trouble?

Occasionally you'll see articles in newspapers and magazines comparing the cost of homeownership with the cost of renting. Owning a home almost always comes out ahead.

However, there are so many assumptions in these comparisons that they are really of little value, except perhaps as a pattern for an individual to do a personal assessment using the facts and figures that are real to him. What's right for an individual or couple, to buy or to rent, is totally dependent upon the unique situation of that person or couple. One tenant may invest savings so shrewdly that his profits far outpace those of a homebuyer who puts exactly the same amount of money into the downpayment on a home. And some homebuyers have been known to buy white elephants that actually depreciate in value.

In general, homeownership *is* a good deal. *How* good a deal it really is, however, depends on how well your home satisfies your personal goals. Which is the result of how well you know those goals and how well you buy. Evaluating your personal goals is up to you; the next fifteen chapters will help you with what and how to buy. When you finish the reading and the worksheets, the odds for your success in the real estate marketplace will be increased, since you'll be armed with a powerful weapon—*knowledge*.

For More Information

"Selecting and Financing a Home," U.S. Dept. of Agriculture Publication #174M, is a brief comparison of renting with buying, how to figure what you can afford, what to look for in homeowner's insurance, etc. It is available from Consumer Information Center, Pueblo, Colo. 81009. Price: $3. Also available from the Consumer Information Center is "Rent or Buy?" Publication #173M. Price: $3.50. It tells how to compare costs and returns of renting with those of owning a home, and includes charts for estimating the monthly costs of each.

10

The First-time Homebuyer's Ten Greatest Fears (and How to Conquer Them)

Karen and Bob can afford a home, but although they tell friends they'll be buying any day, they have yet to venture out of their apartment to go househunting. Donna's accountant has been urging her to buy, but Donna doesn't appear to be listening to his advice, although she concedes it is sound. Gary has had his eye on a brand-new condominium complex in his neighborhood that would be perfect for him and his 6-year-old daughter. He's gone through the model apartments several times but can't bring himself to speak to any of the sales staff there.

Unlike the confirmed apartment dweller who prefers to rent, all of these people genuinely want to buy a home, but can't seem to take that step that will lead to ownership. Perhaps not even totally conscious of their fear, they find excuses of all kinds for not buying, and offer what they consider sensible rationalizations to friends. But they are scared right down to their socks about the whole homebuying scenario.

Why shouldn't they be? And why shouldn't you if you recognize yourself here? A house (or condominium or cooperative or mobile home) may be the largest single purchase you ever make. Paying for it will take the better part of the rest of your life. So approaching the process with a little honest fear is only natural. But when that fear gets in the way of allowing you to buy a home you truly want, or from making the progress with your life you think that purchase represents, then you have a problem and not simply a fleeting attack of the jitters.

Let's examine the major fears of homebuying and -ownership. By taking them apart they should fall apart, and you will see that buying a home is just another of life's stages that you will get through. You may even enjoy the process, if only in retrospect. And no nail biting while reading this!

Fear No. 1

Is a home really a good investment? What if I buy and then the economy collapses?

Media and anti-administration critics are continually forecasting total economic collapse, but that hasn't happened yet, no matter how bad times have been. So you might as well be enjoying a home while you wait for fiscal Armaggedon.

Also, homes are not subject to the high sensitivity that short-term investments such as stocks are. They do react to the overall economic climate, but not so quickly and so radically as stocks. Naturally all homebuyers hope their purchases will reward them financially in days to come, but the first reason for buying is to get shelter. In times of recession most people hang on to their homes until the market improves. There is no panic selling of family residences.

You should keep an eye on the economy (bad times often present excellent opportunities to buy). But don't let periodic downturns alarm you into thinking it's all going to tumble down, taking you and your house with it. If you buy wisely—and reading this book demonstrates your seriousness in learning about the real estate market—your investment will be safe from the natural ebbs and flows of the economy.

Fear No. 2

I'm confused about what to buy. There seem to be so many different styles of housing around these days.

Yes there are, and isn't that wonderful? The diversity and the wide range of prices are bringing homeowning opportunities to many more Americans. Whether you buy a house, condo, co-op, or any other style of shelter depends on your own situation—what you can afford, the size of your family, commuting time, and other ingredients that make the home you select just right for you.

An important point for first-time buyers to remember is not to assume automatically that "home" means suburban house on a quarter- or half-acre lot. In fact, if you do allow yourself to think exclusively in that vein, you may well price yourself out of buying.

Those single-family homes in desirable suburban locales are not the most affordable for most people these days.

Keep your mind open to other housing styles, and don't dismiss any of them until you have done some investigating. You say you wouldn't live in the city? Drive through the city nearest you and you will probably spot some enclaves that have revived since the early 1970s and are now very attractive. In fact, you may not be able to afford some of those houses. But a few blocks away may be another good-looking neighborhood with homes also on the way back, carrying slightly lower price tags. You may also see stable neighborhoods that have never declined, with congenial, proud residents eager to welcome you to their community. Tell everyone you wouldn't be caught dead living in a mobile home? Have you visited any of today's new mobile home parks? They are virtually indistinguishable from those attractive suburban streets you may not be able to afford, yet mobile homes cost only a fraction of traditional single-family houses. Drive through a few parks some weekend for an eye-opening experience.

Visit model apartments or new or converted condominiums and cooperatives in your locale, too, to get an idea how that style of ownership operates and whether you think you would fit in there. No need to worry about the stability of that form of ownership. Condos and co-ops are now firmly fixed on the American housing landscape and will be around for many, many years.

Think also of the people who are living quite happily (and profitably) in lighthouses, converted churches, lofts of all sizes, and just about any other structure with a roof and a foundation. Go on house tours. Visit open houses. Take a look at any and all structures that are called "home" by some members of your community. After conducting all those investigations you should find yourself drifting back to one particular favorite. Perhaps it's a housing style you like, or perhaps the only one you can afford. But the decision of what to buy will be made. Then you can concentrate on the many varieties of that particular style until you come up with *the* home.

Fear No. 3

I'm so afraid I won't qualify for a mortgage that I'm afraid to apply for one.

Lenders say that 85 percent of all mortgage applications are approved, so yours is likely to be one of the fortunate ones. After all, banks and similar financial institutions are in the business of lending money, and unless the country is sailing through some very troubled economic waters, making mortgage money more or less readily available is their job.

There are six factors that will enter into your ability to get a home loan: income, job stability, credit references, amount of downpayment, assets, and purchasing a home with a good resale value.

If you are a very young first-time buyer, you should know that lenders also take into account "career potential." This means that if you are just out of school and earning a not-very-grand salary, the lender may still see you as an excellent income prospect for the future. He or she will weigh your career field, expected salary growth, and time involved in reaching those plateaus and may well grant you your loan.

If you are nervous to the point of paralysis about securing mortgage approval, take some preliminary steps to see how you might rate with a lender. Visit a local bank or savings and loan association and talk to the mortgage officer. Better yet, visit three institutions so you can acquaint yourself with various financing programs and do some comparison shopping that will lead you to the best deal for you. Ask the officer if you would qualify for a home loan with your income, and in what price range you should be looking for a house. No lender can make a firm mortgage commitment without a formal application (done after you have found the house you want), but he or she can tell you if you're in the ballpark vis-à-vis securing a loan.

Next, try to obtain a copy of your credit report, an important document the lender will want to scrutinize. Check the Yellow Pages under "Credit Reporting Services" and make a few phone calls to see which bureau has the report on you. Call that office and ask for a copy of your report, which you should have no trouble obtaining for a small $5 or $10 charge. That sheet will show your credit history for the last seven years (longer if you have filed for bankruptcy), and some facts that may surprise you. Perhaps there is an error you should correct, or a point that needs elaboration. Incidentally, this is not a credit "rating." The bureaus make no judgments on the files they keep; they just release the data they have collected, and the prospective lender makes a decision based on that information.

Once you have done some of this homework, and are aware of just what a lending institution is looking for in mortgage applicants, you should no longer fear the process. And remember that 85 percent approval rate!

Fear No. 4
Financing has me totally confused. I don't know where to begin figuring out how mortgages work.

Today's home financing picture is very different from the some-what placid times we enjoyed as recently as the mid-1970s. Today's househunter must study (1) what types of mortgages are available, (2) which is best for him or her, and (3) how to get that loan. Remember that even a fraction of a percentage point in interest can translate into your spending—or saving—several thousand dollars over the life of a loan. So being an informed shopper becomes vitally important.

The mortgage officers at the lending institutions you visit can explain how mortgages work and which kinds of loans those institutions offer. Your real estate agent can also tell you a bit about financing, although that is usually not their area of expertise. You might also contact your local FHA and VA (if you qualify) offices for booklets explaining how buying a home works with those programs.

But bear in mind that bank officers and realty agents may not be willing to spend much time with you. They may have their own pet financing programs, or ones they choose to stay away from. So finding out what's best for you is going to be pretty much up to you.

Read all you can about homebuying and financing in books and magazines. Pay special attention to daily news stories in newspapers and on radio and television. These programs will have current information about homebuying patterns and statistics that can help you *now*.

You might also purchase a paperback book containing amortizing mortgage payment tables, put out by any number of publishing houses. These books consist of nothing but tables that can tell you at a glance what your monthly mortgage payment will be for a mortgage of *X* dollars at *Y* percent interest rate. It will be a small price to pay to save yourself time—and mistakes—in scribbling your own calculations.

Mortgages can be confusing, but the area is not an impenetrable maze. There are many dewy-eyed househunters who, two weeks into looking for a loan, are spouting *amortization, points,* and other terms that may now be incomprehensible to you. You will learn quickly, no doubt because it's your own hard-earned money you will be parting with.

Fear No. 5

What if I start househunting and then learn I'm a few thousand dollars short of the downpayment? Are all downpayment require-ments alike?

Downpayment requirements will vary from one property to the

next but generally fall between 10 and 20 percent of the purchase price. A real estate agent can acquaint you with requirements in resale houses in your area, and you can tell from the large display advertisements local builders run in newspapers what they require as downpayments for new homes.

There are ways around not having enough money to put down. If you can afford to carry the monthly payments, being a few thousand dollars short shouldn't deter you from buying.

First, you can see if you can borrow the extra amount from relatives, or perhaps take out a bank loan (although some bankers frown on borrowing for downpayments). You can ask the seller to extend a small loan to you in the form of a second mortgage for that amount. You can look specifically for FHA-insured or VA-guaranteed loans, which have low and sometimes no downpayment requirements. Also, if you fit the income requirements, and if the plans are still in effect, you can purchase a house under state-sponsored mortgage programs, which also carry very low downpayment requirements (and lower-than-market interest rates). Check with the governor's office to see where the Housing Finance Agency (or Mortgage Finance Agency) is located in your state.

Finally, you can purchase private mortgage insurance especially designed for the first-time buyer having a hard time putting together the dollars needed for a downpayment. This is a plan that allows you to put down as little as 5% on the home you buy. The insurance costs 1 percent of the mortgage amount, payable at the closing, and ¼ percent which becomes payable every year on the outstanding balance. The payments stop after ten or twelve years, when it is felt the loan no longer needs to be insured. You can ask your real estate agent about this, or contact one of the companies offering the policies. The nation's largest private insurer of home loans is the Mortgage Guaranty Insurance Corporation (MGIC), based in Chicago and with offices in several other cities.

Fear No. 6

What if I put down a deposit on a house and then change my mind? What if I change my mind after signing a contract?

Don't sign until you feel quite certain you want the house. It's always a good idea to "sleep on it" (wait at least one night) before making an offer, even if an aggressive sales agent is telling you that there are two other buyers "interested" in that same house, each with his or her checkbook out and pen poised.

When you *are* ready to buy, use professional services to protect your interests. Contract and closing practices vary widely across the country. In some areas the real estate agent usually draws up the contract; in others (especially the Northeast) contracts are drawn by lawyers. But wherever you are, you can make your commitment to buy subject to the advice and approval of several professionals: a lawyer, an engineer or house inspection firm, and of course your lender.

Even if the sales agent tells you, "My office policy is to make offers *only* with a signed contract in hand," stand firm. Tell that individual you will write an *earnest money* check for $500, which he can show to the sellers as he makes your offer. If the sales agent insists on the written offer, you can agree to sign a *binder* or *offer form* that will spell out the essential terms and conditions of your offer. Real estate legislation in most states requires a sales agent to present *every* offer made in writing to the seller.

To assure yourself that this binder *cannot* be interpreted as a contract of sale, however, have your sales agent type the following sentence above your signature (or add your initials beside it): "This agreement is subject to a contract to purchase being drawn or approved by the buyer's attorney within five business days of this date and signed by all parties involved in the sale."

With an earnest money check and this offer form in hand, the sales agent will present your bid on the property to the seller. If the seller refuses and no mutually agreeable figure can be reached, you will *by law* be entitled to your money back. If and when a mutually agreeable selling price is reached, the binder, signed by both parties, will take the property off the market and give you and the seller a few days to work out all the details of the purchase fairly. You can hire a lawyer to write or review a contract to purchase, even if lawyers do not usually handle closings in your area of the country. (Their fees, by the way, vary significantly, so shop around before you make your choice.)

Negotiating verbally with an earnest money check or, if necessary, with an offer form subject to legal counsel will prevent you from signing your name under clauses and contingencies you do not understand. Also, you may keep buyers' heebie-jeebies from ruining your deal. A day or two after an offer is accepted, many buyers (probably a good majority, in fact) get cold feet. "What are we doing? Did we pay too much for this house? Can we really afford to make the payments? I'm not sure our furniture will fit in the bedroom!" If you get these feelings, work through the numbers again, with or without the sales agent; and walk through the property again, measuring rooms if you must. You have time before your deal is cast in stone.

Even after your contract to buy is signed, however, it should allow for at least two contingencies before it is binding upon you. The first is financing. You cannot buy unless you can get the money to do so, and your contract should say that. If you can't get adequate financing, you will get your deposit money back and be free of your commitment to buy.

The other important contingency is professional inspection of the structural elements and working systems of the property. You do not want to buy a house with a buckling foundation wall, or one in which the plumbing has deteriorated so the best you'll get is a trickle of lukewarm water in the upstairs shower. If you hire a home inspection firm and their report shows a serious flaw or flaws, you can get out of your contract and have your deposit returned. If you still want the house, you can require that the fault be repaired by the seller or you can renegotiate the purchase price, taking into consideration the cost of repairs.

Other contingencies to meet your special needs or apprehensions can be written into a contract by your attorney. Once all of them are satisfactorily met, however, it's all over but the shouting (and the paperwork). The property will soon be yours.

Fear No. 7

I've been living in an apartment and don't know anything about home maintenance and repair.

There appear to be three types of homeowners: those who seem to do all the work around a house themselves, those who do some and farm out the rest, and those who call in repair people for everything. You may think you will belong to the latter group, but when you buy you will probably surprise yourself with your abilities—and your interest. Now that you're in your own home, puttering around may be enjoyable. One look at a repair person's bill may make you decide to enjoy yourself.

Generally, buyers find they grow into becoming responsible homeowners the way one grows into other roles. You don't have to learn everything at once, and you will be pleasantly surprised at how much help is out there: from relatives and friends, your new neighbors, the people at the lumberyard, the paint and hardware stores, and members of your civic association. All will gladly pass along tips on where to find craftspersons, how to repair widgets, and other little complexities of life you will run into at your manor. And of course there are a few hundred books on the market about various aspects of home repair.

There is no need to know every intricacy of what makes a heating plant or a plumbing system work. You may not know just exactly how your car operates, but you can still be a good and intelligent driver, can't you? Just learn enough about your home to recognize a problem when it occurs, and either fix it yourself or call in expert help to do the job. You may fall into the role so easily that your next house may be one you will build yourself!

If you are truly concerned about maintenance, consider buying a condominium or cooperative, or a relatively trouble-free mobile home. Or how about a two-family house with a relative, friend, or co-worker, so you can share worries about leaky roofs?

Fear No. 8

What if I buy a home and then find it's too expensive for me?

That shouldn't happen. Unlike a landlord, who frequently does not care how much of your income you have to spend to pay the rent, a mortgage lender will be very careful that the house you buy will not cost you monthly payments of more than 25–30 percent of your gross verifiable income (overtime is not counted).

Of course, the lender will not know that as soon as you are in the seven-room house you are going out to charge three rooms of new furniture. Or that you'll need another car that will saddle you with an extra $200 a month in payments. The lender is not going to put you on a budget. Managing these new expenses is going to be up to you, and that is sometimes difficult for the first-time buyer. It can take time to get used to monthly mortgage payments, real estate taxes, water and sewage bills, gas and electricity charges, perhaps condo and co-op maintenance fees, and then the ordinary expenses attached to setting up a home—purchasing trash cans, rakes, a lawn mower, etc. There is exultation in owning a home, too, that makes one want to rush out to buy furniture, carpeting, draperies, and every gadget there is to make that castle more attractive.

So you will have to budget, especially the first year or two, until you get the hang of those regular expenses. That may require some changes in your life-style. An emergency repair job may cost you that annual Mexican vacation one year. Something always seems to be going kaput in a home, and repairs may take little dribs and drabs out of your savings at fairly regular intervals. That is to be expected. If you have had your home inspected by an engineer or house inspection service prior to buying, you should have a fairly clear picture of the shape it's in and what repairs, if any, will be needed. That should give you an opportunity to save up for any major expenditures. In all, unless you drastically change the way you live, take on more and more expenses, or get fired from your job, the house you buy should be one you can afford. Your mortgage holder will see to that.

Fear No. 9

What if I buy and then don't like the house? Or I get transferred out of town and must sell? Can I be stuck?

If you don't like your new home, and have given yourself sufficient getting-acquainted time, you can sell it and move. The average American moves nearly ten times in a lifetime, so unless you are 85 years old, the home you are now buying is likely to be only one stop along the road for you. It's wise to be serious about homebuying, but not so serious that you feel you must spend the rest of your days in that first home. Times change, people change, neighborhoods change, lives change, and all of that contributes to today's mobile society and to the steady buying and selling of homes. And you will probably contribute your share to that housing activity. But be sure to hold on to your home until you find a buyer willing to pay the price you want. Try not to let your dissatisfaction lead you to a premature sale.

Unless you are in a very mobile job—one year here, another year there—it may be wise to buy, and then sell your home when you are transferred. Even one year in a house or condo may be worth the investment. Do some number crunching to compare the cost and benefits of renting with the cost and benefits of buying to see whether ownership would make better financial sense, even for the short term. If you do buy and are transferred, try to secure as many benefits and as much housing assistance as you can from your company. Employees don't like moving around so much these days, so corporations are bending over backward to keep them happy when they must be transferred. Let your company try to make you happy.

Fear No. 10

What if I get married?

On the surface, this is a curious question. We don't believe there is any state law prohibiting single homeowners from marrying. But there are nuances here understandable to any unmarried would-be homeowner. Until the mid-1960s, single men and women usually did not buy a home until they married. Since then, thanks in great measure to the advent and success of the condominium, they have entered the homeowner ranks in dramatic numbers. Today, single persons buy huge houses and tiny condos. They buy farms and lofts and mobile homes and any style home that families buy, and why not?

Still, for some unmarried persons there is hesitation about buying a home, despite prodding by relatives, friends, accountants, and the media. What if I buy this house I'm so crazy about and the woman I eventually marry doesn't like it? What if he sees my house and thinks I'm too independent, too inflexible? This small studio co-op is all I can afford, and it isn't large enough for two. Should I go ahead anyway?

Sure, go right ahead. When you marry, housing decisions will be made by the two of you in the same way you make other decisions about your life together. Perhaps you will sell one home and live in the other. Maybe you will sell both and buy a new property together.

The important point to realize is that it's not smart to let your marital status determine whether you will own the home you want *now*. Your income is a factor. Your career situation may be a factor. But whether you are married or not? Nonsense. There are some single persons who, figuratively speaking, never unpack their suitcases. They believe real life doesn't begin until they marry, and so they spend ten years, twenty years, or perhaps the rest of their lives making do with odds and ends and bricks and boards long past the time those economies are needed. Remember the old saying that "life is what happens to us while we're making plans for the future," and act accordingly.

On the more practical side, if you do decide to unload one home to buy another, or to move into the other person's home, try to buy the new place without selling the old one. Unless you're truly pressed for money, or unless the house is far away, it's a good idea to hold it. It's so easy to sell real estate and sometimes so difficult to buy. Try to rent the house. If it's a large structure, see if you can divide it into two full apartment units, bringing you even more income. The rental monies and tax advantages of owning an income-producing property will make that dwelling an excellent investment for both of you.

Have the fears abated a little? Good, they should have. But no doubt dozens of questions remain, and new ones may have occurred to you. The following chapters in this section will take you step by step through the homebuying and selling process, from judging locations to working with a realty agent to financing and to closing, and dozens of points in between. By reading those pages and doing some of the suggested exercises, you will be better prepared and even more confident for stepping out into the marketplace.

11

End-of-the-Century Homeownership: What Can You Buy?

The wealthy have always built castles. Others have lived as best they could, often with a dream of someday owning a place of their own. There was a time when single-family houses were essentially free; you staked out a claim and built your home. That opportunity, however, gasped its last breaths almost a century ago, leaving farms, farmhouses, and a few mountain cabins as its legacy.

With the shift of population to the cities beginning at the turn of the century, apartment living became more common. Even then a few creative souls carved out the first cooperative ownership plans and set the precedents for the conversions that are agitating tenants today. In smaller towns (now our mid-sized cities), two-, three-, four-, and even six-family houses stood in for apartment buildings. Many small business owners simply lived over their stores.

In the 1930s, housing construction, like everything else, slowed down, but the introduction of FHA-insured mortgages kept the middle-class dream of owning a single-family home alive. After World War II, that dream began to blossom, as sprawling tracts of look-alike houses were built for the parents of the baby boom generation. And then in the sixties, condominiums! A possible giant that is today still but a growing child.

Homeownership is alive and well as the twenty-first century approaches. Its forms, however, are more varied than anything imagined in 1885. Let's take a look at them.

Directory of Common Post–World War II
Home Styles

Cape Cod: Most commonly built in large look-alike tracts soon after World War II. Usually these are small, square houses. If upstairs bedrooms have been added, they have pitched roofs and dormers and are often hot in summer and cold in winter.

Colonial: The darling of the late 1960s and 1970s. Two stories, often four bedrooms and two-and-a-half baths with an eat-in kitchen and a family room on the main floor. The extra-large ones may be difficult to resell if the trend to smaller living spaces continues.

Contemporary: Most popular in the West and Southwest. Features include cathedral ceilings, lots of glass, and stone and/or wood construction. Many do not have basements. Somewhat more difficult to sell in the Northeast, where traditional designs are heavily favored.

Ranch: As applied to housing, the name means any house built on one level. Popular during the 1950s and 1960s, but still a standby style especially in luxury homes. Tract ranches were usually 5½ rooms (three bedrooms, living room, dining area, and kitchen), and most had only one bath. More recent models have another bath and a family room. Ranches from the 1950s with do-it-yourself basement family rooms do not command top sales dollars.

Expanded Ranch: This is a ranch floor plan with extra bedrooms added upstairs in Cape Cod style with dormer windows. Often has as many as five bedrooms. Heating and cooling the upstairs area may be a problem.

Raised Ranch or Bi-Level: A house designed in response to the national call for "family" rooms in the mid-1960s. The entry foyer is between floors. Upstairs, a traditional ranch; downstairs, a family room, extra bedroom, laundry room, utility room, and garage. No basement, very little storage. One of the most difficult styles to sell.

Split-Level: The "in" style as the popularity of the Cape Cod began to fade. Like the Cape, it was built in huge look-alike developments. The main level has a small kitchen, living room, and dining area; a half-flight up are the bedrooms and a half-flight down the family room and the garage. This style is disliked by many young families and older buyers because of the ever-present need to navigate stairs.

Tudors, Normandy Castles, Dutch Colonials. Virtually always one of the standard four-bedroom, two-story "colonial" floor plans with a flashy facade designed to attract buyers and raise prices. Size may become a problem in resale too.

Cape Cod

Colonial

Contemporary

Ranch

Expanded ranch

Raised ranch

Split-level

Tudor

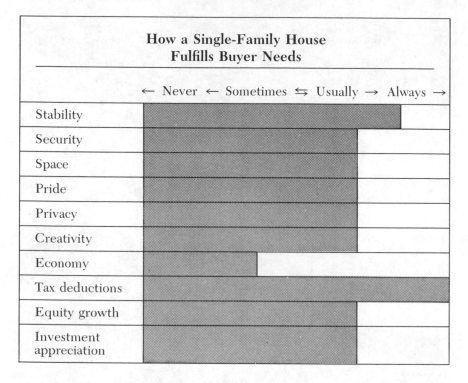

The Single-Family Detached House

In all but our very largest cities, the single-family house surrounded by its own land is still the favored dream. In a National Association of Realtors poll, three out of every four respondents chose this housing form. People feel that it best satisfies their desire for privacy, space, autonomy, and creative expression. It is also the form that requires the greatest time commitment, however, and it is usually, but not always, the most expensive to maintain.

Single-family houses have been around in this country since log cabins and sod huts, yet many single-family housebuyers think only of the "development houses" of the past thirty years or so, and thus miss out on many fine and economical housing options. Older, individually constructed houses in midsized cities tend to be less expensive than their suburban counterparts. (Also less energy-efficient, but increased heating bills might well be compensated for by reduced gasoline bills for the car.) And townhouses—tall, narrow buildings built on every inch of available land so that the wall of one actually touches the wall of another—are making a comeback in popularity.

In the opposite direction, country property is still less expensive than "prestige" suburban housing, and usually comes with more land. A little creative time spent on raising vegetables or chickens, boarding horses, or keeping bees and a thorough enjoyment of the sound of crickets on a summer evening or the sight of a rabbit crossing the lawn while you drink your breakfast coffee might well be worth the extra time and money spent commuting.

And of course some new single-family houses are being built despite the economic woes of the early 1980s. Luxury homes are still luxurious, but the market for middle-class new homebuyers is changing. Newspaper articles are appearing with headlines such as "HOMEBUILDERS SCALE DOWN FOR AFFORDABILITY." Those headlines are verified by a HUD study showing a trend toward decreasing size and fewer amenities. Less than one in five new homes now has four bedrooms, and the two-bedroom house is making a strong comeback. Even the number of bathrooms is being decreased!

Probably the most economical single-family housing option, however, is also the most often overlooked: homes that come from a factory, currently called "manufactured homes." Yes, they were once called mobile homes. Today, however, they often arrive in sections to be assembled and permanently set on a privately owned piece of land. And their cost is 40 percent or so less than that of comparable houses built "on site." (Much more information on this in Chapter 24.)

In real estate offices across the country, there is now a strong interest in nondevelopment houses at virtually every income level. Why this change when the "typical" American buyer of the last three decades has preferred to live in Happy Acres? Primarily it's a response to too many people looking for not enough places to live. But high prices, unstable interest rates, and cost-of-living increases also contribute to the change. People are seeking answers, often creatively and unconventionally, for their housing needs.

Multi-Family Houses

If alive today, few architects would want to take credit for their role in building the multi-family "homes" of the early twentieth century. They are unlovely boxes. Most of them, however, are still standing, structurally sound, and occupied.

In many cases these houses have become "investment properties," owned by absentee landlords. Given the current movement back to the city, however, and tax incentives for the renovation of income-producing property, they may well represent an

How a Multi-Family House Fulfills Buyer Needs

	← Never	← Sometimes	⇄ Usually	→ Always →
Stability				
Security				
Space				
Pride				
Privacy				
Creativity				
Economy				
Tax deductions				
Equity growth				
Investment appreciation				

excellent first-home buying option. Prices are relatively low when compared to single-family houses or condominiums, and renting the unit not occupied by the owner can help make the mortgage payments and pay expenses. For tax purposes, depreciation and deduction of maintenance expenses help to lower the dollars an owner must pay to Uncle Sam.

Multi-family houses also present the opportunity for families or friends to pool financial resources and buy property together. Mortgage payments, taxes, and maintenance expenses can then be shared, but it is likely that income-producing property tax benefits will be lost unless at least one unit is rented.

Not all multi-family houses are simply stacked-up flats. Side-by-side duplexes and triplexes have become popular over the years, and new ones are being built even in prestigious suburban towns. Also, some very old and very large Victorian-style single-family houses have been converted to multi-family units, sometimes to be resold as condominiums, but almost as often to be held by an owner-occupant who rents the remaining units for income. In larger metropolitan areas, what were once townhouses are being renovated to include an owner apartment and one or two rental units. The in-

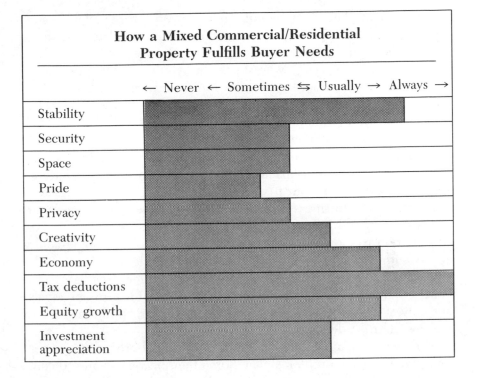

come from those units often pays mortgage, taxes, and expenses while the owner lives "free."

Ownership of a multi-family house is simpler than ownership in a cooperative or condominium, and much more autonomous. You as owner are a small landlord. You may make whatever "creative" changes to the property you can afford (within the law and your lease agreement with your tenants), and you may sell when and to whom you choose.

Living Above the Store

As a young married man with an infant daughter, an ambitious grocer bought a tiny neighborhood store in the early 1940s. Above the store was a four-room apartment into which the family moved. With no rent to pay and food available at wholesale, they lived inexpensively while the business grew and prospered. Soon there was another home and another grocery store.

During his career, continued real estate purchase and sale took this man through ownership of several rental houses, three small apartment buildings, two supermarkets, an exclusive single-family house, several vacation homes, and several pieces of commercial property. Today he lives "comfortably," owning three Florida condominiums, a cooperative, several parcels of land, and an oceanfront summer home in Connecticut.

Of course not everyone who starts out by "living above the store" will travel this Horatio Alger route, but mixed commercial/residential property can provide a young professional person with an excellent start toward homeownership and investment goals.

Properties are available across the nation. Barber shops, real estate agencies, dress stores, pharmacies, paint stores, etc., occupy ground floor space, and upstairs there are apartments, or at least an apartment. This is not luxury living, but it can be a fine place to start. And if the business does well, another home can be purchased in a few years and the original apartment rented.

A slight variation on living above the store is the single-family house with a professional wing or with professional offices in the basement. Psychologists, nursery school teachers, pediatricians, dentists, lawyers, and beauticians, to name but a few professionals, not only start out this way but choose it as their optimum place of business and residence.

Bringing a business into a residential neighborhood, however, sometimes creates problems. The home then becomes a mixed commercial-residential property that usually violates the zoning regulations. A zoning variance, however, will solve the problem. If the neighbors don't object to the property use, it is usually granted.

Condominiums

Now we move into the realm of the invisible. When you own a condominium, you own air space. But wait! That's not as bad as it sounds. The exact amount of air space you own and its exact location within tangible walls is recorded in your local government records office, and you receive a deed to that air space. No one else can occupy it.

As bonus investment protection *and* as required by law, you as a condominium unit owner also own an *undivided interest* in the *common elements* of the property in which your unit exists. Common elements are everything not specifically owned by any individual unit owner: the land, the walls, the plumbing and wiring within those walls, the swimming pool, the parking lots, the recreation room, lobby and hallways, the roof, and the windows, just to start the list. Theoretically, all the unit owners in the condominium community use these elements in common.

Your undivided interest in the common elements is an interest that cannot be separated or severed from the others. You do not own a certain number of bricks in the walls of your building, you own a certain share of each brick and the same share of each grainy bit of mortar that holds them together. Usually you do not even own your patio or your balcony. Such areas are called *limited common elements;* the condominium community owns them, but only the individual owners of a particular unit can use them. In other words, only you can light up the hibachi on your patio and only you can park in your garage space.

But perhaps we're getting ahead of ourselves. What does a condominium look like anyway? The question is a bit like asking "What does a dog look like?" Are you going to describe a Saint Bernard or a toy poodle? Condominiums come in a seemingly endless variety of shapes and sizes. Some are apartment units in luxury high rises; some are units in long rows of two-story buildings that resemble public housing; some look like a part of the set for a movie (*The Great Gatsby? Star Wars?*); some are the two halves of an "English Country House" in a community of look-alike, close-together English country houses; and some are subdivided rooms in a renovated and remodeled Robber Baron's house, guest house, or carriage house.

Condominiums are usually apartments, but that designation leaves a lot to human imagination and ingenuity. And some condominiums are *not* apartments. There are mobile home condominium communities, and commercial shopping center condominium communities, and professional office condominium communities, and even stateroom-on-a-ship condominium communities!

But let's stick to homeownership. When you buy a condominium you own real property. You can mortgage it exactly like a single-family house, and you pay real estate taxes on it to your local gov-

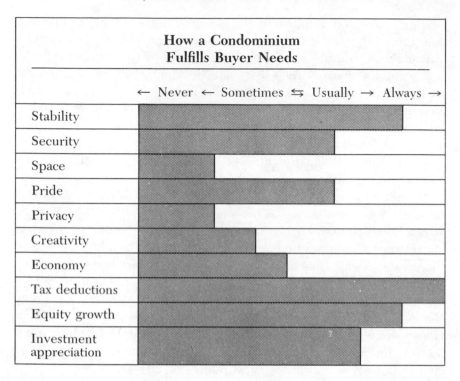

ernment. You can also use all the tax deductions available to single-family homeowners on your federal income tax return.

Unlike a single-family home, however, you are not responsible for outside or structural maintenance work. On the other hand, you cannot significantly alter the landscaping or make any structural changes in your property.

The common elements of a condominium are almost always controlled by an association of unit owners, which is established when the property is declared a condominium. (The legal document that creates a condominium is usually called the *Declaration*.) This association is run by a *board of directors* (in some areas called a board of managers) that is elected by the unit owners from among themselves. The board of directors supervises the maintenance work and rules on any requests for decorating or remodeling changes. You could put up a wall to divide a large bedroom into two small bedrooms inside your unit without the board's permission (you control the inside space), but you could not change the lighting fixture next to your front door or paint that door burnt orange without applying to the board.

Living in a condominium, you have complete freedom from cutting grass, raking leaves, and shoveling snow, but you pay for this freedom. Condominium communities require a monthly maintenance fee from each unit owner to keep the community running. The number of votes in the unit owners' association assigned to your unit in the Declaration will determine the portion of the condominium's annual expenses that you must pay. This fee is smaller than in cooperative apartment buildings because there can be no mortgage on the common elements of a condominium and because all local real estate taxes are paid by the owners of the individual units. No portion of a condominium maintenance fee is tax-deductible, however.

Because the common elements of a condominium cannot be mortgaged (unlike a co-op, where loans can be secured by the building), major repairs or improvements, such as the addition of a tennis court or the replacement of a worn-out elevator, must be financed by special assessments to the unit owners. If the majority of the members of your unit owners' association vote *yes* for an improvement that you do not want, you are still required to pay your share of the special assessment. If you don't have the money to meet the assessment, you can take out a second mortgage or a home improvement type loan based on the equity in your unit.

Before you buy a condominium, it is important that you understand the bylaws and house rules under which you will live. Among the regulations that have been upheld in courts across the country are the association's right to do the following:

- Prohibit pets or restrict their kind and size.
- Restrict ownership to a certain age group. (This includes the right to prohibit children, except in California.)
- Prohibit drinking alcoholic beverages or smoking in the common areas.
- Strictly regulate subletting or the renting of units on a weekly or monthly basis. (This rule is especially important if you buy a unit in a prime vacation area.)
- Require that the board of directors have a right of first refusal on the sale of any unit.

A right of first refusal stipulates that the board of directors will have the opportunity to match the agreed-upon sales price of any prospective buyer and thus to buy the apartment and stop that sale. Usually it is written into a condominium's bylaws in an attempt to keep the community homogeneous. It is prohibited, however, in any condominium community financed with HUD funds, and prospective buyers cannot obtain FHA or VA financing to buy a unit in a condominium where the board has the right of first refusal.

Although you own real property in a condominium, your investment is very much intertwined with that of every other unit owner.

Is it safe? Most likely. In fact, being a condominium may even *improve* its chances for appreciation. Condominiums are the fastest-growing type of housing in the country today. Most of the wrinkles in state condominium laws have been worked out, and in most states consumer protection is good, especially in states where condominiums are very common (New York, Michigan, Virginia, Florida, Hawaii, and California, to name a few). And perhaps most important, investment appreciation seems very likely since condominiums have been accepted by the general public as an appealing alternative to single-family homeownership.

Condos appeal to the young couple buying their first home and to the older person trying to shed the demands of home maintenance. They have special appeal to singles (especially single career women) and divorced people. Some are being purchased purely as investment property, some as second homes, and some as the life-style of choice even by the two-parent, two-child "typical" American family.

Cooperative Apartments

People who "own" co-op apartments don't actually own real property at all; they own shares of stock in the corporation that owns the building in which their apartment is located. Their right to occupy a

particular apartment and use the common areas of the building is guaranteed by a *proprietary lease* (sometimes called a *Certificate of Beneficial Interest*). To maintain that right, however, they must also pay a certain portion of the cooperative's expenses, which usually include a mortgage on the building, real estate taxes, repair and fix-up costs, heat, water, etc.

But "owning" a co-op is almost like owning real property, especially in the eyes of most lenders and the federal government. Loans to buy a co-op apartment are written much like mortgages despite the fact that they are personal loans secured by stock in the corporation. That stock is assigned to each apartment when the cooperative is created. The number of shares attached to a given apartment determines voting power at stockholder meetings *and* the apartment's share of the annual expenses. It can be changed only by the unanimous vote of the shareholders.

The Internal Revenue Service also treats co-op owners pretty much like single-family homeowners. Section 216 of the IRS code allows deductions on individual federal income tax returns for each tenant/shareholder's portion of the municipal taxes and the mortgage interest paid by the corporation, as well as the interest that is paid on the individual's apartment purchase loan.

There are restrictions and qualifications, however, that must be met by a cooperative corporation to assure tenant/shareholders of their tax deductions. Best known among these is the 80/20 rule. Briefly, it requires that 80 percent of the gross income of the cooperative be derived directly from the tenant/shareholders. (This does not preclude subletting; during a sublet the tenant/shareholder is still paying a share of expenses.) In any given year, if more than 20 percent of the cooperative's income is derived from sources other than the shareholders (from the renting of commercial space on the ground floor, for example), every tenant/shareholder will lose the homeowner-type deductions.

Among the other government regulations on cooperatives are the requirements that only one class of stock be issued by the corporation and that each stockholder be entitled to occupy an apartment in which to live. Only individuals, lending institutions that acquire the stock by foreclosure, and the sellers of the building to the cooperative corporation can hold stock. These regulations effectively keep big business and real estate syndicates out of the co-op scene.

A cooperative is run by a board of directors just like any other corporation, even though a management company may be hired to

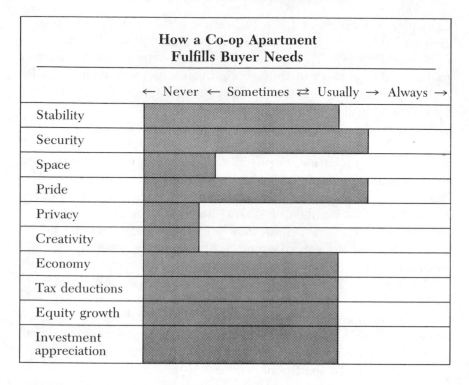

How a Co-op Apartment Fulfills Buyer Needs			
	← Never ← Sometimes ⇄ Usually → Always →		
Stability			
Security			
Space			
Pride			
Privacy			
Creativity			
Economy			
Tax deductions			
Equity growth			
Investment appreciation			

collect "rents" and supervise maintenance. Members of the board are elected from among the residents, but rarely receive salaries.

Generally, buying a cooperative means a commitment to a community lifestyle. You may well overhear an argument in your neighbor's kitchen, you will share the cost of repairs if a hurricane strikes your area, and bylaws and house rules will determine whether you or your neighbor can keep a dog or even live in the building if you have children under a certain age. Even though you "own" your apartment, you may live in it only if you abide by those rules.

In order to assure the financial stability of the community, the bylaws of most cooperatives also reserve to the board of directors the right to evict any tenant/shareholder who is not paying the monthly maintenance fee assigned to his apartment. That apartment can then be sublet until the stock is sold to another party. Does this sound harsh to you? Perhaps it is, but the rule is an effective deterrent to tenant/shareholder defaults, a string of which might increase the size and burden of maintenance fees to the other tenant/shareholders and thus start a domino effect of defaults eventually causing the whole building (corporation) to default on its financial and tax obligations.

The bylaws of most cooperatives also reserve to the board of directors (or in some cases a majority of the stockholders) the right to approve or reject the sale of stock (and thereby the sale of an apartment) to a potential purchaser. This clause has been tested in court cases, and the rulings have upheld boards' rights to refuse sales for any reason *or no reason*, except that a refusal cannot be voiced as an objection to race, color, creed, or national origin. Most tenant/shareholders support this clause even though it might one day affect the sale of their own apartment. They feel it assures the security and compatibility of the cooperative community.

Co-ops are most common in New York City, but Chicago, the greater Miami area, San Francisco, Washington, and Buffalo all also have rather significant co-op populations. There is a smattering throughout the rest of the country, especially in Connecticut, Illinois, Massachusetts, Michigan, New Jersey, and South Dakota. Most are older buildings converted from rental apartments, often with the cooperative corporation's assumption of excellent long-term financing on the property.

The existence of this below-market-rate financing (let's say a twenty-year self-liquidating first mortgage at 7½ percent with twelve years of its pay-out period remaining) helps to keep maintenance fees down. When a building is converted, tenants (especially those in rent-controlled areas) are usually offered "insider" prices on their apartments which range from 40 to 60 percent off market value, making those apartments some of today's best buys in real estate.

For More Information

"The Home Buying Veteran," VA Pamphlet 26-6, is a good general overview of homebuying and is available free to anyone. Call your local Veterans Administration office.

"Questions About Condominiums," a free HUD pamphlet, is available from U.S. Dept. of Housing and Urban Development, Washington, D.C. 20410.

Also recommended are: *The Complete Guide to Co-ops and Condominiums*, by David T. Goldstick and Carolyn Janik, Plume ($7.95); *American Shelter: An Illustrated Encyclopedia of the American Home*, by Lester Walker, Overlook Press, 1981; *A Field Guide to American Architecture*, by Carole Rifkind, New American Library, 1980; and *The American House: Styles of Architecture Coloring Book*, by A. G. Smith, Dover Publications, 1983.

12

Location: How to Pick Your Piece of the Earth

"It will determine the potential appreciation of your home," says an article in a slick magazine. "It will affect the settling of a new house and the potential for basement water problems in a house of any age," says a home-fix-it newspaper column. "It's gonna make a difference in how much taxes you'll pay, and how long you stay in the house, too," says your mother-in-law. And your real estate agent hands you a photo of a rather ordinary split-level saying, with a smile, "You realize, of course, that you'll have to pay a little more for this house because of its prime location."

Location, real estate's *sine qua non*, can make or break the value, longevity, and desirability of a house and affect all the people who call that house their home. No other real estate factor equals its importance, and nothing else should be considered as carefully when choosing property of any kind.

But the real estate term *location* means more than the piece of the earth described by metes and bounds in your deed or staked out by a surveyor's red-flagged sticks. That's just a *lot*. *Location* is that lot, and the neighborhood around it, and the town in which the neighborhood lies. You may not be able to afford all the house and location you would like, but a knowledge of why one location is more valuable than another will help you get the most for the money you can afford.

On a grander scale, location even includes state and area of the country. You may be making such a grand choice depending upon your attitudes, career, age, or circumstances beyond your control.

This chapter, however, is limited to the location choices most of us make most often: town, neighborhood, and lot.

Choosing Your Hometown

Today, few Americans grow old in the neighborhood where they were born. Those who do often remark "You can hardly recognize the place anymore!"

That we live in an age of change and movement is an oft-repeated fact. Less often discussed, however, are the means of gaining some sense of security and happiness in such a world. Certainly housing is one avenue to that security and happiness; location is the pavement on the road. Now, let's look at the factors in choosing among local towns.

Taxes

As inevitable as death, so they say. But the services you get and the amount you pay for those services are neither inevitable nor equal. Property tax is still the primary source of revenue for the American municipality, whether it be a metropolis or a blink-and-you've-missed-it village. The character of the community's real estate is a major factor in determining the tax structure.

Everyone pays property taxes. Well, *almost* everyone; some individuals are fortunate (or smart) enough to get tax abatements. The rest of us send in our tax dollars in various ways. Tenants pay in their rent, homeowners and condominium owners pay directly or through their mortgage lender, and co-op owners pay in their maintenance fees. Paying is a given. The real questions are, How is the amount of taxes decided upon, and what do we get for our tax dollar?

There are two determinants of the amount you must pay to your town: mill rate and assessed valuation. A mill is one-tenth of one cent. In terms of money, it is the actual dollar figure you pay on each $1000 of the assessed value of your property. So if your home is assessed at $100,000 and your town's mill rate is 23.7 you must pay $23.70 for each one thousand dollars of assessed value. (Multiply 100 x 23.7 to give you a tax bill of $2370 a year.)

But this is almost too simple for the government, right? Just to complicate matters a little, many (if not most) municipalities express their mill rates in terms of rate per *one hundred* dollars of assessed valuation. In the case of our example, then, you would pay 2.37

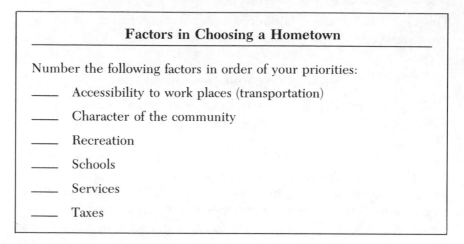

Factors in Choosing a Hometown

Number the following factors in order of your priorities:

_____ Accessibility to work places (transportation)

_____ Character of the community

_____ Recreation

_____ Schools

_____ Services

_____ Taxes

dollars for every 100 dollars of your assessment. To figure your tax bill, you would ask yourself: how many $100 units in $100,000? Answer 1000. Then you would multiply 2.37 times 1000 and come up with the same answer, $2370.

But before you go forth to find the town with the lowest mill rate, get the vital statistics on assessed valuation. Not every town bases its mill rate on an assessment of 100 percent of fair market value. Town A might have a mill rate of 23.7 on 60 percent of fair market value assessment while Town B has the same mill rate on 100 percent of fair market value. You will pay considerably lower taxes for the same amount of house in town A.

There seems to be a nationwide movement, led by large, heavily populated states like New York and California, to base all property taxes upon 100 percent of fair market value, determined either by professional assessments or simply by the actual sale price of the property at the last change of hands. But movements such as this take time to make their way across a country as vast and varied as ours, and there are still places where homeowners are paying 11.5 mills on a 40 percent assessed valuation established in 1975! So call the town tax collector's office or ask real estate agents for tax structure information on the towns that interest you. If you should discover that the low taxes of a particular town are based upon an evaluation done eight or nine years ago, be wary. Another assessment may be in the works and you may face a significant jump in taxes soon after you buy a house in that town.

Residential property taxes, however, are not the only revenue source for a municipality. Income is also generated by taxes on business and industrial property. A town with a high proportion of business and industry to residences is therefore likely to have a lower overall tax rate, since taxes upon the nonresidential structures help to offset the cost of services to community residents.

A few of our largest cities also have sales taxes and personal income taxes. But don't pat yourself on the back too quickly for avoiding these taxes by choosing to live outside the city limits. You'll pay the city's sales tax on the shopping you do there. And if you happen to work "in the city," you'll pay the city's personal income tax, too. You should consider these taxes as a part of your cost of suburban living. Add them to the municipal, county, and state taxes that you pay, and you may find that your suburban tax bill is not as comfortable as you thought.

"Will the taxes go up?" is the homebuyer's second question right after "What are the taxes?" And the answer is almost always "Oh everything is very stable here. We don't expect any big tax jumps." But do some investigating on your own. Answers to questions about stable taxes fall into the same category as responses to questions about good schools. Everyone has them.

Some basics to consider:

• Is the town about to undergo a reevaluation of its property taxes? Will there be a reassessment? It's rare for taxes to go down in such situations.

• How do the present and projected school population relate to the school plant facilities in the town? Will the town need more teachers or even a new school in the near future? (Expensive!) Or is the population stable or diminishing? Can a school be closed, perhaps rented to a recreational organization such as a YMCA? Can fewer teachers be hired?

• How much open space exists? How is it zoned? New single-family housing developments, condominiums, high rise co-ops, low-cost housing, planned unit developments, and the conversion of industrial space into rental housing can increase the school population and the demand for municipal services more than the added tax dollars they generate. Thus, higher taxes for everyone. New office buildings, shopping centers, industrial plants, and commercial recreational buildings, on the other hand, can cushion the tax demand on individuals.

• What shape are the town buildings and equipment in? A new town hall or a new police station can cost plenty. Even fire trucks and police cars can increase the taxes somewhat.

• What's the town's track record like? Have tax rates been relatively stable over the past few years? Have there been any scandals regarding mismanagement or misappropriation of municipal funds? How does the balance sheet look? Is the town financially healthy?

Schools

Back in the eighteenth century, the founding fathers decided to leave the matter of education to the local communities. Since then the states and even the federal government have gotten into the act to varying degrees, but essentially the character and quality of American schools is still determined by the people of the community around each school.

If you are a single person buying property, or a couple who does not plan to have children, you may wonder about this long section on schools. But don't skip to the next section too hastily. You may not care about the schools, but the schools *will* affect the taxes you pay on your property. Also, the odds are excellent that any potential buyer of your house will be concerned with the schools. Good schools almost invariably equal a better selling price for a home.

Among the first questions that a parent asks a real estate agent is "How are the schools?" That question, however, is really wasted breath. The answer is always good, fine, or excellent. Rather than ask so general a question, ask for some specifics:

• How many elementary schools are there in town?

• Are the children bused? Why? (Rural nature of the town or for racial balance?)

• How are the grades grouped? Kindergarten to 6 in one building, 7 to 9 in junior high school, and 10 to 12 in high school was the traditional grouping for many years. Today, many communities are using school buildings to group children more closely by age. Kindergarten to 4, 5 to 8, and a four-year high school has become an especially popular pattern. Some parents prefer a different grouping, however.

• What's the average class size in elementary school?

• What special programs are offered in elementary school?

• What subjects do junior high or middle school students study? At what grade can foreign language study begin? Are there advanced math courses for bright students below the high school level?

• How do local pupils rate on standardized tests as against other area towns? Other areas of the state or nation?

• What courses are offered at the high school level? (You can usually get a printed course of study booklet that is given to students.)

- What courses are required for graduation?
- What percentage of each high school class graduates?
- What do graduates do after graduation? Where do they go to college? Professional training school?

Most important of all, ask about the amount of writing done in the classroom. Virtually every school study recommends more writing in our schools in every subject and at every grade level. Teaching by requiring students to write, however, takes more time than filling in the blanks in lesson books, and only the finest schools and finest teachers do it consistently. The amount of writing being done in a school system is a good indication of the quality of the education going on there.

If schools rank high on your list of factors in choosing a town, we strongly recommend that you visit several schools in the towns you are considering before you make a commitment to buy a home. Principals are usually happy to discuss their schools and their programs with prospective parents, and you will surely get a tour of the plant facilities. Try to sit in on a class or two if you can, and be sensitive to what is happening. Is there an emphasis on learning to think or on learning "right" answers? Are the students treated as individuals? How much freedom is allowed in the classroom? What's on the bulletin boards? And listen in on whatever snatches of student conversation you can catch.

After you have asked questions of real estate agents, local residents, and school administrators, and after you have visited several schools, give due respect to your gut feelings. Don't be overly influenced by reputation or by what others have told you to expect, since reputation often lags behind reality. A school system may be declining rapidly, yet still basking in its past success; more frequently, a system that is making impressive improvements may suffer under a mediocre reputation.

Services

People are always surprised when a service that they took for granted in their old hometown is not provided by their new. But the grisly fact of the matter is that you get more for your money in some places than in others. Among other things, find out about:

- *Refuse collection.* Some towns provide it; others don't. If yours doesn't, you will have to make regular trips to the town dump or pay a private collector for garbage pickup. Cost is usually between $10 and $20 a month; add it to your annual taxes when comparing one town against another.

• *Sewers*. Generally large cities use sewers, and rural areas use septic tanks. In the suburbs you may find both in the same town. Is there a sewer use fee? Add it to your taxes. Are sewers projected for the neighborhood that interests you and will you be required to pay a sewer assessment and a hook-up fee? Will town sewer installations be added to everyone's tax bill in the near future?

• *Water*. Is city water free (included in your tax bill), or do you pay the city for the water you use? Do you pay a private water company? If the property uses well water, is the water pure and plentiful? And don't be too anxious to add disadvantage points to the house in the next town that pays $35 a quarter for water use; the pump on a well draws electricity, so the water isn't really "free," is it?

• *Road service*. How well will your streets be plowed in winter? Sometimes you can get a clue by how well they are maintained during the spring, summer, and fall.

• *Police protection*. What's the crime rate like? Can you go out safely at night? Are break-ins common? Does the town maintain rescue vehicles, or must you pay for private ambulance services? How large is the police force in relation to the population? How does this compare to other areas?

• *Fire department*. Is the fire department full-time or volunteer? Most cities use full-time personnel; most suburbs and rural areas use volunteers or a combination of full-time, part-time, and volunteers. How well are they equipped? How is equipment paid for: by taxes or by contributions?

• *Library services*. A town's library services are often a clue to its character. How large is the library system in relation to the town? Does it belong to an exchange library group? Does it feature any special collections? Is there a children's library? Are there many library activities, or is the building limited to books and quiet reading?

• *Social services*. Does the town sponsor programs for senior citizens, teenagers, and children? Are family counseling services available? (In rural areas, such services are often provided on a county basis.) What special services for the poor are offered?

Recreation

As a factor in choosing a hometown, recreation may or may not be important since people readily cross city, state, and even national boundaries in search of fun. Thus your personal needs and lifestyle will determine how much attention you give to recreational facilities in and near the towns you are considering.

Of course, there are some recreational factors that increase property value in a town whether you use them or not. An example is a lake within the town borders, especially if there is a beach maintained for the use of residents and their guests. Or a marina in a seaside town "for residents only." Or a municipal golf course that would attract Arnold Palmer. Or even a municipal ski lift or toboggan run in a mountaintop town. Any such factor that makes living in a particular town "special" will usually increase the price of houses there.

Some people don't mind that their town has few recreational facilities. If there are facilities available in a nearby town, that's good enough for them. In fact, facilities outside the town may be preferable since they allow easy access for residents without the noise and traffic of fun-seekers coming into their town.

In evaluating the recreational opportunities offered within a town, consider how they are used every bit as carefully as what they are. Everyone asks, "Are there parks in town?" What they should ask is:

• Are there enough fields to allow little league and youth soccer seasons to run concurrently?

• Are tennis courts open on a first-come, stay-as-long-as-you-like basis, or is there a reservation system?

• Are scouts or other community groups allowed the use of the parks for overnight camp-outs or rallies?

• Are there any indoor municipal recreation facilities?

Accessibility to Work Places

How long are you willing to travel, twice a day five days a week, in order to get to and from work? The connection between hometown and work place has become a major factor in choosing where to live. Most people are unwilling to go beyond a one-hour commute (which is actually two hours a day).

Access to work places in general is also a major factor in determining property value. Towns surrounding major corporate headquarters usually rank high in desirability. Second in line are towns along major interstate highways or on rail commuter lines that provide access to multiple work places. Dollar value appreciation in these towns is especially likely if the corporate population of a state or area is growing. On the other hand, the shutdown or relocation of a major employer can devastate property values in the towns where employees own homes.

Transportation within the residential community has less effect on property value, even though it might be very important for you.

Thirty years ago real estate agents wrote "two blocks from bus stop" on their listings as a positive feature, but not so today. City dwellers expect that public transportation will be available, and most suburbanites have resigned themselves to having at least one car per adult resident.

The Community's Character

Communities have personalities just as individuals do, and no two are quite alike. Choosing a hometown is a little like choosing a mate or a friend: the personality of choice need not be *like* yours, just compatible!

Do you want to live in an area with many types of people, or are you more comfortable with people pretty much like yourself? Do you want lots going on, lots to do, or is a Sunday picnic in the park your big day? Would it bother you to know that 20 percent of your community's population changes each year because of company transfers? Would you hesitate to make friends knowing the likelihood of corporate transfers?

And how about your hobbies and interests and those of your family? If yours is an artistic world, are there artistic, musical, or active theater groups in the area? If religion is important to you, how far will you have to travel to attend the services of your choice? Is there an active congregation of like faith in the community? If you are a gourmet, are there enough really good restaurants within easy traveling distance?

Such factors have nothing to do with tax rates and municipal balance sheets but are essential fiber in the community's character. And they are as important to your happiness as good schools and services are to potential value appreciation. This is an area where

---

Checking Out the Towns

Rate between 1 (worst) and 5 (best) how well each of the following aspects of each town meets your personal needs and goals. You can then compare towns by (1) comparing totals, (2) comparing one factor across the board (for example, schools), and (3) picking your three most important factors (see the chart on page 187, totaling them for each town, and then comparing how the towns rank against each other in terms of your personal preferences).

Choice Factors	TOWNS								
Accessibility to the work place									
Local transportation									
Character of the community									
Recreation (space)									
Recreation (activities)									
Schools									
Municipal services									
Taxes									
Special considerations									
Shopping									
Medical facilities									
Accessibility to places of worship									
Child care facilities									
Opportunity for post–high school education									
Totals									

feelings enter into choices and where real estate's rational numbers are not primary.

Most people looking for houses within a forty-mile radius of where they are currently living have little difficulty assessing the character of the communities they are considering. Character becomes a problem in the company transfer or the long-distance relocation. If such is your situation, you will never be quite as secure in choosing your hometown by character as one of the "natives" might be, but there are aids to getting the feel of communities.

Realty offices are a good place to start, but be sure to choose one that belongs to the local Multiple Listing Service (MLS) so that you will get the widest possible perspective. To get a general overview of several communities, it's also usually better to choose one of the larger firms in the area.

Where transferees are abundant, many real estate firms have special programs for placing out-of-state buyers. Some offer prepared booklets describing the character of each community they serve, its median house price, a profile of the school system, a listing of recreational facilities, and information on taxes, potential growth and development, local industry, special interest groups, and ethnic festivals. Other firms show films that take the prospective buyer on a tour of local communities while seated in the firm's reception room.

In an office with well-trained agents, a prospective buyer will be asked to fill out a family-interest questionnaire. The agent will then try to advise the buyer on which communities in the area best fill those needs. In some high-tech offices, this family profile is typed into an office computer, and a list of towns is produced in seconds.

If your real estate firm does not offer these services or if you prefer to do a little research on your own, ask the real estate agent to allow you to look through the MLS listing books (or sheets, or cards) for all the towns that the office serves. Listings are arranged in price order virtually everywhere, and most people turn immediately to their price range. *Don't*. Instead, look at all the properties available in each town and make comparisons. Try to get a socioeconomic overview of the area. Notice which towns have the widest range between the least expensive and the most expensive listings, and note in which price range most houses for sale fall. Notice those towns that are more or less homogeneous, with most houses for sale at pretty much the same price. Notice where condominiums are prevalent and where houses on five acres appear. Which towns have the most listings? The least? Do these findings coincide with the populations of those towns, or is the town with the smallest number of active listings especially desirable and the town with the largest number undesirable? (Ask the agent why.)

Your second stop in evaluating community character should be the planning or zoning board office, usually located in the town hall. There you can request to see the town's *master plan*. Although the information is free and readily available, few buyers actually check it. The master plan is an x-ray of the town. On the map you will see all the current streets with their zoning indicated and all proposed zoning and development. Future highways, open spaces, and the potential for high-density housing or commercial development will be apparent with but a few minutes of study. One word of caution, however: zoning can be changed, so don't assume that every line on the master plan is carved in granite.

Once you have narrowed your choice of towns down to a few, visit the library of each one. Tell the reference librarian that you are considering buying a house in the town and would like some information on the community. The library may well have a community profile that has been prepared by the League of Women Voters, the Jaycees, or some other civic group. It will usually have material on local history and activities.

Check the local newspapers. Don't get the area's "big name" paper; get a community weekly. A paper small enough to care about school problems, zoning board meetings, the doings of the mayor's office, the achievements of local personalities, and who won the little league championship. Ask the librarian for back issues, one a month for six months. You'll really see what's going on in the town.

The Neighborhood Counts

The essential element of neighborhood is nearness. Whether you are talking about a city block, a builder's tract, a condominium community, a walled private association of luxury houses, or a rural road, like it or not the houses around your house are your neighborhood. Let's look at some aspects of the house-neighborhood connection.

Relative Size and Style

People tend to feel most comfortable in neighborhoods of homogeneous socioeconomic makeup, and houses sell best when they fall in the middle of a neighborhood's price range. This is true whether we are talking about a tract with only four different models or a grouping of suburban houses that were built at different times, in different styles, and of different size.

The extremely large house surrounded by smaller houses will not appreciate as much as it would if it were located in a neighborhood of houses like itself. Neighboring houses seem to dictate the price of your house. A house with a two-story, $30,000 addition may only bring $4000–$5000 more when sold than its additionless twin down the street. You may get a bargain by buying the biggest house in the neighborhood, a great deal of space and amenities for the money, but remember that you will not sell it for a whopping big profit. Most prospective buyers want their property value secured by being surrounded by other houses of comparable value.

Generally, the smallest house in the neighborhood gets a somewhat better price than it would bring in an area of houses its own size. The reverse of the large house, its value is pulled up by the price of neighboring properties. Be aware, however, that it might take a little longer to sell the smallest house. Some buyers are intimidated by the thought of keeping up with the Joneses. Others are unwilling to pay extra for a prestige neighborhood and a smaller house. The "right" buyer, however, invariably comes along eventually.

Boundaries

"Well, we live on the edge of our neighborhood," says one Missouri homeowner. "The high school is behind us and then there's a street that's mostly old houses converted to doctors' and lawyers' offices. It makes it really nice and quiet."

It may indeed, but edges of a neighborhood are not usually good housing choices if you are considering profitable resale. Price security resides in the center of a like grouping of homes. Even a huge condominium community is affected by a nearby office building or industrial plant. The condos on the outer edge will resell for less than those in the middle of the community.

If yours is a moderate-sized house on the edge of a neighborhood of moderate-sized houses that abuts a neighborhood of Tudor castles, your house will always look a little dwarfed by its fancy neighbors in the next neighborhood. After nearness, socioeconomic sameness is most important in creating a sense of grouping. It forms an almost visible dividing line, and it is best not to be near the line. Thus an elegant and luxurious contemporary will sell for less than its like-styled neighbors if around the corner from it stands a group of post–World War II Cape Cods.

But there's an exception to this rule. Houses on the edge of neighborhoods that are bounded by woods, parks, or golf courses will sell *better* than those in the middle of the neighborhood. Such natural boundaries and open spaces are especially appealing to buyers.

Maintenance

A working woman from Memphis remembers the awful time her family had selling their home. "We were next door to this house where both people worked and no one did anything to keep up the house. Paint was peeling from all the trim, the screen door on the front hung at a crazy angle from one hinge, and the lawn was a weed patch that was hardly ever cut. Houses exactly like ours on the next street over were selling in a matter of weeks for $150,000, but ours was on the market for months and we finally took $129,000. Sometimes real estate agents would make an appointment, and we'd be all ready, only to see a car slow down in front of our house and then drive away. Sometimes the agents called and apologized for not coming in, usually they didn't. No one ever said it was the house next door that kept them away, but I knew it was."

Unfortunately you can't force your neighbor to cut the grass or paint, so be wary of buying next door to a handyman special with a junk car parked on the lawn. Safety lies in finding a neighborhood where each person is especially proud of his or her home.

You may think that maintenance is not an issue in a condominium community since it is done professionally. But condominiums have personalities and images too, and shoddy, haphazard maintenance can ruin resale value. Be sure your condominium is run by a board of directors that oversees and insists upon careful maintenance.

Some single-family houses are located in private associations which might own a clubhouse, golf course, swimming pool, and sometimes even the roads. There may be rules in these associations about home maintenance and intense pressure to comply. "The rules are for the benefit of all," say the neighbors.

Good maintenance can add many thousands to the value of older homes, especially if there is a movement toward refurbishing throughout the neighborhood. Least affected by the maintenance of the neighboring houses are country properties where considerable land separates dwellings.

Lifestyle

Neighborhoods often develop a kind of tone or harmony of lifestyle that individuals within them accept as "the way it is." See if you can detect a neighborhood's tone and if you feel comfortable with it.

Are children's toys left in front yards or on the sidewalks? Are children allowed to play in the street? Is there graffiti on the stop signs? Are rural mail boxes dented and rusted? Do pets run free, or are they carefully walked and gutter-trained? Are a majority of the yards fenced? Or are property boundaries not particularly noticeable? Are car parts or broken-down washing machines rusting in backyards, or does Lawn Doctor arrive each week to be certain that not a weed protrudes from between the Belgian-block curbing? Do plastic deer decorate front lawns, or do stone pillars flank driveways and split-leaf red maples brighten manicured lawns? It's difficult to place economic value upon neighborhood style. But it's important that you be aware of it in your househunting.

Travel Patterns

When choosing a neighborhood, consider your travel patterns. How will you get to work and where will you do your shopping? Travel those routes at peak hours and get a feel for the driving you will be doing. Can you handle it on a regular basis? How about the route to schools, churches, and the activities your family likes to do? Choosing the wrong neighborhood location for your interests and lifestyle can commit you to hours in the car every week.

If you have three children under 5 years old, consider carefully before choosing a house in a development five miles from the nearest corner store, even if the price tag is $5000 or more cheaper than the same-size house closer to town. A ten-mile round trip every time you run out of milk will not increase the harmony of your home life.

On the other hand, if *real* deer in your backyard at dusk and the sounds of birds rather than traffic are important to you, you may opt for extra driving time as a price well worth paying. Just be aware that you are making that decision.

Traffic Patterns

Early in their marriage, Joe and Carolyn Janik rented an apartment on a quiet Sunday afternoon. Before dawn on the Monday morning after they moved in, they were astounded to discover that their bedroom window was but a hundred feet from the major truck route through New Haven, Connecticut. The experience cost them a year sprinkled with nights of interrupted sleep, but the lost sleep was a fine investment. They were careful not to make such a location error in any of the five houses that followed.

You can avoid the error without the bad experience. Visit the neighborhood you are considering on different days and at different times of day, especially the common rush hours. What looks like a quiet street at 1 P.M. may be the short-cut home for half the town at 5 P.M. And houses on busy streets do not sell well.

Sounds and Smells

While you are visiting to monitor traffic patterns, be sensitive to everything around you. Sounds from a nearby highway will lower property value, as will heavy air traffic overhead or the noise of a working rock quarry just over the hill.

And check smells. They are invisible and sometimes carry over long distances. Living near a chemical plant may make life in your house unbearable on a warm summer day. Likewise with the town sewage processing plant or even the town dump.

Take nothing for granted. Spend some time driving around appealing neighborhoods without the real estate agent. (Agents have a habit of choosing the loveliest approaches to property that is for sale.)

Talk with the Neighbors

One of the best ways to get a feeling for a neighborhood is to talk with the people who live there. Walk the streets on a sunny day and strike up a conversation with anyone you see raking, gardening, walking a dog, or minding children. In fact, talk with the children. You may be surprised at how forthright and honest they are.

When talking with adults, ask nonthreatening questions—you do not want to appear as though you are passing judgment on the neighborhood. Start with specifics and let the conversation drift, carefully controlled, to the topics and opinions that you want.

The Lay of Your Land

"The land and all that is attached to it" is the generally accepted definition of real estate, and the land should be your concern, even before the house that stands upon it. Unfortunately, this is rarely the case with homebuyers. They fall in love with a house first and then look at the lot upon which it is built. In fact, walking the lot lines is a sure-fire sign to sellers that a buyer is seriously interested in their property. You will probably fall in love with the house first, especially if it is in a preferred town and neighborhood, but be aware of the importance of the lot, too. The following are some factors to consider.

Shape

Generally rectangular or square lots with good frontage on the road and good depth behind the house are best. Pie shapes, triangles, and multi-angles always require explanations and usually hurt resale value.

Be wary of "flag" lots. A flag lot is a landlocked piece of property that has access to a road by a right of way over another piece of property or by ownership of a narrow strip of land for a driveway.

Nine Nonthreatening Questions to Ask the Neighbors

1. Where do children usually play in this neighborhood?

You may be surprised at how much information this question will produce. Empty lots, parks, cut-throughs to the bike trails in the fields (you hope your prospective house isn't on a cut-through), how many children there are in the neighborhood, the general age range, how well behaved they are, teenage problems, community recreation programs. And these are only the topics that come up most frequently.

2. Where's the best place to get groceries in this area?

You'll be told the quickest routes to the best shopping areas. This is a good lead question for information on neighborhood traffic patterns.

3. Does the dogcatcher come by often?

This is an indirect question. By not asking "Do pets roam free?" you'll get a more honest answer since your respondent doesn't have to defend his choice of pet-keeping practices. And the question is a natural lead to a discussion of the neighborhood's personality.

4. Does the town allow basement sump pumps to drain into the storm sewers?

You'll know all about the water problems in the area from the answer to this question. Expect everything from "Gee, I don't know, no one has a sump pump" to "No they don't, but . . ." followed by a dissertation on how various neighbors solve their water problems. This approach is much better than asking "Are there basement water problems in this area?" because that question makes people defensive.

5. Is there any chance of getting into a carpool to the Big City from this neighborhood?

This question often leads to a discussion of the neighbors, where they work and what they do. You can also get into the accessibility of public transportation, commuting time, etc.

6. Do you know if French or Spanish is offered in the elementary school?

People love to talk about their schools, but if you ask, "How are the schools?" they'll usually reply, "Excellent." The trick is to inquire about specifics and open a conversation that leaves room for complaints as well as praise.

7. Have the tax assessors been around yet?

"What tax assessors?" says your prospective neighbor, look-ing at you curiously. To which you can always reply, "Oh, I must be getting this town confused with another we are con-sidering." If, however, your question touches a button in your neighbor, you will get an honest reply about impending tax policies and potential reassessments.

8. How's the food at the China Royale?

Pick any restaurant that you notice in your tour of the town. This question usually leads to a discussion of good places to eat, which can in turn lead to other recreational activities, or to physical fitness facilities, or even to diet and health clubs.

9. Have there been any other houses sold in the neighborhood recently?

This question usually leads to a discussion of what was sold, at what price, how long on the market, and to whom. With a little careful steering the discussion can move toward what was the original price of the house or houses in a relatively young development. Knowing original prices gives you an idea of how much negotiating room you might have. This discussion is also an excellent way to judge a neighbor's perceptions of home value appreciation in the area.

Even if it's a $400,000 house on 5 acres, the fact that it is behind a furniture store will hurt resale speed and value.

Size

Lot size in relation to property value is a slippery thing, governed more by neighborhood and area than by any rule of proportions. A quarter of an acre is a large lot in a city; an acre is the norm for more expensive housing in many suburbs.

Large pieces of property that cannot be subdivided rarely add to the value of a house. For example, the pretty Tudor home on Lyons Road would sell for $84,000 on a half acre since all of its neighbors have half acres. The fact that it has seven acres of land fanning out behind it and its neighbors on both sides, some of which is swamp and some rock and virtually undevelopable, will not increase the resale value of the Tudor by a penny. It may, in fact, hinder resale since the owners are paying property taxes on all that land. Owners of some such lots have dedicated (given) their excess land to the towns in which they live for "open spaces." They thus reap income tax benefits and reduce their local property taxes while assuring themselves that the land will remain in its natural state.

Contour

Level land is usually best. Houses built on steep slopes are often hard to sell. Buyers are especially wary of houses built below the level of the road, where driveways slope sharply downward. Land that slopes down toward the house also invites difficult-to-correct basement water problems. Land sloping gently away from a house is a plus and often allows for a walk-out basement.

When choosing your lot, be aware of the area's contour as well as your particular lot's contour. Flood plain maps made by the U.S. government are available in many town halls and will show you the contour of the land throughout the town. You will want to avoid buying land that is at the low point of the town or neighborhood. In spring thaw or major storms (hurricanes, for example) water will follow the easiest course to the lowest point of land. You do not want these storm waters cascading through your living room.

What's Beneath the Grass?

This is a question that is almost never asked. But what's below the surface can affect you more than most people would like to imagine. Was the area once a farm? A garbage dump? A forest? A swamp?

These become essential questions prior to purchase if you are considering a house that uses a septic tank for waste disposal, since the composition of the earth will determine how well that tank and its leach lines will drain. Especially poor drainage could mean a nonworking system, which taken to its farthest limit could mean an uninhabitable house.

In some developments built over the past fifteen to twenty years, municipalities have required that the results of *percolation tests* be recorded in the town hall. (You'll have to snoop around for them; they could be in the building inspector's office, the tax assessor's office, or some other creative category.) In a "perc" test, a hole is dug on the property and water is poured in to test the rate of absorption. Sometimes notes are made on the composition of the earth to the bottom of the hole (clay, shale, gravel, rock, etc.). If your town has perc test information for your lot, it's worth asking for.

What's underground will also affect how a house settles. Houses built on rock will settle little. Houses built upon landfills may settle unevenly, especially if the fill was tree trunks and other debris collected as a development was cleared and constructed. You should watch out for fill lots if you are considering a house at a low point in a development, usually the youngest houses in the neighborhood. As a general rule of thumb, choose high ground if you can.

Views and Things

Every real estate salesperson sells views, even if the view is a glimpse of the ocean at high tide. A genuinely beautiful view *is* worth money; the trick is to determine how much money. That's a subjective judgment at best.

Woods and landscaping are also worth extra, but again, how much is up to you. Streams are a detriment, especially if one bisects the property, leaving a part of the backyard on the other side of a bridge that you have to build. Lake frontage and ocean frontage are positive factors. Mountaintop is a plus unless the road to your mountaintop is especially steep or narrow, or in poor shape. Property lines that border open spaces are a plus.

Position

Corner lots, the most desirable location for business, are usually not desirable in residential real estate. They are too exposed and require trees or fencing for privacy. Cul-de-sacs are popular with families with young children and are especially salable if the road widens to a circle for a turnaround.

Choosing Among Your Choices

You may now be thinking, "Well, a backyard abutting a golf course may be a lovely option for someone in the Phoenix area, but it's hardly a factor to be considered on my househunt in Detroit."

Granted! No two persons are going to have exactly the same choices. Recreation, for example, can mean deer hunting or the opera. Your lot may include two acres of fruit trees, or it may be a shady square behind your house just large enough for a group of lawn chairs, or it may be the land exactly taken up by your co-op building. We can't speak personally to every individual, but *you* can select those factors that are pertinent to your lifestyle and your available choices.

No one must stay in one location just because he or she is accustomed to being there. Make modern mobility and changeability a plus in your housing options. Look at all the locations available to you and evaluate them. What is best for you will not necessarily be best for another. The choice *is* yours.

Location: Some Positives and Negatives

Town

Positives	Negatives
Good schools: small classes, special programs, wide course selection in high school	School problems: overcrowded classrooms, double sessions, sparse budget for extras, high drop-out rate
Low taxes Good commuting with a wide employment choice nearby	High taxes Isolation, poor transportation facilities, depressed area with few job opportunities
Community pride	Dirty streets, high crime rate
Good recreation: parks, tennis courts, facilities for children, theaters, restaurants, etc.	Poor recreation: "Nothing to do"
Municipal services, many and well done: snow removal, road maintenance, refuse removal, city sewers, city water, police, fire and rescue squad	Poor municipal services: Few services, the necessity of paying for private services

Neighborhood

Positives	Negatives
Socioeconomically homogeneous	Wide range in house value and style with commercial properties mixed in.
"Neat as a pin"	Poor maintenance: unkept lawns, peeling paint, trash and junk cars visible
Trees, good landscaping, gentle hills, cul-de-sacs, curved streets	Flat land, all-alike houses, rectangular all-alike blocks, no shade trees
Proximity to parks and open spaces; between one and five miles from a shopping center	Close proximity to commercial or industrial development, or to housing that is considerably lower in price

Lot

Positives	Negatives
Views—pleasant	Views—unpleasant
Trees, shrubs, flowers, carefully planned foundation planting	Bare grass, no foundation planting
Level lot, or gently sloping; high ground preferred	On the lower side of the road with steeply sloped land; cliffs, gulleys, or hills behind house; low point of the area
Mid-block, mid-neighborhood	Corner lot, edge of neighborhood
Regularly shaped lot	Irregularly shaped lot
Backyard line abuts park, woods, or open spaces	Backyard line abuts commercial property, schoolyard, high-density housing, or lower-priced neighborhood

13

How to Househunt
(With and Without an Agent)

The newspaper's Sunday real estate section is often reserved only for housebreaking puppies unless household members happen to be looking for a new place to live. Then it becomes the most important section, read and reread, decorated with red underlining and scribbled notes, filigreed with cut rectangles and torn circles, and carefully coddled in the kitchen until the next Sunday.

That newspaper is the start of the househunt for most homebuyers. They run out to open houses, call on "for sale by owner" ads, and verbally dance with real estate agents trying to get addresses for "drive-bys" without giving their names. At worst, such activity is a waste of time, telephone tolls, and gas; at best, it is a warm-up for the real hunt to come.

To avoid the waste and the warm-up time:

• *Don't begin househunting by inspecting "for sale by owner" properties*. Most are overpriced, and in order to know by how much, you will need experience in the local marketplace.

• *Don't call real estate agents asking for drive-by addresses*. You'll be running from one end of town to the other to see only the facade of a home and its neighborhood. That can be accomplished in an office through photos and by taking an overview tour of neighborhoods that might interest you.

• *Don't make an appointment to meet an agent at an advertised property for a showing of that house only*. Especially in the beginning of your househunt, you will need comparison properties.

• *Don't drive fifty miles to attend a model open house at a builder's new tract*. You may well fall in love with the house, but you'll be a stranger in town with no idea of relative property value or local color.

Most people start househunting with high hopes, a sense of antic- ipation and adventure, and a determination to get a good deal. Most buy only after they have become, at various times, both disillu- sioned and exhausted. Which is all right (househunting is hard work), *if* dashed hopes and fatigue don't draw you into a purchase unsuited to your needs. The following are some very specific hunt- ing techniques that will minimize your fatigue and help you keep your wits about you during this ever-so-important adventure.

Use Professional Services

Listing contracts state that the seller pays a sales commission to the broker. There are whispers, however, that it's the buyer who actually pays since the commission is added on to the owner's price. Those whispers are wrong, or at least wrong most of the time.

The fact of the matter is that few properties sell above the compa- rative fair market value of similar properties. In other words, except in special situations that will be discussed later in this chapter, you pay about the same whether a seller uses a broker or not. It is financial foolishness therefore *not* to take advantage of the services offered to buyers by real estate firms, especially since there is neither cost nor obligation. Be sure you do the following:

1. *Get qualified.* Agents in every real estate office will have infor- mation on lender loan requirements. The job of evaluating how much of a loan a prospective buyer can carry and realistically esti- mating his or her maximum monthly payment for the loan, taxes, insurance, and maintenance fees is called "qualifying the buyer." You *want* to be qualified, so don't withhold information on your income and long-term debts. Let the agent make calculations and come up with a monthly figure that you can afford. In fact, let several agents in different offices go through the same process. Their calculations should come in quite close. If they don't, someone has made a mistake; check further. This kind of prepurchase evaluation can save you a lot of time wasted looking at properties in the wrong price range or, worse yet, in awaiting a mortgage approval that could be refused.

2. *Get local information.* Every real estate agent should be inti- mately familiar with the areas in which he or she actively sells property. Information on taxes, schools, neighborhoods, recreation,

A Guide to Evaluating Real Estate Agents

Since competence in any job cannot be judged by a yardstick (or even by a computer), every evaluation is subjective. Bear in mind that the agent you judge as top-notch might well get a different rating from another buyer. You can do your evaluating by simply giving each agent you consider a mental plus or minus for each factor on the following list. Or you can be more mathematical (although not necessarily more accurate) by rating each agent from 1 to 5 on each factor and then adding up the points. Remember that 5 on the plus column is the highest grade while 5 on the minus side is the lowest. Zero is no opinion or no information.

Factor	Plus Points	Minus Points
Community knowledge	Local resident for two years or more; community involvement.	Lives outside the area in which he or she works; new to the area.
Professional experience	Three or more years' experience in residential real estate sales.	Less than three years' residential work; primary involvement is in commercial or other real estate field.
Commitment	Full-time agent; earns his or her living through real estate.	Part-time agent, sells houses only on nights, weekends, and vacations.
Competence	Takes the time to qualify buyers and shows properties in their price range.	Does not qualify buyers; shows properties above buyers' stated range.
	Plans showing routes carefully; has preinspected most properties.	Gets lost *en route*; has not seen properties prior to showing.
	Thorough knowledge of financing options and local lender policies.	Cannot answer buyer's questions about financing.

Factor	Plus Points	Minus Points
Ethics	Is mindful of the information on the family profile when selecting properties for showing.	Shows properties that do not fit buyers' needs or goals.
	Alerts buyers to problems in location or condition of the property.	Neglects to mention known problems; for example, the proposed highway 100 yards behind the house or the water stains on the basement walls.
	Respects the fact that buyers might be househunting in other towns with other agents.	"Bad mouths" other agencies and locations.
	Allows a property to "sell itself"; gives buyers thinking time.	High sales pressure: "There's someone else seriously considering this property."

etc., should be easy conversation, not "well, I can find out for you" research. Use the agent's knowledge to help you choose among towns and among neighborhoods within a town.

3. *Get street maps and printed information.* If you ask, most agents will give you a street map of the area in which they sell. *Ask.* The map will be invaluable for return drive-bys (without the agent) and for exploration of surrounding areas. Many local organizations (ranging from the League of Women Voters, to the Cinema 6 down the street, to local weight loss clubs, to nursery schools) leave flyers, pamphlets, and booklets in real estate offices. Take them home and read them. Even the driest text becomes interesting when it affects your life in a given place.

4. *Use Multiple Listing Service tools.* The orderly arrangement of listing sheets on nearly all the property for sale in a given community, by price, with pictures, and with all pertinent sales informa-

tion, is the hallmark of Multiple Listing Services across the country. If you work with a real estate firm that belongs to such a service, your househunt will be less tiring and more thorough. In these offices, ask to see the listing books. Virtually all agents will allow you to look through them, *if* they are asked. So sit in the agent's office and look at pictures. You may just see something interesting that the agent missed, and certainly you will satisfy yourself that you are not missing anything or being shown only those properties that the agent thinks right for you.

5. *Use comparables.* One of the best things an agent can do for prospective buyers is to tell them at what price similar properties have recently sold. Most real estate firms have such information on file. Ask to see the "comparables book" or "comparables file" as you begin to hone in on a particular neighborhood. Those listings of comparable houses that have sold within the past year, with both asking price and actual selling price indicated on the sheet, should prevent you from overpaying.

6. *Use family profiles.* Not every real estate agent takes the time to do a family profile, but the best ones do. Such profiles will differ in format from one office to another, but they should all include the number of people in the buying family, their names, ages of the children, and even their pets. Each person's particular interests and hobbies should be listed, and a three-part "Needs and Wants" schedule should summarize the family's housing goals. For example:

Must Have	Would Be Nice	Do Not Want
Three bedrooms	Fireplace	Busy street
Eat-in kitchen	Two-car garage	Split-level
Basement	Formal dining room	Sloping lot

If you find that agents in your local area are not using such family profile sheets, write up one of your own for yourself. Take it to your library or office, make some photocopies, and then give it to every agent that you work with. The agent won't get you mixed up with other customers, and you won't have to repeat yourself quite so often.

7. *Ask for agent evaluation before you see a property.* It is not unreasonable to expect that an agent will have inspected a property before showing it to you. He or she should be able to answer your questions about neighborhood, lot, floor plan, condition, decorating, etc. And after working with you for a while, the agent should know

your preferences and eliminate undesirable properties without dragging you through them.

8. *Use builder's open houses*. After you have made several househunting expeditions in a given area and are beginning to get a feel for price and value, visit some builder's model homes. You may be dead set against buying a new house, but such visits are a good means of comparing new cost against the value of a resale house. You'll also get some ideas for decorating, appliances, lighting fixtures, floor covering, etc.

Be Loyal but Demanding

Finding the right real estate agents for you may take a little time. You will need a different one for each local area (it may include from one to five towns) since the agent's familiarity with the "turf" is one of his or her major services to you. You will also want someone with whom you feel comfortable, and even more important, whom you trust. The necessity for competence and efficiency goes without saying.

Once you find an agent who is doing a good job for you, stick with him or her. In areas where multiple listing is commonly used, your agent can show you any property advertised by any multiple listing member office. When you see another agency's ad in the newspaper for a property that "sounds good," call *your* agent. He or she will probably have information on it and will be able to take you there. Even when a property is not listed on a multiple listing service, most brokers are happy to co-broke, that is, to allow another agent to show their listing for a split commission.

By thus remaining loyal to your working agent, you will save yourself countless phone calls from every agent in the area who gets your name, to say nothing of stops at properties you have already seen or do not want to see.

You may also save yourself from involvement in a lawsuit. Here's how a suit often begins:

Dick and Jane have been working with Emma Goodhouse for three weeks, and they have been very satisfied with her efforts to find them a place to live. On a Sunday afternoon on the way home from brunch at a friend's, they pass a new condominium development with banners and balloons flying and Grand Opening signs everywhere. Dick and Jane had not even thought about buying a condo, but they decide to go in just for fun. They are

What's in a Name?

Are you "better off" with a real estate broker or a Realtor? Well, every Realtor is a real estate broker, except when the Realtor is really a Realtor-Associate licensed salesperson who calls himself a Realtor in common practice. *Not* every real estate broker, however, is a Realtor. Confusing? Yes, it is. Let's sort out the tangle:

Real estate broker. Defined as any person, firm, or corporation who for a fee or commission seeks to sell, buy, exchange, or lease real property. Every state has strict licensing laws for real estate brokers, requiring many hours of classroom study and/or years of experience as a real estate salesperson. A real estate broker must also conduct business in compliance with all state real estate laws. Only a licensed broker can enter into a contract to act as an agent in handling real property.

Real estate salesperson. A person licensed by the state to work in real estate *under the supervision* of a licensed broker. A salesperson cannot enter into a contract to sell property, act in an agency capacity, or collect a commission for his work; those roles are reserved to the broker under whose supervision the salesperson works. In actual practice, however, most of the people who will show you houses are salespersons, and almost universally they are also called *sales agents, real estate agents,* or just *agents.* They do indeed work on a commission basis, but the commission is paid to the broker, who then pays the sales agent a share.

Realtor. The word is a registered trademark of the National Association of Realtors (NAR), a trade organization founded in 1908. Every broker who joins the organization must subscribe to its code of ethics. The vast majority of Realtors who conduct business in residential sales are also members of a local Realtor Board's Multiple Listing Service (MLS) and agree to share access to their listing and split commissions under agreements arranged among their membership. Licensed salespersons employed by a Realtor may also join NAR. They are given associate membership, but in common usage among buyers and sellers they too are often called "realtors."

Realtist. A real estate broker who is a member of the National Association of Real Estate Brokers (NAREB), a trade organization founded in 1947 with the stated purpose of promoting the rights and opportunities of minorities in real estate. Realtists are active in 46 states. Some Realtists are also Realtors.

Independent broker, fee broker. A state-licensed broker who does not belong to a trade organization. Many, but not all, such brokers work for a flat fee rather than a commission, hence the name "fee broker." Independent brokers can make arrangements to share listings and commissions with other brokers. They can also employ salespersons to act as their representatives in showing properties and seeking listings.

---

greeted at the door of the sales office by a young man who hands them his business card and asks them to sign the "guest" book. He then shows them through the beautifully decorated and furnished models. Dick and Jane like what they see.

The next day Jane calls Emma Goodhouse and says, "We passed this condo community yesterday and we liked it. Would you take us through?" She doesn't tell Emma that they already had a tour because she is feeling a little guilty about not calling her first. Dick and Jane buy a condo. Two days after the contract is signed, the manager of the listing agency handling condominium sales calls Emma Goodhouse. Their agent showed Dick and Jane through that condo community on Sunday, he says. The agency therefore refuses to share commission. Emma Goodhouse sues for her share of the commission, saying that she, not the young man, was the procuring agent of the sale. Closing is delayed as the lawyers argue.

This scenario occurs all too often and is not limited to new properties. Sometimes one agent shows buyers a property that doesn't interest them. Three weeks later another agent convinces those same buyers to look at it again. The second time through they like it and buy it. The legal question is: "Does the first agent deserve part of the commission?" The answer is often "yes," but each case is decided individually, and court time can delay a sale.

The obvious solution to legal tie-ups is not to get involved in them. Remember: do not walk upon the grounds or through the building(s) of any property for sale unless you are willing to buy that property through the agent who is accompanying you, if you do decide to buy.

Do not, however, take agent loyalty beyond rational limits. If your agent is on vacation for two weeks and you drive by a house just listed that is very appealing, go for it! Or if you fall in love with a for-sale-by-owner house that is not priced above market, buy it! Your hardworking agent will not get paid, but that's the business. Agents are very accustomed to such ups and downs, and a smart agent will come back for the listing when you're ready to sell.

Also, *don't be loyal if loyalty is not merited*. You owe nothing to an agent who is not doing a good job or who is simply not competent. Find another agent. When you get to the negotiating stage of your purchase, you want the best people on your side.

Discrimination

Discrimination is not a nice word, but it still exists despite extensive government, professional, and civic efforts. Race is the most obvious basis for discrimination, but religion, national origin, sex, marital status, and any number of other factors may predispose an agent to show or not show certain properties to certain people. Such activity is called "steering" and is against the law.

If you suspect that you are being steered, because of some factor other than your ability to afford the housing, you can quietly make enough noise to change the situation. If the agent in question is a member of the NAR, contact the local Realtor Board first (listed in the phone book). You can find the Board's exact name by looking at the agency ads in the Yellow Pages, since every agency that belongs will say so in its ad.

The NAR's Code of Ethics strictly forbids discriminatory practices. Disciplinary action is taken against offenders, and most Realtor Boards will assist buyers in finding an agent who will work with them and make every effort to provide equal housing opportunity. If you are unsatisfied with the action of the local board or do not understand its procedures, you can contact the National Association of Realtors, 430 North Michigan Ave., Chicago, Ill. 60611. Their phone number is (312) 329-8200.

An investigation will surely follow. Meanwhile you might continue your efforts to find a home by using independent brokers not associated with any professional group or by seeking out Realtists, a group founded with the specific purpose of working toward fair housing practices. This professional organization, however, is much smaller than the NAR, and its membership is concentrated in cities.

If you wish to pursue your action against discriminatory practices further, you can notify your state real estate commission. Proven cases of discrimination can result in suspension or loss of license for the agent(s) involved. Sometimes just the threat of reporting such practices to the real estate commission can put an end to them.

If you feel that a real estate agent has participated in housing discrimination against you, you can also contact Fair Housing in Washington, D.C., by calling (800) 424-8590. Another source of help and advice is your local Community Housing Resource Board, a group composed of citizen representatives, civic groups, and local governments, and committed to working for compliance with the Fair Housing Act of 1968.

The Logistics of the Hunt

All right, you're not embarking upon an African safari. There are, however, some rules for easier, more successful hunts:

1. *Do the in-office work first.* Get qualified, talk about your family profile, and look through the listing books. Don't waste your time running off to see houses when the agent doesn't really know what you can afford or what you want.

2. *Limit the number of properties per trip.* Five properties in five different locations on one day is plenty. At seven, features will get confused and fatigue will color your perceptions.

3. *Give a day to each area.* Don't cross and criss-cross your own tracks trying to see the "best" houses in three towns or even at the points of the compass in the same town. Limit yourself to a workable area so that you can get a good idea of comparative value. Your agent should limit your trip to properties that can be lined up in a circular route out from the office and back. Save the super-value in Boonesville for another day when you can see other properties in Boonesville.

4. *Go in the agent's car.* Let the person who is supposed to be showing you the area do the driving. You can take notes, mark your street map with comments or price ranges, or just observe. You can also ask questions. Following an agent in your own car may give you more privacy to talk over what you have seen, but it cuts off the opportunity to ask questions as you think of them. Save the private

How to Find a Good Agent

Personal referral. This is the best method. Ask friends who have recently purchased a house, "Who was your agent? Were you satisfied?" Show them the agent evaluation chart on page 202 and ask them how that agent would rate.

Local newspaper articles. Not everyone knows someone who just bought a house in a given area (especially if you are house-hunting on a transfer). If you don't know a soul, watch the local papers. From time to time, you will see pictures of sales agents who have made the million-dollar sales club or who are being given recognition for other achievements. They are probably competent agents (it's hard to argue with success). Call the agent's office and ask for him or her personally. Make an appointment for a get-acquainted interview.

The referral service. All of the national franchises (Century 21, Realty World, Better Homes, Gallery of Homes, Electronic Realty Associates, to name a few) refer buyers from one office to another. Many independent agencies also belong to referral services such as Nationwide and Home to Home. If you use one of these franchises or services, you will receive some printed information and will be assigned an agent in your new location. That agent may or may not be "good," but the firm is almost invariably reputable, and training programs are often extensive. Judge the individual agent for yourself.

Open houses. Attending open houses takes time, but you will meet and get to talk with the agents who are running the open house without incurring any obligation to work with them, even for a short time. Ask questions! You will leave the open house with a sense of their personality and at least a gut feeling about their competence.

Response to newspaper advertisements. This is how the majority of buyers find agents. It is also the most chancy method because most firms assign their agents "floor time." Any prospective buyer who calls in response to advertising during that time is "theirs." Unfortunately, floor time is not assigned on the basis of competence, so you have an equal chance of getting the person who shows up once a week as the person who spends six days a week working at her job. A slight improvement on calling blind is to respond to the ad by asking for "the listing agent on the house (describe the house) that you advertised in yesterday's paper." The agent who responds will at least be familiar with the property that caught your interest.

Your cousin Vinnie. Working with relatives is tough in all situations, but extra tough during the already stress-filled house hunt. If you possibly can, avoid relatives and "old family friends."

conversation for the dinner table. Following the agent can also be dangerous if you are struggling to stay close in an unfamiliar area.

5. *Don't buy at first sight.* You may fall absolutely in love with a dream home, but give your head a chance to advise your heart before you sign a contract. Our first impressions are often influenced by what we want to see as much as by what we actually see. If you have doubts about this, try the following exercise:

After you see a property that you like, go home. If two people are involved or have seen the property, go into different rooms. Each of you should then try to draw, from memory, the floor plan of the property that you "love." Put in doorways, windows, closets, stairs, kitchen appliances, etc. Limit your drawing time to 20 minutes. Then compare your drawings. If you are buying alone, put the drawing aside until tomorrow. The following day return to the property and compare your drawings with reality. You'll be surprised at how many differences there are and how many questions come up.

6. *Allow for a long second visit.* If you have enough interest in a property to return to it a second time, do a careful and thorough inspection. It will require all of an hour.

Househunting with Children

The best advice we can give you is: *Don't take the children on your househunts.* They will be bored, intimidated, cranky, and tired before most expeditions are over. Often they will both annoy and distract you as you are forced to play the double role of homebuyer and parent. In your own fatigue and exasperation, you could well decline a property that would meet your needs and be a good investment, too. Less likely, but with worse consequences, you might decide to buy something you don't really like. No matter what the circumstances, be sure that before you buy you make at least one inspection of your future home without the children.

In reality, however, sitters cancel or cannot be reached when you need them, and some appointments simply cannot be broken. So when you must take the children along, be aware of their special needs and watch out for situations that might be dangerous to them. You may well be able to go for four to six hours on a cup of coffee, but your children can't and shouldn't. Don't hesitate to ask your agent to stop at a fast food restaurant for a hamburger at lunchtime or at an ice cream store in mid-afternoon.

It's never a good idea to leave a sleeping toddler in the car while you inspect a property. But if you must, leave windows open in the summer and closed in the winter. And hurry—waking up alone in a strange car in a strange place is terrifying for a small child.

If young children accompany you inside the house you are inspecting, keep them close by your side. Unfamiliar stairs are dangerous for toddlers, as are perfumes, cleaning chemicals, and pills that are left about by the owners.

Most dangerous for children of all ages, however, are household animals. Most sellers are sensible enough to cage or tie dogs, but children will put their fingers through protective bars and approach a tied dog even when the animal is barking. Many children will pounce upon a sleeping cat or chase a walking one. When thus scared most cats hiss and run, but occasionally one will scratch or bite.

Many children (and adults) also let indoor cats out, which can cause much heartache for the sellers until their pet is found. And speaking of being let out, there must be a whole society of gerbils and hamsters in the world who have "escaped" while their owners' houses were on the market. And we won't even talk about the piranha in the fish tank or the python in the pretty painted box.

Children should be kept close at hand not only for their own safety, but also out of respect for the sellers and their belongings. It is very upsetting for the sellers' children to come home and find that their toys have been played with by a child they never saw. Yet many househunting parents will send their child or children into the sellers' children's room to play while they inspect the remainder of the house. Think of the situation in adult terms: how would you feel if several sets of valuable stamps ready to be mounted in your collection were spilled across your desk? Or what if your best china had been rearranged in the china cabinet?

Leaving children to play outdoors doesn't work very well either. Toddlers feel deserted and often cry. Older children usually mope around picking at things, or worse, they explore the garage or tool shed. And any "attraction" on the property becomes a potential hazard; the bubbling brook with tadpoles, the pond with a rickety boat dock, the bull in the pasture next door.

One of the worst scenes routinely plays when parents find an interesting property and return to the real estate office. The adults sit down to ask questions while the children create waterfalls at the cooler, turn over ashtrays on each and every empty desk, play "Go Fish" with the real estate forms in the closet, or fall asleep in the broker's chair. As we said, try not to bring the children.

Househunting without an Agent

Once you have been out househunting with an agent several times and you feel that you know the area and its comparative housing values, there's no harm in running down the for-sale-by-owner ads in the newspaper. The trick is not to waste a great deal of time chasing after the hopeless cases.

How Much Do You Want for It?

The knottiest problem with owner sales is overpricing. Most people love their homes, and everyone wants to make a killing in real estate. These two factors together tend to create incredible asking prices. You want to separate the gold-mining sellers from honest sellers at the telephone stage.

When you call on an ad, you are seeking two essential points: the price and the street address. You'll be given plenty of information on style, number of rooms, the remodeled kitchen, etc. Listen and then tell the seller that you will call back if you want to see the property. And don't forget to give your name it makes sellers feel less nervous and will earn you recognition and welcome when you call back.

With the address in hand, get out the street map that you got from your agent when you first started your househunt. If you've been marking it up, as you should, you'll have price ranges indicated for most areas of town that you can afford. Find the location of the house you just called about. How does the asking price for this property compare with neighborhood value? If it's more than 20 percent above fair market value, don't even bother to go out to see it. The odds are overwhelming against getting the sellers to come down to a realistic price. It will take months on the market with no serious offers before these sellers see the light.

Being Shown Through

The situation is awkward at best. The person who answers the door is host, real estate agent, and seller all in one. Sometimes wearing so many hats leads to inane conversations:

Seller: This is the living room.
Buyer: Very nice.
Seller: This is the dining room.
Buyer: Very nice.
Seller: This is the kitchen.
Buyer: Um-hummm.
Seller: This is the blue bathroom.
Buyer: Yes, nice blue tile.

Don't get caught up in such nonsense. Ask questions right from the start. Even if you know you're going to hate the house, you can gather information on the town and the school system. Ask why the owners are selling. If you get an honest answer to this question, it may help in negotiating later. And if you feel that you must make conversation or comment on the property, compliment some personal possession in the house, a painting, a rug, a new kitchen appliance, the baby pictures on the dresser. Don't comment on the condition of the property or the price at this stage.

Serious Consideration

If you like a for-sale-by-owner house and think a price agreement is within reach, your next step is to gather information. Call and make an appointment for a second visit, but prepare an information sheet on the property before you go. Model it, if you like, after the real estate listing sheets you have become familiar with, and fill in all the information you already have. (Some sellers give out information sheets that may answer most of your questions.)

When you arrive for the second visit, do an inspection of the house and its working systems first. Don't let your thoroughness embarrass you. Do exactly what you would do if a real estate agent were by your side and the owners away from home. And ask more questions.

If you are still interested in the property after doing your inspection, sit down with the sellers and fill in the blanks on your information sheet. You should ask about taxes, heating costs, age of the house, size and boundaries of the lot, etc. But go slowly. It is better at this point *not* to make an offer. A little delay, a time when you "think it over," will increase seller anticipation and add weight to the "well-studied" offer you will make.

Your offer should be about 10 percent below fair market value. Remember, we said fair market value, *not* asking price. Face-to-face negotiation between buyer and seller is always difficult, and anything below that figure may end in emotional rejection. Your primary tool in keeping negotiations rational and friendly will be your knowledge of comparable sales that you gathered while working with real estate agents. Bring typed or clearly written sheets (one for each comparable house) with you to your first negotiating session. Your objective is to prove fair market value and then to show the seller the advantages to selling at 10 percent off that value. The advantages? Quick sale, no further disruption to family life by showings, no commission to pay.

Don't expect immediate acceptance. Everyone wants to haggle a little. A good second offer from the buyer is usually the fair market value minus the usual real estate commission in the area. In response to this, the sellers will say (if they are smart) that there is then no advantage in selling without a broker since the commission is being deducted without any of the broker's services.

The conclusion of negotiations in the happily-ever-after version of this story is that sellers and buyers agree to split the real estate commission and set the selling price between market value and net-to-owner-after-commission. Extras, closing dates, and financing can be worked out then and there or with the attorneys who will draw the contract to buy.

Unfortunately, these deals don't always have a happy ending. Because they are new to the marketplace and still have high hopes for top money, many owners are adamant about their asking price. If you come up against such a stone wall, don't beat your head against it no matter how much you love the house. Write your best offer on a sheet of paper with your name and phone number and tell the sellers to call you if they change their mind. Go back to your hunt.

Do not return to this property with an agent when and if the sellers decide to list with a real estate agency. Remember that if you walk through it accompanied by an agent, the seller might be obliged to pay a commission if you eventually purchase the house, even after the listing expires. This fact would keep the price up and discourage a sale to you. Instead call the sellers from time to time and ask them how they are doing. But don't make another offer; that should come from them. If they come down a little, you might come up a little; that's how the game is played.

Protecting Yourself

Whether you use an agent and pay no attention to local newspaper ads or embark upon a combination of househunting with and without an agent, it is essential that you remember a basic premise of the marketplace: *No one will watch out for your money and your happiness as well as you will*. No matter how competent and kindly an agent seems, thoroughly inspect any property that interests you. No matter how sweetly the grandmotherly seller assures you that the woods behind the house will always be woods, go to the town hall and find out who owns them and how they are zoned.

In taking such protective steps, you are not passing negative judgment upon the people with whom you are working. You are simply acting in a businesslike manner. Buying a home is a personal *and* an investment purchase. A businesslike manner is essential to your success.

For More Information

The National Association of Realtors distributes a number of booklets and pamphlets through its member offices. If the firm you are working with does not have material on the Realtor's role, code of ethics, etc., call the local Realtor Board office and ask what reading material is available. Some Board offices stock pamphlets, and some have libraries.

If you are interested in specific research on real estate practices and the history and function of Realtors, you can write or call: Beverly Dordick, Librarian, Herbert U. Nelson Memorial Library, National Association of Realtors, 430 North Michigan Ave., Chicago, Ill. 60611, (312) 329-8292.

The National Association of Real Estate Brokers will send you information about their trade organization and help you to find a Realtist in your area. Write or call: National Association of Real Estate Brokers, 5501 Eighth St. N.W., Suite 202, Washington, D.C. 20011, (202) 829-8500.

Your state real estate commission will send you, upon request, information on licensing laws and real estate law in your state. The commission is listed among the state agencies in your phone book.

14

Features to Watch For
and Watch Out For

When the confetti of house hunting facts and fantasies finally clears, there are only two reasons for buying: shelter and investment. Shelter translates into comfort and convenience "How happy will I be living here?" Investment translates into tax advantages and potential appreciation "How much money will I make when I sell?"

All of us, of course, would like the house we choose to rate high in both categories, but such good fortune is not easy to come by. We're limited in our choices by money, job, family, and personal needs, and most of us must make some compromises. The big, four-bedroom colonial in a community of three-bedroom split levels, for example, might be a spacious, comfortable, and even luxurious place to live, but the money invested in it will rarely appreciate as much as money invested to buy a house in a neighborhood of similar houses. In such a situation, you would have to choose between the quality of your shelter and the potential of your investment.

But location is not the only important factor in determining satisfaction and investment appreciation in a home. There are many others. Real estate agents call them "features" and every residential property has a potpourri of features: architectural style, floor plan, window style, kitchen plan and convenience, basement, garage, bathrooms, etc. Some features add to comfort and enjoyment, some add to resale value, some to both. Some features are negative qualities to some buyers and positives to others.

To buy wisely and well, you must know why you are buying and what to look for. The *why* is a matter of evaluating your motivations.

Is shelter and comfort your primary goal? Or is investment potential paramount? Most people who buy a house that they plan to live in for twenty years or so choose comfort. Most who buy planning to move within five to seven years choose investment potential.

Once you know your own priorities, your next step to successful house hunting is to recognize which housing features will add resale value and which will detract, which features will add to your living comfort and which will cause inconvenience.

Unfortunately, we can't give you an exact list of good and bad features since every property, every buyer, and every selling situation is unique. But we can point out things to think about and we can give you a general idea of the most common homebuyer and homeowner responses to the most wanted and most disliked features. It all boils down to a househunter's shopping list. Let's start outside the house and then move inside.

Views and Landscaping

What's it worth to catch a glimpse of something beautiful from your windows—a view of the ocean, a hilltop that overlooks the city lights, a sunny valley at the edge of the mountains? Sometimes it's worth a lot and sometimes not very much.

Views are one of those features that turn property appraisal from a job to an art. No one can be certain exactly what a given buyer might be willing to pay for the view until that buyer makes an offer. The market for a house with a view must be tested, and this is usually done by listing the property at a price that is higher than market value.

Sometimes such house-and-view packages sell quickly (the view was valuable). But sometimes they stay on the market until the owners reduce the price to a level comparable with other houses of approximately the same size (the view was not valuable).

If you should fall in love with a house with a view, try to buy it without paying for the view. Get comparables and make your first offer at a price slightly below the market value for a similar house without a view. If the sellers hold firm on their price, however, you will then have to decide exactly how much that view is worth to you.

The word *view* is generally applied to the distant horizon, but in fact your windows may look out on a great deal of beauty close at hand. What's a stream or a pond worth? A forest that will always remain natural? A rose garden? Orchards?

The beauty of what you are buying is a known quality; the investment potential will always be something of a question. Therefore, always try to buy property with unusual landscape features as though it were on an ordinary lot. If you must pay for the beauty, raise your price gradually until the view becomes more painful to your purse than pleasing to your eye.

Siting

Which way is north? You may not be expert at finding your way with a compass, but you can get the answer to that question. And the answer will affect your heating bill and your disposition.

Which rooms will have morning light? Which will bask (or bake) in the afternoon sun? How many windows between you and the north wind? Are there rooms which will remain dark most of the day?

Siting is a shelter feature. Although it will affect your comfort and cost of living, it will very rarely affect the value or potential appreciation of a house.

Style

To be stylish is to be attractively individual while still conforming to the prevailing taste of the times. The rule applies to houses as well as people. A house that is totally different from its neighbors is often difficult to sell. It stands out like a sore thumb, and few buyers have the courage to claim it as their own.

Thus a stone and glass California contemporary may boost your self-image, but it will be difficult to resell if it is located in a neighborhood of clapboard Cape Cods. In the same vein, Spanish-style ranch houses don't sell well in the Northeast; a colonial saltbox style would probably sit long on the market in Florida; and a Victorian farmhouse replica would hardly be the style of choice in Phoenix.

Usually, style will positively affect investment potential if it harmonizes with the area, and negatively if it jars the eye. If resale value and speed are unimportant to you, you can feel free to choose the unusual or offbeat; if investment appreciation and resale ease are essential to your purchase, stay within the prevailing style limits in the area.

Construction Materials

Brick houses are considered desirable across the country. Wood is also acceptable everywhere, although it is somewhat less desirable in areas where termites are abundant. Vinyl or aluminum siding over a wood frame may or may not add to resale value, but will probably save you maintenance time and money.

Stucco is an attractive and widely used building material throughout the South with good buyer acceptance. In the North however, stucco houses are often hard to sell since their unjointed surfaces are subject to cracking from the changeable weather. Stone and granite facades, on the other hand, have expansion space and rarely cause problems. They are usually impressive and attractive, and a selling plus.

New and experimental construction such as vinyl-sheathed underground houses or foam-insulated dome houses usually appeal to adventurous people. Unfortunately even sky divers become conservative when hunting for a house, and most experimental structures are difficult to resell.

Driveways

Blacktop or concrete driveways are most preferred and add to resale speed and value and to owner convenience. Crushed bluestone is acceptable, especially in tract developments where blacktopping the driveway is not included in the price of the house. Gravel driveways, however, are usually a resale and convenience *minus*. Most buyers and owners object to the mud in wet weather and the dust in dry. They are also more difficult to clear in the winter and require some time each spring to pick the stones from the lawn near the driveway.

A large turnaround area or a circular driveway certainly adds to owner convenience, not to mention safety, but rarely affects selling price. An especially long or steep driveway may not significantly affect resale value, but will usually increase the length of time needed to sell the property.

Garages

The attached two-car garage has almost become a standardized part of the "American Dream." Some suburban condominiums even feature garages that are almost as big as the apartments.

Generally, a garage located to the side of a house brings the best buyer response. An extra eight or ten feet in its width or length (the so-called oversized garage) will almost always be considered a plus toward quick resale, but will rarely affect the selling price. Such space is a significant positive feature in terms of owner comfort, however, since it'll give you a place to put the lawn mower, the garden equipment, the bicycles, the picnic table during the winter, and the sleds during the summer.

Garages located under the house are less desirable. Many owners complain about drafts in the rooms above and about higher heating/

cooling costs. And most object to the fact that getting in from the garage means climbing a flight of stairs. Those stairs may not sound like much of a problem until you imagine yourself carrying six or eight bags of groceries from the car to the kitchen.

Detached garages are unpopular in the North (no one wants to shovel through a foot of snow to the car) and carports are regarded with a glance and a nod but not a penny extra in offering price. In the South, however, carports are acceptable shelter for the family autos and detached garages are a plus.

Decks, Porches, and Patios

A place to sit or eat outdoors (but near the house) is almost always a plus for both resale and comfort. In fact, roofed and screened porches and glassed in "solar" additions have become two of the most popular home improvements in recent years.

Windows

Self-insulating windows and sliding glass doors are often considered such positive features that they are specifically mentioned by brand name in advertisements. Some homeowners who have them, however, claim that old fashioned storm windows are better at keeping out the cold. In some very cold areas or on the northern exposure of some houses, owners have installed conventional storm windows over self-insulating windows, and most buyers consider the installation a positive feature.

In the North, houses with neither self-insulating windows nor storm windows lose points. In the deep South, however, screen windows without storms are acceptable. Southern oceanfront properties often feature hurricane shutters to protect both the window glass and the interior of the house or apartment. They are a buying plus but do not raise the value.

Entranceways

Front doors add little to comfort and convenience. After the first few weeks in a house, the new owners almost always use the back door or garage entrance. The front entranceway, however, is an important factor in the salability of a house. It strongly influences a buyer's first impression, and first impressions are hard to dispel.

The "best" front entranceways have wide stairs and a large sheltered or roofed landing. Heavy wooden or steel front doors are currently fashionable; glass and aluminum storm doors have become a fashion faux pas.

Back entranceways, on the other hand, don't have much effect on salability, but they certainly do effect the sanity and comfort of their owners, especially if children or pets live in the house. The "ideal" back door opens into a mud room, a back hallway or cubicle where there is space to hang coats, remove wet or muddy boots and mittens, or wipe dirty paws. In many well-planned houses this back hall is adjacent to or combined with the laundry room (which saves transporting the dirty clothes, rugs, and rags).

Back doors that open directly into the kitchen can be bothersome because of the increased traffic and clutter that they generate, but they are preferable to family room back doors, especially if a patio or outside eating area is serviced by the door. Sliding glass doors are popular and won't hurt resale one bit.

Floor Plans and Traffic Patterns

Mention floor plans and most people think of black and white line drawings hanging in the sales offices of new condominiums or in the model homes of new tracts. But those line drawings are eventually transposed into real living space and the heavy lines, double lines, arcs, and circles become walls, windows, doorways, and bathroom fixtures. The floor plan then becomes a map of the living area and an excellent means of assessing space and traffic patterns.

If you are buying new construction and such a floor plan is available to you, trace your way through your daily routine and a special situation (a party, for example) on it. Where will you come in from work? Where will you hang your coat? Where can you read quietly while the children play video games?

If you are buying property with no floor plan available, draw one of your own. Indicate rooms, doorways, and windows, but don't try to be an architect. Do this even though you can actually walk through the rooms of a house that is already standing. Few people really try out a house when they first inspect it. Most "tour" as observers and guests. That's fine for the initial "just looking" stage, but hardly adequate for a house under serious consideration. If you draw and take home a floor plan, you can live in the house mentally. We guarantee questions will pop into your head. Among the most important traffic pattern questions are the following:

• *Are there any rooms that must be walked through in order to reach other rooms?* The kitchen is an acceptable walk-through room and is often located at or near the activity center of the house. All other walk-through rooms are detriments to a sale. Be especially careful to avoid floor plans where you must walk through one bedroom to get to another bedroom. Such houses are very difficult to sell.

• *How does one get from the kitchen to the backyard?* This question is especially important for young families with small children to watch. But even singles and couples will want to go from the lawn chairs to the refrigerator, and an easy traffic pattern adds much to one's "love of home."

• *How will guests enter the house?* Most homebuyers prefer some kind of foyer or front entrance hall in which to greet guests. From there the movement into the living room should be a natural, easy one. And then from the living room, how would a guest get to the dining room? And finally, where is the powder room or guest lavatory? You might also try to imagine how people would mix during a party, if parties are a part of your life style.

• *What is the traffic pattern between the family living area (kitchen and family room) and the most often used lavatory?* Some lavatories are located off the foyer, which may be convenient for guests but is inappropriate for the family, especially when muddy children who are told to wash their hands walk through the dining room to the lavatory.

• *What is the traffic pattern for bringing groceries and merchandise into the house?* If you park your car in the driveway, how difficult will it be for you to get packages into the house? Watch for stairs!

• *What's the distance and traffic pattern between the family room and the kitchen?* Some people like them adjacent or actually the same room; others prefer a good separation.

• *Are any of the hallways particularly long or dark?* Many buyers object to long hallways. Lighting from skylights or high windows can eliminate this objection.

Kitchens

Eat-in kitchens appear on the must-have lists of most homebuyers, and a charming, sunny kitchen can tie up a deal. In contrast, long, narrow "pullman style" kitchens are least popular and will often keep a house on the market a long time.

Center islands and center island stoves are positives, as are sinks (especially double sinks) under a window. Counter space is important and gourmet cooks will look for a minimum of four unbroken feet of working area.

Abundant cabinet space is a feature always mentioned in a sales pitch, and when there's plenty of space the cabinet doors are always opened to demonstrate. Many buyers forget to look for a broom closet, however, and many houses don't have one. Ask yourself where mops, buckets, brooms, cleaning agents, and the vacuum cleaner will be kept. Some substitutes for the broom closet are the back hall coat closet, the laundry room, the garage, and the pantry.

Bathrooms

Early in this century a real estate agent might have said, "It's hard to sell a house without a bathroom." Today he or she will say, "It's hard to sell a house with only one bathroom." Many owners of older houses have remodeled or added on to their homes in order to provide at least the extra half bath now so much in demand. Two-and-a-half baths seems to be everyone's dream figure, but beyond that you're getting into either a castle or a boarding house.

Bathrooms with outside windows are far more appealing to buyers than interior baths with vent fans. But better an interior extra bathroom than none at all.

Walk-in shower stalls are preferred to shower-over-tub arrangements, but most people want at least one bathtub in the house. Ceramic tile is preferred to Formica, fiberglass, or vinyl paneling around the shower and on the bathroom walls. Bathroom vanities are becoming a must in fashionable houses. Double sinks are a plus, as are full-wall mirrors behind the sink/vanity. Wallpaper is preferred to paint, but fish and sea shells are definitely out.

Laundry Facilities

A washer and dryer hook-up in the basement is better than no facilities at all, but it won't help a resale and you, the owner, won't enjoy carrying the laundry up and down the cellar stairs. The most requested laundry facility is a separate room near the kitchen. When these rooms are large enough to accommodate an ironing board or a sewing machine, they become a major selling point for the house.

Laundry facilities in the kitchen behind sliding or folding doors don't seem to hurt resale value, but most homeowners who have them don't like having dirty laundry in the kitchen on washday.

Some avant-garde houses feature laundry rooms near the bedroom area, even on the second floor. Most homeowners who have such facilities are pleased with them, but most buyers are a little wary.

Closets

The more closets the better. Large bedroom closets are a selling point and a better living feature. A walk-in closet in the master bedroom is on practically everyone's want list. But don't limit closet count to the bedrooms. Look for the following:

- a foyer or front hall closet in which to hang guests' wraps
- a linen closet (an ideal situation is one closet for sheets and bedding and another in the bathroom for towels)
- a broom or utility closet (the best location is near the kitchen)
- a back door closet or at least a place to hang family coats and store boots, etc.

Bedrooms

We'd all like the bedroom spacious and sunny. Unfortunately such rooms seem to rank on the luxury level when it comes to home construction, and it's rare to find more than one per house. If you must settle for "cozy" rooms, look for good wall space for furniture arrangement and easy access to a bathroom. A separate dressing area in or adjacent to the master bedroom is sometimes found in more expensive houses and is very well received by prospective buyers.

Attic additions or Cape Cod–style bedrooms with sloping ceilings and dormer windows are not buyer favorites, but they rank higher in appeal than basement bedrooms, which no one seems to want.

Family Rooms

Today family rooms are more important than living rooms, and sometimes larger. In fact, the larger the family room is, the better for both resale and lifestyle. In the South and West, family rooms are being combined with kitchen and eating areas into "great rooms," which most buyers seem to like. In contrast, basement family rooms are out of style and almost a detriment to a sale. Most buyers and owners alike prefer lots of glass and sunshine. In the North, fireplaces are a major plus.

Paneling is still popular, but some homeowners prefer conventional wallboard that can be painted or papered. Others are choosing the new wood slats (actual boards cut thin for application to walls with bonding cement), artificial brick, or even vinyl panels. More important than wall covering material is good taste and plenty of room for furniture.

Living Rooms

In a house without a family room, the living room should be as large as possible. But in houses with family rooms, most buyers are more concerned with the location of the living room than with its size. They want the living room to be formal, and out of the path of day-to-day family traffic. If everything else is all right, small is not necessarily bad. Living room fireplaces usually bring a smile, but rarely bring a penny more in offering price. (They are also seldom used by most homeowners.)

Dining Rooms

The formal dining room is still a "necessity" in higher priced homes. However, it is becoming a plus but not a must in less expensive dwellings, especially in new construction where dining areas adjacent to the kitchen have become features and in condominiums where one eating area serves as both family table space and formal entertainment space.

When a formal dining room is a part of the floor plan, it should have a direct doorway to the kitchen and another to the foyer or the living room. If it is separated from the kitchen by stairs or a hallway, most buyers will object, sometimes strongly enough to turn away from the house. Homeowners also usually admit that such arrangements are inconvenient. Dining "L"s are less favored by buyers than separate dining rooms, but if they are well located most buyers do accept them. They are always mentioned in negotiations as a minus, yet it rarely has much effect on selling price.

Attics

The old-fashioned walk-up attic (with real stairs), where Norman Rockwell might paint a little girl opening her grandmother's trunk is probably the most useful kind of home storage space. But it's hard to get unless you choose an older home. Today's attics are far less accessible. Pull-down stairs in a hallway are acceptable to most buyers and do provide a means of getting to the Christmas decorations. Less appealing to buyers and downright inconvenient to homeowners is attic access through a trapdoor in the ceiling of a bedroom closet.

Basements

Where they are commonly used (primarily in the North), basements are high on the buyer's demand list and high on the homeowner's convenience list. Above all, they should be dry; and good lighting is an added plus. Also very desirable is a direct exit to the outdoors.

In homes that do not have basements, a utility room for the furnace, water heater, air conditioner, etc., is usually located on a lower level or in a back corner. The larger it is, the better.

Using a Features Checklist

It's all right to get caught up in admiring other people's home decorating during the beginning stages of a house hunt, but once you are actually choosing your future home, you must try to evaluate it in terms of *your* lifestyle, needs, and goals, not those of the current owner. A checklist will help. The following one is merely a suggestion. Change it to suit you and your family.

	Your Ideal	*Actual Features*
		Address: _____
		_____

View:		
Landscaping:		
Siting:		
Style:		
Construction materials:		
Driveway:		
Garage:		
Deck, porch, patio:		
Windows:		
Entranceways: Front:		

	Your Ideal	Actual Features
Back:		
Other:		
Floor plan and traffic pattern:		
Kitchen:		
Bathroom:		
Laundry facilities:		
Closets: Bedroom:		
Linen:		
Utility: Coat: Bedrooms:		
Family room:		
Living room:		
Dining room or area:		
Attic:		
Basement:		

15

What's Wrong with It?
A Home Inspection Primer

If you are having a house custom built for you or are buying a builder's "spec" house, skip this chapter. Inspecting to see if the newly-finished construction conforms to the plans and contract specifications is entirely different from inspecting to see if an owner/ occupant is indeed selling you a "healthy" house. New home buyers should read Chapter 22.

If you are interested in buying historic property or in buying a "handyman special" and doing extensive rehabilitation, you might read on to familiarize yourself with the major concerns of keeping a house standing and working. But you'll also need to study Chapter 35 and read a good many other books, pamphlets, and research material in order to assure your success, or at least reduce your risk. Inspecting a structure when you *know* major problems exist is again different from inspecting a home that is apparently being comfortably lived-in.

This chapter is for prospective buyers of homes that are neither especially weary nor completely untried. And its purpose is not to give you x-ray vision, but to tell you where to look and what to look for as you walk through your prospective home.

If you still want to buy after your inspection, you can go on to negotiating and contract signing. You can write yourself a chance to reconsider even after contracts are signed, however, by making the purchase subject to a satisfactory report by a professional home inspection firm. Some lenders even require a professional inspection before approving a mortgage loan. If you do not want to pay the price for such an inspection and it is not required, but you are

Absolutely Necessary Home Inspection Tools

Flashlight. Your primary tool. Don't put your faith in a small light. Get a big beam.

Pocketknife or ice pick. Necessary to test the soundness of the wood that holds up your prospective house.

Marble or small ball. Determining whether the floors are level is child's play.

Magnet. Primarily for older houses where cast iron plumbing is still a possibility.

Compass. You'll want to know how the house is sited when checking for energy efficiency.

Binoculars. You might not be able to get *on* the roof, but you can still get a pretty good look at it.

Old clothes and rubber-soled shoes. To do the inspection right you'll most likely have to crawl and climb.

Pad and pencil. Home inspection and evaluation is not a time to trust your memory, no matter how fine it may be.

worried about one or more particular aspects of the property, you can make your contract subject to inspection of particular features, such as plumbing, heating, or the roof, by a professional in the field.

So we're really talking about two inspections in this chapter. Your own "should we buy this" inspection and a follow-up "second thoughts, professional help" inspection. Go along on the professional inspection—virtually all the inspection firms not only allow but encourage it. You'll learn a lot.

We'll start your personal prepurchase inspection in the basement and work your way up and then out. But first, just a word for condominium and co-op apartment buyers. You may have a little difficulty starting at the bottom and working through your buildings. To inspect the basement and other common areas of a building you will probably need the permission of the Board of Directors, or at least the building superintendent. The extra effort required, however, should not deter you from doing the inspection. A home inspection service can do the job, but you'll understand better what it's talking about in its written report if you've been on the tour yourself.

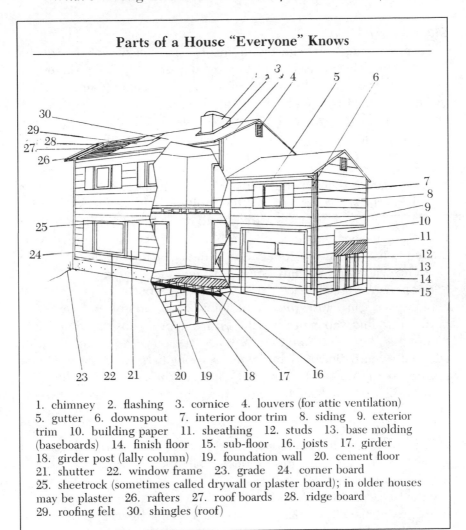

Parts of a House "Everyone" Knows

1. chimney 2. flashing 3. cornice 4. louvers (for attic ventilation)
5. gutter 6. downspout 7. interior door trim 8. siding 9. exterior
trim 10. building paper 11. sheathing 12. studs 13. base molding
(baseboards) 14. finish floor 15. sub-floor 16. joists 17. girder
18. girder post (lally column) 19. foundation wall 20. cement floor
21. shutter 22. window frame 23. grade 24. corner board
25. sheetrock (sometimes called drywall or plaster board); in older houses
may be plaster 26. rafters 27. roof boards 28. ridge board
29. roofing felt 30. shingles (roof)

Reprinted with permission of S. Zimmerman.

Foundations

The *foundation* refers to any construction that is below or partly
below the ground level and upon which the house is built. It may be
a concrete slab, walls and a crawl space, or a full basement. The
most common materials used in today's construction are concrete,
concrete block, and cinderblock. In historic properties, stone is
most common.

The Concrete Slab

To prevent termite infestation and dry rot, all wood parts of the house should be at least 6 inches off the ground. Slabs should be poured over a layer of crushed rock and a permanent vapor barrier (usually a polyethylene plastic sheet). Hairline cracks in the slab that are visible as you walk about outside are not usually a cause for concern. Major separations or extensive crumbling are.

The Crawl Space

A foundation that lifts the house 18 to 36 inches off the ground is called a *crawl space*. It is most often built of concrete block or cinder block. The floor of this area is frequently the ground itself, a situation that can cause serious moisture problems, especially if ventilation is inadequate. At least one foundation wall-ventilator should be built in at each corner with all four being kept open all year round.

Keeping the crawl space dry is of utmost importance, since a wet crawl space can cause *joists* (subfloor beams) to rot and can send harmful ground vapor up into the entire house, causing mildew and dampness. A wet or damp crawl space can often be corrected with adequate ventilation and by laying a vapor barrier of polyethylene plastic on the exposed ground. Insulating directly under the floor above will prevent heat loss from the living quarters and cut down on condensation.

If a crawl space is floored and heated, venting is unnecessary. Heating does not require separate registers for the crawl space. The passage of hot water heating pipes or air ducts through the area is usually sufficient.

Crawl spaces are difficult (actually uncomfortable) to inspect and they are avoided on many inspections, both by the prospective buyer and the professional inspector. Don't avoid it. Wear your oldest clothes, crawl in with your best flashlight, and look around. Be sure the home inspection firm you hire does so also. Look for standing water on the ground, especially near the walls and in the corners. Poke at the beams above your head with an ice pick. The pick should *not* sink into the wood. If it does, get a professional to check for dry rot and termites. Look about also for rodents' nests and/or droppings. The little beasts love the darkness and privacy of crawl space.

The Basement

Most basements today are seven feet high, plenty of room to stand and walk about. Inspect yours carefully, for you will be able to see

more of the working systems of the house on this level than anywhere else. And you can gather information about construction,
settling, and water—the kind you want (drinking) and the kind you
don't want (ground water seepage).

Contrary to popular opinion, concrete is *not* waterproof. Water
can seep through it in the same way that smoke passes through
fabric. And block construction is even less waterproof. The dryness
of a basement really depends upon the water table in the area and
the grading outside the house.

Basement dampness (as opposed to standing puddles of water) is
often due to condensation. The cool air in the below-ground area
cannot hold as much moisture as the heated air from the house in
winter or from the outdoors in summer. The rising of ground moisture through the basement floor is another cause of that cold feeling
and musty smell. This problem, however, can often be corrected by
a dehumidifier.

Seepage from outside ground water is a much more serious problem and can undermine the structural soundness of a building. First
check for water in the corners. If that's where you see it, the seepage may be due to the faulty positioning of a downspout. Your water
problem could then be solved by moving, extending, or fixing the
downspout. However, those puddles can be due to a collection of
ground water around the footings, a very serious problem which can
cause uneven settling. If you see water, suspicious stains, or a newly
painted floor and cracks in the foundation walls, you might want to
continue your house hunting elsewhere. At the very least contact a
professional engineer and get an evaluation of the problem. (Call the
town hall and ask for the town engineer or building inspector if you
know of no one else.)

Look also for stained areas on the basement walls. Moisture, after
it has dried, leaves a yellowish-brown marking. If you see an even
line at the same level all around the basement, it is probably the
high water mark. The house ships or has shipped a good deal of
water!

Flimsy white fuzz growing on the walls is called *efflorescence*. It's
caused by moisture mixing with acids in the concrete and indicates
moisture behind the wall. If it's slight, no harm. If it's heavy, check
further unless you want to risk the expense of installing drainage
tiles around the house soon after you move in. And beware of newly
painted, bright and shiny basement walls. Why did the owners take
the time to paint their basement? How many water stains, how
much efflorescence has been covered over?

If there's a sump pump in the basement, ask the owner how often it works. Some only turn on once or twice a year, others work during and after every rainstorm. And ask where the pump drains. A dry well at some distance from the house is good. Even better, if allowed by the town, is a storm sewer system, since the water is permanently taken away from the foundation. A pump that takes the water up and out through the basement window doesn't accomplish much. The act is something like bailing a leaking boat, since the water is still on the other side of the wall.

Basement water problems are one of the homebuyer's greatest fears. If you suspect them, even if you can't exactly pinpoint the reason for your suspicions, it's a good idea to call in professional help. A home inspection firm may confirm your suspicions, and a basement waterproofing company will give you an idea of how much the repair will cost (if you're still interested in buying the house).

Even more serious than basement water problems, though less often noticed and taken seriously by nonprofessionals, is uneven settling of the house. Every new house settles somewhat, and there are usually some hairline cracks in the foundation whether it is a slab, crawl space, or full basement. These are acceptable. But if a footing sinks, leaving the support of the structure uneven, the soundness of the house and every working system in it can be endangered.

Look for large cracks in the foundation walls that can be seen from both inside and outside the basement. The condition is particularly serious if the cracks extend from the top of the wall to the bottom or if they form an open V. A house with this kind of settling problem will have doors and windows that bind and diagonal cracks in the wallboard or plaster, especially above doors and windows.

Some of these same symptoms may also be caused by buckling of the basement walls. Repairing this problem is very expensive. Either the basement must be rebuilt or buttresses must be used to shore up the weak points.

When the basement is poorly constructed, more often than not the rest of the house will have problems. If there seems to be a lot of unexplained things wrong upstairs, go back down to the basement and check the walls again. Get a plumb line if you must and determine if what looks straight really *is* straight.

While you are in the basement, you should check for evidence of wood decay, dry rot, and termites. As in the crawl space, take your ice pick or pocketknife and poke at the wood joists, especially where they are in direct contact with the foundation walls. These contact points between wood and concrete are the most vulnerable to all wood deterioration problems. Problems exist if your blade slips into the wood or if you encounter a spongy rather than a solid resistance.

When you have finished testing the soundness of the wood, look for water stains on the joists. Leaking pipes not visible in the living areas (they're behind the wallboard) may cause stains on basement wood. If ductwork is visible in the basement, look for rust stains or discoloration. Check also for broken or punctured ducts unless you particularly want to heat your basement while heating your house.

And finally, look at the cellar stairs. Many are open on both sides. If there isn't at least a handrail all the way down, don't buy the house until the seller installs one. Doctors in every hospital in the country can tell you about the concussions and broken bones suffered by people in a hurry who fell off the side of the cellar stairs.

Termites

Termites are alive and well in every state except Alaska. Their communities are healthier and their population growth most rapid in the Sunbelt, but every house should have a termite inspection before it is purchased, even if it's in Maine or Minnesota. Indeed many lenders require professional inspection. In any case, we do *not*

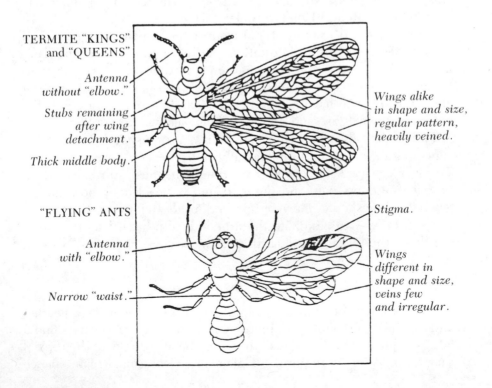

TERMITE "KINGS" and "QUEENS"

Antenna without "elbow."

Stubs remaining after wing detachment.

Thick middle body.

Wings alike in shape and size, regular pattern, heavily veined.

"FLYING" ANTS

Antenna with "elbow."

Narrow "waist."

Stigma.

Wings different in shape and size, veins few and irregular.

suggest that you do it yourself. The following information is just some background, in case the ravenous insects ever chew their way into your life.

Wood is the staple of their diet, but termites also need water to survive. Their quest for water is often a giveaway to their presence. To get it they must maintain contact with the soil. The chore is easy when construction wood rests on the ground, more difficult when a foundation lifts the house away from the earth.

Why can't they just crawl down the six inches to the ground, get a drink, and crawl back home? Most termites cannot tolerate exposure to light and drying air. In order to go for water, therefore, they must build tunnels from the ground to the wood parts of the house. If a house is a home to termites, you might well see mud tunnels, half-rounds the diameter of a pencil, on the foundation walls.

Swarming is another sign of termite presence. It most often occurs in the spring but can take place at any warm time of the year. If you are witness to a swarming, you'll see a mass of insects suddenly emerge from the wall of the house or from a nearby woodpile. This is the mating flight of the termite kings and queens. Soon after the act, the newlyweds shed their wings, and dried wings on window-sills or door jambs are dead giveaways to a recent flight (and to termite infestation). Don't mistake termites for flying ants: Catch some in a jar and examine them against the drawings on page 235.

Most cases of termite infestation can be eradicated and the damage repaired. And most extermination companies will give a guarantee against the insect's return. But before you have the job done or allow the seller to have it done for you, find out what chemicals the exterminator will use and how the chemicals will be applied.

Two chemicals, chlordane and aldrin, are suspected of causing cancer and are banned from virtually all uses except termite control. To be safely used for termite extermination, these substances must be used outdoors *only* and pumped into two-foot-deep holes in the ground. They should *never* be sprayed inside the house. If they are, there is no way to eliminate the human health hazard short of tearing down the building and carting it away.

The Working Systems

You need a license to be a plumber, an electrician, or a heating and cooling contractor, and unless you have all three licenses and a fair assortment of other skills, you won't be able to do all the repairs that a home might require. So plan on an occasional maintenance bill in your life as a homeowner. But it doesn't take a license or even specialized training to spot when something in a house is in trouble. Let's take a lay-person's look at the working systems.

Electrical

Do you know the difference between an amp, a volt, and a watt?

"A watt?" you say.

OK, we're not much into electricity either. You need to know the minimum electric service recommended for today's lifestyle is 240-volt, 100-ampere service. You don't need to understand that, just ask if the house has it. If your castle comes with an electric stove or oven, an electric clothes dryer, or central air conditioning, it will need to have 150- to 200-ampere service (but still 240 volts).

In the not-too-unlikely event that you ask the real estate agent or the owner about the electrical service and get a glazed look in response, go to the main electric board (the place where the fuses or circuit breakers are located) and look around with the help of your flashlight. The electric capacity is usually printed somewhere there.

Since most of the electrical work in a house is behind the wallboard, you won't be able to inspect very much. And if you could, would you be able to tell the difference between a size 10 wire and a size 14? Or know which should go where?

You'll probably have to confine your electrical inspection pretty much to counting outlets (there should be one for every twelve feet of wall, more in the kitchen), throwing the light switch in every room to make sure it works, and checking in the backs of closets and behind couches and things to be sure there aren't exposed wires or extension cords holding five or more plugs. (By the way, if you throw a light switch and nothing happens, check the table lamps before you panic. The switch may control a socket and the lamp plugged into that socket may be turned off at its switch, or the bulb may be burned out.)

Check to be sure the doorbell or doorbells ring. If they don't, have the seller do the repairs before the closing. You won't need that little bother in the disarray of moving in.

Needless to say, if anything that you see worries you, mention it to your home inspection service or get a qualified electrician to do an evaluation.

Heating

There are three main concerns about a home heating system. Is it safe? Does it provide enough heat? And how much does it cost?

Some Words You Thought You'd Never Need to Know

Bleedout. A term indicating that effluent from a septic system is rising to the surface rather than draining into the earth.

Bridging. Usually, criss-crossed pieces of wood wedged between supporting beams. They reinforce the beams and distribute the stress.

Circulator Pump. The pump on a hot water furnace boiler that moves the water through the heating pipes and radiators.

Eave. The extension of a roof beyond the walls of a house.

Efflorescence. White, fuzz-like powder that forms on basement walls when moisture is present behind the walls.

Effluent. Treated sewerage from a septic tank, usually 99 percent water.

Fascia. A flat horizontal board enclosing the area under the eave.

Flashing. Material used at roof angle changes or joints to prevent leaking.

Flue. The passageway in the chimney through which smoke rises to the outside air.

Girder. A main supporting beam of the house.

Grade or grade level. The line of the surface of the ground.

Jamb. The side of the doorframe that faces the opening.

Joists. Beams that rest on the outer foundation or walls to support the boards of a floor or ceiling.

Lally Column. A steel column filled with concrete that supports a girder or sometimes other floor beams.

Leader. A downspout.

Pilaster. A reinforced projection of the foundation wall that gives additional support to a floor girder or strengthens a length of wall.

Potability Test. A test done on the water to determine if it is suitable for drinking.

Riser. The vertical part of a step.

Sash. A window.

Sheetrock. Plasterboard or drywall.

Soffit. The visible horizontal underside of an eave.

Splashblock. Stone or concrete formations under the downspouts to take water away from the foundation.

Sump. A pit in the basement floor or crawl space that collects water to be pumped out.

Tongue and Groove. A type of interlocking-boards construction.

Tread. The horizontal part of a stair.

Vent Pipes. Pipes that allow gas to be vented outdoors from the plumbing system.

Window Well. An excavation around a cellar window.

Determining safety is a job for the experts. Proponents of every kind of heating method tout its safety. But no matter which system you have, you should shine your own trusty beam of light upon it. If you see soot or blackened areas that might indicate a fire, ask questions! There may not have actually been a fire, but the unit could be working marginally or very inefficiently.

You should turn on the heat even if you are inspecting a house in July. Once you turn it on, go to the farthest room from the furnace and wait. A circulating hot water system should change the temperature of a room within fifteen to twenty minutes and it should do so without excessive clanging and banging. A hot air system will change the temperature within five to ten minutes.

Once the heat is on go from room to room and check each heating register. Do you feel heat? You don't want to find out in January that the back bedroom or the hall bath doesn't ever get warm. This check of individual registers is especially important if your prospective house has electric heat, since a heating unit might be inoperable without any external evidence and without affecting the remainder of the system.

As good a way as any to check the system's efficiency and the weather tightness and insulation of a house is to ask for the total amount of the heating bill for the previous winter and the name of the fuel supplier. Then call the oil or utility company and ask what a typical bill for a house of your square footage would have been for the previous winter. Most companies will have this information and you'll be able to see exactly how your dream house measures up.

While you are in the basement or utility room, it is a good idea to shine your light on whatever heating pipes or ductwork you can see. Are they insulated? Leaking? Rusted? Punctured? Call in a professional if you see anything suspicious.

Hot Water

Tap-ready hot water is a luxury that virtually everyone in this country regards as a necessity. But how do you get it? Or more specifically, how is it provided in the house you are about to buy? Ask someone.

In houses with circulating hot water heat, a "continuous hot water" supply is sometimes listed as a feature. It may or may not be a feature you want. Hot water holding tanks in these systems are usually small and often run out of hot water while you are still luxuriously soaping in the shower. If you're a bath person, you may never get the water hot enough for a good old-fashioned soaking. Once the holding tank is emptied, the supply is indeed continuous, but the furnace doesn't have enough time to heat the water satisfactorily before it passes into the system. Also remember that with a hot water system tied to your heating system, you'll have to keep your furnace running all summer.

Free standing hot water heaters are another story. If the tank has a capacity of 40 to 80 gallons, you aren't very likely to run out. Heating your hot water electrically, however, is expensive. Gas is cheaper at this writing, but not available everywhere. If you're into avant garde devices, you might look into solar-heated hot water.

Besides the cost of operation, the cost of replacing a hot water heater must be considered when you are evaluating a house. Until a homeowner walks into the cellar one day to find puddles or a flood, he or she is unlikely to know that the life span of most hot water heaters is only eight to twelve years. Some heaters do live longer and display no signs of illness until the day they leak. If you happen to be away on vacation at the time, the leak will continue to drip (or pour) and the tank will continue to refill (unless you had shut down the system before you left.)

In any case, ask how old the unit is and shine your inspection light about it carefully. If it's ten years old and you see one tiny glint of water, try to negotiate either a price reduction to cover the cost of a new tank, or, much better, the installation of a new one paid for by the seller *before* closing.

But inspecting the hot water system doesn't end in the basement. Go to each of the faucets in the house and turn on the hot water. How long does it take to get there? You should not have to stand around for a full two minutes with the water running. Also, is there enough pressure? What happens if you add some cold water to a mixing faucet? Do you get warm water or does the cold water take over completely?

A weak hot water system should not stop you from buying a house that is otherwise acceptable. It certainly should be a negotiating point, something that can be mentioned just in case the owners try holding out for more than you are willing to pay.

Plumbing

Your plumbing experience may be limited to pouring Drano into your kitchen sink, but take heart, only plumbers and house inspection engineers know much more. Besides, the first steps in a plumbing inspection are obvious. Check the drains to see that they are not clogged. Check around whatever pipes you can see (including those within kitchen and bathroom cabinets) to determine if they are leaking. And look for stains in the sinks, which indicate leaky faucets.

Check water pressure by opening the kitchen faucet and then going to a bathroom (preferably an upstairs bathroom if the house has more than one floor) and opening that faucet. You should get more than a trickle. You can add to the stress test by flushing the toilet while the two faucets are running. If the water flow is reduced to connected droplets, call a plumber and find out why before you buy.

In older houses where cast iron plumbing is still in use, water pressure is sometimes poor because mineral deposits have collected in the pipes and reduced their diameter. You can test for cast iron pipes by using a magnet in the basement or wherever pipes are exposed. The magnet will be attracted to cast iron; it will not be attracted to copper.

If the water pressure is poor and the pipes are cast iron, you may start to wonder if you should really buy. How much will replacement of all the plumbing cost anyway? Well, you may not have to replace all of it. Deposits build up faster in horizontal pipes than in vertical pipes. You may be able to restore good pressure at a much lower cost by replacing the horizontal pipes only. Get two or three professional opinions and estimates.

Cast iron pipes or a combination of cast iron and copper drain, waste, and vent pipes were used in house construction long after copper water pipes became standard. Such drain pipes usually function adequately, but the plastic piping now being used in new house construction is actually superior.

If you are concerned about the condition of the drain and waste pipes, partially fill the tub. At the same time that you open the tub drain, flush the toilet. The system should handle the combination without a problem. If water backs up, find out why.

In doing your plumbing inspection, watch out for hidden leaks, most commonly found under tubs or stall showers. Look at the ceilings below the bathrooms for discoloration or for a fresh coat of paint that has been "feathered in" to the rest of the ceiling paint job. If you are suspicious, or just plain careful, stop up the shower drain, run the water until two inches or so has collected in the bottom of the stall, turn off the water, and remove the stopper. If there is a leak in the shower floor or drain system, it will usually appear when this much water drains at one time.

If you are a city person with the amenities of city water and city sewers at your house, you can stop reading this section now. If a country place is your dream house, however, you have more to think about, namely getting your drinking water and getting rid of waste.

Let's start with drinking water. Bad water is one of the few reasons to walk away from a house that you absolutely love, at any price, unless you don't mind buying your drinking and cooking water in gallon plastic jugs at the grocery store.

When a well is polluted or inadequate, the habitability of the house becomes very questionable. Yes, you can try digging a deeper well or digging in another location, but there are no guarantees that the problem will be solved. And the cost! If you were to buy a property just below its market value, put twenty thousand dollars into getting clean water, and then decide to sell, your twenty thousand dollar investment will net you not one penny in return. Buyers expect clean water—they will not pay extra for it.

If you are buying a house that uses well water, *get the water tested*. Many lenders will not write a mortgage loan without a water test, it's that important. If you are in an area where wells are common, the bank or the real estate agent will be able to give you the names of testing labs. Their reports will usually tell you the bacteria content of the water and the mineral content also. If the water is particularly "hard," you may need a water softener.

Besides getting the water tested, you might also call the town health officer or board of health and ask if there have been any recent well water problems in the area. And of course you can always try reading back issues of local newspapers.

Right after the quality of the water in importance comes the supply. An English teacher, his wife, and their three children live in a house in Connecticut where the well runs dry by the fourth of July every year. It doesn't bother them much, however, since they have by then closed up the house and moved to their camp counselor jobs in the Berkshire hills. However, it might bother most other people.

When water is obtained from a well, subsoil conditions and seasonal water levels are always something of an unknown. There *are* established patterns, however. Talk with the neighbors and with town officials. Also, call well-digging companies and ask how deep wells in the area usually go, what types of soil and rock are encountered, and how good and reliable the water supply is. If everyone agrees that there is no problem, there usually is no problem.

Well water must be pumped into a house, and well pumps have an expected lifespan of about ten years, although some last much longer. Find out how old the one in your prospective house is. You can have someone (the house inspection firm, a well-digging company, a local plumber) test for gallons-per-minute being pumped, but you can also test the supply of the moment by simply running the water for ten minutes or so. Open several faucets. Does the supply seem adequate? Or does the water pressure fall after a few minutes?

Inspect the interior storage tank for the well water also. Rusting is a sign of marginal condition.

The other end of a private water system is waste disposal, a septic tank or cesspool. But you don't always have both ends. Some suburban locations have municipal water supply but private sewer systems. A very few have a municipal sewer but private water supply. Waste disposal is not quite as difficult a problem to correct as poor water supply, but a malfunctioning septic system can be a hole in the ground into which the owner pours money.

A dry season, when the well is gasping and coughing, is the time when waste disposal problems are hidden. And vice versa, when there's plenty of water flowing from the tap and rain upon the land, the septic tank effluent may be bubbling merrily to the surface and gathering an umbrella of gnats. Since you can't ever really see what's going on in such a system, you should use a professional inspection, either through a home inspection firm or a septic/cesspool service. These professionals can put dye tablets into the system and then run water through it to see if the dye surfaces.

It's a good idea to ask the seller for a record of tank maintenance. And try to get an indication of where the tank and leach lines or dry well are located. Even if everything is fine when you close on the property, you may have a problem a year or two later and you'll be saved a lot of expense if you know where the system is laid out under the ground. Some towns require that every builder file a *plat plan* showing the location of the septic tank. If you run into septic tank problems after you buy, ask the town clerk if such maps were required in the town at the time that your house was built and where they are kept on file. Do this *before* you pay someone to poke around your yard with a long, thin steel pole.

The Cooling System

In some parts of the country, cooling equals or surpasses heating in importance. Test air conditioning equipment just as you tested heating equipment: turn it on. Then ask for the bills for the previous year.

In the South, an all-in-one heating/cooling system called a *heat pump* is popular, and its growing use attests to its efficiency and economy. In more northern areas, however, such systems usually cool effectively during the summer but cannot be relied upon to heat through the entire winter. For more information on heat pumps, write to: Better Heating-Cooling Council, 35 Russo Place, P.O. Box 218, Berkeley Heights, N.J. 07922. There are four booklets available: "Reliability"; "Serviceability"; "Cost of Operation"; and "Installation and Comfort." At this writing each costs a dollar.

The Interior

Don't be fooled by decorating! Many buyers pay too much for "pretty" houses. Look at the structure, the floor plan, and the working systems; everything else can be easily changed and will be if you live there any length of time.

The Kitchen

Few kitchen floors are carpeted, so this is a good place to test for uneven settling. Place a marble in the center of the floor and see if it rolls. A casual meandering is of no significance, since no floor is *perfectly* level. But if the marble takes off toward a corner like a greyhound at the track, go back outdoors and look again at the foundation or go down into the cellar and check the floor joists. If the marble rolls in other rooms too, or if you're nervous about the floor tilt, get the opinion of a home inspection firm or a qualified builder or carpenter.

Spots in the floor that creak when you step on them are common in old and new houses. Theoretically they can be found in every room but are most often heard in the kitchen because of the lack of carpet and upholstered furniture. Usually creaky spots are of little significance. The person putting down the floor probably missed the beam when nailing, thus leaving some wood unsecured. But if the floor feels spongy along with the creaking, check for rotting wood.

While you're in the kitchen, turn on and use all the appliances that remain with the house, even if the seller is sitting at the kitchen table. Try out the range, oven, diswasher, garbage disposal, exhaust fan, refrigerator, and even the washing machine and clothes dryer if the listing says they stay with the house. Poor condition of these units may not stop you from buying, but they sure are negotiating points that may result in lowering the price.

The Bathrooms

Look for cracked and broken tile and crumbling or missing grout. Water seeping into such holes can lead to major repairs not only in the bathrooms but also in the ceilings or subfloors below. If the house has an interior bathroom, check the ventilation fan. Always flush the toilets. Some require a formula of holding down the lever for X number of seconds while watching the water level in order to get an adequate flush. Can you live with the formula, or will the toilet need repair or replacement?

Floors

Where you can, use the marble test. Where there is wall-to-wall carpet, you won't be able to see much unless you can persuade the seller to allow you to lift a corner somewhere. Hardwood floors of tongue and groove construction are still most highly valued, but you will find plywood subfloors in many newer houses where wall-to-wall carpet was included in the original purchase contract. They are perfectly acceptable, but you'll have to buy new carpeting from time to time.

As you walk through the house looking at floors, look also at the baseboards. Moldings should not have separated from the floor. If they have, it could indicate shoddy construction, green lumber, uneven settling, or a combination.

Walls and Ceilings

Look for the diagonal cracks already mentioned. In theory there should also be no popped nails, and the taping of wallboard should be invisible. Plaster walls should not be crumbling or full of unpatched nail holes. And long cracks in plaster ceilings are suspicious. Plaster ceilings *can* fall down and the mess is horrendous. Negotiate about these flaws, but they are not worth losing an otherwise good deal.

Windows and Doors

Are there storm and screen windows? How old are they? Are all the pieces for all the windows present? Do they *work?*

Move each window up and down. Binding and sticking may mean uneven settling or just poor window construction. Some windows may even be painted shut. Note any that are and ask that the seller free them up before closing. When you check the house just before the closing to see that any requested work has been done, open all the windows. Banging and pounding to break a painted seal sometimes breaks the glass (or even the wood). You shouldn't have to do such repairs when the problem was caused by someone else's carelessness.

If the house has self-insulating windows (the kind pictured in magazines with two feet of snow outside and a naked baby playing by the windows inside), find out their age. These windows can lose insulating ability with age, especially if the seals are broken. Peeling paint, cracked or checkered wood around the glass or on the sill, and the presence of a black mold that looks like lake bottom mud are all indications that both moisture and air are passing through the windows.

Fireplaces

Do they work? And do they work without filling the whole house with smoke? You may feel funny about starting a fire in August, but it's the only way you'll be sure you won't be cleaning up soot in December. And we're not referring to the little bits that Santa dislodges.

The Attic

Get into the attic even if you have to squeeze through the back corner of a bedroom closet. There's much to be learned.

First shine your flashlight at the rafters. Look for water stains—the wood will be darker with an irregular edge to the shading. The most common locations for leaks are at the chimneys or vent pipes and along the roof line of an addition or change in the angle of the roof.

You will probably be able to observe the insulation in the floor of the attic. Just because it's there, however, does not mean that the entire house is insulated in a like manner. Fiberglass attic insulation is a common homeowner project. Ask about the insulation in the remainder of the house. Testing can be done by a home inspection firm or a heating contractor.

Attic ventilation is extremely important, yet is often minimal. Moisture caught in the attic can cause the rafters to rot and allow the growth of vile smelling fungus. Simply keeping the attic well ventilated will reduce this moisture build-up in the winter, and also reduce heat build-up in the summer. So be sure that vents are open and kept open all year round. If ventilation is inadequate, consider installing roof vents.

And while you're in the attic look about for bats or evidence of mice or squirrels (droppings or shredded materials in the corners). They can do serious damage.

The Exterior

Always inspect the exterior in daylight. This may sound elementary, but you'd be surprised how many people sign contracts to buy after completing an inspection at 9 P.M. Let's start at the top and work down.

The Roof

Asphalt shingles are the most common roofing material, and their life span is approximately sixteen to twenty years. If your house is over fifteen years old, look for barren places on the shingles where the granular mineral coating is worn away. If there are many, you will need a new roof in a very few years.

If you can get up on the roof, look at the *flashings*. These are angled barriers designed to keep water from seeping into the attic at points where two roof angles meet or where something like a chimney or vent pipe protrudes through the roof. Ideally, flashings should be inspected and sealed every year; they rarely are. But if your attic leak is due to the poor condition of flashings, the problem is easily solved.

Gutters and downspouts are needed to control the flow of rain water or melting snow off the roof. Most are now made of aluminum and require little care beyond clearing them of leaves and debris. Wood gutters require annual maintenance to prevent rotting. If the house has wood gutters, inspect them carefully and consider negotiating for the installation of new metal ones.

Downspouts take the water from the roof to the ground at acceptable places. Without them, a person standing at your front door in a storm would be drenched by run-off from the roof. The general rule is one downspout every thirty feet.

After you get down off the roof, walk around the perimeter of the house to be sure that extensions to the downspouts and/or concrete splashblocks take the water away from the foundation. A broken downspout simply collects water and deposits it at a particular point along the foundation. Thus you might get roof water into your cellar.

The Siding

The siding is what you see when you look at the outside of a house. It is usually brick, vinyl, aluminum, stucco, stone, or wood. Wood is the most common.

As you walk about the exterior, look for signs of deterioration no matter what the siding is. Blistering and cracking paint may mean a poor paint job or it may mean moisture caught in the wood, which will eventually mean a new siding job. Long cracks in the stucco could mean it cannot tolerate the changes in temperature of the area's weather or the particular angle of the house's siting. Crumbling brick and mortar needs no explanation, it needs repair.

The Trim

It's currently fashionable to paint the trim of a house (soffit, fascia, corner beams, and window moldings) a different color from the siding. These are usually areas where paint wears and peels rapidly, and such peeling turns some buyers away thinking the house is in need of repair and repainting. Often, only the trim needs repainting. The job is bothersome because most of it has to be done from a ladder and done very carefully. But new trim paint can make a wallflower house into a neighborhood beauty.

Porches, Patios, and Decks

Check that they are structurally sound and have handrails where necessary (more than four steps). Cracks between concrete steps and the house should be sealed.

Garages

Is the floor cracking? Does the water that drips off wet cars drain *out?* Do the windows work? Is there a fire-shield on the door leading into the house? Do the garage doors open easily?

The Land

Observe the drainage. Good grading takes water away from a foundation. A house in a hollow is likely to have basement water problems.

The Home Inspection Service

Until the late 1960s the rule in real estate was *caveat emptor,* or let the buyer beware! But as the decade turned, buyers began winning suits in the courts against sellers and/or real estate agents who misrepresented or failed to disclose negative aspects of properties. At about the same time, home inspection services and home warranties became popular.

Today sellers are usually aware that if they are asked about water in the basement, they had better reply truthfully or face a potential lawsuit that could award damages or rescind the sale. And buyers are indeed wary. More home purchase contracts are signed subject to professional inspection than not.

But what do you get when you hire a home inspection service at a cost of between $100 and $300? For the most part these firms are completely unregulated. Some are one person operations, others are multi-office chains operating within one state, and others are members of large nationwide groups. Some of the inspectors are licensed professional engineers, some are retired handymen, some down-on-their-luck builders, some none of the above. How do you know which service to hire? It's not always easy to choose, but before we pick a firm, let's look at what inspection services usually offer.

Professional Inspection Pluses

• *Experience.* The person who does the inspection has inspected a great many houses. Your experience is limited by the number of home purchases you have made. No amount of reading and study can completely make up for actual experience.

• *Perspective.* The professional inspector is not emotionally or financially involved in the sale. His or her vision is therefore more rational, if not necessarily more careful.

• *Plan.* The home inspection firm provides a check list for the inspection. If the list is followed, the inspector is unlikely to overlook anything.

• *Standards to judge by.* The inspector knows the life expectancy of the working systems and the structural materials in the house and can make value judgements as to their quality and condition.

• *A written report.* An excellent negotiating tool or a way out of the contract if there is truly something wrong with the house.

Home Inspection Checklist

Foundation

       Slab   *Crawl*   *Basement*

    Walls:

    Water/moisture:

    Sump pump:

    Ventilation:

    Condition of exposed wood:

        exposed plumbing:

        exposed heating equipment:

    Stairs:

    Termite inspection:

Working Systems

    Electrical:

    Heating:

    Hot water:

    Plumbing:

        Well:

        Septic or cesspool:

    Cooling system:

Interior:

    Kitchen:

    Bathrooms:

    Floors:

    Walls and ceilings:

    Windows and doors:

    Fireplaces:

Attic

    Water stains/moisture:

    Ventilation:

    Insulation:

    Pests:

Exterior

    Roof:

    Gutters:

    Downspouts:

    Siding:

    Trim:

    Porches, patios, and decks:

    Garage(s):

    Land:

What the Inspection Won't Do
• *Guarantee anything.* If you want a warranty, you'll have to pay more.
• *Make your decision.* Hiring an inspection firm gives you a professional opinion of the property's condition. It will not tell you if the house is a good deal or whether or not you should buy it.

How to Choose an Inspection Service
Do not ask the seller or your real estate agent to recommend one. Even the best of these people will call an inspector who won't make too many waves in the deal.

Ask for referrals from friends or business associates. In large corporations, personnel offices will often supply the names of inspection firms who will work completely in the interests of their transferred employees. If you don't have a corporation behind you or friends in the area, ask your mortgage lender or your lawyer for a recommendation. The lender wants you to have a sound house with no sudden financial catastrophes. The lawyer has no stake in the success of any particular deal. If all else fails, use the phone book and tell the inspection firm that you are responding to their advertisement. At least then they will know that they owe no loyalty or favor to the real estate firm or the seller.

The Home Warranty

The home inspection company usually offers a home warranty plan. Read its fine print carefully before paying a penny extra for it. Most plans are very limited warranties, and most have a deductible that the buyer must pay for *each claim.* The amount of the deductible ranges from $100 to $250. At present $100 is most common.

Many structural elements such as the roof or exterior walls are simply not covered and there may be upper limits on how much the warranty will pay even when something *is* covered. It may be written that structural element coverage extends to 50 percent of the cost of repair to a maximum of $1000. But the collapse of a basement wall or a roof will cost you much more than that.

The working systems of a house are usually covered by the warranty, but they are depreciated. For example, a water heater may be depreciated at the rate of 10 percent per year. If you buy the house in year seven and the water heater springs a leak six months

Evaluating the Problems

Like the lights on a traffic signal, some housing problems call for a full stop (red), others require you to proceed with caution (yellow), and still others require an acknowledgment of their presence but no real delay (green). Of course every "rule" here is subject to extenuating circumstances. What's most important is that you put the problems you have found into some perspective. With some faults you may want to walk away from the county's finest bargain, with others you may have the time, money, and motivation for repair work.

Red Lights
 Unsafe or inadequate drinking water.
 A nonfunctioning or malfunctioning private sewer system (septic tank or cesspool).
 Location in a flood plain. (The United States Geological Survey has mapped most flood plain areas in this country. If your property is on low land near a river or stream, investigate. Federal flood insurance is available to residents of flood plain areas. Most lenders will not write a mortgage without it.)
 Uneven settling or a buckling foundation.
 Uncontrollable basement water problems.

Yellow Lights
 Peeling, cracking, or bubbling exterior paint.
 A roof "almost" in need of repair.
 Deteriorating gutters and downspouts.
 Leaks in the roof at the flashings.
 Excessive moisture in the attic due to poor ventilation or inadequate insulation.
 Pests (termites, bats, mice, squirrels, roaches).
 Inadequate electrical service. (It can be brought in at a cost.)
 Inadequate heating plant. (Negotiate the cost of a new furnace).
 Inadequate insulation.
 Plumbing pipes or fixtures in need of repair or replacement.
 Leaks around the bathtub or from under a stall shower.
 Windows in need of repair or replacement.

Green Lights
 An aged or inadequate water heater.

> Nonworking appliances. (Built-in ranges, ovens, dish-washers, etc.)
> Hairline settling cracks in the foundation.
> Leaky faucets.
> Dirt, grime, and eyesore decorating.

later (now year eight), the warranty company considers 80 percent of the useful life of that water heater to have passed. They therefore will pay only 20 percent of the cost of replacement. And that's *after* you pay the $100 deductible. Will you get anything? It's unlikely.

Non-Inspection Warranties

Like life-insurance without a physical, there are home warranty programs available without an inspection. Usually they are sold to the *seller*, who then offers the warranty as an incentive to buy. These plans are usually even more limited than the inspection-plan warranties. They're generally all right, however, as long as they don't cost the buyer anything. You may or may not get something from the insurance, but don't let it lead you to a false sense of security. Inspect the property *thoroughly*, whether it has a warranty or not.

Some Cosmic Thoughts

If there's not a perfect person on this side of heaven, there's also not a perfect house. Choose the faults and favors that you can live with and then work at making the living arrangement work. After all, that's what "living happily ever after" is all about.

For More Information

The Small Homes Council—Building Research Council at the University of Illinois at Urbana-Champaign has a number of booklets on home maintenance and planning available. For a free publication list, write to: Small Homes Council, University of Illinois at Urbana-Champaign, One East Saint Mary's Road, Champaign, Ill. 61820.

"To the Home Buying Veteran," VA pamphlet #26–6, has a good section on home inspection. You don't have to be a veteran to get one. Call your nearest Veterans Administration office listed in the phone book under U.S. Government.

The following three booklets are available from the Superintendent of Documents, U.S. Government Printing Office, Washington, D.C.

"Basic Housing Inspection," Public Health Service publication #2123.

"Finding and Keeping a Healthy House," U.S. Department of Agriculture, Forest Service Publication #1284. (Everything you want to know about termites.) "Wood Decay in Houses, How to Prevent and Control It," U.S. Department of Agriculture, Home and Garden Bulletin #73.

How to Inspect a House, by George Hoffman. Dell Publishing Co. $4.95. This book is technical but comprehensive. Well illustrated.

16

Condos and Co-ops—
Some Special Considerations

It's almost an epidemic in some parts of the country: condo/co-op fever! If you think you've got it, a dose of knowledge and consideration will help you recover stronger for having been through it. Maybe richer too.

First go back to pages 170–177 and read again what makes a condo a condo and a co-op a co-op. Then check the index and read each entry where we talk about special condo/co-op procedures or problems within the process of buying and selling a home.

All right, you understand the theory and your want-to-buy fever is still raging. Except that you have two small questions: "What's it really like to live in a community where you own a good deal of space and things (like walls, pools, and parking areas) with a lot of other people?" and "Would buying such a home *really* be a good investment?"

The take-two-aspirins-and-call-me-in-the-morning answers to these questions are: "It's just like living in an apartment except that you have some say in how the place is run" and "Buying a condo or co-op is just like buying any other home. Of course it's a good investment."

"But hold on!" you say. "This is my life savings that I'm putting into this purchase. Can't you do a little better than a take-two-aspirins answer?"

Yes, and we've gathered the extras in this chapter so that those caught up in the fever can immerse themselves in it and those who are not can skip on. Let's look at life in a shared-space ownership community. How do you pick a good one, and how do you sell it profitably?

Life in the Apartment You Own

Who's Responsible for What?

If you're a new condo or co-op owner and had been a tenant most of your life, you may be tempted to call the super to complain about the dripping faucet in the bathroom that is beating out the five-second intervals of your insomnia. Bad luck! You're now a homeowner and the leak is most likely all yours to fix.

Although the ownership form is different, most condos and co-ops across the country are run pretty much alike when it comes to maintenance responsibility. Generally, if the problem originates *inside* your living space, it's yours.

To illustrate, let's assume that we're talking about a plumbing leak that is now staining your carpet and walls. What a mess! Now you're really upset. *They* better fix this problem and *they* better pay you for the damages to your carpet and the new wallpaper you're going to need!

Before you call a lawyer, you had better read your proprietary lease (for a co-op) or your declaration and bylaws (for a condo). The following responsibility *usually* applies, but some legal documents differ:

1. It is the responsibility of the co-op corporation or unit owners' association to find the cause of a major leak.

2. It is the responsibility of the corporation or association to repair the condition if it is caused by factors in the main or branch pipes serving the apartment. (The leak would then be inside the walls. The dripping faucet is still your responsibility.)

3. The corporation or association must not only repair the pipes that are leaking, they must also replaster or repair the wall that was broken through to get to the pipes. They are not responsible, however, for your carpet or wallpaper unless you can prove that the leak and/or the damage was the result of negligence. For example, the leak was allowed to continue for over a week despite your daily phone calls and written notices.

4. It is your responsibility to give access to your apartment in order to get the leak fixed. If you refuse to allow workers in to fix the problem, you could be held responsible for the cost of repairs to all apartments involved!

5. If the workers must break through a wall in your apartment in order to get to leaking pipes that are staining someone else's walls, you must allow them access. The corporation or association is then required to repair your walls and leave the area broom clean. In

most cases, however, they are not required to pay for redecorating that wall. (Sometimes they will volunteer to do so. Sometimes you can get them to do so by proving that there was another, easier way to get to the pipes.)

6. If you don't want to risk paying for such responsibility, check your homeowner's insurance policy to be sure that it includes a contingency for redecorating costs in the event of such a necessary breaking of walls between apartments.

So are your responsibilities those of a tenant or of an owner? Not exactly either, yet both. When you think about it, *proprietary lease* (the term used in most co-op purchases to name the instrument that guarantees occupancy of a particular apartment) is really a self-contradicting term. Proprietary connotes ownership, lease connotes tenancy. And contradictory as it is, that term pretty much sums up your life style as the owner of a co-op or a condo. Some of your responsibilities are those of an owner, and some are those of a tenant.

Maintenance of all the common areas in a condominium or co-op community is the job of the unit owners' association or the corporation; maintenance of your living space and the appliances within it is all yours. No landlord will fix your refrigerator or paint your apartment once every five years. But you won't have to shovel snow from your driveway. The chart on pages 258–259 lists some common problems and their usual responsibility. To be certain of the situation in your particular condominium or co-op, however, you'll have to check through its legal documents.

So maintenance is a split deal. How about insurance?

A good question. Think about these situations: Your cleaning person slips on the oriental rug in your bedroom and ends up in the hospital with a herniated disc. Or she slips on a banana peel in the hallway leading to the front door of your apartment. Again there is the question of what is a common element and who is responsible for it. Generally, inside your apartment is your responsibility, outside is the responsibility of the association or corporation. You therefore should carry comprehensive homeowner insurance and the association or corporation should carry insurance against fire, casualty, and liability just as any rental apartment building owner would carry.

Special use of the common elements also sometimes causes problems in shared-space homeownership. The corporation or association is responsible for maintaining these facilities, but the individual user is responsible for observing the house rules, for normal respect for property, and for clean up after special use. If you decide that you would like to hold your daughter's wedding reception in the magnificent lobby of your building, for example, you'll have to get permission from the board of directors. While the reception is in full swing, you'll want to be certain that no one gets carried away with smashing champagne glasses for good luck. And after it's over, you'll have to take down the decorations, empty the ashtrays, and wash the floor, or pay someone to do so.

The same principle applies to children and pets. Whereas the association or corporation is responsible for keeping the grass cut, they are not responsible for refilling and reseeding the hole Rover dug while you were talking with Tom and Pete about the World Series. The association or corporation is responsible for keeping lobby windows clean; you, however, must pay for replacement of the plate glass your little leaguer threw a ball through.

Getting Things Changed

The power of ownership is commonly misconceived by new condo or co-op owners. Each seems to think that a say in the running of the place comes with his or her ownership of a unit. Few realize exactly how the community really functions.

The vast majority of condominium and cooperative communities are run more like miniature republics than true democracies. That is they are run by representatives elected by the unit owners, not by a "vote of the people" on each issue. These representatives are called the *board of directors* or *board of managers*, and in a very real way

Who's Responsible for What		
	Corporation or Unit Owners' Association	*Apartment Owner*
Repairing damage to a wall or landscaping after a hurricane or tornado.	✔	
Pumping out a flooded basement	Depends on whether basement is shared space	
Sweeping a patio reserved to the use of one unit.		✔

	Corporation or Unit Owners' Association	Apartment Owner
Repairing cracked or heaved concrete on a patio reserved to one unit.	✔	
Removing graffiti from the blacktop of one parking space.	✔	
Repairing damage from a small fire *inside* the garage of one unit.		✔
Landscaping in front of your unit.	Could be either	
Landscaping near the entrance gate.	✔	
Keeping the hallways clean.	✔	
Landscaping in an interior surrounded completely by one unit.		✔
The dishwasher breaks and floods the kitchen and dining area.		✔
A tree is struck by lightning and crashes through your window causing rain damage inside.	Probably both to different degrees	
Raking leaves, cutting grass, shoveling snow.	✔	
Redecorating interior.		✔
Painting exterior.	✔	

they absolutely run the place. They hire the maintenance staff or management company. They prepare the budget and allocate funds, write checks, and handle the day-to-day management problems. Only in the smallest condos and co-ops do all the unit owners have a say in decisions.

If you buy into a condo or co-op community that is run by a board of directors, therefore, you will be more governed than a governor. If you do not like the way the place is being run, you can vote for new board members, run for office yourself (most communities are always looking for people to serve on the board), or lead a palace revolt.

A palace revolt will most often occur when someone wants a bylaw changed and can't convince a majority of the board to side with his or her position. It is like a referendum and a petition combined. To lead such a movement you must take your case to the other unit owners, more or less on a one-to-one basis.

Let's say for example that you want the no-pets bylaw changed to allow one cat to an apartment. You must state your position in writing and then gather signatures representing votes (in some communities, actual proxies). The vote on changing the bylaw will take place at the next scheduled meeting of the shareholders or unit owners. Remember, however, that you must enter your petition properly on the docket of new business for that meeting. If it's not there, all your signatures may be for naught, and the board can ignore you.

If you are determined on leading a rule change movement, be sure also that your signatures represent a majority of shares or votes rather than simply a majority of owners. The two are not always the same, since different units carry different numbers of shares.

Shares in the corporation or votes in the unit owners' association are assigned to each unit when the co-op or condominium is created. Larger and more desirable apartments are almost invariably assigned more votes. (They also pay a larger proportion of maintenance costs, just as larger detached single-family houses in a community pay a larger share of taxes.) In the matter of any controversial rule change, the owners of the more desirable units therefore have somewhat more power.

Let's see how this works. You duly enter your petition for a rule change about cats on the new business docket for the upcoming unit owners' meeting and you fully expect to win. Your building has 100 units and the owners of 51 of them have pledged their support. (In fact a friend is already keeping little Balthazar for you!) But alas! when the subject comes to a vote, you lose! You counted apartment *owners,* not votes.

The behind-the-scenes story is that many of the larger apartment owners refused to sign your cat petition unless small dogs were also included. You wanted no part of yappy dogs, so there was no real coalition of pet fanciers. The larger apartments carried more votes, so those who objected to all pets and those who refused support unless dogs were also allowed combined forces to defeat those who wanted cats and those who did not object.

This story is in many ways a prototype for the individual unit owners' role in governing the community. Life in a large condo or co-op often resembles working in Congress. Things get changed slowly and usually by behind the scenes work and negotiation. There are always factions among the unit owners, but group loyalty switches depending upon the subject. Compromise is a way of life and the people most successful in condo and co-op living are those who are willing to give a little to get a little.

But there is one aspect of condo and co-op life that is harder to change than getting a constitutional amendment ratified by the states: share or vote allocation. In all but a minute number of exceptional cases, the shares or votes assigned to an apartment when the co-op or condo is created can be changed only by *unanimous* vote of the shareholders or unit owners. For all intents and purposes therefore, it is unchangeable. Why? Think about the following example.

In Surfsound Village, top-floor apartments 314 and 315 were identical except that 314 had an ocean view and 315 looked out on a state highway. When the co-op was created, 314 was assigned a larger number of shares than 315 because of its greater desirability. Its owners therefore paid slightly more for the apartment when they bought it and they paid slightly more of each year's annual maintenance expenses than did the owners of 315.

When Surfsound Village was ten years old, the vacant lot between it and the ocean was purchased by a developer. A twenty-three story time-share resort hotel was built there. Meanwhile, traffic on the state highway had diminished drastically since an interstate had been completed nearby.

"Sounds great," you say. "Less traffic and a high-priced, luxury neighbor! Everyone in Surfsound Village should be happy, right?"

Wrong. The twenty-three story building totally blocked the view of the ocean from the east units of Surfsound, including 314. In fact, not only was there no view, there was also no *sun*. The siting of the high rise cast little three-story Surfsound into the shade. Owners began listening to commercials for household sprays to rid their corners of mold and mildew!

At the annual shareholders' meeting, the owners of 314 voiced their objections to paying a higher proportion of the building's maintenance fee than 315 and other west-facing units. Their apartment was no longer more desirable, they said. In fact, 315 was now the more desirable unit. The owners of 314 requested that the share allocations be changed.

"Well, that sounds fair," you say. "After all, things have changed."

True, they have. But try to convince the owners of 315 that they should pay more of the maintenance fee! That's what share allocation change comes down to—*money*. If 314 has its share allocation lowered, someone else (or several other owners) will have to have their share allocations raised to compensate. Few people will vote themselves a higher bill out of consideration for the other guy. And remember, the approval must be unanimous.

Be sure to check the share or vote allocation of your unit before you buy. Compare it to the share allocations of other units and consider whether or not it seems fair. Remember that share allocation will be a factor when you sell your unit. (Think about the owners of 314 trying to sell their sunless unit with its extra-high maintenance payment.)

Serving the Community

Very few condominium or cooperative communities pay their directors any salaries. Usually the job is voluntary, often learned while being done. Unfortunately, it often falls to the same people year after year because no one else will step forward.

If you feel strongly about your community or wish to protect your investment in it, don't let false modesty or lack of experience keep you from getting involved in its management. There are checks and balances in the system that will keep you from major (and costly) errors, and you will learn a great deal during your time in office.

If you are hesitant to step into the large shoes of a member of the board of directors, try heading a committee (recreation, grievances, newsletter, etc.) Even if you never do serve on the board, your experience on the committee will bring new influence to you, to say nothing of the potential for new friendships.

The Managing Agent, Management Company, and/or Superintendent

Some new condo or co-op owners confuse the roles of the board and the management company. In general, the board hires the management company. The management company or managing agent then hires the super, the doorman, the outdoor maintenance crew, the indoor maintenance crew, etc. The management company will also:

- Collect maintenance fees from the unit owners.
- Collect rental payments from concessions such as laundry machines, vending machines, pool chair rentals and supplies, etc.
- Keep track of expenditures.

• Prepare and submit accounts to the board.

• Act as a point of contact between the municipality and the condominium or co-op.

In very small condos or co-ops however, the board may take over the management company's functions. They may hire a super, arrange for snow removal and grounds maintenance, and appoint one of their members to disperse funds for day-to-day expenses. In a larger condo or co-op, if the snow is not shoveled from your parking space you should complain to the management company; in a smaller building, to the person in charge of hiring the snow removal contractor. Find out who's responsible for what *before* you need to complain. It's much to your benefit to know how and by whom your community is run.

Renting and Subletting

Sooner or later, the question of renting or subletting one's condo or co-op unit becomes a concern. In some communities it causes more concern than in others. Co-ops are especially likely to have stringent rules about subletting, often including board approval of the prospective tenant. Board approval of the tenant is not nearly so common in condominiums, but control of the rental term is often written into the bylaws, with six months being a common minimum. Sometimes the restriction is written as a maximum of two or three rentals in any given year. These rules are usually written and enforced in an effort to keep the condo or co-op community residential rather than transient.

People who buy into a condo or co-op community should be (and usually are) made aware of such restrictions on rentals. They therefore tacitly subscribe to these limitations when they make their purchase.

There has been some controversy in recent years, however, over bylaws passed in some communities that flatly prohibit rentals. If tested, such bylaws are usually found to be unenforceable, for in the eyes of the law in most states they are seen as an unreasonable restraint or alienation.

Courts generally recognize a condominium's or co-op's rights to place reasonable restrictions on renting individually owned or held units. This right is based upon the principle of the common good or interest of the owners in the condominium or co-op as taking precedence over individual profit motives. The common interest theoretically is to maintain and preserve the character and proper operation of the community.

Many state laws allow condo associations and co-ops to insist on prior consent to a rental or sublet, but provide that it may not be withheld "unreasonably." If you do get into a battle over a rental or sublet, you will probably need an attorney to define "unreasonably" in your area, and perhaps to argue your case.

Picking a Good Condo or Co-op

You've already read about the importance of location and condition, floor plan and features, so we won't go through all that again. Let's focus on some factors unique to shared space ownership.

The Financial Health of the Community

Your apartment may be as neat, clean, and well maintained as a hospital, but if the mortar is crumbling between the bricks outside, if the trim paint is flaking off, or if the lobby looks crumby (literally, full of crumbs), the value of your property will be lowered.

"Sure, everyone knows that," you say. "But when you go out to buy a place, you avoid the ones where the association is lax about maintenance. It's just a matter of using your eyes!"

Visual inspection is extremely important, but with a condo or co-op purchase your eyes won't tell you everything. That paint may indeed be peeling because no one has bothered to notice, or cares about it if they have noticed. Or it may be peeling and flaking because there are no funds for repainting!

Lack of good maintenance can indicate financial problems, and financial problems will probably mean higher maintenance fees in the very near future. Higher maintenance fees not only mean that it will cost you more to live in the same space, but that your property will have lower resale appeal. Buyers look not only at what they are getting for their money but also at how much it will cost them on a month-by-month basis. Smart condo and co-op buyers look at what it will cost this year and what it will probably cost in later years. The community's financial statements are the crystal balls in which you'll find that information. Read the box on page 265 carefully! And remember even a condo or co-op community with good exterior maintenance can be in financial trouble. Don't let appearances fool you.

Owner/Resident-to-Tenant Ratio

If you are buying a condo or co-op as your home, you will want to buy in a building or complex where most of the other residents will also be owners. In established co-ops this is rarely a problem since

What to Look For in a Financial Statement

Cooperatives.

These financial statements are far more complicated than those of condominiums because loans can be obtained by mortgaging the real estate (buildings and land) owned by the corporation. These mortgages are the most important factor in estimating future maintenance fee increases or decreases. There may be first, second, and even third mortgages on the property. Some may be self-liquidating (the monthly payments completely pay off the loan) and some may be interest-only notes (the principal will probably have to be refinanced.) If your co-op has a self-liquidating mortgage, your maintenance fee payments may go down when the mortgage is paid off. Look for the date the payments end in the financial statement. If your building has an interest-only note, however, one that will be refinanced at a higher rate of interest, your payments may well go up.

Check also for major expenditures for repairs or improvements. How are these financed? Are any major expenditures anticipated in the near future? Have there been any recent special assessments to shareholder/tenants?

Condominiums The common elements of a condominium community cannot be mortgaged. Major repairs and improvements must be paid for by special assessments to the unit owners. Therefore, it is much more important that a healthy condo community have a contingency fund for emergency expenses and a reserve fund for future improvements or repairs. A portion of each unit owner's maintenance fee should contribute to these funds.

Read through the financial statement to see if there have been any recent special assessments. Be sure that you are not assuming your seller's assessment! Ask members of the board and the management company if any major changes or repairs are being contemplated. How much will they cost? How much money is being held in reserve for them? How much more will be raised through special assessments?

The Services of an Accountant.

The fee that you might pay an accountant to explain all the pluses, minuses, brackets, and subtotals in a financial statement is usually well spent. You'll sleep better at night if you understand what you are getting into.

residency is usually a prerequisite of purchase and there are strict rules about subletting. In a co-op conversion, you will need to take more care since the conversion sponsor may be unable to sell some of the units, which will then continue to be occupied by tenants. Some sponsors also sell blocks of occupied units to investors at huge discounts. These investors then become in effect, absentee land-lords. The more owner-occupied apartments in a conversion, the stronger your deal is likely to be.

Condominium units are more often bought for investment than cooperative apartments and the rules for rental are more often lenient. Some condo communities therefore have a high percentage of tenants.

It's an old saw in real estate that owners are the best occupants, and the reason behind the adage is obvious: it's their money, their pride, their future appreciation. So before you buy a condo or co-op ask a member of the board or a representative of the management company what the ratio of owner/residents to tenants is. Too many absentee investor-owners may sway important decisions at a unit owners' or shareholders' meeting.

Buying in a To-Be-Built or Unfinished Community

Chances are you'll be offered a package that's hard to refuse while you're seated in the sales office looking at the architect's drawings for Happy Hilltops. The price for comparable space seems to be $10,000 or more lower than anything else you've seen. And the brochures state clearly that there will be no maintenance fees until the entire community, including the recreational facilities, is complete. All maintenance is to be done by the builder. What a deal! There are five hundred proposed units. It will take at least three years to get them all done. No maintenance fees for three years! Getting in on the ground floor price! Choosing your own colors! Having everything brand new!

Before you reach for the nearest pen to sign on the dotted line, think about the following points:

1. You are buying or at least making a commitment to buy based on pictures and words. You won't and can't have the opportunity to walk in the space of your unit until just before the closing.

2. You don't know when your unit will really be ready for occupancy. Builders are notorious for being late. Six months is closer to a norm than an exception. Will you have a place to live while you're waiting?

3. You don't know how the grounds and the roads will be maintained between the time you move in and the time the community is completed. You may live in a sea of mud for many months.

4. You don't know when the promised recreation facilities and parking lots will be completed. These are often (in fact usually) the last things built. What if the builder goes bankrupt before completion? Who will pay for these facilities? Will you ever get them?

5. You don't know what the maintenance fees will be when the responsibility for maintenance is turned over to the unit owners' association.

There really are bargains and benefits to be gained by buying while a community is still on paper or in its very early stages. Most builders start their prices low to attract buyers and then raise them as the complex becomes more and more desirable. If you think this kind of deal is for you, read Chapter 22 on having a house built for you so that you'll be sure to have as strong a contract as possible in order to protect your interests. Then check your builder's reputation. Is there a record of previous bankruptcies? Ask your mortgage lender to run a credit check on the builder. Can you visit another condominium community the builder has already built? If so, by all means go there and talk with the residents. What kind of problems did they have? Were their units completed near the promised date? Was maintenance well done while construction was still under way? What is maintenance costing now?

If you're still interested after such a visit, there are a few more points that should be secured. Ask at what point in the development of the condominium community a unit owners' association will be established. How much power will it have while the community is still under construction? When will it take over management of the community? Will it be allowed to choose the management company? You do not want a long-term contract with a managment company chosen by or owned by the builder. Ask, and be sure it is written somewhere, exactly how many units there will be in the community. You do not want additional development added to your working unit owners' association. And finally ask what the estimated monthly maintenance fee will be once construction is complete. Compare this figure with other, similar working condominiums in the area. If it's much lower or much higher, be suspicious and ask for specific reasons for the expected difference in operating costs.

Some Problems in Selling

Several factors can affect your sale of your unit. Your undivided-interest-ownership in shared space in a condominium or your ownership of corporate stock rather than real estate in a co-op, the sheer size of the community, the existence of bylaws, and sometimes the delay before occupancy is possible can all cause problems. It's a good idea to know about and consider these problems before you *buy* a condominium or co-op so that you don't go into the purchase thinking that you can just sell profitably and move with the freedom of a tenant.

The Right to Assign Your Purchase Contract

If you are buying a to-be-built condominium or an apartment in a co-op conversion, the right to assign your purchase contract or subscription agreement is an insurance policy worth fighting for. Assignment means the right to sell or transfer to another party the right to buy the property referred to in the contract as it was signed by you. This means that someone else can fulfill your contract at the price and terms you agreed to.

If you should be transferred while awaiting completion or occupancy of your unit, or if some major family event such as a birth, a death, or a divorce should make the purchase no longer feasible, the right to assign your contract will allow you to sell and move even though you have not yet closed. Since prices usually go up as completion approaches, assignment could even turn a quick profit for you.

Here's how it works: Six months after the date of your purchase contract but still six months before the probable occupancy date, you are told that you've been transferred two thousand miles away. In the six months that have passed the builder has raised the price on apartments by $3000, and you have an ideal location. For $1000 or even $1500 you can sell someone the right to buy your unit at your price. You're happy to get out of the deal and the buyer is happy to get something of a bargain. The only party who might be unhappy is the builder or sponsor who lost a potential purchase by your buyer.

Since builders would rather sell at the higher price themselves in good times or hold you to your contract in bad, you will not find the right to assign your purchase agreement in the contract you are first offered to sign. Have an attorney write it in for you. The builder may voice some objection at first, but the point can usually be negotiated.

The Logistics of Showing

Whether you advertise "by-owner" or through an agent, selling an apartment can call for some extra steps and precautions. Think about:

1. *Finding the unit.* Be very specific in your directions. Apartments tend to look alike and buyers (and even some agents) can become easily discouraged if they feel lost in a maze.

2. *No "For Sale" sign.* Some condos and co-ops prohibit them. Be sure your apartment number and name are clearly visible on your door or mailbox.

3. *Showing the common elements.* Be sure to include the name of the super, some other employee of the management company, or a volunteered member of the board of directors on your real estate agency listing sheet. The agents who show your unit will want to contact this person to show the basement, the pool-house, the meeting rooms, etc.

4. *The professional inspection.* An appointment for a professional inspection prior to purchase includes your apartment *and* the common areas. Check the time and date with the super since the inspector will spend time in the basement, elevators, hallways, recreation facilities, meeting rooms, etc.

Board Approvals

Virtually all co-ops require approval by the board before a sale can be closed. The board can deny approval for any reason or no reason as long as the denial is not based upon factors prohibited by civil rights legislation.

Tell your prospective buyers what the board considers important. What kind of people live in the building? Old? Young? Professional? Artsy? Will the buyers need personal references? A financial statement? Last year's tax return?

Because condominium units are owned "fee simple," it is more difficult to justify board approval of a sale and few condo communities have such requirements. More common is a right of first refusal reserved to the board. In this situation the board can match the price offered by a prospective buyer and take the sale from him or her. Even when a board decides not to exercise this right, considering it can delay a sale for weeks and even months.

If your condominium bylaws include a right of first refusal, tell your prospective buyers about it. Explain that it was written in to protect the life style of the community and that it will protect their interests also. They will be more likely to wait for a board decision if they understand why they are waiting. (Remember, by the way, that no condominium financed all or in part with HUD funds can include a right of first refusal in its bylaws.)

The Question of Children

Can a condominium or co-op set minimum age requirements for residency?

Until recently the answer was "yes" throughout the country. In fact "adults only" and "retirement community" were among the advertised features of a large number of condos and co-ops. But that's no longer the case in California, which was the first state to pass legislation that prohibited condominiums from excluding children. Will the pattern of such legislation spread to other states?

There are powerful arguments on both sides. "Children are people," say the proponents of the California system, "they cannot be denied their right to live in a community just because they are children." "We have the right to the quiet enjoyment of our privately owned property, *without children*," cry others.

Who's right? How can the problem be solved? The argument is rumbling like an active volcano in several states. It may go all the way to the Supreme Court one day, and there's no way to predict the outcome.

For More Information

"Tax Information on Condominium and Cooperative Apartments," IRS booklet #588, is available free from your local Internal Revenue Service office.

17

Negotiating for the Best Deal

With apologies to Charles Dickens, negotiating is:

- the best of times and the worst of times;
- a time of wisdom and a time of foolishness;
- a time of belief and a time of incredulity;
- a time of Light and a time of Darkness;
- the spring of hope and the winter of despair;
- a time when you have everything before you, and a time when you have nothing before you.

Yes, it's a tale of two parties and at some point in the negotiating process most buyers and most sellers think (at least momemtarily), "Good grief! I could write a book!" Some do.

In general, however, most Americans have little experience in this slippery and sensitive art. Really, we don't get much chance to practice since we don't bargain in the open marketplace over the price of lettuce or a handmade rug. In fact, cars and houses are the only negotiated items many Americans ever buy. Since they are also the two items in which we invest the largest sums of money, it's no wonder we get angry, fearful, defensive, and insecure when we start talking price. No wonder also that the most prevalent disability in the real estate marketplace is cold feet.

But take heart. Even if you don't have the talents of Henry Kissinger, you *can* proceed through the negotiating stage of homebuying both professionally and profitably. There are really only two essential points to remember:

1. Know what you are doing and why you are doing it.
2. Don't let your feelings overrule your good judgment.

Sounds simple, right? And it is, except when each of those points becomes a five-hundred-piece jigsaw puzzle and someone accidentally pours the pieces of both puzzles into one box. But sorting things out is one of the goals of this book, so let's look at the pieces.

Steps in the Negotiating Process

We're not going to list "find the right property" here since we've already spent eight chapters talking about it! Let's just say that you should *not* begin negotiating for a house until you are rather certain that you want to buy it, that it will meet most of your needs, and that you can probably afford it.

Establishing "Fair Market Value"

In most real estate textbooks, "fair market value" is defined as the highest price a ready, willing, and able buyer will pay and the lowest price a ready, willing, and able seller will accept. In other words, it is the proverbial "meeting of the minds." To be completely accurate, fair market value cannot be established until a property is actually sold. But the trick of a fair market value estimate is to come as close to the figure for which you could turn around after the closing and sell the house again quickly. (Quickly in real estate is two to three months.)

Make your market evaluation by comparing the property you want to buy to similar properties that have been sold in the area during the past year. You'll already have a feel for the price from the house hunting you've been doing. When you're ready to start negotiating, ask your sales agent to show you comparables. *Comparables* in a real estate office refers to the listing sheets describing properties that have recently been sold. These sheets contain all the pertinent information on the property, the original asking price, all price reductions, the actual selling price, the date of the closing and the date of the original listing contract (how long the property was on the market).

Virtually every real estate office that belongs to a multiple listing organization will have a comparables file or a computerized comparables book. Even so-called independent agencies that do not share listings will keep a file of properties sold by their own offices and agents. The single-office file works out well in the largest cities where many brokers are independents and tend to work only in tightly defined neighborhoods rather than trying to cover the entire city. It also works well in condominium or co-op sales where one or two real estate agencies usually handle all the sales within a particular building.

Once you have the comparables, make a list of selling prices and addresses of the properties that you consider similar to "yours." Get photocopies of these listing sheets if the agent is willing and permitted to give them to you. Take them home if you can. You will want to compare and rate each property against "your" house on a point-for-point basis.

When you finish this homework, you'll know exactly what other people in the area have had to pay for a certain amount of house in the same neighborhood or a similar neighborhood. From here, stepping along to an evaluation of what "your" house is worth is relatively easy.

Once you have established what you think is a fair selling price for the property, compare it to what the sellers are asking. If your evaluation price should be higher than the asking price (a phenomenon that rarely occurs), don't get out your pen to sign an offer. Look again at the property, the neighborhood, the location, the lot, the time on the market, local conditions, everything. You may have missed something *very* important. If everything checks out, then act quickly. The sellers may just have underpriced their property and you will want to buy before word gets out and another buyer or two appears to start a bidding war.

It is much more likely, however, that the asking price will be more than your estimate of fair market value. This is what negotiating is all about. Try a little role playing for a moment. Why do you think the sellers set the price so high? Try to anticipate what they will say in response to your offer. Is there new carpeting? A remodeled kitchen? Beautiful landscaping? A swimming pool? Prepare yourself to take the position that money put into a property for amenities that make life nicer for the owner does *not* always add to the resale value of the property.

In order to give your good judgment something tangible to hold on to when the going gets rough (which it often does), buy a small notebook and make it your negotiating diary. On the first page record the addresses and prices of your comparables. On the next page record your ideal price (the dollar figure for which you would like to "steal" the property), your fair market value estimate, and your absolutely "top dollar" price.

Why would you ever pay a "top dollar" price higher than the fair market value of the property, you ask. Because until the contract is signed, fair market value is still an estimate, and even professional real

Questions to Ask Before the First Offer is Made

How long has the house been on the market? The longer the time, the more likely that negotiation will bring down the price.

Have there been any price reductions? Price reductions indicate a need to sell and/or a rethinking of property value.

Have there been any previous offers? Don't be intimidated if offers higher than the one you intend to make have been refused. Time has a way of changing things.

How long have the sellers owned the house? At what price did they buy it? Short-term ownership usually means a smaller profit margin and therefore less negotiating room.

What improvements have the sellers made? How much did they cost? Don't feel you need to add the cost of improvements to your fair market evaluation. Many improvements never return their original cost. Some (additions which disrupt the traffic pattern, for example) actually lower the property value. You want this information before you start negotiation. Later, when the seller tosses it out as a reason for a high price, you should be able to reply with facts and figures on the value of improvements vs. value in the neighborhood.

estate appraisers can differ in their fair market value estimates. You must therefore leave yourself a margin of error, a realistic dollar space that will keep you from becoming too rigid during the negotiations.

You might want to discuss your evaluation of fair market value with your real estate agent. Ask his or her opinion of the property's market value, and if he or she is willing to give it, note it along with the other information on page one of your diary. But don't be overly influenced by this number. Remember the agent wants to make a commission by *selling* the property.

Most important of all, do not reveal to the agent the information that you wrote on page two of your diary. Your "top dollar" and "steal" figures must be kept to yourself. Think of the negotiation as a poker game. You would hardly expect to win if you showed your cards to someone else at the table! And you won't win in real estate if you tell anyone more than is necessary. If, for example, you tell a real estate agent that you want to make an offer of $75,000 but that you can pay $80,000 or $82,000 if you have to, it is extremely likely that you will buy the property for between $80,000 and $82,000.

Evaluating the Selling Situation

Before you make your first offer on a property, it is important that you have a feel for the mood of the local marketplace. If it's a fast market (sometimes called a seller's market) where properties are moving quickly and if "yours" is a desirable house with wide potential market appeal, you will want to start your negotiations fairly close to market value. You don't want to lose the property playing games over price. Such a tactic could allow someone else to step in with a more realistic offer and walk away with "your" house.

In some special situations, relatively rare, a house or location is so "hot" that simultaneous offers are made. Sometimes the best of these is simply accepted. More often the sellers negotiate with all prospective buyers simultaneously. They are out "for the kill."

As the buyer in such a situation, you want to do everything possible to increase your chances of getting the property. These tactics will help:

• Come in with your best figure, but be willing to move up another $500 or $1000 if the house means a lot to you. Do not, however, get caught up in auction fever and bid the house up far above its market value.

• Ask for as few extras in the sale as possible.

• Make the closing date as agreeable to the sellers as you can.

• Have conditional loan approval from a lender, if you can get it.

• Make your offer on a contract form that you have signed. The bidding war is the exception to the rule about never using a contract to make an offer. In this situation, a contract which the sellers might sign on a high that has been orchestrated by your very competent real estate agent will seal the deal for you. This contract, however, should contain a "review clause," that is it will establish the price and the fact that you agree to buy and the sellers agree to sell to you, but it will reserve to you the right to take the contract to your lawyer to review and perhaps even change some of the terms and wording.

If the market is soft, however, (sometimes called a buyer's market), or if the seller is under need-to-sell stress, or if the house is not particularly appealing to most people (they can't see the potential that you see, or their needs are different from yours), you can move more slowly and negotiate over a wider range. In these situations, it's possible to get a much better deal with a little patience and perseverance.

Making the Initial Offer

Occasionally you will be advised that 10 percent below asking price is a good initial offer. Don't believe it. There is no universal "good" initial offer based upon asking price. Why? Because there are so many variables in real estate and because sellers rarely set their asking prices with consideration to market value or other rational thought processes. They are out to get the most they can for their properties, and many have emotional ties to "home" that turn Cape Cods into castles.

When you consider that each and every piece of real property is absolutely unique, as is each and every selling situation, you can understand why rules of thumb in real estate are very dangerous. But if you must have a guideline, a first offer that is 10 percent below *your fair market value estimate—not* the seller's asking price—will keep you from insulting the seller. It will also keep you from having your first offer snapped up because it was higher than the seller's what-we-hope-to-get-for-this-place price.

When you finally do have a figure in mind for your first offer, there's still an unanswered question. How do you go about *making* the offer?

When professionals—the apartment house buyers, the shopping center developers, the traders—deal in real estate, they rarely set a word on paper before there is agreement on price and terms. All negotiating is verbal. Everything is discussed, sometimes over hours or days, sometimes over weeks or months. After there is mutual agreement between sellers and buyers, everything is written up by the lawyers into a contract to purchase, which everyone then signs. It's neat and clean. Ah, but the procedure is usually somewhat different in homebuying.

Many residential real estate agents pull out the contract forms as soon as the word *offer* is mentioned. They fill in the blanks with names and addresses, numbers and specifics. They ask you for an earnest money check (usually a minimum of $500, more often $1000 in today's market). And they want you to sign the contract *before* they will present the offer to the seller. If you do this, and if the seller likes your first offer and also signs the contract form, you have bought a house.

There's no time for rethinking, no time for fine-tuning the agreement. Even if pressure is exerted by the real estate agency, even if

---

Consumer Protection for Contract Signing

Negotiating with a contract signed by the buyers has become so prevalent as the *modus operandi* of many residential real estate agencies that some states have passed consumer protection laws regarding contracts for the purchase of real property. (There are even special condominium and co-op laws.) These laws differ from state to state, and usually allow anywhere from three to fifteen business days during which a buyer (or sometimes either party) can void a signed contract and be refunded all monies deposited. Many states, however, have absolutely no consumer protection legislation regarding real estate contracts. To find out what, if any, protection exists in your state, you can call or write your state real estate commission. Addresses are listed on page 351. Phone numbers are listed in your phone book under the heading for your state government.

---

they tell you that this is the only surefire way to keep someone else from snatching this fabulous property away from you, you should avoid this procedure.

"What's the alternative?" you ask. Well, it's not likely to be an all verbal deal such as the town's real estate tycoon might make. Most residential real estate agents will refuse to present a verbal offer that is not accompanied by an earnest money check and specific information on financing and closing date. A buyer's saying "Call and ask them if they'll take $50,000" is just too vague for their business. That buyer could be asking that same question of seven different agents about seven different properties, a situation that holds the potential for myriad problems. "Ask him if he'll take . . ." is the opposite extreme of presenting a signed contract with the first offer. We don't recommend *it* either.

You can present a written offer which includes an offering price, a closing date, financing information, a list of contingencies, and an earnest money check *without signing a legal contract to purchase*. Most real estate offices and Realtor Boards have in their supply closets short offer forms, often called *binders*, which, ironically, are nonbinding agreements. These forms can be used when a buyer will not negotiate using a signed contract. We recommend that you use one of these forms, *but* (and note this most carefully) be absolutely certain that your particular offer form, short form, binder, or whatever it's called, contains a statement to the effect that the agreement is *subject* to a mutually acceptable contract-to-purchase to be drawn within three (or five, or any mutually agreeable number) business days and signed by all parties involved in the transfer of the property. If this kind of statement is not on your offer form, have it typed in above your signature. If you don't take care that this protective statement is written out on your offer form, that piece of paper could turn into a legally enforceable contract.

It's very possible that you may run into a real estate agent who says, "You must negotiate with a signed contract. Everyone does. It's office policy." *Don't be "everyone."* Everything in real estate is negotiable, including the way in which you choose to negotiate. If you present a written offer with an earnest money check, even if the offer is a nonbinding agreement, every state requires that the agent present that offer to the sellers.

But the paper upon which you write your offer and its terms is only half the problem in making a residential offer; the other half is the earnest money check. Most real estate agents ask that the check be made out to the broker-of-record in their firm or to the firm name. When you do this, add the words *trustee* or *fiduciary agent* after the broker's or firm's name in order to protect your money. Your check must then be deposited as money held in trust.

Real estate law in every state provides that this earnest money will be returned to you if the offer is not accepted and a contract-to-purchase is not entered into. The return, however, may take some time, especially after the check has been deposited in the broker's account. And unless you have thousand-dollar bills lying around ready to deposit in brokers' accounts, you may find that your return to house hunting is tied to that broker until you get your money back. You may even be prevented from making an offer on another property in another area because you haven't gotten that money back yet. It's a dependable way for raising blood pressure.

The best way to avoid this kind of entanglement is to give the agent an earnest money check and specify that it is *not* to be cashed or deposited in any account until there is an agreement on price. Do not say, "This is a paper check; we don't have the money in the account yet." Simply say "we do not want this check to be deposited in any account until there is an agreement on the price." The agent can show the check to the sellers as a demonstration of your good faith, which is what earnest money is all about, but your money is not tied up unnecessarily.

Before You Start Negotiating	
Do you have . . .	
The selling prices and addresses of comparable properties?	
Your own fair market value estimate for the property?	
A notebook in which to keep a negotiating diary?	
A *written* list of items on the property that need or will soon need repair or replacement?	
A list of negative market features?	
An accurate estimate of how much monthly payment you can afford to carry? In other words, how much you can afford to pay for the house?	

An earnest money check is standard procedure when working through a real estate agent. Do not, however, give an earnest money check directly to a seller, not ever. If you are dealing with for-sale-by-owner sellers who insist upon earnest money before a contract can be executed, write that check to their lawyer or yours, and write *fiduciary agent* after the lawyer's name. This money will then go into a trust, or escrow, account until the negotiations are complete, the contract signed, and its contingencies met. If the deal falls apart, you'll get it back. But if you give earnest money directly to the sellers, you may never see it again, or you may have to go to court to get it back.

So you've signed a nonbinding offer form and written out your earnest money check. Now what?

Don't expect this first offer to be accepted. Everyone wants to haggle over price. Try to be calm, and wait to see what the seller says.

The Counter-Offer

The counter-offer is the sellers' response to your first offer. Sometimes it names the actual amount that they want for the property, but not usually. Most sellers still have some room in their first-response prices, even when they say "not a penny less." You now must work toward a meeting of the minds.

In your negotiating diary record your first offer, its terms, and its contingencies. (You can shortcut the writing process here by having the agent give you a copy of the offer form after it is completely filled out and signed.) Then, when you get the counter-offer, record not only its facts and figures, but what the agent says the sellers said. Do they want a quick closing? Is this their bottom price? Are they anxious to sell? Don't take a word of what you hear as gospel truth, though. In negotiating, you must always keep testing for what's "real" and you must never drive anyone into a corner from which there is no escape.

The counter-offer is usually returned to you on your original offer form with numbers crossed out and new numbers written in and initialed.

Your Second Offer

The second offer should not be your top dollar, but it should approach your market value estimate. Have the agent write out a whole new offer form. Do not work with scratched out figures and initials on the old sheet, since this only confuses people.

In your negotiating diary, write down the facts of this second offer and any asides that are mentioned by anyone. Keeping such a written account of who said what and when may well prevent arguments, misunderstandings and denials later. It will also give you a chance to review what happened.

Working Toward Agreement

Most houses are sold upon or before the buyers' third offer. Sometimes, however, the negotiating goes on for many days. The procedure is always the same, offer, counter-offer. You and the sellers are making adjustments, circling about each other, trying to find a place to meet. A good real estate agent can be invaluable!

Resolution

Once price and terms are agreed upon, the contract should be drawn. Procedures vary across the country. Sometimes real estate agents routinely draw contracts, sometimes buyers' and sellers' lawyers get involved, sometimes lender attorneys review contracts before they are signed, sometimes title companies or closing agents

When the Seller Says Your Offer Is Too Low

Topics to Talk About

Comparables and fair market value. Have addresses, descriptions, and sale prices written down. You want to convince the sellers that they're seeing too much of a castle in their home.

Condition. What needs repair and/or replacement now and what is likely to need it in the near future. A written list, especially a long one, is a good negotiating tool.

Negative market appeal of the property. Talk about anything that is likely to narrow the number of potential buyers for the property, even if that factor makes it just perfect for you. Some examples are: a busy street; on the down-side of a hill; proximity to an industrial complex; and a strange floor plan.

Soft area real estate market. You might say something like: "With the clothespin plant in town shutting down, there seem to be more houses for sale than there are buyers. We foresee the possibility of property values going *down* during the next several years."

Topics to Avoid

Poor taste in decorating. You'll only anger or insult your seller. Just plan to do it over after you move in.

Comparison to another property you are considering. The obvious answer from the seller is: "Well, if you like that one better, why don't you buy it?"

Financial problems. The phrase "we cannot afford any more" must be reserved for your last offer, when you really can't. At this point seller financing at a lower rate of interest sometimes pops up in conversation or real estate brokers offer to cut their commission by a thousand dollars or so to put the deal together. If you play this card too early, however, when you still can afford another thousand or so, you weaken your negotiating power because the seller begins to worry about your ability to qualify for a mortgage. Remember, sellers do not want to take their properties off the market only to have a deal fall through several weeks later.

help with the contracts. No matter what the standard procedure is in your area, however, read your contract carefully before you sign it. If there is something in it that seems strange to you or that you do not understand, do not sign until you understand it. Do not accept "Oh, that's just a part of the standard printed contract. No one pays any attention to it around here." If something is printed in a contract and you sign your name to it, you will be held to the agreement. Keep in mind that items can be crossed out of a contract as well as added to it.

If you are at all apprehensive, remember that you always have the right to request the assistance of an attorney, even if it is not customary procedure in your area. You are, after all, entering into a binding contract that involves a lot of money.

Some Success Secrets

Know Value

"That's no secret," you say. "You've already said 'know the market' at least half a dozen times!" Yes, and we'll probably say it six or seven more times. There's nothing more important to successfully buying and selling real estate than knowing the market.

As you negotiate, it will help you to bring the sellers' price down by showing and telling them what comparable houses have sold for. Of course the real estate agent should be doing this for you, but don't ever count on anyone else to fight for your money as diligently as you.

Don't Be Rigid

Just as a seller might say "we won't take a penny less," you can say "we won't pay a penny more." This is not to mean, however, that you should not pay $80,500 for a property if that figure happens to be a compromise between your top-dollar $80,000 and the sellers' bottom-dollar $81,000. Don't lose a property that you really want over a few dollars a month, which is what financing the extra $500 would cost you.

Set limits, but don't be so rigid that you can't respond or rethink a decision. Never say: "never"; "absolutely not"; "this is the only . . ."; or "Take it or leave it." Such phrases slam the door on a deal.

Don't Show Your Hand

Don't tell *anyone* what you will do next. Act as though you fully expect your offer to be accepted. If you don't, it won't be.

Ask for Concessions and/or Extras as You Increase Your Bid

When you present your first low bid, don't ask for any extras. If it is accepted, you'll have plenty of money to buy them. Then each time you increase your offering price ask for something more. Anything listed as negotiable on the listing sheet is fair game, and you can try for almost anything that you see: draperies, chandeliers, carpeting, appliances, lawn mowers and equipment, lawn furniture, sometimes even living room or dining room furniture. Most people, sellers included, like to see themselves as good, generous people; few want to project a negative or stingy image. So play a little on human psychology while negotiating. Ask as you offer.

The sellers may say "no" to your bid, but "yes" to your request for extras *at their higher price*. But when you increase your price again, even if just a little, those extras are already part of the deal in both your minds. Here's a scaled-down example of how it may go.

Buyer: We'll come up to $84,000, but we would like the living and dining room draperies and cornices to be included.

Seller: The absolute least we'll take is $86,000, but we will include the drapes at that price.

Buyer: Let's split the difference. How about $85,000? The seller, after a little deliberation, agrees and the drapes and cornices go with the house.

Here the draperies were earned through negotiation. The buyers probably would have ended up at $85,000 anyway, yet it might have cost them $4000 to have comparable draperies custom-made.

Never ask for all the extras at once, however, It's too overwhelming, especially with a low first offer that you are gradually increasing. Once a seller says "no," which is easy to do when the requests seem too numerous for too little money, it's harder to get a reversal than it is to get something new added later. Remember negotiating is a give and take process. And remember also negotiating's oldest maxim: *Ask for more than you want, offer less than you are willing to pay*.

Use the Closing Date in Your Negotiations

Time is money, so the saying goes. In negotiating for a home, time can be worth money if you use it as a tool. Try to find out early in the game what the sellers want time-wise as well as price-wise. Do they need a quick closing because they are carrying two mortgages? Do they need time to find another house? Do they need flexibility in closing date because they are having a house built and don't know exactly when it will be completed? Compare the sellers' needs to yours. How flexible can you afford to be?

With your original low offer you will be asked to name a closing date. If it works for you, name one that is not likely to be to the sellers' liking. If they need a quick closing, set your offer-date for three or four months in the future. If they want a distant closing, ask for one in four to six weeks. Then as you make responses to their counter-offers, you can increase the bid by very little cash but sweeten the deal by moving the proposed closing date into line with the sellers' needs. It's almost always worth money.

On the other hand, if closing date is very important to you, work toward your ideal date in your negotiations. But be prepared to offer more money to get the date you want.

Use Financing in Your Negotiations

Now we're really talking money. If you plan to pay cash for the property or if you have a tentative mortgage commitment from a lender already, use your strong financial position as a negotiating tool. If you bid a little low, tell the agent to explain to the sellers that this is a no-risk offer. There is no mortgage contingency. No waiting to see if the buyers will qualify for a loan! It's a strong card, if not a trump.

You can also try a low bid on a house if your prospective financing does not require the seller to pay points to the lender in order to get the loan. (One point is one percent of the face amount of the loan, paid at the closing.) The charging of seller points is a fairly common practice in times of tight money and a tight real estate market. It is best avoided, however, even if the purchase price must be lowered by the amount the seller would pay in points, with the mutual agreement that the buyer is to assume all payment of points. Why? Taxes. The points a buyer pays to get a loan are usually considered interest paid in advance and are therefore deductible on federal income tax returns. If the seller pays points, however, the IRS considers them an expenditure but not the payment of interest. The amount is therefore subtracted from the profit the seller has made from the sale, but that profit is usually carried on into another house investment with the payment of taxes being postponed. The sellers get no immediate tax advantage for paying points. They therefore are much more interested in how many dollars they will actually *get* from the sale of the house than in the numbers on the contract, and most would rather lower the purchase price than lay out cash to pay points to a lender.

In times when mortgage money is generally available, seller points are rarely mentioned. Even FHA insured mortgages now allow the paying of points to be a negotiated item, the buyer or the seller may pay. As of this writing, however, VA guaranteed mortgages still limit the number of points that can be charged to the *buyer* to one, requiring that the seller assume payment of any additional points generally being charged by area lenders. As a matter of practice, however, the purchase price of a house sold with a VA mortgage contingency is very often increased to compensate for the points being charged to the seller.

Know When to Stop

Some deals just can't be made, so don't beat a dead horse. If your sellers are not ready to sell at a reasonable price, start looking elsewhere.

Keeping Emotion Out of Negotiation

When emotions take control, many real estate agents run for cover. They know that words can fly like spears and carefully constructed deals can fall to rubble as though hit by cannonballs.

Act rationally is essential advice in real estate, but it's also hard advice to heed when you are negotiating for a home. Let's look at the most common emotions that carry away both buyers and sellers.

Love

"Some day my prince will come . . ." was a popular tune in the 1940s, giving voice to the dream that there was a perfect mate out there for each of us. With the divorce rate at almost 50 percent in the 1980s, we know that dream isn't necessarily true. But by the same token many of us go right on dreaming that there's a perfect house out there for each of us, somewhere. When buyers think that they have found theirs, they usually pay too much for it.

Love the house you are negotiating for, but try not to fall head over heels for it. If you start thinking that you'll never find another house as good anywhere, you might as well forget about negotiating effectively. Try to remember that there are other houses, just as there are other potential mates out there, that are just as good and maybe better.

If you don't get the house you want at a fair price or at a price that you can afford, it may take you a while to get over your love affair.

But you will, and there will be another place for you. If you have the luxury of time, it's a good idea to let some pass before going out house hunting again after a negotiation falls apart. You don't want to buy on the rebound if you can avoid it. A mistake purchase which then prompts the buyer to sell the property soon after buying is expensive, just like divorce.

Anger

If you're playing with home, love, and money, can anger be far behind? The emotion makes its appearance in most real estate negotiations at some point or another. Think of all the possibilities: the buyers can get angry at the sellers, the sellers can get angry at the buyers, they both can get angry at the real estate agent(s), and the agent(s) can get angry at them. And that's just business anger. In-house, the buyers can get angry with each other, the sellers can get angry with each other, the agent can fight with his or her spouse or boss over "nothing and everything." And we have not yet mentioned the possibilities for aggravation with loan officers, home inspectors, exterminators, in-laws, children, neighbors, dogs, cats, and competing real estate agents.

It's easy for us to say "stay calm, stay rational," but the fact of the matter is that it's hard to do. However, words said in anger can really hurt negotiations. So we've gathered a few suggestions for avoiding this particularly dangerous emotion.

• *Keep a negotiating diary.* Record facts, messages, bids, etc., as they are communicated to you, with the date and time alongside. This little book can settle arguments before they really get rolling.

• *Use time for cooling off.* If you feel yourself (or your spouse) about to scream, say "I'd (we'd) like to take some time to think about this before saying anything more." Hang up the phone, leave the room, or leave town for the day if you have to.

• *Define the cause of your anger.* People sometimes find themselves furious, yet don't know why. Ask yourselves, "What got this started?" Once you answer that question, it's easier to go quietly on to, "How can we settle this?"

• *Stick to the point.* If you are negotiating over closing date, don't let who's going to fix the broken toilet get into the discussion.

• *Don't slam doors and burn bridges.* It's hard to come back from "Stuff your stupid house!"

• *Don't accuse.* Saying "This is all your fault" accomplishes nothing. Ask instead "How did we get to this point, and where should we go from here?"

• *Don't lie*. Not even white lies. If you said something yesterday and changed your mind overnight, say so. Don't deny what you said. And especially, don't fib about your financial situation. No, it's not even permissible to "forget" something. Nothing sours a deal faster than contradictions about money.

• *Don't pound your fist on the table*. Your point can be made better by writing it down or by speaking very softly so that your listeners have to listen harder.

• *Don't say anything when you're really mad*. Nothing about anything.

Pride

Many a deal has been lost over a comment like, "No way! I won't come up another $500 and let them win! They're not going to have the last word! No way!" Result: no sale.

Negotiating is not a game of winning or losing. It's a coming together. You have to be able to give up a little to get a little. If you are determined to go about proudly bragging about your deal, you may never make that deal.

Possessiveness and Greed

When people sell their home, they're giving up a part of their lives. Some of those roses in the back yard were watered, metaphorically at least, with their sweat. It is therefore sometimes emotionally difficult to part with the property. Some sellers fight to keep every stick that is not nailed down and expect to be paid dearly for every one that is. This could be called possessiveness.

When people buy, however, they want the most for their money. "That should go with the house" is the usual attitude since they are thinking of out-of-pocket expenses for everything that doesn't go with the house. This could be called greed.

There's no right answer here. If you get into an argument over bits and pieces, ask yourself if possessiveness or greed aren't factors. Sometimes just recognizing feelings helps to resolve the issue.

Prejudice

"Those damn Patagonians in their tuxedos, they think they're hot stuff!" "The sellers are just like the rest of the Westphalians, stubborn, stubborn, stubborn!" If you catch yourself thinking thoughts like these (and who among us doesn't at one time or another), do not voice them. A single insult can kill a sale.

What if . . .

You tell the real estate agent that you want to make a certain offer. He or she says "I'd be embarrassed to make an offer that low. It's out of the question."

Tell the agent that you want to make the offer *in writing* and that you are willing to give an earnest money check. Real estate laws in every state provide that a licensed agent *must* present every written offer. In most states the penalty for noncompliance is loss of license.

The seller says "no" to your first offer and does not make a counter-offer.

This does not necessarily mean that the seller is unwilling to negotiate. It does mean that he or she does not want to start working toward a meeting of the minds with your offer at one end of the spectrum and the asking price at the other. The middle point is too low. Try making a second offer closer to your evaluation of the property's market value. But leave yourself some room to come up, because you'll most likely have to.

Fear

Believe it or not, this is the big emotion. Fear devastates negotiating power. It creeps in, however, not as one major fear, but as many small fears. One fear seems to give birth to another until they dance in a circle about the deal. Look at some of them!

- There's another party interested in the house! They're coming to see it tomorrow!
- What if we can't get a mortgage?
- What if we're paying too much?
- What if there's a water problem in the basement?
- What if we make our offer too low and they get insulted?
- What if I lose my job?
- What if the local economy goes sour? The national economy?
- What if the sun doesn't come up tomorrow?

The best way to avoid getting caught in a circle of fear is to go back to the facts and figures. Review the listing, comparables, and your finances. Is the market in the area really so hot that someone else is likely to "steal" the house from you? How long has it been on the market, anyway? How long have you had your job?

Try not to worry needlessly, or about things you cannot influence. You may not be able to see it behind the clouds, but the sun will come up tomorrow. If it doesn't, don't read any further.

A Meeting of the Minds

When everyone finally agrees upon price, closing date, contract contingencies, and what goes with the house, shake hands and go out to buy a bottle of champagne. But don't uncork it yet. The contract must be signed, the contingencies must be met, and the closing must take place before the house is yours. After the last check is passed across the table and the last paper signed, you can bring out your wine and some glasses for the celebration.

18

The Contract and the Closing

For five dreary, disillusioning, disappointing days you've been walking through other people's houses. Your return flight home is booked for the day after tomorrow. You've been thinking about that a lot lately and you've begun thinking that perhaps you don't want this promotion and transfer anyway, especially if there's not a decent, affordable place to live in this whole damn city!

But suddenly, now, right this minute, your heart is beating a little faster. Yes, this split level house is lovely. You like the way the sun shines on the breakfast nook, you like the wide-open stairway down to the family room, you like the fieldstone fireplace in the living room. There are enough bedrooms and a two-car garage. You want this house, you can afford it, you tell your real estate agent.

She cancels the rest of the day's appointments from the phone in the kitchen of "your" house and drives directly back to the office. Before you have hung up your coat, she returns from the supply cabinet with several sheets of legal-size paper printed on both sides, each identical to the others.

"This is a standard purchase contract," she says. "We'll just fill in the blanks and present your offer to the sellers."

Even if this agent has been the personification of honesty during your past week working together, she just lied to you. There is no existing sheet of paper anywhere in the United States that is a "standard purchase contract." A legally binding real estate contract can be written on a 3 × 5 card or on ten pages of agate-printed, watermarked paper. It can be full of blank spaces where words have been whited out, and/or black bars where they have been deleted with Magic marker, and/or row upon row of typed-over XXXXXXs. The margins can be crowded with words, phrases, sentences written perpendicular to the text, and innumerable, illegible initials. Or the contract can be freshly typed, not a word preprinted and not an extra space anywhere.

There is some information that must be included in every contract, but any given contract *can* include almost anything. Let's quickly run through the essentials first and then spend some time talking about what you might want in *your* contract.

What Every Contract Must Have

Date

To be a legal instrument, a contract must be dated.

Names

These are the full names of *each* and *every* buyer and seller. Do not accept "Mr. & Mrs. John Jones" or "John Jones *et ux*." (which means *and wife*). Someone might legitimately ask "Which wife?" It's a good idea to have addresses here too. For example: "John T. Jones and Mary K. Jones of 25 Stoney Road, Quarryville, Texas, herein called *the purchasers*."

The Price

The full amount of the purchase price must be named; it's what you are agreeing to. Some people who draw contracts will also tell you that this figure should be broken down into how much cash the buyers have and how much mortgage money they will need. More about this later under "Mortgage Contingencies."

The Address of the Property Being Sold

A street address is usually acceptable. Unless, of course, there are no numbers on the houses, in which case you'll need at least a block and lot number from the local tax map (it's a good idea to have this anyway). If you're buying a condo or a co-op, be sure the apartment number, and building number if necessary, appear in the contract along with the street address. If there's time and if someone is willing to search it out, a "metes and bounds" description of the property is the epitome of legal safe harbor.

The Date and Place of Closing

This is often changed by mutual agreement later but a named place and time to transfer the property is an essential part of an agreement to purchase.

Signatures

Each person buying the property and each person who currently owns the property must sign the contractual agreement. A missing signature can invalidate the entire agreement.

Other Considerations, Clauses, and Contingencies

The Kind of Deed That Is to Convey Title

We're into the realm of lawyers here. But some kind of conveyance of title should be named in your contract. A *warranty deed,* for example, guarantees good title. However, few sellers, their attorneys, or the printers of contract forms want to go so far. A *bargain and sale deed with a covenant versus grantor's acts* represents less liability to the seller since by it the seller maintains only that he has done nothing to damage the marketability of the title. A "just plain" *bargain and sale deed* offers no protection to the buyer, but remember, title insurance does. If you are concerned about the kind of deed being used in your area or in your particular contract, you should talk with a local attorney.

Mortgage Contingency Clause

Unless you have the full cash purchase price in hand, you will have to borrow money to buy the property in question and your contract should be subject to your being able to get this money. Then, if you can't get the money, you are legally released from your contract to purchase and you will get all of your earnest money back.

The best way to write a mortgage or deed-of-trust-loan contingency into a contract is to account for the source of each and every dollar of the purchase price. For example:

Purchase price: $100,000
Earnest money paid upon signing a
nonbinding agreement to purchase $1,000
Additional earnest money to be paid within
three days of the execution of this contract 9,000
Gift monies to be paid in cash at the
closing (gift letter* attached) 20,000
First mortgage in the amount of 70,000
                                              $100,000
    for a term of ____ years at an interest rate
no higher than _____

---

*A gift letter is simply a letter from relatives or anyone else saying that they are making you a gift of so many dollars before the date of the closing.

It is very important that the length of the term of the mortgage and the maximum interest rate that you want (and can afford) be spelled out in the contract. If your contract just says "mortgage in the amount of $70,000" and the bank turns you down, the seller or someone else (the real estate broker, for example) can offer to give you a mortgage loan of $70,000 for *five* years at *18 percent*. You would be legally committed to accept it and buy the property (which of course you couldn't do) or *lose your deposit monies*. Granted, this is not likely to happen when dealing with reputable, respectable people, but not all people are reputable and respectable.

Some agents like to write "prevailing rate" into the blank after "at an interest rate no higher than _____." It's better to write in the rate *currently* prevailing. Then if rates suddenly take a jump you can go with the higher rate if you choose, but you do not have to.

The mortgage contingency clause should also have a cutoff date. Allow yourself plenty of time to get a mortgage commitment. Remember, it is hard *not* to justify an extension of the allowable time period if you have acted in good faith and made honest efforts to obtain financing but are being held up by bank red tape or backlog.

Termite Inspection Contingency

You want the right to have the house inspected for termites. If they are present, you can void the contract or you can negotiate with the sellers to have them exterminated, the damage repaired, and termite barriers installed. The seller usually pays for such repairs.

Home Inspection Contingency

You want your contract subject to an assurance that the plumbing, heating, electrical systems, and appliances are in working order and that the house is structurally sound. You can negotiate over who pays for the professional inspection, but most buyers would rather pay and have the inspector working *for them*. You can also negotiate over repairs. Sometimes repairs are made at the seller's expense, sometimes there is a price reduction to cover the cost of the repairs, and sometimes the buyers walk away.

The Promise of Clear Title

You will want a clause in your contract stating that the seller provides title that is free and clear of all liens and encumbrances. (Such problems are sometimes called "clouds on the title" in legalese.) You can negotiate over who will pay for the title search to determine if it is clear, and of course you can negotiate to accept some or all of the liens or encumbrances, if you choose to do this.

The Right of Assignment

Arguments sometimes develop between buyers' and sellers' attorneys over the right of assignment. If this right is written into a contract, it allows the buyer to assign the contract and all its terms and agreements to someone else before closing. (This is sometimes done quite profitably. See the condos and co-ops chapter, p. 255.)

When a contract is assigned the sellers must sell to a party other than their original buyer, a party of the buyer choice. Since the sellers have no control over who this party might be, most seller's attorneys prefer to write in a no-assignment clause and furthermore, to make the contract binding upon the heirs of the buyer in the event of unexpected death. You can negotiate over these clauses. Don't sign anything to which you have objections or reservations!

Escrow Monies

"Who holds them?" is often a negotiating point among buyers and sellers who make their livings in real estate. Each wants the monies held by someone who is likely to be "on their side," just in case the deal gets messy somewhere along the line. But sometimes it's hard to define who's on whose side and/or what an "uninvolved party" really is. Lawyers or lenders are usually preferable to real estate brokers, who have commission money at stake.

The other question that often comes up in big deals is "Who gets the interest on the escrow monies?" In this age of high interest rates, every escrow account should be interest bearing, even if the money is held only for a month or so. Everyone agrees on that. But buyers always think that they should get this interest since it's their money that is being held until closing day. Sellers will argue that once all the contract contingencies are met, the escrow monies rightfully belong to them (and there's legal precedent for their position).

The question is obviously open to negotiation, and it should be settled *before* the contract is drawn. The contract should then state clearly who holds the escrow monies and to whom the interest on those monies will be credited.

Closing Costs

As we've said again and again, in this world of real estate just about everything is negotiable, including who pays for which of the closing costs. In some areas of the country there are "common practice" codes, but these differ not only from state to state, but also from city to city. If you adhere to them, you could theoretically pay for a title search as a seller in one city and pay for a title search as a buyer in another city, all on *one* move.

Remember, however, that common practice is *not* law. Even in a town where the buyer traditionally pays for the title search, or some other item, the seller can offer (or be persuaded) to do so as an incentive to the sale. And vice versa. Everything is negotiable.

There's a list of common closing costs in the last section of this chapter. Find out which apply in your area and negotiate over who pays them. Then specify who pays for what in your contract.

Personal Property

Lawyers will tell you that everything that isn't nailed down (*attached* to the building) is personal property and *not* real estate. It's a good guideline, *but* some sellers think nothing of pulling out built-in (and therefore attached) dishwashers and detaching and removing all the lighting fixtures the day before the closing. Many more sellers (in fact close to a majority) remove drapery hardware, which is attached to the walls by any definition. An argument at the closing table almost always follows.

The best contracts will have a personal property addendum attached. On this sheet of paper everything that even vaguely resembles personal property or anything about which there might be a question is listed under one of two headings: *included in the sale* and *not included in the sale*. Both the buyers and the sellers should sign this page.

Liability and Maintenance

Most contracts contain a statement that liability for damage from fire, storm hazard, or act of God remains with the seller until the closing of title. In other words, you should receive the property in essentially the same condition that it was in when you signed the contract. If a tree falls and breaks a huge hole in the roof, it must be repaired to your satisfaction. If this is not possible (in a fire, for example), you have the right to walk away from the deal with the return of all your deposit monies being held.

When the buyers use an attorney, he or she sometimes adds a line to the liability clause that reads something like this:

> Seller agrees to cut grass, maintain landscaping, and provide for snow removal until closing of title, and to deliver the premises in question in broom-clean condition.

Broom-clean means empty of trash and clutter, but not necessarily spotless.

Adjustments

An agreement should be reached and recorded in the contract as to how taxes, water and sewer charges, fuel, premiums on existing transferable insurance policies, utility bills, interest on mortgages when assumable, and rent (if there are tenants involved) are to be divided between buyer and seller on the date of the settlement. This written agreement can save innumerable arguments at the closing table and sometimes even prevent lengthy delays of the closing itself.

Day-of-Closing Inspection

A good contract will provide that the buyers be allowed to inspect the property on the day of the closing, *before* the closing takes place. Everything then should be as it was promised.

It's a good idea to include this clause even if you know you won't be there to do this inspection. You can designate an agent (anyone, even a friend or relative) to do it for you. If you have no such agent, include the clause anyway. Just the possibility that someone will walk through the property an hour before the closing is enough to keep many sellers a little more honest.

Other Clauses

Ours cannot be a complete list because anything can be written into a contract, theoretically at least. Don't hesitate, therefore, to ask that any request or agreement be reduced to writing. The printed word can be much more effective than aspirin in the relief of headaches.

The Closing or Settlement

In the real estate world the word "closing" generally denotes the formal process by which title to real property passes from the seller to the buyer. In some areas of the country, this process is called "settlement" rather than closing. By whichever name it goes, however, it has many different faces.

In some regions, notably the Northeast, the scene of a closing might be a bookshelf-lined room in a lawyer's office, a room with a long table in its center surrounded by highbacked oak chairs and no windows. This room would be crowded with people: the sellers, the

---

Selecting an Attorney

Where to Get Some Names:
  local bar association
  neighborhood legal-aid office
  lenders
  real estate agents
  friends, co-workers, your future neighbors
  ✔✔REMEMBER to ask for the names of attorneys with substantial real estate experience, especially in local residences.

Questions to Ask the Lawyers Whom You Call:
  What is your fee for reviewing contracts and giving advice (flat fee vs. hourly rate)?
  What is your fee for being present at the closing?
  What is the usual role of an attorney in residential closings in this area? If the attorney does the mechanics of the closing, will he or she represent both parties? Is this acceptable to you?
  Is there a package fee for closings? That is, one flat fee for the entire closing procedure no matter how many hours involved?

  ✔✔REMEMBER that lawyers' fees are not set or regulated in any way. You can shop for the best deal. Don't be shy about asking "How much do you charge for . . ." but also consider the value of reputation and experience. The "right price" for legal services is the price that is satisfactory to you.

---

sellers' attorney, the buyers, the buyers' attorney, the lender's attorney, a representative of the title insurance company, and the selling real estate agent. (Sometimes even the listing real estate agent shows up.)

In contrast, the scene of a settlement on the West Coast might be a small office with a desk and floor-to-ceiling windows. One person will be working alone there, an escrow agent. No one else need come, and they don't.

Between these poles are many, many possible closing scenarios. Depending upon local custom, settlement may be conducted by an escrow agent, a lending institution, a title insurance company, an escrow company, a real estate broker, or attorneys for the buyers and sellers. And even the words of the settlement/closing procedures will differ from one area of the country to another since terminology, like procedure, is a matter of local custom.

Does all this sound confusing? It is, but there is a stabilizer. In response to buyer and seller confusion due to the diversity of closing procedures across the country, and in response to the prevalence of some unethical practices and paybacks, the federal government has stepped into real estate. In 1974 RESPA, the Real Estate Settlement Procedures Act, became law. That act now governs most of the steps in the transfer of real estate and protects the homebuyer with its disclosure requirements. No longer can innocent buyers go to a closing having invested their last dime in their home purchase only to be slapped with closing costs of $1500 or more *that were never anticipated!*

Under RESPA, if you apply for a loan to purchase real estate, the prospective lender is required to provide you with a good faith estimate of the costs of settlement services (closing costs) and a copy of the HUD booklet titled *Settlement Costs* within three business days after written loan application. The lender is also required to inform you as to which documents and services must be presented or completed before the closing. If the lender designates that you must use specific settlement service providers (lawyers, title examiners, title insurance companies, surveyors, etc.), you must be given their names, addresses, and telephone numbers and an estimate of the cost of their services. You must also be informed as to whether each of these designated providers has any business relationship with the lender.

Finally, if you request it, one business day before settlement the person conducting the settlement must allow you an opportunity to see the HUD-designed Uniform Settlement Statement. This discloses whatever figures are available at that time for the settlement charges that you will be required to pay. At the settlement meeting, the completed Uniform Settlement Statement will be given to you. If there is no actual settlement meeting in your part of the country, this completed form will be mailed to you.

A blank copy of the Uniform Settlement Statement appears on pages 304–305. Look through it, but don't let it intimidate you. Remember, someone else will be responsible for filling in all the blanks with the appropriate figures. You need only familiarize yourself with it so that you will be able to check through the numbers at the closing.

"That's fine for closing costs," you say, "but I'd like to know what's going to *happen* at the closing. If every city and town has its own little variations on custom, how can I find out?"

The answer is so simple it will surprise you. *Ask*. Your real estate agent, your prospective lender, and your lawyer are all excellent sources of information about local closing procedures and customs. Ask them to describe exactly who does what at the closing, where it takes place, who must be present, and how long it will take. RESPA assures that you will know fairly accurately what the total cost will be.

You can even ask your questions about the closing *before* you find *the* house. Make them a point of conversation with the real estate agent as you drive together between showings. Information such as this is always valuable, even if it does nothing more than ease tension and apprehension. As the Boy Scouts say, "Be prepared."

Closing Costs

We can describe and explain the most common closing costs here, but we cannot make you any promises. Doubtless some costs will apply to your purchase, doubtless some will not. Therefore, familiarize yourself with all of them so that you can talk intelligently with your lender, lawyer, or closing agent and pin down exactly what does apply to you. For the sake of clarity, we'll generally follow the order of their listing in the Uniform Settlement Statement:

Items Payable in Connection with the Loan

1. *Loan origination fee.* This covers processing costs. It may be stated as a percentage of the loan or a flat fee.

2. *Loan discount fee (points).* This is a one-time charge to "adjust the yield" on the loan (that is, make it more profitable to the lender). One point is 1 percent of the loan. Buyer, seller, or both may pay points.

3. *Appraisal fee.* This is the charge to have the property professionally appraised. Most often paid by the buyer, but it can be paid by either party by mutual agreement. The appraisal fee is sometimes included in the mortgage insurance application fee.

4. *Credit report fee.* This fee is sometimes paid upon making written loan application rather than at the closing. In that case, whether you get the loan or not, it is nonrefundable.

5. *Lender's inspection fee.* This fee is usually applicable only to new construction, where representatives of the lender must make several inspections at various stages of the building process.

Closing Day "Don't Forgets"

Electricity. Arrange to have the meter read on the day of the closing and an account established in your name. If you make these arrangements a week or so in advance, there should be no interruption in service.

Fuel. If the house is heated by oil, have the oil company measure the oil in the tank the day before closing, if this is agreeable to the seller. Otherwise make some other agreement and stick to it. If gas is the fuel, have the meter read on the day of the closing and an account opened in your name.

Water. Have the meter read. Water companies and municipal water departments are notoriously lax about meter reading so make these arrangements several weeks in advance and follow up after the closing to be sure the meter was, in fact, read.

Before-closing inspection. Do it if you can, even if the sellers have been acting like long-lost college buddies. Make a list of any problems or questions.

A *certified check*. This should be written for the total amount of cash still due (the cash above the amount of the mortgage loan and the escrow monies being held). Make the certified check payable to yourself. Then if something happens and the property doesn't close, you still have your money. You can endorse it over to the lender, the lawyer, the seller, or the closing agent when all is well.

Extra money in your checking account. Closing costs can usually be paid by personal check, but verify this with the closing agent several days in advance. If certified checks are necessary, have them made payable to yourself. And be sure you have some extra money in your account; something unexpected often comes up.

A *copy of your loan commitment letter*. If there's a mistake or misunderstanding with the lender, you should have this letter to verify your position.

A *copy of the contract to purchase*. You'll want your own copy at hand just in case something "doesn't sound quite right" to you.

Your hazard insurance policy or policies. Many lenders will not allow the property to close without paid-up fire and hazard insurance policies and flood insurance if required.

Personal identification. Sometimes a closing agent will ask for personal identification to verify that you are the people you say you are. A passport is always acceptable, if you have one; a driver's license is usually adequate.

Your bottle of champagne. Don't forget the glasses.

6. *Mortgage insurance application fee.* This fee covers the processing costs for an application for private mortgage insurance. Sometimes it includes the appraisal fee and sometimes it is paid in advance of the closing.

7. *Assumption fee.* This fee is charged for the processing work in connection with a mortgage assumption.

Items Required by the Lender to Be Paid in Advance

1. *Interest.* Usually the buyers must pay, at the closing, interest on their loan for the period of time between the closing date and the date that the first scheduled loan payment is due.

2. *Mortgage insurance premium.* The first premium is often paid in advance, at the request of the lender. It can cover several months or a full year.

3. *Hazard insurance premium.* Lenders often require payment of the first year's premium at the closing. Or they require that you bring a paid-in-full one-year policy to the closing with you. They may even keep a copy. In certain areas of the country, you may also be required by Federal law to carry flood insurance.

Reserve Funds Deposited with the Lender

1. *Hazard insurance.* Some lenders require a certain amount of money to be held in reserve in order to pay the *next* insurance premium. Try to negotiate the payment of interest on your reserve fund.

2. *Mortgage Insurance.* Some part of the premium is sometimes placed in a reserve account rather than paid in advance at the closing. This is preferable to full payment in advance, especially if you can negotiate to have interest paid on the reserve funds.

3. *Taxes.* Many lenders (in fact, *most* lenders) require a regular monthly payment to the reserve account for city and/or county property taxes. They may also require an amount equal to six months' (more or less) taxes to be paid at the closing and held in an escrow account. Again, try to get the lender to pay you interest on the money being held.

Homeowner's Insurance

In securing a mortgage for your home you will find the lender will require you to take out a homeowner's insurance policy, which you no doubt would do anyway. You can go to any agent (a representative of a specific insurance company) or broker (one who sells insurance for several different companies) to take out any type of policy you want, just so your home is protected. Lenders have a few minimum requirements; coverage above that is up to you.

Broadly speaking, the basic homeowner's package consists of coverage for at least 80 percent of the replacement value of your home, plus coverage for your belongings at whatever value you place on them, plus $25,000 to $100,000 liability coverage to protect you if you are sued. But there are many variations on that package, and you should investigate all of them.

The Fair Access to Insurance Requirements plan (FAIR) is in effect in twenty-six states, offering insurance to those who have difficulty getting protection for a high-risk property or one situated in a high-risk area. Your real estate agent can tell you more about FAIR.

If you live in a condominium or cooperative you will need two policies: one purchased for the entire complex, where you pay your prorated share of premiums through your monthly maintenance fees, and the second as coverage for your own unit and its possessions.

You can find insurance nowadays against practically every calamity that could befall your home, except nuclear power plant disasters. As you are reading this, however, someone may be writing out the first of those policies. Here are some other kinds of protection for you and your home:

Fire, flood, and earthquake. Fire protection usually goes along with homeowner's coverage. Earthquake is usually a separate provision, with coverage running $150 or so in annual premiums. The average homeowner's policy does not include coverage for flood damage, which comes as a dismal surprise to many unfortunate homeowners. And as you have seen from news reports over the last several years, flooding is not a rare phenomenon. To see if your community is eligible for coverage under the low-cost National Flood Insurance Program, you can contact your agent or broker, or phone toll-free (800) 638–6620. Or write National Flood Insurance Program, P.O. Box 34222, Bethesda, Md. 20817.

Floaters. This is additional coverage attached to your regular homeowner's policy for items of special value, such as jewelry, furs, expensive collectibles, and antiques.

Job insurance. This was developed during the recession of the early 1980s. Lenders and some homebuilders offer the policy, which provides that if the major breadwinner is laid off, the policy will pay up to twelve consecutive months of mortgage installments. Premiums range from $175 to $250 for twelve months coverage and from $140 to $200 for six months.

Mortgage life insurance. This is a policy that provides funds to pay off a mortgage if the principal wage earner dies during the term of that loan.

Title insurance. Title insurance is almost always a requirement for closing on a home. Usually it protects only the lender against unclear title to the property you are buying, something few buyers realize. If you want protection, you will have to take out an owner's policy for a small additional charge.

Other creative options. And then there is insurance for damage in your home caused by ghosts, insurance in the event your house is hit by a satellite, and various other sorts of protection for your castle. For information about this complicated field, one where we may all be tempted to become "insurance poor," it is suggested that you read one of the several good consumer guides to buying insurance available on the stands and in libraries. You can also call your State Insurance Department to see if they have printed material or can answer your questions.

Another source of information is the Insurance Information Institute, the educational arm of the industry, at its toll-free hotline—(800) 221-4954.

Two booklets:

"Condominium Insurance: A Guide." 28 pages. Write Condominium Insurance, Publications Request Desk, Corporate Relations, F-6, Kemper Group, Long Grove, Ill. 60049. A single copy is free. Please send a self-addressed, business-size envelope and 37 cents postage.

"Home Insurance Basics." Free from the Insurance Information Institute, 111 William St., New York, N.Y. 10038.

Form Approved
OMB No. 2530-0006

A.

U. S. DEPARTMENT OF HOUSING AND URBAN DEVELOPMENT

SETTLEMENT STATEMENT

B. TYPE OF LOAN	
1. ☐ FHA 2. ☐ FmHA 3. ☐ CONV. UNINS.	
4. ☐ VA 5. ☐ CONV. INS.	
6. File Number:	7. Loan Number:
8. Mortgage Insurance Case Number:	

C. NOTE: *This form is furnished to give you a statement of actual settlement costs. Amounts paid to and by the settlement agent are shown. Items marked "(p.o.c.)" were paid outside the closing; they are shown here for informational purposes and are not included in the totals.*

D. NAME OF BORROWER:	**E. NAME OF SELLER:**	**F. NAME OF LENDER:**

G. PROPERTY LOCATION:	**H. SETTLEMENT AGENT:**	**I. SETTLEMENT DATE:**
	PLACE OF SETTLEMENT:	

J. SUMMARY OF BORROWER'S TRANSACTION		**K. SUMMARY OF SELLER'S TRANSACTION**	
100. GROSS AMOUNT DUE FROM BORROWER:		**400. GROSS AMOUNT DUE TO SELLER:**	
101. Contract sales price		401. Contract sales price	
102. Personal property		402. Personal property	
103. Settlement charges to borrower (line 1400)		403.	
104.		404.	
105.		405.	
Adjustments for items paid by seller in advance		*Adjustments for items paid by seller in advance*	
106. City/town taxes to		406. City/town taxes to	
107. County taxes to		407. County taxes to	
108. Assessments to		408. Assessments to	

(Form Continues on Next Page)

109.		409.	
110.		410.	
111.		411.	
112.		412.	
120. GROSS AMOUNT DUE FROM BORROWER		**420. GROSS AMOUNT DUE TO SELLER**	
200. AMOUNTS PAID BY OR IN BEHALF OF BORROWER:		**500. REDUCTIONS IN AMOUNT DUE TO SELLER:**	
201. Deposit or earnest money		501. Excess deposit (see instructions)	
202. Principal amount of new loan(s)		502. Settlement charges to seller (line 1400)	
203. Existing loan(s) taken subject to		503. Existing loan(s) taken subject to	
204.		504. Payoff of first mortgage loan	
205.		505. Payoff of second mortgage loan	
206.		506.	
207.		507.	
208.		508.	
209.		509.	
Adjustments for items unpaid by seller		*Adjustments for items unpaid by seller*	
210. City/town taxes to		510. City/town taxes to	
211. County taxes to		511. County taxes to	
212. Assessments to		512. Assessments to	
213.		513.	
214.		514.	
215.		515.	
216.		516.	
217.		517.	
218.		518.	
219.		519.	
220. TOTAL PAID BY/FOR BORROWER		**520. TOTAL REDUCTION AMOUNT DUE SELLER**	
300. CASH AT SETTLEMENT FROM/TO BORROWER		**600. CASH AT SETTLEMENT TO/FROM SELLER**	
301. Gross amount due from borrower (line 120)		601. Gross amount due to seller (line 420)	
302. Less amounts paid by/for borrower (line 220)	( )	602. Less reductions in amount due seller (line 520)	( )
303. CASH (☐ FROM) (☐ TO) BORROWER		**603. CASH (☐ TO) (☐ FROM) SELLER**	

Previous Edition is Obsolete

(Back of Form Continued on Next Page)

HUD-1 (5-76)

L. SETTLEMENT CHARGES	PAID FROM BORROWER'S FUNDS AT SETTLEMENT	PAID FROM SELLER'S FUNDS AT SETTLEMENT
700. TOTAL SALES/BROKER'S COMMISSION based on price $ @ % =		
Division of Commission (line 700) as follows:		
701. $ to		
702. $ to		
703. Commission paid at Settlement		
704.		
800. ITEMS PAYABLE IN CONNECTION WITH LOAN		
801. Loan Origination Fee %		
802. Loan Discount %		
803. Appraisal Fee to		
804. Credit Report to		
805. Lender's Inspection Fee		
806. Mortgage Insurance Application Fee to		
807. Assumption Fee		
808.		
809.		
810.		
811.		
900. ITEMS REQUIRED BY LENDER TO BE PAID IN ADVANCE		
901. Interest from to @ $ /day		
902. Mortgage Insurance Premium for months to		
903. Hazard Insurance Premium for years to		
904. years to		
905.		
1000. RESERVES DEPOSITED WITH LENDER		
1001. Hazard insurance months @ $ per month		
1002. Mortgage insurance months @ $ per month		
1003. City property taxes months @ $ per month		
1004. County property taxes months @ $ per month		
1005. Annual assessments months @ $ per month		
1006. months @ $ per month		
1007. months @ $ per month		

(Form Continues on Next Page)

1008.	months @ $	per month	
1100. TITLE CHARGES			
1101. Settlement or closing fee to			
1102. Abstract or title search to			
1103. Title examination to			
1104. Title insurance binder to			
1105. Document preparation to			
1106. Notary fees to			
1107. Attorney's fees to			
(includes above items numbers;)			
1108. Title insurance to			
(includes above items numbers;)			
1109. Lender's coverage $			
1110. Owner's coverage $			
1111.			
1112.			
1113.			
1200. GOVERNMENT RECORDING AND TRANSFER CHARGES			
1201. Recording fees: Deed $; Mortgage $; Releases $			
1202. City/county tax/stamps: Deed $; Mortgage $			
1203. State tax/stamps: Deed $; Mortgage $			
1204.			
1205.			
1300. ADDITIONAL SETTLEMENT CHARGES			
1301. Survey to			
1302. Pest inspection to			
1303.			
1304.			
1305.			
1400. TOTAL SETTLEMENT CHARGES (enter on lines 103, Section J and 502, Section K)			

HUD-1 (5-76)

4. *Special assessments*. Like the tax escrow account, this money is held in escrow to make payments due either at intervals throughout the year or annually. Usually the fees represent special-improvement assessments such as sewers or sidewalks but they can represent neighborhood or homeowners' association dues. Again try to get interest on escrow monies, or, better yet, negotiate with the lender to allow you to take responsibility for paying the fees yourself. If your credit rating is good, most lenders will listen.

Charges for Title Services

1. *Settlement or closing fee*. This is the fee paid to the closing agent. Who pays it (buyer or seller) can be negotiated before the contract is signed.

2. *Abstract or title search, title examination, title insurance binder*. (A title insurance binder is sometimes called a commitment to insure.) These are charges made for title search and guarantee services. They may be paid to one provider or several depending upon local practice, and who pays them may be dictated by local custom or an agreement negotiated before the signing of the contract.

3. *Document preparation*. There may be a separate fee for final preparation of legal papers. Be sure you are not paying twice for the same service, for example, preparation of the mortgage.

4. *Notary fee*. This is a fee paid to a licensed notary public to authenticate the execution of certain documents.

5. *Attorney's fees*. If the services of an attorney are required by the lender the fee will appear on the Uniform Settlement Statement. If you have privately hired an attorney to represent you, that fee will not necessarily appear. It is usually due and payable, however, at the closing, so find out how much it will be in advance.

6. *Title insurance*. A lender's policy may be required; an owner's policy may be offered as an option. The premium for each is a one-time charge. Sellers sometimes pay for an owner's policy to be given to the buyer as a part of their assurance of clear title. Buyers usually must pay the fee for the lender's title policy, but often only the amount of the mortgage, not the purchase price of the house, need be insured. Of course, who pays for what is open to negotiation.

7. *Government recording and transfer fees*. Fees for legally recording the new deed and mortgage are usually paid by the buyer and can be fairly large. They are set by state and/or local governments. City, county, and/or state tax stamps may also be required and carry a fee.

Other Settlement Charges

1. *Survey.* This is often required by the lender and usually paid for by the buyer. Sometimes money can be saved by simply updating the previous survey, made when the seller bought the property.

2. *Pest and other inspections.* Fees for these inspections are usually paid in advance of the closing and directly to the providers. Sometimes, however, the amount of the fee is reimbursed to the buyer by the seller as a part of the closing agreement.

3. *Broker's commissions.* The seller traditionally pays the real estate broker's commission at the closing. If the buyer made a special agreement in the contract or hired a buyer's real estate agent, however, the buyer will pay the required commission at the closing.

4. *Other fees.* Because of the diversity of settlement procedures and the uniqueness of every property and every transaction, you may encounter other fees not mentioned here. If you have questions about them, ask. And if you feel uncomfortable about the answers, get professional help.

Going Home

It's yours now. Your own home. Put your name on the mailbox. Relax. Try not to think about money.

19

A Basic Guide to
Home Financing

When the house hunt and the negotiations are done, the third of
the three big dragons that you must battle before "living happily
ever after" still looms ahead: getting the money. (Unless, of course,
you're independently wealthy and intend to pay cash for your little
bungalow.)

Occasionally your real estate agent will fight that dragon for you.
Some firms have mortgage applications in their files from all of their
favorite lenders. Some will introduce you to a mortgage broker who
will find you a loan (for a fee). Some giants in the business will even
lend you the money to buy. (Another branch of their corporation
just happens to be a finance company.)

But often you will be left completely on your own, holding a
contract that says you must have a mortgage commitment in four
weeks. Whether you get help or not, one fact remains as constant in
home financing as it is in the real estate marketplace: *You will be
more motivated to look out for your own interests than anyone else*.
And in financing, as in everything, you'll do a better job if you know
something about the field.

Now we can't make you an expert in twenty minutes' reading time.
Volumes have been written upon the subject of financing, most of
which turn the average reader away before he or she reaches page 3!
We can, however, give you an overview. Enough knowledge to make
some comparisons between lenders and loans, to sense when something doesn't quite ring true, and to know what questions to ask. If
you're feeling uneasy about the financing choices being offered to you
or the fine print in a particular mortgage agreement, consult a real

estate attorney. And be sure that attorney is a reputable, *local* attorney who knows local practices and local lenders. *Local* is as much a keyword in financing a home as it is in finding one.

Let's begin with an introduction to the language of home finance.

The Words Demystified

Mortgage

The word mortgage comes from the Old French meaning *dead pledge*. As serious as all that! In the simplest terms, it is a loan that is secured by real property. In other words, if you don't pay back the loan, you will lose the property.

In the real world, however, legal procedures and practices don't allow anything quite that simple. Since you never gave up title to the property when you took out the mortgage loan, the lender who wants to foreclose on that loan must go after and get that title before taking possession of your home. This can take a few months or, much more often, a few years.

The complexity of foreclosure procedures have, in fact, stimulated the creation of a whole new type of home financing in which failure to pay can mean rather quick eviction and loss of your home. The idea started on the West Coast and has moved rather rapidly across the country. It's called the *trust deed*.

The Deed of Trust, or Trust Deed

This is not a mortgage because you can't pledge property that you don't own as security for a loan. That's right, when you finance through a deed of trust, you do *not* take title to your home.

The deed, which is the legal instrument that grants title to the property, is held by a third party (not by the lender, and not by the borrower). Usually this is the title insurance company or the escrow company that handles the closing.

As long as you make the payments you promised, the net effect of using a deed of trust to finance your home is the same as having your home mortgaged. You can live in it, make additions and improvements to it, and claim all the homeowner tax benefits allowed by law. If you don't make the payments, however, the sword of the lender has a keener edge.

Read carefully. In deed of trust financing, you are called the *trustor*, ironically, one who trusts! The firm that holds title to your property is called the *trustee*, one who is trusted. And the lender is called the *beneficiary*, the one who benefits from the arrangement if you don't pay!

Each state where trust deeds are used has its own procedures, spelled out in nice legalese, for what to do when a borrower defaults. They are almost invariably faster than mortgage foreclosures. In California, for example, your house can be offered for sale ninety days after a notice of default is filed. You can stop the sale then *only* by paying off the entire amount of the loan, plus interest, and any costs that have been incurred in the default proceedings.

Because words and usage change slowly, many, many people (professional and otherwise) continue to use the word "mortgage" when talking about home financing, even in states where trust deeds are routine. No one says, "I'm trust deeding my home for $100,000." We also will use *mortgage* to refer to the means of financing a home throughout this book. Remember, however, to find out exactly what legal instruments will be used to get you the money that will allow you to take possession of the house you choose.

Mortgagor and Mortgagee

Always confusing! The lender of the money is the mortgagee. The borrower is the mortgagor, the one who offers up his property as collateral for the loan. The mortgagee is the one to whom the mortgage is given. The mortgagor is the one to whom the mortgage *loan* is given.

Mortgagor   Mortgagee

S. Zimmerman.

Second Mortgage/Second Deed of Trust

In case of default, loans are paid off in numerical order from the proceeds of the sale of the property. The first mortgage first, then the second, and so forth. The lender who holds a fourth mortgage on a piece of property is paid off with what's left after the three lenders who have precedence have been paid. The odds for his full repayment are usually slim, and his interest rate, therefore, is usually high.

Home improvement loans are often written as second mortgages. And sometimes you can get a vacation loan or a college tuition loan by using a second mortgage on your home. Some buyers try to get their downpayment money, or part of it, by arranging private second mortgages with family or investors. Most institutional first mortgage lenders frown on this practice and many, including the federal government (FHA and VA), strictly prohibit it. There is, however, some common practice of deception where buyers bring in "gift letters" for a part of the downpayment and then, after the closing, have their "gift" written as a second mortgage. The practice is illegal.

Principal

This is the amount you borrow at the outset. Later, the amount you still owe, the amount upon which interest is calculated.

Interest

Interest is the charge levied for borrowing money.

Rate of Interest, or Interest Rate

This is a stated percentage of the principal that is used to calculate how much interest is due and payable.

Term

Term is the life span of the mortgage. It could be three years or thirty, or any other length of time you and the lender can agree upon.

Amortization

Amortization is the process of gradually paying off the principal by making regular installment payments.

Negative Amortization

The practice of *adding* to the principal of a loan when (1) its monthly payments are insufficient to pay the interest due or (2) on a regular monthly program is called negative amortization. In other words, each month you owe more money, not less. Negative amortization can occur in adjustable loans that have a provision for a stable monthly payment despite interest rate escalation. (See page 321.) It also occurs in reverse annuity mortgages which are designed for retired homeowners (see Chapter 40). The possibility for negative amortization must be agreed to by both the lender and the borrower when the mortgage agreement is signed.

Appraisal Fee

A flat fee usually charged by the prospective lender, the appraisal fee pays an independent appraiser or the lender's representative to inspect the property to be mortgaged and to estimate its fair market value. The fee is nonrefundable even if your mortgage loan application is refused.

Loan Origination Fee

This is an extra charge, paid in cash at the closing, that covers the lender's administrative costs and often makes the loan more profitable to the lender. It is either a flat amount, say $900, or a percentage of the face amount of the loan.

Points

These are also called discount points. This fee has nothing to do with a discount for you. It's a discount on the value of your loan. Think about this: if you must pay a lender $2 in order to borrow $10, you have really only borrowed $8! This example is, of course, exaggerated for effect but add some appropriate zeros and you may just feel resentful about points. Sometimes points are called prepaid interest.

Points are most commonly charged when money is tight; the tighter the money, the more points. One point is 1 percent of the face amount of your loan. The fee is charged and paid in cash at the closing.

There is one small saving grace: tax deductions. If the charging of points is common practice in your local area as a part of the cost of a loan and you don't pay more than is "usual and customary," you may deduct this fee as interest paid in the tax year in which you pay it on your federal income tax return.

Loan Application Fee

Not to be confused with the loan origination fee, the loan application fee is a stated amount (usually between $50 and $100) which the lender charges all of its customers for the privilege of filling out the application form with the opportunity (but not the guarantee) of obtaining a mortgage loan. Like the appraisal fee, it is not refundable even if you are turned down.

There are whispers in the real estate business that high loan application fees discourage homebuyers from shopping around among lenders for the best financing. After all, who would want to pay six or eight $50 fees at six or eight different lenders just to get *one* mortgage commitment.

The truth of the matter is, however, that you *should* shop for your loan and you needn't spend *any* money to do so. You can get all the information you need to know about home financing programs by simply asking questions, and you do *not* have to apply for a mortgage loan to ask those questions. You should know which lender has the best (and cheapest) program for you long before you fill out an application and pay the application fee.

Prepayment Penalty

This is a named amount or percentage of the principal to be paid to the lender if you should decide to pay off your mortgage loan early. When a prepayment penalty is written into a loan, it is usually in effect for only one to three years and often it is waived if the house must be sold because of a business transfer. But ask about it before you sign any papers. You do not want to be paying a prepayment penalty when you sell your house seven years from now.

Required Downpayment (Loan-to-Value Ratio)

Few lenders will lend the full value of a property unless they have special guarantees such as the Veterans Administration offers. It's just too risky. If the borrower should default in the early years of the mortgage, foreclosure, fix-up, and resale costs could result in a loss on the mortgage loan. Lenders therefore require a cash downpayment, usually 20 percent of the appraised value of the property. In other words, the lender will give a loan that is 80 percent of the value of the property. When mortgage insurance is purchased by the borrower, the loan-to-value ratio might be increased to 90 percent or even 95 percent of the appraised value thus requiring a downpayment of only 10 or 5 percent.

Mortgage Insurance

Mortgage insurance does *not* refer to a term life insurance policy that will pay off the balance of the mortgage debt in the event that an owner dies. Mortgage insurance will guarantee that your lender will not lose money if you default and a foreclosure becomes necessary. There's no benefit in it for you except that lenders will write mortgage agreements with as little as 5 percent downpayment when the loans are insured.

Mortgage insurance comes from two sources: the federal government (FHA programs) and the private sector (primarily thirteen companies, members of the Mortgage Insurance Companies of America, a trade association). It costs you, the buyer, money, usually a fee at the outset and a percentage of the face amount of the loan added to the monthly payment. Some private mortgage insurance programs are written so that the insurance and its premium drops off after a given number of years when enough equity has been accumulated in the property to make insurance unnecessary.

Disclosure Requirements

In 1968, the federal government enacted the Truth-in-Lending Act, which was revised and updated in 1982. That law requires that every lending institution provide its loan applicants with complete and accurate information about the *real* cost of borrowing money.

These disclosure statements are supposed to be written in clear language, but somehow they never seem to be very readable and they get downright hairy when such factors as adjustable rate loans, indices, and rollovers are included. If you don't understand everything, *everything*, spend a few minutes with your attorney or financial advisor *before* you take a pen into your hand. Or you can have the real annual percentage rate of the loan recalculated for you by the National Consumer Law Center. There is a $20 fee as of this writing and you must send a copy of your financing documents to: National Consumer Law Center, Attention: Amortization Check, Suite 121, 11 Beacon Street, Boston, Mass. 02108.

Assumable Mortgage

Wouldn't it be nice to find a 7 percent mortgage from the good old days (mid 1970s) that you could just take over the payments on by paying the seller his $20,000 or $30,000 equity? Dream on. In the first place, housing appreciated at such a mind-boggling rate in the late 70s that virtually everyone who bought during that period of time now has considerably more than $20,000 or $30,000 equity. And in the second place, most lenders stopped voluntarily writing "assumable" loans in the late 1960s!

The federal government requires that its guaranteed and insured loans (VA and FHA) be assumable, but it allows lenders to require that all other mortgage loans be due and payable upon sale or transfer to a new owner. These loans cannot be assumed. Keep reading.

Due-on-Sale Clause

When new mortgage money became almost impossible to get in 1980, consumers and real estate professionals (especially those in our western states) cried "Foul!" State laws were enacted which invalidated the due-on-sale clause and made virtually all mortgage loans assumable. Then the *bankers* cried "Foul!" The argument went all the way to the United States Supreme Court, which ruled in the summer of 1982 that a state could not regulate a federally chartered lending institution. Due-on-sale clauses were and are therefore valid at all federally chartered lenders (the vast majority).

In states where due-on-sale clauses have been legislated invalid, you might still be able to find a mortgage loan written by a state chartered lender that is assumable. Paying off the equity of the seller, however, will probably require that you take out a second mortgage loan and the total of first and second mortgage payments may add up to be higher than it would be if you simply went the route of a new first mortgage at the current rate.

If you're intent upon finding an assumable mortgage, you should buy a good calculator (the kind real estate agents carry that calculates interest and principal payments) and you should line up some professional counselors who will help you evaluate and compare your financing options.

The Call

When a call is written into a fixed-rate long-term mortgage, that mortgage is a wolf in sheep's clothing.

To call a mortgage means to demand payment in full. Certain dates are usually specified upon which repayment can be required, often at three, five, or seven year intervals. If you sign your name to a mortgage agreement that contains call dates, you are agreeing that you will pay off the entire remaining principal of your loan on any of those dates that the lender might request.

In times of unstable mortgaging conditions, this agreement is dangerous indeed. What if your lender calls your mortgage at a time when there simply is no new mortgage money to be had? When no other lender in town is lending? Will you be able to pay back the entire remaining principal of your loan? And if you can't, will you lose your home to foreclosure?

Some lenders include provisions in a call clause that allow the borrower to refinance the principal balance at the current rate of interest at the time of the call. This kindness may save your home, but it changes the mortgage agreement you signed from a long-term fixed-rate loan to the potential equivalent of a roll-over (explained in the next section).

If you see a call clause in your mortgage agreement, have it struck out. If the lender won't agree to strike it out, look for another lender or at least a more secure mortgage loan program.

Equity

Finally! Something positive. Equity is the cash value of your property over and above the money owed on it (mortgages, second mortgages, judgments, liens, etc.). Almost invariably the amount grows over the years; it is the proverbial nest egg. You can borrow against it for almost any reason and it may be a source of income for you when you sell the property.

Equity is the basis for seller financing. If you don't need all the equity you have accumulated in your residence, you can lend some of it to the buyer, perhaps as a second mortgage with very favorable rates. Or you can invest it elswhere and collect a stipend for your retirement years.

Loan Types and Features

Less than ten years ago real estate writers wrote books in which the mortgage chapter was among the shortest. Then there were only two kinds of home financing worthy of discussion: government-backed loans and "conventional" loans. To get either one you almost always went to a savings bank or a savings and loan association.

But everything changed as the decade rolled over into the 1980s. There are so many loan types today that bankers and brokers identify them by their initials. And there are dozens of different lenders in the marketplace including municipalities, pension funds, commercial banks, credit unions, finance companies, and even private citizens.

We'll try to sort out the alphabet soup for you by identifying and describing the most common loan types. Oh, and remember, when we say "mortgage" we mean mortgage or deed-of-trust loans; the programs for repayment are identical, only the names and foreclosure procedures differ.

The Fixed-Term, X Percent, Self-Destroying Loan

This is what used to be called a conventional mortgage when it was obtained from a lending institution without federal mortgage insurance. Today it is being called the long-term, fixed-rate mortgage, and it is still the most sought-after form among homebuyers.

The life of the mortgage is long, usually twenty, twenty-five, or thirty years and there is no call provision in the mortgage agreement. If you make your payments regularly, you can keep that mortgage as long as you own the house or until you pay it off. The interest rate on the day you make your first payment will be the interest rate when you make your last payment. The total amount of principal and interest in payment number one will be the same as payment number 230 or payment number 459. (Your total monthly payment, however, could go up if real estate taxes go up.) On a thirty-year loan, when you make payment number 460 you will own the property free and clear.

With tongue in cheek we've dubbed the loan "self-destroying" because the payments it requires eventually eliminate it. Among real estate professionals, bankers, and investors, such an agreement is called an amortizing or, more frequently, a self-liquidating loan. It offers maximum payment stability.

The FHA Variation

Until recently, all home mortgage loans insured by the Federal Housing Authority were long-term, fixed-rate, self-liquidating mortgages with interest rates set by the government (usually below the going market rate.) All that has changed, however.

Besides the fixed-rate, fixed-term loans, FHA adjustable rate mortgages have been established (more about them later), and more important, the government no longer sets the interest rate on its FHA insured loans. The rate is allowed to float with the market and may vary from city to city, even from one lender to another. So you must now shop for an FHA loan just as you would shop for an uninsured loan.

In the good old days, the relatively low government-fixed interest rate on FHA loans prompted lenders to charge discount points in order to make these loans profitable. The government responded by limiting the number of points to be charged the buyer to *one*, but it did not limit the number of points that could be charged a seller. An "FHA buyer" therefore often cost the seller several thousand dollars in mortgage points, an amount that was as often as not added to the purchase price. This inflating of the dollar figure that the seller would accept with an FHA mortgage caused a good deal of dickering, disillusion, and just plain anger, not to mention the number of deals that fell through because of it.

But all that is also history. With the elimination of government-regulated interest rates has come the elimination of point regulations. Today there is no limit on the number of points that can be charged to an FHA home buyer. In fact, the same lender may "price tag" different FHA mortgage arrangements with different numbers of points.

What remains of the old system is the insurance and the loan limits. Even the loan limits, however, have been softened. Once an FHA loan had a set dollar limit nationwide, for example, $67,000 maximum loan for a single family house. If the house you wanted to buy cost $100,000, with an FHA mortgage you would have to put down $33,000 and you were *not* allowed to take out a second mortgage to do so. Today the maximum loan amount is set in a range ($67,000 to $90,000 as of this writing), the exact figure for any given geographic area being determined by the average cost of a home in that area. Because FHA loans, theoretically at least, were established to help moderate income buyers, these loan limits are invariably at the lower end of the housing price scale.

So what's left of the old FHA loan system? The insurance. Because the Federal Housing Authority insures these mortgages, buyers can obtain the loans with minimal downpayments, sometimes as little as 3 percent of the purchase price. If the buyer defaults, the FHA insurance assures the lender of recouping the outstanding balance of the loan. But this insurance costs the buyer a fee (½ of 1 percent of the principal as of this writing) which is included in the monthly payment.

Even with all these changes, however, FHA loans are generally a good deal for homebuyers with minimal downpayments. But remember there are still strict income-to-carrying costs regulations and you must qualify to get the loan.

So where does one get an FHA loan? *Not* from the FHA. You must go to an approved FHA lender. But rest easy, most lending institutions are FHA approved. In fact, many lenders are now applying for a new special status which allows the lender to act on an FHA loan application (according to FHA guidelines, of course) without sending that application through the FHA-approval maze. Once this special status for lenders becomes not so special, that is, once most lenders have it, getting an FHA insured loan will take no longer than getting an uninsured loan. In the past, five or six weeks waiting time for approval was not unusual, even when uninsured loans were being approved in two to three weeks.

What all this change means is that FHA insured loans have become more like conventional bank loans. In fact, almost no one talks about conventional loans anymore.

The VA Variation

Loans guaranteed by the Veterans Administration are long-term, fixed-rate, self-liquidating mortgages and there is no insurance fee. The upper limit on the amount of the loan is flexible, dependent primarily upon the buyer's ability to carry the monthly payments. As of this writing, the origination fee to the buyer is still limited to *one* point, but there are rumblings of change in the future.

You must be an eligible veteran to obtain a VA loan or the widow of a veteran who died of a service-related injury. To check if you qualify, call your regional Veterans Administration office, listed in the phone book under United States Government. The VA also operates a free home counseling service at most of its regional offices. And it has a number of "good advice" booklets available. For more information, you may write: Veterans Benefits Office, Veterans Administration, 2033 M Street N.W., Washington, D. C. 20421.

VA mortgage loans are also made by "approved" lenders, but in times of very tight money or in areas where loans would not otherwise be available, some mortgage loans are made directly through the Veterans Administration.

At one time a qualified veteran could obtain a VA loan only once in his lifetime. The rule, however, has been changed, and repeat VA loans *are* available *if* the first loan is entirely paid off. The program effectively forces a choice between the benefits of loan assumability and the ability to reuse the program, for if you allow your VA mortgage loan to be assumed, it has not been paid off. You therefore cannot get another VA loan.

The Graduated Payment Variation

The FHA, the VA, and some private lenders all offer graduated payment mortgage loans in which both the term and the interest rate are fixed but the monthly payment changes over the years. It is lowest at the outset when the homebuyer theoretically has the lowest income and the most expenses. And it increases each year for a specified number of years (usually between five and ten). At that point, the payment remains fixed for the remainder of the term. The fixed payment that is finally reached is somewhat higher than one would calculate for the loan at the term and interest rate named because the later payments must compensate for the lower "early years" payments.

Adjustable Loans (commonly called ARMs for Adjustable Rate Mortgages)

Books and magazine articles published in 1981 were predicting the demise of the long-term, fixed-rate mortgage loan. Everything was to be "adjustable" in the future, they said. But the homebuying public didn't like the idea and the fixed rate loan has survived, albeit at a somewhat higher initial rate of interest than the ARMs now being so highly promoted.

What's the possible lure of an adjustable rate mortgage? It's that "teaser" interest rate. The interest rate at the outset of the mortgage may be from one to three or more points lower than a fixed rate loan. But beware, it can jump and jump over the following years! Remember, lenders are in the business of lending money to make money, and some ARMs are structured so that predetermined jumps in the interest rate will compensate the lender for that lean first year.

But we're getting ahead of ourselves. Let's look point by point at the most common possibilities for change in an adjustable loan:

1. *Rate changes.* Interest rates may go up or down. Rate changes are usually linked to a specified or chosen national index. You can and *should* ask your banker how this index has performed over the past months before deciding whether or not to hitch your monthly mortgage payment to it. Be sure that rate *decreases* as well as increases are linked to the index you choose; adjustable mortgages need not be adjustable one way only. Try also to have a rate-change ceiling *written* into the adjustable mortgage agreement. For example, if you start out at 12 percent, you might agree with your banker that your rate of interest will never go above 16 percent no matter what the national index does.

2. *Time interval of rate changes.* You don't want a mortgage payment that goes up and down every month or two. Even tenants have more stability than that! It is important therefore that you establish, *in writing*, exactly at what interval the adjustments will be made. Certainly the minimum interval should be six months; a year is better, especially if you suspect that rates might go up. Some agreements specify changes at two, three, or even five years.

3. *Amount of monthly installment payment.* The greatest fear of

homebuyers facing an adjustable loan is monthly payment increases. They fear that they might not be able to afford the huge jumps if interest rates were to "go crazy." And if they couldn't afford to pay the higher monthly mortgage payment, they could theoretically lose their house. In response to this concern, some lenders will set limitations (caps) upon the amount that monthly mortgage payments can be increased. Some even offer "fixed-payment" loans. They adjust the loan in other ways to compensate for the shortfall in the payment. Keep reading.

4. *Amount of principal.* If you agree to an adjustable rate loan with a *fixed* monthly payment (one that will not change over the term of the loan), you could, theoretically, owe more money than you originally borrowed when your mortgage matures in twenty years. It's true! If rates continue to increase or remain for a long term at a point higher than the rate at which you took out the loan, the extra money owed above each fixed monthly payment is added to the principal of the loan. This practice is called negative amortization. And then, of course, you also pay interest on the amount that has been added. The situation pyramids. If the lender is agreeable, ceilings on the maximum amount of increase of the principal can be written into the loan agreement.

5. *Term of the loan.* If the idea of owing more than you originally borrowed when your mortgage matures scares you, consider owing the same amount for longer. Instead of thirty years to pay out your mortgage, it may take you up to forty years of exactly the same monthly payments.

6. *Combination adjustments.* In some agreements the monthly payment remains fixed but both the principal and the term can be adjusted to compensate for short fall. This becomes more and more like paying rent.

Graduated Payment Adjustables

When a graduated payment schedule similar to that of a graduated payment fixed-rate mortgage is added to an adjustable mortgage loan, the relationship between the amount of your monthly payment and the gradual paying off of your loan is tenuous at best. How much does your current monthly payment fall short of the actual payment needed to pay out the loan in its stated term? How is that shortfall being handled? Does it increase the term, the principal, or the future amount of your monthly payment? And what happens to your graduated payment schedule if interest rates rise suddenly and stay high for two or three years?

Think about it: adjustable rate, adjustable term, adjustable principal, and adjustable monthly payment. You are truly at the mercy of the computer. To sleep at night, you must always believe that the right numbers are being fed into that computer and that its digestive system is working perfectly.

FHA Adjustable Rate Mortgages

FHA insurance of adjustable rate mortgages was approved by Congress in the fall of 1983, but the program did not become immediately available to the public since the rules under which the mortgages were to be offered had to be formulated and approved by Capitol Hill. As of the summer of 1984, FHA insured ARMs will have:

1. An annual adjustment of the interest rate.
2. Caps on the maximum allowable interest rate increase, currently no more than one percentage point each year.
3. A maximum allowable rate increase of five percentage points over the entire life of the loan.
4. No negative amortization allowed.

According to HUD, these rules have been designed "to remove some of the risks to mortgagors associated with the use of an ARM." Remember the mortgagor is the homebuyer. The HUD restrictions effectively protect the homebuyer and put some of the risk of future interest rate hikes back on the lender.

ARMs in the Future

Since it looks as though adjustable mortgages are here to stay, and in fact, will probably become the lending medium most prevalent in end-of-the-century homebuying, there has been a cry for a firming up of their variables and a clarifying of their options. A subcommittee of the House of Representatives held hearings on the problem during the summer of 1984.

At one of those hearings, David O. Maxwell, chairman and chief executive officer of Fannie Mae (Federal National Mortgage Association) said, "Existing disclosure requirements do not help consumers understand the many features of ARMs. Explanations of the terms and provisions are highly technical and confusing, and basic features of the loan agreement are often buried in the documentation."

The government is responding, though slowly, it seems. Among the suggestions now being considered by our legislators are:

• required interest rate or payment caps

- limits on initial interest rate discounts (the "teaser" rates)
- limits on negative amortization
- uniform disclosure forms

Which of these suggestions will become regulations remains to be seen. Meanwhile shop for ARMs carefully and if you don't understand *everything* in the written loan agreement, get professional help before you sign.

More Creative Financing

During the past five years or so, when a real estate agent talked about creative financing he or she usually meant seller-assisted financing. But there are other alternative financing methods, some new and creative, some not new at all. We can't possibly get into all the variations here, so we've selected those that have been around for a while and/or those that seem likely to be around for a while longer.

Straight Mortgages

Straight mortgages are commonly used in commercial real estate, rarely in home financing, and even more rarely when the home is financed by an institutional lender. Your most likely candidate for a straight mortgage money lender is the homeseller.

This is the simplest of all mortgage agreements. The borrower agrees to pay back the amount he is borrowing on an agreed upon date sometime in the future. Meanwhile he pays interest on the money. The interest can be paid monthly, quarterly, semiannually, or annually. When the term of the mortgage is up, the entire principal is due and payable. Your payments have *not* reduced the amount you borrowed. Some real estate professionals and borrowers call this arrangement an interest-only mortgage.

Balloons

Bright colored things that go pop! No, seriously, balloon mortgages are somewhat risky because on a given date they do exactly that, pop.

When you take out a balloon mortgage, you agree to make a given monthly payment which will amortize your loan over, say, thirty or even forty years. But on a named date five, ten, or any named number of years in the future, the entire unpaid balance of the loan (which is usually almost all of it) becomes due and payable. In other words, pay up, refinance, or lose the property.

Balloon mortgages are a good way to keep monthly housing costs to a minimum if you are rather certain of a company transfer or self-initiated sale well within the period of the balloon.

Roll-Overs

You might call the roll-over a mixed breed, a cross between a fixed-rate long-term loan, an adjustable rate loan, and a balloon. Indeed a kind of shaggy dog.

When you take out a roll-over loan, you make payments at a fixed rate of interest that would amortize that loan over, say, thirty years. The catch is that at the end of a named period of time, usually three, five, or seven years, the entire balance of the principal is due and payable just as in a balloon. But here's the roll-over and adjustable-rate part. The borrower has the option at that time to renew the loan at the *current* rate of interest, usually for a term of the same length as the first roll-over term. There are usually no additional fees for this refinancing, and the borrower continues to make payments that will eventually liquidate his loan.

The roll-over offers the borrower the security of knowing that some form of financing will be available when the roll-over date comes up no matter what the national economic picture. The interest rate of that financing, however, is completely beyond his control, unless, of course, certain caps and conditions are written into the loan agreement.

Wraparounds

Wraparounds, sometimes called all-inclusive mortgages, have been around since the depression days of the thirties but usually surface as a popular means of financing only in times of tight or expensive money. They are really a kind of second mortgage, but offer maximum safety to the second mortgage lender and usually an excellent rate of return. They can save the borrower money too.

To understand how wraparounds work, think of a great green python wrapping around a home mortgage, swallowing it whole, and then waiting contentedly until that first mortgage is gradually digested. You prefer working with numbers, you say. OK, here goes.

Beauregard has just inherited a good deal of money and has decided to sell his house. There's a $75,000 balance on his mortgage on that house and its appraised value is $100,000. After two weeks on the market at an asking price of $115,000, he is offered $110,000 by an up-and-coming young physician named Sandra who has excellent income but only $10,000 ready cash. She might be able to get a new first mortgage with private mortgage insurance, but the interest rate and the cost of the insurance is high. A wraparound would be beneficial to both Beauregard and Sandra.

Beauregard has his attorney write up a wraparound for $100,000 at 11 percent interest (a full point below the going rate for a first mortgage in the area). He notifies Sandra that this financing is being offered "subject to" a first mortgage on the property at 8 percent interest with a balance of $75,000. Thus she is informed of the existence of that first mortgage, but she is *not* responsible for making payments on it. She makes her monthly payments directly to Beauregard, who uses a part of each payment to make his old mortgage payment and *keeps the difference*. (Very profitable!)

Sandra benefits by getting financing for her purchase at a rate below market and she protects herself against mortgage problems by having a clause written into the mortgage agreement. In the event Beauregard fails to make payments on the first mortgage, she may assume those payments and pay Beauregard only the difference between that payment and the scheduled payment on the wrap.

Beauregard benefits by lending $75,000 *that is not his* at a rate of interest 3 percentage points above the rate that he is paying for the use of the money! And if Sandra defaults on the second mortgage (the wraparound), he can reclaim the property and continue to make the first mortgage payments.

Wraparounds can be the financing of choice in certain circumstances; even some banks and savings institutions write them occasionally. But they are not for novices. If you are considering entering into a wraparound as a borrower or a lender, get yourself the finest legal advice you can find. And most important of all, read the first mortgage carefully. *You cannot use a wraparound mortgage when there is a legally enforceable due-on-sale clause in the first mortgage.*

Zero Interest Rate Mortgages and Buy-Downs

Both of these creative financing plans are the brain children of builders facing the dismal homeselling market of the early 1980s. As times have gotten better, they have virtually disappeared. We include them here only because times might just "go bad" again someday, and then the plans will resurface.

In a zero interest rate situation, a builder offers to finance the new home he is selling for a short term, usually three to five years, at no interest. Usually the buyer must put down at least 50 percent and the periodic payments (monthly or quarterly) which will pay out the entire balance of the purchase price are very high. Such a zero interest rate plan is an option usually open only to the wealthy. And beware. Sometimes the builder raises the price of the property to carry the cost of lending the unpaid balance. If there is such an increase, it is *not* tax-deductible since it is not interest.

In contrast, a buy-down has its primary appeal to people of more modest income. In times when money is expensive, the builder goes to a banker and pays a lump sum in cash to induce the lender to offer two or three years of financing at an interest rate several points below what is generally being charged. This is perfectly legal. The builder is essentially paying interest in advance.

The danger for the homebuyer is that the interest rate may jump like a firecracker once the buy-down period is over. If qualification to carry the mortgage payments was marginal or if the buyer hits upon hard times, he could be unable to meet the payments at the new interest rate and could possibly lose the property.

Should You Ever Consider Refinancing Your Home?

YES, if . . .

You have an adjustable rate mortgage without a cap on the interest rate and adjustables *with a cap* or fixed rate mortgages are available in your area without extraordinary points or mortgage origination fees.

You have a fixed rate mortgage and

(1) interest rates are currently two full percentage points or more below the rate on your mortgage,

(2) the amount you must pay in points and/or origination fees will be "made up" in savings at the new interest rate within three to five years, and

(3) you plan to continue to own the property indefinitely.

You have a balloon mortgage which will come due within the next three years and interest rates are currently at particularly favorable levels.

You are now paying off more principal than interest in your monthly mortgage payment and you have calculated that a higher annual interest payment (tax deductible) combined with the investment of a portion of your equity elsewhere will be financially rewarding, *despite the costs incurred by refinancing.*

NO, if . . .

You can get a second mortgage for needed funds while keeping a low-interest-rate (below 10 percent) first mortgage.

You plan to sell your property within five years. (Even if you are paying as much as three full percentage points more than the current rate, it is unlikely that you will recoup the up-front costs of refinancing before you sell.)

You have an adjustable rate mortgage with a cap and fixed rate mortgages are only a point (or two or three) below the rate at which you originally took out your adjustable rate mortgage. (*Unless* you are willing to pay several thousand in up-front cash for the security of a fixed-rate/fixed term loan. But remember, it will take years and years before you make up your refinancing costs through interest-rate-incurred savings on your monthly payments.)

OR, if you're still at "maybe" . . .

Many lenders across the country are now providing a free service for their borrowers. They will run a mortgage through their computer and tell the homeowner how much faster he or she can pay off that loan by increasing payments $10 or $20 or so a month, and how much interest will be saved with higher payments. Bi-weekly payments are another possibility. Check with the lender holding *your* mortgage.

Growing Equity Mortgage

Growing equity mortgages are often called GEMs. A GEM is a fixed-rate loan which banks are often willing to write at a below market interest rate because its term is relatively short. When you mortgage with a GEM, your payment *increases* each year (usually by 3 percent or so). All of the increase, however, is applied to paying off the principal. As a result, the loan is usually paid out (and the property all yours) in about fifteen years.

Shared Appreciation Mortgage

Consumers did not like SAM, and as of this writing it's hibernating. Briefly, the lender offered interest rates at considerably below the market and sometimes added the enticement of low monthly payments in return for a share in the capital appreciation of the property upon its sale. Usually the lender wanted a 30 to 50 percent share of the profit. And often the homebuyer was required to sell at the time specified in the agreement. If he didn't, he could be liable for the dollar amount of the lender's share of the new appraised value. It's as sticky as flypaper!

Shared Equity Mortgage (Partnership Mortgage)

In this type of creative financing the mortgage loan is one of the ordinary kinds made by an ordinary lending institution, but the borrower/homebuyer has an absentee partner (one who does not live in the house). This partner usually provides all or some of the downpayment money and sometimes helps with the monthly payments. Such a partner can be an investor paired with the homebuyer by a real estate broker's computer. Or, much more often, the partner can be a relative of the homebuyer.

"What's new about that?" you ask. "Mom and Dad have been providing downpayment money for decades."

True, but only recently (December 1981) has the Internal Revenue Service recognized that such generosity can also be an investment. There are some good tax breaks available here for the partner, and the homebuyer doesn't fare too badly either. But wrinkles are still being ironed out of the tax procedures and many questions still do not have clear answers. You will need the advice of an attorney and a tax counselor on this one. Especially with such questions as "How much rent does the homebuyer pay to the investor for the use of the investor's share of the house?" And don't forget the basics like: Who decides when to sell the property? And for how much? And how is the capital gain divided between the homebuyer and the partner?

Shared equity financing *can* work, but be sure to get competent professional advice in drafting the written agreement.

The Reserve Account Mortgage

This is another innovation for homebuyers who have little or no downpayment. In this financing plan, *someone* (it could be the seller, the builder, the real estate agent, a relative, anyone) deposits a named amount (let's say 5 percent of the appraised value of the property) into an interest-bearing account with the lending institution that will give the mortgage loan. This money cannot be withdrawn since it is used as a kind of temporary equity fund on the buyer's behalf. If the homebuyer defaults on his loan, the lender can appropriate the reserve account monies to defray foreclosure costs. If, however, the homebuyer makes his payments on time for a number of years (let's say three or more), the money in the reserve account will be released to the person who originally deposited it, *with interest*.

Reserve account loans can be arranged with little or no downpayment, they usually do not require private mortgage insurance, and their interest rates are comparable to other available mortgages. There is usually, however, a point or mortgage origination fee.

Some experts are predicting that reserve account mortgages will be the most popular home financing plan of the decade. Time will tell.

What's Ahead?

Who knows! There are almost as many predictions as there are experts. But be assured that as long as people want to buy houses, they will actively seek ways to finance their purchases. And as long as the lending of money is profitable, there will be lenders exploring ways to lend money to homebuyers. Those plans that benefit both borrower and lender, or those that are about equally painful to both, will most likely survive. Judge among them carefully, and read the next chapter to find out how and where to get your money.

For More Information

"The Mortgage Money Guide," published by the Federal Trade Commission, is an excellent overview of currently available mortgages. To obtain a copy, request booklet 418 M from Consumer Information Center, Pueblo, Colo. 81009. Price: 50 cents.

"Fannie Mae's Consumer Guide to Adjustable Rate Mortgages" is a clear and comprehensive explanation of adjustables. It can be obtained free from: Federal National Mortgage Association, Fannie Mae's Consumer Guide to Adjustable Rate Mortgages, P.O. Box 23867, Baltimore, Md. 21203.

The New Mortgage Game, by Robert Irwin (McGraw-Hill, 1982), is an excellent in-depth guide to financing real estate, although some rules, regulations, and statistics in this book are now out of date.

Inexpensive books containing mortgage payment tables showing the monthly payment necessary to pay out your loan at different interest rates and over different terms are available at most book stores. Look in the business section. Be aware, however, that when the variables of adjustable rate mortgages enter the picture the numbers you see on the page may not be exactly those presented to you by your lender.

Getting the Money

The days of applying for your first home mortgage loan at the savings bank where you used to deposit the rolls of quarters saved from the tips on your newspaper route are *not* gone! Local savings banks still give preferential treatment to their long-time depositors. But there are also many other possible lenders in today's home financing marketplace. And a little shopping time might just save a good deal more than all the rolled quarters you ever dreamed of.

First you need to know who these lenders are and what they are offering. Then you must choose the best mortgage plan for your particular needs. And finally you will want to be prepared for the mortgage application interview.

Where to Hunt Mortgage Money
Mutual Savings Banks and Savings and Loan Associations

Mutual savings banks are becoming fewer as some of their number convert to stock companies and others are absorbed through mergers. They, along with savings and loan associations, were once the foremost source (in some areas the only source) of home financing in the nation. The financial fluctuations of the early eighties, however, almost put many of them out of business.

Savings banks are healthier now and lending again, but more cautiously. Most would prefer to write shorter-term loans (car loans, for example, or second mortgages), but the demand for mortgage money is still great. And if there is a demand, business will usually try to fill it (profitably, of course).

Savings banks are usually quieter than their big commercial brothers, but don't fail to check them out even if you're attracted to the bigger newspaper ads or jolly radio jingles of other lenders.

Commercial Banks

New to the home mortgage field, commercial banks have money to lend and sometimes very favorable terms to offer. Don't overlook them.

Credit Unions

Credit unions are another newcomer to the home mortgage field, although they are still much more involved in home improvement loans and second mortgage loans.

Finance Companies

When they are affiliated with or wholly owned by large real estate agencies or franchises, home financing *is* their business.

Government Agencies

When mortgage money is not otherwise available, the Veterans Administration will make direct loans to qualified veterans. The Farmers Home Administration (FmHA) has several direct loan programs available in rural areas.

Mortgage Bankers

Mortgage bankers are companies that qualify applicants, find the best available loans, fund the initial loan, and then sell to or place that loan with another lender or investor.

You've probably heard, for example, that life insurance companies hold large portfolios of home mortgages. But why don't you ever hear of anyone applying to an insurance company for a loan? Because the insurance companies buy the vast majority of their mortgages in the secondary mortgage market, often from mortgage bankers. And insurance companies are but one example of the huge lending business. Mortgage bankers are an important part of it.

Even after a mortgage banker has sold or placed your loan, you will usually continue to make your monthly payments to that mortgage-banker company. They collect a servicing fee, which is profitable to them.

Mortgage Brokers

A mortgage broker is a person or company who, for a fee, will find a lender. (They become more numerous in times of very tight money.) They do not, however, lend money and you must still pay all the application and processing fees for the mortgage loan. Those fees are *in addition* to what you pay the mortgage broker to find you that loan.

Sellers

Sellers are rarely the first mortgage lender of choice. Most sellers want their money much sooner than the usual thirty years. They are, however, a good source of second mortgage or short-term loans.

Questions to Ask the Lenders
When Shopping for a Loan

Mortgage shopping is truly a time to "let your fingers do the walking." It is most effectively done by phone, especially in the early stages of comparing one lender to another.

When you call each lender, ask to speak to someone about a new mortgage. When you are connected, introduce yourself and say that you are planning to buy a home soon and that you would like some information about home financing.

Except in times of incredibly tight money, loan officers are happy to talk with prospective borrowers. Lending money, after all, is the business of the bank. If the bank doesn't have any borrowers, it doesn't have any customers. And then it can't make any money.

Think of yourself, therefore, as a customer. Ask the following questions pleasantly, slowly, and clearly. And be sure you understand the answers. If you don't, stop and ask the loan officer to explain further.

1. *What types of financing are available?* You want to know if the lender is offering both fixed rate and adjustable plans. Are FHA and VA mortgages available? Is private mortgage insurance being used? Are balloons available? Roll-overs?

2. *What are the current interest rates for each type of loan?* You will be surprised at how much interest rates can differ among different mortgaging plans, to say nothing of how much they differ among different lenders.

3. *How long a term are you offering on the various types of mortgage loans?* Ask if the term is fixed on adjustable rate loans or if

it can be lengthened if your payments fall short of the required amount at a higher interest rate. Ask if there is a lower rate of interest available for shorter-term loans; sometimes fifteen- or twenty-year mortgages rate a quarter of a percent or more off the going rate.

4. *What is the minimum downpayment required for each type of loan?*

5. *Is there a limit on the loan amount?* Some lenders set limits on the amount of money they will lend on residential property; others limit their loans only by a loan-to-value ratio. Government agencies do set limits on the loans they insure.

6. *What guidelines does the lender use for loan qualification?* Is the lender holding to the old 25 percent of your gross income for housing costs rule-of-thumb or has the number inched up closer to 30 percent. Or is the lender using the more modern income-to-monthly-debt-payment ratio? More about this under "How Much Can You Borrow?"

7. *Are points being charged? How many for each kind of mortgage?*

8. *Is there a loan origination fee? Does it differ for the different types of financing?*

9. *Is there an application fee? How much?* Remember these are nonrefundable and cannot be applied to any other expense.

10. *Is there an appraisal fee? How much?*

11. *Is there a credit check fee? How much?*

12. *Are there any other fees?*

13. *Is there a prepayment penalty on any of the loans?* This is an important question if you face the possibility of transfer or if you think interest rates might go down in the near future and you might then want to refinance.

14. *Does the lender have preferred customer benefits?* Some lenders actually lower the interest rates on mortgage loans if the borrower makes use of other banking services being offered—charge accounts, savings accounts, checking accounts, etc.

15. *How long will a mortgage decision take after application is made?* This question may become crucial if you need a quick closing. Some lenders will give you an answer in a week or two. Three to five weeks is a more common waiting period, however, especially in a busy market.

16. *How long will a mortgage loan commitment be effective?* Some banks will make a commitment for ninety days, with renewals available. Some will make commitments for up to six months, especially on

new construction. The question of how long the commitment holds may become crucial if you are scheduled for a distant closing date, or (more likely) if your closing should be postponed several times.

17. *Does the interest rate remain constant on the loan commitment?* Some lenders are willing to give a borrower a commitment for a mortgage loan, but that loan will be written at the interest rate prevailing at the time of closing (somewhat risky in a time of fluctuating interest rates). Some lenders will guarantee the rate, but if rates go down before you close, they will hold you to the original rate. To get a better deal, you will have to reapply for a loan somewhere else, and application fees may well wipe out the interest rate advantage! And then there are banking's "good fellows." These lenders will guarantee the "best" rate. If interest rates go up before your closing date, they will stay with the rate at which they make their commitment to you. If interest rates are down on your closing date, however, they will write your mortgage loan at the lower rate.

18. *Is there a late payment fee?* You may hesitate to ask this question for fear it will make you look bad, but remember you are just a voice on the phone, not even an applicant yet. And it's better to know, just in case. . . .

To mortgage shop effectively, you should call at least six lenders in your area (more if you have the time and are determined to get the best possible deal) and ask each one the same questions. Once you've done so, however, you've accomplished nothing. Nothing, that is, unless you summarize and compare the data you have collected. This takes still more time and patience, but it's very unlikely that anyone else will do as good a job as you yourself.

On pages 336–337 is a model for an individual survey sheet. Add any other questions you may think of and make one up for each lender you plan to call.

When you have completed your survey, make up a comparison sheet of the best loans for your needs (there's a model on page 338). *Now* you can talk knowledgeably, realistically, and unemotionally about which lender has the best loan program for you.

A word about "unemotionally." Ideally, mortgage shopping should be done while you are still hunting for the right house. If you wait to begin your mortgage shopping until you are under time pressure to get a mortgage commitment for your dream house, you will not shop unemotionally. In fact, the very first plan someone offers to you with the words, "I'm sure we can get this for you . . . " might sound pretty good.

The Mortgage in Your Life

"What's the best mortgage loan?" may turn out to be one of the questions that characterize this decade. In the mid 1980s it's not unusual for one lender to offer five, seven, ten, or *more* different mortgaging programs at interest rates that might range over three full percentage points. And is there a town in the nation with only *one* lender within easy reach?

If the homebuyer isn't exactly a kid in a candy store, he or she *is* a person faced with decision. And it's a decision among many possible choices. Besides as much knowledge and understanding of the programs as possible, the most important key to the right decision is changing the question. Ask instead: "What's the best mortgage loan *for me?*"

A loan program just right for Dick and Jane may be all wrong for Jennifer and Keith, and vice versa. While everyone would like to turn back the clock to the good old days of 8 percent loans, there has been one positive benefit from the financial turmoil of 1980/81: home mortgaging is no longer a one-lane road. So shop not only for the best interest rate and cash outlay, but also for the best terms for your particular needs.

Just like deciding which house you want to buy, deciding which mortgage you want to buy it *with* is ultimately a decision you will have to make *for yourself*. Yes, gather all the advice, professional and otherwise, that you can, but think your own thoughts and make your own choice. The following sketches are just a few illustrations of how and why some homebuyers choose particular programs.

Fixed Monthly Payment: Adjustable Interest Rate,
Adjustable Principal, Adjustable Term

Why would anyone choose a mortgage where the interest rate could go up at any time resulting not in a higher monthly payment but in more money owed to the lender and/or a longer time to owe it? Read on.

When Marilyn and Peter were ready to buy a home, interest rates were high and home prices rather depressed. Together the couple had saved a rather large downpayment, but they needed to live securely on Peter's salary alone. Marilyn was pregnant and wanted to give at least ten years to raising a family before even considering another job. The couple therefore was seeking the most house they could buy for the lowest possible monthly payment, a payment which would remain constant for at least ten years. At that point, if

Model For Lender Survey Sheet

Lender_____

Address_____ Phone_____

Types of financing:

Questions:

Current interest rates					
Term					
Minimum downpayment					
Limit on loan amount					
Loan qualification guidelines					
Points					
Loan origination fee					
Application fee					
Appraisal fee					
Credit check fee					
Other fees (list)					
Prepayment penalty					
Preferred customer benefits					
Time needed for decision of lender					

Questions:						
Length of loan commitment (number of days)						
Renewable?						
Rate guarantee on commitment (if any)						
Late payment penalty						

Notes and comments: _____

_____

_____

_____

_____

Summary:
The best offering(s) for us seems to be:

Cost of obtaining the loan: (add together all the fees payable at the closing) $ _____ $ _____ $ _____ $ _____

Monthly cost of carrying the loan: (Use mortgage tables to find the principal and interest payment at the named rate of interest for the named term. Or enter the lender's figure for fixed payments on an adjustable loan. Add mortgage insurance premiums, if any.) $ _____ $ _____ $ _____ $ _____

Model for Lender Comparison Sheet

	Cost of obtaining the loan	Monthly carrying costs
Lender 1_____ (name)		
Loan_____	$_____	$_____
Loan_____	$_____	$_____
Loan_____	$_____	$_____
Lender 2_____		
Loan_____	$_____	$_____
Loan_____	$_____	$_____
Loan_____	$_____	$_____
Lender 3_____		
Loan_____	$_____	$_____
Loan_____	$_____	$_____
Loan_____	$_____	$_____

Marilyn chooses to return to work, they might just consider buying a larger or prettier house.

"OK, a mortgage with a fixed monthly payment is a must, but why not a fixed-rate mortgage?" you ask. Because the interest rate on the fixed-rate loan was two full points above the current rate on an adjustable loan. Choosing a fixed-rate loan therefore would mean that the couple could afford to borrow less money. Also Peter was betting that rates would come down.

If interest rates do come down while Marilyn and Peter own their house, the extra in their fixed payment will be applied to paying off the principal of their loan. If rates go up, however, Marilyn and

Peter won't feel any pain until they sell their house in ten years. At that time they will owe more than they would have owed had they been making payments on a fixed-rate loan. "But," says Marilyn, "we're quite sure that the house will have appreciated enough to cover the extra money owed and still give us a nice profit."

Fixed Rate, Long Term

This is the financing plan for security and stability. Chuck is 38, Sylvia 40. They have three children and four cats. Chuck is an engineer with a major corporation. He has done well over the past twelve years, but he feels strongly that there is little opportunity for further promotion. He'll get some raises as time goes by, certainly, but no big salary jumps. Since Sylvia has recently returned to work as a secretary, their combined salaries qualify them to carry the higher payments on a bigger house. They do not want to face the possibility of still higher payments in the future, however.

They have chosen a fixed-rate, long-term mortgage at 1½ percentage points above the prevailing rate for an adjustable loan because they want the security of knowing what their payment will be and how much they'll owe at the end of ten, twenty, or twenty-nine years. They have no intention of selling their home or moving in the forseeable future. "We might just stay here long enough to pay off the mortgage," muses Chuck.

Yes, if interest rates on fixed-rate loans should ever drop three or more points, Chuck and Sylvia would probably refinance. But neither of them thinks the possibility too likely.

Adjustable Rate, Fixed Term, No Negative Amortization

For some people such a loan means living dangerously. "What if rates go up and we can't afford to make the payments?" they ask and bite their fingernails. And it's true, they're in trouble.

Leonard, however, isn't worried about monthly payments. Only 20 percent of his gross salary goes towards housing costs since he rents out one room of his house (with kitchen privileges). "If the rates go up, I can afford it" he says. "And if they go down I get a break without all the hassle and expense of refinancing."

But Leonard is less a gambler than his bravado makes him out to be. He chose his adjustable-rate loan carefully. After doing some rather thorough research, he found a lender who was willing to tie the interest rate on his adjustable rate mortgage to a national index that had performed consistently for over two years. Interest rates tied to it were well below the prime lending rate. Yes, his interest rate might go up, but he was pretty sure that he'd be getting a better deal than most people. And he liked the idea that his payments were gradually diminishing the principal. If he stayed in the house, he would one day own it free and clear.

On the other hand, there was the possibility that he might not stay. And this adjustable-rate mortgage held a bonus there too. *Because* the rate was adjustable, the lender had been willing to make the loan assumable. If Leonard were to decide to sell in a time when mortgage money was hard to get, he could advertise his assumable loan with its interest rate tied to a very well-behaved index. Or, still better, if he didn't need all of his equity from the sale, he would have the opportunity of writing a wraparound mortgage agreement since his original loan contained no due-on-sale clause. That could be very profitable indeed.

Ten-Year Balloon with a Forty-Year Payout Schedule

"Anyone who chooses this loan has to be crazy or a crap shooter!" you think. "Good grief! On a forty-year payout, you've barely made a dent in the principal at the end of ten years. You'd have to repay almost the whole amount you borrowed in one lump sum. What if you couldn't refinance? You could lose the house!"

All true, but losing the house is unlikely. Some arrangement for refinancing can usually be made. You may not like the rate and terms, but some arrangement. . . .

John and Carol are not worried about refinancing, however. When they bought their 5-bedroom house their children were ages 15, 12, and 6.

"How nice it will be to have a guest room" thought Carol, but she really meant "a guest room at a price we can afford!"

The forty year payout schedule brought their monthly payment on a 5-bedroom house to a figure lower than the thirty-year monthly payment on a 4-bedroom house. And the balloon payment requirement was not a cause for concern.

"Look," said John, "in ten years our older children will be 25 and 22, adults, on their own. That leaves three of us in a 5-bedroom house. We'll rattle around like marbles in a coffee can. I figure we'll keep this house somewhere between six and eight years. Then we'll sell and move into something smaller."

The ten-year balloon with a long payout schedule is also appealing to young executives who are quite certain that they will be transferred well within the term of the balloon.

Fixed-Rate, Graduated Payment VA Loan

Eddie and Sue were high school sweethearts; now they're both dentists. And both of them went through dental school on army scholarship programs. The army paid for their educations, and they each owed the army a three year enlistment. Now that they're back to civilian life, they're heavily in debt to the dental equipment companies who helped them to furnish their mutual office in their home town, and they also want a home of their own.

A year into private practice, their savings amounted to pocket change but their income, right from the start, was excellent. Either one of them would have qualified for a no downpayment VA mortgage. They chose the graduated payment plan because they believed that their practice would continue to grow and their incomes to increase. Life was lovely indeed.

You don't have to be a dentist to choose a VA or FHA mortgaging plan (although you must be a qualified vet for VA or the widow of a veteran who died of a service-related injury). If you will only take care to choose a house that you truly can afford, you can buy it with nothing down (VA) or as little as 5 percent down (FHA). And if you prefer not to use a government-backed plan, you can get a graduated payment privately insured mortgage through a great many lenders, again with as little as 5 percent down.

Assumption with a Second Mortgage

Helen and Norman stumbled upon an assumable mortgage from a state-chartered lender at 8 percent with twenty-three years left on its term! The problem? They had $30,000 in downpayment money and the seller had $50,000 in equity, which left Helen and Norman $20,000 short of the assumption. The seller offered them a wrap-around mortgage at 11 percent (the going rate for new fixed-rate financing was 13 percent).

Instead, Helen and Norman chose to assume the 8 percent loan and finance the additional $20,000 through a short-term second mortgage for five years at 15 percent. Things would be tough for those five years, they figured. Almost all of Helen's income would go toward paying out the second mortgage. But after it was paid, they would live easily for the next eighteen years *with an 8 percent loan*. The big reduction in housing costs would come two years before they needed money for college tuition. Perfect timing.

The problem with most short-term second mortgages is the high monthly payment required. If you can come up with the money,

---

Comparing Loan Offerings

"It's a Question of Savings"

When comparing one mortgage with another remember to weigh the monthly carrying costs of your loan against the up-front cost of obtaining that loan. Let's look at one simple example.

One lender (let's call him Red) is offering you a fixed-rate loan at a ½ percent lower interest rate than anyone else. That ½ percent for you on your $50,000 mortgage means approximately $19 a month savings. But Red is charging 3 points at closing whereas his closest competitor (let's call him Blue) is charging only a $250 loan origination fee. Three points equals $1500. At closing, therefore, Red's loan costs $1250 more than Blue's loan. At a rate of $19 a month savings, it will take you roughly five and a half years just to get even. (And that's not even considering tax angles or what you could have done with an extra $1250 on closing day.)

Is it worthwhile to go with Red's lower interest rate? Probably, if this is your dream home and you intend to stay there into retirement. Maybe, if you're pretty sure you'll stay until your seven-year-old goes to college. No, if you think your company will transfer you within five years or if you are buying a starter home which you plan to sell when you upgrade in a few years.

---

however, the assumption with a second mortgage is usually much cheaper in the end than the wraparound.

The GEM

The growing equity mortgage (GEM) is not for everyone since payments increase *every year*, and that's not even considering the possibility of property tax increases. You do, however, own your property free and clear at the end of fifteen years or so.

Martha saw the GEM as the perfect plan for her. At 38, she had just finished her MBA, had a new job with a major corporation, and had been divorced for two years. Child support payments from her business executive husband would cease when their youngest child graduated from college at 22 (not quite coincidentally in fifteen years).

During that time, Martha felt that she would be in line for pay increases at work and probably at least one promotion. At age 53, she figured, she would be free to enjoy the good life with only the maintenance fee on her condominium and its real estate taxes as her housing costs.

But what if something disrupted this well-defined life plan? Job loss, transfer, illness, remarriage? Well, if life doesn't go quite as scheduled, you can handle a GEM just like any other mortgage. No mortgage agreement is carved in granite. If increasing payments become a burden, Martha can refinance with a fixed payment, or even a graduated payment loan. If life changes call for a move, Martha can sell the condo and pay off the mortgage.

Questions the Lender Will Ask You

When you've done all your homework and chosen the lender and the loan, the tables turn. Now you want very much for the lender to choose you. In other words, you want to qualify for your mortgage loan.

Sitting across the desk from a loan officer is unnerving to everyone (even if the applicant is buying his or her fifth home, each a little better than the last). You will feel more comfortable in the applicant's chair, however, if you know in advance the questions that will be asked of you and have the answers at hand. Let's go through the most common qualification questions.

Your Name, Etc.

"My name!" you say. "Good grief! We're starting at the preprimer level."

Pardon. No insult was intended. We just wanted to remind you that you should enter the full *legal* name of each and every co-owner of the property on the application form. If your legal name is Casimir Jones and you write Casey Jones on your mortgage application, the approval process can be held up for days upon days as computers doing credit checks and employment verifications print out their inability to find a Casey Jones in their memory banks.

And don't forget to include the name, address, employment information, and all other pertinent answers to the following questions for your spouse or any other person buying the property with you. Mortgage qualification must weigh the incomes of all prospective owners equally.

How Much Mortgage Can You Afford?

Even in this age of computers, every mortgage loan is still individually approved or disapproved. There is always an element of subjective judgment in that decision. The following qualification guidelines therefore are just that: *guidelines*. They differ from one lender to another and often from one mortgaging situation to another.

Gross Income Formula
This is the old-fashioned way but it is still used by some hometown lenders. Ten years ago most lenders would lend two times an applicant's gross annual income. For example, if you made $20,000 a year, you could get a mortgage loan of $40,000. In the past few years, however, many of those lenders that are still using this qualification formula are allowing 2½ or even 3 times gross annual income.

Income to Housing Costs Formula
In this qualification procedure, the anticipated housing expenses are computed. These include mortgage payment, real estate taxes, fire and catastrophe insurance, and mortgage insurance, if any. To qualify with many lenders, the total monthly figure for housing expenses must not exceed 25 percent of the gross monthly income of the applicant(s). For example, if you make $2000 a month, your housing expenses should not exceed $500. As a result of the housing and interest rate spiral, however, some lenders now approve loans when housing costs amount to as much as 29 percent of monthly income.

Income to Long-Term Debt Payment Formula
Today's newest and most widely used qualification guideline evaluates a broader financial demand upon the borrower. Rather than monthly housing costs alone, all of the borrower's long-term (ten months or more) debt payments are calculated. Included are car payments, large outstanding charge account balances, child support payments, and alimony payments. To qualify with most lenders, the total monthly payment for housing expenses *and* long-term debts should not exceed 36 percent of the gross monthly income of the applicant(s). Some lenders go to 39 percent; a few hold out below 36 percent.

How Much?
As you calculate how much mortgage you can probably afford, please remember that a mortgage lender is *not* concerned with how comfortable you will be living in the home you want to buy. The lender is concerned *only* with protecting his loan, his goal being to write a loan that will be repaid *on schedule* and without the threat of foreclosure. If you are a good credit risk, a loan with a rather high monthly payment may well be approved. Remember, therefore, that you too must make a loan decision. Ultimately *you* are the person who must decide how much of your income you are willing to commit to housing.

Your Dependents
The lender wants to know how many people must live on the income that you are reporting.

Your Employment
List the current employer of you and your spouse or co-owner. If you have been employed there for less than a year, the lender will probably ask for previous employment. In some situations, you will be asked to list your complete employment history. Try to have the name and telephone number of the person to contact for employment verification with you when you fill out the loan application. Also have your social security number and payroll number.

If your income includes commissions, bonuses, or overtime, be sure that the person who will verify your employment is aware of these income sources. You do not want a flat hourly wage reported as your total income. And if a part-time job is a regular part of your life and its salary will help you to qualify for your loan, by all means list it on your application form.

And for young marrieds: remember that the loan officer interviewing you is *not* allowed to ask if "the little woman" intends to continue working if and after the couple decides to have children.

If you are self-employed, the employment verification process is a little more complicated. You will have to provide proof of income to the lender. Sometimes copies of two years' federal income tax returns is sufficient. Sometimes the lender will ask for the name of your accountant.

Other Income

You can list child support, alimony, or public assistance payments. And how about rental income from your vacation home? Money you make from the purchase and sale of antiques? You may think of garage sale antiquing as a hobby, but if you do it regularly and sell much of what you buy at a profit, it's a business. Do you lecture occasionally? Collect royalties? Take care of children in your home on school holidays? "Other income" is just that, *other* income; list all of it.

Your Assets

You may not think that the six rooms of furniture and two cars you own are relevant to a mortgage loan, but in marginal decisions, they are. The lender wants to know that you will not be faced with a sudden, heavy debt loan right after you take on your mortgage payments.

And it goes without saying that the balance in your savings account(s) and any securities (stocks and bonds) should be listed. Have your bank account and brokerage firm account numbers available to speed up the verification process.

If you own other real estate, list it under assets. If that real estate is a home you are selling, say so and bring the name of the mortgage holder and your account number. If you have a buyer for that home with a signed contract, say that too, it counts for a big plus. If your other real estate is an income property, be sure to list the monthly or annual income from it. It will count toward your loan qualification.

Don't forget any mortgages or second mortgages that you hold. List the monthly or annual income. And trust accounts from which you collect interest income, or trust accounts that will be turned over to you at a certain age. Do you own oriental rugs? Steuben glass? A magnificent stamp collection? They are all assets.

Your Debts

You will be asked how much you owe and to whom. Have account numbers with you to speed up the verification process and to assure accurate reporting.

Don't be tempted to "forget" or accidentally omit any debts. Almost all lenders use credit check agencies and your forgotten debt will probably show up on your credit report. That will look very bad indeed.

If you are turned down for a loan because of the information provided by a credit reporting firm, you can ask the lender for the name of the firm (you have the right to know). You also have the right to contact that firm and inspect the credit information which it provided to the lender. You can correct any errors. If there is a dispute, you have the right to enter information (your side of the story) into your credit records.

The Address of the Property You Are Buying

Be sure you have the *right* address! Your lender will use the information on your mortgage application to arrange an appraisal of the property. You do not want the delay, confusion, and expense of having the wrong property appraised.

At some point, but not necessarily when you first apply for the loan, you will be required to give the lender a copy of your signed contract to purchase. Also have available the phone number of the current owners (and their names) if they are still living in the house. If the house is vacant, you will need to give the lender the name and phone number of your real estate agent. The lender will contact that agent to get access into the property for the appraisal.

Your Downpayment

The amount of your downpayment is crucial to your loan approval—usually the higher the downpayment the easier the approval. But be sure that you can account for the source of the money.

If you are selling one house to buy another, the downpayment usually comes from your equity in the property you are selling. You have the strongest hand when you already have a buyer and a signed contract. Bring a copy of that purchase contract with you and include it with your loan application papers. If you do not have a buyer for your old house, bring a copy of the real estate listing sheet with you to help establish the value of the property and your equity in it. A copy of your last municipal real estate tax bill is also helpful, especially if the assessed valuation is realistic.

If you are buying your first home or if you are not using your equity as a downpayment, the loan officer will want to know where you are getting the money. Ideally you will be able to point to an entry or two that you have listed under assets. But what if those assets happen to be $10,000 or so short?

You might be getting that $10,000 through a second mortgage loan. Some lenders allow part of the downpayment to come from a second mortgage loan, some do not. It's a good idea to ask ahead of time if you think you might need such a loan. Or you might be

When a Lender Evaluates a Mortgage Loan Application: Some Plus and Minus Points

When it comes to making a loan decision, *nothing* is carved in stone. The following are some "usual and customary" lender predispositions which may help you to evaluate your own strong and weak points. Don't take *any* of them so seriously, however, as to keep you from making application for a loan that you *can* afford to carry.

Employment

Plus

long-term, steady employment (regular increases in income are a double plus)

job changes in which your income and job description improve

possibility for future advancement or income increase

stable, respectable employer, the larger the better

Minus

frequent job changes without advancement or salary increase

high percentage of income from commissions or bonuses

large income fluctuations over the past several years

self-employed in a new venture

excessive moonlighting (two or three jobs needed to meet qualification guidelines)

Money

Plus

large downpayment—the larger the better

good credit rating (you have paid out previous loans on schedule)

a history of regular savings (especially at the institution to which you are applying for the loan) large net worth (stocks, bonds, cars, boats, other real estate, furniture, jewelry, collectibles, etc.)

Minus

little or no cash reserve

bad debt history (if there was a valid reason for some late payments—illness or job loss, for example—explain it to the loan officer in advance)

heavy, long-term debt load

no previous borrowing record (in this country, it's *not* always a good idea to pay cash)

The Property

Plus

good location—a neighborhood appreciating in value

new or relatively young home

Minus

rundown neighborhood

the largest or most expensive house in a neighborhood

property in need of major repairs

The Borrower

Plus

between 25 and 50 years old

well-educated; good career training

married (despite laws against discrimination, single women, single black men, and two people of the same sex buying property together complain frequently of loan discrimination)

Minus

unskilled laborer (even though current salary may be high)

young people (early 20s), even when a large downpayment is available getting your necessary $10,000 as a gift from relatives or as an interest-free loan to be paid back at some future unspecified date. If this is the case, you will need a gift letter from those relatives. Nothing fancy, just a typed and signed sheet saying that on the closing date you will have $10,000 as a gift from them.

One of the best possible loan application plus points is to have all or part of the downpayment on deposit with the lender to whom you are applying for a loan.

The Commitment Letter

During your loan application interview, ask how long a decision will take. Most lenders know pretty accurately, and some will act within very short periods of time (fourteen days, for example) for a fee. If your purchase is time-sensitive, tell the loan officer. Some lenders will do their best to act quickly upon applications that have imminent closing dates, even without a fee.

Once your loan is approved, you will receive a commitment letter from your lender. Send a copy to your real estate agent and to your attorney or your closing representative. The commitment letter states that the lender is willing to lend a specific amount of money to be repaid over so many years on a particular piece of property. The commitment is good for a specified period of time, usually ninety days. Often it is renewable. Try to pin down the interest rate, or better yet, try to get a guaranteed best rate if you can.

If your mortgage application is refused, go to the lender personally (not on the phone) and ask why. The lender is required by law to tell you. If you are given valid reasons why the lender feels you are a poor risk, you may be able to remedy the situation before applying for a loan with another lender. If you feel that you are being discriminated against, you can take appropriate action (see box).

Loan Discrimination
What Can You Do?

The federal Equal Credit Opportunity Act makes it illegal to deny a mortgage loan because of the borrower's race, color, religion, national origin, sex, marital status, or income from public assistance. Other laws prohibit the denial of a mortgage because of the location of the property, a practice commonly called redlining. If you think you have been unfairly denied a mortgage loan, you can complain and you can get help. Advice on how to proceed is usually available through the Consumer Affairs Division of your state's attorney general's office. The following federal agencies will investigate your complaint and take appropriate action:

When the lender is a federally insured savings and loan association (FSLIC stickers in the window):

    Federal Home Loan Bank Board
    1700 G Street N.W.
    Washington, D.C. 20552

When the lender is a federally insured national or state bank (FDIC stickers in the window):

    Federal Deposit Insurance Corporation
    550 17th Street N.W.
    Washington, D.C. 20551

When the lender is a national bank (*National* in its name or the letters N.A. for *National Association* after its name):

    Comptroller of the Currency
    490 L'Enfant Plaza
    Washington, D.C. 20219

When the lender is a bank holding company or a state-chartered commercial bank that is a member of the Federal Reserve System:

    Board of Governors
    The Federal Reserve System
    21st Street and Constitution Avenue
    Washington, D.C. 20551

Often a call to an executive of the bank will quickly right a wrong. Explain that you feel you are being discriminated against and why. Tell the executive that you would like to give the lender an opportunity to review your application again before you contact the appropriate agency. If you feel uncomfortable making such a call, ask your real estate agent, your lawyer, or someone from your state attorney general's office of consumer affairs to place the call for you. Making such a call will usually get results much faster than actually filing the complaint.

21

How Uncle Sam Can Help You Buy a Home

Yes, the government can make a homeowner out of you—find you a house, offer you lower-than-market mortgage interest rates, and perhaps even provide a fix-up loan for the property. It can do everything but help you furnish the place.

Ask the average househunter about government assistance in homebuying and the answer will probably be "FHA" and "VA" and perhaps "public housing." But there are other programs. Some have lasted decades; others come and go as financing for them comes and goes—and as presidents come and go. Some names may be familiar to you. Others come as (good) news.

Because of that continuing fluctuation of economic climates and political administrations, the househunter's smartest move is to keep in touch with federal, state and local housing offices. The programs are there. *Someone* is getting the money. It might as well be you. During your househunt the names and phone numbers of these offices should be as familiar to you as the name and number of your local real estate agent. As you will see from the following pages, funds disappear quickly to an eagerly waiting public, so keeping on top of what's coming out of Washington or your state capital or city hall could bring you just what you are looking for in housing. Hesitate too long, and whoops—the money's gone.

Why feel disheartened that you are priced out of the homebuying market when an auction of government-owned homes might win you a structurally sound house, requiring only minor fix-ups, for under the going market price?

Why sit in a slump in your rural community when there's a government program designed especially for those who need financial help to buy in the country?

It's true that some of these programs have income requirements—the rich need not apply. But the maximum income allowed is not always that low. And some programs are for everyone, no matter what their income.

Let's start with Washington, D.C., the source of most of the nation's housing programs.

Federal Programs

The office of the federal government that handles just about all matters pertaining to housing is the U.S. Department of Housing and Urban Development or, as it is more commonly known, HUD.

This agency was created during President Lyndon B. Johnson's administration to implement the part of his plans for the Great Society that pertained to housing. The agency shrunk as economic times became harsher and subsequent administrations placed less importance on housing issues. Still, while there is not as much money floating around these days as there seemed to be in the late 1960s, and fewer imaginative programs too, the well hasn't totally run dry. You may be able to find a perfectly adequate house for yourself here. It won't be as easy a sale as you might transact with a private owner, but if money is a problem for you, the folks at HUD are good to know.

So the first order of business if you are a *serious* househunter with money concerns is to contact your regional HUD office. Addresses can be found in Appendix A.

Call (check the telephone book under "U.S. Government") or drop in at the office nearest you and ask about housing programs in your area. Request any printed material those offices may have, too. And ask if there's anything in the pipeline that will be coming up in the next several months that could help you buy. After you've talked to one person there, call him or her in a couple of months to see what's new. Continue to keep in touch. As mentioned, when monies do come up they are spent quickly, so it's important to be right there when disbursements begin. The househunter on a very tight budget must expect to spend perhaps a year, or longer, in looking for an affordable property. So one phone call probably won't do the job for you (unless you've had a particularly unusual stroke of luck!).

Urban Homesteading

This is a program we'll consider under federal programs, although it is usually carried out by participating states, following HUD guidelines. It's the popular "A house for $1.00" plan you've read about over the last ten years.

Urban homesteading is a variation of the original Homestead Act of 1862, which allotted large parcels of land at $.25 to $2.50 an acre to homesteaders who agreed to develop them. The purpose was to open up new frontiers. Today, the focus of homesteading has become our nation's cities—fixing up urban homes, improving the quality of life in those communities and, not incidentally, getting the properties back on tax rolls.

In 1973 Annie Mae Barksdale and her 13-year-old grandson won in a drawing a small brick rowhouse in Wilmington, Del., which, along with sixteen other homes, formed the nation's pilot homesteading program. Annie Mae Barksdale became our first modern-day homesteader. The seventeen homes were drawn from two hundred homes that had been taken over by the city for nonpayment of taxes. They were in areas where property values were stable or increasing, or where most of the residents owned their homes.

Wilmington's experiment was successful, and soon homesteading programs were in effect in Baltimore, Washington, Philadelphia, and a score of other cities. Today, some ninety municipalities nationwide participate in urban homesteading. The program has changed a little over the years, however. Today's homes can be sold for a few hundred dollars or as much as $75,000 (multiunit dwellings), although $15,000 is the more usual figure. In some locales homesteaders must purchase as a community group and rehabilitate predominantly multifamily buildings. Rules vary from one urban area to another. But the primary purpose of homesteading remains fixing up dwellings to bring in ratables; the secondary aim, bringing affordable housing to more Americans.

In the main, and allowing for regional variations, here is how the program works:

1. HUD-owned single-family and multifamily homes, taken back by the government through FHA and VA foreclosure, are transferred to certain agencies of local government.

2. The local government sets up a homesteading program, perhaps adding some of *its* houses taken back for nonpayment of property taxes or water bills or some other cause.

3. The localities arrange to sell the properties at a nominal sum to homesteaders who agree to fix them up (usually within six months)

and live in them for a minimum of three consecutive years. After the homesteader has met those requirements he or she is given full title to the property. This differs from outright auctions of government-owned property where title is granted at the closing and there are no strings attached to the purchase.

4. The localities consider the applicants. They are interviewed to see if they can live up to what you might call the challenge of the project, for this type of homebuying would definitely entail more than buying a home from a private seller. Credit reports are checked, too, to be sure the prospective homesteader is not in default on other properties in town.

5. Applicants are taken around to see the available houses. Sometimes a match is made right there. The lottery that has become so associated with urban homesteading is usually utilized only for the more desirable homes that everybody wants, or when there are many qualified applicants for particular properties.

6. Winning applicants may then be required to have a contractor submit bids to the appropriate city agency showing what renovation work is likely to cost for that house. The bid must be approved.

The careful screening must work well, for this is a program where less than 3 percent of the participants have dropped out over all the years it has been in operation. Still, there is no free house (except Annie Mae Barksdale's), and a house bought for, say, $15,000, is not going to be in mint condition. Perhaps the city is trying to upgrade an entire neighborhood, so the location won't be all that great either. The spirit of urban homesteaders makes anything possible, however. In Baltimore the entire Otterbein section—104 homes—was saved through homesteading and that is now one of the city's more attractive neighborhoods. In fact, more than 300 homes in Baltimore have been rescued in this manner, making that city the most successful of all the program's participants.

So homesteading can work, but if there is a program in your community, be sure it is a job you would want to undertake. The government can usually (depending on the economy and current administration) help with a low-rate mortgage, but the huge stumbling block for many would-be homesteaders is the often substantial rehabilitation money they must come up with. Sometimes the city will offer a companion home improvement loan, but more often the buyer is left to scout around at local lending institutions. That can be difficult money to borrow if you don't even have title to the property you want to fix up. So borrowing for improvements is the primary problem here. A second concern is whether you can carry both mortgage and home improvement loans. If there is no mortgage because you won a home for practically nothing, no problem. But if your house cost $35,000 and you'll need another $20,000 worth of repairs, can you carry the payments for both those loans?

Then there is the actual rehabilitation. A sizable number of those who did fizzle out with this program simply couldn't handle what was a gut rehab project along with working at a fulltime job. They became simply swamped. You can expect to be busy dealing with contractors, securing permits, coping with house inspections, and doing as much work as you can yourself from dawn to far beyond dusk.

All of which is not to discourage you. After all, the percentage of those who do toss in the towel is certainly low. The overwhelming majority find that all the sweat, tears, paint, and plaster dust is well worth the trouble, for they now have a home they probably would not have been able to afford through any other purchasing method.

For more information about urban homesteading—and a realistic look at what's involved here—you can contact your regional HUD office or your local housing agency. Or write HUD in Washington for its free booklets, "Urban Homesteading Fact Sheet" and "Directory of Urban Homesteading Sites." The address is Office of Urban Rehabilitation, U.S. Dept. of Housing and Urban Development, Rm. 7168, 451 7th St. S.W., Washington, D.C. 20410.

As we move deeper into the 1980s, the urban homesteading program may remain stable or it may virtually disappear. It's certainly worth inquiring about, though.

HUD Auctions

These are sales of homes taken by the federal government, again through foreclosure. The program is different from homesteading only in that these homes are sold individually at auction or through sealed bid and not as part of a homesteading package. You may see advertisements in your local paper from time to time for HUD homes that look something like this:

LOOKING FOR A HOUSE?

THE U.S. GOVERNMENT HAS HOUSES IMMEDIATELY AVAILABLE FOR SALE

All bids should be mailed to HUD Property Disposition P.O. Box 888, Canal Street Station New York, N.Y. 10013

Since most of these sales are handled through local housing offices, and are sometimes sold along with locally owned properties, they are explained in more detail later under "City Auctions."

Want to Buy a Lifeboat Station?

This next suggestion is certainly no way to *concentrate* your househunt, but if you are searching for an unusual property that you know you will have to wait months, perhaps years, to come across, or if you are interested in buying with a few friends a large structure that you'll convert to loft space or some other joint-ownership use, it might pay to keep an eye on what's coming up with the U.S. General Services Administration. This is the federal office that, among other responsibilities, is selling pieces of property (land and/or buildings) no longer needed by the government. It's an ongoing program, but a special five-year push began in 1983 to *really* knuckle down and bring in some money here.

By trying to sell unwanted and unused properties the government hopes to realize some $17 billion during that five-year program. The usual procedure has been that the unwanted properties are first offered to state governments, either free or at nominal cost, and then to the public at large. But the federal government, like the rest of us, wants to make money these days. So now the properties are being sold at current market value. Most local governments probably won't be interested if they now have to pay for what they want, so the GSA is counting on the general public to buy.

There is certainly a diverse group of properties here, from acres of land, some of it in desirable locations, other plots of seemingly little worth, to buildings such as a lifeboat station, a farmhouse, an abandoned radar installation, a former ranger station, a laboratory, and so forth. Real esoterica.

If you are interested in what will be coming up in these sales, not just during the five year push, but with regularly scheduled sales thereafter, you can contact the GSA office in your locale. There are offices in Atlanta; Auburn, Wash.; Boston; Denver; Kansas City, Mo.; New York; Philadelphia; San Francisco, and Washington, D.C. Ask for a copy of "Buying Government Surplus Property" and then ask to be put on that region's regular mailing list. You can also obtain the GSA's monthly catalog of its nationwide real estate sales by writing to: Properties, Consumer Information Center, Dept. J., Pueblo, Colo. 81009. Ask for "Sales of Federal Surplus Real Estate."

You can also keep an eye open for advertisements in the backs of magazines and in newspapers. Local real estate brokers will also be engaged in selling the properties since some sales will not be at auction or through sealed bids, but will be handled as any ordinary transaction, with a seller (the federal government) and a buyer (maybe you?).

Remember, however, that there will be no bargains here; the government is trying to earn as much as it can from these properties. Remember too that you will be dealing with developers and other high rollers for the more desirable goodies. Still, if you have a little vision and a lot of persistence, you might pick up a terrific little lighthouse for yourself. Or maybe that ranger station sounded good. . . .

Farmers Home Administration (FmHA)

You're familiar, of course, with FHA-insured and VA-guaranteed home loans, but you may not have heard of this program. No, you don't have to be a farmer to buy. You don't even have to promise to raise tomatoes in the backyard.

There are many qualifications for purchasing a home under this plan, but if you do qualify you can find an excellent deal for yourself. The loans are fixed-rate, long-term mortgages at lower-than-market interest rates, which in hardship cases can drop, through a complicated formula, to as little as 1 percent.

You must buy in a community with a population of ten thousand or less, though in some instances twenty thousand or less is allowed. These must be rural areas—no small bedroom suburbs of ten thousand qualify. As a spokesman for FmHA put it: "If you're flying across the country and you look out your window at some little patch of a few houses surrounded by open country, then that's the kind of community we're talking about." That is a broad definition, he concedes, adding that rural communities that qualify *can* be found not too far from cities, although they certainly won't be what we think of as suburbs.

Only year-round houses can be considered, so you can't buy a vacation home under this program. New homes can't be larger than 1,200 square feet; existing structures no more than 1,400 square feet.

As important as the profile of the community is a look at the would-be homebuyer. If you are interested in this program, you must have been unable to obtain a mortgage elsewhere, usually because your income is not high enough or you lack a downpayment. There are definite income ceilings, too, although those requirements are likely to vary from one community to another. Nat-

HAVE YOU . . .

Contacted your regional HUD office, queried them on available housing programs in your area, and procured from them the name and phone number of local (state and municipal government) agencies you can call?

Called those offices to acquaint yourself with programs to assist househunters in your area?

Queried the local office of your U.S. senator about housing assistance in your state?

ARE YOU . . .

Reading the news pages of local newspapers regularly to see if there are any new housing programs coming up that you might qualify for?

Checking the advertisements in those papers to see when government-sponsored sales of homes are to be held? These may be quarter- or half-page ads, or they might be minuscule notices buried near the classified ads.

Calling all of the above-mentioned government offices every few months or so to keep apprised of any new housing appropriations?

---

urally, though, you can't be rich, rich, rich and expect to qualify here. Companion home improvement loans, and construction loans for new homes are usually available too.

For more information you can contact the Farmers Home Administration in your area, or write Administrator, FmHA, U.S. Dept. of Agriculture, Washington, D.C. 20250.

State Programs

These will vary from one state to another, depending in most instances on the aggressiveness of the state in securing monies from HUD, or in drumming up its own funds.

One program shines above all others, however, because it's a good one and because it's in effect in every state except (at this writing) Kansas. In the last several years fully one-third of all first-time buyers have purchased their homes under its auspices. It goes by different names in each state, but generally is referred to as a "state-sponsored low interest mortgage program." This program, like a number of other housing and non-housing government benefits to the public, might have gone through the paper shredder by the time you read this. But then again, it may still be around. It's worth your checking, as you will see as you read on. Sometimes a government program is killed, but already appropriated, unspent monies remain in local coffers for some time after the plan's official demise.

The agencies who run this program are quasi-autonomous arms of state government, and go by the name of "Housing Finance Agency," "Mortgage Finance Agency," "Housing Finance Corporation" or some similar designation. Funds come from the sale of tax-exempt state bonds, sold following federal guidelines. Mortgages are offered by participating banks and savings and loan associations.

The program is directed at first-time buyers (although sometimes those who haven't owned a home in the previous three years will also be able to qualify) and offers thirty-year mortgages at lower-than-market interest rates (sometimes as much as three points lower) and lower downpayment requirements as well. One delightful aspect of the plan is that no matter how low mortgage rates fall, those offered here will be still lower. So if the prevailing rate is 8 percent, you'll still be paying a lower figure. The gap is larger for higher rates, so if loans are going elsewhere for, say, 14 percent, you can expect to pay 10 or 11 percent under this plan.

Houses are usually available only in selected neighborhoods, and you must plan to live in the home to qualify. Some are single-family houses, others contain three or more full living units. There are usually, but not always, income requirements, but they are not inordinately low. A family earning over $30,000 a year could qualify.

Two points to make you move with haste:

1. When new money available to would-be buyers is announced, it disappears very quickly to eagerly waiting applicants; you have to work fast here.

2. As mentioned above, the program is always in danger of disappearing from one government cutback or another. So you had better contact your governor's office within the next hour or so to see where the appropriate agency is in your state and to ask questions pertaining to your situation and the neighborhood where you would like to buy.

While you have the governor's office on the phone, you might also inquire about other state-sponsored homebuying plans. There may be one coming up—or rapidly disappearing—where you live, and you may just be able to latch onto it. In New York State, to take one example, there are the widely known, limited-profit cooperatives known as the Mitchell-Lama program. That plan has allowed some 80,000 residents living in nearly 140 separate developments to own their homes, but without making the profit that usually falls to homeowners when they sell. With Mitchell-Lama co-ops, the homeowner gets back his original investment when he sells (and that is a small amount of money compared to the price of co-ops on the open market), plus a fair interest on that invested money. Your state may have other programs designed specifically for its residents. But you must ask. And keep asking periodically.

Local Programs

Now we come down to where you live, little old Hometown, or Big City, U.S.A. You might call your local housing office (if your community is truly minuscule you'll probably be referred to a county agency or a regional HUD office) to inquire about housing programs for which you might qualify.

To take one example of how local authorities can sometimes benefit the bargain-hungry househunter, a couple of years ago the city of Baltimore sold 524 abandoned houses for $200 each. They were offered on a first-come, first-served basis to buyers who would agree to complete renovations, bring them up to building code standards within two years, and then live in the houses. There were no other requirements, such as income. The city of Philadelphia allowed more than 600 residents to become homeowners under an innovative plan that made Philly the first city in the nation to use public employee pension funds for residential mortgages within its boundaries. The mortgages were offered by the Board of Pensions and Retirement and allowed Philadelphians to buy at interest 2 points below the going rate.

So you see, cities develop experimental programs from time to time that may practically drop a house in your lap. This is a good reason to keep in constant touch with your local housing office or Community Development Agency (local arm of HUD in many communities).

City Auctions

Municipalities come by houses or apartment buildings, or slivers of land, through nonpayment of taxes or water bills, condemnation, or urban development. In order to get those buildings or lots back on the tax rolls, they—or the liens against them—are sold at auction or through sealed bid, or occasionally by means of a lottery. Larger municipalities wait until they have a package of several buildings and hold a sale a few times a year. In smaller communities the houses will more likely be sold as they come up. HUD foreclosed properties can also be included in these sales. If you buy one of these homes you may have to pay the back taxes, although sometimes the minimum, or floor bid, is set at a figure that automatically includes all delinquencies. Even if all liens are presumably removed when you buy, it's still wise to obtain a title report and title insurance.

You are usually allowed to inspect the houses prior to the sale, and indeed the booklet or fact sheet describing the properties, or the newspaper advertisement announcing the sale, may include the street addresses (although sometimes it's just the lot number and the neighborhood, which won't help you much in determining the exact building). If you *are* permitted inside and are seriously considering a purchase, take an engineer or house inspector with you to give you a rough idea of how much rehabilitation work is needed. There is a wide range of houses sold at these auctions. Some are in good shape and the owner lost the building only through some personal misfortune. Others have been abandoned for some time, perhaps vandalized or totally stripped of many of their interior fixtures.

You may find a bargain or you may not. Naturally the more attractive the house the more buyers (some of them clever speculators) will be bidding on it. Opening bids can be as low as $500, or as high as $50,000 for some multifamily buildings. Renovation may be a problem for you too. As mentioned in talk of the urban homesteading program, if you can't come up with a home improvement loan— and be able financially to carry those payments along with a mortgage—you may not be able to fix up the house. And if you can't repair it enough to meet code standards you may find yourself falling behind in mortgage and home improvement loan payments and real estate taxes and then, lo! You'll lose the house and it will show up again in next year's city auction.

If you are a successful bidder you will usually have to put down a deposit, which is considered part of the downpayment. Procedures vary considerably from one locale to another. At closing you usually owe the difference between that deposit and 25 percent of your winning bid. Closings usually occur about three months after the sale. Sometimes the municipality offers an attractive low-interest mortgage.

Folks who have lost their homes usually can redeem them within a certain period of time after the sale. It may take as long as two years for clear title to pass on to you.

Notice of these sales can be found in local papers under headings such as "Public Notice" or "Foreclosure Sale." You can also contact your housing agency to see what may be coming up. On the county level, it might also pay to get in touch with the sheriff's office to see about foreclosure sales being handled for banks and other lending institutions. Some househunters find this sort of sale a little off-putting since they are buying a home over someone else's bad luck or hard times. Others say *someone* is going to purchase the foreclosed house and it might as well be them. If you are specifically interested in this kind of sale you might also get in touch with lending institutions directly. Talk to the senior loan officer and ask for a list of foreclosed properties. There may be none at the moment, but you can request that they inform you as properties come up for foreclosure. These, too, can be redeemed, so what you buy may not truly become your home until the present owner has forfeited his or her chance to make up mortgage payments, taxes, and other delinquencies.

All of the foregoing is not *guaranteed* to get you a home at a price you can afford. But wouldn't it be foolish to ignore Uncle Sam in your househunting? This isn't the arm of the government that takes your tax dollars, or the arm that sends out the "Greetings" letters. It's one that may have news you actually want to hear, and may reward you for persistence and hard work by making a homeowner out of you. And you will indeed have deserved that prize!

22

Having a House Built Just for You

Once upon a time in the land of NotSoFarAway there lived three brothers. For many weeks each of the brothers had spent every Sunday morning reading the real estate section of his newspaper and every Sunday afternoon reading and rereading copies of *Good House, Better Home*, and *The Best of Everything*. Each of the brothers, you see, was determined to own the most beautiful, most comfortable, most awe-inspiring, brand-new castle the family had ever seen. And each set out to do so, in his own way.

Ralph bought a lot and hired an architect. Rodney came upon a builder opening a tract called Deerhart. Roger bought a piece of unused farmland and decided to build-it-himself.

Before a year had run its course in the land of NotSoFarAway, each brother had suffered severe pains in his head, each had fought lien dragons, each had sworn fearsome oaths while biting bullets, and each had sweat beads of blood (not to mention the tears). Each had thought of giving up, and each had wondered why he ever got into his mess anyway. But in the end, each brother stood before the door of a brand-new, awe-inspiring castle.

Whose was the best? Ralph, Rodney, and Roger each thought it was his.

The moral of the story: *There is no easy way to get a brand-new, built-just-for-you castle*.

But wait! Don't close the book! There's no *easy* way but there *are* ways. There are ways, that is, if you have the three magic ingredients: *time* (yours), *money* (yours and your lender's), and *determination* (yours and your workers').

Seriously, every year thousands of people do custom-build successfully and perhaps this house-acquiring method is right for you, too. We told our story only to caution you to think twice (or three-times-twice) about having a house built for you if:

• You don't have a good deal of personal time to devote to the project of getting things done, all the way from the first thoughts of the house to moving in.

• You face time pressure to move out of your present house and into a new one.

• You are bothered by uncertainty about how much things cost now or may cost in the near future.

• You can't sleep at night after buying a negotiated item (like a car) because you worry for days about whether or not you "got a good deal."

• You have a difficult time supervising people, communicating your ideas, saying *no*, asking that a poorly done job be done again, or discussing money.

• You have little or no interest in attending to details.

• You give in to pressure, social, emotional, or financial.

• You and your spouse (or co-buyer) consistently disagree on items or topics significant and insignificant. And/or either of you tends to point the finger of blame at the other when things go wrong.

• You dislike making decisions.

• You are not quite sure, exactly, what you *really* want in a house.

You're still reading! Which means, of course, that you're still interested in seeing an idea transformed to a drawing and then into a building. OK, let's look at the process.

Buying a building that you can see, touch, hear, and smell is a complicated enough procedure, but creating the building you are buying is an aesthetic (and sometimes maddening) experience. Almost every person who has done it will say to a novice who is considering doing it, "Don't do it! It was awful!" Yet many, many of these same people will custom-build again. Why? Is it a moth–flame attraction? Or do they feel the self-assurance, skill, confidence, and maybe even exhilaration that having had the experience instills?

There is absolutely no question that experience is the best preparation for buying a built-for-you house. But how do you get experience until you've done it? Of course, you find substitutes. Sometimes you can get experience vicariously and sometimes you can lean upon the experience of the professionals that you hire. Still, in every house-building effort, you will encounter situations in which you must make the decision to strike out along one path or another, even at the risk of making expensive mistakes.

Mistakes in house building, however, are not only expensive, they are often long lasting, if not permanent. So you will want to avoid as many as possible. Having a map of the paths available to you, with intersections and dangerous curves marked, diminishes somewhat those risks. This chapter is such a map. To the extent that we can enter into your unique house-building project, it is a collection of vicarious experiences and forewarnings.

How to Get the Plans

When many people unfamiliar with house building think of house plans, they envision blueprintlike floor plan drawings. They forget that a house is a three-dimensional entity. Floor plans indicate the division of space in terms of width and length only; house plans that are accurate and workable must also include drawings of elevations and cross sections. Nor can floor plans be simple single-line drawings. They must also include the conventional symbols and dimensions for doors, windows, plumbing, heating and electrical systems and appliances, certain structural elements, and more. And if you have beautiful, accurate, and complete plans, you *still* don't have enough to start building your dream house.

Besides drawings, you will need "specs," more properly called specifications. These are lists and directions for everything needed to complete the house from its roof shingles to shower nozzles, from door knobs to the kitchen floor to the furnace in the basement. These specs should be as *specific* as possible, noting size, quality, material composition, style, and naming brand names.

Without drawings and specifications, your dream house won't even get to the hole-in-the-ground stage. Virtually all local zoning and building codes require that drawings and specifications be submitted to various local government departments and approved before a building permit will be issued. And virtually every lender will require a set of drawings and specifications to examine and appraise before granting you a construction loan. Take heart, however. There are several sources of plans for every budget.

Stock Plans

You've seen them in every home magazine. In fact, you've seen whole catalogues of house plans on the magazine stands. "Send $110 for a complete set of working blueprints!" the ad reads.

"Why not?" you say. After all, you love the drawings of the house in the magazine and the price of the plans certainly seems reasonable.

Actually stock plans are an excellent buy. *If*, that is, they are exactly what you want. But changing the size of the building, even slightly, or rearranging its interior floor plan may be difficult and costly. Even small changes like moving a window or dividing a bedroom into two bedrooms may require the services of a drafts-person or drafting service or entail the risk of "leaving it up to the builder." The primary advantages of stock plans are their low cost and easy availability. The stock plan catalogues themselves can even be a source of many good ideas during the planning-to-build stage.

There are, however, several disadvantages to using stock plans. Consider the following:

• *Inconsistent quality.* Some mail-away plans are excellent, others are not. You have no way of telling which you'll get the first time you order from the catalogue.

• *Drawn to inappropriate building codes.* The plans that you get from a company in Virginia may not meet the building codes of your hometown in Utah.

• *Specifications not included, incomplete, or inadequate.* Sometimes you can get a specifications list, but you must specifically request it, and there is usually an extra charge.

• *No quantity takeoffs.* Quantity takeoffs estimate how much of each building material is needed to construct the house. This information is absolutely necessary for accurate estimates of the cost of construction and the prevention of delays because of the need to reorder. Sometimes materials lists are available with stock plans at an additional cost. Get them, they will save you many times their price tag.

• *Cost of construction is not estimated.* Construction costs vary from one area of the country to another, so even plans that include a cost-of-construction figure are often inaccurate. It is easy, therefore, to waste money ordering plans for construction that you cannot afford. You can, however, do your own very rough estimate of costs by calling building supply companies or homebuilders in your area and asking for the current estimated cost per square foot of new home construction. Multiply the square footage of your prospective house plan by this dollar figure.

• *Plans not adapted to the site.* Some houses simply can't be built on a slope, for example, while others almost cry out for one. When you order stock plans, it becomes your responsibility to choose the right plan for your lot, not always an easy task for an amateur.

Abbreviations You May Find on Your Plans

Asph.	Asphalt	Ht.	Height
Bldg.	Building	L.	Center line
B.R.	Bedroom	L.P.	Low point
Br.	Brick	L.R.	Living room
B.S.	Bevel siding	Lt.	Light
Cem.	Cement	Mldg.	Molding
D.C.	Drip cap	Mull.	Mullion
D.G.	Drawn glass	No./#	Number
D.H.	Double hung	Obs.	Obscure
Diag.	Diagonal	O.C.	On center
Diam.	Diameter	O.C.	Outside casing
Dim.	Dimension	O.S.	Outside
Div.	Divided	Pl.	Plaster
Dn.	Down	Pl.	Plate
Do.	Ditto	Cond.	Conduit
D.R.	Dining room	Cop.	Copper
Dr.	Door	Corn.	Cornice
Dr.C.	Drop cord	Csmt.	Casement
Drg.	Drawing	C.T.	Crock tile
D.S.	Downspout	Crys.	Crystal
Ea.	Each	Pl. Ht.	Plate height
El.	Elevation	R.	Radius
Ent.	Entrance	Rm.	Room
Ext.	Exterior	R.W.	Redwood
Fin.	Finish	Scr.	Screen
Fin. Ceil.	Finished ceiling	Sdg.	Siding
Flash.	Flashing	Specs.	Specifications
Fl.	Floor	T and G	Tongue & Grooved
C.I.	Cast Iron	T.C.	Terra Cotta
Clg.	Ceiling	Th.	Threshold
Clr.	Clear	Typ.	Typical
C.O.	Cased opening	Ven.	Veneer
Conc.	Concrete	V.T.	Vertical tongued
Cond.	Conductor	and G.	and grooved
Ft.	Foot/Feet	W.	Wide
Ftg.	Footing	W.C.	Wood casing
Gar.	Garage	Wd.	Wood
G.I.	Galvanized iron	W.G.	Wire glass
Gl.	Glass	W.I.	Wrought iron
Gr.	Grade	WP.	Waterproof
Gyp. Bd.	Gypsum board	Yd.	Yard
H.P.	High point		

Reprinted with permission from Draw Your Own House Plans, *Mike and Ruth Wolverton (TAB Books).*

Draw Your Own Plans

You've looked at floor plans till they are coming out of your ears and none seems quite right, so why not do your own? After all, you could combine the best features from a variety of drawings in the catalogues.

This hardly ever works, but the experience of trying may give you a better idea of what you want and what you can reasonably have. You can fiddle around with rough sketches to your heart's content, but if you are serious about drawing your own plans, there are two essential steps you should take before you approach a contractor for a bid:

1. Read the local building code for residential construction (usually available in your building inspector's office). If you get through this and still want to draw your own plans, ask your buildings department personnel if a Plan Check Correction Sheet is available. It will help you.

2. Learn something about architectural drawing. The symbols and abreviations are a language in themselves. Among the several books available on this subject, *Draw Your Own House Plans*, by Mike and Ruth Wolverton (TAB Books, $13.95), is comprehensive and readable.

Even if and when you have completed what you think is a perfect set of drawings, you will more than likely still need some professional help. Building code officials are almost always wary of home-drawn plans and some states even require that all house plans be drawn and signed by an architect. If you take your plans to an architect, you can usually negotiate a flat fee to redraw them with corrections to meet building codes and perhaps a few aesthetic suggestions too.

If you are not required to have an architect's signature, you might consider taking your home-drawn plans to a draftsperson or a drafting service. These people are in the business of drawing plans and making up specifications lists. You can get the five to ten sets of drawings you'll need from them. Usually a good drafting service saves you more than its fee in corrected mistakes and headache prevention.

Buy a Local Stock Plan

Walking through builders' model homes or through custom homes under construction (if the general contractor will allow it) is an excellent way to get a three-dimensional feel for space and traffic flow which no amount of peering at floor plans can give you. And if you stumble upon a plan that really appeals to you, you may just be able to duplicate it upon *your* lot.

Ask the general contractor who allowed your walk through or the real estate agent in charge of the model for the name of the architect who designed the house. If he gives you a local name, call the firm. (Local can mean anything from in the same town to in the same state or region, depending upon how much long-distance calling and driving you are willing to do.) Tell the designer of the house that you have seen it being built by Soandso on Suchandsuch Street in Nicetown. Say you are planning to build yourself in *Yourtown* and ask if you can buy the plans.

Most architects retain the copyrights to their work and many will sell the plans to you at a reasonable cost. Of course, the architect will probably refuse your request if you are asking for the plans to a Texas version of Falling Waters, but there is rarely a problem in copying builders' tract houses.

The obvious advantage to using local stock plans is that they conform to local building codes. Quality is also usually consistent with the reputation of the local architect, and sometimes you can get the opportunity to walk through an already-built house based on *your* plan. For an hourly fee paid to the architect for a few hours' work, you may even be able to get the him or her to meet you at your building lot and help you modify the plans to suit the site.

Generally the cost of plans bought from a local architect is somewhat higher than that of mass-produced mail-order plans. Usually the extra money is well spent, however, since the plans are better suited to the area and can be modified by their originator to suit your site and lifestyle.

Using a Builder's Package Deal

This is the most common way in which to-be-built house construction is sold in this country. It features "free" plans and "freedom from care" about details of construction. Or so the sellers say.

There are several ways to get "free" plans from a builder. We say "free" because you are actually paying for the plans, you just don't know how much. Their cost has been figured into the package price for building that particular model either on the builder's tract or on your lot. To get such plans you can:

• *Go to a tract or planned community (like Deerhart) that is in the process of being developed.* Usually the builder has from four to ten different models that he will build upon a given lot in his tract.

• *Go to a tract of unique and custom homes.* You'll probably find a trailer-office on site. When you climb inside expect to see rolled sets of blueprints scattered about. You'll probably be shown a few as samples of the builder's work or he may even show you through a completed house or two. If you choose to select a lot in the tract, you'll more than likely be invited into town to the builder's office where dozens of plans will be available to you. Builders of custom homes want each house in a given development to look unique (they get more money for them that way), so you won't be shown anything that is already standing in the neighborhood where you are buying. After you select your plan, the builder will do a work up and quote you a figure for building that particular house on the lot that you have selected. Please realize, however, that there is no competitive bidding on this price. If you want that house built on land in the tract being developed, you will have to pay that builder's price without ever knowing if anyone would have built it for less. If you are going to buy a to-be-built tract house, either custom or one-of-five, compare several developments and builders in your area to be sure you are not grossly overpaying for what the builder promises to build.

• *Go to a large custom-building company.* You'll see their ads in the newspapers: "WE CUSTOM BUILD ON YOUR LOT. COME TO OUR OFFICE AND CHOOSE FROM OVER 500 STYLES." Each of the models in the office catalogue will have a package price listed. "You'll have the least amount of custom-building worry," the salesperson will tell you. "Choose your colors, put down 10 percent, get a mortgage commitment, and you can move in in three months." Maybe.

If you are buying a builder's package, be aware that every change you make, even if it's substituting a stainless steel kitchen sink for a procelain one, will cost you money. Go over the specifications therefore with the finest-tooth comb you can find, *before* you sign the contract. Then visit the building site often and be sure you are getting what was promised and not easy substitutions. Be aware also that some builders impose an extra charge for working on a difficult lot.

Hire an Architect

There are relatively few houses in this country that were designed by an architect *for* a particular client. Why? Partly because many people are intimidated by the thought of approaching an architect. The word architect is tied in their minds with the word wealth.

Not necessarily so, say architects across the country, many of whom believe that they actually *save* their clients more than they are paid.

If this is true, or even nearly true, why hasn't word gotten out and why aren't there lines outside the doors of architects' offices? There are several reasons. Even if the architect doesn't cost the home-buyer a penny, even if he or she in fact saves money, building with an architect entails other demands and a good deal of commitment. You are going to have to devote time, work, and care to the project if you want a custom-designed house. And even before that, you are going to have to spend a good deal of time just finding the "right" architect.

Finding "your" architect. Just as some doctors don't do surgery and some cleaning people don't do windows, some architects don't do houses. (Churches, schools, office buildings, and hotels are usu-ally more lucrative on a time-spent-for-payment basis.) You can get a list of those architects in your area who design houses by calling the local chapter of the American Institute of Architects (AIA). If you are having trouble getting names, write to: The American Institute of Architects, 1735 New York Ave. N.W., Washington, D.C. 20006. They will send you the names of local architects and the name, address, and phone number of your local chapter.

You might also get the names of architects from real estate agents, building materials dealers, builders, and acquaintances who have already built their own custom homes. Be sure to drive by some of the houses designed by the architects that are recommended. Occa-sionally you'll even see large display ads in the local papers for planned communities to be built. The name of the architect often appears in the ad. If there is a model open, visit it. There is no better way to preview an architect's work that to walk *through* it.

Once you have a list of names, how do you choose among them? If you've fallen in love with one of the houses you've visited, you might well make an appointment with that architect. If you are unsure, however, interviewing is probably the best method of selec-tion. Unlike your first meeting with a doctor or lawyer, it doesn't cost you money to talk with an architect. No obligation or fee is incurred until a contract is signed.

You will meet the architect in his or her office, look at pictures of the kind of work he or she does, and talk about the kind of house you have in mind. It is most important in these interviews that there is truly an inter-viewing. Both architect and prospective client should get a feel for each other's personalities. You will need to work closely together and it's almost an absolute prerequisite that

---

Architect Shopping:
How to Have an Effective First Interview

What to Tell the Architect

Tell how much you can afford. Indicate how much space you need.
Describe your building site.
Describe the kind of house you want. Contemporary? Traditional? Lots of glass? Energy-efficient? Conducive to additions at some time in the future? In other words, share your dreams.
Tell about yourself, your family, your lifestyle. If you are to have a custom-designed house, the architect must know you.

What to Ask the Architect

What houses have you designed in this area? Look at plans. Get addresses. It is important that you like the kind of work your architect has done.
Are you interested in working on the design for the kind of house we would like? The architect should say more than "yes," he or she should tell you why and perhaps how money can be saved.
Can you design a house such as we want within our budget? A key question!
What is your fee and how is it to be paid? Difficult questions to ask, but absolutely necessary.
What is included in that fee? Drawings only? Specifications and materials takeoffs? Selection of the general contractor (putting the plans out to bid)? Construction supervision?

---

you like each other. You must also trust and feel comfortable with the person who will design your home.

How to hire and pay your architect. After you choose an architect, the next step is to draw up a written owner-architect agreement. This will state in writing what you want the architect to do and how you will pay him or her. You can get some sample owner-architect agreements from your local chapter of the AIA or by writing to the Washington office. Request these forms: B 141   Owner-Architect Agreement; B 161   Owner-Architect Agreement for Designated Services; and B 727   Owner-Architect Agreement for Special Services. Read them carefully, but remember your contract with your architect is a contract between two parties. You can change any aspect of the printed form by mutual agreement.

There are several ways in which you might work with an architect. Services may or may not include:

• drawing plans and specifications lists

• putting the project out to bid to several general contractors and/or helping the owner to select a general contractor

• obtaining all permits

• obtaining all lien waivers

• acting as an advisor to the owner during construction or as an arbitrator between the owner and the contractor in the event of disputes

• making periodic inspection visits to the site to check on the quality of the workmanship

• sometimes (though rarely) acting as a general contractor and doing all the subcontracting plus supervision of the construction process

How much you must pay your architect and how and when you pay him or her will depend upon which services you choose and upon your mutual agreement. Some generally accepted payment practices are:

• flat fee for plans and specifications

• flat fee retainer, plus hourly rate, plus expenses

• percentage of the project cost (usually 6 to 15 percent; this arrangement may or may not contain a top-limit cap)

• any method you both agree upon

Who owns the plans? If you have a house custom designed for you, the architect in most cases still owns the plans and may sell them again. You may, however, arrange by mutual agreement to buy the copyright to the plans so that no other house quite like yours will ever be built again. But it will cost you more, and are you really sure it's so important?

What if you change your mind? If you suddenly decide not to build or not to use your architect's plans, you can cancel your contract. You will be required to pay, however, for the services rendered to that point in time.

How to Get the Money to Build

Mortgage Commitments

If you choose to have a house built for you on a builder's tract or you use one of the huge package building companies, you will have just a little more financial fuss than if you were buying an already built house. Most builders who are developing tracts already have commitments for financial backing during the construction process.

When you sign a contract to buy a house that is to be built for you, you will be required to put down some earnest money. (The most common amount is 10 percent of the purchase price, but that figure is negotiable.) Try to have a clause written into the contract that requires the money to be held in an escrow account and try to have the interest on that account credited to you. You are talking a considerable amount of money here over several months. Using an escrow account is an important protective device for your earnest money investment. If you don't use such an account but give the money directly to the builder and, let's say, he goes bankrupt, you will lose some or all of it.

Once you have a signed contract, one that is contingent upon your being able to get a mortgage, take that contract and a set of drawings and specifications to your lender. Now you will be asking for a mortgage commitment based upon the value of the house when it is finished, but you won't borrow that money *until* it is finished. The bank may have an appraisor look at your plans and take a trip out to inspect the lot you have chosen. The appraiser will most likely take another trip out to inspect the house when it is finished (but before the closing), for which there will probably be a charge. But essentially you will have little difficulty getting the mortgage commitment on your new construction. After all, not a penny of the bank's money leaves the bank until the house is standing and in move-in condition.

The catch in getting a mortgage commitment on construction to-be-built is time. Most houses take four to six months from digging the foundation to seeding the lawn, and most mortgage commitments run for ninety days. Try to get a six month commitment even if your builder is promising you the construction will be complete in sixty days. Or at least try to have a renewal clause written into the commitment letter. And, if you don't mind asking for just a little more, try to have the interest rate in the commitment letter fixed.

Many lenders, however, will not commit to a loan four to six months away at a rate fixed on the date of the commitment letter, but insist on making their mortgage commitment "at the prevailing rate at the time of closing." Prevailing rate commitments are somewhat more risky to the buyer since you could be in for a higher payment than you expected, but it *is* a commitment to finance. And who knows, the rates might go down. Dealing with the unpredictable mortgage money scene is just another of the risks of new-house construction.

Construction Loans

Getting a construction loan is somewhat different from getting a mortgage. You do not borrow a lump sum which you get all at once at the closing and then pay back over a period of years. Instead, after examining plans, an upper limit to the amount you will need to borrow for your construction is decided upon between you and your lender. The money is disbursed in installments as designated stages of construction are completed.

When your house is finished, the construction loan must be repaid, usually by taking out a mortgage loan. Who collects the construction loan money and who pays the workmen depends upon your construction method:

1. *If you use an architect,* the architect may draw the construction loan payments and disburse the monies either to the general contractor or directly to the subcontractors.

2. *If you use a general contractor,* your lender may disburse lump sum amounts to him; he in turn will pay his various subcontractors. Or by agreement with your general contractor, you can pay him and the subcontractors individually and directly. This method gives you tighter control of the money, but also requires more work, time, and responsibility on your part.

3. *If you do your own subcontracting,* you *must* pay your suppliers and subcontractors directly. Be sure to get lien waivers or paid-in-full statements when you pay these bills. Your lender may require them.

4. *In some states lenders require the use of a fund control company.* You must pay for this service but are free to shop for the lowest rate. The fund control company acts as an escrow agent, collecting monies from the lender and disbursing them according to a prearranged agreement and schedule. The supervision of disbursements is thus independent of both the lender and the owner.

When you apply for a construction loan you will need a complete set of drawings and specifications along with an accurate estimate of cost or a general contractor's bid that you have accepted. Be sure that you include all your costs in your loan application. Design costs which you pay to an architect are considered a part of the cost of the house (even by the FHA), as are survey fees, soil tests, permit fees, etc. The more cost you can document, the more money you will probably be allowed to borrow. Get as much as you can, you may need it all.

In processing your application, the construction loan lender will be concerned with the following points:

1. *Do you have a mortgage commitment?* Since the construction loan is short-term financing, it must be paid off with the interest accrued when the building stage is complete. This is usually accomplished by taking out a long-term mortgage. Sometimes the construction lender and the mortgage lender are one and the same institution, but not always. It is important therefore that you secure a mortgage commitment as early in the construction process as possible.

2. *The accuracy of the cost estimates and the feasibility of the construction.* Since a construction loan is a means of *creating* value, the lender wants to know that what is created will indeed be valued at or near his expectations, not below and not far above. Why not far above? Well, if the lender agrees to a construction loan of $100,000 and the project ends up costing $150,000, where will the extra $50,000 come from? A project that breaks down in mid-construction because of lack of funds can be a financing disaster. Often bank appraisers carefully examine plans and visit the building site before and throughout the building process. The appraiser wants to assure the lender that you are not planning to build on the unstable side of a cliff or that you are not building a structure completely different from the plans that you submitted.

3. *Compliance with zoning and building codes.*

4. *The reputation of the general contractor.* Lenders are more likely to lend when the builder is someone they recognize as reliable. They do not want to deal with a builder who routinely goes broke in the middle of a project. Lenders are also wary of owners who plan to do their own subcontracting. In fact, you may have considerable difficulty getting financing for such a do-it-yourself homebuilding project. It won't hurt, however, if you've built a house once before, have a steady job, have more income than you need, have lived in the community a number of years, and have few long-term debts.

5. *Your financial status.* Custom building almost always costs more than you expected. It's no one's fault, really, hidden or unexpected "things" just come up, or sometimes owners just can't resist adding luxuries. The lender, however, will want to know that you have the resources to cover extra costs.

How to Get it Built

What makes building a house an undertaking that most people avoid and that virtually everyone regards with some apprehension? There's no one answer to that question. The reasons behind the headaches, ulcers, and arguments of home building are many. The project is large, in physical size and in cost, and mistakes can be both dangerous and expensive. It occurs over time (several months at least) and requires a commitment of time from the owner-to-be (some people would say the better part of twenty-four hours a day!). It's dependent upon the talents and training of a large number of people, groups, and organizations. It is subject to local governmental legislation, inspection, and approval. It is dependent (usually at least) upon borrowed money. Progress is subject to the availability of building materials. Despite the interdependence of the construction process (a given job often cannot be done until another is finished), most of the work is done by independent, unrelated, and self-employed subcontractors. Owners at times get involved in the construction process and make last-minute changes. And then there is the weather—a force beyond everyone's control.

Stepping in to conduct and coordinate all this is the general contractor (some people still call him the builder, even after he finishes his work). The competence of this person will make a tremendous difference in the building's progress as well as the quality of the finished product.

Choosing the General Contractor

If you are determined to do your own subcontracting, skip from here to the section titled "Being Your Own General Contractor." But remember that what you skipped is still in the book, just in case you change your mind later. If you decide to buy a package plan house on a builder's tract or from a large building company, you will not be able to choose your contractor. He will be the developer of the tract or someone assigned to the project.

For those who must choose, choosing is not always an easy matter. It is easiest, however, if you are working with an architect. The architect puts his design out to bid, usually to several contractors with whom he is familiar. It's fairly safe to take the lowest bid in this situation since the architect has already screened out those contractors likely to be unreliable. Most general contractors also make an extra effort to work at maximum efficiency on an architect-supervised project since they want the opportunity to bid and work on future jobs from the same source. Sometimes an architect will advise an owner to choose a particular contractor familiar with the kind of construction that the project requires. You are by no means required to hire a recommended person in such a situation, but it usually pays to listen.

If you are looking for a builder on your own, it's harder. Although plumbers, electricians, and heating and cooling contractors are licensed in most states, there are few requirements for becoming a general contractor. You must use standards of judgment, therefore, beyond the simple possession of a license. "How long has he been in the business?" is an excellent criterion, for homebuilding is a field where survival of the fittest pervades. You might also ask "What has he built?" and "For whom?" Go to look at these houses and, if possible, ask questions of the owners.

After you have a list of prospective contractors, you should give each a set of plans and thus "put the project out to bid." Be aware, however, that the lowest bid may not be the best, especially if it is considerably lower than the other bids. Now you must again check reputation and references or you will always wonder "Will the workmanship be shoddy? How can he do it for so much less than anyone else?"

Unfortunately, choosing a builder is sometimes a matter of default. No one else is available or no one else wants to work on so unusual a project, or so far out of town, or whatever. But again, think twice before hiring the only guy who'll do the job. Are you sure the design is workable? Can you check this contractor's references? Why is there such a scarcity of contractors at this time?

Fees and Payments to the General Contractor

As with the architect, any payment arrangement that is mutually agreeable is acceptable. The most usual methods of payment are:

1. *Lump sum.* This is by far the most common payment procedure. The contractor bids a fixed sum to construct the project. This fee includes the cost of materials and all subcontracting, plus his profit. If the owner makes changes during the course of construction, the cost of the changes is added to the lump-sum figure. Some lump-sum contracts contain a provision for inflation of materials costs during the construction process. Try to put a dollar figure cap on this possible escalation of cost. Remember what happened to oil prices in a few short months in the 1970s?

2. *Cost plus.* The contractor is paid the actual cost of materials and labor plus either a fixed fee or a fixed percentage of the cost of the project. This method does not place an upper limit on the cost of the project. If the subcontractors that the general contractor hires are the most expensive persons for the job in your area, you will pay

Mechanic's and Materialman's Liens

Every company that furnishes building materials and every subcontractor hired to work on the construction of a house has the right to be paid for his materials and/or work. If he is not paid, or not paid-in-full, he can impose a lien on the property, which becomes an encumbrance. Sometimes such liens can be foreclosed in much the same way as a mortgage.

There is no uniform law among the states concerning liens. In some states they even take priority over construction mortgages and the periods during which they can be filed vary from months to years. It's no wonder then that lenders ask to see lien waivers or paid-in-full statements from subcontractors and materialmen before disbursing the next installment of funds.

Waiver of Lien

A lien waiver is a signed statement voluntarily giving up the right to file a mechanic's or materialman's lien during the statutory period allowed in the given state. Usually suppliers or subcontractors will not sign such a waiver unless paid in full. Signed waivers therefore are the best evidence to the lender that "all is going well."

---

top dollar, whether it could be done less expensively or not. In the percentage payment situation, the more the project costs, the more the general contractor makes. Since it is an invitation to price padding, you need to supervise this payment arrangement closely. Ask to see paid receipts from the subcontractors all along the way.

3. *Maximum total*. The maximum total cost of the project is agreed upon between the owner and the general contractor. This maximum total includes the general contractor's fee. If, however, he can get the project done for less, the owner and the contractor, by agreement, can either split the savings or the general contractor may keep them as extra profit. This payment method is an invitation to using cheaper materials and least expensive labor.

At what point or points in time a general contractor's fee is paid is dependent upon the agreement between the owner and the contractor. Few contractors, however, will wait for payment until the end of a project. Most are given an up-front fee and then a certain amount each month as the construction loan funds are disbursed. Usually the owner keeps about 10 percent of the total cost of the house back, however, until *all* the work is finished to his satisfaction. Sometimes this money is even held until the statute of limitations period for filing mechanic's or materialman's liens has run out in order to be sure that all the subcontractors have been paid.

Your Contract With the General Contractor

Whether you select a builder's tract house, a catalogue package plan, or have your house designed by an architect, your contract with the general contractor should include all of your drawings and specifications. Without drawings and specs the contract is a flimsy piece of paper from which no one could judge if the agreement had been fulfilled. The contract should also include your method of payment and the agreed upon sum, and it should list the contractor's duties explicitly. Is he, for example, to disburse money to materials suppliers and subcontractors, or are you? A list of those items that you will supply outside the contract, lighting fixtures, for example, should be attached or included.

It is important that your contract name a date of completion, but don't count on moving in on that day. Most home-building projects run late, some by as much as six months! In some contracts, penalties are named to be paid to the owner by the general contractor if the project is not completed on time. It's not a bad idea to include such a penalty clause, but again don't count on getting this money. Most contractors can give good and valid reasons for the delays, thus negating the penalty payment requirement.

You can get a sample owner/general contractor contract from the American Institute of Architects or from your local chapter office. Ask for *A 201 General Conditions of the Contract for Construction*. It may well act as a guideline in forming your own contract.

The general contractor that you select may have his own contract ready and waiting for you to sign. Bear in mind as you read through it, however, that as in house buying, there is no "standard contract." You can write in or cross out anything. It's probably a very good idea to talk with a lawyer before you sign any contract with a general contractor, especially if you have not had the benefit of direction from an architect.

Visiting the Building Site

No matter which construction mode you choose, the more often you can visit your building site and the better you get to know the workers, the better are your chances of getting a quality-built house. This is true no matter how many supervisors or workers you have on the job.

Being Your Own General Contractor

There is no test or license that qualifies one to build a house, and there are people about who feel qualified to take on the task when or if they have owned a house for ten years and done all the general handiwork about the place. Or they bought a handyman special, fixed it up, and sold it for a handsome profit. Or perhaps they worked as a carpenter (more accurately, *for* a carpenter) summers while attending college. Or even when they have a friend or co-worker who built his own house and talks about it all the time.

Well, you could probably say that all these experiences add to one's knowledge of home ownership and perhaps even of home-building. But jumping from any or all of these levels of expertise to acting as your own general contractor is a little like feeling qualified to conduct the New York Philharmonic because you have played second tuba in the Smartsville Community Orchestra for six years.

So why do people take on this nerve-shaking, marriage-stressing, time-consuming, exhausting, and humbling job? Money. By acting as your own general contractor, you can save thousands of dollars on the cost of your home. Some experts put the figure as high as 25 percent. On the other hand, you might also *lose* thousands, too, in errors of judgment and downright mistakes for which there is no one to blame but yourself.

Before you put on your contractor's hat, think about what you would do if:

• The foundation hole is dug three feet nearer the front property line than it was supposed to be. The house will now be two feet over the zoning setback line. By the time you discover the error, the subcontractor who dug the hole has moved all his equipment to a job he is working on in the neighboring town. He can come back next week, he says. The footings were supposed to be poured tomorrow.

• Just after your house is framed, you have three consecutive days of heavy rain. A subcontractor is scheduled to start work nailing exterior siding to the framing on the fourth day. It's sunny, but everything is wet. The subcontractor tells you that if he and his men don't start your job *that day*, he will take another job and will not be available for three weeks. Do you let him work on the wet framing wood?

• You can't put up the interior sheetrock (wallboard) until the building inspector inspects and approves the wiring that was done by your electrician. You wait at the site the entire day of the inspector's appointment but he doesn't show up. The next day at the office a co-worker tells you that he saw your building inspector on the golf course yesterday. Meanwhile your sheetrock man tells you he can't wait any longer, you'll have to get someone else.

• The bathtub must go in before the tile. The day after the tile man leaves, you take a walk around your nearly finished house and notice a chip out of the porcelain in the tub. It looks as though someone dropped a hammer or other heavy tool. You talk with the tile man and the carpenters who were working there the day before. No one dropped anything, they all say. How much will it cost to rip out the new tile, install a new tub, and redo the tile? Do you cry or scream?

• It turns out that you shortordered the brick for the chimney by approximately one hundred pieces. You go back to the materials supply company only to find that they are sold out of that particular brick. Special order will take two weeks and no brick in stock matches the one you were using. Your mason must take another job, but he promises to come back to finish your chimney just as soon as he has a free day.

• Your finish carpenters and electricians are scheduled to install the kitchen appliances on Tuesday, but all of Monday passes and the appliance store does not deliver the double wall oven, countertop range, and dishwasher you ordered. You call them, furious. "Sorry, ma'am," says the voice on the phone, "it was a mistake. Our delivery truck will be in your area again next Monday and they will be sure to have them then." Your carpenters are leaving Friday and you don't know *when* you can get the electricians again.

Anyone who has ever built a house could fill a book with stories like these, some even worse. So if you are determined to do it, be prepared to devote much of yourself to the job of being your own general contractor. It's an undertaking that requires time, patience, time, tact, time, perseverance, time, determination, time, knowledge, and *time*.

After reading all this, you still want to go ahead. OK, but before you jump in with both feet:

• Go to your library and find everything you can on housebuilding. Bring it home and *read* it.

• Talk with your insurance agent about insurance for your construction site. Theft or damage? Workers compensation? Liability?

• Visit building supply companies in your area. Who has the best prices? Who will help you do "take offs" (estimates of how much of a thing you will need)? Who has the largest in-store inventory (special orders delay construction)?

• Start compiling lists of competent subcontractors. You should have two or three names for each professional group that you will use.

• Talk with a lawyer who is familiar with new construction contracts about safeguards in your contracts with your subcontractors.

• Decide on bathroom and kitchen fixtures and appliances early. Special orders can take many, many weeks.

• Be sure that you have a place to live during construction. It always takes longer than you think, sometimes by many months. Do not sell the house you are living in "out from under you" or you may find yourself living in a motel room with your furniture in storage and your serenity in shambles.

• Pray, if you are so inclined.

Some "Finishing" Thoughts

There is a good deal of work on your house that you will not be able to do (even if you "build it yourself") because you do not have the equipment (digging your own foundation hole, for example, or grading) or because you do not have the license required by your local government to do such work (installing wiring, or plumbing, for example). Many homeowners, however, do save some money by doing finishing work such as painting and floor sanding themselves. Some owners even swing their own hammers.

If you want to go even beyond doing your own subcontracting to hands-on participation in the construction of your home, you could save even more money. First, however, read the next chapter on homebuilding schools, kits for houses, and housing that is delivered in modules to be put together.

Finally, when you move into your new house, don't expect paradise. Every new house has problems, whether its construction was architect-supervised, conducted by a huge homebuilding firm, or subcontracted by the owner. Keep a list of the faults you find (the window in the back bedroom will only go up halfway, the downstairs bathroom door won't lock, etc.). In most states the builder is required to return to fix these problems for one year after construction is complete. Or you may even consider a longer homeowner's warranty program (discussed on p. 249). But remember if you do your

Some People in Your Housebuilding Life

Architect	Kitchen planner
Surveyor	Interior decorator
Draftsperson	Materials suppliers
Banking loan officer	General contractor
Bank appraiser	Construction manager
Building inspector	Insurance agents
Architectural review board	Landscape architect
Board of adjustment	

Subcontractors

Foundation excavators	Roofing contractors
Concrete footings firm	Exterior painters
Foundation builders	Interior painters
Carpenters	Insulation specialists
Heating & cooling contractors	Leader & downspout company
Electricians	Septic tank company
Plumbers	Well diggers
Dry-wall installation specialists	Grading & outdoor finish crew
Window specialists	Nurserymen and landscape crew
Tile specialists	
Flooring specialists	Floor sanding & finishing specialists
Carpet installers	Clean-up crews
Cabinet makers	
Masons	

own subcontracting, *you* are the builder. You will have to call back subcontractors to redo their faulty work. *If* they will come.

Is it worth it, this custom building? Most people who do it say "yes." But that "yes" usually does not come until a year or so after they have moved in.

For More Information

How to Get It Built, Better—Faster—For Less, by Werner R. Hashagen. Available from the author at 7480 La Jolla Blvd., La Jolla, Calif. 92037. This is a comprehensive and very readable guide. Price: $16.

A clean-up crew is yet another subcontractor, absolutely essential.

Be Your Own House Contractor, by Carl Heldmann, Garden Way Publishers, Charlotte, Vt. 05445. Contains detailed step-by-step instructions for the first-timer. Price: $6.95.

509 Practical, Money-Saving Tips for Homebuilders, by Alan D. Roebuck, TAB Books, Blue Ridge Summit, Pa. 17214. Hints, tips, shortcuts, and ideas. Price: $9.95 paper.

From your local HUD office: "FHA Description of Materials Form (New Housing Construction)." This lists *everything* in detail. Use this form as a check against your specifications list. It will help to assure that nothing is left out.

From the Small Homes Council, University of Illinois, One East St. Mary's Road, Champaign, Ill. 61820: a catalogue upon request, which contains a complete listing of books, pamphlets, technical reports, instruction sheets, and research studies. Most are inexpensive. Most pamphlets and technical reports, for example, sell for 50 cents each with volume discounts available. The following list is just a sampling: *Basic Construction and Materials Take-off*, a textbook for a course taught by the council, $12.00; "Current House Construction Practices," a compilation of articles by the council, $3.00; "A2.0 Business Dealings with the Architect and the Contractor," 50 cents; "C5.32 Kitchen Planning Standards," 50 cents; "D7.0 Selecting Lumber," 50 cents; "TN #1 Prevention and Treatment of Construction Damage to Shade Trees," 50 cents; "Instruction Sheet #20 Wall-Panel Construction Using Double Header," $1.

From the Society of Certified Kitchen Designers, 124 Main St., Hackettstown, N.J. 07840: "Directory of Certified Kitchen Designers." A state-by-state, city-by-city, nationwide listing. Free.

From the American Institute of Architects, 1735 New York Ave., Washington, D.C. 20006, (202) 626-7460: "You and Your Architect," by David R. Dibner (free); and "Architects Bite!" a pamphlet that dispels some strange ideas about architects (free).

"Homeowner's Glossary of Building Terms," Publication #603H of the Consumer Information Center, Pueblo, Colo. 81009.

"House Construction—How to Reduce Costs" ($2.50), of the Department of Agriculture, Office of Government and Public Affairs, Publications Division, Washington, D.C. 20250.

"Why Are New House Prices So High, How Are They Influenced by Government Regulations, and Can Prices Be Reduced?" Free from General Accounting Office, Distribution Section, 441 G Street N.W., Rm. 1518, Washington, D.C. 20548.

"Designing Affordable Houses" ($1.75). Available from HUD, Superintendent of Documents, U.S. Government Printing Office, Washington, D.C. 20402.

23

...Or Building It Yourself

Can you build your own home? Should you attempt it?

Some of you reading this will be quite confident indeed about your own abilities. Others have the dream, but gulp at the enormity and complexity of the job. And more than a few of you pay no mind to your own doubts. You swallow hard and decide to plunge in, because the only home you can afford will be the one you build yourself.

With the exception of the supremely confident, you are all going to be in for a surprise. You *can* build a house even if the last time you picked up a hammer was to put together a halfway decent bookcase five years ago. Not even a bookcase to your credit? You too can build a house. Read on.

Building it yourself can save you 20 to 60 percent of the cost of a home, depending on how much of the work you do yourself and what percentage you farm out to professionals. Besides the cost saving, doing it yourself will bring an enormous sense of accomplishment, which is why a growing number of Americans who can well afford to have a home built for them decide to deal with the 2 x 4s themselves. Those who have undertaken this, the ultimate do-it-yourself job, say they now feel they can do anything, which is a pretty nice way of looking at the world.

Once you have the land, the style of home you erect can be just about anything you want, thanks to the increasingly attractive array of homes for self-builders these days.

You can design and build the house with no help from contractors or housing manufacturers or architects. Or you can have an architect design the place for you, and then you build. Or you can turn to the factory-built house, which is likely to be your choice. After all, most novices scarcely know where to begin building a house. The factory-made home practically takes them in hand and *shows* them. Figures vary from one source to the next, but broadly speaking, something like 40 percent of all new homes are factory made these days. That is because they are less costly than traditional site-built, or stick-built, houses. Those savings are passed along to you, particularly if you are doing the building yourself. These are good, solid houses too. One couple who purchased a $75,000 home package from a manufacturer spent another $125,000 to "polish up" the house. They conceded that they did not save any money having the house come from a factory, but they liked the efficiency of the process and the quality of construction possible in a factory, quality they said they might not see in on-site construction today.

The first step in talking about factory-built housing is getting the terminology straightened out, for even within the trade the semantics can be confusing:

• *Manufactured homes*. This nowadays refers to mobile homes that are put together in a factory and delivered to the building site, where they are assembled. They come in one, two, or three units. Manufactured homes are built according to federal HUD standards, while other forms of factory-built homes are made to comply with state building codes.

• *Precut homes*. These are more commonly called "kit homes"; they are houses that start out as pieces—sometimes hundreds and thousands of them—manufactured in a factory and then delivered to the site for assembly. Sometimes the pieces form little more than a shell; other manufacturers deliver homes more complete, but still usually exclusive of heating, wiring, and plumbing.

• *Modular/sectional homes*. These are also put together in a factory but are 95 percent complete when they leave that plant, right down to the plumbing fixtures, kitchen appliances, flooring, and the like. A modular home can sell for over $250,000, so keep in mind throughout this chapter that factory-built does not necessarily mean cheap.

• *Panelized homes*. These fall somewhere between precut and modular, offering more than the former, but a less complete package than the latter.

Modular homes, because they are usually delivered in two halves to be put together on the site, require special tools and a number of workers. Not to mention requirements that the site be large enough to accommodate delivery of the house and that it be level too. This is more than a mom and pop job, and indeed most modular homes are purchased by builders for their own developments. Modulars are also used for hotel/motel units and for multifamily housing, where the units are stacked on top of one another. You as a neophyte are more likely to purchase homes in the precut category, which we will call "kit" homes from now on. The term annoys some in the industry ("sounds like a toy instead of a house," remarked one marketing man), but it seems to have taken root in our housing lexicon. Kits include just about any design put out by those manufacturers, including the popular log and dome homes. The kit folks are flexible, too. Many manufacturers will allow buyers to submit their own plans, and they will put together a kit following that style.

Kits vary widely from one manufacturer to the next and, as stated above, while the quality may be uniformly good, the amount of house you buy can run from little more than a frame to a far more complete product. That's why shopping the market here is so important.

Your home—something like a 40-ton pile of materials—is sent by flatbed truck from the plant. If your site is more than seven hundred miles or so from the manufacturer, delivery will be by rail. Sometimes there are two or three shipments. All of the material is color-coded and accompanied by blueprints and a catalog so that you can more or less easily see what goes where. Some manufacturers also provide on-site assistance for the novice, for which you might have to pay $100 a day. Besides offering entire houses, most kit manufacturers sell home additions too.

What the House Is Likely to Cost

Prices vary widely, according to the style of home selected, completeness of the package, the materials you use and, most important, how much of the work you do yourself. We'll assume you own the land on which you will erect the house.

Kit homes can run from $15,000 to well over $100,000. You can even spend that six-figure number for a fancy two-story log home. No, that isn't cheap, but let's see how you can make *your* kit house more affordable.

First, you will be saving several thousand dollars by not hiring an architect to design the house. Next, you must look at how much of the work you are willing to do yourself. Even if you farm out the entire project, from contractor to painter of the interior walls, you still can save something like the 3 to 7 percent a developer would make in building and selling a home. You should be able to make your savings more substantial than that, however.

Let's say you purchase a $40,000 kit package. Here are some extras that will add dollars to the price tag:

$ 700	clearing the site
3,000	well
4,000	septic system
6,000	full basement ($2,000 if you opt for just a foundation)
3 to 4,000	utility line hookups if there are no utility lines on the land

Then what about a road if there is none leading to the house? Will you want to improve the basic kit package—substitute better-quality kitchen appliances, perhaps, finish the exterior with stone siding, improve insulation? What about what the kit doesn't provide? What if you have to finish floors yourself? Many kit packages suggest you purchase some materials from local lumberyards and hardware stores. How much will that come to? What about tools, and the cost of buying or renting what you do not have? And then there's the heating system, plumbing, and electrical hookups.

You can see how a $40,000 kit home can add up and we haven't even considered your calling in a professional contractor to lend a hand for a few days, or to bail you out completely if you find you just can't do the job.

To repeat, you can and will save money if you want to do so, but you can see that the savings will come from "sweat equity"—yours. Otherwise the house can, as you have seen from the experiences of the couple a few paragraphs back, easily go well over any budget price. This caution is for those who are building to save money, of course, not for owner-builders who can afford overruns.

Those who have gone the do-it-yourself route (known as DOY in the trade) have been, almost to a man and woman, satisfied with the finished product. The annoyances that do crop up are in the area of a piece or two missing from the package, which can usually be sent along in the next shipment, and aggravations with local subcontractors. And of course, there are frustrations with one's own mistakes, almost all of which can be covered up quite neatly.

Points to Ponder

If you are thinking at this point that a prefabricated house may indeed be the solution to your housing needs, here are a few points to mull over while polishing up the old tool chest:

1. *Check the company you are considering.* The ones we will mention in this chapter are reputable and have manufactured thousands of homes. But perhaps you are engaging someone new to the business, or a company *you* have never heard of. No matter what firm interests you, ask to see their homes in your area. If it requires a thirty-mile trip to the nearest site, make that journey. See what a prefab looks like, if you haven't before (you almost certainly have, but didn't know it). Talk with the owners of that house. Talk cost, which they probably won't mind. And learn from the mistakes they will tell you they made.

2. *Be sure you know what you are getting for your money.* What services will the sales representative provide? Is there any follow-through after delivery of the package?

3. *All things being equal, consider the kit manufacturer closest to your home.* You will pay for materials according to miles traveled to the site. You should know, however, that several of the larger manufacturers have plants around the country, so if the company headquarters is in the Midwest and you live in Georgia, you may still come out all right, price-wise, if they will be shipping your home from their Arkansas plant.

4. *Ask about a lower purchase price if you buy in the off-season,* when things are presumably slow at the factory.

5. *Problems can loom peculiar to the style of home you choose.* For example, if you want a log home, think about building it yourself and lifting those logs, which weigh hundreds of pounds apiece. You can lift bricks alone, but erecting a log home will take help from a spouse or a friend or two or three. If you are interested in a geodesic dome you may have trouble finding contractors or subcontractors. "Sixteen roofers came out," said one dome owner. "Most of them said, 'Hell no, lady. No way.' "

6. *Think about the resale value of the house.* What matters here is that the home you are planning to erect fits into the neighborhood and landscape, not that it is precut. The house should be in the same price range as the others, and not so much a tribute to your unique style that it will sit on the market for years when you want to sell. That happens sometimes with homes architects build for themselves. Quite understandably, those homes are statements, and the men and women designing them incorporate every feature they have ever desired to come up with their dream home. But unless they are fortunate enough to find a soul whose taste meshes with theirs, the houses are likely to sit unsold sometimes for years. Heed that caution.

7. A *special alert* to those interested in putting up a dome home: More than one owner of those distinctive houses has had to plant a huge hedge around his property to discourage gawkers. Some planned communities have banned domes. Be sure before you order materials that you can indeed put your dome where you wish.

Finding the Prefab Home for You

Here are some companies that offer precut homes of many different designs, from Cape Cods to bows to ranches to A-frames—including one, two-, and two-and-a-half stories. All offer printed material to acquaint you with their housing styles:

Acorn Structures, 930 Main St., Acton, Mass. 07120 (617) 369-4111.

Kingberry Homes/Boise Cascade, 1501 Johnson Ferry Rd., Suite 222, Marietta, Ga. 30062 (404) 977-0036.

Scholz Homes, 3103 Executive Parkway, Toledo, Ohio 43606, (419) 531-1601.

Stanmar Homes, Boston Post Rd., Sudbury, Mass. 01776, (617) 443-9922.

Techbuilt Homes, 585 State Rd., North Dartmouth, Mass. 02747, (617) 993-9944.

Yankee Barn Homes, P.O. Drawer A, Grantham, N.H. 03753, (603) 863-2940.

For still more information, the National Association of Home Builders offers the illustrated booklet "Guide to Factory Made Housing," which explains the housing style and lists names and addresses of manufacturers. Send a check or money order for $8, plus $2 for handling to NAHB, 15th and M Sts. N.W., Washington, D.C. 20005, attention: Publications Orders.

Two popular styles of kit homes are log and dome houses. Here are some of those manufacturers. They offer free brochures, but you can expect to pay $3 to $6 for catalogs:

New England Log Homes, 2301 State St., P.O. Box 5056CJF, Hamden, Conn. 06518, (800) 243-3551.

Real Log Homes, Box 202, Hartland, Vt. 05048, (800) 451-4485.

Ward Log Homes, Box 72, Dept. 411, Houlton, Maine 04730, (207) 532-6531.

Daystar Shelter Inc. (dome homes), 22509 Cedar Dr. N.W., Bethel, Minn. 55005, (612) 753-4981.

Monterey Domes, Inc., Riverside, Calif. 92517, (714) 684-2601.

The Federal Department of Agriculture's Forest Products Laboratory, P.O. Box 5130, Madison, Wis. 53705, publishes free booklets on the construction and preservation of log homes.

Log Homes, a publication subtitled "The Complete Guide to Buying, Building and Maintaining Log Homes," is available for $10.95 from Home Buyer Publications, Inc., P.O. Box 2078, Falls Church, Va. 22042, (703) 241-5560. For $1 the company will send you a list of log home builders in your state. Credit cards accepted.

You can also check your Yellow Pages for listings under "Buildings—Precut, Prefabricated and Modular" and "Log Cabins and Homes."

Finally, there is the book, *Building a Log Home from Scratch or Kit*, by Dan Ramsey (TAB Books, Inc., 1983, Blue Ridge Summit, Pa. 17214, $17.95, hardcover).

Paying for a Kit Home

Manufacturers usually ask for 25 percent down at the time the order is placed, the balance paid C.O.D., although each company is different and some may ask for three-stage payments, the initial one being as low as 10 percent. All require full payment on delivery of materials, however, except in a very, very few instances where the owner-builder can show a letter of commitment from a lender so the company knows the money is on the way. Subcontractors can be paid in stages, of course, but they too will want all their money by the time the job is finished.

The Barrington model by New England Log Homes, Inc. is priced from just over $27,000. *Reprinted with permission of New England Log Homes, Inc.*

So your house must be paid for in up-front money. You will need a construction loan and then, when the job is finished, a mortgage. Financing can sometimes be a problem, although the situation is easing a bit as the precut home becomes more visible on the housing landscape. Note, too, that most of these homes are built to FHA and VA specifications.

It isn't the house that's the problem. It's you, the inexperienced builder. You may have to shop around quite a bit to find a lender willing to believe in you and your ability to build a solid house.

Some kit manufacturers will help you find financing. By all means ask the sales representative with whom you are dealing. New England Log Homes, for example, which at this writing is the leading log home manufacturer in terms of sales and dollar volume, helps put buyers in touch with lenders in their area. A spokesperson for the company added, however, that they consider log homes somewhat easier to put together than other precut styles, and lenders may agree. "It's simpler to build a log home," said the spokesperson. "When you put up the exterior walls, you've also put up the sheetrock, framing, and insulation in one step. There's less you can do wrong."

You might also try the Farmers Home Administration to see about securing a FmHA-backed mortgage, which is available in communities of under 10–20,000 population and to certain low- and moderate-income groups (income ceilings vary according to family size and change regularly). If you qualify you can secure one of these loans at very favorable interest rates.

Besides being nervous that you won't finish the job, or that you will make a mess of it, lenders are also, quite understandably, concerned that you might fall off the roof of the house and incapacitate yourself (or worse). There, too, the house would not be finished, and then what would they do? Take back a hole in the ground with a few beams poking up?

Here are pointers that can help your cause when you go hunting for financing:

• Dress neatly and businesslike. You want to reassure the lender that you are indeed a serious person. Clothes do not make the man (or woman), of course, except to bankers.

• Bring with you detailed cost estimates for the project, a building schedule, and plans. Put everything in file folders. Scraps of paper, ideas in your head, and scribblings on envelopes tend to frighten lenders.

• Remember that if you are building a house that's too far out, design-wise, the bank may also give you a cold shoulder. And, of course, price-wise it should be within your income range to pay back, just as buying any conventional house should.

• A lender might be greatly reassured if you have a partner (or spouse or friend) who will be building with you, so that if one falls off the roof, the other can shed a few tears and carry on. Bring that partner with you to the lending institution.

• A certificate from an owner-builder school showing that you have completed its course can help (more about them later).

• Consider an insurance policy covering your ability to finish the project. Lenders would like that too.

You may have no trouble with financing in the Midwest or the West, where rugged build-it-yourself types presumably abound and sweat equity projects are more common. You may even have an easy time of it in the effete East, if you follow the above suggestions and take any assistance passed along to you by your kit manufacturer. You may even, in fact, choose a home according to the level of financing assistance offered by that company.

Finally, if you're interested in building a dome house, you might want to write for a copy of "Dome Home Mortgage White Paper" to prepare yourself for facing a mortgage lender. The report is free from the National Association of Home Builders' National Dome Council, 15th and M Sts., NW, Washington, D.C. 20005. You'll also be sent a list of banks that lend money for dome homes.

"But Can I Really Build it Myself?"

Sure. The kit you are sent, as mentioned earlier, will be elaborately set up to assist you in putting together the materials. You may be better off hiring a professional at least to stand by until you are finished with the erection of the frame, but many DOYs sail right through that too. You can call in a local contractor, or a company representative.

Naturally, you will have prepared yourself for this mammoth project well before the first shipment of materials begins winding toward your building site. There are dozens of homebuilding books on the market, some of them mentioned at the end of this chapter. We are assuming that you own the land. If you don't, read over Chapter 44 for specifics on buying acreage on which to build. The kit manufacturer you are interested in can help in directing you toward—or steering you away from—land unsuitable for his product. That could be land that is not level or a lot too small for the trucks delivering the building materials. Assume you will need a site wide enough to accommodate the turning radius of a 40- or 50-foot multiwheeler. There are many other points to consider when buying land, of course, such as access roads, utility lines, zoning for residential properties, etc. Chapter 44 will help, and so, too, will Chapter 22, which talks about having a home built for you.

Talk to neighbors, too, as you think about building. One woman, building her first home, a summer place at the shore, called the local senior citizens office that offers volunteer help from retired persons to those setting up their own business. She asked if they had any carpenters, plasterers, etc., on file. They did and she will follow their guidance when she starts work. She was also told by locals in that area that there are "a lot of old-timers who will get a kick out of helping a young woman build a house." Great. She'll take advantage of *their* goodwill too. And keep the beer and sandwiches coming.

How long will the project take? A modular home, the ones that arrive at the site in two or three parts virtually 95 percent complete, can be put up in a day or two. Precut, or kit, homes can be completed in four to ten days with a crack team doing the work. The average neophyte doesn't work that quickly. One couple and a few of their friends erected an 800-square-foot house in eighteen months of weekends. Another man is still building his weekend home after fourteen months. But it's ninety miles from his principal residence and he can only work weekends. Still another owner-builder, working fulltime on the construction of his primary home, had the house completed within four months, although he subcontracted for electricians, plumbers, and a few other workers who were working on the place along with him. A woman began a ranch home in June and finished the following March, working only on weekends with family members and friends helping sporadically. So there are many ingredients to the time factor, the principal ones being how much time you can spend on the project and how far you are from the building site.

What About Builders' Schools?

School is an excellent idea for the inexperienced would-be builder who has both the time and money to spare. Actually it isn't that much of an expense when compared to the cost of the project you are undertaking.

Schools for owner-builders have been cropping up regularly in the last decade as interest in DOY projects grows, right along with mortgage interest rates and prices for traditional, site-built homes.

Learning how to build a house can't be confined to a classroom. Students at Heart-wood Owner-Builder School in Massachusetts get plenty of hands-on experience. *Reprinted with permission of Heartwood Owner-Builder School.*

The finished product, built by several classes. *Reprinted with permission of Heart-wood Owner-Builder School.*

The schools offer hands-on experience in the building trades, as well as a well-thought-out curriculum that can include many special courses in areas of particular interest to the student—cabinetmaking, for instance, or solar installations. Some schools feature courses in building additions to one's house.

What's an owner-builder school really like? Let's take as an example the first of the schools—the Shelter Institute in Bath,

Maine—begun in 1974. Over 6000 students have completed courses there that are offered year round. A sampling of workshops includes drafting for blueprints; wood model framing; sighting solar angles and plotting obstacles; and wiring skills. The Shelter Institute, like many other schools, offers a "super-compressed" two weeks of classes six days a week, as well as shorter one-week courses, evening classes, and one-day workshops.

Each of the schools is different in curriculum, but all teach beginners how to build a house, not just in classrooms but on actual building sites where the students don't just watch, they build. An important aspect of that studying is just becoming familiar with building terms and tools.

Costs range from around $200 to $600 for the complete home-building course (usually there's a lower combination rate for couples). Sometimes lodgings are included in the price. If not, students are given directories of nearby private homes and motels where they can stay.

Whether you go on to build your own home after "graduating" or not, you will leave these schools with confidence. The business of building a home will be demystified. You will feel more secure talking to those in the trade, with the folks at the lumberyard, with contractors and subcontractors. And since confidence is such a large part of getting any job done, your tuition is likely to be dollars well spent. Go for it, if you can.

The following is a partial list of owner-builder schools:

ALASKA
Matsu Community College, University of Alaska, P.O. Box 899, Palmer, Alaska 99645, (907) 745-4255.

ARIZONA
Arcosanti Workshops, 6433 Doubletree Rd., Scottsdale, Ariz. 85253, (602) 948-6145.

CALIFORNIA
Owner Builder Center, 1516 Fifth St., Berkeley, Calif. 94710, (415) 526-9222.
Owner Builder Center of Sacramento, P.O. Box 739, Fair Oaks, Calif. 95628, (916) 961-2453.

COLORADO
Colorado Owner Builder Center, Box 12061, Boulder, Colo. 80303, (303) 449-6126.
Denver Owner Builder Center, South Golden Road, Golden, Colo. 80401, (303) 232-8709.
Durango Owner Builder Center, Box 3447, Durango, Colo. 81301, (303) 247-2417.

CONNECTICUT
Building Resources, 121 Tremont St., Hartford, Conn. 06105, (203) 233-5165.

FLORIDA
Owner Builder Center at Miami-Dade, 11011 S.W. 104th St., Miami, Fla. 33176, (305) 596-1018.

GEORGIA
Georgia Institute of Home Building, 5 Dunwood Park, Atlanta, Ga. 33038, (404) 393-9788.
Georgia Solar Coalition, Box 5506, Atlanta, Ga. 30307, (404) 525-7657.

HAWAII
Pacific Owner Builder Center, 4562 Aukai Ave., Honolulu, Hawaii 96816, (808) 523-8056.

ILLINOIS
Home Building Institute, 2424 N. Cicero Ave., Chicago, Ill. 60639, (312) 745-3901.
Owner Builder Seminars, 409 Gartner Rd., Naperville, Ill. 60540, (312) 355-6128.

KENTUCKY
Urban Shelter School, 1252 S. Shelby St., Louisville, Ky. 40203, (502) 636-3663.

MAINE
Cornerstones Energy Group, 54 Cumberland St., Brunswick, Me. 04011, (207) 729-6701.
Shelter Institute, 38 Center St., Bath, Me. 04530, (207) 442-7938.

MASSACHUSETTS
Heartwood Owner Builder, Johnson Rd., Washington, Mass. 01235, (413) 623-6677.

MICHIGAN
Michigan Owner Builder Center, 1505 E. Eleven Mile Rd., Royal Oak, Mich. 48067, (313) 545-7033.
Riverbend Timber Framing, 415 E. Adrian, Blissfield, Mich. 49228, (517) 486-4044.

MINNESOTA
Minnesota Trailbound School, 3544½ Grand Ave., Minneapolis, Minn. 55408, (612) 822-5955.
Owner Builder Dome School, Natural Spaces—Rt. 3, North Branch, Minn. 55056, (612) 674-4292.

NEW YORK
Earthwood Buildings School, RR1, Box 105, West Chazy, N.Y. 12992, (518) 493-7744.
Eastfield Village, Box 145 R.D., East Nassau, N.Y. 12062, (518) 766-2422.

Owner Builder Center of New York, 160 West 34th St., New York, N.Y. 10001, (212) 736-4909.

NORTH CAROLINA
New Homestead School, Rt. 1, Murphy, N.C. 28906, (704) 837-8873.

VERMONT
Yestermorrow, Box 76A, Warren, Vt. 05674, (802) 496-5545.

VIRGINIA
Spectra School, Flint Hill, Va. 22627, (703) 675-3288.

WASHINGTON
Northwest Owner Builder Center, 1139 34th Ave., Seattle, Wash. 98122, (206) 324-9559.

Here are two more sources of information: "The Owner/Builder Schools" directory is available for $2 from Home Again Publishing, Village Station, P.O. Box 421, New York, N.Y. 10014, (212) 473-5583.

And for more reading on the subject, there's "Owner/Builder Quarterly" magazine, available by calling (800) 547-5995.

Finally, if you are too far away from any of these schools, look to trade schools in your area that may from time to time offer building courses, or at least a specialized course in one aspect of the operation.

Those who have taken courses at owner-builder schools have been overwhelmingly pleased with the course of study and with what they have learned. Disappointments are few and are concentrated on the distance you'll have to travel to the job site and sitting through some classes and subjects that hold little or no interest for you. Otherwise—money well spent.

Then There Is the Yurt

Never heard of it? Building a yurt is probably not a serious resolution of your housing dilemma, but it could be an interim solution, depending on your current personal situation.

Yurts are Mongolian tent homes in use since the days of Genghis Khan. You stand more of a chance of seeing one today in such old movies as *The Conquerer* with John Wayne than you will anywhere near your community. A yurt resembles a cupcake, with the icing coming up to a rounded point. In early days the covering for the tent would have been leather or felt. Today, yurts have wood frames covered with vinyl-coated canvas. The roof is a spoke-braced cone with a Plexiglas skylight in the center. Since there are no windows, the skylight provides the only source of light. Yurts have good wall insulation and plywood floors. They range from about 13 feet to 32 feet in diameter.

Yurts have no electricity or water. They are heated by woodburning stoves and lit by kerosene lamps. Most have been built on or near college campuses to house students for a semester or two as part of a "life experience" study. There is a bathroom near the yurt compound and a place to do laundry—a regularly constructed dormitory, for instance, or other college building.

Yurts can cost as little as $500 or as much as $5000, depending on the quality of materials selected. They are portable, so you can literally fold your tent and steal away in the night.

What might work for you is erecting a yurt—and it takes just a weekend—in the backyard of your folks' home or one of amenable friends, using their plumbing and cooking facilities. If you are going to be in the vicinity for awhile—perhaps finishing college, or taking a special course, or jobhunting—you may find living alone in the yurt preferable to staying in the main house.

The only problem you may have here is from your municipality, which may have a strict zoning code. Then again, maybe the code does not concern itself with backyards. Or perhaps because the yurt has no electricity or plumbing it will not be considered a true residence.

"Building a Yurt" by Leonard Charney (Macmillan, $3.95, paperback) will take you step-by-step through the project.

Building Codes, a Building Permit and Inspections

Just a reminder: No matter what sort of house you build, it will have to meet the building code requirements of the municipality in which it is erected. To get a building permit you will have to have your plans approved by an arm of local government, and construction will have to pass specific inspections by a municipal building inspector. These requirements and inspections may cause delays, so allow for them.

For More Information

Two U.S. government pamphlets that will interest you are: "Wood Frame House Construction," Publication #177M (1981, 223 pages, $7.50) and "House Construction: How to Reduce Costs," Publication #172M (19XXX, 16 pages, $2.50). For copies of either, write to Consumer Information Center, Pueblo, Colo. 81009.

How to Build Your Own Wood-Frame House from Scratch, by N. H. Roberts, TAB Books, Blue Ridge Summit, Pa. 17214. Price: $11.95, paper.

509 Practical Money-Saving Tips for Homebuilders, by Alan D. Roebuck, TAB Books, 1982, Blue Ridge Summit, Pa. 17214. Price: $14.95, hardcover; $9.95, paper.

24

Today's Not-So-Mobile
Mobile Homes

Please don't call them trailers anymore. Even mobile home is becoming increasingly inappropriate as the industry undergoes dramatic changes that will permanently alter America's conception of that housing style. These days mobiles are more accurately called "manufactured homes," an umbrella term describing many styles of housing constructed in factories, then shipped in sections to home sites where they are assembled.

We'll continue to call them mobile homes here, however, until the industry resolves its terminology problem. And even though less than 2 percent of all units are ever moved from their original site, which again questions the term "mobile."

Mobile homes are given a special chapter, apart from the remainder of manufactured housing, because for many homebuyers mobile home "communities" represent an attractive and increasingly popular alternative to more expensive site-built housing. The homes are less costly for developers, too, and so are expected to represent a sizable chunk of the new-home market in coming years.

If you visit any of today's contemporary mobile home communities, you will notice little difference between those parks and suburban neighborhoods of traditionally built single-family houses. There are wide, treelined streets in each, attractive homes set back on small, nicely landscaped lots. Mobile homeowners frequently add their own extras, too—blacktopped driveways, carports, decks, and the like—making them even less distinguishable from conventional housing. In all, a far cry from the old "trailer courts" of the 1930s and 1940s that littered our highways when mobiles were introduced.

More than 10 million Americans live in mobile homes today. Just under half of those homes are in special mobile home parks. The others are on private sites, usually in rural areas and small towns.

Why are mobiles so popular?

• For economic reasons. Although you *can* spend well over $100,000 for a mobile home in a four-star park, the homes usually run much, much less. A new larger-size mobile can cost almost 40 percent less than a new site-built home.

• The units are safer than ever before, and no longer need to be thought of as tin firetraps. Mobile homes are the only form of housing in the United States where construction must comply with uniform federal safety standards. More about them later.

• New design features bring today's models even closer to the look of the traditional single-family home. Wood and stucco exteriors are replacing metal siding in some areas of the country. Pitched roofs, eaves, and overhangs take away that trailer look, and inside a mobile can boast a cathedral ceiling, bay window, fireplace, wet bar, and sunken living room.

• Mobile homes require little upkeep, a factor that appeals especially to older buyers. Exteriors are permanently finished and interiors may be completely paneled and carpeted.

• There is privacy and security in a mobile home park, since there is usually only one entrance. There is a greater distance from one's neighbor than with a condominium or cooperative apartment.

• Mobile parks foster a special sense of community among residents. There are often regular social events, perhaps a clubhouse, pool, and tennis court for residents.

• There are tax advantages equivalent to those of single-family homes, condos and co-ops. The interest on the personal loan or mortgage secured is tax deductible, as are real estate taxes, if any, on an individual unit, or one's share of that tax if it is apportioned among all residents.

This is not a housing style without problems, of course. Mention mobile homes and many Americans (ones who often have never seen one of the brand-new mobile communities) still wrinkle their noses. One retired Californian, living in a top-quality park in a resort community in that state, carries a picture in his wallet of his plush mobile to show relatives and friends in his former hometown. "You say you live in a mobile home and they just don't know what it really looks like," he says with a sad smile.

The image of the mobile home resident as a transient lingers too. But a survey conducted by Rutgers University found that mobile home residents in New Jersey moved every 7 years, compared with 5.5 years for families living in other housing. Other studies have also shown mobility rates among these residents closer to those of the population at large. And since mobiles aren't moved much anymore, today's buyers plan to stay just where their home is installed, not to hitch it behind the family Dodge when they decide to move.

Some communities feel that mobile home parks lower property values and contribute to suburban sprawl. That resistance is gradually easing, too, principally because of the magic word, ratables. Park owners pay real estate taxes to local governments on their communities, of course, and now a growing number of mobile home owners pay property taxes on their individual units, just like traditional homeowners. The attractive appearance of today's mobile home communities helps with acceptance too.

Finally, more and more local and state governments are mandating that higher-priced suburban areas provide affordable housing so that families in broader income ranges can live in those communities, another development that should see the appearance of mobile parks.

Just What Is a Mobile Home, Anyway?

By legal definition a mobile home is a motor vehicle, not real estate. A true mobile has a license tag attached to its siding in some discrete location and it has a ditch dug underneath its body to accommodate axles. If the axles are removed some states no longer consider the homes potentially movable and they are then considered real estate and their owners must pay property taxes. But that definition is now applicable only to older style units. Today's newer models are set in permanent foundations.

A mobile home is put together in a factory—there are dozens of manufacturers around the country—and then trucked in sections to the home site where it is assembled. That trip is usually the only one the mobile makes.

Besides buying into a mobile home community, you can purchase a model from a manufacturer and set it on a lot you own, unless prohibited by zoning laws in your community. These are being eased, too, to bring affordable housing within reach of more househunters. There is more about manufactured homes on private lots in the preceding chapter.

A word of clarification here, too. A mobile home should not be confused with a motor home. The latter has an engine and riders can

Contemporary mobile home, a far cry from yesterday's "trailers." *Reprinted with permission of Manufactured Housing Institute.*

Cathedral ceiling highlights interior of this double-width mobile.

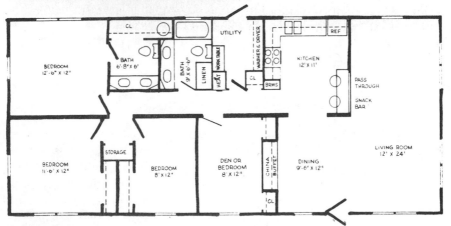

Double-width mobile—24′ × 49′, 1,176 square feet.

move freely between the driving and living areas. That is not true with a mobile home. A Winnebago, for example, is a motor home, not a mobile home.

Sizes and Prices

The historic mobile unit, the one in existing older parks, is the so-called single-width model. It measures 8 to 14 feet wide and 40 to 80 feet long. Those units can sell brand new for from under $20,000.

Two or more single-width units can be joined together to form what we see in the newer models—double- and even triple-width mobiles. For these you can expect to pay from $25,000 to well over $100,000 in top quality parks.

No matter what you pay, all mobiles come with appliances and frequently carpeting, paneling, and draperies. You may also be able to purchase furnished models. The sales price usually includes transportation to the site and installation.

That's new mobiles. The cost of buying an existing model varies widely. You can purchase a single-width unit in an older mobile community for under $5000. The quality of the park determines the sale price. As with any homebuying, however, you can expect that a rundown mobile in Fancy Acres Park will cost more than a gorgeous, immaculate model in Al's Trailer Court out on Highway #1. Naturally, that handyman's special would be a better investment for you than the spiffy home at Al's. Remember those three magic words in real estate—location, location, location—apply to mobile home parks just as they do to traditional neighborhoods.

There's a scam in mobile home sales to keep an eye open for— inflated prices of new models, allowing for kickbacks to dealers or developers. Bargain over the price of a home just as you would with a car, offering less than the sticker price. The FHA is now working to try to curb padding abuses.

Construction and Safety Standards

To ensure safer homes, in 1976 the U.S. Department of Housing and Urban Development promulgated uniform construction standards for the mobile home industry. Among regulations for the homes: two exterior doors remote from each other; smoke detectors wired to the electrical system with audio alarms outside each bedroom area; tie-down systems that anchor the unit; an electrical system that conforms to the one for on-site homes; and an increase in the fire-retardant rating for the surfaces of the furnace and water heater compartments and the area adjacent to the cooking range.

Mobile homes used to be considered fire traps, but studies in recent years have shown a steady decrease in mobile home fires, no doubt due to strengthened construction codes. Fire fatalities are now down to about the rate of those in single-family homes.

Single-width mobile homes, and even double- and triple-width mobiles on permanent foundations, are more prone to wind and storm damage than site-built homes. Problems with those units, the industry claims, are because of improper installation rather than from defects in the model's manufacture. If properly anchored, single-width mobiles should not be particularly vulnerable to damage from the elements.

Remember in your mobile shopping, however, that homes erected prior to 1976 are not subject to HUD safety standards, and neither are multifamily mobiles or units for the handicapped.

Renting vs. Buying

In some mobile parks you will buy your unit, while renting the ground on which it is installed. You will be expected to pay a "pad fee" or "land rent" to the owner. That amount covers utilities, water, trash collection, snow shoveling, and the like. The charge can be from $50 to $300 or so a month, depending on the location and quality of the park. Like other forms of rent, that figure can be expected to rise. However, in communities with rent control legislation you will have the protection of those regulations.

In other parks you buy not only your mobile but also the land under it. Those are the communities that so resemble the traditional suburban neighborhoods. Here you will be expected to pay your own real estate taxes for your unit, just as any single-family home-owner would. Mobiles in those communities are always double- and triple-width models. Single-width units are found in rental parks, although you may rent the land in some communities with double-width mobiles too.

You might also buy into a community that operates under the condominium form of ownership. Here there will be an owners' association you must join and a monthly maintenance charge to pay for your share of services and repairs to the complex. As with other condominium purchases you will own your own unit plus an undivided share in the common areas. Common areas may or may not include the land under your home.

A growing number of park owners are in the process of converting their communities from rentals to condominium ownership. Chapter 6 in Part I, "Conversion: Does It Spell Opportunity or Eviction?" offers suggestions if you find yourself in that situation.

Where the Mobiles Are

Can't find the newer mobile home communities in your area? They are off the main highway these days, frequently unmarked, hidden behind lavish landscaping, or otherwise difficult to spot. They can be in urban, country, desert, or waterfront locations. You might call your state mobile home association (nowadays probably called the manufactured housing association or some similar name), located in the state capital. They will probably offer a directory of parks statewide. You can also contact your state mobile home *owners* association, representing park residents, which may be located anywhere in your state.

If you are looking to relocate to a retirement mobile community, where one must be at least around forty-eight years of age to buy, you might consult *Woodall's Retirement Directory*. That book, published by a company that has been covering mobile homes for many years, is available for $7.95 from Woodall's, 500 Hyacinth Place, Highland Park, Ill. 60035. The book covers only Alabama, Arizona, Arkansas, California, the Carolinas, Florida, Georgia, Louisiana, Mississippi, and Texas. It includes details on facilities in mobile parks, recreation, prices and addresses, as well as data on climate, terrain, etc., in each locale.

There may be only a few first-class mobile communities in your region, unless you live in the South or the Southwest, where many of the top-grade parks are clustered. If you do find luxurious communities in your area, and they are still building on, you will have a good chance of finding a spot for your new home. Frequently, however, those communities are not adding new spaces and have long waiting lists for admittance. When your name does come to the top of the list, you will have to buy a resale mobile there.

Getting the Best of Both Worlds

If you are on a very tight househunting budget, try to find a mobile community where the owner expanded from the older, single-width section to add double-width fancier models on newly acquired land. If you buy one of those small units, you will be living in an attractive community and will have full access to any of the recreational and other amenities the owner may have added to upgrade the quality of the park for the newer buyers. In fact, you will have everything the buyers of those newer models are getting—including the fancy name of the park—but will have paid only a fraction of the price for your home that they did.

Some Problems with Mobile Home Living

Like any other housing style, mobile home living has its own set of aggravations and concerns you should bear in mind when shopping:

• There are practical considerations. Most of the homes have no basements, attics, or crawl spaces, and usually no garages, so if you are a pack rat or if you have a growing family, storage may be a problem (although cabinet and closet allocations inside the units are adequate). In older communities you may not even have a carport for your automobile.

• Those used to private homes, and even some former apartment tenants, may have to adjust to community life. Park residents are usually quite friendly, and many communities offer an active social program. All that bonhomie may be too much of a good thing for some. Then, too, you are a homeowner, but you also belong to a community, and must make decisions and concessions for the common good, just as you would in a condominium or cooperative complex.

• There may be those old, feudal landlord-tenant disagreements. You own your home, but you may rent the land, making you both a homeowner and a tenant. Rents for your space will probably rise from one year to the next. Some developers are less interested in top-flight maintenance and management than others. If your park is in a particularly desirable location, you may have another set of worries. One park operator, with a community of four hundred families, sold half his land, which had become extremely valuable when a huge office park complex rose nearby, to a commercial developer for a shopping center. Two hundred families were evicted. They had to move their homes to another location—if that was possible. The two owners of another park told its residents that they were retiring, and "phasing out" the park. Those horror tales occur more often in parks of single-width size than in the newer communities where mobiles are on permanent foundations, but they do illustrate one concern in renting, not owning, the land on which you set your home.

Financing

This is a side of the mobile home picture that is changing too. Single-width mobiles on rented space are considered personal property and not real estate. You would finance the purchase with a personal loan, usually at a percentage point higher than the prevailing mortgage interest rate. The loan would run ten to fifteen years. Downpayment requirements vary, but are usually low.

If your mobile purchase includes the land, you can probably secure a long-term mortgage, like any other homebuyer. The FHA, the VA, and the FmHA now also support mobile home financing. The dealer you buy from may also offer financing, but it's best to shop around before immediately accepting his terms.

Buyer's Checklist

When you go mobile home shopping, be sure to:

1. Talk to as many people as you can in the mobile community that interests you to see if they are satisfied with life there (maybe they will know of a better-run community a few miles down the road!).

2. Be careful about new communities under development that promise pools, clubhouses, co-op gardens for residents, and the like. With a cost overrun, and sometimes without one, the developer may decide to drop those amenities in favor of adding more mobile units. Those nice extras will get no further than the sales brochure.

3. Make sure pets and children are allowed, if that applies to you. In adult communities can your grandchildren, or any other young people, stay longer than a few weeks if the occasion arises?

4. Ask if there is an entrance fee to the community. In some states these are outlawed.

5. Look closely at the makeup of the community. Does everyone appear to be at or near retirement age and you are twenty-seven years old? Is there a profusion of tricycles and other children's toys about and you are a quiet-seeking fifty-seven? Too much of a lifestyle or generation gap may make you uncomfortable if a park consists almost exclusively of any one group—and you're not a member.

6. Have your lot ready when you plan to have your home delivered. This will require working closely with the park owner.

7. Get everything in writing. If you *think* the lot will be sodded, ask, and if that is so, get it in the sales contract. If you're assuming

that the home comes with the brand-name appliances you saw in the model, don't take that point for granted. Get it in writing. Remember your order goes from the park owner to the dealer to the manufacturer to the shop supervisor to the quality control inspector to the shipping clerk, probably back to the dealer, and then to be set up on your lot. There are plenty of chances for slipups, so if you want even the tiniest detail—*especially* the tiniest—changed from the model home, that notation should go into the contract before that paper leaves the sales office.

8. Ask how many changes you can make to the mobile you are considering. Will you be allowed, according to park regulations, to install awnings, a carport, a deck, and any other extras you would like? What will they cost?

9. See about a warranty that should come with your unit. Who is going to make repairs when they are needed?

10. Talk to the park owner about garbage disposal, parking, transportation to shopping, and schools in the community.

11. Ask about utilities. Do you pay your own bills or are they part of the ground rental fee?

12. Bear in mind that if you are unhappy with your choice—either the home or the mobile community—you will almost certainly have to move, without your mobile.

13. Do an analysis if you are considering purchasing an expensive mobile home. Would it be a wiser investment to buy a site-built house, considering price, appreciation, and other factors?

When You Want to Move

You will probably have to sell your unit when you want to move rather than transport it to another site. It costs hundreds of dollars to move a single-width mobile, if you can find a spot to put it. House movers usually will not touch double-width (or larger) homes, which are risky because they are just bolted together.

Will you get back your investment, and then some, when you sell? Single-width mobiles in less attractive parks depreciate the way an automobile would, so you are not likely to recoup your original investment there. But residents of attractive, higher-priced parks, whether of single-, double-, or triple-width sizes, are increasingly seeing their homes appreciate in value, which translates into a profit when they sell. The Foremost Insurance Company of Grand Rapids, Michigan, the largest insurer of mobile homes, reports homes in the better parks have been increasing in resale value by at least 5 percent a year, and as high as 15 percent a year in California during those times when runaway housing prices hit that state. So if you choose your mobile home *community* wisely, you can expect to sell your home at a reasonable, perhaps even dandy, profit.

For More Information

The National Federation of Mobile Home Owners, Inc., is at 3375 34th St. North, Suite 202, St. Petersburg, Fla. 33713.

The Manufactured Housing Institute, a group that includes manufacturers of mobile homes, offers free printed material for shoppers. Write 1745 Jefferson Davis Highway, Arlington, Va. 22202.

"Mobile Home Financing Through HUD" and "How to Buy a Mobile Home" are available free from your regional HUD office. Or write to HUD Publications Service Center, Room B-258, HUD, Washington, D.C. 20410. The financing booklet is Publication No. HUD-265-F(5); the one with buying tips is Publication No. PA-607.

"Tips on Buying a Mobile Home" is available at no charge from the Council of Better Business Bureaus, Inc., 1150 17th St. N.W., Washington, D.C. 20036. Please send a stamped, self-addressed #10 envelope. Try your local BBB office before writing.

The Foremost Insurance Company offers at no charge "Buying Mobile Home Insurance," "Tie-Down Guide," and "Safety Guide." Write Marketing and Communications Department, Foremost Insurance Company, 5800 Foremost Dr. S.E., P.O. Box 2450, Grand Rapids, Mich. 49501.

25

For Sale by Owner

For every person who successfully sells his own home in this country, there are nine and a half people who sell through a professional broker. Yet if you drive through a suburban town on any given spring morning, you'll see almost as many "For Sale by Owner" signs on the lawns of single-family homes as real estate agency signs. How then can that 9.5 to 1 ratio be accurate? The explanation is easy: most people who try to sell their own homes fail.

Even doing everything right will not guarantee you a successful homeowner sale. Too much depends upon the market mood in your local area, the desirability of your property, and luck. But doing everything right *will* improve your odds many, many times. And if you win against those odds, your efforts and your risk investment can be worth thousands of dollars. The essential element in doing everything right is the effective use of the tools and tactics of the real estate professional.

How to Set the Price

Most for-sale-by-owner houses, condominiums, and cooperative apartments are overpriced. Why? Primarily because emotions rule whenever people talk about "home." Sellers forget that they are selling shelter (a dwelling) and want to get paid for their prize rose gardens, the custom draperies on their windows, and the memories that fill their rooms almost as tangibly as the furniture. Often they fantasize their property as universally appealing and therefore set out to make "a killing in the market."

On the other hand, buyers, no matter how caught up in the fantasies of a dream house, tend to see each property as an item for

---

Why By-Owner Home Sales Fail

Overpricing

Poor marketing

Lack of financial savvy

Poor negotiating techniques

Legal tangles

Bad luck

---

sale. Besides wanting to love the house they buy, they want to get the most for their dollar. With but a few exceptions, they will walk away from an overpriced property without even making an offer.

The result? The for-sale-by-owner home stays on the market until the sellers become discouraged or exhausted. It is then listed with a broker, either at a more realistic price suggested by the listing agent or at its original high asking price which is then gradually reduced as selling pressure builds upon the owners or as they become more aware of property values in their area.

To avoid the delay, frustration, and inclination toward failure inherent in overpricing, you must estimate the fair market value of your property *before* you put it on the market. A professional appraiser would tell you that the fair market value of any property is the highest price that a ready, willing, and able buyer will pay and the lowest price that a ready, willing, and able seller will accept. And, for a fee, he would inspect your property and give you a written statement as to what he believed that magic number to be.

This method of determining fair market value is excellent (especially if two independent appraisals are made), but expensive. Each appraisal will cost you several hundred dollars, and ironically, you can get virtually the same information free.

Careful inspection of the property, knowledge of the local real estate market, and information on the cost of new construction are among the appraiser's tools, but his most essential and most heavily weighted tool is his comparables file. It is his key to fair market value and it can be yours.

Comparables (called comps in real estate offices) are properties similar to yours that have been sold in the past year or so. In an area which uses a Multiple Listing Service (MLS), a comparables file (or in some larger cities, a comparables computer printout book) is a collection of the listing sheets on all the properties that have been sold during the past year or so within a given area (that covered by the local Realtor Board). In areas that do not use MLS, a comparables file is the collection of all the properties listed or sold by any given real estate firm. In either case, those listing sheets contain all the information previously used in marketing the properties plus the actual selling prices and the actual dates of sale. This information helps to determine the value of a property that is about to be put on the market by indicating the exact price at which similar properties have recently sold.

"Fabulous," you say. "But how can I possibly get access to a comparables file?"

The answer may surprise you. Real estate agents will not only bring comps to your home but will also give you their personal estimate of the market value of your property. The service is called a competitive market analysis and it is free. Free because it gives real estate firms the opportunity to introduce themselves, valuable to you because it provides you with accurate competitive sales information without obligation.

Thus, to determine the fair market value of your property, you should call three to five different real estate firms with offices relatively close to your home. Tell the sales agents that you are planning to sell your home, and ask for a competitive market analysis to help you in determining its value. Virtually all efficiently run real estate offices will welcome your call. Make appointments with each agency on a different day or at least several hours apart.

After showing the agent through your home, sit down with him or her and compare your property with the comparables selected. Ask the agent why those particular listings were selected and ask what he or she thinks are the most important points of comparison. Ask what the agent thinks are the strongest selling points of your property, and the weakest. Finally ask at what price the agent thinks your property will sell. When you have three or more opinions, you should begin to see them cluster. If any agent is far too high or far too low, disregard that figure; it is probably inaccurate.

Call in and talk with as many agents as you must to satisfy yourself that you know the market value of your property. And remember, your own evaluation of the information on the comps is as important as anything an agent can tell you. So look them over carefully.

While each agent is in your home, he or she will also try to "sell" his agency to you. Listen, but do not sign anything. Listening to the agency sales pitches is a valuable part of your premarketing experience because you may indeed need professional help in selling your home at a future date. The market analyses are a good time to evaluate the services offered by various firms and the personalities and competence of a number of agents. But when, or if, a listing contract form is drawn from the sales agent's briefcase, simply state that you plan to talk with several different agencies before making any decisions about selling your home.

Besides determining the fair market value of your property before putting it up for sale, you will also need to decide upon an asking price. Not even a candidate for patron-saint-of-home-buyers would consider putting her property on the market at exactly the price she hoped to sell it for. Negotiating is an accepted and expected part of buying real property. The trick is to set an asking price that leaves you room to negotiate down toward your estimated fair market value figure without naming a price so high that it turns prospective buyers away.

Here again both the comparables and the real estate agents who bring them to you can help. While you are examining the comps, make a mental note of how much disparity you are seeing between the original asking prices and the actual selling prices. This negotiated gap often varies from one community to another. In some areas you will find homes selling rather consistently within one or two thousand dollars of asking price. In others, a five or ten thousand dollar difference is the accepted norm. To further complicate matters, however, norms which have been established in a community for years can change radically in response to national and/or local economic conditions.

So talk with the real estate agents when you invite them into your home; they are closest to the pulse of the market. Ask: How active is the market right now? How long does it usually take to sell a house? How much negotiating space is usually necessary? If you ask the same questions of every agent, you will get a professional overview of the market through a number of different eyes. Like their estimates of value, the agents' answers should cluster around certain themes and figures, but take the time here to pursue any offbeat comments that seem to have a chance at validity. A new or different idea could be on the leading edge of a coming trend.

You will be tired of talking with agents and hearing about the special services and listing benefits offered by their firms by the time you complete your several premarketing interviews. You will, however, have an excellent idea of the value of your property. Remember when you set the asking price, however, that in reality you have extra negotiating room built into the fair market value figure that you decide upon. For example, if you decide that $100,000 is the value of your property and you put it on the market for $104,000, you can sell that property yourself for $97,000 and still be $3000 richer than if you sold through a broker who charged a 6 percent commission. With that broker, a sale at $100,000 would net you only $94,000.

The chief sales advantage that an owner-seller has, therefore, is his ability to sell below market value and still come out with a greater profit than when working through an agent. To do this, however, one must be confident that he does indeed know market value, and one must believe that a bird in hand is indeed worth two in the bush. The chance to sell at slightly below market value but with greater net profit than by selling at market value with an agent is often turned down when greed whispers in the ear of a homeowner. Enough said.

Fixing Up the Property

"Cleanliness is next to Godliness" goes the old adage. In residential real estate sales, it's also next to more money. Dirt and clutter turn away more potential buyers or lower the negotiated sales figure more often than any other single factor. So get on your softest, oldest jeans, roll up your sleeves, and clean your house as though you were expecting *Better Homes and Gardens* to feature it in their April issue. Pay particular attention to the following:

1. *Bathrooms*. Fix dripping faucets! You'll also have to get the grime out from between the shower tiles. And be sure the room smells sweet, especially if it's windowless.

2. *Kitchens*. Your prospective buyers may never want to "eat off your floor," but they'd like it to look as though they could. Keep countertops free of clutter and the sink spotless. Clean the insides of the oven and dishwasher and make the stovetop shine. Put a tablecloth on the kitchen table and perhaps a vase of flowers, or, at the very least, keep it clear of dirty dishes.

3. *Hallways*. Wash away fingerprints, peanut butter and jelly stains, and crayoned murals. If the walls are beyond recapture, you'll have to paint or paper. People feel closed in by hallways, and there's nothing else for them to look at or for but the dirt.

4. *Bedrooms*. Clean out the closets; everyone will open them and they look bigger when nearly empty. Store extras under the bed; no one looks there.

5. *Living and family rooms*. Remove excess furniture. We tend to feel comfortable with the clutter of our lives and therefore not to see it. Try to get a sense of spaciousness. Less is often more.

6. *Basements*. Vacuum soot away from around the furnace and sweep or vacuum the floor. Get rid of cobwebs between the beams in the ceiling. Wash the windows! And stack all stored items that you can't sell or give away neatly together. Try to get a feeling of space and light.

7. *Every room*. Be sure all light switches and light bulbs work. Clean the windows. Check that door knobs are secure (you do not want one to fall off in the hand of a prospective buyer). And remove all clutter.

8. *Outdoors*. Clear away any junk: tires, garden tools, unused and dilapidated children's gym sets, rusting lawn furniture. Clean gutters and downspouts. Trim hedges and shrubs, especially those along a walkway. Seed the lawn if necessary and possible. Be sure to clean up all dog droppings regularly.

In virtually every home there are also some spots that need more than just cleaning, and the question of how much repair and redecorating a seller should do always comes up. The answer is slippery and very dependent on how handy one is and how much time and money one wishes to devote to preselling cosmetics. Decorating is not as important as cleanliness, but consider the following:

1. *Painting ceilings* (especially the kitchen). A freshly painted white ceiling adds light to a room without calling attention to itself.

2. *Touching up woodwork*. If you kept your paint, you can fill in chips and cover ground-in dirt with relative ease. If you don't have the original paint, an entire paint job takes a good deal more effort but adds a well-kept feeling to the rooms.

3. *Having carpets cleaned*. They'll look almost new for a while. If carpets are extremely worn and if they cover hardwood floors, consider tearing them up and having those floors refinished professionally. Although bothersome in terms of inconvenience and expense, this improvement will repay itself many fold. Buyers are inordinately discouraged by worn carpet and inordinately impressed by highly polished wood. Do not, however, install new carpeting even if your nearly dead carpet rests only on subfloor. Some buyers will walk away from a property because the living room wall-to-wall does

---

The Risk Investment in a
Selling-It-Yourself Effort

Advertising costs. These could run several hundred dollars.

Marketing materials. Brochures, signs, etc., under $100.

Fix-up costs. About the same whether you sell yourself or use a broker.

Time. Most appointments can be made evenings and weekends but someone must be available to do the showing.

Safety. Only a little preparatory work and stubbornness required to assure minimal risk.

---

not match their furniture. It is far better to leave the worn carpet in place, let your buyers complain about it, and then lower your asking price somewhat as a concession. For aesthetic appeal, you might cover the worst worn spots with area rugs. They are pleasing to the eye *and* you can take them with you after you sell.

4. *Painting outside trim*. Trim seems to crack and peel before shingles. Sometimes a house that on first impression looks as though it needs a complete paint job needs only trim work. This is worth doing. Repainting the entire house is another question. If you have the time and/or cash, go ahead; statistics indicate that you'll probably get your money back, plus a little. If ready cash is a problem, however, use the need for exterior painting as a negotiating point and be prepared to lower your price.

Market It Professionally

When you set out to sell your own home, you are competing with well-established and usually well-respected local business firms (real estate agencies) and their highly trained, well-funded, and carefully organized sales forces. If you want to fare well in this match, you must present your home as professionally as possible.

Much work must be done before you announce that your property is for sale. First, of course, set the price and fix and clean. Then prepare your marketing tools.

Directions to the Property

Begin by getting together clear and accurate directions. Many a by-owner sale dies before its first breath because the potential buyers get lost on their way and simply give up. *Do not let anyone get lost*.

Buy a street map of your town and spread it out upon the kitchen table. Mark the location of your property. Then find a *major* thoroughfare on each side of town, north, south, east, and west, and mark the location of a landmark or intersection on it that virtually everyone would recognize. Trace the route from it to your property. Now go out with a companion and drive each route. Note cross streets, traffic lights, odometer readings, landmarks, anything that will make your directions mistake-proof. When you return home, type or write out the directions from each approach. Make several copies, one for each phone extension, and a few extras. When potential buyers call in response to your advertising, give directions to them very slowly and then ask them to read those directions back to you, "just to be certain."

Your Sign

Besides good directions, you will need a sign both to advertise your property for sale and to reassure potential buyers that they have indeed reached the right place. The signs that most homeowners set out are best seen by the neighbors across the street. Do not paint your sign on one side of a board and then nail it to a tree or a post in the ground parallel to the road.

To be read most effectively by passing motorists, a sign should be two-sided and perpendicular to the road. Two feet by three-and-a-half feet is a good size. Quarter-inch plywood can be used and nailed to boards at either end which can then be driven into the ground. Use stencils (available at stationery stores) when you paint your sign so that your lettering will look as professional as possible. That lettering should be black, red, or another dark color; the background any color that is lighter and doesn't clash. (If you should have leftover house paint, you can create a sign that "matches your house!") But keep it simple. You need print only three lines: For Sale; By Appointment Only; and your phone number.

Newspaper Ads

The real estate classified section is the broker's primary marketing tool and it will also be yours. But this is one sphere in which you should not try to compete. Real estate agency ads are written both to advertise the company name and to entice people to call the office, but not necessarily to sell the property being advertised. You, on the other hand, are trying to sell your home, not hook customers.

You do not want calls from people who think yours is their dream house but could not possibly afford to buy it, and you do not want calls from people looking for a colonial when you have a split-level. Your advertising copy therefore should be short and straightforward (this actually sets it apart from the broker's ads). Here's a sample:

> *Kensington:* ranch, 3 bedrooms, 2 baths, family room with fireplace, full basement. ¾ acre lot. By owner, $84,500.   555-1234.

No matter how long or short your ad, always include:
- the town, and neighborhood or community, but not the street address
- the style of the house, but without adjectives such as "gracious," "rambling," "huge," "authentic" (save these for the phone)
- the number of bedrooms and the number of baths (this gives potential buyers an idea of size as well as shape, or style)
- one or two (certainly no more than three) special features, but avoid jargon like "custom kitchen"
- the size of the lot—most important in both weeding out and attracting buyers (some like a lot of land, some a little)
- the price—*an absolute must* (newspaper readers simply will not call on for-sale-by-owner ads that do not include price; but do not add qualifiers such as "*asking* $84,500" or "$84,500 *firm*"—this information belongs at the negotiating table)

If you are selling a condo, co-op, or an especially unusual piece of property, you may want to include some additional specifics such as "patio plan," "high-rise penthouse," "renovated 1790 farmhouse with two contemporary additions," "converted loft," or anything else that helps to give the potential buyer a concept of the kind of property you are selling in as few words as possible.

Don't worry about not including information on your dining room, laundry room, foyer, garage, deck, and vegetable garden. You will stimulate more phone calls by leaving questions in the minds of house-hunters than by an overkill in print. And once you have them on the phone, you can talk about your property to your heart's content.

Place your ad in local newspapers, especially weekly community publications. Money spent on advertising in the major newspapers of metropolitan centers fifty miles or more from your home is usually money wasted since most successful owner sales are to local residents. People moving long distances (especially transferred corporate executives) virtually always work with real estate firms.

When the Phone Rings

During the first days that your ad "hits the papers," your phone will ring circles around itself. But don't get too excited, about 75 percent of the calls will be from real estate agents looking to list your property. Tell them:

1. You've already decided upon an agent to handle your home if you do not sell it yourself. (You chose one from among those who did competitive market analyses.)

2. You are serious in your intention to market your own home but you will be happy to show the agent through the property and talk with him or her about the agency. (A chance for another opinion on probable selling price, a chance also to evaluate another agent, and most important, a chance to show your property to an agent who will then have personal knowledge of it, if and when you do list it with a broker.)

3. You are not interested in working through a real estate office at this time.

If an agent should say to you, "I'm working with this excellent couple that I'm positive will love your home!", do not allow him to bring his customers to your property, even if he tells you he can get $10,000 more than you are asking. Those same prospective buyers may see your ad in the next day's paper and call you themselves. However, if a real estate agent walks them on your property with your permission and then sells the property to them, you most likely will have to pay commission (see Open Listings in the next chapter).

Only under one very specific circumstance should you bend this no-professional-showings rule, and then only with a written agreement. If an agent calls you to say that he is working with transferred buyers who have only one week to find a home, you should allow the showing. It is unlikely that these buyers will have the energy or inclination to run down for-sale-by-owner ads, and because of their time pressure, they are excellent prospects. The opportunity therefore should not be missed.

Have the agent come to your home, alone, prior to the showing to get his copy of an agreement (which you can write out or type yourself), such as:

> With my consent, Mr. Alan Alert of Pushtoshov Realty will show my property located at (your address) on (date) to (name of prospective buyers). In the event a sale should be agreed upon and closed at $84,500 or another mutually agreeable price, I

will pay a commission of 6 percent of the actual selling price to Pushtoshov Realty. This agreement is valid only for the one day indicated.

(Alan Alert's signature) (Your signature)

(Date)

Insist that the name of the prospective buyers be entered into your agreement in order to validate beyond doubt the "transferred executive" story.

You may legally name a figure higher than your for-sale-by-owner price in your 1 day/1 buyer showing agreement: this to help compensate for lost net income due to commission. And most important, be sure that the words "agreed upon and closed" are in your showing agreement since you want to pay commission only if the property does actually close. Make two copies of this agreement; one for Pushtoshov, one for yourself.

Does all this sound to you like a lot of trouble for one single showing? Honestly, it's not, especially if you compare it to the legal entanglements you might be caught up in over a commission suit!

Your Telephone Marketing

What about the other 25 percent of the phone calls, the ones from prospective buyers? The manner in which you handle them could be a determining factor in your success or failure. It could also get you into trouble or keep you out of it.

• Answer the callers' questions and talk about your property enthusiastically, but ask for their names early in the conversation.

• If asked, give the callers your street address and directions to the property, but remind them that you will show your home only by appointment. Then stick to this stubbornly. Even if Betty Crocker comes to your door, tell her she is welcome to make an appointment for later in the day or on Saturday. (This rule is for your own safety.)

• Ask for the phone number of anyone who makes an appointment. Say, "Just in case we should need to cancel or postpone the appointment for some reason, may I have your phone number?" Then verify the name and phone number of your callers in the phone book. If there is no listing, or if the number is wrong, check with directory assistance. The operator will tell you if there is an unpublished entry for that name or if there is no phone service listed. If you're running into trouble, call the party back and ask questions.

A Model Flyer

$84,500   44 Winding Road   Hopewell, Massachusetts   L-shaped ranch.   Frame with cedar shakes.

6½ rooms: Entry foyer 4 x 8; LR 15.6 x 12; Dining area 12 x 11.9; Kit with dishwasher & garbage disposal 12 x 11.9; 3 BDS, 12 x 14, 10 x 12, 10 x 11; Ceramic tile bath.

Garage: 1 car oversized.

Basement: Full, dry with paneled family room, bookshelves, storage cabinets. Washer/dryer hookups, workshop.

Bilco doors to backyard.

Water: city.   Sewer: septic tank and leach lines.

Plumbing: copper.   Electricity: 220.

Storms/screens: Aluminum.   Heat: Oil-forced warm air.

Lot: ½ acre plus.   Built: 1966.   Zone: Residential.

Assessed at: $79,000.   Taxes: $1,800.

Included in sale: W/W carpeting; custom draperies; TV antenna and rotor; treehouse.

Membership in association with lake privileges passes with title.   Dues $125 year.

FOR SALE BY OWNER: (Your name)
                                    (Your phone number)

Flyers and Other Papers

If you househunted with a Realtor when you bought the home you're now selling, you probably remember sitting at your kitchen table with copies of MLS listing sheets spread out before you. These sheets are a marketing advantage for professional brokers since they allow the buyers to take home both the pertinent information on and a picture of each property that interests them. You can compete quite inexpensively with this marketing tool, however, by making your own flyer. Use the sample format above or structure your flyer to resemble the MLS sheets in your area.

Take a photograph of your home and glue it above the typed information. Then make as many Xerox copies as you need. (Start with a batch of twenty-five; you can always make more if you need them.) Even at 10 cents a copy, a hundred copies will cost you only $10.

Flyers should be kept on a foyer table or in any spot where they are easily visible, and they should be given out freely. (You can even give them out to your associates at work or in your church or recreation club "just in case" anyone should have a friend looking for a house.) Several other home-related papers, however, should be kept together in a drawer where they are readily available but not obvious and should be shown only to people seriously interested in buying. Gather those items in the following list that apply to your property:

• *Survey*. You may have paid for and received a survey map showing your property lines and the exact location of all structures on that property when you bought your home. If so, dig it out. Buyers are impressed and many questions can be cleared up with a drawing that words would only cloud.

• *Association rules and fees*. If you are selling a detatched house in a development where an association of homeowners owns recreation facilities such as a lake or a golf course, have information about the association and the facilities readily available.

• *House rules*. If you are selling a condo or co-op, prospective buyers will need to know if their lifestyle will fit into the community. Also you must inform them when a co-op board of directors has the right to approve or disapprove the sale of your apartment.

• *Names of condo or co-op board executives*. Phone numbers should be available also. Many buyers will want to talk with board members before buying.

• *Financial statement*. Condo and co-op financial statements are essential to calculating future maintenance costs. Have the past year's statements available and be ready to explain monthly maintenance cost increases due to major expenditures such as a new elevator, new roof, or heating system repairs.

• *Utility bills*. Serious buyers will want to know heating, water, sewer, and refuse removal costs.

Showing Your Home

Don't show the property you are selling in the same way you would show your newly bought home to your grandmother. If you think about it, you will feel a little silly standing in the middle of a room furnished with a sofa, two chairs, end tables, lamps, and a coffee table while you say "This is the living room."

Greet your customers at the door, introduce yourself, and say "You must be John Smith." Let the first person you meet introduce you to the others in the party. As you walk through the rooms point out items of interest ("We installed a trash compactor last year" or "This bedroom catches the afternoon sun") and ask questions ("Where are you folks from?" or "Do you have children who will be attending the schools?") In other words, use your showing time both to give information about the property and to get information about the prospective buyers.

You will know early in the showing whether or not your customers are interested. People who like the house tour much more slowly, ask more questions, return to rooms a second and even a third time, often trying to imagine their furniture placement, ask to see basements and attics, and almost always walk around outside the house to look at the foundation and see the property lines.

For your safety, it is best to have two people at home during showing times, but only one person should actually conduct the tour. The other person should remain quietly (reading, watching TV, etc.) in a room that has a phone. If you are nervous about showing to particular customers or if you must show alone, you can tell a neighbor or friend the time at which a showing is scheduled and arrange to have him or her call you approximately half an hour later as a check that everything is going well.

Try to keep children in one room (the family room or a basement playroom is best) during a showing. Keep pets under control; a snarling German shepherd or a jumping mini poodle can turn off even the most enthusiastic househunters. And, if you can, schedule appointments one-half hour apart. Nothing stimulates an offer as quickly as the knowledge that someone else is looking at the house.

Financial First Aid

The thought of getting a mortgage is far more intimidating to most homebuyers than the actual work of finding a property that meets their needs. Often in for-sale-by-owner situations, customers decide to buy and are then stopped cold when they come up against the question, HOW? You can improve your chances for a sale that will actually close, therefore, by having financial information available and offering it to those customers that you think are most interested in your property.

To do this, first read the home financing section (Chapter 19) in this book carefully. Then survey your financial local market by calling between five and ten lenders and asking:

1. What types of home-purchase financing do you offer?
2. How many points are you charging?
3. How much downpayment is required for the various loans? (This will be expressed as a percentage of the appraised value.)

4. What qualification guidelines are used in deciding upon loan approval?

5. How long after an application is filed is a loan commitment made?

Once you have this information for each of the lenders on your list, type a sheet or sheets headed: FINANCING INFORMATION FOR THE (YOUR NAME) HOME, (YOUR) ADDRESS, (YOUR) PHONE NUMBER. Enter the information for each lender as follows:

Nickel Savings & Loan Association
(Address and phone number)
• Thirty-year fixed-rate loans at 14 percent interest with 20 percent down and 3 points origination fee.
• Thirty-year AML (adjustable mortgage loans) at 12.75 percent interest with 20 percent down and 1 point origination fee.
• Loans with 5 to 10 percent downpayment can be arranged with private mortgage insurance.
• VA and FHA loans available.
• Qualification requirements: generally total monthly payment must not exceed 30 percent of monthly income.
• Loan processing time: usually three weeks.
At the end of your lender list, include the following information:

Just as an example: If this property were purchased at $84,000 with a thirty-year fixed-rate mortgage at 14 percent from Nickel S & L, the monthly payment would be: Principal and interest payment on a

Loan of $67,000	$793.95
Taxes ($\frac{1}{12}$ of $1,800)	150.00
Insurance (approximate)	21.00
	$964.95

To afford this property by Nickel's qualification guidelines you must have a monthly income of approximately $3,216 or an annual income of approximately $38,600.

There is no guarantee that this information will keep unqualified buyers from making an offer on your home, but it will help by making them aware of the financial obligation involved. When all is said and done, it's not the price of a home that people can or cannot afford, it's the monthly payment.

In times or areas where home sales are slow and difficult, some sellers try to attract buyers by offering what is being called "creative financing," which usually means seller financing of part or all of the loan. Generally, however, seller financing is not a good deal for the seller. (Why? You'll have to read Chapter 28.) But it is an option, especially if it's the only viable way to get the property sold. If you want to offer help with financing, say so at the very end of your Financial Information Sheet but do not give any specifics. Exactly how much seller financing you are willing to give should be a part of the negotiation on price and terms.

Also, if your mortgage is assumable, say so on your Financial Information Sheet and indicate the interest rate: assumable mortgage at 8½ percent. Do not indicate the principal balance on paper, however; let prospective buyers ask about it and be prepared to talk about second mortgages or wraparounds when they do.

Negotiating Techniques

If you get a phone call from a prospective buyer that starts out, "We'd like to make you an offer of $_____," no matter how low that offer is, reply "Thank you. Why don't you come to our house and we'll talk about it over coffee." Avoid telephone negotiating, especially in the initial stages, it is much too easy for either party to hang up the receiver and kill the deal dead.

When the buyers are at your home and seated around a table, start the negotiating by asking how they arrived at their offering price. The common replies are "It's what we think it's worth" or "It's what we can afford." Most likely neither of these statements is true. In reality, they have offered you their ideal price, a starting price in the negotiating process to balance your ideal asking price.

Do not try to discuss their offer or their reasons. Use that information as a lead to "OK, but let us tell you how we set the price on this house" and tell them about the real estate agents that you invited in for competitive market analyses. Mention the actual selling prices of comparable properties (especially if they are on the high side of what you really want). Then disguise your first counteroffer by saying "Of course we won't be paying commission, so we could afford to sell this property at $_____." The figure you name should be approximately 3 percent off your asking price. If the buyer is smart, he will say "Well, the real estate commission in this area is usually 6 percent" and make another offer somewhat higher than his original one. And thus you find yourself in the midst of negotiation.

Words Sellers Wish They Had Never Said—and Why

"Look, if the Joneses could get $57,000 for that place down the street, we can get at least $75,000 for our house."

IT TAKES NINE MONTHS TO SELL THEIR HOUSE. THE SELLING PRICE: $63,000.

"We don't want anything to do with real estate agents, my cousin's husband told us exactly how to sell."

THEIR HOUSE SELLS IN FOUR DAYS. FIVE WEEKS LATER THEY DISCOVER THAT THE SAME MODEL THREE STREETS OVER IN THE DEVELOPMENT SOLD TWO MONTHS AGO FOR $9,000 MORE.

"Are you kidding? $81,000! I don't care if it's your best offer. We're asking $86.5 and we know this condo is worth between $82 and $84."

FOUR MONTHS LATER THE APARTMENT IS SOLD THROUGH A BROKER FOR $82,500. BUT THE COMMISSION COSTS THE SELLERS $4,950.

"Let's buy it! We can probably get a hundred thousand for ours so we'll only have to carry an extra $15,000 on the new mortgage."

THEIR OLD HOUSE SELLS AFTER EIGHT MONTHS FOR $89,500. COMMISSION LOWERS THEIR NET CASH TO $84,130. THESE BUYER/SELLERS THEN CARRY A NEW FIRST MORTGAGE THAT HAS A $15,000 HIGHER PRINCIPAL AND A 3 POINT HIGHER INTEREST RATE THAN THEIR OLD MORTGAGE AND A $17,000 SHORT-TERM SECOND MORT-GAGE. THEY EAT SPAGHETTI A LOT.

Of course you will already have read the negotiating chapter in this book (Chapter 17) so you will know all the fine points of adjustment. Remember not to slam any doors. If things seem to be at a deadlock, you can always say, "Let's both think about this for a while. How about getting together again on Tuesday?"

The buyer may even call you before Tuesday and offer you an acceptable price on the phone. If he does, pause a moment or two and then reply, "I think we could live with that. Why don't I have my lawyer draw up a sales contract? Then we can get together in his office and go over it." Don't ask for deposit money; that will come upon signing of the contract.

The Role of Your Lawyer

Before putting your home on the market, you should arrange for an attorney to represent you if you are successful in the sale. Many people use the same attorney who handled the closing when they purchased the property. If you do not wish to do this, or if attorneys generally do not close property in your area, select an attorney who has a reputation for working with real estate. A great divorce lawyer is not necessarily a great real estate lawyer.

Your lawyer will not only protect your interests by drawing a tight contract, but also will play some of the roles generally assumed by a real estate broker. Help with further negotiation is one of these; financial qualification is another.

If your buyers are also using an attorney, have your attorney contact theirs to gather employment and credit-check information. If they do not use their own attorney, have yours call them directly. Gather enough information to be relatively certain that these buyers can afford to buy your property before you sign a contract.

Also be sure that you, your buyers, and the attorney(s) work out closing dates, contract contingencies, and any other aspects of the sale. One special aspect that should be included in every contract is a list of exactly which items of personal property are included in the sale and which are not. (Among the most common articles of contention are washing machines, draperies and drapery rods, chandeliers, portable dishwashers, microwave ovens, lawn furniture, mail boxes, and window air conditioners.)

Time on the Market

How long should you market your own property? There is no definitive answer, of course; so much depends upon market conditions, patience, perseverance, need to sell, and buyer response. As a general rule, however, sellers who wish to get their property sold as quickly as possible should not continue their for-sale-by-owner efforts beyond four to six weeks. During that period of time you will have pretty much exhausted the pool of active local buyers and you will need the help of real estate agents to bring in transferred business people, prospective buyers from nearby towns, and those local would-be buyers who simply will not get out to look at property unless prodded and chauffeured by a sales agent.

So prepare to list your home with a local broker, but do not feel as though you have failed. You are about to tap a much larger buyer pool with professional marketing help. The work you have done to date has been excellent preparation for the next step in your selling experience. Read the next chapter.

For More Information

Your local Board of Realtors usually has a variety of free pamphlets available on home fix-up and marketing.

IRS Publication 523, "Tax Information on Selling Your Home," is helpful.

Selling Your Home, by Carolyn Janik, Collier Books (1980). Price: $4.95.

26

When a Broker Sells
Your House

First, before you sign anything that even vaguely resembles a listing contract, you must take a mental leap. Stop calling the place you live in "your home" and start calling it "the house." You are about to sell a piece of property through a professional agent whose primary goal is to make as much money as possible, as quickly as possible. You will be most successful in achieving exactly this same goal, to your benefit, if you can separate the property you are selling from your sense of self-worth and from your memories of the time you have spent there.

If you cannot or will not make this separation, you are inviting an emotional bruising and you are handicapping the agents who will work to sell your property. Just one short story will make the point as clear as a $12 a stem crystal wine glass.

The house was a twenty-five-year-old, lifetime-single-owner Cape Cod on a busy state road. One of those properties that usually get nicknamed "a dog." It was also overpriced by $10,000. Yet a young, ambitious, aggressive sales agent convinced a prospective buyer that it was worth a bid. That bid was $13,000 under the asking price, but, as the agent believed, only $3000 under market value, and therefore well worth considering. She gathered together an impressive array of comparables, the earnest money check, a signed offer form, and some extra pens and set out to present the offer in the seller's living room.

First she showed them the comparables, carefully pointing out the actual selling price of each and how each was similar to or better than the property they were selling. Everything seemed to be going well; the husband and wife were listening earnestly. Then the agent brought out the offer form and the earnest money check and named the offering price. There was silence for the briefest fraction of a second before a verbal explosion began rebounding off every surface in the room. The wife was doing all the talking.

"What?! That's an insult, an absolute insult! This is my home! We built this house, we painted it, we've taken good care of it. It's a good house. It's never been any trouble to us. Anyone would be proud to own a house like this. Your buyers are blind! You just go back and tell them no! Absolutely not! And we never want to hear from them again."

The real estate agent made the error of trying to explain some basic principles of fair market value. She was directing her talk to the man, who was sitting quietly. The woman left the room and returned holding a broom over her head as one might hold a sledge hammer.

"You get out of here!" she screamed. "You and your offer and your stupid buyers!" She swung the broom down, hitting the sofa cushion next to the agent and then swung it up over her head again. "Get out of here! Just get out!"

The agent got out. That house sold five months later for $500 less than the offer she had taken to those sellers that day. And this is an absolutely true story.

The Broker-Sales Agent Connection

There is widespread confusion in the media and among buyers and sellers as to the differences ("Are there any differences?") between a real estate broker and a real estate sales agent. There are differences.

Every state from Alabama to Wyoming requires that anyone who acts as an agent in the sale of real property be licensed, and every state has two types of licenses: a broker's license and a salesperson's license. Only a broker can enter into a contract to handle the sale of property for its owner. A sales agent can act only for and under the supervision of his or her employing broker.

But no one seems to be able to tell the ducklings from the ducks. The major source of this confusion lies in the fact that hardly anyone sees a broker any more. The vast majority of the men and women who show houses and seek listings are sales agents. Most brokers are busy managing their offices.

Real estate law states that under a listing contract a broker establishes a fiduciary relationship with the seller, that is a relationship of trust. The sales agent might sign at the bottom of your listing agreement, yet that contract is not valid until a broker of record in the firm also signs. The sales agent may promise you advertising, but the broker will decide which houses are advertised. The sales agent may offer to take $500 less commission during a negotiating session in order to put together your deal, but the offer won't hold up unless his or her broker will approve it. A sales agent might show you a check for $1000 when making an offer for a buyer, but that check must be made out to the real estate agency or the broker. Only a broker is allowed to hold earnest money in escrow. And only a broker can collect a commission. (Usually, after a commission is paid, it is split according to prearranged agreement between brokers and sales agents.) And perhaps most important, a broker is entirely responsible for the marketing of your property. If one of her sales agents is guilty of a wrongdoing, the broker is also guilty!

Keep in mind therefore that although you may be enchanted or impressed by the personality and efficiency of the sales agent who is seeking your listing, you are in fact hiring the broker or the real estate brokerage company that she represents. Get to know that firm before you sign anything.

Factors in Determining the Right Broker for You

Office Location

When you get ready to choose the real estate agency that will market your property, think local. Don't be swayed by television advertising promising that pictures of your home in Fargo will be sent to ready, willing, and able buyers in Albuquerque, Seattle, Bangor, Rochester, Baton Rouge, and Kansas City. Those pictures may indeed be sent, but no one ever bought a house from a picture!

Real estate is a local business, and the marketing of your house is best handled by local people, people who know your area well. Choose an agency, therefore, that has an office in your town, or if it's a rather large town, on your side of town. Agents will be much more likely to show your property if it is close to their office than if they have to make a rather large loop, out of their way, to include it in a tour.

The Nature of the Business

Only slightly less important than the location of the agency is its specialty. If you are selling a house, you want an agency that deals primarily in houses, not an appraisal firm that carries a few listings on the side. If you are selling a co-op or a condo, you want a firm that deals in apartments on a homeowner basis, not a commercial firm that usually sells apartment buildings. If you are selling a multi-family house in the center of a midsized city, you want a firm that works with city buyers, not one that gears itself to $150,000 houses on two-acre lots.

Choose an agency that routinely handles your kind of property. You will then be assured of the best possible exposure because the advertising for the majority of the agency's listings will appeal to your kind of buyer. In other words, many ads for a particular kind of property means many prospective buyers for that kind of property.

Cooperation

Unless you want your property marketed in a special or unusual way, you should also choose a real estate agency that will cooperate with other agencies to get your property sold. The most common form of cooperation today is the Multiple Listing Service (MLS) subscribed to by Realtors. The member agencies of a Realtor Board agree to share their listings (with the commissions to be split between the selling firm and the listing firm). Information on all properties for sale is printed on a standardized form, usually with a picture of the house, and distributed to all members.

Some of our largest cities and some of our most rural areas, however, do not have Realtor Boards. In these areas certain groups of brokers will usually agree to cooperate with each other. Listings are not always distributed among offices, but word gets out and few sales agents hesitate to call another office to say "I have a customer in the $80,000 price range, may I show your house on Dogwood Terrace?"

Training and Competence

The competence of a real estate sales force can vary tremendously from one firm to another and even within the same firm. Since you want the most competent group possible to market your property, choose a firm where the vast majority of its agents are full-time people, earning their livings as real estate agents. (Not chemistry teachers who work after school, weekends, and during vacations!)

Many excellent firms allow licensed agents who wish to work part-time to act as referral associates only. This arrangement usually works well since the people who answer the phones and service the listings are full-time professionals familiar with the day-to-day changes in the marketplace.

Most of the large franchises (Century 21, Realty World, Electronic Realty Associates, to name but a few) have training programs that are required for all sales personnel. These courses are generally good agent preparation and help prevent your carrying incompetents or newly licensed and untrained salespeople on the back of your selling attempt. Perhaps the best program for sales training however, is that of the Realtor Institute. You might ask the agent trying to persuade you to list with his or her firm how many members of the staff write GRI (Graduate Realtor Institute) after their professional names.

Financial Savvy

Relatively new among the services offered by real estate firms is slick, high-powered mortgage assistance. What used to be a piece of good luck for buyers, a sales agent who knew financing and was willing to help them, has become one of the dividing lines between a first-rate agency and the others. Some top firms have separate mortgage assistance departments, some simply train each and every sales agent thoroughly in all aspects of home financing. Ask the agent from a firm that you are considering how buyers are helped with their mortgages and how agents are trained to do this. It may mean the difference between a sale that closes and one that falls apart because the buyers couldn't get a $5,000 second mortgage! Some of the largest firms and franchises now also offer equity loans to sellers who list with them. More on this in Chapter 27.

Goodwill

One of the primary sources of broker headaches is sales-force turnover. Fifty percent of newly licensed sales agents leave the field during their first year, and half of those who stick out year one leave before year three is complete. Even among experienced agents committed to their careers, there is a good deal of office hopping in search of greener pastures and occasionally an ambitious agent who leaves to start his or her own firm.

To transpose this broker headache into your own state of consciousness, ask: How do I know this agent who wants my listing for six months will still be in the area next August? In fact, how long has she worked here? Worked in real estate? With what kind of reputation?

Reputation, that's the essence. Because sales agents work with a certain amount of anonymity (under the name of their broker) and because they tend to be more mobile than the broker who must maintain an office, their reputations are harder to pin down and to rely upon. Rely therefore upon the reputation of the broker. He or she is ultimately responsible for everything that will occur in the marketing of your property. Well-established brokers in the community take great pains to maintain the goodwill that they have forged over the years. Again, choose locally and choose a firm headed by a man or woman known in your community.

Commissions

There is no standard commission for the sale of a house. Six percent has been traditional over several decades, but the law states that each listing contract is unique and that any commission can be agreed upon. Some agencies ask for 7 or 8 percent and may or may not offer more services; some agencies will handle a listing for 4 or 5 percent and do as good a job as the 6 percent agency. Commission is a point you must negotiate and evaluate.

Be careful, however, that you don't sign yourself out of the best possible marketing for your property in an effort to get a bargain. Especially in times when property is selling poorly, fee brokers and discount brokers seem to proliferate, and many sellers sign contracts with them only to be sorry long before the contract term runs out.

A discount broker will advertise that all sellers will be charged only a 2 or 3 percent commission. Great, if that commission is to be paid only upon closing, but the problem is usually getting the property sold and closed.

Most discount brokers will not cooperate with other brokers. They can afford to market at 3 percent because they plan on keeping the entire commission. In contrast, a multiple listing or cooperating broker may well split his commission 50/50 with another agency that sells the property he lists. So the discount broker really loses nothing at 3 percent commission while the seller loses the wide exposure of having her house marketed by every agency belonging to a multiple listing association.

Some discount brokers will tell sellers that they cooperate willingly with every other broker in town. This may be true in theory, but agreements between brokers are individually negotiated. The discount broker may be willing to cooperate, but no other broker may want the 1 percent commission share he offers, and they in turn may offer him only 1 percent of the commission on their listings. The result: no other firm will show the discount broker's properties, and he will show few of theirs. Cut-rate firms, therefore, are not usually a good deal; you can do as well advertising on your own.

On the other hand, sellers who deal with fee brokers often consider submitting horror stories to top national magazines. Now listen carefully: The typical fee broker advertises that he or she will handle the sale of your home for a set price, let's say $700. That sounds pretty good when you calculate that 7 percent commission on your $100,000 house would come to $7,000 dollars. But, for $700 most fee brokers and their sales agents will not show your house! Instead they will deliver a sign to your property (you put it into the ground), advertise the property, answer the phone calls, give directions to your house (by phone), make appointments for you to show your property to the prospects, and "help" with negotiating.

"Well, what do you expect for $700?" you say. Not much, but the problem is that the $700 usually must be paid upon signing the listing contract and is not refundable if the property is not sold. Some fee brokers charge a lower fee, say, $500, upon signing and then a sliding scale additional fee (say, $700 more if the property sells under $70,000, $900 if between $70,000 and $90,000, etc.) upon the closing of the sale. In contrast, the commission broker gets nothing for his efforts if your house is not sold during the term of the listing contract.

Fair Housing

By law, when you list your house with a real estate broker, you make a commitment to fair housing. Title VIII of the 1968 Civil Rights Act prohibits discrimination in residential housing on the basis of race, sex, religion, or national origin. You cannot legally ask a real estate agency or the members of a Realtor Board to bring only fair-haired Russian women or not to bring any dark-haired Catholic men to your property as prospective buyers. And the Civil Rights Act of 1866 (the date's correct, enacted after the Civil War but recently reaffirmed by the Supreme Court) further prohibits all racial discrimination in the purchase, sale, or rental of real or personal property.

The 1968 Civil Rights Act exempts single-family homeowners (and multifamily homeowners if the house has no more than four units, one of which is occupied by the owner) from fair housing compliance if the property if being sold without the assistance of a real estate broker. The 1866 Act, however, exempts no one.

Contracts That Will List Your Property

Exclusive Right to Sell

The contract most often used and most preferred by real estate brokers gives the broker the *exclusive* right to sell the property during the term of the listing. If any sale occurs, even if parents sell the property to their grown children, the broker is due his or her commission. The exclusive-right-to-sell contract does not, however, prohibit the broker from sharing the listing with other brokers, in fact most MLS groups require exclusive-right-to-sell contracts before accepting a property for general distribution. An owner can request that his property not be listed on a multiple basis, in which case only the one broker named in the contract and his or her sales agents can advertise and show it.

Exclusive Agency

Few home sellers are familiar with the exclusive agency listing and few real estate people are likely to volunteer information. The exclusive agency listing gives one broker the exclusive right to act as the seller's agent but reserves to the seller the right to procure a buyer through his or her own efforts and in that case not to pay a commission to the broker. Some Realtor Boards accept exclusive agency listings for distribution on MLS.

Open Listing

An open listing contract gives a broker the right to act as the seller's agent but reserves to the seller the right to employ other brokers or to sell the property himself or herself without the payment of a commission. A seller may sign any number of open listing contracts with different brokers all to run concurrently. There is never any commission splitting among competing brokers in an open listing situation; each is working for the whole pie. Open listings therefore are never distributed by MLS. Their term should be short (usually weeks) and the contract should contain a clause stating that the open listing is automatically terminated if and when the seller should sign an exclusive right to sell or an exclusive agency listing with any real estate broker. Read pages 424–425 and 474–475 for creative uses of the open listing.

Verbal Open Listing

Many states require that a listing be in writing to be enforceable. In those states that do not have this requirement, a few scattered brokers will still allow their agents to show properties on a nod or a handshake in the hopes that frequent showings will eventually win them a written listing. This is risky business, the kind that invites lawsuits. If one of these verbal listing showings should result in a sale, how much commission is due? When is it to be paid? Much better that you should get everything established in writing before an agent brings anyone to your property.

Net Listing

Net listings are illegal in most states. Where they are still allowed, a seller can name a price to a broker as his net requirement. The broker can then sell the property at any price above the net figure and keep the excess dollars as her commission. For example, if the seller wants to net $80,000 from the sale of his property and the broker sells that property for $99,000, the broker's commission is $19,000. Stay away from this kind of arrangement!

Signing the Listing Contract

No matter what type of listing you choose (see Contracts That Will List Your Property on page 441), you should remember that you are signing a legally enforceable document. Be sure that it contains the following:

1. *The date.* This should be the day upon which you sign it.
2. *Identification of the property for sale.* A street address will do but block and lot number on a tax map is better; the apartment number and name of the condo or co-op is essential for shared-space housing.

3. *Identification of the sellers.* The first and last names of everyone who owns an interest in the property. This is especially important when parents and children own a house together or when divorce is imminent or accomplished.

4. *Identification of the real estate broker.* This can be expressed as the name of the firm but the listing contract must be signed by a broker who is authorized to represent that firm.

5. *The price at which the property is offered for sale.* The price may be changed through negotiation, but if a buyer offers you the full amount specified and meets all the other conditions of sale, the property is considered sold; that is, the broker will maintain that he has done his job and that you owe the commission agreed upon.

6. *Any special conditions regarding possession or financing.* These items may be as important as the price in determining when a property is sold.

7. *A list of items included in the sale.* Many contracts contain preprinted lists. Read through them carefully and cross out any items that your property does not have. A water softener, for example, or an air conditioner.

8. *A list of items not included in the sale.* Be specific and thorough. Do you plan to keep your dining room chandelier, your patio furniture?

9. *The amount of the commission.* This is usually stated as a percentage of the sale price of the house. Less frequently a flat fee is named or a combination of fee and percentage.

10. *A statement that commission is to be paid upon closing.* This clause protects the seller from being required to pay commission if a buyer tries to back out of a contract.

11. *An expiration date.* Every listing *must* have one. It should be a named, specific day, June 11, 1985, for example. Do not accept "three months from the date of contract."

12. *Signatures.* The signatures of everyone who owns an interest in the property must appear on the listing along with that of the broker employed by that listing. The signatures need not be witnessed or notarized.

Some contracts also include a carry-over or protection clause stating that if the property is sold to anyone who viewed it with a licensed real estate agent during the period of the listing, a commission is still due to the listing broker. This clause should have a time limitation; three to six months is generally acceptable. It is written into a contract to protect the broker against the collusion of a buyer and seller to agree upon a lower price after the expiration date by eliminating the commission.

Some listing contracts also state who will hold the earnest money. Try to have it held by your lawyer or an escrow agent, not the real estate broker. (The lawyer won't have a commission owed him in the event something goes amiss.) If the broker is to hold earnest money, be sure that you write "fiduciary agent" after the firm name or broker's name on your check.

Most agents will try to convince sellers to sign a listing for six months. Don't do it. Six months is a long, long time, especially if you are not satisfied with the marketing of your property. Sign for three months. With a little luck your property will be sold by then. If not, you'll know exactly how well the agency is performing and you can choose to renew the listing on a month-to-month basis or to try out another agency.

After you and the broker have signed a listing contract, *be certain* that a copy is delivered to you. You may well need to refer to it during the time of the contract.

Preparing the Listing Sheet

The information your listing agent writes upon his listing worksheet is the information that virtually every prospective buyer will see before coming to your property. It is the information that will be used in writing the advertising for your property, and it is the information by which other agents will decide whether or not to show your property. Make it as accurate and appealing as possible. You will need to gather virtually all the items discussed in the "Flyers and Other Papers" section of Chapter 25.

On your listing, be sure to state room sizes (measure them or have the agent do it). Checkmarks or Xs in the blanks after dining room, kitchen, etc. are disconcerting; they tell nothing. Know your real estate tax bill; the agent will ask for it. And be sure that any special features are mentioned on the listing sheet. For example: beautiful hilltop view; new 60-gallon hot water heater; exterior painted last year; 22 by 14 deck off kitchen. These items attract the attention of both buyers and other agents and bring about more showings.

Go over the directions to the property with the agent. Be certain they are clear and accurate and that they do not take prospective buyers past any not-so-desirable places such as the municipal sewer treatment plant which happens to be a half mile from your property.

And be absolutely positive that your names are spelled properly and that your phone number is correct.

Once your listing is printed and distributed (within a week), ask the agent for a copy. Check it for errors, typographical and otherwise; no one will do this as thoroughly as you. If you find them, have your agent send corrections through the MLS or whatever inter-office system is used. If there is a major error such as a wrong address, a picture of your next-door neighbor's house instead of yours, transposed room sizes so your living room reads 12 x 12 and child's bedroom 22 x 14, or slab instead of full basement, insist that a new corrected listing sheet be printed.

The Photo

In the real estate marketplace, the old cliché "a picture is worth a thousand words" might well be changed to read "a picture might be worth ten thousand dollars or ten weeks' marketing time." You cannot sell your property unless prospective buyers come to see it, and nothing brings more buyers out than a good picture.

If the MLS or office photographer took your house picture on a gray day, or from a bad angle, or when the garage doors were open, the garbage can out front, and two tricycles and a wagon on the lawn, ask your broker to have it retaken and a new listing sheet distributed. Also if you listed your house in February and the photo shows it snow-covered, have a new photo taken in April. People aren't so interested in houses that they think have been around "forever."

The Sign

To have one or not to have one. . . . Most people do and usually it is a good idea. It helps agents locate your property and occasionally it stimulates a buyer inquiry. It is not necessary, however, that you leave the sign with a sold sticker pasted across it on your lawn for the two months between signing the contract and closing. This is *just and only* advertising for the real estate agency. Have it removed as soon as the sale is certain.

The Lock Box

Also called a key box in some areas, this device looks like a large padlock. The loop is designed to go over a doorknob and then lock securely inside the cast iron body of the box so that it cannot be removed from the door except by someone with a master key. The master key opens and lifts off the front panel of the box where the key to the house is kept. Every working sales agent and broker member of a Realtor Board has a master key. This system allows agents to show a property when the owner is not at home.

Some sellers object to a lock box fearing that they will lose control of who enters their homes, and to some extent, the fear is justified. In the vast majority of instances, however, the lock box works well and there have been very few problems with its use. For those sellers who do not wish to use it, a key can be left in the listing real estate office.

The Realtor's Open House

Early in your listing term, most agents will suggest that an open house for sales agents be scheduled. You will be asked to leave the property for a half day, invariably a week day, while your listing agent plays host or hostess to groups of other agents from cooperating offices.

Open houses such as this are well worth their trouble. Cooperating agents will speak more enthusiastically of a property they have seen and as a result your sales exposure will increase.

Showings

If you decided to list your house with a broker without first making a for-sale-by-owner attempt, please take a few minutes now to read through Chapter 25 anyway. The sections on setting the price and fixing up the property apply equally to those who sell on their own and those who sell with a broker and they are very important to your success.

All agent-assisted showings should be by appointment, but it is better if you can arrange to be out while the property is being shown. If not, try to stay in one room and do *not* follow the agent, pointing out selling points as you go. Everyone feels uncomfortable when this happens and most buyers think the seller is overanxious. They will, therefore, make a lower first offer if they do want the house.

If an agent schedules a repeat showing to a very interested party, it is even more imperative that you leave the property. Repeat showings usually precede an offer, but they are long. The buyers often tour round and round the house several times, reentering rooms and imagining the placement of their furniture. Sometimes they even measure windows, climb into attics, test plumbing, and poke into the corners of closets and basements. All of this is discomforting to a seller. Go out, even if you watch from behind a neighbor's curtains! And don't worry about there being no one at home to answer questions. If there are any, the agent will call you.

Public Open Houses

Agents sometimes promise to hold a public open house as a lure in persuading a seller to list with their firm, yet extremely few properties are ever sold at or through an open house. The open house as a marketing tool is much more effective in getting the names of prospective buyers; in other words, in procuring new customers for the agent who conducts it. Meanwhile, the doors of your property are opened to anyone who wishes to walk through. There is no attempt to qualify these people; some agents don't even ask their names until they are about to leave. And who's to say that any name given is real!

If an open house is very successful (lots of people going through), it is an invitation to trouble. The agent assigned to the house cannot possibly accompany every person walking about the property and the opportunity to steal presents itself even to the most God-fearing among us. If you *must* have an open house, put away or tie down everything of value.

Showing a Vacant House

This is a ball game unlike any other and presents special problems. We've reserved a section for it in the next chapter.

When You Get an Offer

Negotiating often triggers food binges, increased smoking, more than a drink or two, and/or consecutive headaches. Perhaps it would be stretching things to say it need not be so, but certainly it need not be as bad as many people make it. Patience, a surefooted knowledge of the value of your property, a poker face, and a positive attitude, will all make the going easier.

Unless you are very lucky, the first offer that an agent presents to you will not be at your asking price or probably even at your fair market value price. You then begin your negotiating by listening and asking questions. After you listen to everything the agent has to say, ask: How soon do the buyers need the house? What kind of financing will they apply for? What kind of job(s) do they have? Can they qualify for the mortgage they will need? What did they like most about the house? What did they like least?

You want all this information before you make a counteroffer, for you are seeking to ascertain the buyer's goals and expectations as well as his qualifications to buy your property. Be sure you have read Chapter 17 on negotiating from a buyer's point of view and then address the price the agent has named.

• If it's an extremely low offer and you do not feel a compromise price will approach your fair market value figure, say something like, "This first offer price is too low to merit a counteroffer. We are willing to negotiate, but not until a more reasonable offer is made." This approach is better than the often-used response of reducing the asking price by $500 because it tests the sincerity of the buyers by putting the ball back into their court, as it were, and asking them to make a "reasonable" offer. You might suggest to the sales agent that he or she show the buyers some comparables.

• If the original offer is below your ideal selling price but within striking distance, make a counteroffer halfway between what you want and what you are asking.

• If the agent returns with a second offer still below your idea of fair market value, suggest that she go through the comparables file with you and show her how you established the market value of your property. Make another counteroffer just a bit on the high side of the price you would accept.

• If the agent returns again saying that her buyers cannot go higher, try to negotiate with occupancy and financing terms. This is where the information you gathered during the first negotiating session comes in. If the buyers are selling a home and need extra time, you might hold firm on the price but extend the closing date to three or four months. If the buyers need housing immediately, you might come down slightly for a sixty- or ninety-day closing but hold firm on your price for a thirty-day closing. If two or three thousand dollars separates you and neither party wants to change his or her price, offer to hold a short-term, interest-only second mortgage for the amount in dispute.

• When you name your rock bottom figure as a counteroffer, be prepared to stand firm on price. Offer instead to add some of the "not included in the sale" items on your listing form: draperies,

---

Why Negotiations Fail

The buyers cannot really afford the house. The sales agent was showing them properties above their price range with the hope that perhaps they could negotiate a bargain. Or the sales agent never properly qualified them.

The sellers are not ready to sell. They still have emotional ties to the property as "home" and want to be paid top dollar. Or they simply do not yet want to move out despite the fact that they have put the property on the market.

Someone is given an ultimatum. For example: "It's $75,900 and a sixty-day closing or nothing. Don't bother to come back here with anything else!" or "Either you leave the dining room chandelier or we don't want the house!" Statements like these leave the other party no space to make another proposal.

A buyer or seller takes a statement made during negotiations as a personal affront and refuses to negotiate further.

There is racial, ethnic, or other social hostility toward the buyers. Unfortunately there is a fine line between selectiveness and discrimination, and until people judge each other as individuals rather than by stereotypes, we will continue to have some problems in this area.

---

carpeting, appliances, chandeliers, a riding mower, patio furniture, whatever.

Never get angry, never say never, allow time between negotiating sessions, and think creatively. There are many ways to make a deal.

The Contract to Buy

Many real estate firms train agents to bring a standard contract (signed by the buyers) to the sellers with the earnest money check, and to encourage the sellers to sign as soon as an agreement on price has been reached. This is not always to the benefit of the sellers. There is no such animal as a standard contract; each transaction is unique. And even if you think yours is package-plan typical, it is still

"What Ifs?" for Sellers

What if you decide that you don't want to sell your home six weeks into a six-month exclusive-right-to-sell listing contract?

You can withdraw your listing from the MLS. All marketing activity will be stopped. You are still bound, however, by the terms of your listing contract with your broker; if you should sell your property before the expiration date of that contract you will owe a commission.

What if you decide you don't want to sell two weeks after you sign a contract to buy with a ready, willing, and able buyer?

If that buyer wants your house, he can sue for specific performance, which is a court ruling that you must carry out the terms of the contract you signed (sell him your house). And even if the buyer merely shrugs his shoulders and walks away disappointed, the broker will undoubtedly sue for his "earned" commission.

What if a co-worker tells you his cousin's sister-in-law is looking for a house just like yours but would like to save the commission for a lower price and you still have three weeks before your listing contract expires?

If you have an exclusive-agency listing, you can sell your property to a buyer that you procure yourself without paying a commission. Show your house to your co-worker's cousin's sister-in-law at a reduced price. If you have an exclusive-right-to-sell contract, however, you can invite your co-worker and his distant relative to dinner at your home but it would be better if you didn't discuss the sale of your property until *after* the listing expired. Meanwhile if a real estate agent brings a buyer to the scene who offers you your price and terms, you must sell to *that* buyer or pay the broker's commission.

What if your hot water heater springs a leak and floods your basement (or your septic tank backs up), and you have an appointment to show your house that afternoon?

Cancel it. Plead the bubonic plague or at least that you are ill. (You *are*, at the sight of the flood!) Do not show a property while a catastrophe is in progress. There is no way to reclaim that potential buyer; he will always associate the property and the catastrophe.

What if a real estate agent appears at your door with two potential buyers in tow and says "I know we don't have an appointment, but we were driving through the area and my customers saw the For Sale sign . . ."

Unless your place is an unqualified "mess" or someone is indisposed, let the agent and the buyers in. Buyers, house-hunting with an agent, who stop in response to a real estate agency sign already like the property from the outside. You are halfway to a sale.

What if you return home late in an afternoon to find mud tracked across your ivory carpet, cigarettes in your sink despite the No Smoking signs, and no agent's card left anywhere that you can see. You also can't find the wristwatch you thought you left on the dresser.

Don't touch anything. Go to a neighbor's house and call the police. Many states require fingerprinting of all real estate agents. Thefts or disrespect for property are extremely rare among real estate agents, but anything can occur. Also call your listing agent, report the state of affairs, and ask if any other firm made inquiries about your property that day. The incident will be reported to the Realtor Board. The penalty for theft, misrepresentation, discrimination, and other acts in opposition to the state's real estate laws is loss of license in addition to any criminal prosecution that is warranted.

a good idea to have it checked through by an attorney before you sign. Remember thousands and thousands of dollars, maybe your life savings, are at stake. In any case, don't sign anything before you read Chapter 18, "The Contract and the Closing."

Once your contract is signed, the house is almost sold, but not quite. You will go through a waiting period until the contingencies are met. The most common contingencies are mortgage or financing approval and a professional home inspection. If the financing falls through, you can suggest that the buyers try another lender. The one that holds your mortgage or trust deed is an especially good choice if that loan is written at a below-the-current-market interest rate (lenders like to get rid of these unprofitable loans). Or you can again offer to hold a small second mortgage at interest only for a few years, counting on house appreciation and the buyers' increasing income to alter the qualification picture.

If a problem turns up because of the house inspection, you may have to reopen negotiations. Let's say, for example, that the inspection report indicates that the roof will need to be replaced within a year or two. "Well, the house doesn't need a new roof now," you may argue, but the buyers will think otherwise. Usually a settlement of $500 or $1000 off the agreed-upon purchase price will quiet the buyers and keep the deal together. (Be sure you pay your real estate commission based upon the adjusted price.) If something absolutely must be fixed, a termite infestation for example, you may just have to fix it.

Try to keep the deal together. Houses that come back on the market (BOMs, or bombs, as the agents call them) don't usually do too well.

Where to Complain

If you are not satisfied with the way your broker is handling your property or if a sales agent has caused damage to your property or distress to you, your family, or your neighbors, you can complain and in most cases have the wrongs righted. If the broker is a Realtor, you can file a complaint with the local Realtor Board. And whether a Realtor or not, you can file complaints and charges concerning licensed real estate agents with your state real estate commission. Most states carry some kind of bond or liability insurance. There is a state-by-state list of real estate commission addresses in Appendix B.

For More Information

Consult your state Real Estate Commission. Many states have free or inexpensive pamphlets on licensing laws and real estate procedures.

Consult your local Board of Realtors. The amount of printed information varies from one board to another. Ask for whatever is available.

Selling Your Home, by Carolyn Janik, Collier Books, is helpful. Price: $4.95.

Selling Your Home With an Agent, by Edith Lank, Reston Publishing. Price: $12.95 hardcover, $9.95 paper.

27

When You Must Sell One
Home to Buy Another

Usually only the young and the very old escape. The young buying into homeownership, the old selling out of it. In between, a change of house (or condominium, or co-op) catches us into tandem cycles of buying and selling, sometimes with excruciating emotional and financial consequences.

There are always problems. The essential question is how to minimize them, and the essential step to that accomplishment is recognizing why the problems occur. For most people, they grow out of the two major activities required in changing one owner-occupied residence for another: liquifying assets (getting the money out of one property so that you can put it into another) and coordinating occupancy (the big switch of families and furniture). This process is often a chain reaction with time and money as the activating forces.

S. Zimmerman.

Except Buyer A, each of these buyers is dependent upon cash from the buyer before him in order to buy "up" or "new"; but each is also dependent upon the ability of the owner after him (the one living in the property he is going to buy) to move out, or in the case of new construction, upon the completion of work by the builder. A failure or a delay anywhere sends ripples in both directions through the chain.

The Home-Switch Situation

Expect the ripples; rejoice and congratulate yourself if they don't occur. During the process, try to stay calm (or hang loose). The problems are always resolved somehow, and there will be fewer permanent consequences if everyone remains as rational and open to new ideas, options, and compromises as possible. Seven of the most common sell/buy situations follow along with insights for the sellers and buyers who must work their way through them.

The Corporate Transfer

This is the best of all possible worlds, financially, that is. Most companies offer to buy, at fair market value, the home of their transferred employee, or in some cases, to lend him or her (without interest charge) the equity in that home and manage the property after the family moves out. Manage usually means maintain it and pay mortgage installments, insurance, and taxes until it is actually sold. Most companies also have a specified period of time during which they will pay living expenses while the family househunts and/or awaits closing.

If you are a selling transferee, therefore, you will know exactly what equity you have in your property as soon as the company finishes its fair-market-value appraisals. And you will know that the cash you need will be available for the closing date of the property you are about to buy. Your problems are not financial.

They are emotional. Most transfers are made over relatively long distances and the uprooting process is all the more painful when a family is housed in temporary quarters in a strange town. It is important, therefore, that you consider the closing date in your choice of home. Those properties most likely to be available exactly when you need them are vacant resales, new houses complete or on the verge of completion, the homes of people departing on a transfer, and to a lesser extent, the homes of those who have already purchased another property. Avoid those properties where the owner wants to sell his or her home before seeking another or where the owner is having a new house built and the construction has only recently begun (even if the builder swears on his driver's license that he will have the job done on time). Also avoid the purchase of new construction that is anything less than virtually complete and in need only of finishing touches.

On the other hand, if you are buying the home of a transferee, you can be relatively certain that the property will close and be available for your occupancy on the date specified in the contract. You can also usually get reasonable delays of the closing date if you need extra time.

Changing Jobs

If a change of job and employer prompts your long-distance move, you will have a financial cushion also, but not so fine a one as the transferred employee. Few companies will buy a new employee's old residence; most, however, will pay moving expenses and provide some financial support for living expenses while awaiting a closing in the new location.

A long-distance job change often separates a family. Typically, the wife and children remain behind to sell the house while the husband goes on ahead to his new job. Free time at the new location is often spent househunting, so selection of a new home usually follows hard on the heels of signing the sales contract on the old.

Most change-of-job buyers want quick occupancy of the new home in order to get the family back together. If this is your situation, try to select from the same selling situations recommended to the transferee, and avoid those situations where delays are most likely.

If you are buying the home of a person who has changed jobs, you can usually expect an on-time closing. In fact, you should plan to close on time, for these sellers are usually both anxious and in need of their equity. They will not take requests for delays of a month or two in good spirits.

Stepping Up

During the 1960s and 1970s people stepped up to larger and larger houses almost as routinely as they climbed the corporate ladder. This trend has been somewhat curtailed by high interest rates and a much reduced inflationary spiral in house prices, but stepping up still occurs at least once in most homeowners' lives.

Because emotions are given more weight when a move is not absolutely necessary, many homeowners looking for a larger house are also looking for a dream house. They are intent upon finding their dream or at least an acceptable substitute before they put their present home on the market. Once they find such a property, they will sign a contract to buy. This contract almost always commits them to the purchase, whether or not their old house is sold before the closing date. In other words, they are in a "must sell" position.

If you are selling because you are stepping up to your dream, try to get a closing date on that dream several months in the future. It is much easier to wait out extra time in your old house than it is to make mortgage payments on two properties and a bridge loan. And price your old house close to its market value in order to stimulate a quick sale. If, however, no ready, willing, and able buyer appears before the closing date for your new house arrives, try to be patient and continue to live in that old house at least until you have a signed purchase contract. Occupied houses generally sell more quickly. You can also help to facilitate a sale by removing most bric-a-brac and all extra items of furniture to your new house in order to give a look of spaciousness to your old.

If you are buying a house from sellers who have already purchased another house, you have a strong negotiating hand. Your first offer should be at a low price with a distant closing date. If you follow this by slight increases in the offering price and offers to close sooner and sooner, you may well save yourself several thousand dollars. Once the contract is signed, however, be prepared to close on time. Sellers carrying the payments on two properties will not be happy about a request to delay an agreed-upon closing date, especially if the sale price was dependent upon a quick close. They might well take steps which would force you, the buyer, to choose between closing on the appointed day and forfeiting all escrow deposits.

Building The Dream House

Most builders will tell you that they can build a house in 90 to 120 days. But rarely, so very rarely, is a house really ready for occupancy 90, or even 120, days after ground breaking. And even more rarely can a buyer do *anything* to speed up the process. Actual closing dates usually run one to six months, or even nine months after the date in the contract.

If you are selling your old home while having another built for you, allow plenty of time beyond the paper closing date on the new property for the closing on the old. You can calculate a rough estimate of how much extra time you'll need by talking with people who have already had homes built by your builder. (This advice is especially appropriate if you are buying in a development. Patterns of both quality and completion time are amazingly consistent.)

The risk of setting too early a closing date on your old house is that you'll be forced to move out of it with nowhere to move into. Such a situation could intensify the emotional stress of a move and cost you a bundle in extra living expenses and furniture storage.

In contrast, the risk of setting too late a closing date is small. Once you have a contract of sale on your old house, the process of getting a loan for your equity in it is a veritable breeze. With such a bridge loan, you can close on your new house and begin to decorate it and/or to move your personal belongings into it. If your two properties are not too far apart, you might well save more than the interest charge on that bridge loan in reduced moving expenses.

Before you decide to *buy* a home whose seller is "having a house built for him," ask what the closing date is on that new construction. If you can, get the address of the property and drive by. Do not expect a closing within sixty days unless the house being built is actually nearing completion.

Any selling/buying chain reaction with new construction as one of its elements is likely to have delays. Awareness of this situation, however, can work to your advantage. Negotiate and allow for extra time between the contract signing and the closing date.

The Safe Switch

Many conservative home sellers and most of those not caught up in the fantasy of finding a dream house contend that the best house-switching procedure is to sign a contract to sell before you sign a contract to buy. Usually these sellers are out looking at possible purchases while their homes are on the market but restrain themselves from making any firm commitment to buy. Once they accept an offer on their old house, however, they are in a must-buy position. Like the transferee, they must choose among the properties available at the moment.

If you choose to sell on a safe switch, be sure that you keep current with all the properties for sale in your price range. Once you are made an acceptable offer, you can in turn make an offer on the best available house and adjust the closing dates on both properties as much to your advantage as possible. If you should receive an excellent offer on your old house at a time when there is absolutely nothing on the market that you want to buy, you will need to decide between refusing that offer and accepting it with a request for a distant closing date (four to six months). To do this is to gamble. You are betting your equity that an acceptable property will come on the market during that time. Usually it's a good bet. Be aware, however, that a buyer can go to court to force a seller to close on his property in accordance with the contract even if the seller has no place to go.

If you are buying a property in a situation where the sellers "are not certain of their future plans," be aware that you may not be able to move in exactly when you choose. Even if you were to get a judgement of specific performance against them, the process could take many months. On the other hand, of course, these same sellers might go out, find another house, close on it, and move out in plenty of time. This one is hard to predict.

The Empty Nest

The decision to sell is often difficult for the proverbial empty nesters, but once made, the sale itself usually follows quickly and with fewer problems than most. The children who once played soccer in the living room have left, often the house has been redecorated, and just about as often its owners have some extra cash (perhaps for the first time in their lives). Usually these sellers are looking to step down to a smaller, easy-care residence (often a condominium or co-op apartment).

In many instances, the question "Where are we going after we sell the house?" is already answered. An intended retirement condo may have been purchased years ago. Or perhaps a smaller house is being built, but these sellers expect to spend the summer (or winter) at their vacation home so the completion date of the new house is not crucial. Even when another house has been purchased and closed upon, the double payments are often easily within the income of the sellers. Moving-out problems, therefore, are rare.

If you are selling in order to move down in size and are especially flexible on your closing date, you can use that date as a point of negotiation in determining the sale price of the property. Find out whether your buyers want a quick or a distant closing. Start with an inclination in the opposite direction and negotiate toward their ideal date while keeping your price relatively firm.

If you are the buyer in this situation and know that the sellers have "somewhere to go," you can be relatively safe in assuming that the property will close on or near the appointed day. That date won't be worth much to you as a negotiating tool, however, so try instead for a purchase money mortgage at a below-market interest rate. If your sellers are taking their senior citizen's homeowner tax deduction, they may view such financing as an attractive way to invest some of their tax-free profit.

Occasionally some empty-nest sellers get sentimental and just cannot bear to part with their home, even though they have signed a contract of sale. They consciously or subconsciously set up all kinds of impediments to the closing. Usually the threat of legal action to get a judgement of specific performance and/or pressure by the real estate broker for payment of the commission will shake these sellers up enough to precipitate a closing.

Divorce

Some real estate agents routinely break out in hives at the prospect of presenting an offer on a jointly owned property to a divorced or divorcing couple. Negotiating is difficult even when a selling couple is working together; when each pulls in a different direction and also against each other, the negotiating task for the agent is something like juggling eggs.

If you are divorced or divorcing and selling your jointly owned property, try to set out some guidelines for a price acceptable to you both and the approximate time each of you needs between the contract signing and the closing. Do this when you list the property for sale. Then, when you do find a buyer, try to stick to the guidelines. Meanwhile make plans and take steps toward your future housing goals.

If you are buying a property involving a divorce, get everything in writing and signed by both selling parties. And be sure that you have a place to live beyond the closing date named in the contract. Given the emotional and financial variables of a divorce situation, delays and postponements are just about even money bets.

Some Problems and Some Solutions

Push comes to shove when:

• The closing date on your new house is two weeks away and you have a mortgage commitment. You must also have the cash from your equity in your old house in order to close, but there is no buyer in sight.

• The closing date on your old house is one week away, scheduled for the same day as the closing on your new house. Your movers have reserved the date, your buyers have a mortgage commitment and are ready to move in, and you plan simply to carry your equity check from one closing to the other. Then the sellers in your new house inform you that they will not be able to move for two more months.

• You are carrying two mortgages and a second mortgage equity loan and the balance in your cash reserve fund has just dropped into two-digit numbers. You still do not have a buyer for your old house.

None of these nightmares nor the thousand other possible combinations will vanish if you turn over in your sleep, but there are some things-to-do that might help solve or at least ease your problems.

The Guaranteed Sale

Some of the nation's large real estate firms and at least two national franchises (Electronic Realty Associates and Century 21) offer guaranteed sales plans. The advertising for these plans goes something like: *List with us and we will guarantee that your house will be sold in ninety days or we will buy it!* Does that sound great to you? It's not as great as it sounds.

The price at which the real estate firm will buy your property is between 10 and 20 percent less than its market value. (One or two outside appraisers are usually hired to determine the fair market value figure from which the 10 to 20 percent discount will be made.) And worse yet, you must still pay a commission to the broker even though she is also the new buyer.

To say such an arrangement is costly is a kindness. Before you enter into it, try reducing the asking price on your property below its market value by 2 percent. If this doesn't bring an offer in a month, reduce another 5 percent. Even allowing for negotiating space, you should still do better than a fixed discount of 10, 15, or 20 percent.

Meanwhile, if your listing expires, you can offer the same or better discount as a for-sale-by-owner price at less expense to yourself since you will not be obliged to pay commission. (Unless, that is, you should happen to sell to someone who originally saw the house with a sales agent and your listing contract has a hold-over clause.)

The Bridge Loan

What is usually called a bridge loan or interim financing is really a loan of the equity you have accumulated in the property you are selling. Many experienced sellers routinely take out such a loan to facilitate a closing on the property they are buying before they close on the property they are selling. This tactic enables them to decorate and move odd pieces of furniture in, and it guarantees them a place to live after the closing on the old house.

When sellers have a qualified buyer and a signed contract, interim financing is easy to obtain. Often the lender giving the mortgage loan on the new house will write the interim financing as a personal

Five Incentives to a Quick Sale

1. Reduce the price.

An asking price at market value will get you a selling price below market value. Not the best deal, but definitely a way out of a problem situation.

2. Offer a $2000 cash decorating rebate to the buyer paid at the closing.

This incentive works more effectively than a $2000 price reduction because the buyer can spend it.

3. Offer a $500 bonus to the selling real estate agent.

Some brokers and Realtor Boards prohibit such sales incentives, but many do not. Check yours.

4. Get FHA and/or VA preliminary loan approval for your property.

Your buyer will still have to apply and qualify for the loan, but you will know exactly how much financing each government agency will approve on your property. You can set the process of getting such approval into motion at the office of any lender who writes FHA-insured and VA-guaranteed loans. There is a fee ($110 as of this writing), but the approval will save time besides attracting buyers and is well worth that fee.

5. Have your property professionally inspected.

Get a written report and if possible purchase a warranty policy. Many inspection companies offer such a maintenance and repair guarantee on all mechanical systems and major structural elements for a one-year term starting on the day of closing. A written inspection report and a warranty policy quiet buyers' fears by assuring them that they are indeed getting a good house.

note due on the closing date of the property being sold. The closing agents do the paperwork and repay the interim lender. In fact, a bridge loan is nothing but paperwork when the lender on the new house also holds the mortgage on the old house.

When sellers apply for a bridge loan without a buyer for the property they are selling, most lenders place a lien on that property, which makes that bridge loan a kind of second mortgage. When the amount of the equity loan is large or when the lender has some doubt as to whether the eventual sale price of the house will actually repay the amount borrowed, the loan may well be written as liens on *both* the old house and the new.

Points and origination fees on interim financing are not uncommon; they make the loans more profitable for the lender. Or bridge loans may be discounted. Despite the term, this practice does not save you any money; it costs. In financial circles, discounting is the practice of calculating the interest on a loan in advance by having the amount of the loan written for a greater dollar figure than the cash you actually receive. For example, you need to borrow $50,000. You will get that $50,000 but the loan papers say you borrowed $50,700. You repay $50,700.

Some lenders require monthly payments on interim financing, others allow the interest to accrue until the time when the borrower repays it. Of the two methods of payment, the second is preferable since cash is likely to be scarce for a borrower who has no buyer in sight.

A great many different types of lenders write equity loans: banks, finance companies, mortgage brokers, even some large real estate firms. The availability, the interest rates, and the particular terms of these loans, however, vary with the lender, the financial marketplace, and the area of the country. If you are having trouble finding interim financing, talk with the sales agent who sold you the new property. Almost always that agent and her broker cannot collect their commission until the closing actually takes place. That fact will stimulate considerable efforts to secure financing on your behalf.

Time Is of the Essence

This legal term is abused and ignored more often than it is used effectively. When written into a contract, as it is in some states, or when served as a special notice to either party, it means that a specific date is an essential part of the contractual obligation and that failure to act upon that date is therefore a breach of contract. When served to buyers, it can result in the loss of deposit monies if they do not close on the appointed day, or even a court judgment for damages which could include the amount of difference between their contractual purchase price and the price at which the seller must sell in order to move the property quickly.

When the sellers default after they have been notified that time is of the essence, their failure to close and vacate the property can free the buyers from their obligation to buy a property without loss of their escrow funds. Or these buyers can go to court for a judgment of specific performance which will force the sellers to sell their property according to the terms of the contract in question. This process, however, can take several months.

These possibilities and penalties have the sound of big weapons, but often "time is of the essence" as a legal tool is just sword rattling. Think about these examples:

1. *Time is of the essence served to a builder who has not completed the house he promised to have ready a month ago.* "I can't make the date," says he. "If you want your deposit money back, you can have it." (He is now signing contracts to build the same model for $7000 more and would love to be able to sell your house at the new price to someone else.)

2. *Time is of the essence served to a buyer whose mortgage commitment has not yet come through.* "I can't close on that date because I won't have the money," says she. "You, however, are not entitled to keep my deposit money if I can't buy." (She's right. When you allowed the contract cutoff date for the mortgage commitment to pass without notifying the buyer and putting your property back on the market, you gave mute consent to an extension. You must now wait for the lender's reply.)

3. *Time is of the essence served to sellers who won't move out on time.* "All right, take back your deposit," they say. "We'll just put our house back on the market since we have no place to go anyway." (You, the buyer, don't want your money back, you want that particular house.)

Variations of these vignettes could fill several more pages, but by now you do get the idea, don't you? It is usually not only better but also often essential to work out compromises than to rely upon "time is of the essence." If no compromises can be reached, however, you can go to court (or threaten to do so) to enforce specific performance of the terms of the contract or to file suit for damages.

But we are now truly in the realm of the law. If you and your real estate agents are tossing about terms like "time is of the essence" and "specific performance," you need a lawyer, no matter what the conventional real estate closing practices are in your area.

Occupancy Before Closing

Let's assume that your buyers want to move into your old house as soon as possible, but you can't move out because the vacant house *you* are buying is tied up in legal and financial paperwork. You might consider applying to your sellers for occupancy before closing.

Or on the flip side, you are financially strapped by carrying two houses. You now have a buyer for your old house and she is anxious to take possession, but the closing will be held up at least six more weeks for processing of the mortgage application. You might well consider arranging for her occupancy before closing with the payment of per diem rent to you.

In situations like these an addendum is usually attached to the contract stating that the buyers accept the property in the condition that it is in on the day of occupancy and that all maintenance responsibility for the property is theirs as of that date. Be sure everyone involved in the sale signs this addendum and be sure that you maintain your insurance policy on the property until the closing. Since you still own the property until then, the buyers usually pay you a per diem rent for their time in your house.

Occupancy After Closing

One method of getting sellers to move out more quickly is to insist upon a closing near the date specified in the contract and then to allow them to remain in the house with the payment of rent to you, the new owner. (The per diem rate is usually quite high.)

The risk in this situation is to the buyers: will the property be turned over to them in the same condition that it was on the day of closing? To protect against the possibility of damages, a part of the sale price of the house (say $10,000 to $20,000) is not paid to the sellers at the closing, but held in escrow by an attorney or other fiduciary agent. The per diem rent is deducted from this fund along with the cost for repair of any damages that might occur between closing and the former owner's vacating of the premises.

Sometimes occupancy for a few days after closing is granted to a seller who is having difficulty coordinating his move. Some cash is still held in escrow, however, and there is still a per diem rental fee.

Generally it is preferable to pass title and occupancy together. But if the closing cannot take place without some adjustments, the adjustments should be made. The only imperative rule is to use an attorney in writing the compromise agreements in order to avoid misunderstandings or misuse of privileges.

Month-to-Month Tenants

When you're at the end of the money, where do you go? You might try talking with the lender who holds the mortgage on the house you are selling. Sometimes a suspension of payments can be arranged until the property is sold.

Or you might try renting on a month-to-month basis to tenants who will allow real estate agents to continue to show the property. The obvious advantage of the rental is income; at least part of the mortgage payments and other expenses are being met by money other than yours. A secondary advantage is occupancy and maintenance. Even if the furniture is not lovely, a house shows better lived in (as long as the tenants keep it neat and relatively uncluttered, that is). And if you can get the tenants to do the yard work (even if it means agreeing upon a slightly lower rent), you'll come out ahead in money and preventive medicine (fewer headaches, backaches, and vile moods).

But—there is always a "But" in real estate—renting on a month-to-month basis has disadvantages too. What if the tenants are not cooperative with real estate agents who want to show or are showing the property? What if the tenants turn out to be untidy, or downright dirty? What if they do not want the house to be sold since they like living in it and therefore badmouth the property to prospective buyers? And what if occupancy becomes a problem? Will you really be able to get the tenants to move out on closing day?

And then there is one more silent, invisible, but very real problem in choosing to rent. You can lose your homeowner capital gains tax deferment. In other words, you may have to pay taxes on a profit that you only saw on paper! Before renting, therefore, be sure to talk with a tax attorney or accountant.

If you do rent, remember that you cannot give month-to-month tenants an option to buy and still keep your house on the market. When any party holds an option on a property, no one else can buy that property until the option expires.

You should also avoid, if possible, a right of first refusal. Under this agreement, your tenants would have the right to match an agreed-upon purchase price from another buyer and buy the property. This situation is a negative one for the seller because most sales agents avoid showing properties which have a right of first refusal specified in the listing contract. (And if you have one, it must be stated clearly on the listing sheet.) Why this avoidance? Sales agents know that they will lose their customers (usually in anger) if those customers go through the process of negotiating a sale only to have another party take the property at their price!

Selling The Vacant House
Being human, sellers often find it difficult to resist moving into their newly purchased home even though they have not yet found a

buyer for the one they are selling. It is not until the movers pick up the last few pieces of furniture that these sellers notice how very shopworn their old house looks when empty. Suddenly the popped nails in the drywall behind the sofa stand out like notes on a musical staff, the worn places in the carpet wind among the indentations left behind as reminders of where the furniture stood, and every room echoes, yes, exactly like an empty house. Inevitably the same thought strikes virtually every seller: Good God! No one will ever buy this place!

If you plan to move out before selling, check the following points carefully:

1. *Decorating*. While you were still living in the house, a thorough and meticulous cleaning was all that was necessary for marketing. With an empty house, you will probably need to do some redecorating. Take heart, however, repair and fix-up costs can be a downward adjustment on the selling price of the house for tax purposes if and when they occur within ninety days prior to the signing of the contract of sale. It's not a *great* deduction, but it *is* a deduction.

Paint is your cheapest redecorating tool and it effectively covers much wear and tear. If you decide to wallpaper, keep your choice of patterns quiet and neutral, the kind of thing that will appeal to the largest possible number of people. Tear up very worn carpeting and have the floors beneath it refinished or, if you have only subfloors beneath your carpeting, install new wall-to-wall. (Choose neutral colors even if the lime green is on sale for half price!) And leave curtains or draperies on the windows throughout the house in order to cut down the echoing and to give the illusion of occupancy from the outside.

If you have some spare furniture (chairs, a couch, tables, lamps, even beds) leave them in the house. When prospective buyers look at an empty house, they always imagine their furniture as taking up much more space than it actually does. A few visible pieces left behind help to put furniture in perspective with room area. Also the lamps are essential if the house is to be shown in the evening.

The kitchen and bathrooms are worth some extra time and money since they are among the primary selling points of the house. Consider a new kitchen floor, countertops, appliances, even cabinets if you're good at do-it-yourself projects. You may have to confine bathroom improvements to new wallpaper, a carpet for the floor, and perhaps a ready-built vanity and sink unless you're really willing to go all out and sponsor new tile work.

An investment of $1500 to $2000 is not out of line in an effort to sell a vacant house. Borrow the money if you must. If you don't and the house does not sell, that amount and more will be gobbled up by mortgage payments, taxes, and insurance, not to mention the cost of maintenance. Remember, once you move out, the goal is to sell quickly.

2. *Maintenance.* You will have to return periodically to dust and vacuum, or hire someone to do so. And you will have to keep the lawn mowed, the hedges trimmed, the walks and driveway shoveled in winter, and the leaves raked in fall. If you have moved a relatively long distance, you would probably be well advised to hire a maintenance firm to do this work. Your broker can help you find one.

If your house is for sale through the winter, you can save some money by shutting down the heating system and draining the water from the pipes to prevent their freezing and breaking. Do not, however, turn off the electricity; lights are needed to show the house in the evening and to inspect the basement.

Although few people would believe it, a vacant house for sale over the summer is a more difficult problem. Since windows are usually kept closed and locked and since no one wants to air-condition an empty house, the property shows as hot and stuffy. You or someone in charge must also look out for mice, squirrels, bats, ants, and other pests. Any sign of such infestation will turn many buyers away. And put up No Smoking signs in obvious places; stale tobacco odors are nauseating.

3. *Showings.* When selling a vacant house, it is essential that you allow the broker to use a lock box. Many sales agents will not make two out-of-the-way trips to a listing broker's office to pick up and return keys, and you want every possible showing to take place.

In some areas, listing agents find a showing book effective in a vacant house. This is nothing more than a guest book (that can be purchased in any stationery store) in which each showing agent is asked to sign his or her name, the agency name, the date, and the time of showing. Listing agents can then phone these showing agents to gather customer opinions and comments or to try to stimulate an offer by giving advance notice of price reductions or special terms.

Business cards are a problem everywhere. Usually agents will leave their cards on kitchen counters, on foyer tables or shelves, or even on living room window sills. Dozens of such cards scattered about the house do not impress a potential buyer with the desirability of the property! You can somewhat alleviate, if not eliminate, this problem by having a basket or box on the kitchen counter with a small note reading "Cards, please." Leave two or three in the basket so that those who come in will add theirs to the pile, but don't let the basket get too full. Have the listing agent collect the cards at regular intervals, or if you can, collect them yourself. Those cards will provide you with information on who is showing the property and how often, information you might want to consider if your listing contract approaches its expiration date.

After-Thoughts

In reading this chapter, did you experience fleeting feelings of confusion? After all, just about every section discussed both buying and selling!

We understand the problem. But re-read slowly; the confusion will clear. Selling one home to buy another is, in fact, complicated and sometimes confusing. You are Janus, facing two directions at the same time. It's a difficult role. But take heart, it *will* end and spring *will* arrive.

For More Information

No one seems particularly anxious to tackle this problem in print but there are some additional tips in the next chapter.

28

Savvy, Luck, and the Moods of the Marketplace

Good times and bad times in the real estate marketplace are two faces of the same coin. That coin comes up heads or tails and somebody wins: usually the good times for sellers are bad times for buyers; and vice versa. But even in the worst of times for buyers or sellers, there are choices and strategies that may tap Lady Luck on the shoulder and persuade her, at least for the moment, to flip the coin in your favor.

S. Zimmerman

"OK, that's possible," you're probably thinking, "but, it's a bad time for everyone when the national economy is about as active as a hibernating bear."

Well, you're wrong. And wrong in a way that precisely illustrates how a prevailing market mood influences the vast majority of the general buying and selling public. When the press and the other media are bemoaning high interest rates, tight money, and a real estate market as soggy as Virginia's Dismal Swamp, smart and perservering buyers are hunting out and arranging financing on homes and investments at bargain prices that may well establish their fortunes—permanently, on high, dry land, with a view!

But buying, selling, and financing in a dead market are among the more sensitive manipulations of dame Fortune. Let's start on some simpler levels: the season of the year, local demographics, and fashion. We'll end with money problems and some suggested solutions.

The Real Estate Year

It's not always possible to choose when you will begin and end your buying and/or selling efforts, but even if you can't pick your time, an awareness of the effects of the season on the real estate marketplace will assist your shopping or marketing tactics. If you can choose your time and you choose carefully, you may unexpectedly find several thousand-dollar bills in your pocket.

Mid-November to New Year's

Imagine the real estate marketplace as a huge shopping mall. From the middle of November until after New Year's Day there's hardly a car to be seen in the parking lot. Even salespeople and administrators are scarce. Everyone is at the mall across the highway buying clothes, perfumes, jewelry, giftware, and appliances, or attending gala parties (some of which are called real estate conventions).

January and February

The salespeople and administrators are back to work at our imaginary mall, but they don't have a great deal to sell or an overabundance of customers. Except in the southernmost parts of the nation, winter slows the pulse of the real estate market. There is usually a quickening about mid-January when the sellers and buyers who held back over the holidays enter the market. By the end of the month, however, most agents are fighting off winter doldrums. They fight until the end of February.

March, April, May, and June

The real estate marketplace is as crowded and active as it will get in the course of any given year.

July and August

The entire nation goes on vacation, or so it seems. Our real estate mall is not as empty as it was during the holiday season, but the pace is slow, even lazy.

September, October, and early November

Activity is brisk, if less frantic than spring. These are good months for both shopping and selling.

Resort Areas

With the exception of the universal inactivity at holiday time, the above information does not pertain to the nation's vacation areas. Winter is the busiest time near both the ski and sun resorts. Late spring and summer are busiest in most coastal regions and lakeside communities.

Seasonal Tips for Sellers

1. In most areas of the country, the best time to list a home is late February to early March. These three or four weeks anticipate the spring onslaught of buyers. The appearance of a new listing encourages not-yet-too-busy sales agents to make an effort at preinspecting the property. As customer activity increases, those same agents tend to show most frequently and enthusiastically those properties with which they are already familiar.

2. If you choose to sell by owner, it is better to enter the market when activity is near its peak. You want prospective buyers, not agents. (You'll be able to tell the approach of peak time by the increased advertising in the real estate section of your newspaper.)

3. Competition from other properties for sale is also highest in the spring since housing inventories usually rise with increased listing activity during this season. If you want a quick sale, therefore, price your property near its market value. If you are seeking top dollar, give it a try in early spring; you may just attract someone who loves your house and is willing to pay extra for their love. If you

originally list high and do not see much activity, mid-May is a good time for a price reduction. You'll still catch an active market.

4. Try to avoid signing a listing contract in July or August. So many buyers and sales agents are on vacation (either literally or mentally) that the enthusiasm usually associated with a new listing just doesn't materialize. If you must list in summer, sign for as short a listing term as your MLS will accept (ideally to expire the first week of September), and then either change agencies or sign an extension premised upon the fact that a new photograph will be taken and your house will appear as a new listing. Also have your listing agent schedule the MLS open-house-for-agents in September—the second week is best.

5. If you list in the fall, list close to market value. You want your home sold before mid-November. Price reductions in November rarely bring about a sale unless they are significant enough to attract everyone's attention (which usually means selling below market value).

6. If you must list during the holiday season, your best marketing thrust is to attract the attention of as many sales agents as possible, hoping that they will stir up and bring around whatever customers they have. If your listing broker is willing (and you might just choose the one who is), you might consider holding a holiday open house. That is, instead of the normal two hours for a tour, invite agents for coffee, eggnog, and holiday foods. Besides printing notice of your holiday open house in the MLS bulletin, the broker should send invitations to the nearest and most active cooperating real estate firms. Yes, this does cost money (you might agree to split the cost with the broker); but the exposure is usually worth the expenditure.

7. Try to avoid winter listing if you live where snow and ice are prevalent, especially if you have a steep driveway. If you have basement water problems, you may also want to avoid a spring listing.

8. In vacation areas, you will usually get the highest price in the time period just pre-season, usually from people who want to use the property that same year. "In-season" is your next best selling time. If your budget and circumstances will allow you to wait almost a year, it is better not to sell at the end of a vacation season; prices will be at their lowest.

Seasonal Tips for Buyers

1. Generally you will be asked to pay top dollar in March, April, and May, the months when sellers are most optimistic. If you are in

a position to wait a bit, try window shopping in the spring. Keep a list of all the properties that you find acceptable and return to do your buying in the summer. By mid-July many sellers get disheartened as activity dries up. This is an excellent time to bargain for a lowered sales price.

2. December is the real bargain time in the real estate marketplace. There will be fewer properties to select from, but most sellers want desperately to sell. If you can find a property that has been on the market, overpriced, since August or September, December is the time to begin slow, studied negotiating with an offer well below market value (especially true if the property is vacant). Many sellers wrongly fear that there is no hope of a winter sale, and that fear gives smart buyers a strong playing hand.

3. Watch the January listings closely. In most parts of the country, there is a flurry of activity about mid-month. You might just get first crack at a beauty.

4. Inspect and follow listings that come on the market in June. Often overpriced on the crest of the spring's activity, these properties are price-reduced when activity diminishes in the heat of the summer sun. By August, any offer may sound appealing to their sellers.

5. You will usually get the lowest price on vacation properties at the tail end of the season. Be aware, however, that you will take on the expense and trouble of closing up for the off-season while having had none of the pleasure of using the property that year.

The Local Marketplace

There was a time when the area around Cape Canaveral, Florida, saw housing demand far exceed supply as the government sank its dollars into space exploration. Prices were soaring until someone put a pin in the balloon by moving the central control center of the space launch program to Houston. Suddenly it was hard to sell a house at any price.

The people of Seattle remember a similar story. And ask homeowners in Detroit about sales during the depression of the early 1980s when many older people who wished to retire to warmer climates simply decided to stay put, knowing they could neither sell nor rent their houses.

On the other hand, Hoboken, New Jersey, just across the Hudson River from Manhattan, was once the butt of cocktail party housing jokes. But the laughter has stopped and heads now turn to catch bits of conversation about a renovated townhouse for sale or a renovated building reopening as a condo. Albuquerque, New Mexico, once just a town whose name no one could spell, is growing like a well-fed tomato plant. And the Lafayette and Soulard areas of St. Louis, once eyesores composed of vacant and crumbling buildings, are being restored to beautiful and very desirable historic neighborhoods.

There's hardly an area of this nation that doesn't have a story or two similar to these. Before buying or selling property you should make yourself aware of your local happenings and housing trends. This knowledge will give you perspective, which in turn may save or make you money. Every local area has a real estate pulse of its own and the tempo of that pulse is regulated by an economic law as old as human need, supply and demand.

When housing supply is greater than demand, properties sell slowly, prices are soft, and we call the time a *buyers' market*. When housing demand is greater than supply, properties sell quickly, prices are firm, and we call the time a *sellers' market*.

Tactics for the Buyer in a Sellers' Market

1. Use several real estate agents. New listings are distributed among the sales personnel of a listing broker's office, or offices, several days before they appear on the MLS. If you have an agent working for you in each of several different firms, you'll get more chances at first showings.

2. Get to know the market value of property in your area well enough to make a decision to buy (and at a fair price) overnight. You do this by shopping extensively and by familiarizing yourself with the actual selling prices of similar properties that have sold during the past six months.

3. If you get into a bidding war with another buyer, don't let competition fever carry you past the fair market value of the property. Try using the closing date as a part of your negotiation. If you lose the property to a higher bid, let it go and look for another. You should not overpay, even in a sellers' market.

4. Run down all "For Sale by Owner" properties in your price range. In a time of escalating prices, some sellers unknowingly set too low an asking price.

5. Watch your local newspapers for new co-op or condominium conversions, new condominium communities under construction, and the start of new single-family tract developments. You may have to wait a while for occupancy, but the first few buyers in any project that is just getting underway usually get the lowest prices.

Tactics for the Seller in a Buyers' Market

1. Be certain of the market value of your home. If you are not satisfied with the figures you get from several competitive market analyses, pay for an appraisal (you can use it in your negotiating later).

2. Make your property more attractive than its competitors. Add an appliance, a microwave oven for example, or paint the exterior in a fashionable and attractive color combination.

3. Try a widely distributed open listing (see Chapter 26). This tactic is neither well known nor often used, but it is very effective. Its success is predicated upon two factors, however: (1) your property must have been listed and distributed throughout the member offices of a multiple listing service for several months so that a standard listing sheet complete with photograph and property specifications has been readily available to all sales agents in member offices, and (2) you must call the broker-owner or office manager of *every* agency that showed your property during its multiple-listed time and arrange for an office-generated open listing that would guarantee the sales agent who actually makes the sale 50 percent of the office commission. By effectively doubling* the potential commission that an agent will earn by selling your property (without spending an extra penny yourself), you will get more, many more, showings. And since the broker (or firm) gets the other 50 percent, they too will usually accept readily, if not enthusiastically, such an arrangement. Some firms will even advertise an open listing under these circumstances. What you have done is to increase competition, with the added incentive of greater reward for the winner.

4. Know when you are approaching the must-sell point. In the stock market, investors routinely bail out at a loss in order to liquify their investment and go on to something better. The same principle can apply in real estate. Except in rare circumstances, lowering the price will sell the property. Therefore if the emotional and financial strain of holding it is too great, sell at a loss, if you must, and move on.

---

*When exclusive listings are entered into a multiple listing arrangement, any sales agent member of the multiple listing service can sell the property. When a sale is consummated, the commission is split between the listing broker and the selling broker. The usual split is 50/50 or 60/40 with the 60 percent going to the selling office. The commission due to each firm is then split again between the broker and the salesperson. The man or woman actually doing the leg work to sell your property therefore, is working for approximately 25 to 30 percent of the commission.

The Swings of Fashion

In the 1960s, two-story, thirty-year-old houses in midsized cities were hard to sell. "Everybody" wanted a split level in the suburbs. Today, those same two-story houses, now over fifty years old, are in demand again! And in the same vein, condominiums, barely known by name in the 1960s, are now more popular than suburban split levels.

To all the factors we have already discussed, therefore, we must also add fashion and public taste as yet another determinant of market value. If you are buying a home that you hope to sell at a profit within the next five years, you must maintain a sense of what is in demand in your area. Choosing a twenty-five-year-old ranch-style house with a do-it-yourself basement recreation room over a two-year-old condominium with the same square footage may cost you as much as $10,000 in profit. However, if you are buying a home that you plan to live in for the next twenty-five to thirty years, you can safely ignore fashion and choose exactly what pleases you.

"But how can I possibly know what will be in demand five years from now?" you ask.

Your question is a valid one and its answer, of course, is slippery. You can't, not for sure, anyway. Any look to the future is crystal ball gazing. There are, however, hints, signposts, and actual aids to the forecasting.

The federal government and many private sector groups, such as the National Association of Realtors, the National Association of Home Builders, and Advance Mortgage Corporation, conduct and publish frequent surveys focused upon various aspects of housing across the nation. Statistics such as the median price of newly constructed houses, the proportion of singles in city & suburban condominiums, and the availability of fixed-rate mortgages are usually published widely in the press. Watch for them! The numbers may not foretell the future, but they will give you clues.

Local fashion is a little harder to pin down. Which are the fashionable towns, or sections of a town? Prices will always be higher there. Ask the question of every real estate agent you work with and then do your own research. Which are the best schools? Where are the best recreation facilities? Where are the finest shops? Which areas are best maintained? And finally, what are future zoning plans?

While working on fashionable location, don't overlook housing style. Contemporary houses with huge glass walls, cathedral ceilings, and great rooms instead of separate living and family rooms are

Housing in the Crystal Ball

The nation's population is shifting to the South and West, with some growth continuing in New England and along the Northeast corridor (Boston to Washington). With growing population, the demand for housing tends to remain high; with diminishing population, there is more likely to be greater supply than demand. (Beware of overbuilding, however, which might well flip the supply/demand ratio even in areas of rapid population growth.)

Across the nation, there is a continuing growth in the number of single-person households and in the number of single-parent households. Both statistics bode well for the increased popularity of condominiums and cooperatives.

The tendency to smaller family size continues along with a trend to smaller living area in new-home construction. The five-bedroom colonial and its four-bedroom twin may be white elephants on the market within the decade.

Conversion of rental apartment buildings to condominium or cooperative ownership continues. More city dwellers will own their own homes in the future. Improved upkeep should accompany pride in ownership.

There is increased interest in the restoration, renovation, and rehabilitation of older properties. These will become more valuable as a sense of neighborhood ("the people on our block" kind of thing) returns to American life.

Americans are living longer and older citizens will make their needs felt in the housing marketplace. Transportation and shopping facilities will affect the value of a property. Safety and security may become lead sales items. And freedom from maintenance chores will further strengthen the condominium and cooperative marketplace.

fashionable in the west and southwest; they are hard to sell in the northeast where colonials with fireplaces and formal dining rooms are most desired. Basements are in high demand in the northern part of the country, virtually disregarded in the south. Houses of stucco are preferred in some parts of the country, brick in others, and cedar shakes or clapboard in still others. Ask every real estate agent you work with what his or her buyers most often look for in a house. Keep a list of the answers you get, making a checkmark each time any item is repeated. An outline of local fashion will begin to appear for you.

Hurricanes, Chemicals, Nuclear Accidents, and Other Disasters

Several years ago people living in the vicinity of Love Canal in upper New York state discovered that seepage from toxic waste was endangering their lives. The members of the community banded together and launched an aggressive campaign for government help. They drew excellent media coverage, which increased their bargaining power, and the community convinced the government that they indeed needed and deserved help. After a danger zone was fenced off, the houses within it were bought from the residents with government funds. Their owners thus had the money and the freedom to buy property in another location.

But what about the people who owned property on the other side of that fence, or for that matter, anywhere in town? Who would buy their houses? And more recently, who would buy residential property around Three Mile Island after the nuclear power plant accident there? Or near any of the sink holes of Florida? Or even on the fashionable and expensive California coast, which the weather seems to be eating away?

Real estate has been promoted as the safest of possible investments and usually it is. But nothing is forever. Land and housing value can be changed dramatically and significantly by a local disaster. And property in an area of long-term danger may indeed become unsaleable.

In such a situation, your first step should be to gather individual property owners together into a group that will act as a unit. The pressure of numbers is strong and pleas for government help should be made both through conventional channels and through the publicity pressure of the media.

But what if all efforts for assistance have been turned down and you personally cannot continue to live with the disaster circumstances? And further, what if you cannot sell your property at any price?

At this point you will need the assistance of a competent tax attorney. Federal income tax laws do not allow tax loss deductions on a personal residence. It might, therefore, be advisable to move out and turn your residence into an investment property by renting it for a year, at *any* price. (According to the IRS, however, you must rent at *fair market value*. But fair market value usually means the best price you can get after making a reasonable effort.) After a period of renting you could then decide upon foreclosure or abandonment as a means of ridding yourself of the burden of the property. Foreclosure will usually qualify you for a capital loss; abandonment may qualify as a loss against ordinary income.

But not all disasters carry the long-lasting real estate stigma associated with toxic waste seepage or a nuclear power plant accident. Often hurricanes, tornados, earthquakes, and even floods strike an area once, wreck havoc, and never recur in the century that follows. If such is your situation, consider rebuilding. Disaster funds for loans are usually available. A few years after rebuilding, the properties in the area are usually worth more than they were before the disaster. If you sell immediately following a disaster, expect an extremely low price.

On the other hand, buying after a disaster may be an excellent investment for the adventurous. Prices will be very low, rebuilding funds will most likely be available, money can be saved by doing some of the work yourself, and potential appreciation is fabulous.

The Question of Money

Owing money is the American way. Some of us owe less than others, but virtually everyone who owns property owes a bundle. We put as little cash down as possible and borrow the rest, basking happily in the sunshine of tax breaks, leverage, and anticipated appreciation. So when the well goes dry (when lenders stop lending or when the cost of borrowing goes up so high that it becomes economically impossible to buy), everyone cries.

In the early 1980s home loan interest rates almost climbed through the zero in the 20-percent marker. After wringing out their handkerchiefs, the buyers and sellers and brokers and sales agents in the real estate marketplace began to look about for ways to keep that market open. Creative financing was one answer. The term, of course, is a euphemism; most of the time it really means seller-assisted financing which virtually always diminishes the seller's profit.

Purchase Money Mortgages

A purchase money mortgage (or trust deed) is a promissory note with a lien on the property accepted by the seller in lieu of all or part of the cash price agreed upon in the contract of sale. It can be the first and only lien on the property or it can be second to another loan by a lending institution. Purchase money mortgages are common in commercial property transactions; they are rare in residential real estate, except when tight money and/or high interest rates put pressure upon sellers.

Since few people not in the business of lending money want to wait twenty or thirty years for the repayment of such a loan, most purchase money mortgages are written for short terms (three to five years is common) with interest-only payments due during the term of the loan and a balloon payment of the entire principal due upon maturity. The interest rate is usually several points lower than the current rate for home mortgages as an inducement to the sale. However, purchase money mortgages are a viable option only when the sellers do not immediately need the entire cash equity they have accumulated in their property.

Very often sellers do not realize that they are actually selling their homes at a discount by offering to accept a purchase money mortgage at below market rates. Usually the cash they do not get could be invested at a more profitable rate of return. Also sellers do not take into account that the payment due at the end of the term will probably be worth less in real (noninflated) dollars than it was at the time the note was written. To calculate how much a purchase money mortgage mortgage will cost you (the seller), you must know and use principles for compounding interest and for discounting the future value of money. The numbers needed to do this calculating change with the economic mood of the times, but you can get them along with expert help in doing the calculations from any established lender. The best place to inquire is at the lending institution that currently holds the mortgage on your property.

Once you know how much the purchase money loan will cost you (it might well be in the range of $13,000 to $15,000 on a five-year $100,000 loan), consider reducing the price of your property by almost that amount for a cash sale (the buyer finds his own financing).

As another alternative to a purchase money mortgage, you might try approaching the lender who holds your current mortgage for the offer of a slightly-lower-than-market-rate mortgage loan for your buyers. The lender benefits by getting rid of your low rate and unprofitable loan for a new one at a better (if not top dollar) rate. This type of financial arrangement is being called a "blended rate" mortgage.

The Mortgage Assumption

"Assumable mortgage" is a star-spangled advertising phrase in times of tight money. Its future, however, is limited. VA and FHA mortgages are assumable; most others are not.

Most buyers trying to assume a ten- or fifteen-year-old mortgage stagger at the equity of the seller and need secondary financing to make the assumption. Often it is not economically feasible to make such an arrangement. Most mortgages cast after 1970 contain due-on-sale clauses which the Supreme Court has ruled are enforceable at all federally chartered lending institutions. Loans from state-chartered lenders also contain the due-on-sale clause, but some states have overruled the clause to make loans from their state-chartered institutions assumable, much to the distaste of the lenders. The controversy continues, but the future looks bleak for widely available assumptions; even the federal government may succumb to lending-industry pressure against assumable loans someday and cancel the clause in FHA and VA-backed loans.

The Wraparound

Especially popular in the western part of the country, wraparound financing is beneficial to both the buyer and the seller. It is possible, however, only when the seller does not immediately need all of his cash equity and when his mortgage does not contain a due-on-sale clause. The financing technique is explained in Chapter 19. You will need a good real estate attorney to assure that everyone's rights are protected in the financing arrangement.

The Land Contract

Commonly used when mortgage money is difficult to get, the land contract allows a buyer to take possession of a property after making a downpayment to the seller and agreeing to make monthly principal and interest payments to that seller on the balance of the purchase price. Title to the property, however, remains with the seller. It is usually mutually agreed upon that the buyer will procure financing from a lending institution as soon as possible. Sometimes an interest rate is named in the contract at which the buyer must procure financing as soon as it is available. Sometimes a cutoff date is used (say, three to five years) by which point in time the buyer must arrange other financing. The buyer then pays the balance due the seller and takes title to the property. If a buyer defaults on his payments under a land contract, he can be evicted. The property still belongs to the seller who also keeps all monies paid to date.

Mortgage Insurance for Sellers

As a direct result of the prevalence of seller-assisted financing in the early 1980s, the nation's largest private mortgage insurance company, Mortgage Guaranty Insurance Corporation (known as MGIC or "Magic"), instituted the first program to safeguard sellers against financial loss due to the default of their buyers. For a small premium (less than the cost of FHA insurance) the sellers are insured for 20 to 25 percent of the loan balance and all foreclosure fees (the premium is usually paid by the buyers).

However, this homeseller insurance policy may only be procured through a MGIC-approved lending institution which must also take over management of the loan, that is, collecting payments, apportioning funds to the tax escrow account, providing statements of account to the buyer and the seller, etc. There is, of course, a charge for this service, but who pays it (buyer or seller) is up for negotiation.

For more information, ask your real estate agent for the names of local lenders handling the program or similar programs sponsored by other mortgage insurance companies. Or write: Homeseller, Mortgage Guaranty Insurance Corporation, 270 East Kilbourn Ave., Milwaukee, Wis. 53202.

Selling Gimmicks

When people are really desperate to sell, they reach for whatever handles they can grab; some secure, some attached to the goal they seek only by tape and paper clips. The more unusual tactics, however, often make the newspapers, and some even become accepted practices.

Auctions

A voluntary auction is not the same as a foreclosure sale. The auctioneer invites bids but is not required to accept them. There is usually a floor bid for starters and the sellers usually reserve the right to accept or reject the top bid.

Since the members of an auction audience are almost invariably seeking a bargain, few top bids approach fair market value, and sometimes there are no bids at all. For you, the home seller, an auction may or may not get your property sold. It probably will not bring you a good selling price.

If you are a buyer, however, an auction could allow you to purchase a property at a significant discount. But be sure that you inspect all the properties that you plan to bid on thoroughly before the auction date. If your top bid results in a sale, you will be asked to sign a contract and to leave a substantial deposit (at least $2000) in cash or a cashier's check. You will then be required to bring in additional monies (usually to total 10 percent of the purchase price) within a given number of days (usually ten), and you will probably be required to close within four to six weeks, sometimes even sooner. Financing is often arranged and approved on the spot. If you decide to back out, you will lose your cash deposit, at the least.

Probably the best bargains at auctions are builder's "spec" houses in a development and condominium units in a newly constructed building. Loan carrying costs on such completed construction are expensive to the builders, many of whom will choose to cut their profit margins substantially for a quick sale. However, all federal and state laws relating to full disclosure and consumer protection must be complied with in an auction sale.

As a savvy buyer at a builder's auction, you should bid only on those properties that are complete and ready for occupancy. A builder's promise to finish other houses or units in a comparable manner is hard to enforce and a low auction price is an invitation to cost and quality cutting.

Raffles

Is there a real estate broker anywhere in the United States who has paced a path in his carpeting while worrying that house raffles will cut into his business? It's hardly likely! A few sellers have been successful with this tactic, many more have run into serious problems, and the vast majority are not interested in trying. But a few words for those of you who are curious.

In a house raffle, the seller sells his property to a charity at a price near fair market value. The charity then sells raffle tickets on the property, usually at $100 a ticket. The number of tickets to be sold is usually limited, but that limit is set to provide a healthy profit for the sponsoring organization.

The problems? Promotion costs and activities. Selling enough tickets. And most important of all, federal and state raffle laws. The raffle cannot be promoted nor can tickets be sold through the

United States mail. And state raffle laws vary across the country from loose to labyrinthian. If your raffle violates the law, you could conceivably lose your property or, at the very least, tie it up in legal ribbons for many months.

And for buyers: If you buy a house raffle ticket and win, remember that you will be required to pay income taxes on your winnings. Those taxes will have to be paid in cash on the following April 15th, which could mean that you will have to mortgage your new property or sell it to get the tax money out!

More Bargains for Buyers in a Soft Market

For the adventurous, and for all those potential buyers who refuse to sit on their hands bemoaning the state of the economy and the coming of doomsday, there are some special situations in a soft market that can be stepping stones to fortune. It takes courage to buy when everyone else is waiting and worried, but it is usually much more rewarding than buying when crowds are lined up at sellers' front doors.

New Houses

A lot of building contractors went out of business during the tight money of the early 80s. Many sold completed houses at, near, or below cost. Others offered "buy-downs" on mortgage interest rates that cost them thousands of dollars.

Usually new house prices are firm, but nothing is firm in bad times. If you are good at do-it-yourselfing, try offering a low price on an almost completed house where you feel relatively certain you can do the finishing work. A quick closing is worth a lot to a builder. Or find out what the buy-down is costing the builder (your bank will tell you), and do your own loan shopping. If chances for a loan look good, offer the builder a price several thousand dollars below the net amount he would receive after paying for the buy-down. Then, if necessary, negotiate upward slowly.

Conversions

Sponsors of condominium or cooperative conversions caught in mid-stream by a recession are in pain. Usually they want desperately to move their unsold units and turn the building over to the Homeowners Association.

A smart buyer can sometimes purchase two, three, or a block of these units at prices up to 50 percent and more off their market value with seller financing at below market rates for five years. Such a buyer can live in one unit and collect rent from the others, with all kinds of tax advantages. A slightly negative cash flow, if it exists, will usually be wiped out at tax time.

There is a risk, of course, in that the financing comes due in five years. But one plays the odds (odds which have historically proven to be excellent in favor of the player) that before the five-year term is out, he will be able to sell the investment units at substantial profit. And what better way to watch your investment than to live in the same building?

Multifamily Housing

Multifamily houses very often involve seller-assisted financing even in good times.

Living on the premises affords the best control of your investment. You can also act as your own super and keep maintenance costs to a minimum by doing repair work yourself whenever possible. When you are ready to move on, the property will most likely take longer to sell than a single-family house or condominium unit, but your profit and tax savings will be substantial.

PART III

Managing the
Special Situation

29

Home Improvements: Don't Pick Up That Hammer Until...

It is said you're never finished when you own a home. "Tell me about it," you grumble as you look around your own place. The roof waters the plants in your living room nicely when it rains, you could use a second bathroom, and your mother-in-law is moving in and space must be found—or made—for her and her accumulated possessions.

The need for fixing up—whether you call it repairs, remodeling, renovation, rehabilitation, or restoration—never stops. Some jobs, like the roof, are necessities. Others—a wine cellar, a sauna—are done for your own use and enjoyment. But all require work and perhaps some degree of concern on your part, whether you do it yourself or hire others. And whatever you undertake will cost money, sometimes more than you dreamed.

Before you pick up a hammer or telephone, it is important to give that improvement serious thought. In fact, planning can be more important than where the money is to come from. Frequently, arranging financing is relatively easy, or at least follows a set procedure. But how to judge the value of a home improvement job, and how to proceed with the work is, for many homeowners, sailing into totally foreign—and frequently unfriendly—waters, no matter how many years they have lived in their castle. Whether you are paying $300 to have some trees pruned on your property, or $50,000 for a full-scale addition, take the time to think through exactly what you want done. This is your home, of course, but it is probably also your biggest investment. You won't want to make one wrong decision or one blow with a chisel that will lessen the value of that investment.

Homework

To clarify the project in your own mind, ask yourself a few questions. Why are you undertaking this job? Is it work that truly needs to be done for maintenance of the property or is it an amenity to make life a little more pleasant for all of you—a patio, say, or an exercise room or a few stained-glass windows? Or is it perhaps a trendy development you're going along with just to be in super style, such as a hot tub? How will the improvement look in relation to the other homes in your neighborhood? How will it affect the value of your house? Will it be worth more, will it make no difference at all, or will it, in fact, make your home potentially difficult to sell? Will you get all or part of that investment back when you want to move? Here's a guide to help you answer those questions.

Talking About Values

No matter how much you care about the remodeling project you plan, it is wise to give a few cold and calculating thoughts to the day when you will want to sell and how that improvement is likely to set with prospective buyers. This is what we mean by protecting your investment and, if you can, helping it to make even more money for you.

Let's separate the more common home remodeling jobs according to their value. Value is a somewhat slippery term here and changes quickly and effortlessly, following the fashion of the time and alternating from one neighborhood to the next. However, the following home remodeling projects have stood the test of several years' analyzing and have been judged by appraisers, homebuilders, realty agents, and others in allied areas to fit into the following categories.

Remodeling projects that can return more than you paid for them when you sell if *the job is done well*. Interestingly, these two projects are both relatively low-cost ones. If you paint the outside of your home spending, say, $2000, you may well be able to tack another $3000 or $4000 on to the asking price when you sell. Exterior appearance is that important. Also on the outside, inexpensively upgrading the existing landscaping, if there is any, will also make your home more attractive and can bring you back far more than you spent. Don't go overboard with exotic landscaping, however; that's a wrong move.

Remodeling projects that should at least return your original investment, or a sizable chunk of it. First comes the two most popular home improvement projects—a new or updated kitchen and a second, and possibly third, bathroom. Both are extremely desirable features in any home and should pay for themselves when you sell. If you don't go overboard on the kitchen. Professionals say kitchens are the most overimproved area of a house. You can improve a kitchen to the point where you spend almost what you paid for the house! In that event you are certainly not going to see your original investment returned when you move.

Energy improvements and installations run the gamut. Improvements such as thermal or storm windows and upgraded insulation can indeed return your cash outlay. Solar heating or hot water systems don't quite make it yet, probably because their initial expense takes a longer time to recover.

A third or fourth bedroom can be a wise investment only if you do not have to go through another room to reach the new one. Layout counts here. Fifth bedrooms are not so popular in these days of small families, unless that space is in a former garage, in the basement or some other area where it can easily be turned one day into a self-sufficient apartment, zoning laws permitting.

Then there are the smaller improvements that are relatively inexpensive, yet contribute enormously to the good looks of the house. Their low cost can easily be recouped. In this area, for example, would be a $300 or so skylight to illuminate a dark stairwell, or a $40 to $50 vanity cabinet to cover sink pipes in the bathroom.

Remodeling projects not likely to return much, if any, of your investment (but here, too, they may make the home more attractive, which translates into more salable). You may be surprised to find aluminum siding in this category. Some folks like it, but a fair number of others loathe it, so don't count on recouping money spent here. Also in this frequently hazy area are tool sheds, gazebos, hot tubs, and Jacuzzis. Wall-to-wall carpeting may well be ripped up by someone not enthralled with the hot mustard shade you chose, or by a buyer with pets and/or allergies, or by someone who just plain prefers the look of polished hardwood floors.

The basement "rec room" is as out of fashion as the 1950s, but a family room is still a selling point, if it is adjacent to the main living area, and not downstairs or in an attached garage.

Some improvements go from popular to who-needs-it as one moves from one section of the country to another. Take central air conditioning. If you install a system in your home in Tucson a buyer

What's Hot and What's Not

Fads come and go. Fashions change too, although a little more slowly. The following design and architectural features are showing up increasingly in house blueprints and in simpler home improvement projects. Will the newer styles be around for a while? Well . . . maybe.

Hot	*Not Hot*
Greenhouse/solarium/conservatory	Sun porch
Decks and patios	
Skylight	Dormer
Exposed interior brick wall	Inexpensive paneling
Stained glass windows	Louvered windows
Dining space open to the kitchen	Formal dining room
	too far from
	the kitchen
Basement efficiency apartment	Basement "rec room"
(a/k/a "that little old taxpayer in	
the basement")	
Wood fencing painted white (think	Chain link fencing
of Kentucky horse farms), natural	
wood fencing left unpainted	

won't bat an eye. It's expected. Put it into your Minneapolis house and the buyer still may not blink and will rarely thank you with a higher check for the house. How often is the system used in colder climates? More than one new owner of a centrally air conditioned home somewhat north of the Mason-Dixon line has taken a look at the first summer's electric bills and laid the system to rest. They purchase a few room air conditioners and that's that.

The jury is still out on the value of greenhouses, probably because those spaces are open to such wide interpretation. The newer style ones, also called solariums or sun rooms or conservatories, are frequently solar-heated and are quite attractive indeed. One of these would probably increase the value of your home if it can be used for extra living or dining space and is not just a small outbreak from the kitchen only to accommodate plants and vegetables.

Also in this murky category is a new roof or sidewalk, a paved driveway, and other jobs required to keep your property from falling

The greenhouse, an increasingly popular home improvement, is not just a room for plants. *Reprinted with permission of Sun System Prefabricated Solar Greenhouses.*

to pieces in front of you. A buyer won't be impressed if you show her those bills. She expects a good roof and a decent sidewalk and is not about to pay extra for them, although your improvements should make her feel better about your house.

Remodeling projects that may well hinder your ability to sell when you want and at the price you want. The two home projects here are swimming pools and tennis courts. Buyers may not want either and will not pay more for them than other houses in the area are commanding without those amenities. Exceptions are communities where everyone seems to have a pool and court. Then by all means join the crowd if your house will not be overwhelmed or overimproved by their addition.

The Cardinal Rule

In home remodeling it's "Don't overimprove." Don't fix up your home to the point where it becomes worth $140,000 in a neighborhood of $100,000 homes. You won't get your price when you sell. Househunters looking for a $140,000 home are going to search in $140,000 (or more) neighborhoods. But, as with every rule, there are exceptions. Your home is indeed your refuge and your castle, and if having a pool or a lavish kitchen is what will truly make you happy, then go ahead and start building. (It does make better sense, though, for you to plan to stay in that house for several years to take advantage of that expenditure.) And be aware of the problems you may be faced with when you put the house on the market and find buyers not the least bit grateful for the investment you made. However, what you've spent in that major remodeling project will also increase the cost basis of your home for tax purposes. So that will reduce your capital gains tax when you sell.

Tastes differ, too, of course. As mentioned earlier, carpeting the entire house wall-to-wall may be a lavish gesture on your part that will go unappreciated by the next buyer, as may aluminum siding. One man, proud of $1500 worth of dropped ceilings in his 10-room city house, was appalled when the eventual buyers offered quite a bit lower than he was asking, telling the real estate agent that, among other things, they'd have to rip out all those panels because they wanted the high, open ceilings above. And they'd probably have to do some replastering after those anchoring beams were yanked, they added. The man didn't speak to the buyers throughout the closing ceremony (but notice he did take their bid!). So the moral here is don't expect everyone to appreciate your improvement, unless it's one of the more popular kitchen/bathroom/extra bedrooms, noncontroversial ones.

When You Need More Space

Perhaps your intended project is more than a new hot water heater or installing fire alarms. You need an extra bedroom for a new baby, or a bed/sitting room with bath for an elderly parent or parent-in-law who is moving in. Where is the room to come from?

First, take a look at existing space before thinking of getting into major construction. You may find what you need in unused or underused areas around the house as it is now. Many architects, appraisers, and others in the building and buying field say that many, many home additions are just plain dreadful. They are poorly planned, they look like afterthoughts, and they have bad traffic patterns that make life in those rooms something like a French farce. It may be fun to spend a couple of weeks in the summer in a beach or lakefront house that is poorly designed, where you can have a few giggles because you all have to walk through Karen's bedroom to get to the only bathroom, or Tony has to be the last one to bed because his is the last bedroom in a chain of sleeping quarters with no other entrance. But no one wants to live like that in a permanent residence. So layout is extremely important in figuring where to find or make more space.

That's why looking at what you have may work well. Presumably your house has already been designed by an architect and works well, traffic-wise. So perhaps you could convert the attic into an extra bedroom, if there is a staircase to reach it that doesn't mean going through someone else's room. Converting a garage is less costly and a better-designed improvement than constructing a new addition alongside the house. So is closing in a side porch, where there, too, you already have a roof and a foundation. Utilizing a basement for living space or carving a small area for a powder room from the side of a large living room make better sense for present use and future sales potential than building new areas. And they're cheaper.

If you must construct new space, building up is less costly than building out into a new addition. Plumbing and other mechanical systems need only be extended and not installed new. So you might use the "air rights" over your house to put up that room and bath for Mom (if stairs are no problem), rather than adding a costly wing on a new foundation.

Another suggestion here on the subject of an aging parent moving in. You could also consider erecting a "granny cottage" on your property, if there is room. This is a housing development that arrived just a few years ago from Australia. It's a prefabricated unit of less than 1000 square feet which is erected on your lot for under $20,000. It contains one open room, a kitchen, and bath. This alternative housing for an elderly parent is still new, but so far zoning officials have been amenable to its use—if it is for a parent and if it is dismantled if no longer needed. For more information, contact the American Association of Retired Persons, 1909 K St. N.W., Washington, D.C. 20049.

Once you have a good grasp on the work you want done, do some rough pencil sketches to get something on paper. Try to get a ballpark figure for what it is all likely to cost. Now you're at the point where other persons and agencies will come into the picture. Some are necessary, others will be your own choice to make the improvement as fine a job as possible. A few, sadly, may, with all kinds of rulings behind them, turn a firm thumbs down on your dream project.

And yes, a major remodeling job will probably trigger a tax reassessment of your property.

Condominium Owners Association/Cooperative Board. It's your home, but you're not always free to make any changes you want. Consult these groups if the work you plan makes touching base compulsory. In garden community condos, for example, you may not be allowed to change the exterior paint color of your unit, or construct a patio, or even install awnings.

Building Inspector/Zoning Department. How will your community feel about the changes you propose? What do zoning laws say about the two-car garage you plan? Or the rental unit? Or the greenhouse on the roof? Zoning laws in many communities can be extremely strict and pretty inflexible too. Your local building inspector will acquaint you with the rules in your town, will tell you how to go about applying for a variance if one is needed in your situation, or how to apply for permits if you plan to do the work yourself (permits are usually required when any structural work is planned or when the basic living area is altered). There are a few unclear areas here, too, however. For example, greenhouses, while they do frequently require structural alteration, are sometimes not considered separate rooms and a license is not required to go ahead and install one. Over the last several years a small but significant number of homeowners has been converting part of their houses to full apartments that they rent to relatives or on the open market. This is frequently being done in communities strictly zoned for one-family housing. Officials often look the other way since, after all, homeowners and their new tenants, vote and the new units help ease the housing crunch in those towns. Whether you decide to convert within or outside the law is up to you, but do be acquainted with what's on the books in your town and talk to fellow townspeople who have made that alteration to their properties.

Sometimes your city or town hall can poke its nose into even the smallest home improvement job. In some communities building a treehouse is verboten. Exposing an interior brick wall may have to be done by professionals, since some plaster is fire retardant and must not be removed without a permit. The contractors could compensate for the loss of the plaster's fire retardant properties.

Engineer/Home Inspection Service. These individuals or companies can tell you whether you *can* tear down that kitchen safely, or whether the walls can bear the load of a third story. And which *are* the loadbearing walls, anyway? You will get a guesstimate of what the job you plan is likely to cost and all of that will be in writing so you can show it to contractors when you start taking bids. The cost here is usually a flat fee of $40 or $50 an hour, or it is based on square footage of the projected job.

Architect. You want to add an extra bedroom, but you don't know just where. Or you're converting the ground floor to a full apartment for your daughter, but you don't know what constitutes a good layout. By all means have an architect (unless you truly trust your builder's expertise and taste) do the planning so you can avoid a design mish-mash that will have you kicking yourself every time you walk by it. An architect is especially important if you have purchased a large, old house and are planning a major rehabilitation. Many a rehabber has put a kitchen in dark room X downstairs and the bedroom above it in cheery room Y, only to find a year later it would have worked better the other way around: a cheery kitchen and a dark, quiet bedroom. An architect will charge either a flat fee or a percentage of the job and is well worth the expense if you are entering into any project above, say, $15,000.

Real estate appraiser. What is your home worth now? What is the improvement you're planning likely to do to that value? This man or woman can tell you. The flat fee here is in the $100 to $200 range, and if you'd like the name and address of a licensed appraiser near you you can contact the Society of Real Estate Appraisers, 645 N. Michigan Ave., Chicago, Ill. 60611, (312) 346-7422.

Designer/interior designer/decorator. There's a lot of overlapping here, but in general the designer does pretty much the same work as an architect, but he or she does not have the architect's special training. You can hire a designer when new construction and furnishings are called for, since the designer will have knowledge of space planning. He or she will be able to tell you where a new interior staircase should go; where to construct a loft or loft bed space; how traffic patterns would flow if you put the room you are planning just where you want. Fees here are considerably lower than for an architect. Decorators (and designers too for that matter) can suggest treatments for walls and windows, how to gain more storage space, how to partition rooms, as well as offering basic decorating advice such as the choice of color, paint, wallpapering, etc. Prices for decorators range from the top-of-the-line craftspeople whose work you see in decorating magazines and who have professional credentials, to the inexpensive neighbor just getting started, to your local department store, where there may be no charge for decorating advice with a certain minimum furnishings purchase.

If I Had a Hammer . . .

Should you tackle the job yourself or call in the pros? The answer should depend on
- how much time you can devote to the job
- whether you will have friends or relatives to help you
- how much you want—or need—to save the cost of a contractor
- your expertise or willingness to learn the job

Outdoor decks continue to be a popular home improvement, ranging from the simple (left) to the more elaborate tri-level (right). *Reprinted with permission of Western Wood Products Association.*

Doing it yourself can save you anywhere from 10 to 30 percent of the cost of a remodeling job, and that is the important, ever-rising labor expense. Cost aside, you may well want to spend a couple of weekends constructing a patio. If you choose to do at least some of the work yourself, try letting the contractor handle the major construction, then you do the finishing—staining, painting, wallpapering, carpeting, hanging of doors, and any unusual window treatment. You'll still save a nice bit of cash.

Doing it yourself means dealing with local agencies for permits, inspections and, where necessary, certificates of occupancy. In some communities you will not be allowed to do electrical, plumbing, and heating work on your own, but must call in licensed electricians, etc. In any event, it's wise to leave those important jobs to the ones who know them best, even if no one at town hall minds your doing it yourself. These are potentially dangerous installations, not just while doing the work, but for years later while you are living in the house. This is money well spent.

Dealing with appropriate agencies takes time, and so does working with subcontractors, all of which may affect your decision to do it yourself. Keeping an eye on subcontractors is important to see the job done well, not so much to keep them from running off with the silver as to see that they follow instructions, especially if what you

The Top Twenty-Five Do-It-Yourself Projects

1. Interior painting
2. Wallpaper hanging
3. Exterior painting
4. New or additional weather stripping, caulking, and sealing
5. Lighting fixtures
6. Kitchen faucet
7. Burglar/fire protection devices
8. Bathroom faucet
9. Lockset
10. Additional insulation
11. Shelving
12. Ceiling fan
13. Remodeled bathroom
14. Wall paneling
15. Carpeting
16. Remodeled kitchen
17. Additional electric circuits
18. Moldings
19. Floor tiles
20. Storm windows/doors
21. Fence
22. Bathroom vanity
23. New roof
24. Waterheater
25. Patio/outdoor deck

Source: *Building Supply News*

want done is complicated or innovative or both. Leaving a list of instructions as you dash off to your 9 to 5 job is a gamble you are very likely to lose.

Also to be considered when working with subcontractors is workers' compensation insurance. In fact, before starting any job where you bring in outside help, family included, it's wise to check your homeowner's insurance policy about coverage in that area.

A growing number of homeowners are picking up the hammer themselves these days, thanks to a fluctuating economy on the one hand and a heightened interest in the home and home improvement projects on the other. There may well be courses you can take in local schools and colleges to guide you through the job you plan. And, of course, there are hundreds of home improvement books to turn to for help. Two particularly good ones are the Time-Life and Sunset Books series on home remodeling projects.

Homeowners who are also remodelers say that dealing with local businesspeople can be more helpful for the neophyte than heading for the larger discount stores on the main highway. Local hardware, paint store, and lumberyard folks can offer more guidance to long-time local customers than some of the biggies. You may pay a little more at Main Street Hardware, but if you need consistent direction, spending that extra few dollars may be worth it. And you may still save money over bringing in a professional.

Choosing a Contractor

Nooooooo, you muse, I don't think it's in me to build a bathroom. I'll go with the contractor. If you do decide to call in the pros you should know that this is a field where the fly-by-nights abound. In fact, a check of local consumer protection agencies and Better Business Bureau offices puts home repair complaints second only to auto complaints. If you want to come out of a home improvement job with your health, your sanity, and your marriage intact—and your house in pretty good shape too—there's plenty of homework involved here. This is not a case of simply sitting back and letting the guys who know the job take over.

How would you feel if the company you hired walked off the job of adding on to your house, leaving one wall open and exposed to the elements? It has happened. What if the contractor built a wall over the fireplace opening? One did. Shoddy work, no-shows and outright scams proliferate here.

Some of the popular recorded ripoffs:

The "While I'm in the Neighborhood" Ploy
This is especially popular for use with retired persons living alone (it gives them no chance to consult other members of the family in the house). The contractor knocks on the door and says "I was in the neighborhood doing some work on Randolph Street and noticed you have some loose shingles on your roof. I can fix them while I'm here for $50." When he gets to the roof, he finds lots more wrong, of course. Frequently, the "contractor" will open the roof in a few spots, pour down some water and then lead the homeowner upstairs to see the badly damaging leaks. "That water is dangerous to the electrical wiring," the charlatan explains grimly. "You could have a fire anytime." Many, many homeowners understandably quake at the word fire and hasten to pay the phony $1000, $2000, $3000, or whatever he asks to make repairs. In cash, of course, and he'll be happy to drive you to the bank.

This can be avoided by checking the credentials of anyone applying to do work at your place, and noticing if the panel truck has the contractor's name and address or merely the words "carpentry—painting" or the like. It should be pointed out, however, that legitimate workmen take advantage of being in a neighborhood to drum up more business and they, too, may well come to your front door saying "I was in the neighborhood doing some work on Randolph Street. . . ." Just be careful to check references and talk to the owner of that home on Randolph Street.

Bait and Switch

The contractor offers a product at an astoundingly low price. When you call, he points out the flaws in that product, or says it wouldn't fit your home, and directs you to a higher-priced model.

Downgrading

The contractor will sell you—and charge you for—one model or brand name item and then install an inferior and lower-costing one.

The "City Inspector"

A man comes to call claiming to be a housing or building inspector for your community. After a cursory look around, he informs you that your home needs repairs and then recommends a firm to do them—his.

And new ripoffs are being thought of daily in the area of solar energy as nefarious contractors get a better handle on that aspect of home improvements.

Properly scared? Here's how to go about choosing a good man or woman for the job, one who won't leave you a nervous wreck, with an incomplete job or one that has to be done over. One who won't force you to head for a lawyer's office, at a lawyer's fees, for a potential lawsuit. The house where the workmen left the wall exposed? The woman there was hospitalized with pneumonia. More bills. And it was months before she truly recovered.

You may need just a carpenter. Or you may be looking for a general contractor who will oversee the entire project, subcontracting plumbing, heating, electrical, and other specialized work to others. For ease in reading, we'll simply use the term "contractor." The admonitions and procedures for hiring are similar:

1. How to find a contractor? It isn't wise simply to turn to the Yellow Pages. Remember, the phone book isn't a screening mechanism. It's better to ask relatives, friends, neighbors, and co-workers for suggestions. The personal experience of a satisfied customer is the best reference. Perhaps your local building inspector, or a bank, may

have some suggestions. If your community has a civic association, ask a few of those members. They are usually quite amenable to passing around the names of good workers. Recommendations from a lumber yard or hardware store frequently turn out to be those merchants' best customers, so that isn't a particularly helpful source.

2. It is best to deal only with licensed contractors, who can at least be traced if anything goes wrong. Some people just starting out, while perfectly competent, often cannot afford to put up the required performance bond of several thousand dollars, and so remain unlicensed. If you deal with these workers, it's even more important that they be referred to you by homeowners who have been satisfied with their work.

3. Get at least three estimates (the bank that grants you a loan if you need one may require two anyway), and be sure to tell each contractor the same story about what you want so you can properly evaluate each estimate. The low bid is not necessarily the best one. Try for the middle one. You might also ask if the contractor charges for estimates, before he or she comes to call.

4. By all means bargain over the bid, especially if you like one contractor, but another has come in with a lower figure. Ask if he or she is willing to match that price.

5. Ask for references not more than two years old. This can result in a contractor referring you to a job he or she did for cousin Vinnie and various assorted relatives, but still it's worth visiting those sites to see what kind of work that individual does. Ask the homeowner if he or she has been satisfied with the job. Did the contractor listen to directions or just go ahead with the work the way he or she wanted? Did he or she clean up at the end of each day? After the job was completed?

6. Check out anyone you are considering with your local consumer protection agency and your local BBB office to see if there are any complaints against him or her in their files. If there's nothing on the books, remember that doesn't mean he or she is a sterling individual. It just shows that if there were any dissatisfied customers they did not formally complain to those offices. Or perhaps it's a shoddy company that changed names when things got too hot for them. At least by checking you'll learn if the firm you are considering is the biggest ripoff artist in the county and was prominently featured on *60 Minutes* last fall. The really bad guys are sure to have a file.

7. Does the contractor carry liability and workers' compensation insurance? Ask to see proof.

Your Contract and What It Should Contain

Maybe you won't be offered a contract by the individual or company you plan to engage. If not, it's wise to pick up a simple form at a stationery store and fill it in yourself. Oral promises carry no weight in a court, if it should come to that. Here's what that agreement should contain:

The name, address, and license number of the contractor.

A full description of the work to be done, including brand names and model numbers of products you want. If you're expecting a GE refrigerator, for example, and a Cheapee is installed, the contractor may well shrug and point to the lonely word "refrigerator" in the contract. All warranties and guarantees should be included as well.

A start and completion date for the project, and, if you can, a day-to-day dollar penalty for work that goes beyond that date.

Proof of insurance for workers' compensation, liability and, property damage coverage.

A statement that you will not be responsible for payments to his subcontractors or suppliers. Some states require that subcontractors be paid, no matter what the contract says, so you may still be held liable here.

Assurance that the contractor will obtain the necessary permits.

A payment schedule. Never, never pay all or most of the money up front. Unscrupulous contractors can make a nice living collecting such monies from any number of homeowners, and then never beginning, or finishing, the job. A good payment plan is 15 percent at the start of work, with another 15 percent paid when the job is finished. The balance can be staggered at intervals in between. Try to hold back as much as you can till the end, to give you any leverage you may need to see that the job is done and done properly.

All blank spaces filled in with a phrase like "Does not apply." Never sign a completion certificate for a job until you are satisfied. Keep all receipts, check stubs and other proof of payment. Finally, remember that if you don't pay your contractor he can file a mechanic's lien, which is a claim on your property.

8. Will the contractor be responsible for obtaining necessary permits for work to begin?

9. Will the contractor do the cleaning up or is that up to you? We're not just talking about sweeping up here. If a wall, is opened up, will you be expected to have it replastered?

Because of the increasing number—and ingeniousness—of home repair frauds, several states now have laws governing remodeling contractors that afford maximum protection to consumers. Also, a Federal Trade Commission rule allows you to cancel a contract within three days of signing, and get back any downpayment in full, another security net for you.

The truly nervous might also look into protection offered by Home Owners Warranty Corp., 2000 L St. N.W., Washington, D.C. 20036. As you may know, this group sells insurance against defective workmanship and materials in new homes. It has now begun offering similar coverage for remodeling jobs done by its affiliated contractors. If you have a problem, the company first asks the contractor to fix the job. If that fails, HOW will bring in another contractor. Rates are about $175 to $200 for projects costing up to $5000, with the premium rising $3.50 or so for each additional $1000.

If the Job Is Botched

You're furious, you're sick, and you don't know where to turn. Everything has gone wrong and we're not talking about weather delays or the contractor taking off and goin' fishing more than occasionally. Serious problems are evident and it's his fault. If you do find yourself in this unfortunate situation, you do have some recourses:

• You can keep after him to make repairs.

• You can contact your local consumer protection agency. You will need to send a comprehensive, sensibly written package to that office, which includes a cover letter explaining the problem and giving the contractor's name, address, and license number. Attach photocopies of the contract, of any other correspondence you have had with that individual, and of receipts for any payments you have made. They will tell you how to proceed next. (You can, and indeed you should, notify the BBB of your experience, but remember that that office has no legal powers.) You can also contact your state's Contractor's License Board.

• You can take the contractor to Small Claims Court if the job cost $1500 or less.

• If you have the HOW insurance policy, you can turn to that office for redress.

• You can consult an attorney and consider suing the contractor.

You shouldn't have to come to this grief, however, if the homework you put into finding a contractor is at least as detailed as your plan for the improvements.

Finally on this subject, contact your local Internal Revenue Service office to learn how the cost of major upgrading projects can be taken off your capital gains tax at the time you sell your home.

For More Information

Your city or state consumer affairs agency will no doubt offer printed material at no cost informing you of protection laws in your area when dealing with contractors, and advising you on other aspects of home improvement vis-à-vis the well-informed buyer.

The National Association of the Remodeling Industry (NARI), 11 E. 44th Street, New York, N.Y. 10017, the largest professional association in the home remodeling industry, will send you free printed material to guide you in the choice of a contractor and through other home improvement decisions.

The American Association of Architects, 1735 New York Ave. N.W., Washington, D.C. 20006, will send you a list of member architects in your locale who do remodeling, renovation, or restoration projects. No charge.

If your house is just plain old, and not historic, you can write for "Renovate an Old House?," a 21-page booklet available from the Superintendent of Documents, Government Printing Office, Washington, D.C. 20402. Ask for Home and Garden Bulletin 212. Price is $3.00.

30

Thirteen Ways to Finance a Home Improvement

You need a new heating plant. Or storm windows. A new sidewalk. Another bedroom. A new roof. A powder room. A new driveway. Electrical smoke alarms. Exterior siding or a paint job. Insulation. New wiring.

You would like a patio. A skylight. Paneling. A laundry room. Central air conditioning. A sauna. An inground pool. Landscaping. Awnings. An open porch enclosed. A greenhouse. A new kitchen. A replacement for the falling-down tool shed.

It's always something with a house as we strive to turn our leaky little nest into a modest version of Windsor Castle. Where does the money come from for all those necessities or goodies? Usually it's in the form of a loan, since most of the items mentioned above are a little pricey, and many of us don't have the cash on hand. Saving until you can pay for the improvement you want doesn't always make the best financial sense if what you want is costly. If you are dreaming of a $10,000 kitchen, for example, and figure it will take you three years to accumulate that amount, by that time the kitchen may well cost $12,000. You'll never catch up. Better to borrow, you reason, and have the job done now, even though that $2000 you are supposedly saving will go toward interest on the loan.

Emergency repairs or new installations may also force you to consider a home improvement loan, since those jobs cannot be put off until the checkbook is in better shape.

Once you decide to go ahead with an improvement, there are a few golden rules to bear in mind. This is an area, after all, where very big bucks could be involved. Every bit as much attention should be directed to finding a home improvement loan as you paid to finding the best home mortgage.

Golden Rule No. 1
Don't borrow unless you have to.

Any loan, no matter how excellent the terms, is going to cost you money. If you have the cash, use it. If you have $7000 in savings in a bank or savings and loan association, take it out and forego the 5½ to 9 percent interest, which is far less of a loss than incurring a high double-digit interest figure for a loan would be.

One exception to the pay-cash-if-you-can rule is government-sponsored loans and those offered by some utility companies, which can carry interest rates of under 5 percent. If you qualify for one of them it would naturally be wiser to let your $7000 stay in savings in one form or another and continue earning you interest of at least 5½ percent. Take the lower-cost loan. You will still come out ahead.

Golden Rule No. 2
Get estimates of the work to be done before seeking the loan.

Indeed, some lenders will require that you present them with two or three written estimates as a condition for their considering your application. Besides, shopping around for the best deal is only good business sense. You may be quite surprised at the range of price quotes you receive for the same job. It's far smarter, too, to be certain you need $12–14,000 when you stop in at a potential lender than to ask vaguely for "around $20,000."

Golden Rule No. 3
Shop around for the best borrowing terms.

Making the rounds here means covering a wider variety of loan sources than when you were looking for a mortgage. As you will see, your loan *could* cost you anywhere from 3 percent to over 20 percent in interest. For example, $10,000 borrowed for ten years at 6 percent will cost you a total of $13,200. With that same amount at 20 percent, you will pay $22,560!

Convinced of the worth of investigating all sources? Here are places to look:

1. You can ask relatives for a loan, which would almost surely be offered to you at below-market interest rates.

2. By borrowing against a passbook savings account, you will be charged around 3 percent against an account earning 5½ percent

interest, bringing your loan charge to an inexpensive 8½ percent or so. Obviously this will work only if you need just a few thousand dollars. You are not likely to have $15,000 or $20,000 sitting around in a passbook account.

3. If you have a whole life insurance policy you can borrow against that at a low rate. The face value of the policy is, of course, reduced by the amount of the loan. So if your policy is for $100,000, and you borrow $15,000, it is then worth $85,000. You can make up the borrowed amount by increasing your regular payments.

4. Check your broker to see if you can borrow against *securities*, again at terms more favorable than those of many banks and S&Ls.

5. Don't overlook your credit union, if you are a member of one. Always an excellent source of financing, at very attractive terms.

6. The contractor you plan to engage may also offer you financing. That can be either better or worse than what you will find elsewhere, so don't blithely accept his terms without doing some homework on your own. In hard economic times, a contractor may be able to secure a loan with a lower-than-market interest rate with a lender he does business with, perhaps telling that institution he will lose the sale if he doesn't make his rates competitive. So the lender drops the interest figure a fraction of a percentage point or so. On the other hand, you give up important leverage when you finance through a contractor. Since the loan is usually paid to the contractor by the lending institution, you have no power to withhold payment if you are not satisfied with the job.

7. If you are looking to make an energy-saving improvement, contact your local utility company. Many around the nation offer no-interest or very low interest loans for certain improvements and installations for good customers (usually defined as those who have not received a shutoff notice for the preceding year). There are no income requirements here. Monies borrowed—usually up to around $5000—can be used for storm windows, insulation, clock thermostats, and other conservation devices. The payments are added to your utility bill, spread out over however long the loan is to run. If you are over sixty-five years of age, check into special loan programs for seniors.

8. You can apply for an unsecured home improvement loan with your local bank or savings and loan association. Terms and amounts that can be borrowed vary from one institution to another, but generally you can expect to be able to borrow as much as $15,000 or $20,000, for five or ten years at a fairly high interest rate, usually 1½ to 2 points over the current rate. With this type of loan you do not

offer your house or other assets as collateral. You are judged for eligibility solely on your ability to pay (job security, good credit history, income), just as you would be in applying for a mortgage or auto loan. Approval for these loans usually comes within forty-eight hours, whereas with a home equity loan, where your house is usually pledged against the amount borrowed, the procedure is more time consuming.

With the unsecured home improvement loan, the lender may well want to see those three written estimates for the job.

9. You can look to the government for a home improvement loan. Although many programs have dried up since the early 1980s, there are still some around that offer excellent terms for borrowers. Chief among them is the FHA Title 1 improvement loan. Terms here vary depending on whether economic times are good or bad. The largest program of its kind under the federal umbrella, Title 1 offers HUD-insured loans of up to $15,000 for fifteen years at an interest rate that is usually a point above the prevailing rate. There are a number of restrictions here, however, the principal one being that the loan must be used to improve the livability of your home and cannot be used for any freestanding improvements or installations. So no swimming pools, or even carpeting or new appliances. Not all banks offer FHA loans—they don't like to be bothered with the paperwork involved—so you will have to search for one that does. Do make the effort. The deal here will be worth it, particularly the long repayment schedule, which you will not find with unsecured home improvement loans offered by other lenders.

Then there is the Farmers Home Administration (FmHA). You don't have to be a farmer to take advantage of this program, but you do have to live in a rural community with a population of 10,000 or less, though in some instances 20,000 or less is allowed. No suburbs, strictly rural. The home improvement loans (mortgages and construction loans are available too), are at lower-than-market interest rates, which in hardship cases can drop, through a complicated formula, to as little as 1 percent.

There are several restrictions to these loans (you must have been unable to obtain a loan elsewhere, for instance), and there are very definite income requirements, but if you qualify you can come out with an excellent deal. For more information, you can contact the Farmers Home Administration office in your area, or write Administrator, FmHA, U.S. Dept. of Agriculture, Washington, D.C. 20250.

While on the subject of numbers and initials, there is also the federal government's Section 203 (k) program. This was designed to assist in the financing of rehabilitation of one- to four-family residential properties. A 203 (k) mortgage can finance the purchase and rehabilitation of a dwelling, a refinancing/rehabilitation transaction, or it can be used solely to finance rehabilitation.

This program can be particularly valuable for those who purchase an older property in need of practically a gut rehabilitation. Typically in this instance the homeowner must secure financing first to purchase the home, again to start the rehab work, and then again when the job is completed to pay off the interim loans with a permanent mortgage. Often the interim financing (the acquisition and construction loans) involves relatively high interest rates. With Section 203 (k), however, the borrower can secure just one loan, at a long-term fixed rate, to finance both the acquisition of the home and the rehabilitation construction. Amounts that can be borrowed vary from one locale to another, but generally run as high as $90,000 for a single-family residence. For more information about this program, contact your local HUD office.

Remember, however, that the availability of government loan assistance is very much dependent on the administration in office and the overall economic climate.

Moving down to the state level, just about every state now offers loans for renovation and rehabilitation at below-market interest rates through its Mortgage Finance Agency or Housing Finance Agency or some similar agency. You can call your governor's office to obtain the name and phone number of that quasi-autonomous office in your state. Monies are derived from the sale of tax-exempt bonds, which allows the agencies to offer both mortgage and home improvement loans. Loan terms vary widely from one state to another. In some areas only certain neighborhoods will qualify, and there may be income requirements for borrowers. But the terms are excellent. Who wouldn't want a loan at 3 percent, which is how low some interest rates can be. Here, too, programs are subject to cancellation at any time.

Then there are programs on the municipal level, sponsored by cities for special improvements to certain blocks and neighborhoods they are trying to upgrade. Most of these programs are offered by the municipalities in conjunction with federal or state government plans. Call City Hall to see what's available where you live. And if you have a Community Development Agency (CDA) office in your city, give them a ring too. They're a sort of liaison or filter between HUD in Washington and your local government. The news will be the same whether you call CDA or City Hall, but it's wise to keep in

The Cost of a Loan

Let's say you need $10,000. Here is what you can expect your monthly loan payments to be at terms quoted to you by lenders:

	5 years	10 years	15 years
12 percent	$220	$141	$118
13	225	147	124
14	230	152	130
15	235	158	136
16	240	164	143
17	245	170	149
18	250	176	156
19	255	182	163
20	260	188	169

touch with all bases. While money from Washington for housing programs has dwindled to a great extent, every now and then a new program does crop up, with funding disappearing very quickly to waiting and well-qualified applicants. It'll pay you to be right there when those monies come in. Reading about new programs in your local papers may be too little effort too late.

10. Finally, in terms of borrowing small amounts of money, you can borrow from a finance agency. We've left this for last because interest rates here are very high. Finance companies should be considered the source of last resort, used only for emergency repairs and improvements where borrowing is available from no other source.

If you need a fairly large amount of money—$20,000 to, let's say, $100,000 or more—you will probably be better off applying for a loan against your home. The repayment plan is longer, allowing you lower monthly payments. And, of course, many lenders will just not let you borrow more than $15,000 or so, making the secured loan the only way to obtain the larger amount of money you need. Here are several sources of those loans:

11. You can refinance your existing mortgage, but only if the time is right for such a potentially drastic action.

Refinancing works like this. Suppose you have a $70,000 mortgage on a home that is currently worth $95,000. You are paying an interest rate of 9 percent. Now you need $20,000 to finish off an attic and add a bathroom up there to accommodate a growing family. The object of refinancing in this instance would be to take that old loan, add the new one for $20,000, and then write up a whole new mortgage combining the two figures. So now your mortgage will be at $90,000 and the interest rate is . . . But wait a minute. The interest rate will be 15 percent. Why should you turn in $70,000 at 9 percent for $90,000 at a whopping 15 percent? Aha, smart you. That is when refinancing makes no sense at all, and over the last few years this has been true indeed for those lucky souls holding low-interest mortgages dating from pre-1978. If you find yourself in this situation it would be smarter to leave your existing loan alone and take out a $20,000 loan at the best rate you can find. Even if you still wind up being charged 15 percent, it will be 15 percent only for the smaller amount and not the entire $90,000.

However. If you bought your house when interest rates were high and have been thinking of refinancing now that they have dropped a bit—and a drop of at least two points is necessary before refinancing makes any sense—then you might want to tag on a small home improvement loan to the new mortgage you will have written.

In your mathematical doodling, remember that in refinancing you will also have to pay loan origination fees, points, title searches, and all the rest of the costly procedure you went through the first time around that went under the heading of closing costs. That amount is usually 3 to 5 percent of the cost of the loan. Prepayment penalties might cost you too. (This is why it makes no sense to refinance until interest rates are at least two points lower than what you are paying now—your saving will just be eaten up in new processing fees.) You will have to figure out just what you will be spending, or saving, here. Perhaps it will all be foolish and extremely costly. In that event you might turn to:

12. The second mortgage has long been the traditional source of money for major home improvements. As you would do with a first mortgage, you borrow a specified amount and repay at a fixed rate of interest, usually for ten or fifteen years but some lenders are now financing longer-term second mortgages. You will have to add to that amount loan fees for having your home appraised, a title search, and any other loan origination charge the lender will make, so in effect you are paying closing costs again.

In shopping around you will probably also come up with the variable-rate second mortgage. Which is the better loan then, the fixed-rate or the variable?

The answer depends to a great extent on the state of the economy when you are applying for the loan. If interest rates are high (and they are expected to remain so through the 1980s) while the rest of the economy is in good shape, then the variable becomes more attractive, especially since interest on these loans is generally re-computed only every six months or at the end of the year, since there is no prepayment penalty and since most have caps now. If you see interest rates are about to skyrocket you can always renego-tiate the mortgage.

Second mortgages generally carry high interest rates, but the vari-able loan is usually offered at an attractive figure, at least a couple of points below the current market rate. All things considered—and, of course, that's just what you will do—your best bet is likely to be the adjustable, not the high-cost fixed-rate loan.

13. Then there is the home equity loan, also known as the line of credit. These vary widely from one lender to another, but are based on the principle of a revolving line of credit that is sometimes se-cured by the value of your home, sometimes not. If you are a recent first-time homebuyer, of course, you probably have no substantial equity in your home and so this access to a home improvement loan is likely to be closed to you for a while (although some intrepid lenders are making home equity loans to new buyers and to renters, requiring them to pledge, instead of homes, time deposits and other investments as security).

Banks, savings and loan associations, brokerages, and finance com-panies all offer these loans, although not every one of them in every state.

Once your home is appraised, or, less formally, "inspected," and your application for the credit line checked in the way it would be for any other loan or for a mortgage, you are granted a line of credit that can be as much as 70 or 80 percent of the equity in your home (the market value, less the balance due on your mortgage and any other lien). You are then given a special checkbook and can write checks against that amount any time you choose. Need $5000 for Bobby's tuition next fall? Write a check. Waiting for the contractor to take a look at the kitchen remodeling job you'd like done? The checkbook is there when terms are agreed upon.

The beauty of the home equity loan, therefore, is that:

• You don't have to go into a lending institution every time you need a loan; you just turn to your checkbook, a year from now or ten years from now.

• It works well if you do not know exactly how much money you are going to need—that kitchen job, for example. You don't have to borrow more than you will have to pay for the job.

• The loan can last a lifetime, or at least as long as you are in your home. In fact, lenders advertise the credit line as "the only loan you'll ever need."

The initial cost is usually a one-time fee of 2 percent or so of the value of the loan, plus an annual charge that runs $35 to $50. Sometimes, however, there is no annual charge, and an upfront fee of just $200 or so. The interest rate on money borrowed is usually two points above the prevailing rate, but here again terms differ from one lender to another. One point about the credit that remains the same is that you are charged interest only on the amount you borrow, not on your balance in the account. Keep that $50,000 or whatever the amount untouched year after year and pay no interest. (Don't keep it untouched too long, however, or the bank will contact you in a year or two about your intentions.) The loan term can run for five or ten years or any length of time determined by the lender. There are other variations here too—some lenders require the homeowner to have an annual income of at least $20,000; others call for $35,000. Some require a minimum loan of $20,000 or $50,000 or whatever amount they call for. Some interest rates will vary during the term of the loan; other lenders allow minimum monthly payments, with the principal paid at the end of the loan.

Bad features to a line of credit? Yes, especially for those with fingers itchy to get to checkbooks. For some there will be the temptation to write a check for a vacation, or for new clothes. Some say there is an advantage in using the checkbook as your only source of credit—you know at a glance just how much you are spending and how much you owe—but on the other hand it is important to remember that this is a loan where frequently your home is used as collateral. Miss a few payments, and the lender can declare you in default and you risk foreclosure. That won't happen if you fall behind in your Mastercard payments. Only you know if all that ready money handed to you in a home equity loan is a little too much money for you to handle.

All of the above-mentioned suggestions are legitimate ways to finance a home improvement, but as you have seen they can vary in cost from low, single-digit interest rates on unsecured loans to high, fixed-rate interest where your home is security. Only by studiously questioning prospective lenders and reading all you can on the subject can you be assured of a loan that will not take the edge off your enjoyment of that remodeling project.

31

How to Choose (and Profit from) a Vacation Home

"Our country place." "We'll be at our beach house." "I have this little ski condo."

If owning a house is the American dream, then surely having a second, or vacation, home comes next on the aspiration list. Many a vacationer has returned from a rented bungalow or hotel room in a resort community with visions of having his or her own place there. Nothing fancy, of course, just a beach shack or a one-room condo or perhaps a time-share. The traveler carts home not only souvenir items and a few rolls of film, but also brochures touting new developments and realty agents' business cards and brochures.

The traveler is hooked.

It is not difficult to understand the allure of wanting to own property where one has spent a happy holiday or perhaps many years of vacations. Why continue paying hotel bills? Why spend a few thousand dollars for a season's cabin rental every year? Why eat all those expensive restaurant meals? And maybe a little tax shelter too.

There are any number of other reasons for wanting to buy this type of property, of course:

• There is, in many of us, the desire for a place of our own away from the hubbub of our workday life, a spot where one can escape on weekends to unwind and put the pieces back together before the next week's assault.

• There are status reasons for wanting a second home. *Everybody* has a place on the island. *Everyone* is at the lake in August. And the mini-second you can afford it, by George, *you're* going to own a home in that hot spot too.

• There are those who buy with the expectation that the second home will one day become a fulltime retirement residence.

• Some buy only for investment. They'll stay at that cute little chalet a week perhaps, but count on renting it the rest of the year, and taking advantage of available tax breaks. Everybody buys with the hope that they are making a good and sound financial investment, but this group pays more attention to that aspect of the purchase and less to the let's-all-have-a-good-time part.

The Market Overall

Just under 5 percent of the population owns a second home, and that property can be any style of residence. Beach houses, mountain cabins, and ski condos most often come to mind, but the hideaway can also be a farmhouse, log cabin, or a converted one-room schoolhouse. It can be a time-share anywhere in the world. It can be a campsite, bought and paid for, on which you plop a tent or pull in with your Winnebago. A second home can be a city pied-à-terre for those who spend most of their time in the country. In fact, it is any dwelling that you do not, for voting and tax purposes, consider your principal residence.

The second home market is subject to even more fluctuations than the primary home market. As you might expect, in a bad economy there is little sales activity here (aside from the ultra-high-priced homes, since if one has plenty of money it is possible to ignore any economic vagary). For the average second home, there's little mortgage money around in bad times, too, since banks then prefer to concentrate on customers looking for a principal residence. You may have to seek out seller financing if you are buying, which can work well if you're lucky and persistent, but can also limit the number of properties available to you. In tough times construction will be down too.

It is important to see the second home market in its own light, not just as an appendage to the primary market. The principal residence is not "senior," with the vacation home "junior." The second home arena has its own ebbs and flows, its own pricing scale, its own financing, and its own tax advantages.

Is This What You Really Want?

Since so much of purchasing a second home is, let's face it, romance and illusion, it is vital to take off the rose-colored glasses and consider this purchase with all the practicality you can muster. A wrong move here and the dream can fade with the drop of a palm leaf.

For one thing, it's important not to make the mistake of thinking that if you're spending $4000 every summer to rent a cabin on the lake, you're foolish not to buy that home and your rental money is just cash down the drain.

Not true. Just because it's a house doesn't mean you have to buy it. Perhaps you can't afford a summer (or winter) home, and that's a pretty good reason for not investing in one. Maybe you won't want to spend holidays in that spot year after year after year. Too, you might have wiser investments to make with any extra cash than plunking dollars down for a summer home. Remember that as an investment, this is a low-yielding one, ranking lower than a principal residence and lower, too, than several other realty buys such as year-round rental properties, commercial properties, and even syndicates. If you want to buy more real estate, you'd do better to look around your own area for a *medium-priced* two-family home to purchase for rental. Or check Part IV of this book for other options for real estate investments. Just don't feel you're a financial lamebrain because you're paying a hotel bill when you vacation in Bermuda and don't own property there.

Here are a few more questions to ask yourself which should help crystallize your motives for buying in this complex and frequently difficult market:

1. *Are you the second home type?* Can you see yourself packing up and spending two weeks every year at Lake Wackeewackee, and perhaps many weekends too? Or will you begin to mutter, "O Lord, I've got to go to that bloody lake again"? If you want to spend your vacation next year in Europe, will you feel guilty about leaving the lakefront home? What if you can't rent it? What if you don't want to? Perhaps your personality is such that you need the stimulation of new people and new places periodically and the thought of routine vacations makes your eyes glaze.

2. *What do you truly want from a vacation home?* We all know what we would like, but let's be coldly realistic here. Do you want to be able to leave your city office at 5 P.M. on Friday and ninety

minutes or two hours later be walking along a beach? Do you want to spend a few weeks in the winter in a milder climate? Are you scouting a retirement home? What you expect of the property will direct you to the appropriate shopping channels. For instance, if you just want to spend your two-week vacation there, buying a second home may be too much of a burden. You may be better off staying at a hotel, or trying a time share, unless the place you buy has a year-round renting potential so that it is occupied, and bringing you money, as often during the year as possible. If you're looking for a retirement home, remember to visit that spot in the off-season to see if you can handle the heat or the deserted appearance or the rains or snows or whatever else characterizes the place when the tourists have gone. The important point is to get your thoughts clear on just what you want and expect from a second home.

3. *Is the property you are considering the very opposite of your personality and lifestyle?* If you live in the city, the idea of hearing nothing but crickets at night may sound sweetly appealing, but once out in the country it may be a different story. Deep down you may be similar to that quintessential urbanist, Woody Allen, with unvoiced fears of bugs, quiet, chainsaw murderers, and other terrors that await those who step beyond city borders. Do you feel you "should" buy a ski condo, even though you loathe the cold weather and feel you look like a sofa in a parka? If you live alone or have small children, being too far into the wilderness may not in fact be safe. Vacation homes in remote areas are inviting targets for vandalism and serious thievery, and can even be taken over by squatters if the house is not visited often by its owner. If you plan on having tenants, prospects may be put off by an isolated location. If you must live in God's country, the house that is at most five miles from town is a better buy than one that is really in the boondocks, come renting or resale time.

4. *How much work do you want to do on a second home?* If you're truly on a tight budget, little bargains that need a good deal of rehabilitation are certainly around for the buying. But ask yourself how you want to spend your getting-away-from-it-all time. Sitting in the sun is the most some people can manage, while others relax by practically rebuilding a house. Which is you—the low-maintenance condo, or the elderly, and always in need of repair, gingerbread?

5. *Are you willing to cope with the bother of maintaining two households, especially if there are children and pets to consider?* Can you handle visiting relatives and friends who will be dropping in throughout the season? Remember that buying a summer

home nearby is a little like hitting the lottery. Cheery (and demanding) relatives will be on your doorstep before the news has traveled 100 yards. Will you enjoy spending your weekends cooking and changing sheets and washing towels for all these good folks?

6. *Can you afford a second home?* Finally, of course, there is the not insignificant question of where the money is to come from for this purchase. The worst scenario here is that you buy by the skin of your teeth, find you are unable to keep up mortgage and tax payments, can't find tenants to tide you over, are unable to sell because of a sluggish market, and lose the property through foreclosure. End of dream.

In sum, it is important to know the real you. This is more necessary with second home buying than in shopping for your main home because your personality and needs come more into play here than with a principal residence. There, affordability, commuting distance, schools, and other hard realities more or less force you to play with the cards you are dealt. Here the bit of gossamer that is your dream often makes up your mind.

If you've given thought to the above questions, have not lost any of your enthusiasm, and, in fact, are even more firmly committed to owning a second home, then indeed this may be an excellent purchase for you. Maybe you know now exactly where you want to buy; perhaps the crystallization process is still taking place. In either event, reading on should continue to clarify the subject.

The Buddy Plan

Don't overlook the option of buying a summer (or winter) home with relatives, friends, or co-workers. You all become tenants in common, with all your names on the deed. You may find that vacationing every second or third weekend at your holiday spot is enough for you. The sharing of ownership allows you more latitude with your own vacation plans, not to mention less of a financial investment and less risk. Single persons in particular might look favorably at joint ownership, since it may well be the only means for them of having a second home. This is one real estate purchase that usually takes a two-career family to afford.

This buying style is common in the second home market and can work very well for all parties. There's more about joint purchasing in Chapter 37.

The Price of Shangri-la

You need to have a fairly good overview of prices of vacation homes in the locale you are considering. You can learn these by reading local newspaper advertisements (subscribe to the paper if you are some distance away) and checking in periodically with area real estate agents. You may not even have to talk to those folks, at least not in the preliminary stages. Most real estate offices in resort areas will have pictures, descriptions, and prices of houses for sale posted in their front windows, so you can easily comparison shop without being disturbed.

The highest prices will no doubt be for traditional homes that are year-round residences. And these will be very high indeed in desirable areas. Condominiums and townhouses in recreational areas are also priced high, unless there is a glut of them in that area, in which case you might benefit from a price war. Somewhat cheaper would be your purchasing a lot, then having a house built on it. Building your own kit home, perhaps a relatively inexpensive A-frame, might be the least expensive way to go.

There are inexpensive—downright cheap—homes around that can be used for vacationing, if you head for the woods and small, off-the-beaten-path villages in counties that have not yet been discovered. It is possible to find a house for $5000 or so. The search for the truly inexpensive can take a year or longer, but then buying a second home often does take more time than picking a principal residence.

Keep an eye open for the offbeat property. Since this is presumably a home for good times and casual living, you can afford to be a little unconventional. Maybe there is a small church, firehouse, train depot, or barn you could convert to housing, perhaps with a small outlay of cash. Don't overlook any structure with a roof and four walls during your househunting. You might also read some of the books that have been published in the last several years on alternative uses for existing buildings to see how many of these properties have been imaginatively converted to residences. Yes, it took buckets of money in some cases, but the concept is there for you to take and adapt to your own budget.

Cost means more than the purchase price of a home, of course. If your Shangri-la is a plane ride away, how many trips can you afford each year, taking your spouse and the kids along? If it's a long drive, what about fuel costs? Overnight motel stays along the way and meals out mean more money. Many savvy second home buyers look no farther than ninety minutes from their principal residence, both

---

If You Are Buying a Lot or "Home Site" in a New Development

There are many caveats to buying vacation land, but one bottom-line test should show you the wisdom of taking an acre in FunForAll Acres. If you're considering buying there, stop in at a real estate office in that area and tell the agent you own a lot in FunForAll Acres you'd like to sell. Does he:

Say no, he doesn't want to be bothered, and quickly show you the door?

Laugh and tell you he has ten lots in that development he's trying to sell?

Say he will handle the sale—and tell you he's sure he can get you $3000 for the acreage that cost you $7500?

Seem genuinely happy to handle the sale—and to put a decent price tag on the land?

The correct answer should be obvious and will tell you in a few brief minutes just how your land ranks at the moment. And any land is only as valuable as its resale potential, unless it just plain makes you happy to own a chunk of the good earth, no matter how much or how little it is worth.

---

for shorter and less costly travel time, the ability to spend more time there, and the ease in keeping watch on the property from their principal home. So if you live in New York and don't have all that much money to spend, the home in the Poconos is a wiser buy, all things being equal, than the one in Florida.

Where the Best Spots Are

They are everywhere. You don't have to buy in the latest "in" community 1600 miles from your home to have made a wise investment. As you have seen from the foregoing, good vacation homes can be found virtually a stone's throw from where you live now. After all, every place is far away to *somebody*.

There are a few basic points to bear in mind when deciding where to buy, however:

1. If you expect to hold onto the house for many years, avoid buying in the latest fad areas, unless you're very sure the fad will become a longer-lasting fashion. This requires keeping an eye on what's in and what's out and what's coming up, but then homework is an important ingredient in any wise real estate purchase. One example of an area that has lost favor slightly over the last few years has been Vail, Colorado. Overbuilding and a little less interest in skiing overall—or perhaps just the growth of smaller, neighborhood skiing spots taking some of the business from the older glamour resorts—has left prices of homes questionable and more than a few unsold properties. All of that may change, of course, but you can see how whimsical the buyer's interest in "the latest" can be.

2. Watch out for overbuilt areas, where your investment may decline over the years. Ocean City, Maryland, and parts of Florida are two examples of a mad rush to build that left far too many condos standing empty. If you buy in such an area, can you sell when you want and at the price you want? Or will buyers be more interested in rushing to the latest condo and not your older model?

3. Check local environmental rulings. Regulations to preserve the environment are keeping more houses and condos from being built in settings that could be considered recreation land or land that should belong to the public. So while overbuilding can occur in some areas, in others there will be no new construction at all. This will, of course, affect prices in such areas for years to come. If you want to buy along the California coast, for example, in an area where chock-a-block oceanfront building is forbidden, naturally you can expect to pay more for such a house or condo when you buy and have a greater treasure when you decide to sell. There is, after all, no more ocean being built. Or Gulf or mountains either.

4. If you are planning to rent out whatever you buy, your strategy must be even more carefully planned than the house bought just for fun (and, of course, prudent investment). Say you like the beach. Which is the wiser investment—buying along the Delaware shore, where the high season runs from the fourth of July to Labor Day and rarely can you rent a vacation home during the other nine months, or buying a shore home close to Atlantic City, where you still have the ocean but the season never ends, thanks to the gambling casinos. A difference of not that many miles geographically, but quite an income range financially. Should you buy in the ski community which virtually closes up when the crocus pops up, or in one that can be touted to prospective renters as having amusements for the

---

Before Buying That Vacation Home . . .

Be sure in your own mind that this is the real estate investment for you. If it isn't one that will bring the most appreciation for your dollars, at least be sure it is one you will enjoy and not tire of.

Study prices and types of properties available in the area in which you are interested. Read local newspapers (subscribe if you live many miles away) and visit real estate offices there.

If you will want a rental income, look for a house or condo, if you can, that affords the potential for year-round rental. Try not to limit yourself to just a high-season rental potential of eight or ten weeks if you expect to make money as a landlord.

Ask your local IRS office for booklets pertaining to vacation houses so that you know before you buy just what tax breaks you are entitled to. There may not be as many as you think.

---

summer as well? There's more about buying with the intention of renting coming up shortly, but in the main the best investment will be a property with a four- or at least two- season rental possibility, not one with an off-season that kills tenant potential for most of the year.

When to Shop

It's best to look for a vacation home during that area's off season. Everyone wants a beach house when the sun is shining and the ocean breezes cool the warmest day. But you will look far better to a seller in February, if the house has been on the market for a while, or if the seller's circumstances are such that he or she must sell during the winter. March to November are real estate brokers' busiest times for these types of homes. So if you can, shop in the other months.

Visit the property during the off-season, if possible, to get a better idea of what life is like there when the crowd is gone. Is there enough activity to bring you tenants if you want to rent during the off months? Is there a college or university that could be a source of tenants during the school year or, if you are in a winter vacation spot, taking summer courses and staying in town? Just how closed down is this town in the off season? Every little shop that shuts its doors when the season is over is one more small barrier to your realizing the highest rental income you can from your property.

Financing

A second home is paid for a little differently from a primary residence. You can expect financing for a second home to be a little tougher than it was when you bought your principal residence, and lenders themselves to be a little less flexible. Downpayment requirements may be higher and mortgage interest rates a percentage point or so higher as well. If thirty-year fixed-rate loans are available for primary homes, twenty-five years (or less) may be tops for vacation homes. You may be required to pay points up front for the loan. Naturally, to make the sale sweeter, you can try to obtain financing from the seller at lower-than-market interest rates. You should also know that many developers of new resort communities offer financing to buyers that includes downpayments as low as 10 percent and interest rates lower than the current market figure.

It's always smart, too, to shop for financing in the community in or near where the home is located, rather than at a lending institution back home. The lender there is more familiar with the area, can appreciate the value of the home you are considering, and will be more likely to take into account your expected rental income from the unit.

The downpayment for a vacation home frequently comes from refinancing the principal home or from a home equity loan. With the former your mortgage is rewritten with a new, current interest rate, which can be good if rates have dropped since you first bought, or totally disastrous if you are trading in your 9 percent loan for one now priced at 14 percent. If that's the case when you are thinking of buying, consider the home equity loan instead. There you tap the equity in your home for a downpayment, taking out what is essentially a second mortgage. The smaller amount you withdraw is financed at the higher rate and you keep your existing mortgage—and its low interest rate.

You might be interested to know, too, that tax law provisions now make it easier to borrow from your company pension benefits when buying a second home.

Renting Your Vacation Home

"Well, we won't have to worry about affording a second home because we plan to rent it and the rent will pay our mortgage and tax bills." Maybe. The National Association of Home Builders estimates that something like 40 percent of the people who have second homes try to rent them at one time or another with varying degrees of success. If you are going to count heavily on seasonal rental, you may be in for a disappointment, depending on where your home is located.

If you are buying a new home, the same may be true. Part of a developer's sales pitch to you may be that he will find tenants for you—for all of you, via a rental pool. But how does he know he can? In some glutted areas, how can you be sure that your lone condo in a sea of thousands will be booked solid for whatever time you want it rented and at your desired price? If you leave the renting to other hands, they may skim a fairly high percentage off the rent for their fee, if they are successful in finding tenants.

Say the mortgage and real estate taxes at your new home come to $6000 a year and you can rent the house at $6000 a season. Will you be able to afford the other costs that go along with ownership, such as utilities, insurance, and repair charges? Homes at the beach, for instance, take a beating during the winter months, and your expenses for exterior maintenance may be higher than for a year-round home inland. If you are many hours from that second home, it is important to have someone who lives there permanently check your property at least once a week when it is not in use to see that blizzards or hurricanes have not caused damage, that the pipes have not frozen, that a tree has not fallen, or any one of a few dozen other calamities has not befallen it. There may be costly telephone calls to workers a hundred miles or more away.

Consider this too: It is difficult to be an absentee landlord when your primary home is many miles or a few states away from that vacation retreat. Who will notice if someone walks away with a couple of wicker porch chairs? Who will clean up between tenants?

A house inspection by a professional engineer or inspection service is important before buying any property, but with a vacation house it is vital. Some vacation homes conceal antiquated wiring, plumbing, and heating systems (if there is any heat at all).

All of this is not meant to discourage you from anticipating rentals, just to bring home to you the reality of such a situation. Renting is an excellent idea for just about any vacation home, since by its very nature you are not going to be there anywhere near even half the year. Just be sure you've done some arithmetic before blithely assuming that tenants will pay all the expenses of your house.

How to Start

First, realize that no one is as eager to rent your place as you are. No real estate agent, no tenant, no developer, no management company. If you're serious about bringing in the bucks through rentals, you're going to have to take control of that aspect yourself. You can engage a real estate agent in that locale, who will charge 10 or 15 percent, a figure that is naturally quite a bit higher than the average 6 percent charged for home sales. You can trust the agent to find a tenant for you, and screen that individual for references, but you should do some advertising of your house or condo yourself as well. Put up notices on your office bulletin board and on any other bulletin board in your community. Advertise in your local newspaper. Try to make the rental sweeter by tossing in beach badges or ski lift passes. If you are using a realty agent, that person will know how to set rents. If you're not, you can get a fair idea of going rates by reading local papers, talking to your neighbors in that community and, again, looking at agents' office windows where properties are advertised for sale or rent.

Here's a checklist of what to consider when you are bringing in tenants:

1. The place should be decently furnished if you plan to rent it year-round. With a one-season house, make-do furnishings are all right, but if you expect, say, a nine-month rental in the off-season and then a high season, three-month rental, keeping the place almost always occupied, then you'd better try to make it as attractive as possible. A decent heating system. Nice landscaping. Furniture that is more than youthful orange crate. It will be assumed that it will be rented fully furnished, too, which includes linen (but not towels), and a range of *basic* kitchen appliances (a toaster, but not necessarily a blender). Dishes and flatware will be expected too.

2. Check your homeowner's insurance policy to see if it makes any reference to renting. If it does not, you may want to have a clause written in that will cover you during the rental period (the tenant should have his or her own liability coverage and coverage for his or her own belongings).

3. You will have to arrange for a local service to cut the grass or

shovel snow, clean the windows, etc. Or you can ask the tenants to undertake those chores in exchange for lower rent charges.

4. Tenants should be given the names and phone numbers of plumbers, electricians, and other repair people they can call when something in the house goes on the fritz. Perhaps you would rather they check with you first by phone before calling in those workers, but for emergency purposes they should still be in possession of such a list.

5. It's wise to have an inventory of the contents of the house before the tenants arrive. If you don't want to be bothered with this admittedly tedious chore, you might take color pictures instead. Shoot all sides of the exterior and grounds, and take pictures of every room from all angles. This, unlike a written inventory, takes little time and could prove invaluable if there is damage to your possessions and you wind up in Small Claims Court or consulting a lawyer.

6. How you will handle the phone bill, whether you will be dropping by occasionally to use the season ticket to the local summer theater, and other miscellany should be worked out by you and the tenants before they move in.

How the IRS Views Your Vacation Home

Coldly and with none of the romance you bring to the purchase. Tax deductions for second home owners are constantly being revised, usually in the government's favor with the tiniest loophole closed against the taxpayer. Even as this book goes to press, changes are afoot. It's best to contact your regional office of the IRS for a copy of booklet #527, which offers a detailed explanation of rulings and allowable deductions, including information about depreciation, deductions for repairs, and renting the property to relatives or strangers.

Time-Sharing

Probably the most important development on the American housing landscape in the last twenty-five years has been the condominium. It is an extremely satisfactory housing style that has, among its other good features, brought homeownership to millions of Americans who might not otherwise have been able to afford a home. The condominium is stable and, when purchased wisely, an excellent investment.

There are time-share resorts for warm-weather buffs and those who prefer to spend vacations bundled up. *Reprinted with permission of Mariner's Boathouse & Beach Resort, Fort Myers, Florida. Reprinted with permission of Samoset Resort, Rockport, Maine.*

The time-share is an offshoot of that concept. It became popular in the mid 1970s, during a housing slump that saw many developers in resort areas take their unsold condos and convert them into a European style of ownership where expensive properties are sold to several buyers who share the facilities. This is enormously profitable to developers, but as a buyer you would do well to hold back your enthusiasm. Where buying a year-round or vacation home condo

---

The Best Time-share

A completed development, not a hole in the ground or a color brochure.

A week (or two or three) purchased in that area's "high season."

In an internationally well-known resort community, to allow you a better opportunity for trading.

Is financed through a local lending institution at market interest rates rather than through the developer, which is usually more costly.

---

can be an excellent purchase, the time-share may not be. It is still fairly new to the vacation home market scene, and while there are many successful complexes, there are dozens of others run by scalawags who will take your money and leave you all with a huge mud hole next to an empty construction trailer. It is important not to think automatically that condo = good buy. Not necessarily true when it comes to this style of condo.

While it is most often an apartment, a time-share can also be a country inn, an ocean liner, a campsite, a hotel room, or even a house in a resort community. It works like this: You and a number of other people buy shares in the same condo unit. Those shares entitle each of you to use that condo for a specified time of the year for as long as you own the unit. Perhaps you decide you want the first two weeks in August. Allowing two weeks usually held open during the year for cleaning and repairs to the unit, there will then be a potential forty-eight other owners of that unit.

Time-sharing, as you can see already, is a complicated ownership picture. Some plans involve shared ownership where each buyer gets title to an undivided interest in a particular unit, plus the right to use it for the specified annual period. This is the "deeded" or "ownership" time-share. Other plans (the "non-deed" or "non-ownership") involve vacation leases—that is, prepaid leases on particular units for the specified annual time. There is no ownership involved here, simply an advance reservation for the same unit for many years down the road. Needless to say it's important to be sure you know which style of time-sharing you are buying. Do you want to own, or would simply having a guaranteed reservation at that spot suit you just as well? Which is better? At this point there is no clear winner, since ownership usually does not bring significant tax breaks during ownership or any noticeable windfall when the buyer sells.

The points to beware of here are many, since the system is still relatively new and experiencing shakedown problems which may or may not work themselves out as it matures. For one thing, who is to say that the place you buy will even be standing in thirty years, not to mention habitable? Time-sharing units will get greater wear and tear than conventional condo apartments, and the physical depreciation may be enormous over the years. What happens if the "vacation club" that sold you your lease goes bankrupt? What happens if the building is eventually condemned? What happens when you want to sell your share and the area is overbuilt or your own building or complex is on rocky financial footing? What happens if you just plain get bored with the place?

Also, bear in mind you will have little to say here about how the community is run, since your overall ownership is minuscule—a small, fractional percentage in one unit, with perhaps a thousand other co-owners in the entire development. Since your investment is so small, it is hardly worthwhile to take yourself off to Baja or St. Thomas or wherever to cast your vote in the annual condominium association election (especially since, if it isn't your week to be there, you will have to stay at a hotel—or in someone else's time-share unit!).

Costs

The price range is fairly wide, based on the attractiveness and desirability of the resort, on the size of the unit you are buying, and on whether you are buying "in season" or "off season." You might be able to purchase a studio apartment in a nice, but not internationally well-known, resort in this country for $2000. A flossy, two-bedroom oceanfront condo in Hawaii or the Caribbean would run closer to $25,000. Generally, though, $5000 to $10,000 is the most common price tag. Maintenance charges, which cover repairs, linen service, administrative services (including a business office), and the like, can range from $100 to $200 a week for each week's stay. You will also probably have to make an initial outlay of $200 or so for your share of the furnishings for the unit.

It sounds pretty good, doesn't it, owning a week in a very desirable resort community for many years at, let's say, just $10,000 plus a $150 a year maintenance fee? But let's look a little closer at that figure. If you invested that $10,000 instead of buying your one-week time-share apartment, you might net 9 percent on your money after taxes. That's $900 of spendable income from your $10,000 investment. Your time-share unit therefore costs you the $150 maintenance fee plus the $900 lost in investment income, a total of $1050 each year. Surely you could rent an apartment—or even stay at a very nice hotel—for $1050 a week in that locale. So when you do some number crunching you see that you aren't *really* getting a top-flight vacation for just $150 a week, are you?

Financing

If you are leasing a unit, naturally there is no ownership involved and you will pay with cash or through a personal loan. If you've bought your unit and will receive a deed in the transaction, in theory you will be entitled to a mortgage, but lenders are still wary of offering loans for time-share units, since the resale potential is still so hazy and the concept itself so new. They are coming around slowly, especially for top-of-the-line complexes, but for now your financing will probably be obtained through the developer/sponsor and, generally speaking, it will be more costly than what you paid for your principal residence. Higher even than a second home that is not a time-share. You will likely find, for example, a sliding scale of interest rates based on the amount of your downpayment. So if the going conventional mortgage rate is 13 percent, and you are putting 10 percent down on your $10,000 time-share, the interest you will be charged for financing the remaining $9000 might be 18 percent. If your deposit is $3000, the rate may drop to around 15 percent, and so on.

Resale

It's bad business to buy a time-share unit with the thought of cleaning up come resale time. True, some units do earn money for their buyers, but those are luxury time-shares in all-season, internationally famous resort communities. On the whole, it is still too early to chart an overall resale pattern for the average time-share. But when you do want to sell, expect to have difficulty finding a buyer at the price you want, and know that appreciation will probably be slight, if there is any at all, especially when brokers' fees and other administrative charges are deducted. You can't make a killing here. If you buy, tell yourself it's a means to a vacation you know will be waiting for you every year. That's your investment, not growing equity.

Special Points to Look Out For

Watch out for the reputation of the developer and management company. Check them out with the local Better Business Bureau and that state's Attorney General's office to see if there are any bad reports on them.

Look out for the community that is not yet built. Can you be sure the pool, tennis courts, and other amenities will ever be a reality? In one time-share resort, an advertised "nine-hole golf course" turned out to be three holes. It was laid out in such a way that the golfer approached the same three holes three times.

Watch out for the "mailgram" and similar letters informing you that you have won trips, toasters, gold bars, and the like just for showing up at a resort community. The prizes most often are not what they seem—cheap junk or "trips" to a so-so nearby time-share development where you will be subjected to a 20-decibel sales pitch throughout your stay, and you will have to pay your own travel expenses besides. You are entitled to the prizes if you go. Just be sure you know about, and can arm yourself against, the day-long sales spiel you will have to endure.

Be sure if you sign any contract that you are allowed to cancel during the so-called three-day cooling off period. Some states do not offer this protection. If yours is one, don't put a pen to anything unless that contingency is written into the document.

You should have a "nondisturbance" and "non-performance" clause in writing which, in the main, will guarantee your right to use the property should the developer default on his bills or be faced with other financial problems.

Swapping

You must sign up for a specified time when you buy your time-share, but that doesn't lock you into that slot in perpetuity. You can exchange slots with your co-owners or even with persons in other complexes and other countries. One of the lures—and salesperson's pitches—of time-share is that you can swap your week for someone else's anywhere in the world.

You may have no problem if you buy in a four-star community that is recognized as a prime resort draw anywhere in the world.

And if the week you own is in high season. But while a time-share in a Tennessee complex near the Great Smoky Mountains may sound perfect to you—and while it may indeed be an excellent, well-run community—the whole world is not aware of the existence of the Great Smoky Mountains. More flexible weeks and ones that would open more doors for you in worldwide trades would be Miami, Orlando, Honolulu, or Palm Springs, to take a few examples. In high season. There are several companies worldwide that handle arranging trades for time sharers. The largest, such as Resorts Condominium International (RCI), based in Indianapolis, and Miami-based Interval, are in contact with hundreds of resorts around the world. Before you buy a time-share that you believe will be your ticket to inexpensive worldwide travel, you ought to have a good idea of your chances of success in trading.

Tax Advantages

If you buy a time-share lease, you will not, of course, be entitled to the tax breaks that go along with home ownership. If you buy your unit outright, you *may* get a few pennies off your income tax bill, but it *will* be pennies since your ownership portion is so small. The IRS is just beginning to explore all the ramifications of time-sharing, and is constantly revising its laws regarding the system. Consult your tax advisor for up-to-the-minute word on any tax benefits or cautions if you become a landlord.

Does all of this sound terribly negative? In a way it is meant to, to point out all the serious issues that should be taken into account by anyone who is swept away by the dream of a week in Paradise *forever* for $10,000. Time-share is still a gamble right now, at least in most complexes. It is even less well regulated than conventional condominium sales, and it took nearly a decade for legislators to concern themselves with abuses in that form of ownership. With time-sharing you are gambling on the developer's skill in building the complex (or in effecting a satisfactory conversion); selling it and managing it properly; holding down expenses and maintenance charges and, in fact, staying in business for the next fifty years or so. That may be too much of a gamble—or you might figure that your investment is low enough to make the roll of the dice worth the chance.

On the more positive side—and there is a sunny side to all of this—it should be repeated that there are some excellent time-share complexes and, as its popularity continues to grow, more good ones will appear on the scene. If you like knowing your vacation spot will be ready for you every year with no hassle about reservations, then time-sharing may look extremely good to you. If you hate restaurant meals and want to make your first and last cup of coffee of the day in your own kitchen, a time-share apartment offers that choice. If you have parents—or children—who live in the vicinity of the time-share complex you may find staying in that community an easier and more pleasant alternative than bunking in with the family. A time-share can be an excellent buy—and even an investment—in highly desirable resort areas where future construction has been curbed because of environmental rulings or because there is just no more available land. Time-shares *can* work. You don't have to be burned. All that is called for here is caution and plenty of homework, analyzing your own motives for buying and studying the resort market virtually all over the country and even throughout the world. A tall order? Perhaps, but then it's your hard-earned money that's at stake.

You might find that a more satisfactory alternative to time-sharing is simply purchasing a standard condo unit outright with a few friends or relatives, splitting ownership, and deciding among yourselves when each group stay in the unit and whether you will rent it when no one is there. This is cleaner and potentially more profitable than the time-share. Such a system of buying has already been catching on in Hawaii in particular, where it is formally known as *hui*. Naturally, joint ownership is nothing new, but some clever buyers, looking at the popularity of time-sharing, are adapting it to even smarter uses.

For More Information

"Resort Time Sharing: A Consumer's Guide," available for 50 cents and a stamped, self-addressed envelope from the American Land Development Association, 1000 16th St. N.W., Washington, D.C. 20036.

Buyer's Guide to Resort Timesharing Price: $7.00; available from the CHB Co. (publishers of a newsletter for the industry), P.O. Box 184, Los Altos, Calif. 94022.

"Ten Timeshare Tips," a free brochure from the Federal Trade Commission, 6th and Pennsylvania Ave. N.W., Washington, D.C. 20580.

A consumer's guide is offered by the National TimeSharing Council, 604 Solar Bldg., 100 16th St. N.W., Washington, D.C. 20036. Send $1 plus a stamped, self-addressed business envelope.

32

Good Grief, You're Moving

You can be delighted and excited at the thought, or you can be digging in your heels, cranky and pessimistic. No matter what your attitude, moving is always a little upsetting, sometimes downright traumatic. There seems to be so much to plan, so much to do—and so much money to spend. Will we sell this house? How will we get along in the new home? Will the neighbors be congenial? How about work? Will we miss and worry about the relatives we're leaving behind? It's no wonder that on life-stress tests moving is right up there with divorce, losing a job, and other heart-thumpers. Twenty percent of us move every year. That's a lot of potentially nerve-wracked Americans.

It is not for us to say whether you should or shouldn't move, and so we won't. But there are two quite different reasons for relocating, broadly speaking, and one of them requires a little more thought than the other.

In the first, you are moving because you want or need a larger or finer house or you want to move closer to your work or are being transferred, or you have some other concrete reason why this move is imperative or desirable. You know where you are going and why.

The second move is a more amorphous one. Life is not good where you are now, and so you will move to where the jobs are (you believe) plentiful, or where the climate is sunnier, or where living is cheaper. This is the tough one. Moving if you are trying to make yourself happier—and not just in your housing situation—requires a little analyzing.

Heading for "The Good Life"

These relocations require tons of planning, at least a year of it to adequately prepare yourself. And planning is more than sitting in your kitchen over a 3 A.M. cup of coffee convincing yourself that life will be better in Tucson or Denver or Montpelier.

There are good reasons for wanting to pick up stakes for another part of the country, one that is not familiar to you and where you know no one, or virtually no one. Perhaps jobs in your field, after you have done some investigating, are better where you want to head. Perhaps your health would improve in a different climate. Perhaps you never liked it where you are now, but for one reason or another you've been stuck there for a while. Even just plain wanting to start over someplace new for personal change or growth can be a legitimate reason for leaving Passaic for Portland, again if the project is well thought out and you are not merely trying to escape problems and inadequacies that will follow you anywhere.

Who should not move? The newly widowed should not consider a change of residence for at least a year after the death of a spouse. They may not believe it, but their decision-making process is a little off kilter during that trying time and major life changes should be put off for a while. Those who are divorced and have custody of their child(ren) should first consult an attorney before considering a move too far away. It might interfere with the other parent's visitation rights.

Some find, too, that a move would be unwise where the children would be adversely affected, or where an aging and ill parent where they are now living requires attention. Moving under those circumstances, when you don't have to, probably would only add to one's troubles.

It's wise to sit back and give all of this some thought. Here's how the homework should go:

Your finances

Can you afford to move? It's a pretty expensive proposition. How much money do you have to fall back on if it takes you a while to find a house/apartment and a job? Is there anyone, a family member for instance, who could help in a financial emergency, or will you be strictly on your own?

Work

Under ideal conditions you would have a job waiting for you in Santa Fe before you left Omaha, or at least some leads and names and addresses of companies and individuals you can contact. You should, of course, know how jobs in your career field are going in the locale that interests you.

Housing

This is a very important consideration. Will you be able to sell your home where you are now? Is housing priced higher where you are heading? Where will you stay if you can't find a place to live immediately?

Finally, in considering any move, you might keep these five caveats in mind:

1. *Beware of* moving lock, stock, and barrel to that "better place" before you have spent some time visiting there. And visiting doesn't mean just one weekend. Vacation there if you can. Spend time talking to residents, merchants, real estate agents. Read the local papers. And, if where you're heading is a seasonal resort, vacation there in the off-season. Vail may be just as lovely in the summer as it is during schuss season, but how about southern Florida in August? Can you take the heat?

If you can't afford a hotel-style holiday, perhaps you could swap your home with an owner in that locale. There's more about this increasingly popular vacation style on page 532.

2. *Beware of* thinking of the sun belt as Valhalla. It is true that jobs and other economic improvements have grown over the last decade in the area that stretches south roughly from Los Angeles to Virginia. But bear in mind that during the economic recession of the early 1980s, Dallas, Houston, New Orleans, and other popular sun belt cities were urging newcomers to stay away. There was no work there, officials cautioned, and newcomers were warned that it was difficult to apply for public assistance too.

Overall, the new news about the glorious sun belt is that many of its communities are experiencing problems that threaten to make them just like the rest of the country: overcrowding, insufficient water supply and other public services and facilities, and unemployment. It pays to consider each town or city separately and thoroughly investigate the one that interests you without automatically thinking it terrific just because it lies below the Mason-Dixon line.

3. *Beware of* believing that life will be perfect once you move to that ideal locale. If you hate winter, you may be thrilled to find it warmer in January where you have moved. If it's too quiet in Smalltown, your new home may be sufficiently bustling and busy. The

---

Before You Move . . .

Mail change of address cards.

Contact local utilities (do you have a rebate coming? a deposit return?).

Discontinue newspaper service.

Arrange for medical and dental records to be sent to those professionals in your new community; if you haven't selected them yet, at least notify your doctor(s) and dentist that you are moving and will be sending for those files.

If you are moving from one fairly large city to another your credit report will probably follow you; in smaller communities you can't be sure. Before you move, write to the credit bureau that services your new community. You can get its name from Associated Credit Bureaus, P.O. Box 218300, Houston, Texas 77218. Ask them to get your file from your old bureau, and include in your letter your current address, date of birth, social security number, and signature. You may have to pay a small fee but should have no problem in arranging that transfer. You can also ask the credit bureau where you are now to give you a summary of your credit history which you can take with you. In that way you can see the information on file. The charge for that will be around $10.

---

move may indeed be better for you in many ways, but it won't approach perfection. You may be just two blocks from the ocean—but you may not be able to find work in your field in that community. The jobs may be plentiful and well paying—but that city is dirty and crime ridden and a few other unwelcome things you hadn't counted on. The suburban setting is as serene as you had hoped—but the commuting is terrible and you can't afford a car. It's important to know there will always be something (or a few things) wrong. That's life.

4. *Beware of* burning your bridges. It may be wiser to rent your home instead of selling it until you're sure the move is working out. The same with subletting your apartment where you are now, instead of letting it go. A leave of absence from your job, if that can be

worked out, is another gentle way of easing yourself out of your old community. Don't badmouth the town you're leaving, either, to friends or relatives who will be left behind, or break up good friendships. Good old Podunk may look mighty sweet to you after several weeks in an Eden where you can't find work and are still living at the YMCA. If you part on good terms with everyone, coming back will not seem so impossible. Which leads to

5. *Beware of* being afraid to go back home. There is nothing wrong with trying a new place, giving it time to work and then deciding "no thanks, not for me." After all, to put it in a lighter vein, if God had wanted us to stay in one place He would not have allowed the creation of moving vans!

The Three Steps to a Successful Move

No matter what your reason for picking up stakes, there is a procedure that, like a wedding, depends on organization for success. Moving can be a mammoth production, and some of us badly need a cruise director type to take us in hand. It's fairly easy to organize yourself, however, since the process can be broken down into *three major steps:*

No. 1: Look into the New Community

Whether you have occasionally visited your new home or whether you know virtually nothing about it, you'll feel a lot less strange about the move if you learn as much as you can about New Town before you pull up behind the moving van. You don't have to leave your armchair to do it.

The newspaper. Try subscribing to the Sunday edition of the newspaper in that community. This is less expensive—and easier to plow through—than taking both weekday and Sunday papers. Reading the paper is one of the best homework steps you can take. It will tell you what houses are selling for and what apartments are renting for. It will, through bank advertisements, give you an idea of mortgage interest rates. It will offer the names of realty agents you can contact now or when you arrive.

You will read about jobs that are available and the salaries. You'll see what nationwide store chains are operating in that community, and in the social pages you will become familiar with the names of schools and social and religious groups you may later want to join.

Perhaps more important, though, you will find in the news pages of that paper a sense of how the community is functioning, and if it is a place on the way up or sliding down. What about crime, for example? Zoning battles? A toxic dump nearby, or one planned? A nuclear power plant? A series of depressing job layoffs in industries vital to the town? An infusion of federal aid coming to perk up the place? Good reading scores in the local grade schools?

Perhaps you have no choice, but must move to that town no matter what you read. On the other hand, a few weeks of reading about life in Upper Succotash may change your desire to move there if you don't have to. A worthwhile investment of $10 or so for a subscription.

(You can find the name, address and, circulation figures of any newspaper in the country by consulting the *Ayer Directory of Publications* in the reference department at most public libraries.)

The Chamber of Commerce. Write the Chamber of Commerce in that town too. They can send you reams of printed material that will round out your picture of the community. Ask for the "newcomer's package." You can also query them about any other matter of special interest to you, such as jobs in your field of interest, schools for the handicapped, golf courses nearby, and the like. These folks are naturally going to be great boosters of the town, so keep their enthusiasm in mind when you are evaluating the package.

The State Department of Tourism. While you have the paper and pen out, drop a line to the Department of Tourism in the state that interests you, at the state capital. You can do this even if you are just moving to another corner of the state you're living in now. Ask for material on your favorite sport or outdoor activity—boating, camping, cycling, etc. Historic sites and parks too. It will be nice to know what's waiting out there for you that's fun.

No. 2: Take Inventory

From the cellar to the attic to the toolshed to the hall closet that hasn't been fully explored since 1976, take stock of all your belongings. Quite a lot, isn't there? Decide what will go with you and what will stay behind, either given away or sold. There is likely to be an initial reflex action here to say determinedly to yourself or someone else in the house "This is a chance finally to get rid of all this stuff."

Stuff can be pitched in any number of ways these days, some of them rather ingenious. It will take a fair amount of organization on your part, however, to determine just what goes where. That holds if you're weeding out a studio apartment or a 10-room, center-hall Colonial. You can make lists if that will help, or you can set aside

---

Settling In

Arrange for automobile license and registration in your new community.

Check to see if there is a professional organization in your career field where you are now, or a branch of your alumni association. You can also look into religious, social, charitable, or sports groups that interest you. There might be a Newcomer's Club, too. Join something. It's the only solution to feeling lonely in a new town.

Call Welcome Wagon. You'll get a basket of free goodies from merchants around town and a talk from the Welcome Wagon hostess about stores and services. She can also answer your questions about trash pickup, night school, political groups, and anything else of interest to you. This is absolutely free.

Some moving companies offer "settle-in" services to make the newcomer feel more at home. Sometimes this is as simple as a flyer with the names and phone numbers of doctors, hospitals, child care services, and the like, but whatever it is it is likely to be of some help.

---

certain parts of the house or apartment to hold items designated for sale or charity. Here are some of your choices:

Charities. You can give unwanted items to Goodwill Industries, the Salvation Army, or other local charities. It's important to allow yourself plenty of time to contact those organizations—don't wait until moving week. They may not want what you have to offer, and in the midst of the activity and tension of moving you will be forced to figure out what to do now with the boys' bunk beds or those three unwanted bureaus.

Classified ads. You can sell what you no longer want through classified ads in your local paper, or with notices tacked up at supermarkets, social centers, the library, and so forth.

Garage sales, etc. You can hold a garage/sidewalk/gate/lobby sale. These have, of course, become enormously popular over the last few years, proving again that one person's trash is another person's treasure. The success of any sale depends in large measure on where you live, when you hold the sale, and how well it is publicized. If you can band together with others on your block, or in your building, the sale becomes that much more attractive to would-be buyers. Naturally you should choose a season when the weather is best and hold the sale on a weekend. Interestingly, it has been found that some holidays attract garage sale buyers (Memorial Day, Independence Day, Labor Day), while others do not (Mother's Day, Father's Day). Many moving companies publish booklets on conducting garage sales that offer help with arranging stock, pricing, publicizing the event, security precautions, etc. Here are some of them:

"79 Ways to Make Money at a Moving Sale." Available from Wheaton Van Lines, Inc., Dept. 51, Box 50800, Indianapolis, Ind. 46250. Cost is $1, which also brings you the booklet "72 Ways to Save Money Moving." Both are free, however, if you contact your local Wheaton agent.

"Pre-Planning a Garage Sale" is available free from United Van Lines, One United Drive, Fenton, Mo. 63026; or call (800) 325-3870.

"Garage Sale Guidelines" is offered by Allied Van Lines, P.O. Box 4403, Chicago, Ill. 60680.

Tag sale. You can hire an individual or company to run a tag sale for you. This takes the work out of your hands entirely and can be useful if you do not have the time to become involved, if you are not sure of the value of your things, or if you feel so attached to them you break down at the thought of them being carted down the driveway (tag sale operators prefer owners to be away from the house on the day of the sale to avoid just that emotion). Not every community or region has an individual who conducts tag sales and her (it's usually a woman) fame is usually spread by word of mouth. A tag sale operator will inventory your furnishings, price them (calling in an appraiser if necessary), arrange them all in the most attractive setting, publicize the sale, and run the operation on sale day, bringing in assistants. Her fee can range from a flat daily fee to a percentage—usually 25 percent—of the sale's income.

Auctioning. You can call in an auctioneer. Here, too, the work is taken off your hands, and the auctioneer can be particularly helpful if you have objects that need appraising or expensive collections. The fee can be a flat rate or a percentage of the day's sales. You might want an auctioneer if you have valuable art, china, or collectibles and just want his or her services for that collection.

Storing. Then there is self-storage. This is a fairly new concept in warehousing your belongings that has become enormously popular and profitable because of its variation from the straight warehouse concept. It works like this: You lease space on a month-to-month basis in buildings—usually converted warehouses in the city, new one-story facilities in the suburbs—broken into several dozen or a few hundred storage cubicles. You can rent a small space, say 6 × 6 feet, for approximately $25 a month. Large units—24 × 26 feet, for example—would rent for around $400. In some buildings you'll have twenty-four-hour access to your belongings; other facilities have set hours. Just about everything but flammable and perishable items can be found in a storage cubicle waiting to be called into use again. So if you're moving from a large to a small space, and can't bear to part with as much as you should, consider self-storage. Besides ordinary furnishings you can stash out-of-season clothing and sports equipment, as well as holiday decorations, luggage, and porch and patio furniture. The units are heated, so you can even practice your tuba or do homework there!

One of the more popular aspects of self-storage is that in the new one-story buildings you can drive right up to the door of your unit any time of the day or night, so that you never feel your stuff is inaccessible the way it sometimes seems with a full-fledged warehouse.

For more information about self-storage (which, incidentally, used to be known as "mini-warehouses"), you can check your Yellow Pages under "Warehouses" or "Self Storage."

Finally, of course, you can store what you won't need now in a warehouse. Those great big barns that you see in cities or along major highways are still very much in business despite the popularity of the newer self-storage units. Indeed, if you are going abroad or otherwise need to store practically a whole house of furnishings, warehousing is the ticket.

Okay. Once you know where everything's going, you can move on to the next phase with a clear idea of what is to be moved.

No. 3: Select a Mover

Choices, choices. If you are 23 years old and are moving the contents of your studio apartment across town, you may prefer to hire a truck or van for a few hours and do it yourself with a couple of brawny friends. If the truck costs $15 to $30 an hour, and you take the guys out for pizza and beer later, your moving expense may be well under $100.

Or you can hire the van and a couple of brawny fellows who come with it and do this kind of work on weekends. Their charge may be $30 or $40 an hour and this, too, is quite a bargain if you are not moving an 8-room house across three states and if you're going to be there to supervise at Old Home and New Home.

If you are moving an 8-room house, you will probably call in a moving company. Great care should be taken before you pick up that telephone because a) moving can be very, very expensive, with the average home move in the $1400 to $1800 range, and b) the field has its share of charlatans. You don't want to wind up with an overinflated estimate, or a no-show mover, or one who seems to drop every barrel marked "Fragile."

You can expect to pay around $500 for a local move with a moving company. An interstate move will run around $1500, although some folks run up bills of $10,000 and more!

Now, some considerations:

Which company? You have a choice of local movers in your area or the large nationwide companies. Naturally, you should check any mover you select with your local consumer protection agency, and make sure that that outfit has authority to operate from the Interstate Commerce Commission (ICC) or from the government agency in your state that regulates moves.

It's smart to get two or three estimates. When you call, a representative from that carrier will come to your place to look over what you plan to move and give you an estimate. For short, intrastate (within the state) moves of under forty miles or so, the estimate is based on the time the move is likely to take. Charges for interstate moves (from one state to another) will be based on the weight of the goods (so many dollars per hundred pounds) and the distance the movers will travel. Be sure you give each mover the same information about what's going and what you are leaving behind so that you can accurately evaluate the figures you are given. Too many different stories and too much changing your mind only confuses both of you—and adds more expense to the move. To be really smart, have all your goods inventoried before the estimators pull up.

Some companies will offer you a binding estimate. With others, the estimate is just that, and the final charge can—and probably will—be higher. If you are given three binding estimates, the choice then is a personal one, unless one mover offers more auxiliary services than another. But what if you get two binding estimates and one nonbinding one? Sometimes the binding estimates are higher, just because they are binding. The nonbinding one may be a better deal for you if it's lower, if you are sure you've told the mover everything that will be going along. Also, if on moving day you add a few more items, especially heavy ones, to a binding estimate, that may throw the movers for a loop, causing delays, more paperwork, and additional charges. Here too the nonbinding quote becomes the better deal.

Timing. Moving companies are busiest April through October, with business peaking from June to September. Try to avoid those times if you can. (And if you do, ask about a discount for moving in an off-season). Movers do overbook during their high season to make up for the slack of the remainder of the year. This practice can, of course, leave you cooling your heels and waiting for a van on one end or the other. Remember when looking over and signing the company's documents that oral promises on pickup and delivery dates mean nothing. Get everything in writing. A growing number of carriers, especially the larger ones, are offering late payments of $100 or so for every day that their trucks are late. This, understandably, has led to better performances by those carriers. If you must move in one of the busier seasons, try to give the moving company plenty of notice—sixty days isn't too much.

Liability. The mover is usually liable for the market value of items damaged or lost, minus depreciation. So if something happens to your $800 home computer, now valued at $500, you would have to pay the additional $300 to replace it. That is where the need for protection comes in. For insurance from the mover you can expect to pay around $5 per $1000 of coverage. There's also "free coverage," which values property at 60 to 65 cents a pound. Also, some carriers now sell protection for the full replacement value of your possessions.

If you are planning to move valuables such as art and antiques, you should call them to the attention of the mover to be sure they are adequately covered. Check your homeowner's insurance policy, too, to see if it, or any riders to it, mentions coverage during a move.

If any dispute arises between you and the mover that can't be settled between the two of you, with many companies you will enter into binding arbitration. That means both of you must go along with whatever decision the arbitrator reaches about your problem. The mover may provide you with a booklet describing the arbitration procedure. Not all of them offer that means of conciliation, but if yours does, and you accept it, you should know that you have given

---

About Stress

If you or a member of your family is having serious problems adjusting to a move, consider consulting a relocation counselor or therapist. It's all right these days to admit that you don't like change and are having a difficult time adjusting to your home and life in a new locale. Even a welcome move brings stress. You can call your local social services or human resources agency for the name of someone who can help.

An alternative: Some newcomers are forming their own groups, bringing in guest speakers or hiring one individual to stay with the group for its duration. While some of those speakers talk about the psychological upheaval of moving, others deal with career concerns or local civic issues. Some newcomers invite speakers to discuss regional cooking and specialty dishes of that area. Believe it or not, even unfamiliar regional food can add to a stressful situation.

---

up the right to go to court afterward. The arbitrator's word is the final one.

If you have any complaints about a move within your state, you can contact your state Department of Transportation.

Complaints about a move to another state should be directed to the Interstate Commerce Commission. Write the ICC, Office of Compliance and Consumer Assistance, Rm. 6328, 12th and Constitution Aves. N.W., Washington, D.C. 20423, (202) 275-7844.

A Satisfactory Move

For a satisfactory move:

1. Watch what you purchase from the mover. Barrels and special protection for china and valuables are fine and necessary, but ordinary cardboard boxes will cost you extra and can easily be picked up at no cost at local grocery and liquor stores. Keep an eye on the mover's packing. An all too common practice is "short" or "balloon" packing—putting too few objects in large boxes and stuffing the boxes with paper. All of that extra weight adds to your bill.

2. Be sure you keep an eye on the weighing of the goods, too, since that will determine your final cost in long-distance moves.

"Weight-bumping"—weighing goods in a truck that is already full with dollies, pads and even a couple of men—is quite common. Naturally that adds substantially to your cost too.

3. Call if your mover is one day late in showing up. Believe it or not, some folks wait weeks for the carrier. Sure, most moving companies will reimburse you for hotel/motel costs and a percentage of food bills, but who needs the aggravation of a long wait? And they won't pay if you have to rent furniture while you are waiting. (All of this delay may be just peachy with you, however, if you are being paid by the carrier for late delivery).

4. It's best to stay with the movers all the way, if you can. If not, at least have someone at either end looking out for your interests.

5. Most movers offer some form of liability protection for your goods. Look into extra coverage—from your own insurance policy or from the government—and what that encompasses.

6. Don't sign any receipt when the movers arrive at your new home until you have examined at least the most important of your furnishings. On the receipt you can note any damage and add something like "approved subject to unpacking boxes." Remember, if anything goes terribly wrong your words on that receipt may be all you have to document your case.

7. Check your apartment lease or call the rental manager where you are moving. Some buildings restrict moving in and out to certain days of the week or within certain hours.

Is Any of This Tax Deductible?

Expenses connected with moving can only be deducted from your federal tax return if you are transferred by your company, with a job waiting for you in the new locale. Even under those circumstances there is a laundry list of restrictions. Check with your accountant or ask your local IRS for a copy of Publication #521.

The Corporate Move

Although most Americans move as a matter of choice, others are told they are pretty much expected to pick up stakes because of their jobs. If you are being transferred by your employer, you have probably been told when you were handed that news that your company will assist you with many of the details of the move. As a rule, a corporation will pay for a few trips to the new locale for you and your spouse to do some house or apartment hunting. They will also pay your moving expenses.

And, depending on the state of the economy, they will do a good deal more to see you happy. During the recession of the early 1980s, many companies offered rent supplements to employees transferring to higher-priced communities. Others compensated employees for the difference in mortgage interest rates between their old and new home for at least three years. As we eased our way out of that recession, a fair number of larger corporations were also buying an employee's home, usually handled through a bank or relocation company, or reimbursing employees for the cost of selling those houses.

Company benefits, therefore, depend on the condition of the economy, whether the employee is transferred from a relatively low-cost community to a higher-priced one, and to some extent on intangibles such as the value of the employee and the desirability or undesirability of the new locale.

With more and more women in the marketplace, in careers and not merely jobs, the male transferee (only about 5 percent of corporate transferees are women) may give pause these days to being uprooted. Is it fair to ask his wife to move? Where will she find work in the new town? To combat that reluctance a growing number of corporations are offering those women career counseling services in the new locale, for which they pick up the tab.

All these tips are mentioned so that you can see what some businesses are doing, how much you can ask from your own, and what you can reasonably expect to receive. The bottom line here is "ask." Relocating is expensive and is likely to cost you something. But if you are worth transferring (and we're assuming here that the company is asking you to move, not the other way around), then they should be willing to pick up the bulk of your expenses and contribute in any other way to an easy transition from Point A to Point B.

Your Home

You're being transferred and you're expected to show up in New Town in three months. What do you do about your house? In an even economy, and certainly in a seller's market, you will have sold your home by then, even if you might have to come back (or one of you stay around) for the closing. But you have other options here:

• Depending on the real estate market, you can request that your corporation take the house off your hands—either buy it outright or conduct the sale for you after you've left.

• You can move, leaving the house empty and in the hands of a local real estate agent.

• You can rent the house until you sell it, or indeed continue to hold the property as investment real estate.

• You can go on ahead, leaving the family behind until the house is sold. (Will the company pick up your bill in New Town for housing during that period?)

What you decide here will depend on economic conditions to a great extent. If you cannot sell at a good price, naturally you will rent the house until the market improves (or unless you can get that decent price from your corporation). If you think you may be coming back to Old Town one of these days, you may likewise prefer to rent. Just remember that the rent money may not cover your mortgage, real estate taxes, and other payments on that home. You may have the expense of carrying some of that property along with your house in New Town. And being an absentee landlord a few cities or a few states away might be a problem for you. A growing number of transferees over the last few years have indeed rented their old homes and rented apartments in New Town besides. Unable to afford homes in the new community, or uncertain about staying there, they have elected to hold on to that profitable chunk of real estate in Old Town.

There's more about the tricky procedure of buying one house while trying to sell another in Chapter 27.

If you are renting an apartment in Old Town, and think you may be coming back in the future, you may want to sublet. Some laws and leases, however, stipulate that the tenant asking to sublet cannot be leaving for another permanent residence.

The Relocation Company

They may have been around for a while, but the popularity of relocation companies has truly blossomed only over the last several years. They come in all sizes and descriptions and can handle a variety of chores connected with moving. The two largest—Homequity and Merrill Lynch Relocation Management—have been joined by hundreds of smaller concerns. The very smallest may be a man or woman operating in a small community with rapid turnover of transferees, who works on a freelance basis for one or two large companies in the area.

The relocation company first talks to the transferee to learn his needs in the new community—neighborhood, size and style of housing, nearness to schools, housing budget, and so on so that it can put him in touch with real estate agents in the New Town (sometimes the relocation outfit is a branch of a real estate agency). The

---

Got a Stamp?

Then there was the Hawaiian who mailed some 8000 pounds of belongings from that island to Massachusetts prior to his family's move there. There were 131 packages that included the furniture, which had been taken apart for ease in shipping. Delivery time: three weeks. Cost: $2500. The intrepid Hawaiian estimated he saved $6000 on more conventional moving costs.

---

company introduces the employee to the community, its shops, cultural attractions, educational facilities, and the like. It will spell out company benefits and policies regarding moves. It will arrange the move, fill the employee in on the tax picture regarding relocations, and in general try to make the experience run smoothly. The employee's corporation, of course, pays for all of this. If the employee decides to rent his house instead of selling, an employee transfer company will frequently find a tenant, collect rent, make mortgage payments on the house, and supervise repairs—but usually at a fee of $1000 or so a year to the employee (unless the company adds this perk to the moving package).

If the relocation officer at your corporation does not mention a relocation company, it's worth querying him or her. Some companies automatically hand over the employee to one of these outfits, while others provide similar services in-house and so have no need of outsiders.

If your employer leaves you pretty much to fend for yourself vis-à-vis scouting New Town, you should know that the larger relocation companies work only through corporations. You cannot call them to take you on as an individual client. This may not apply to the very smallest, one-person outfits, however. If you'd like to make inquiries, you can call the Employee Relocation Council in Washington, D.C. This is an umbrella group of corporations that move their employees, relocation companies, real estate brokers, and others interested in the field. The council's number is (202) 857-0857.

You can also check the Yellow Pages under "Relocation Services." You should, of course, look into any company you are considering engaging, asking for references and checking with the Better Business Bureau in that locale and with the consumer protection agency.

Costs, if you pay on your own, will vary here. A specialist may charge you a flat fee for one or two days' work, or it may be an hourly fee or a package charge for however long it takes the expert to see you settled in. Most spend ten to fourteen hours with a client.

For More Information

The Interstate Commerce Commission offers the free booklet "When You Move: Your Rights and Responsibilities," and also a free copy of the latest "Complaint and Performance Data on Household Goods Movers." Write the ICC, Office of Compliance and Consumer Assistance, Rm. 6328, 12th and Constitution Aves. N.W., Washington, D.C. 20423, (202) 275-7844.

For a free list of directories for various urban areas around the country that will show you what life is like in that city with regard to housing (names and addresses of apartment buildings, rents, amenities, etc.), write Apartment Directories & Guides of America, Inc., 7200 France Ave. So., Suite 238, Minneapolis, Minn. 55435, (800) 438-5927.

The Nationwide Relocating Service has compiled a list showing what an average house costs in 115 cities around the country. It's called "Home Price Comparative Index" and is available at no charge from (800) 323-7097.

"Nice Things to Know About Moving, Storing, Winterizing Home Appliances," a free booklet from the Whirlpool Corporation, will tell you how to prepare major appliances for moving. Write Appliance Information Service, Administrative Center, Whirlpool Corp., Benton Harbor, Mich. 49022.

Finding Your Best Place to Live in America, by Dr. Thomas F. Bowman, Dr. George A. Giuliani, and Dr. M. Ronald Minge. Red Lion Books. Paperback, $9.95. Analysis of eighty major cities as to weather, per capita income, salaries for some professions, marriage rates, and other samplings.

Places Rated Almanac, by Richard Boyer and David Savageau. Rand McNally & Co., $19.95; paperback, $12.95. Again, ratings of places to live and those that are the most expensive, have the biggest tax bites, the worst health care, etc.

Retirement Edens Outside the Sun Belt by Peter A. Dickinson. E. P. Dutton & Co., $8.95. Covers weather, taxes, medical facilities, leisure-time activities, housing, and special services for seniors in spots not normally thought of as retirement havens.

Moving: A Guide to Selecting a School System, by Albert & Marilyn Pautler. Pautler Assoc., 50 Bragg Court, Williamsville, N.Y. 14221. An $8.95 paperback.

American Almanac of Jobs and Salaries, by John Wright. An 824-page survey of several hundred occupations and their pay rates, plus ranking of states according to new jobs created from 1978 to 1983. Avon, 1984. Price: $9.95.

33

How to Move a House
(and Why You Might Want To)

A house is a little like a tree, isn't it? "Plant" one and it will take root in that spot and remain there forever. To move it is unthinkable and would interfere with the natural order of things.

That is not true, of course, but since so few of us ever see a house being moved, the concept is almost an out-of-this-world one. Moving a house as a solution to problems surrounding it would rarely occur to us. Still, more than one bungalow or three-story Victorian gingerbread has been uprooted and moved at night along city streets and local highways at a v-e-r-y slow pace, and then satisfactorily replanted on its new site.

Moving a house shouldn't be undertaken lightly, but there are genuine and practical reasons for considering that measure:

• Perhaps you own a house on land scheduled to be cleared by local officials for, let's say, the purpose of highway construction. You will be paid fair market value for the house, of course, but your municipality will probably also allow you to buy back the structure at a small fraction of its value with the stipulation that you move it. Maybe you do want to keep the house.

• You may want to move your home farther back from the highway or, if it's on the ocean, back from encroaching beach erosion.

• You might want to move a mobile home to a new mobile community or to a private lot. Some house movers won't touch today's larger mobiles, but others will gladly take on the job.

• Your home may be set in the center of a large lot. By moving it to one side of that site you can subdivide and sell the remaining acreage.

• Perhaps you purchased a home from a seller who wants to rid himself of the dwelling while holding on to the land. He may even pay *you* to haul off the house.

• You may own the land, but cannot afford to build the house you want. Or any house. Buying an existing home offered at a bargain price, and moving it to your lot, can make ownership possible by saving you a bundle.

• You may have bought your home from Anthony Lozano, who runs (at this writing) the nation's only "used house" lot, in Manteca, California. Mr. Lozano sells something like fifty houses a year, all of which must be moved to new sites.

• Sometimes a house is moved because the owners (or their exterminator) used toxic chemicals for termite control. When the house itself can be saved, a new foundation can be laid while the house is removed from the site.

Those are probably more reasons than you thought existed for moving a house. But we live in a mobile society these days where it is not only people that move. A house can report a change of address too.

How to Shop for a House to Move

This is certainly an offbeat househunting arena, but if you are strapped for money, yet do have land on which to plop a home, there are several sources that may make a homeowner out of you. The house you find may be free, or it may cost you a token dollar or so, or it may be selling at just under market value. It may be sold on the open market, or through auction or sealed bid. It's worth investigating the possibilities, no matter what the state of your pocketbook. There are some pretty nifty, even historical and architecturally significant, homes that come on the market here, carrying price tags with very affordable figures. The properties just happen to be in the wrong place at the wrong time, or in the way of someone or some project. They don't come around often, to be sure, but persistence on your part could pay off handsomely. And it is the persistent cuss who always seems to come across the "find" or the "unbelievable bargain," right?

To shop:

1. Check with house movers in your area to see if they know of properties that must be uprooted and moved.

2. Call your state highway department and request that they

put you on their mailing list for upcoming auctions of unwanted properties.

3. Call your local or state historical society to see if they have properties they are eager to preserve through moving.

4. You should keep an eye open, too, for local newspaper advertisements offering houses that must be moved, for sale outright or through auction or bid.

5. It's smart to read the news pages of local papers for reports of urban renewal and other projects in your city or the one nearest you (not too far away though). Planned demolition of houses to make room for commercial projects or new residential development may mean you can walk away, figuratively speaking, with a house that had been only waiting for the wrecker's ball. In a New Jersey town, to take one example of how these properties come up, the city fathers offered at auction a house for the price of $40,000. The property had to be moved to make way for a municipal parking lot. The buyer was expected to foot the $20,000 moving fee to bring the home to a city-owned playground. The playground then became the buyer's property. This is not exactly a bargain price for a house that one was expected to move, but then $60,000 is not bad either for an attractive home, plus ownership of the land on which it is to be set, especially in a community where homes are worth at least that much and in some neighborhoods substantially more.

When househunting in this area, bear in mind that, as we all know, there is no free lunch. While you may indeed save thousands of dollars over a traditional purchase, a home acquired in this manner, even if it is handed to you free, is going to cost you *something*. And the charge is likely to run into five figures. We're supposing, of course, that you already own the land for the house. If not, then that's an additional expense, and with land costing what it does these days, your bargain house could wind up costing you as much as, or more than, one bought in the usual manner. It pays to figure out the advantages of moving a property very carefully before congratulating yourself on having found a bargain route to homeownership.

Here are a few points to consider, should you come across a house that's yours *if you will move it*:

1. Be sure, of course, that you have a place to put it.
2. If you must look for land, keep the practical aspects of the move in mind when you are shopping. A mountaintop aerie may make a house mover tip his hat to you and say thanks, but no thanks.

3. Remember that the easiest and most common moves are only a mile or so from where the house is originally situated.

4. Will the house blend in with others on the new block where it is heading, or will it stand out uncomfortably, even unattractively?

5. The age of a house is not a factor, but generally a wood frame home is easier and cheaper to move than one with a brick or stone facade. The latter takes more time to prepare for the move and weighs more, so will cost you more. Some house movers may want to remove the facade before the transport, which can become another complication.

6. Be sure the house is not too large for the route it must travel to the new lot. Edward Monroe, Jr., a third-generation house mover based in Norwalk, Connecticut, cautions: "Many people think if they can drive from one spot to another with their car, they can drive there with a house." Not necessarily true.

7. Mr. Monroe adds that utility charges for moving a house can be higher than the house mover's fee, so whatever quote the mover gives you is not the total cost for transporting the house. And the utility charge is one phase of the move you can't get around. More about that later.

Moving It

So you have a house at point A and the lot ready for it at point B. Naturally this move is not a job for even the handiest do-it-your-selfers, although there might be a tough soul out there who could successfully move his one-room log cabin a few yards. The first step for the rest of us is to check the Yellow Pages under "House and Building Movers." You may have to go into another county, or even several counties away, to find such a listing, since while the profession is an old and enduring one there is not necessarily a house mover within everyone's whistling distance. Try to find at least two companies if you can, however, so you can compare references and estimates. Ask how long the company has been in business. Whom have they moved recently (so you can call that individual)? What does their fee include? How much of the work will be left to you? If you are moving a house of some architectural or historical impor-tance you will want to be sure the mover is sensitive to its fine details. You won't want it to arrive with damage to moldings, stained glass, or the like.

Bear in mind that no special licensing is required for these movers, so it's best to use a company that is bonded and carries enough

Reprinted with permission of Worcester Polytechnic Institute.

insurance to cover you if something dreadful should happen to the house between points A and B. And of course you will want your lawyer to look over the contract presented to you by the mover.

The mover will act as the general contractor for the project. He, not you, will plan the travel route. He will look out for narrow roads, hills, and trees and will measure clearances under bridges and freeways. He will secure the necessary permits from city hall or other appropriate local or state or private agencies. Usually there's a permit to move the house, a demolition permit to remove it from its present site, and a building permit for the new location. Regulations for moving vary from one community to another, of course. You should not have to concern yourself with these details, but in truth in some moves you may have to become involved with small points that will crop up. "Involved" means a phone call here and there or perhaps a trip to city hall. You won't have to help in jacking up the place.

The mover will also inspect the house to see if it can be moved in one piece or if the roof, capes, porches, or other appendages will have to be removed and transported separately. Large houses may have to be cut in half, or dismantled completely to be reassembled at the new site.

If the mover tells you that, yes, your house is going to have to be disassembled, keep in mind that this will be tough on the structure (as it would be on anything or anyone), and it's not likely to be in exactly the same shape on the new site as it is where it's standing now. Still, if you are moving it a great distance—seventy-five miles or so—dismantling becomes far more practical than transporting it virtually intact and trying to cope with permits, road conditions, utilities, and the like for a long journey. And that's not mentioning cost!

Some homeowners opt for dismantling when they see projected bills from government agencies (removal of traffic lights and street signs), cable television companies, and the telephone and gas and electric companies for moving utility lines along the route. Those charges can run several thousand dollars and may cut so into owners' budgets that they decide to go with breaking up the house.

What the Move Is Likely to Cost

House movers' charges vary widely, according to the size of the structure—is it one, two, or three stories?—the distance to be traveled, the complexity of the travel route, and whether it will be moved intact or will have to undergo some dismantling. Whether it's a wood or stone structure will also have a bearing on the cost.

A house mover will probably charge from $4 to $8 a square foot.

Next come the fees to your local gas and electric and telephone companies for raising lines along the travel route. These are not fixed rates and can vary widely from one company to another. They are generally quite high, though, and in fact may be higher than the mover's fee. A guesstimate is from under $5000 to over $10,000.

What happens here is that a crew on a truck rides ahead of the house, lifting or disconnecting (sometimes rerouting) utility wires. Next in this eye-catching procession is the truck towing the house. Behind the house is a similar utility crew putting lines back to rights. Canny homeowners (or perhaps it is the house mover who makes the suggestion) come up with all sorts of alternatives for avoiding this heavy charge. One small vacation home was moved by helicopter to its new site three miles away. The owner of a Michigan home had it moved by barge along Lake Huron from Port Huron to Lexington.

A California couple moved their house by barge too—from Stockton to Tracy, a distance of about 15 miles. An overnight (because of high winds) cruise began at 8 A.M. when the house set sail and ended at the unloading site at 11 A.M. the next day. The lot for the house was only about 800 feet from the river.

The barge trip cost $5000. The owner of the house explained that he opted for river transport when he saw the bill from local agencies for moving the house just a short distance in Stockton.

"There was a bill from the City of Stockton," he recalled. "There was Pacific Telephone, Pacific Gas and Electric, and the cable television company. It cost $5000 for *six blocks* to the river in Stockton. Can you imagine what we would have had to pay if we'd continued moving the house overland for 15 miles?"

The huge home, architecturally a Queen Anne cottage, was acquired at auction for $10,000. The owners had planned to turn the structure into offices, but, according to the Californian, "the city gave them so much of a hassle they decided to sell it." He read the small advertisement announcing the sale in the local paper.

"My wife had fallen in love with that house twenty-five years ago," he explained. "But I farm in Tracy and I didn't want to commute. When we saw it was for sale, she went into vapors." The couple own several hundred acres of land in Tracy, so there was no problem in finding a site for the house.

The very successful transaction cost the couple $10,000 for the house; $5000 for the mover handling the land transport in Stockton and Tracy; $5000 for the utility and other charges in Stockton; and $5000 for the barge trip—a total of $25,000. The house is so handsome and attention-getting that a nationwide paint company is contributing to its repainting in appropriate historical colors.

Admittedly, the Tracy farmer is a savvy individual and armed with skills and experience. He had transported bunkhouses along the river to his farm after purchasing them from a nearby government installation, so river transport came immediately to mind after he saw the expense of an overland move. He was capable of building a full basement for the house in Tracy. Since the house had to travel only 800 feet in Tracy—all on his land—there were no sizable charges from utility and television companies as there were in Stockton.

Still, even if you are a novice and must depend on professionals, you can see that a house now worth well over $100,000 cost nowhere near that to acquire and move (of course the Tracy couple did already own the land for it).

How Long Will It Take?

Permits should eat up only a week or so of everyone's time, depending, naturally, on the efficiency of the agencies involved.

Raising the house from its foundation to prepare it for the move will also take about a week. The mover digs under the house and inserts jacks. As the structure begins to rise, wooden supports are put into place. When these blocks, or cribbing as it is called, become high enough, the jacks are removed and steel girders are placed under the house. Wheels are attached to the girders and the girders are linked to the truck. The tow truck will move the house at about a mile per hour, depending on road (and house) conditions. Local ordinances will probably require the move to take place between 9 P.M. and 3 A.M. so that no traffic is disrupted.

Setting the house down on its new lot and seeing that it functions there is a process likely to take about a week. A new foundation will cost you anywhere from $3000 to five-digit numbers depending on whether you do it yourself or call in a professional, and whether you want the simplest of foundations, a crawl space, or a full basement. The mover will set the house over temporary wood supports, and then the contractor builds the foundation up from those footings, with the mover's supports removed in gradual stages as the foundation work progresses.

Moving a house is likely to be one of the unique experiences of your life. Most of us never see a house moved, which is in itself a sight that is a little mind blowing (if you can bear to look). In your case, it will be *your* house moving slowly along Route 42. How will it take that corner on Abercrombie Road? Will it clear the bridge? Wow!

An experience, yes. And it can be quite a saving, too, in getting yourself a perfectly fine home at a low price, or in saving one you would have lost to erosion or eminent domain or some other natural or man-made catastrophe.

A house is truly meant to stay where it was constructed and should not be moved on a whim. But if moving it means saving it and giving it a new and better life a few yards or several miles away, then go ahead and pick up the Yellow Pages. You're making a smart move in all senses of the word, and you and your home are likely to come up winners.

Raising a House

You may have to move your house while you build a better foundation—because it needs one or because you want a different style from what is there now, because your flood insurance policy calls for certain standards to be met or because your state mandates minimum heights or other specifications. The Coastal Area Management Law in Connecticut, for example, calls for homes along the shore there to be a certain number of feet above sea level.

A house mover will charge anywhere from $2500 to $6000 to raise the structure and leave it in the air while you or a professional lays the new foundation. Then the mover replaces it on the site. This can be an expensive procedure, as you can see, so it's wise to consider the foundation of any "beach shack" you buy *before* you start doing all the fun things like decorating, constructing a sundeck, and so forth.

34

Special Considerations for the Handicapped

Remember *Ironside*, the television series of a few years back? Wasn't it interesting how fairly simple life was, logistically speaking, for "the Chief"? His office was situated in his home (or was it the other way around?), and naturally both were all on one floor. He had an almost always-present attendant to care for him and manipulate the wheelchair.

It was particularly fascinating—and more than a little curious—to see both chief and attendant appear almost miraculously at the door of what had to be the walkup apartment of the low-life villain they were pursuing. How did the two of them navigate all those stairs?

Well that was fantasy, of course, and trifles like getting a wheelchair up three flights have no place in an hour-long, action-oriented television program. It wouldn't do to have the hero quietly pondering staircases for fifty minutes or so.

The aggravations and frustration of those who cannot walk, or are otherwise disabled, are not fantasy, however, and intrude in dozens of great and small ways into their daily lives.

For the Blind

Househunting for the blind, say the blind themselves and the agencies who offer services for them, is no different from househunting for the sighted.

But renting an apartment is another story. Blind would-be tenants may well run into discrimination from landlords who are concerned about the safety of those individuals. They bring up stairs and gas stoves, among other concerns. "Blind people have about the same accident rate as sighted persons," said a spokeswoman, herself blind, for the National Federation of the Blind (1800 Johnson St., Baltimore, Md. 21230). "But landlords will often raise those points, and they don't always do it with ill will. It can be with the best of intentions, and genuine worry about the blind person."

Still, it *is* discrimination, and if you are about to embark on an apartment hunt you should know that federal anti-discrimination laws do not protect the individual against bias because of a physical handicap. Some state laws do offer that protection, but not all of them. Before you visit real estate agents or building managers, better call a local, regional, or national association for the blind and/or your local fair housing office to learn the wisest approach to take with landlords. And, of course, discriminatory practices *can* be fought successfully if you want to take that route to the apartment you want and feel you are entitled to.

When it comes to guide dogs in apartment buildings, most states allow those animals to be an exception to the "no pets" rule a landlord might impose, although the tenant *is* held responsible for any damage the dog might cause. Some landlords charge an extra fee up front in anticipation of possible damage, but some states forbid such charges. Again, your fair housing office will have the information you need in this area.

For the Wheelchair-Bound

Housing problems and concerns are of a different, more complicated nature here. If you are new to life in a wheelchair, or living with someone who is, perhaps the most important point to bear in mind when it comes to your home is *not* automatically to call your local contractor to come over and make changes until you have made a few other telephone calls first.

The same advice holds true if you are going house or apartment hunting.

There is a full network of professionals, many of them disabled themselves, who are there to help you in planning your move or house remodeling. And there's more to it, they say—and maybe you've already discovered—than replacing the front steps with a ramp.

First, you can find assistance at your local hospital or rehabilitation center, and at city or county social service agencies. They can be expected to have the latest information about what is new in the design, architecture, and product areas for the handicapped. Also, several hospitals, colleges, and universities around the country provide a live-in period in a specially designed apartment, so that a disabled individual, and whoever will be living with him or her, can stay overnight or for a few days to become acquainted with new design features and special products and appliances for the handicapped; they also provide some simple, no-cost tips to ease the adjustment in living as well. All of these can later be adapted to one's own home. One of the more renowned residences of that kind is Horizon House, which is affiliated with the New York University Medical Center's Institute of Rehabilitation Medicine (550 First Ave., New York, N.Y. 10016).

Then there are offices and agencies beyond your own locale that can help with virtually every aspect of finding or creating a barrier-free environment, from new products to finding contractors.

One important source of much of this type of information is the National Center for a Barrier-Free Environment (Suite 700, 1015 15th St. N.W., Washington, D.C. 20005).

John Salmen, program director, calls the center a "one-stop shopping service." "We have an information clearing house," he explains. "It provides a wide variety of services to designers, home-

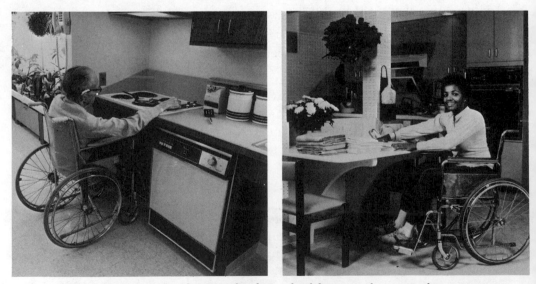

Home adjustments for those confined to wheelchairs involve more than just an outdoor ramp and widening of interior doorways. In the kitchen, stoves (left) can be adapted for wheelchair accessibility. Wall ovens (right) are built in at a low height, and low-counter work space can be either stationary, fold-down, or on casters. *Reprinted with permission of Whirlpool Corporation.*

owners, or anybody involved in the process of modifying or building homes or any other kind of facility to make them accessible."

The center's many areas of assistance include:

• Publications about kitchens, ramps, putting a lift into the house, and so forth. There is a library here of all documents published on the issue of accessibility.

• A technical assistance network—the names of contractors, designers, and architects who have specific experience in barrier-free design in the locale of the individual seeking assistance.

• Knowledge of building codes and standards for all states—requirements for access in multifamily homes, for example.

• Information about products and appliances available for the handicapped. Some of these manufacturers are small cottage industries that can't afford to advertise, but whose products are of great assistance to the handicapped.

• Floor plans, slides, and drawings that have been developed for accessible living.

Mr. Salmen adds, "We also have names of rehabilitation specialists in local areas who will say 'yes, you'll need this, but that piece of equipment will do instead of buying a new door'—that type of thing."

There is a charge for some of the booklets here but the publications list is free. The technical assistance network costs $5 for a list of five individuals in your locale that meet the requirements you requested. If the center can't find five within a certain radius of your home, they'll pass on to you the names of five qualified persons anywhere in the country, without charge. Anyone who can truly not afford to pay will be given any information they seek with no charge.

The Washington center is an important and interesting source of just about every type of information you will need to aid you in barrier-free living, but there are other agencies and offices that can be equally helpful. Most of them have free printed material to acquaint you with what they have to offer before you commit yourself further:

The Veterans Administration, 810 Vermont Ave. N.W., Washington, D.C. 20017.

Paralyzed Veterans of America, 4330 East-West Highway, Washington, D.C. 20014.

Eastern Paralyzed Veterans of America, 432 Park Ave. So., New York, N.Y. 10016.

Able Data offers an index to specially designed equipment for the disabled. Rehab Data supplies listings of printed material on every aspect of physical impairment. Contact both at the National Rehabilitation Information Center, Catholic University of America, 4407 Eighth St. N.E., Washington, D.C. 20017.

The Whirlpool Corporation offers two free booklets: "Aids to Independent Living: Suggestions for Installing and Operating Major Home Appliances for Easier Use by Disabled Persons"; and "Designs for Independent Living: Kitchen and Laundry Designs for Disabled Persons." Write to Whirlpool Corp., Appliance Information Service, Administrative Center, Benton Harbor, Mich. 49022; or call Whirlpool's "cool" line, (800) 253-1301.

How to Create Interiors for the Disabled: A Guidebook for Family and Friends, by Jane Randolph Cary, Pantheon Books. Price: $5.95.

Design for Independent Living, by Raymond Lifchez and Barbara Winslow, University of California Press, 2223 Fulton St., Berkeley, Calif. 94720. Price: $9.95 plus $1.50 shipping cost. California residents add sales tax.

"Kitchens for Women in Wheelchairs," Circular 841. Price: $1.50. Available from Small Homes-Building Research Council, University of Illinois, One East Saint Mary's Road, Champaign, Ill. 61820.

Going House or Apartment Hunting

Naturally anyone in a wheelchair can make use of any real estate agent or building management concern or classified advertisement to secure a home or apartment. But you might save yourself time—not to mention hassles—by investigating what exists in your area to make the hunt a little easier.

Two examples:

Renting
In New York City, which has some 30,000 wheelchair-confined residents and a half million handicapped overall, there is the Housing Data Bank Referral Service, established in 1980 by the Settlement Housing Fund and funded by federal community development monies. The Data Bank has found apartments for hundreds of disabled New Yorkers, designed to meet their specific needs. Of course there are hundreds more registered with the Data Bank, so it cannot come up with a perfectly accessible flat for everyone who wants one. Still, Data Bank provides an extremely useful service to that city.

It's tough—and this applies everywhere in the country and not just New York—to find apartments suitable for the disabled, even in publicly funded complexes. Many have lengthy waiting lists; some do not offer accessibility. New apartment buildings constructed with federal assistance offer the best hope these days of finding a home, since there is now a law that mandates 5 percent of all units in new multifamily complexes of that type, and 10 percent of those in buildings for the elderly, be accessible for the physically handicapped. However—and note this rather bizarre footnote—while the law calls for that particular percentage of barrier-free apartments, there is no rule that the units have to be rented to the disabled!

So you may need a champion to do battle with various bureaucracies for you here. If you are looking to pay open-market rents, contact your local social service agency to see if there is anything like Data Bank where you live. If you are interested in moving into subsidized housing complexes, you can get in touch with your local public housing agency.

Homebuying

This is a slightly different equation. You're likely to find any number of homes within a reasonable radius of where you want to live that could be adapted for wheelchair use. Still, a smart ploy may be to contact Access Real Estate before calling local realty agents.

This is a service that has been in operation for almost a decade now, formed to facilitate real estate transactions involving wheelchair-accessible homes. It was founded by Fred Kolhopp and Richard Weir, both real estate brokers in New York. Mr. Weir is himself disabled.

Access Real Estate is a central real estate registry and referral system that provides handicapped househunters with a listing center for information and the opportunity to buy and sell specially designed homes.

Live in Minnesota and want to move to Arizona? Access can put you in touch with a real estate agent in that locale who has in his listings either (a) a home for sale that has been remodeled for easy wheelchair access or (b) a house suitable for remodeling. Naturally the latter means a ranch-style home rather than a three-story Victorian gingerbread. "Levitt built the best homes for this purpose," said Mr. Weir. "He did a lot of slab building. This is ideal because it's close to the ground, with no rise. When you get into a dozen steps, or even a half dozen, you have more problems." Access offers help with short-haul moves, too, if you just want to relocate in the same community.

There is no charge for this service. All you pay is the regular realty agent's commission for selling your home, and of course no fee at all when you buy.

The agency can also put you in touch with builders who have special experience and expertise in the construction of barrier-free homes. (If you're a veteran with a service-related injury, your VA office can tell you about funding available for having a new home built.)

For more information and/or a free pamphlet, contact Access Real Estate, Sea Realty, 22 Sunset Ave., Westhampton Beach, N.Y. 11978, (516) 288-6244.

Discrimination

If you're buying or building a home, you won't face any, of course. Nor will you in publicly assisted complexes with units for the handicapped (you may not find much bias, but you'll have to do battle with other prospective tenants for those units).

But in open-market apartment buildings you may well find that first, the building wouldn't work for you anyway (remember Ironside visiting those fourth-floor walkups), and second, that the manager does not want to rent to you. It's nothing personal. It's not you actually, it's your wheelchair.

Like the blind, you are dealing here with a federal Human Rights Law that states that one cannot be denied housing because of color, religion, national origin, or sex. But only some states have additional statewide and/or regional laws that prohibit discrimination on the basis of marital status, the presence of children in the family, sexual orientation, political affiliation, and *the existence of a handicap in the applicant*. Even in states that do offer protection by law you can expect to confront bias occasionally or frequently when you go apartment hunting. Indeed there is still plenty of it in areas where it is forbidden according to federal law.

Contact your Fair Housing Council, Open Housing Center, Human Rights Commission, or whatever such an office is called in your locale to see how you should handle yourself in the open marketplace. They can apprise you of laws in your region and can tell you the savviest procedure for answering ads, approaching landlords, etc.

Discrimination, as you may have already learned for yourself, does not always end once you have found an apartment. As happens with other groups that are discriminated against, you may find yourself harassed by management eager to see you move, or denied the use of certain facilities in the building. One seventy-nine-year-old woman confined to a wheelchair filed suit against the cooperative apartment building where she lives, claiming that the management is seeking to evict her because, she was told, her wheelchair makes that fashionable building "look like a nursing home." Management claimed that residents had complained when the woman sat outside in the sun from time to time. At this writing the suit is still pending.

So new and unusual forms of discrimination may crop up from time to time, from one year to the next. It's smart to keep the phone number of that fair housing office handy.

Where the Rehab Money Will Come From

This won't be a long section. There isn't much public money around geared specifically to help the handicapped remodel their homes to make them more accessible. You might contact your regional HUD office, which keeps track of government programs as they come and go. Or you can write for the free booklet "Changing Environments for People with Disabilities," published by the U.S. Department of Housing and Urban Development, which outlines programs available for the disabled. Write to: Special Advisor for the Handicapped, Rm. 10184, HUD, 451 7th St. S.W., Washington, D.C. 20410.

You might also give serious thought to whether you would be better off moving than trying to convert your existing home to one that is totally barrier-free. Here's an area where the consultants mentioned earlier can help.

The handicapped have become quite a vocal presence over the last decade—witness their ongoing fight to make buildings and public transportation more accessible to them—but the money, when it is there, seems to go for jobs or for the aforementioned easier-access facilities, and not for housing benefits. But stay tuned. All that may change as lobbying continues and expands.

The Tax Issue

Whether your remodeling project, or the special installation you made, will qualify for an income tax deduction is a very complex area, much more complicated than how the IRS feels about doctor bills, which leaves little room for negotiation. If the job you're having done will add to the value of your home—a swimming pool, for instance—you may find Uncle Sam not smiling on your deduction, no matter how much the doctor testifies that it is necessary for your health and well-being. You should consult your accountant, of course, on this issue, and you can also ask your IRS office for booklet #907, *Tax Information for Handicapped Persons*.

The Mentally Handicapped

A still fairly new trend in the care of the mentally handicapped is the establishment of so-called "halfway houses" for the mentally ill and "group homes" for the mentally retarded. All of these are existing houses located within residential communities, where a small number of adults or children are provided with a supervised environment that allows them to develop as individuals and increase their social skills. In the case of the mentally ill, the out-of-institution setting helps ease the transition to independent everyday life.

The homes have come in for quite a good deal of controversy, especially the halfway houses for the mentally ill. Homeowners in neighborhoods that have them complain initially—and some continue to do so—of lower property values, of the residents of the homes "frightening" or even "attacking" the townspeople, and have any number of other objections. Homes for the mentally retarded are more readily accepted, because these people's condition is static and irreversible, which allows many of them to hold jobs. However, there is many a town resident who only hears the word "mental" and does not bother attempting to distinguish between the two.

Legislation calling for increasing de-institutionalization of the mentally handicapped continues, so we can expect to see more and more of these facilities. Indeed, many in the field see them as sound concepts for "mainstreaming" more of the mentally handicapped.

The homes are not available in every locale, and they are not common even in heavily populated areas. Still, new ones crop up almost daily here and there, sponsored by various government agencies and church groups. With some facilities the bills are picked up by federal or state programs; in others funding is private and the handicapped individual must pay whatever rate is charged for housing and full board.

For More Information

The National Mental Health Association, 1800 N. Kent St., Rosslyn, Va. 22209.

The National Association for Retarded Citizens, P.O. Box 6109, Arlington, Tex. 76011.

35

The Benefits
and Burdens of Owning an Old
or Historic House

You'll leave others to their chrome and glass contemporaries. Your idea of "home" is an old house. How old? Some go searching for the city or country dwelling that dates to the founding of that community. Others buy "old" houses built as recently as the 1930s, because that's simply the only housing stock in the town where they live.

All who own an old house would agree, however, that yes, they just don't make them like that anymore. Whether the house was constructed for the local tycoon or for the workers at the town mill, there is a durability in building materials and a quality of craftsmanship that rarely show up in the houses we see going up today.

As much as we can accomplish in America—in aeronautics, in medicine, in the arts—we can't build houses like we used to. The number of talented and dedicated craftspeople has certainly dwindled since the country's early days and, let's face it, it's too expensive to use those same construction materials these days. Mahogany-paneled rooms. Intricate moldings. Thick plaster walls. Solid doors. How many luxury-priced homes built in the 1980s list even a few of those quality features?

So the old-house owner, while certainly faced with a few or a few dozen problems peculiar not just to houses but to those that have seen a hundred or more winters, can also take pride in a structure that is unique and truly irreplaceable. We hasten to add that there are certainly mediocre old houses; they are not all glorious examples of Victoriana or the early pioneering days or whenever. But even

571

You're never finished working on them, and they can be a constant drain on the checkbook, but there's something about old houses . . .

the most pedestrian house is likely to be *solid*. After all, it's still here, isn't it, despite a few dozen owners and perhaps a few hundred years?

Some own old houses, while others have homes that are officially designated "historic." The latter may have been named to the National Register of Historic Places, which comes under the U.S. Department of the Interior. Those houses have architectural or historic significance. Frequently houses do not stand by themselves, but are parts of historic districts—Brooklyn Heights in New York and parts of Charleston, South Carolina, to take two popular examples. Some old houses have *state* historic status and others are *local* landmarks. More about landmark designation and what that entails later.

Whether your house is simply an old one out by the highway, or one so historic it is open to the public every weekend "in season," you have special interests that differ from other homeowners. You enjoy benefits—the pride of preserving a bit of your town's heritage, of saving a part of our architectural history, and the joy of becoming involved in the preservation, even the decorating, of old houses. There is a burden too, of course—the expense of maintaining an elderly lady frequently requiring a tremendous outlay of cash for heating and repairs. If your home is a certified "historic" house, you will have to be sure exterior changes are approved, and must follow other guidelines and strictures. *Someone*, it seems, is always looking over your shoulder. Sometimes it isn't a government agency at all, but one or several nosy or crotchety townsfolk.

The highs and lows can run an extremely zigzagged line. An evening's pleasure poring over a book on Early American nails and hinges to see what matches your house can be obliterated the next morning by the muffed job of a painter trying to repair stenciling in the living room. The painter may apologize profusely, however, and opine quite sincerely that your house is one of the best in town. Momentarily lulled, you bring in the afternoon mail to find a bill from a workman who repaired three squeaky stairs in the hallway. $225. Seventy-five dollars a stair!

And so it goes, constantly keeping an eye on what could break next, what needs upgrading next, what you'd *like* to spend a few dollars on next if something else doesn't break down tomorrow.

If you have been living in an old house for several years now and the plaster dust has finally settled, you are probably quite comfortable in your role of lord or lady of that special manor. Poorer, but comfortable. If you are new to old-house ownership, though, or if you are still shopping for a home of a certain age, you should know that you will not have to do battle with zoning boards, craftspeople, tax assessors, *et al*. alone. You have friends out there to help with this rather distinctive housing choice. It's to your advantage—psychological and financial—to join forces with them.

Your Best Allies

Whether you live in an old or a historic house, there are four sources of information, guidance, and handholding you will find invaluable: the National Trust for Historic Preservation, the Victorian Society in America, *The Old-House Journal*, and, for those in and around the New York metropolitan area, The Brownstone Revival Committee Inc. Membership in these groups, or in the one case a subscription to the publication, is nominal when compared with the money you are likely to spend on your home. And that small price can keep you from making some serious and costly rehab errors.

The National Trust for Historic Preservation

This, based in Washington, D.C., is a federally chartered nonprofit organization that encourages public participation in the preservation of sites, buildings, and objects significant to American history and culture. The National Trust also maintains fifteen properties in various parts of the country. Support is provided by membership dues, endowment funds, contributions, and matching grants from federal agencies—including the U.S. Department of the Interior and the National Park Service.

Many people erroneously believe the National Register is part of the National Trust but, as mentioned earlier, that office is a government one, placed under the U.S. Department of the Interior.

You don't have to be an old, or historic, house owner to belong to the National Trust (it's for those owning and/or rehabilitating commercial structures, too). Members also include men and women working in the field of preservation, government officials, local historical societies, and those who just plain like old buildings and the subject of historic preservation.

Joining the National Trust will cost you $15 a year for active membership, $20 for a family, and $25 for associate membership. Membership privileges include receiving a copy of *Preservation News*, the monthly newspaper; *Historic Preservation*, the glossy bimonthly magazine; free admission to the trust's historic properties; various tours, meetings, and regional and local activities scheduled throughout a year; and a 10 percent discount at Trust shops, either in Washington or at local sites.

You can also call the National Trust's offices for guidance in how to go about seeking historic designation for your home or block; for information about craftspeople; for an explanation of historic designation and taxes; and any other questions or problems you may have with the ownership of your home. The National Trust publishes many helpful books and pamphlets too.

The National Trust for Historic Preservation is at 1785 Massachusetts Ave. N.W., Washington, D.C. 20036. The telephone number is (202) 673-4000.

The National Trust also has these regional offices around the country:

Mid-Atlantic Regional Office: Cliveden, 6401 Germantown Ave., Philadelphia, Pa. 19144, (215) 438-2886. Covers: Delaware, District of Columbia, Maryland, New Jersey, Pennsylvania, Virginia, West Virginia, Puerto Rico, and the Virgin Islands.

Midwest Regional Office: 405 South Dearborn, Suite 710, Chicago, Ill. 60605, (312) 353-3419 and 353-3424. Covers: Illinois, Indiana, Iowa, Michigan, Minnesota, Missouri, Ohio, and Wisconsin.

Northeast Regional Office: Old City Hall, 45 School St., Second Floor, Boston, Mass. 02108, (617) 223-7754. Covers: Connecticut, Maine, Massachusetts, New Hampshire, New York, Rhode Island, and Vermont.

Southern Regional Office: 456 King Street, Charleston, S.C. 29403, (803) 724-4711. Covers: Alabama, Arkansas, Florida, Georgia, Kentucky, Louisiana, Mississippi, North Carolina, South Carolina, and Tennessee.

Mountains/Plains Regional Office: 1407 Larimer St., Suite 200, Denver, Colo. 80202, (303) 837-2245. Covers: Colorado, Kansas, Montana, Nebraska, New Mexico, North Dakota, Oklahoma, South Dakota, Texas, and Wyoming.

Western Regional Office: 681 Market St., Suite 859, San Francisco, Calif. 94105, (415) 974-8420. Covers: Alaska, Arizona, California, Hawaii, Idaho, Nevada, Oregon, Utah, Washington, Guam, and Micronesia.

Victorian Society in America

While acknowledging that the true Victorian era spanned the years 1837–1901, the Victorian Society in America has elected to concern itself with homes and cultural life here from 1795 to the end of World War I. Much of this group's work is concentrated on the scholarly aspects of Victoriana—the architecture, interiors, and culture of the time. Membership in the society, which has forty-six chapters across the country, costs $25 a year. Members will receive a copy of the quarterly magazine *19th Century,* the newsletter *"The Victorian,"* which is published six times a year, and other special benefits, among which is the opportunity to attend summer school in the United States or England to study various aspects of the Victorian era. The society will happily answer questions from members and will direct them to appropriate local officials or craftspeople. Want to know how to serve a proper Victorian tea? They'll help there too.

The Victorian Society in America is at East Washington Square, Philadelphia, Pa. 19106, (215) 627-4252.

The Old-House Journal

This journal is published ten times a year, going to some 75,000 old-house owners across the country. And "old" here means any structure built before 1930. Some of the subjects covered: removing exterior paint; draperies and curtains in the old house; how to duplicate plaster castings; hints for the renovator; overcoming musty odors. Besides the nuts and bolts (literally) advice, there are articles on specific houses and neighborhoods, letters to the editor, exchanges of information about products and craftspeople, and advertising. The journal is a very readable, even chatty, publication designed especially for the novice. There's a sort of "we're all in this together and we're bound to make a few mistakes, but don't we love these great old houses" theme running through its pages.

A subscription to *The Old-House Journal* costs $16 a year. Along with a subscription comes information about the office's many pamphlets and books, some of which will be mentioned later in this chapter.

The Old-House Journal is at 69A Seventh Ave., Brooklyn, N.Y. 11217. The telephone number is (718) 636-4514.

The Brownstone Revival Committee

Finally, for old-house owners in the New York metropolitan area (although those farther afield are members too), there is The Brownstone Revival Committee (BRC), with its bimonthly publication, *The Brownstoner*. Membership in the BRC brings other benefits, too, among which is a treasured list of "gems," recommendations by BRC members of local workmen in twenty different areas of home repair, maintenance, and design.

Membership in the BRC costs $25 a year, $15 for renewals. The Committee is at 200 Madison Ave., New York, N.Y. 10016, (212) 561-2154.

Tracking Down the History and Architectural Style of Your Home

"What a lovely house," you exclaim to the real estate agent as she shows you through. "What style is it?"

"Er . . . late Victorian," she replies. Well, the block certainly *looks* Victorian, she reasons.

"What a great house," says Uncle Charlie with a wide grin. "It's a duffelinger with lintelexing subecures, isn't it?"

"Hey, can't put anything over on Uncle Charlie," you gamely reply. Duffel . . . what?

The garden club secretary seats herself on the wicker settee and inquires politely but with more than a dab of curiosity, "Tell me, my dear, now that you've been in the house a few months, does the ghost of Mrs. Carleen DuBuffier Grandstone still prowl the third floor?"

One of the great features of owning an old house is knowing that that structure has a history. Good or bad people lived here. Good or bad "improvements" were made to the house as it evolved into the structure you live in today.

Who *did* build your home, and exactly when? What style is it? Unless it's obviously an adobe or a Carpenter Gothic, and folks who know have told you so, you may have to do some detective work to learn the history and architectural style of your house. This is one of the fascinating aspects of old-house ownership, far more interesting than tracing a 100-year-old sewer line. It can be important as well as pleasurable, since knowledge of just what constitutes your home can assist contractors and others in making changes and improvements to that structure over the years.

If you live in a historic district, the association of homeowners or the local landmark commission or historical society can probably give you the entire history of your home, or can at least tell you how to hunt for that information. Similarly, if there is a town historian, he or she may have the saga of 114 Hill Place since the last brick was put into place.

But what if you can't turn to neighbors for help? There are several sources you can look to for assistance in digging:

• Is there a historical society in your locale? If not, try your state historical society or commission.

• Is there one individual, or perhaps several individuals, in your community who can provide you with an oral history of your house or of the block?

• Can city hall or town hall or the county courthouse help? If your home was constructed before 1850, you're liable to be out of luck, but it's worth checking your local buildings department to see if there is a procedure for finding the information you want. Take with you the block and lot numbers of the house (on your deed). From building permits you should be able to learn the name of the architect, the builder, what the house cost and when it was constructed, the name of the original owner, what the original floor plans looked like, the type of building materials used, and the heating plant, if there was one.

It's not likely you will be given much help by personnel here. But be persistent in asking to plow through old books and maps yourself. If you're going to do the work yourself, the staff may be more helpful.

You can also try the office that handles records of real estate transactions, tracking down the earliest deed to your home. Admittedly, that may not belong to the original owner. Truly early deeds may have been lost or destroyed by fire or flood or some other catastrophe.

• What about the public library? Those folks will be far cheerier in helping you than city hall is likely to be. You can check old photographs and/or newspaper clippings that give you a flavor of the time when your house was constructed, perhaps even provide you with a picture. The library may also have what is known as plat books, which are large-scale maps showing lots and buildings on each block. You already know your lot number and should have no trouble finding your site in these books, which generally go back into the nineteenth century. The books were issued annually, so you've quite a job ahead of you!

• To track down the former owners of your home, you might consider engaging a professional title search company, which, for a reasonable fee, can usually present you with a complete chain of title.

• This is a long shot, but as the saying goes, it can't hurt. Drop in at local stores that sell old prints and postcards of your area, and keep an eye open at regional flea markets for the same bits of history. You may recognize your house or block in a bin of "golden oldies" selling for 25 cents.

If there is no one or no office that can assist you in your search you will have to deduce the history of your home from the structure itself. The house will tell its story quite visibly, but you must be careful to remember that old houses may have been altered frequently over the years, and indeed whole new additions may make the existing structure substantially different from the one that was built there in 1872 or whenever. So each detail must be considered and not the dwelling as a whole. Enlisting the aid of an architectural historian, either on your own or through a state-provided service, can be an enormous help. But you will find the procedure fascinating if you proceed alone, too. Nails and hinges are the best guide to the true age of a house, although here, too, you must be careful, since repairs may have been made with materials older than the house. Windows and moldings are other good indications of when a home was built. No clues are likely to be found from kitchens or porches, which are often later additions.

There are several books on the market that go into the history of old buildings and the materials used in their construction. Some publications that can help you:

What Style Is It: A Guide to American Architecture, a 112-page illustrated book from the National Trust for Historic Preservation. This is a look at building styles in America, in words and photographs, for the last nearly three-hundred years. For a copy, write Preservation Shop, 1600 H St N.W., Washington, D.C. 20006. Price: $6.95 (10 percent discount to members of the National Trust); include $2 for postage and handling. Add tax in California, Massachusetts, New York, and South Carolina. Make checks payable to the National Trust for Historic Preservation.

"Field Guide to Post-Victorian House Styles (1895–1939)," from *The Old-House Journal*, 69A Seventh Ave., Brooklyn, N.Y. 11217. Price: 50 cents.

"How to Date an Old House" also from *The Old House Journal*. Price: 50 cents.

What Does Historic Designation Mean?

Question: I own a very old wood frame house in a small southern city. I'm told it's the oldest house in town. How can I find out if it qualifies for the National Register?

Answer: You can write to your state's historic preservation office or heritage commission or whatever name that office is known by where you live. In fact, each state has a State Historic Preservation Officer (SHPO), and one of that individual's duties is to guide residents through the historic designation process. To learn the name, address, and phone number of that individual in your state, contact the National Register of Historic Places, Heritage Conservation and Recreation Service, Department of the Interior, Washington, D.C. 20243. The telephone number is (202) 343-9536.

In order to qualify for the register, your house will have to be approved by a state review board comprising architects, historians, and probably archaeologists. The house will usually have to be at least fifty years old and have either architectural significance or an association with a historic person or event.

You can also contact municipal officials to try for *local* historic designation, which may be easier to secure.

There are more than 27,000 properties and districts on the National Register of Historic Places, and many more than that have local designation as landmarks or parts of historic districts.

Bear in mind that listing on the National Register does *not* guarantee the protection of your property. It can only provide incentives for your home's preservation and disincentives for its demolition. It *cannot* protect against ultimate demolition. If your home or neighborhood is designated historic by your *municipality,* that will, in fact, have greater impact than federal or state designation. For one thing, with local status you will have less freedom to do what you want with your home and will probably not be able to destroy it. Your local historic district or heritage commission acts like a zoning board. Before any "improvements" can be made that would alter the exterior appearance of your property, and sometimes the inside if it will affect the outward appearance of the house, plans must be approved by the commission. You will probably not be able to secure a building permit until that approval has been received. If the commission does not like your plans, it's usually back to the drawing board until a satisfactory compromise is reached.

If your home is on the National Register, you will not be so tightly regulated, although many houses and neighborhoods come under both federal and state or local designations, so you may still be controlled by tight municipal strictures. In any event, you are certainly free to sell the house whenever you choose and at any price you set. The historic designation does pass on to the next owner, which can aid you in a faster sale or turn away a few buyers. Six of one, half a dozen of the other.

If you have just moved to a historic district, contact your local landmarks' office, or the head of that district, for a copy of the historic district ordinance that applies to the neighborhood. That document will spell out your responsibilities and rights.

If you have just purchased an old home, you should know that historic designation may not show up in the title search. This is still a fairly new phenomenon, with many officials in localities across the country just now getting around to making those appropriate notations on land records. But just try to put up, say, aluminum siding and you'll find out quickly enough that you're tampering with a historic house!

Old-house owners looking to have their elderly jewels officially stamped "historic" should know that the notation can be a burden as well as an enjoyable benefit. It's your home and you can delight in its seal as a historic treasure. But a cloak of responsibility will fall on your shoulders, too, and what seems like a Greek chorus will be continually chanting behind you, "Better not change this" and "Don't even *think* of touching *that.*" Some of the responsibilities you will be taking on will be legally binding ones.

Let's flip the coin. Suppose you *don't* want a historic house but a

Sometimes it's entire neighborhoods, not just one house, that have been restored. Above is a handsome St. Louis community.

local preservation group comes after you to have your home so designated. Your state or local government is interested in preserving the place, too. Can you fight them all? Yes, and probably you can win if you shout long and loud enough at meetings discussing the issue.

Restore, Renovate, Remodel, or Rehabilitate . . . Just What Are You Doing Here?

You'll hear the above terms often, and used interchangeably. Technically, restoring a home means bringing it back to its original appearance, either by removing later work or replacing missing earlier details. Few of us want a true historic piece, however. Central heating *is* nice, and if radiators do not fit in with an authentic eighteenth-century home and decor, well, we'll just try to make them as inconspicuous as possible. We wouldn't care to be without indoor plumbing either, another blow to authenticity.

Renovating a home generally means bringing that structure back to good working condition, with little regard for protecting any particular style. The broad definition of rehabilitation is taking a property and bringing it to livable use, while still preserving those features that are architecturally significant.

Loans For Historic Houses?

Loans for historic homes, better known here as grants-in-aid, come and go as public and private funds dwindle and are replenished. If you think you qualify for help in acquiring, protecting, rehabilitating, restoring, or reconstructing a historic structure or one with the potential for historic designation, contact your State Historic Preservation Officer.

   If you're a city dweller, it would also be smart to check with your local HUD office or Community Development Agency.

You may also come upon the terms conversion, adaptive use, conservation, and preservation. But what everyone will be speaking about, in the main, is taking an old building and making it livable, perhaps retaining some of the original features of that structure, perhaps not.

   What will you do with *your* home? If you have historic designation for the house, you may be restrained by those do's and don'ts. If you simply have an old house, you are freer to do what you want with the property.

   Many buyers look for old houses because they like the details of those dwellings and are loath to begin ripping out and substituting. They prefer to restore. Others find little of architectural importance in the old home they buy and so feel free to sweep out the interior, as it were, and begin rebuilding in just the style they want, giving the inside an almost loftlike, spare look.

   There's a fine line to be walked here, between preserving what is irreplaceable in a home and having the interior and decor *you* want. Fortunately, most old-house buyers are not of the automatic "Let's rip it out" school. What follows are some points to ponder as you walk through the house you have just purchased or are thinking of buying. What should stay and what should go? Just how much should you as a lone homeowner be contributing to the country's architectural storehouse?

   The Secretary of the Interior has developed standards for preservation projects, as well as guidelines for applying them to activities that range from acquisition of the property through rehabilitation. These standards are the official criteria by which work on National Register historic properties is evaluated and eligibility for federal tax credits is certified. Those tax credits are, not so incidentally, available only for investment properties, but they will give you at least a ballpark idea of how the old, possibly historic, house should be approached:

1. Every reasonable effort shall be made to provide a compatible use for a property, requiring minimal alteration of the building, structure, or site and its environment, or to use a property for its originally intended purpose.

2. The distinguishing original qualities or character of a building, structure, or site and its environment shall not be destroyed. The removal or alteration of any historic material or distinctive architectural features should be avoided when possible.

3. All buildings, structures, and sites shall be recognized as products of their own time. Alterations that have no historical basis and that seek to create an earlier appearance shall be discouraged.

4. Changes that may have taken place in the course of time are evidence of the history and development of a building, structure, or site and its environment. These changes may have acquired significance in their own right, and this significance shall be recognized and respected.

5. Distinctive stylistic features or examples of skilled craftsmanship that characterize a building, structure, or site shall be treated with sensitivity.

6. Deteriorated architectural features shall be repaired rather than replaced, wherever possible. In the event replacement is necessary, the new material should match the material being replaced in composition, design, color, texture, and other visual qualities. Repair or replacement of missing architectural features should be based on accurate duplications of features, substantiated by historic, physical, or pictorial evidence rather than on conjectural designs or the availability of different architectural elements from other buildings or structures.

7. The surface cleaning of structures shall be undertaken with the gentlest means possible. Sandblasting and other cleaning methods that will damage the historic building materials shall not be undertaken.

8. Every reasonable effort shall be made to protect and preserve archaeological resources affected by, or adjacent to, any project.

9. Contemporary design for alterations and additions to existing properties shall not be discouraged when such alterations and additions do not destroy significant historical, architectural, or cultural material, and such design is compatible with the size, scale,

color, material, and character of the property, neighborhood, or environment.

10. Wherever possible, new additions or alterations to structures shall be done in such a manner that if such additions or alterations were to be removed in the future, the essential form and integrity of the structure would be unimpaired.

To those words we would add:

1. Get acquainted with your house before starting serious restoration or renovation. Most homeowners find they change their minds several times about how they want the kitchen remodeled, where they want that extra bedroom, or whatever. One of the advantages of not being able to afford to do everything at once is that you can alter plans mentally without making serious financial and/or design mistakes by moving too quickly.

2. Learn as much as you can about old houses and their maintenance and repair so that you are practically as knowledgeable as any architect or craftsperson you may engage. In some instances, you'll have to know *more* than those individuals. Read one or more of the books on the market about remodeling old houses. Take a course. Keep in close touch with neighbors in your same old-house boat.

3. If you're househunting, be sure your love for old houses does not lead you to buy a withering but charming wreck of an old building far beyond your financial capabilities for perking up. Mortgage payments, real estate taxes, fuel bills, plus a hefty home improvement or rehab loan may be far too much debt for you to handle. Better look for a home that's old, but in need of a smaller infusion of funds.

4. Finally, of course, before you pick up even a phillips screwdriver, be sure you know if your house has any historic designation—municipal, state, or federal. That can well affect how much, or how little, hacking away you will be able to do.

Finding Craftspeople and Products for the Old House

Who's going to repair those sagging floors? Can that stained-glass window be fixed? What about the crumbling front porch? Where can one purchase missing hardware?

Whether you are looking for a contractor to handle a gut rehabilitation or are considering a relatively small job such as reconstructing a chimney or repairing a gargoyle, you are likely to be luckier in finding the proper artisan now than you would have been even twenty years ago. If you live in or near a city of some size, or if you are in a historic district, you'll find craftspeople even easier to locate. Some of this gain in the field can be attributed to renewed interest in old crafts dating back to the late 1960s when the nation's back-to-the-city move got underway. Federal tax benefits for renovating historic buildings, granted since 1981, have also been an incentive for the continually growing interest in preservation.

But let's say you're new to your house and/or to your town, or you live miles from any other old house and so are unable to join any old-house network for the exchange of information. Here's where you can turn for assistance:

• If you are a member of the National Trust or of the Victorian Society in America or if you subscribe to *The Old-House Journal* or *The Brownstoner*, you can call those organizations. They'll be happy to steer you to craftspeople in your area.

• Your state, or local, historical society may be able to help, too.

• The American Institute of Architects in Washington, D.C., (202) 667-1798, will provide you with the names of member architects who do remodeling and renovation with an eye on preservation.

• The American Society of Home Inspectors offers a rehabilitation engineering consultation service for old-house owners. The telephone number is (202) 842-3096.

• If there is a historic district near you, or a neighborhood that has seen a revival of interest in buying and fixing up old houses, you might contact their civic association, or even one of the homeowners directly. They are likely to have quite a list of names and addresses of artisans they are using—and they'll also tell you freely which ones to avoid.

• The classified section of your city or state magazine frequently runs advertisements by craftspeople. Be sure to check references.

To repeat a point mentioned several times in this chapter, be sure you and that worker know exactly what is to be done before any irreversible attacks are made on your home. You should not be thinking only of remodeling or preservation here, but also of the market value of your home. A dropped ceiling, for example, no matter how much you pay for it, is not likely to get the reaction from buyers that the house's original 11-foot-high ceiling with handsome plaster medallion would. You'd be wiser to keep the older ceiling, repairing the plasterwork if necessary.

Keep a particularly careful eye on the contractor not familiar with restoration (this is assuming you have not been able to locate one knowledgeable in that area). Many of those individuals will tell you quickly, "That can't be saved," or "They don't make parts for them anymore," because they simply do not know how to tackle the job. Here's where some knowledge on your part may help save that geriatric bathroom or side porch.

Some contractors will not offer a firm bid on old houses because they do not know what they will find once they begin work, and so do not want to lock themselves into a set fee, one that may well be too low, they feel, for the completed job. They prefer to work on a time plus materials basis. This is fine if you have obtained several bids for the job and at least have a ballpark idea of what it is likely to cost. In dealing with old houses, you can usually expect to wind up paying something like 30 percent more than you anticipated. They may have been simple homes then, but they sure aren't now!

Two Mail-Order sources of products for old houses, from massive doors to the smallest lamp finials, are:

The Old-House Journal Catalog of Sources. Price: $11.95 ($9.95 with a subscription to the journal). If not available at your bookstore, write *The Old-House Journal*, 69A Seventh Ave., Brooklyn, N.Y. 11217.

"The Renovator's Supply, Inc." Send $2 for a catalog of all sorts of hard-to-find items for your home. The address is 2612 Northfield Rd., Millers Falls, Mass. 01349. The telephone number is (413) 659-2211.

Financial Benefits of Owning a Historic Home

If your home is listed on the National Register of Historic Places; or if you live in a certified historic district; or if your home has a local historic designation . . . then you may be eligible for a tax deduction or other financial benefits, such as:

Donating an Easement
Donating an easement works like this: You can have a recorded agreement with a qualified nonprofit organization whereby perpetual controls are placed on your property by you to assure the future of the structure. In effect, you will leave the structure just as it is and will maintain it. You forfeit the right to change the property once that preservation easement is granted. For example, you will

not build a greenhouse alongside the house, or put up aluminum siding. You will agree, perhaps, to keep the house residential even though it's situated in a commercial district.

The tax benefits that accrue to owners who donate such easements are complex and varied (and indeed you had better check to be sure they are still in existence as you read this). You can qualify for a reduced assessment on your property, translating into lower real estate taxes. There can also be gift, estate, and income tax breaks. One homeowner agreed to restore the exterior of his house to its original appearance within five years, and then preserve that authentic look. In return, he was able to take a charitable deduction of $20,000 on his federal income tax by donating an easement to the local historical society.

Why the breaks? There is an assumption here that by keeping the house "pure," you are lowering its value, and that's why you are reimbursed by the Internal Revenue Service. Also, easements pass on to the next buyer, which could mean your house will take longer to sell.

But there's plenty to think about before clapping your hands with delight at tax savings.

First, there is the fact that the IRS is beginning to clamp down on easements. "We had been finding some abuses," said an IRS district director. Second, it costs money to save money. You will probably have to have the structure appraised, and there are other charges for the paperwork to process the donation. You can spend $500 or more on all of this preparation.

And you had also better be certain your municipality will honor an easement that is to bring you lower property taxes. One couple in a scenic community was surprised when they gave local groups a facade and conservation easement on their five buildings and several hundred acres of land, and their town refused to consider a reassessment and subsequent reduction in taxes. Town officials said they were unwilling to set a tax-reducing precedent since this was a scenic community and *everyone* could follow that couple's example. Results of litigation following such town decisions have so far been mixed.

There are all sorts of easements, not only ones applying to historic houses. There are ecological and open-land easements, for example. If you would like to know more about those grants and benefits, you can contact the Land Trust Exchange in Maine at (207) 288-9751. They will tell you about nonprofit groups that are accepting conservation easements in your area.

You might also want to contact your local IRS office for a copy of *Sales and Other Disposition of Assets*, Publication #544, which goes into easements.

Tax Credits

The Economic Recovery Tax Act of 1981 provided a significant tax incentive for renovators in allowing, among other provisions, a 15 percent to 25 percent tax credit for the rehabilitation of historic income-producing properties—commercial, industrial, or residential. The credit is deducted from the amount of taxes owed. You won't qualify for this if you have a single-family residence, but if your home has an income-producing apartment unit or two within it, then rehabbing *that part of the house* qualifies for the credit. The rehabilitation must be a substantial one, however. You can't, let's say, just want to remodel a kitchen, or put in another bath. We're pretty much talking gut rehab here.

More information about these narrowly defined benefits can be obtained from your regional office of the National Trust, or your State Historic Preservation Officer.

The Gift of Your Home

If you have a historic house, you might consider the National Trust's Gifts of Heritage program. To be sure your home is maintained in perpetuity, you can donate the property to the National Trust, with the understanding that the Trust will sell it to a qualified buyer. The buyer agrees to a set of protective covenants guaranteeing the preservation of the property. The proceeds of the sale go to the National Trust, supporting their various programs. You as the donor receive a tax deduction based on the appraised value of the property at the time of the donation. You are permitted to remain in the house for your lifetime or, if you prefer, you can turn over title and move out at once. Your regional office of the National Trust has more information about the program.

For More Information

"Organizing for Historic Preservation: A Resource Guide." Instructions on how to form a local preservation group. The illustrated 48-page guide is available for $8 from the Connecticut Trust for Historic Preservation, 152 Temple St., New Haven, Conn. 06510.

Respectful Rehabilitation: Answers to Your Questions About Old Buildings, 192 pages, with illustrations, answering 150 questions about repairs from roofs to basements. Available for $9.95 from Preservation Press (of the National Trust for Historic Preservation), 1785 Massachusetts Ave. N.W., Washington, D.C. 20036. Add $2.50 for postage and handling. Add tax in California, Massachusetts, New York, and South Carolina. Make checks payable to the National Trust.

Renovation: A Complete Guide, by Michael W. Litchfield, John Wiley & Sons, New York. Illustrated. Price: $34.95, cloth. The author, a professional house renovator, offers case studies, charts, tables, and dozens of tips on the rehabilitation of existing structures, rather than just the remodeling of old to new. A valuable how-to for any renovator's library.

36

Buying Real Estate Abroad

Ah, the sun, Ah, the surf. Ah, the snow, the favorable rate of exchange, the friendliness of the people, the foreignness of the place, the sense of truly getting away from it all, the excellent bargain shopping, the opportunity to learn a new language.

Ah, yes. Buying a home abroad does have its appeal, as Americans continuing to purchase homes overseas attest. According to the U.S. State Department, there are now some 1.8 million of us residing abroad, a figure that does not include the military, and also excludes Mexico and Canada.

Who are living overseas?

• Retirees, who choose to move to a foreign country after reaching the magic "sixty-five," either to live in resort communities or in the hometowns where they were born or have relatives.

• Corporate transferees, quite happy to buy homes abroad during their tenure in foreign countries.

• Students and others living in the country of their choice for a short time and not connected with the corporate relocation picture.

• Americans who have purchased vacation homes abroad and spend anywhere from a few weeks to a few months in those houses and condominiums (or houseboats or castles or farms). In this category, too, are those who have purchased time-share units in the hundreds of resorts around the world operating under that concept.

The prices of these small chunks of paradise, as a home abroad is sometimes seen, range from under $10,000 for a time-share apartment or room, to as low as $25,000 for a house (perhaps less for the intrepid househunter) to a high of . . . well, there is no ceiling to the price scale, just as there is none with homes in this country. Got $3 million or so? Surely there'll be something to buy "over there."

Although you can no doubt find an American living just about anywhere under the sun, there are a few countries that attract the largest number of us. First in popularity is West Germany, with just over 300,000 Americans (a figure that does include the military and government personnel). Next comes the United Kingdom with 136,376 American residents; Italy, 110,039; the Philippines, 83,627; Israel, 62,459; and Japan, 62,348.

Besides the attractive surroundings, or being near the rest of one's family, there are other attractions to living in another corner of the world, either part or all of the time:

• A favorable rate of exchange makes some countries quite inexpensive, which is especially appealing to retirees.

• Your property may appreciate in value faster than anything you might have purchased in America.

• The tax benefits can be excellent, too. In 1984, for example, the first $85,000 earned by an American worker wasn't taxable. In 1986 that figure will rise to $95,000. Most countries don't tax residents if they do not live there for more than six months a year. Travel expenses between your property and your home in the United States may be deductible. If your home abroad is your principal residence, and you fulfill the other requirements (age and length of residence in the house), you will not have to pay capital gains tax on the first $125,000 of profit on your property when you sell, the same benefit you are entitled to in this country. For detailed information about your responsibilities to the American government when you buy a home abroad, you can contact your local IRS office for a copy of Publication #54, *Tax Guide for U.S. Citizens Abroad*.

• In most countries there is either no real estate tax or just a nominal charge. In any event, in doing your calculating about an overseas purchase, there is no need to be concerned with this aspect of the sale, one so important in this country where it is not unusual to have a monthly property tax payment higher than the mortgage payment.

• In the main, Americans are welcome abroad, which contributes to the appeal of the home and country selected. By being American they are set apart from the social or caste systems of that country and can be courted because of their differences.

• A home overseas broadens your investment portfolio.

• A vacation property bought today may eventually turn into an excellent retirement home.

• There's the potential rental income from the house or condo when you are not in residence. And as a landlord you are, of course, entitled to such tax benefits as depreciation, maintenance costs, a certain amount of travel to check on your property, etc.

Drawbacks to all of these? A few, of course, and it's up to you to weigh the few clouds against all that sunshine:

• For one thing, you may not be able to purchase a home in the city or country you have in mind. Policies for foreign investment differ, sometimes radically, from one country to another. Sometimes the policies are the same for all, natives and foreigners; in other instances it is only the outsiders who are subject to restrictions. It is very difficult, for instance, for Americans to buy property in the French West Indies. If you have an eye on a townhouse or *pied-à-terre* in one of the more fashionable London neighborhoods, you will probably have to buy your home with a long-term, 99-year lease. Land in choice Belgravia and other West End sections of that city is owned by the Duke of Westminster and his family. You rent from him, although the rental in this case does become a form of ownership.

• Will you be able to rough it, if need be? Americans are used to living with appliances and services that, in the main, work. Water pours from the tap, the telephone gets your message across, food is easily available. How much adapting are you willing to do where you're heading?

• The cost of travel to your home overseas is going to be more than a couple of tankfuls of gas. Will that make a vacation home impractical? If you are moving abroad to live there full-time, will you still need—or want—to return to America periodically? Toting up those air fares will give you some idea of the cost of "commuting."

• The cost of living in the foreign country may well be higher than in the United States. Inflation may be rampant. You may not profit from your investment, or indeed even get your money back, because of currency fluctuations. What would devaluation do to your chunk of real estate?

• The country's political situation may be tense, changeable, eventually perhaps disastrous. What if overnight it becomes unfriendly to all foreigners living there? What if there is a war, a coup? Aside from your life, what would happen to your property? What is the resale value of an American-owned home (or any other for that matter) in a strife-torn country? Great news for buyers who can pick up a chic little condo or even an imposing mini-estate for a song. But what about poor you, the seller?

• You may become terminally homesick—after you've made your major real estate purchase.

• If it's a vacation home you've bought, you may become tired of feeling you must head for that country every holiday.

• Also if it's a second-home investment, who will keep an eye on the place when you're back in America?

As mentioned above, buying property abroad is so different from one country to another it is impossible here to take you by the hand and guide you through a realty purchase in France or Bermuda or wherever you want to take up residence. However, there are a few points that apply across the board when we talk about foreign property:

1. Generally, you will have to do your shopping for a home in that country. Real estate agents here can't help you aside from the few who deal in overseas properties (some names and addresses are listed at the end of this chapter). You may also find a time-share developer here selling properties abroad, but remember one of the cardinal rules of real estate: Don't buy anything you have not seen. Don't buy from a color glossy, don't buy from a fancy brochure or from a movie or because your neighbors raved about the town after they vacationed there last year. That goes for a $20,000 cabin or a $200,000 castle (especially, ironically, the castle, which may be in worse shape than the bargain-basement cabin).

So, in the main, you can expect to be dealing with sales agents in the country of your choice, with virtually no assistance from realty personnel here.

2. Generally, sellers pay real estate agents' commission, but check to be sure that that is the case in the country that interests you. Commissions, incidentally, are likely to run 10–25 percent, versus the 6–10 percent you find here.

3. Generally, closing costs will be higher than what you will have paid in the United States. They run about 15 percent of sale price, compared to the 3 percent to 5 percent charged here. Foreign countries often include, or add in extra, a "transfer tax" or "stamp tax" or whatever name the levy goes by in that country. Check to see who pays what.

4. Generally, as mentioned earlier, you will not have to concern yourself with a property tax charge.

5. Generally, you will have to do a little digging for financing your foreign home. Banks in this country will not offer mortgages for

And Foreigners Continue To Buy Here

Real estate investment by foreign individuals and corporations continues to expand in both the residential and commercial markets. This country offers many benefits to the overseas investor:

A stable political climate.

A plentiful supply of properties, frequently at lower sales prices than what the buyer would have paid in other nations.

A solid real estate ownership picture that always survives periodic downspins.

The availability of mortgage money, at terms frequently more attractive than overseas. Seller financing, for example, is rare abroad.

The liquidity of real estate transactions here. Yes, real estate is not the most liquid of investments, but Americans *can* transfer property more easily than residents of many other countries.

The expectation that real property here will, in all likelihood, appreciate in value.

Good property management here, which is not always the case abroad. This is particularly important for the foreigner who chooses to live here only a few weeks or months each year.

foreign countries, so you will do your mortgage shopping in the country you have chosen. (You can, however, apply to branch offices of American banks in that country. If you are already a customer, you may be able to secure a mortgage rather effortlessly, although, of course, on that country's terms.) Otherwise, finding a loan will depend, as it does here, on the economic climate at the moment, how steep mortgage rates are, and your own qualifications for borrowing. Buying with foreign, not U.S., dollars is preferable. You should know, too, that seller financing, now so prevalent here, is virtually unknown overseas.

And a final, important point: Most banks will finance only 50 percent of the sale price.

Who Can Help You Buy?

So there you are, all alone over there looking for a home. Where can you turn for assistance? Your first, smartest bet would be to check with local real estate agents to see if Americans (or any foreigners) *can* buy property in that country. Are there restrictions to the purchase? Perhaps, to take one example, you want to buy a home in Greece. Did you know that the law there prohibits you from taking any proceeds from the sale out of the country? (Buyers get around this by arranging to sell to another foreigner somewhere else.) Is financing available? Dropping into a few banks may put a lid on your plan to buy. Interest rates may be 18½ percent. And don't forget the 50-percent downpayment you will probably need.

Once you know you *can* buy, you can start looking around. Check the classified advertisements in the *International Herald Tribune*, published daily in Paris, and read the local papers, if you understand the language. Again, keep in touch with real estate agents, and look as well at new construction projects to see what kind of purchase deal developers there are offering. In some countries—most nations in the Caribbean, for example—most of the buying is done by foreigners, since practically none of the natives can afford the properties being offered. So these sales offices will be particularly attuned to outside investors.

Talking about your interest in buying to those involved in selling and financing property in that country will also give you a good handle on how residents see foreigners, Americans in particular. If you're received coolly by those whose business it is to sell you something, multiply that dour attitude by thousands or millions and you get an idea of your probable reception once you move into that country.

Many nations, whether for economic reasons or because of the popularity of American buyers there, or perhaps a combination of the two, go out of their way to welcome tourists or prospective househunters from the United States. Israel, for example, offers many benefits to foreign homebuyers, one of which is a reduction in sale price of up to 30 percent. There are special loan programs available. If you're unhappy with your home, or with life in that country, you are not required to give back any of the government allowances that were made when you purchased. There is no property tax. You can take the proceeds of any home sale with you when you leave the country.

But here, as with all foreign sales, you must weigh heavily the attractions against the potential or real negatives of buying. As a permanent resident of Israel you will be required to take out citizenship after a few years of living there. Inflation is running very high at this writing and, of course, there is the always-tense political situation. Still, the number of Americans and other foreigners moving to that country continues to grow, and so do residential complexes in the section of the country along the Mediterranean Sea from Tel Aviv north to Haifa, where most foreign buying is concentrated.

You can check in with the American Chamber of Commerce in the country of your choice. They can answer questions from the quality of life there to job opportunities—or lack of them. And, remember, American embassy and consulate offices are there if you run into problems with a real estate transaction.

We have found that most foreign embassies, consulates, and government tourist or information offices in America can offer no detailed assistance on buying real estate in their country. But, still, it might be worth a phone call to the one nearest you. You could be lucky! What these offices *can* help you with is settling in once you have bought abroad. Need street maps, tourist data, health information, the lowdown on schools? Ask and you will no doubt be supplied with plenty of answers and reams of printed material. For example, the British Information Service, 845 Third Ave., New York, N.Y. 10022, offers a free booklet, "Residence in Britain," which describes schooling, housing (but not how to buy), and other aspects of life in Britain directed at the newcomer. That's in addition to books and pamphlets of general interest to anyone coming into the country.

Tourist and information offices can also provide you with the names and addresses of real estate agents in their countries who can help you with your search for a home. Many will deal with rentals as well as sales.

Talk to as many Americans as you can, of course, in any country you are considering, preferably some folks who have bought property there. They will tell you what no broker is going to reveal.

Doing all this homework will make you knowledgeable about real estate transactions. But there's one step between toying with the idea of buying and actually signing on the dotted line that will be of more benefit yet.

Testing the Waters, So to Speak

You just know it's going to be wonderful because, after all, you've spent the last six years vacationing there. Or you've been visiting relatives in that particular town since you were 13 years old. Naturally, buying a home there makes sense.

But "visiting" is quite different from "residing." No matter how well you know a locale, if you're a guest in that country—whether staying at a hotel or with relatives or friends—you don't know the country the way an insider does. For example:

• Have you ever shopped for food? Are there shortages of some items? Do you have to queue for hours to buy meat, or bread, or some other product frequently scarce?

• Do you know what to do if your house or condo needs a plumber? Who to call? How to tell if you're being overcharged?

• What about your car, if you have one? Is there a garage for it? What about fuel prices?

• What's the water like? Drinkable?

• Is mail delivery reliable?

• Does the telephone system break down occasionally, or often?

• If you will want household help, is it available?

The answer to these and other questions is to get out of your hotel room or out of Aunt Harriet's chalet and try coping yourself for a while in a house or condo. Whose? How? There are any number of foreign properties for rent or exchange. Perhaps you can even rent a condominium unit for a while in the complex where you think you'd like to buy. Overseas real estate people can help you with short- or long-term rentals. But here are two American companies and one British firm that can find you places, too.

Caribbean Home Rentals, Box 710, Palm Beach, Fla. 33480, (305) 833-4454. This agency has approximately one-thousand listings on thirty-six islands. Prices range from a low of $200 or so a week to a high of $5000 plus for a week in the poshest home in high season. Among the properties this office handles is Princess Margaret's villa on the island of Mustique. Interested?

At Home Abroad, 405 E. 56 St., 6-H, New York, N.Y. 10022, (212) 421-9165. This long-established agency offers many tempting spots for rent around the world. Expect to pay around $1500 for one month. Short- and long-term rentals available.

Villas International Ltd., 213 E. 38 St., New York, N.Y. 10016, (212) 685-4340 or (800) 221-2260. Rental properties throughout Europe, from cottages to castles.

If you think renting may be too steep for your Italian leather pocketbook, try swapping. This is an increasingly popular vacation style, very simple in design.

For a fee of anywhere from $20 to $60 (in rare situations substantially higher) you can list your home in a directory that a house exchange organization publishes once or twice a year. You contact the people in the directory whose homes interest you, and they, in turn, will be writing to you. Members of the swap organizations make their own trades; the organization merely prints the directory.

There are house trades available in almost every corner of the globe, now that the concept has grown so in popularity since its inception in the early 1960s. If you're flexible about the dates of your stay abroad, and are willing to settle for a home in the country of your interest, although not necessarily the town or city you want, you can make an excellent deal for yourself. Your only costs would be airfare to your destination and then ordinary living expenses—food, some sightseeing, etc. All types of residences qualify, from studio apartments to mansions, so don't be shy about trying to swap your 3½-room walkup. Interestingly, many, many Europeans prefer staying in American homes to staying in hotels while they are traveling here. And they will pick a spot they consider a base, making day or overnight trips around an area from there. So you don't have to be in prime tourist country to make a successful swap. Just so you're within driving distance of some tourist attractions. And who isn't?

Swappers frequently trade cars, too, and take on plant and pet care. Usually each homeowner exchanges pictures of the home and family, and makes a few phone calls before the visit, too.

Here are some exchange organizations that can help you make the trade that will give you a *real* idea of what living in Malaga, Montego Bay, or Milan is like:

The Great Exchange, P.O. Box 12028, Glendale, Calif. 91214, (213) 957-0101. Operates in cooperation with Pan American World

Airways. For vacations in New York, London, Los Angeles, San Francisco, and Florida.

Hideaways, P.O. Box 1459, Concord, Mass. 07142, (800) 843-4433.

Holiday Exchanges, P.O. Box 878, Belen, N.M. 87002, (505) 864-8680.

Home Exchange International, 130 W. 72nd St., New York, N.Y. 10023, (212) 864-0639.

InterService Home Exchange, P.O. Box 87, Glen Echo, Md. 20812, (301) 299-4772.

Loan-a-Home, 2 Park Lane, 6E, Mount Vernon, N.Y. 10552. Mail inquiries only. Concentrates on academics on long-term sabbaticals, business executives, and others seeking more than just short vacation swaps. Some rentals available.

Vacation Exchange Club, 12006 111th Ave., Unit 12, Youngstown, Ariz. 88363, (602) 972-2186. The oldest of the home swap organizations carries some 6000 listings in forty-two foreign countries, besides American homes for trade. Some rentals available.

For More Information

"Background Notes on the Countries of the World." Pick the country that interests you. Each of these government-published booklets contains information about that land, its people, political situation, economy, and policy toward the United States. There's also a map, reading list, and the like. Single copies are 70 cents. Available from the Superintendent of Documents, U.S. Government Printing Office, Washington, D.C. 20402.

Travel and Retirement Edens Abroad, by Peter A. Dickinson, Dutton. $12.95, paperback.

Some real estate agents in this country that can help with foreign purchases:

Begg International, 1714 Connecticut Ave. N.W., Washington, D.C. 20009, (202) 338-9065.

Period Houses, 1317 Wisconsin Ave. N.W., Washington, D.C. 20007, (202) 333-6011. Handles the sale of houses in Western Europe dating from the mid-nineteenth century sometimes as far back as the fifteenth century.

Previews, Inc., Greenwich Office Park, Greenwich, Conn. 06830, (203) 622-8600. Luxurious homes here and overseas.

Private Islands Unlimited, (213) 360-8683. Lists islands in any part of the world. A copy of that list is available for $15 by writing PIU at 17538 Tulsa St., Granada Hills, Calif. 91344. For another $10, you will receive pictures and a complete description of any of the listed properties.

37

Joint Ownership—Buying and Selling a Home with a Spouse, Relative, Roommate...

A husband and wife purchase a home together.

Two sisters join forces and buy a condominium.

A couple "living together" decides to buy their apartment in a cooperative conversion.

Three co-workers split the cost, and share ownership, of a vacation home.

Married couples usually purchase a home as "partners," but high housing prices and frequently stratospheric mortgage interest rates have seen more and more relatives, friends, and strangers buying homes together, too. That dwelling can be a two- or three-family house, already made for separate living, or a large older house that can be divided or not. Or the house can be a jointly owned vacation property. Buying a home in this manner makes perfect sense, today's joint buyers reason. After all:

• Those who buy a home with someone else may not have been able to afford one on their own.

• The house and neighborhood chosen together may be far nicer than anything one could have purchased alone.

• A very large house may be far too much room for a single buyer, but still afford privacy and space for several co-owners.

• There is companionship and even security in knowing there are others in the house, even though they may be in separate living units.

Q.: Who's The Best Mortgage Risk?

A.: Single people buying a home together.

Investors Mortgage Insurance Co. of Boston reported in a 1984 study of the more than 400,000 mortgages it insures, that single folks—what the company calls "mingles"—are a lender's best mortgage risk. They beat out the traditional family (husband working, wife at home), who are twice as likely to have mortgage payment problems as two singles. A slightly better gamble is the two-income family, but even they come in second to the singles. Added the president of the company: "When one of the single buyers leaves town, he or she already has an agreement for the other to buy out his or her equity."

• Vacation homes in particular can make good joint purchases. Many would-be buyers feel they have neither the money for a full-time home, nor the inclination to spend all that much time in the resort area.

Since service is their business, builders are, quite understandably, eager to pick up on any trend. The recession of the early 80s kept them from responding in any great measure to the need for *new* homes that can be easily divided, or already come split into separate living areas, but there have been some advances.

What some developers have come up with is a house that allows the owners to share quarters without sharing styles of living. To do this, each home has two (or sometimes three) master bedrooms, each with its own full bath. To ensure further privacy, the master bedrooms do not share any walls. The owners have communal use of a kitchen, living room, and perhaps a dining room, and these, too, are larger than normal size to lessen the chance that presumably different modes of living will collide. There may be separate or communal patios, too, and two- or three-car garages. The houses, which can be detached or part of townhouse developments, are variously known as "tandem ownership homes," or "mingles housing," or "cohabitational units." They are specifically designed for joint buyers who got together and decided owning part of a house was better than no ownership at all.

This could be quite a trend we have here. In fact, the Worldwatch Institute, a research group based in Washington, D.C., speculated in a report on housing trends that such mingles homes could bring

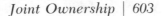

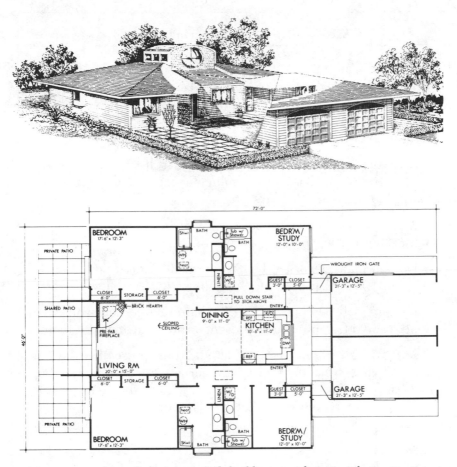

A growing number of designers and builders are directing their attention to "mingles" houses, which feature separate bedroom/bath wings for each co-owner, and community living/dining/kitchen areas. This house, designed by Home Building Plan Service, Inc., in Portland, Oregon, also offers separate and shared patio space, and a garage for each of the joint owners. *Reprinted with permission of Designed by Home Building Plan Service, Portland, Oregon.*

the American family closer together by making it feasible for two or three generations to more easily and comfortably share the same living quarters.

You can find mingles housing in California, Florida, New Jersey, Texas, Colorado, Louisiana, Virginia, and Arizona, with more units opening all the time. There may be one in your area now. To check, you might call your state's homebuilders' association, usually but not always located in the state capital.

Naturally, homes of this size are going to be expensive, but then

Are You The House Sharing "Type"?

So you're all going to band together and purchase a home—either a principal residence or a weekend getaway. Sounds good, in theory. But are you the sort that should enter into a shared-housing situation? There's more involved here than the splitting of a mortgage payment.

Are you reasonably independent and self-sufficient, or are you, perhaps subconsciously, going to depend on your fellow sharers to take care of you?

Are you the sort who needs a lot of time and space alone, more than just having your own room will provide?

Do you plan to work at home, either full-time or only in the evenings? Will that present problems with your fellow sharers?

If there will be children in the shared space, and you have none, can you adapt to their presence and get along with them?

Are you overly concerned about your possessions? In a shared-living situation there is a certain casual attitude that may jar you. It might drive your housemates bonkers, for instance, if you're the type that labels your own yogurt in the fridge, won't let anyone sit in your chair on the porch, etc.

Are you taking this step because you're desperate, either for any living space or for an affordable home (or both)?

Do you actually dislike one or more sharers? Are you joining forces with a family member you never got along with? Watch out. Disaster looms.

Are you and your fellow sharers in more or less the same financial boat? Too much of a disparity in incomes can result not only in one party feeling like poor-Bertha-the-shop-girl, but also in arguments over decorating and improvements.

Are you all straightened out about comings and goings? Do you know that Alex travels a lot and so won't be around if you're looking for companionship and security? Is everyone agreed about overnight entertaining? If it's a vacation home, is there a clear schedule for everyone's visits, including guests' stays?

Are you so concerned with shared responsibilities for the house that you will count how many times you raked the leaves and that Cal changed the hallway lightbulb twice running? Certainly too much work dumped on one sharer is unfair, and a just balance should be struck when it comes to routine maintenance and odd jobs. But if you're going to nickel and dime everyone about the small stuff, you'd better turn down the shared-housing opportunity.

What about the moral values of your fellow sharers? Ethics, believe it or not, has ruined more than one shared-house situation: the Good Guy who wants to pay his just taxes, charge fair rents, not discriminate in renting, etc. living with the Moral Swine, only too eager to cheat city hall, the neighbors, and anyone else if the moment is opportune.

---

again your share of a $180,000 house may be $90,000, or perhaps even $60,000.

Getting down to the specifics of two or more persons purchasing a home together, you will find there are two basic styles of buying real estate under that umbrella: "joint tenancy" and "tenancy in common." (Of course, you and someone else can purchase a home in just one of your names. If you do that there are still points in this chapter you will find of interest and applicable to your situation.)

Joint Tenancy with Right of Survivorship

The distinguishing feature of this buying style is the phrase "right of survivorship." This is how most married couples purchase their homes, but you don't have to be married to buy as joint tenants.

This style of ownership means that both own the property equally, and in the event of the death of one party the survivor becomes the outright owner of the home, without going through probate procedures. This is sometimes explained as the other party "inheriting" the property, but since both own the home equally during their lives, it cannot be passed on in an estate. The survivor simply becomes the outright owner. A joint tenant *cannot* will his or her share of the house to anyone.

Joint tenancy is sometimes called "the poor man's will," since to many couples the fact that property automatically reverts to the surviving spouse seems to negate the need for a formal will. Foolish thinking. In fact, joint tenancy itself should come in for close examination, especially by married couples. That consideration may lead to giving thought to estate planning in general, with more decisions made about property.

If you do have a will, be sure the lawyer knows that you own property jointly with someone else, so that the will does not contradict the disposition of the jointly owned property.

There are benefits to jointly owned property, either by husband and wife or any other co-owners:

• It seems only fitting that married couples should share ownership of real property.

• Jointly owned property avoids time-consuming probate after the death of one of the owners.

• When a co-owner dies and his or her share of the property disappears, usually the home is protected against claims by that individual's creditors.

But there are drawbacks:

• As mentioned above, joint tenancy with right of survivorship is often a substitute for a will, which can cause confusion and a range of other emotions to the deceased's relatives.

• Disposition of the property cannot be controlled by the co-owners. It must revert to the surviving co-owner(s).

• If one of the co-owners wants to sell, the joint tenancy may terminate.

• There aren't many of us with estates large enough to worry about federal/state estate taxes after death, but if you are one of those individuals, what about joint ownership then? Jointly owned property does *not* escape taxes the way it does probate.

Naturally you should check with your lawyer and/or accountant for the many intricacies involved in any joint property purchase. And don't forget the drawing up of a will to clarify your position and wishes.

Tenancy in Common

The next most popular ownership style is this one, where all owners have a partial interest in the property, usually an equal one but not always. (Perhaps one co-owner put up the entire downpayment, for instance, and the others have agreed his share in the property should be larger. This is spelled out in a separate contract.)

On the death of one of these co-tenants, the survivor(s) do not own the entire property, unless the deceased so specified in his or her will. Tenants in common can leave their share of the property to whomever they choose. If they die with no will, that share, and their other assets, will usually be distributed according to that state's intestate succession statutes.

This is a simple joint ownership style and well suited for those buying vacation homes together, or for two or three men or women getting together to purchase a house or condominium. Couples "living together" sometimes opt for joint tenancy, sometimes tenancy in common. Forming a business partnership holds no special tax benefits in buying together.

Naturally, if you are in one of these positions you will see a lawyer to have a contract drawn up spelling out the specifics of your joint ownership relationship. You may never look at that document again, but it's a wise move to have any point of possible conflict right there in black and white. Some points to be brought up and clarified:

1. How is the downpayment to be made? In equal parts, or is one of you going to put up more than the other(s)? How will that affect that person's share?

2. Are monthly mortgage payments to be divided equally, or will one or more of you chip in more?

3. Are there any other unusual aspects to the purchase and running of the house? For instance, if Larry is going to do all the rehabilitation work, he may be exempt from mortgage payments for "x" number of years. If you agree to rent the vacation home during certain months, you may want that put into a contract to be sure the commitment is firm.

4. What happens if one of you wants to sell? Is the remaining owner(s) given first crack at purchasing that individual's share? Does he or she have the right to approve the new buyer? What if a partner files for bankruptcy? If you can, try to avoid renegotiating the mortgage when one of you sells. The "due on sale" clause may become operative. Renegotiating a new mortgage could mean a higher interest rate.

5. You may want other protection in the contract, too, such as what happens if one of you is late with your share of the mortgage payment, or just plain skips off.

6. A contract can also go into maintenance of the common areas of the property, how major purchases (a new roof, new hot water heater, etc.) will be handled, and the like.

As you can see from this listing, there are many sources of potential conflict when two or more persons get together to buy a home.

Zoning Laws and House Sharing

If you plan to buy a large house with Fred and Neal and convert it to apartments, be sure you check first with that community's buildings department and/or zoning board to be sure you can make the conversion legally. You may be house-hunting in an area zoned exclusively for one-family dwellings. You can apply for a variance, but in this instance you are not likely to be granted one.

Besides being a place to hang your chapeau, it is also an investment, a wise one, it is hoped. So, to protect your investment, have a formal contract drawn up to safeguard everyone's interests while co-owning that dwelling.

Life Changes

"Living Together" Agreements

No, they do not have to consider who is going to walk the dog and which one of you will keep up the bougainvillea. We're only talking about real estate here, so let's look exclusively at rented and owned property.

Who owns what and who is entitled to leave a relationship with what goodies when it comes to persons of the opposite sex sharing living quarters (also known as POSSLQ couples) seem to have become increasingly important since 1976. That was the year a court decision ordered actor Lee Marvin to pay his long-time ex-live-in lover Michelle Triola a six-figure sum of money, representing her contribution to their arrangement. The term "palimony" then entered the lexicon, and one wonders if any live-in relationship since has been innocent of concern about possessions.

We now frequently have POSSLQ couples drawing up contracts. These can be oral (but witnessed), but the stronger contract is, naturally, the written one.

This is not at all romantic, of course, but still a coldly written document can spare both parties anger, frustration, expense, and a few other emotions in the event of a breakup. If it's in the contract, that's all there is to it. Case closed.

Contracts can cover the mundane (dog walking), but more often they concern themselves with serious financial matters—whether

Bluenoses and Blue Laws

What goes on behind closed doors will be, to some extent, open information when you buy a home jointly in some communities. It would pay to bear this in mind when you go househunting. For example, cohabitation (more commonly known as "living together") is still against the law in some states, although those laws are not that often enforced anymore. However, make a neighbor cranky for some reason and he may well try to get you out. Buy a house with two other individuals, and then move in a few more roommates and you could be violating dusty and almost-forgotten local ordinances against overcrowding. Neighbors annoyed at too many cars around your house taking up their parking spaces may report you to local authorities.

Moral: When you're planning to buy a house in any but the most traditional fashion, it would pay to conjure up the most conservative of residents in that community. How would that bluenose feel about your lifestyle? About your housemates? If you think there could be a problem, talk with your real estate agent, quite honestly. He or she can advise you of the legality of the joint purchase and what, if any, nuisances you may encounter after you take title.

assets acquired during the relationship, for example, will be shared should the union dissolve.

The couple purchasing a home together has the choice of buying as joint tenants with rights of survivorship, or as tenants in common, which provides no such right and allows both parties to leave their share of the property to anyone besides the live-in lover. If you find yourselves in this house, condo, or co-op hunting situation, you can turn back a few pages in this book for an analysis of both forms of ownership to see which would suit you best. Whichever one you take, the deed or stock shares to that form of ownership, plus a will, should be all you need to cover your relationship from the real property angle. A contract is not necessary.

If you are both living in a rental apartment now, what happens in the event of a breakup is pretty murky, and will vary widely from one end of the country to the other. In general, however, the one whose name is on the lease stands the greater chance of getting to keep the place, so if you're the party whose name is not on the lease, you may want to remedy that. Or you may want to keep your own apartment when you move into his or her pad, and sublet it. A contract can also spell out who gets first dibs on the unit if the building should become involved in a condo or co-op conversion process. See how complicated things can get? If it's an apartment that's truly a jewel—in looks, location, or its low-rent or rent-controlled status, you'd better get thee to a lawyer.

The Premarriage Contract

These documents, also known as "antenuptial agreements" or "marriage contracts," filtered down to the common folk only in the last decade or so. Prior to that they had been the province of the very wealthy who had no desire to part with an unnecessary cent of their considerable fortunes. When an "old family" member married into a "blue book" family (but one with money as well as heritage) there was often the necessity to see that the mingling of the two fortunes was handled properly. That seemed only natural and fitting.

Today, thanks to the increasing popularity of palimony suits, the rise in the divorce rate, and a number of other socioeconomic phenomena, keeping separate what's mine and what's yours is providing nice, steady work for lawyers.

All states recognize premarriage contracts, but they differ as to what those documents should include.

Should *you* consider such an agreement? No, if:

• Your assets are minimal.

• The very idea of a contract makes you stiffen your back and the discussion has already caused hurt feelings and arguments. (On the other hand, there are some psychologists who say if the union can't take a little straight talk about finances, it isn't likely to be much of a success.)

You might want to consider a premarriage contract, if:

• There is a family business to be considered.

• This is the second (or third) marriage for one or both of you and you are concerned about the children from a previous union and their entitlements in the event of your death.

• One of you has an income or assets vastly disproportionate from the other. Perhaps one is in line for a substantial inheritance that he or she does not want automatically to pass on to a spouse. Let's say Aunt Tillie is leaving Ellen her old house on Crabapple Hill. Ellen feels the house, the family homestead, should stay in her family and so, rather than seeing it inherited by her husband, she wills it to her brother, Frank.

If you do decide to consult an attorney about a premarriage agreement, remember that like a couple living together you will have to acquaint yourselves with the styles of real estate ownership and decide which is best for you. And don't forget a will, both of you! A sobbing girlfriend can tell a judge from now until Judgment Day that "Robbie always told me he wanted me to have the condo." But if Robbie dies intestate—that is, without a will—and that condo is in his name it will in all likelihood revert to his next of kin—children, parents, brothers, sisters, etc.

Property Rights in a Divorce

Since we are not taking sides here, we cannot offer specific advice, but we can make two suggestions that apply equally to both parties: (1) Get a lawyer, and (2) try not to share the same attorney.

Settlements in divorce cases are becoming more complicated these days, thanks to any number of factors, from recognition of the rights of fathers as custodial parents to the growing number of women working outside the home, which can affect a financial settlement. If the Jones's divorce should ever come to court, the judge is not likely to issue an automatic decision the way he or she might have several decades ago.

We are not, of course, talking about child custody or division of a business partnership here, but rather real estate ownership, which for most couples translates into the house they share, almost always as joint tenants with right of survivorship. Who is going to be awarded this dwelling, which may have been purchased in 1975 for $35,000 and is now worth something like *$135,000*? You and your lawyer, your estranged spouse, and his or her counsel will make that decision, one that will be reached, it is hoped, without undue rancor.

How you come out in a divorce settlement will depend to a great degree on where you live. Perhaps you reside in one of the eight community property states—Arizona, California, Idaho, Louisiana, Nevada, New Mexico, Texas, and Washington. There, property acquired during the marriage is generally considered to be owned fifty-fifty by each spouse, but with no right of survivorship. Each spouse has the right to will his or her share to any heir they choose. Upon divorce, half of the community property and assets goes to each spouse, unless they have a legal agreement to some other arrangement.

Then there is "equitable distribution," which applies in some forty states. The exact wording of the law varies from state to state, but in the main property here is divided according to each spouse's needs and his or her contributions to the marriage, with no special treatment accorded either women or men. For example, an older woman, trying to get back into the job market after many years' absence, might be awarded the house. There are many complicated stories here and Solomon-like decisions to be made. Take Jane and Al, for example. When they married, Al moved into Jane's house, with her name remaining the only one on the deed. Al was a handy fellow, and made many major repairs and improvements to the place, raising its market value substantially. Who gets what at that couple's divorce?

Perhaps you and your about-to-be-ex-spouse are not able to work out any property settlement without anger and bad feelings getting in the way of constructive resolution. If that is the case, you may want a judge to decide the issue, or you can contact the American Arbitration Association for the name of a mediator skilled in this art to work with the two of you. But you'll have to be restrained enough to be able to accept that person's decision as binding.

Broadly speaking, here is how the family home may be divided after a divorce:

• There is what is called the buy-out mortgage, which can also be called a second mortgage. This is available at banks, savings and loan associations, and any other lender where you would go for a primary mortgage. With this loan you hold on to your primary mortgage and use the second one to buy out your former partner. So now the house or condo becomes yours.

• You can sell the house and divide the profits. Some questions arise here, though, and this is where arguments can come in. Should the split be fifty-fifty or are there other elements to be taken into account? Jane and Al's situation, for example. Or what if Barbara put up the entire $15,000 downpayment when she and Jerry bought their home? Should she get more when the proceeds are divvied up? Unless both parties in positions like this are the souls of generosity and kindness, this is what we need lawyers for, and sometimes judges as well.

• Another solution would be that one party, usually the wife who will stay with the children, remains in the house until the kids are grown or until some other agreed-upon time, and then the property is sold and the profits shared. If you opt for this solution, be sure you can carry the expenses for maintaining the property.

For answers to more complex questions, such as those about tax deductions on real estate in a divorce—house, condominium, or cooperative—you can contact your local Internal Revenue Service office for a copy of Publication #504, *Tax Information for Divorced or Separated Individuals*.

This is a continually changing arena. You may recall a unique property settlement made in 1982, when a Michigan judge ruled that the home of a couple divorcing in that state should be awarded to their three sons, ages 15, 14, and 11. The judge ordered that the parents, who had joint custody of the boys, would spend alternate months with them. That didn't prove too difficult since the couple remained in the same town, she living in an apartment, he with his parents. The two would remain tenants in common on the house until the youngest boy reached 18, at which time the parents would sell the house and split the proceeds. Maintenance for the property would be divided between the two. There was apparently no mortgage.

The case gave some indication of how judges are trying to individualize property decisions in a divorce and even break new ground in an attempt to be fair. But this case showed a couple of flaws, and indeed now, several years later, that sort of property division doesn't seem to have caught on to any extent. For one thing, the decision tied the couple to constant contact and probably more squabbling. The ex-husband conceded that the couple couldn't agree on anything in the first place, which was one of the causes of their divorce, he said. Another problem is that it's darned expensive to maintain two homes, which is what each party was required to do. Now, instead of two households following a divorce, you have three. So while the case was certainly an interesting one, and showed the flexibility and willingness of the court, it does not seem to have set a new standard for property division. Back to the drawing board.

Who Gets the Apartment?

This is another instance of an issue being no problem, and given very little consideration, several years ago. But today an attractive apartment in a community with a low vacancy rate, and a *rent-controlled* apartment at that, is worth fighting for.

You could get that jewel of a living space, if:

• You were living there prior to your marriage and you name is on the lease.

• You are living there now.

• You are paying the rent.

Who gets to keep the apartment in a divorce is a fairly new area of property settlement, and one where nothing but "in all likelihoods" and "probablys" can be used. But, broadly speaking, the one whose name is on the lease stands the greatest chance of winning the unit. Here, too, there can be extenuating circumstances. In some areas of the country, for example, a landlord cannot evict a newly divorced partner and ask for a new lease, even if the original lease was signed by the other former spouse alone. Very, very tricky here. If the apartment matters to both of you, toddle off to a lawyer.

Following the Death of a Spouse

When a husband or wife dies, one of the first thoughts about the house is either "I've got to move away from here" or "I could never leave this home where we lived for so many happy years." Either decision could be the right one, or each could complicate and further confuse the grieving process. Timing is the key here, and all too often both statements are made too soon after the death.

Saying you will not move may be the wrong decision for you, but at least it does not involve any uprooting, burning of bridges, or financial transactions. It's when the newly widowed person decides to sell—too quickly—that the problems arise.

The advice of just about everyone—financial counselors, family counselors, and the widowed themselves who have been through this just plain awful decision—is not to make any move to a new home for at least a year following the death of your spouse. You simply cannot be as rational and coldly analytical of your situation as you should be during those trying times. Alas, this is advice that is often not heeded. The widowed, often in a trancelike state, frequently go ahead and pick up stakes, usually to find themselves a few months after the sale, now alert and questioning, wondering what on earth happened. "What am I doing here?" they muse. "I don't even like the city (suburbs, or country). Why didn't somebody try to stop me?" But of course many somebodies probably did.

Lynn Caine, in her best-selling *Widow* (Bantam, 1975; $1.95), wrote that within three months after her husband's death she had sold her Manhattan apartment and bought a house she hated in New Jersey. The children were pulled out of their New York schools and everyone became suburbanites, a role which, she later conceded, she was not suited for.

If those who have just lost a spouse need another reason for staying put a while, it can be the children. Asking the kids what they think about selling the house is often not done, especially if they're very young, so many parents have no idea what the youngsters are thinking. Jill Krementz, in her book *How It Feels When a Parent Dies* (Knopf, 1981; $10.45), interviewed many young people who had lost a father or a mother. One young boy recalled how his mother had told him about his father's plane crash when the boy was eight years old. "The first thing I asked Mom," he related in the book, "was could we keep Skippy and Shadow, our dog and cat, and could we keep our house, and she said 'Sure.' " So the kids often do care about staying put, at least for a while.

Naturally, this advice is based on the assumption you can afford to stay where you are. If money problems are making you sure you must leave, then taking a less expensive house or renting an apartment makes good sense. Still, don't act too quickly in the panic of seeing no funds on the horizon. Perhaps you can take in a roommate to ease the financial burden. You may be able to convert your house into two (or more) separate apartment units. That rent coming in each month can be an enormous help in meeting household bills. There's more about becoming a landlord in this fashion in Chapter 43.

Contact the social service agencies in your community and/or a regional branch of a widowed persons' group. Those offices can help you be sure you have received any benefits that would accrue to you following a spouse's death, and they can even help you in finding someone to share your home, or in finding a sharer who already has the house or apartment and is looking for a roommate. Support groups can be extremely helpful with the social adjustments of widowhood, too.

For More Information

"Law and Marriage: Your Legal Guide," a 57-page booklet to assist couples with live-in relationships, answering questions about a forthcoming marriage, and dealing with other family matters, is available from the American Bar Association. Cost is $1 a copy, plus $1 for handling. Send check to the American Bar Association, Order Fulfillment, 1155 East 60th St., Chicago, Ill. 60637.

The Living Together Kit, by Ralph Warner and Toni Ihara. Order from Nolo Press, 950 Parker St., Berkeley, Calif. 94710. Price: $12.95.

Joint Property, by Alexander A. Bove, Jr. Fireside. Price: $8.95. Besides real estate, covers other joint-property arrangements such as bank accounts, stocks, bonds, safe-deposit boxes, etc.

Mingles, A Home-Buying Guide for Unmarried Couples, by Robert Irwin. McGraw-Hill. Price: $15.95.

38

Real Estate Gifts and Loans, and Some Thoughts About Estate Planning

Usually the family's gifts to Aunt Millie come in brightly wrapped packages. But now that elderly lady needs a different sort of "present"—help in buying her apartment, which is undergoing a condominium conversion.

Cousin Elise has been a widow for several years and is now remarrying. She and her intended husband will live in her home. She wants to leave that property to her children, but with the assurance that her husband can live there for the rest of his life. She's investigating how that can be done.

Junior could always count on the folks to lend him a dollar or so until the next allowance day. But now Junior is "Jr.," and he is looking for a somewhat more substantial loan—$15,000 to buy a house.

Gifts and loans between family members can become increasingly complicated, and certainly more costly, as the family grows older. And because we're dealing with relatives here, there is also the emotional involvement of lending, borrowing, giving, and taking. If it's friends you're giving or lending to, that is another mind set, with another set of lurking problems.

Family lending, particularly when it involves any substantial amount of money, is more common than loans and bequests to friends, however, and most families *do* want to assist relatives, or at least "do right" by them, if they can afford to do so. Sometimes no money is needed, just a signature on the proper piece of paper guaranteeing backup financial assistance if it is needed.

We're going to take some common gift and loan situations and spell out their benefits and disadvantages to both lender and borrower. We will use family members as examples, because that's the most common transaction in these situations, but naturally anyone you choose can be the recipient in most of these instances.

There are smart ways of giving away money, and of making loans. Just because it's a family affair does not mean you have to forfeit financial savvy and consider the cash down the drain. You can even come out many dollars ahead in some of these transactions. And, of course, you will have given a leg up to a family member, who may not be exactly needy but *is* in need of help, a subtle distinction.

A couple of broad points to bear in mind first:

1. Before taking out that checkbook, be sure you investigate any tax benefits or penalties to you, and to the borrower or recipient of that gift or loan.

2. There is a crackdown underway on the practice of interest-free loans as a tax shelter for the donor. Consult your tax advisor or contact your regional IRS office for the very latest on this changing area.

Now on to some specific information about the most common gifts and loans, concentrating, of course, on the area of real estate.

A Condo for College?

Gads, you say, can't I get away with giving Buddy an electronic typewriter as a graduation present, not to mention my footing the bill for four years at college? Yes, and you probably will, although we won't go into all those neat little extras that will come along the pike between now and his *next* graduation. Still, for some families, buying a home for a college-age child can make excellent financial sense.

It is likely to be a good move, if:

• You can, of course, afford the initial outlay of cash in the form of a downpayment.

• Apartments are scarce in the school vicinity. If they are plentiful and at low rents, that takes away some of the incentive for buying a home.

• Your child is living in a rental apartment in a building that is being converted to a condominium or cooperative.

• You will have two—or even, heaven help you, three—kids at school in the same area at the same time.

• The school is in or near a resort where you and your spouse might consider moving when you retire.

Let's assume your 18-year-old Buddy will be leaving soon for Ivy University, although you can, of course, purchase a house or condo anytime during his school years. The fee for room and board at Ivy is $3000 a year. That's $12,000 for the four years. Perhaps there is a house or condo relatively near the college you can buy for $60,000, with 15 percent, or $9000, down. You secure a 14 percent mortgage with a twenty-five-year payout, to be renegotiated after five years, which suits your purposes fine. You might sell when Buddy graduates. That's a monthly mortgage payment of about $600. But with a whole house, or even a two-bedroom condo, Buddy will probably take in a roommate or two and their rent will help defray your expenses. You'll still be left with real estate taxes, condo maintenance fees, and other bills associated with homeownership, but there is the possible capital gains to consider when you sell, the likelihood that the property will appreciate in value, and right now the usual tax deductions allotted homeowners. You will also be entitled to a depreciation allowance as the owner of an investment property. And you won't have to worry about finding tenants!

A tax lawyer or accountant can apprise you of current specific regulations regarding the benefit of investment property as it applies to your own children and their roommates—charging fair market rent, for example. If you buy a condo or co-op, whether a new complex or a conversion, you will also have to be sure that the sales agreement allows you to rent to students. In fact, for an investment like this a *real estate* lawyer will be the better advisor since he or she will also know the ins and outs of the landlord–tenant relationship.

The cost of room and board at colleges and universities varies widely around the country, of course. Only you know exactly what your child will be paying, what the housing stock is like in the area of the school, and at what price. There are other factors that will enter into your decision to buy:

• What about meals? Will the kids cook in the house or condo, or will they use school meal tickets? Whatever they decide, will that have any measurable effect on the cost of buying the home? Will they take most of their meals in restaurants if they are not inclined to cook and live too far from the campus? Consider that expense, too.

• If Buddy won't be living in a dorm, but in a house ten miles from campus, will you have to buy him a car? Add that cost to your number crunching.

• Who will maintain the place? Make repairs? Shovel snow? Let meter readers inside? Is Buddy a good student but a little, shall we say, impractical when it comes to day-to-day routines?

• If two or three of your own kids will be sharing the house or apartment, will they get along or will there be constant battles, moving in and out, and perhaps, for you, the expense of a dorm room or two *plus* the house?

• Also, if it's your own family in the home, can you afford to furnish the place, even with second-hand odds and ends?

• What about the summer months? Will Buddy be staying in the college locale to work or study? If not, can you find tenants for the summer months so that you have a continuous cash flow?

Finally, if the house or condo market is too expensive where school is, consider a mobile home. That's being done more and more now, too, since an attractive, single-width mobile, furnished, can often be found for under $10,000. That does not apply to all sections of every state, and it's true that the nearest mobile home park of any repute may be thirty-five miles away from your child's college, but it might pay you to do a little investigating. If you spend, let's say, $8000 for the mobile, plus maybe $75 a month in "rent" to the park owner, that comes to $11,600 for the four years. Close to the $12,000 you'd pay on campus, true. But you can sell the mobile and, depending on its condition and the reputation of the park, can either make a small profit or suffer just a small loss for depreciation. You're likely to come away with something in your pocket, which you certainly won't with the dormitory deal. Buddy may or may not be able to squeeze a roommate into the unit, but if he can there's extra rent money for you there, too.

An increasing number of mobile homes (see page 404 for a full discussion) are considered real estate these days, purchased with a mortgage. Naturally, if you buy one of those units—and they are larger than the single-width, approximating the appearance of a single-family home—you are entitled to the full tax benefits of homeownership.

In sum, college costs are so high these days, and likely to rise higher, that more and more parents are looking for just about any way they can to defray those expenses. Buying a home for the college student is a solid, viable alternative to dormitory housing if the parent fits into one of the categories mentioned several paragraphs back. Last year developers in Texas, to take just one example of how this practice is spreading, saw a run on newly constructed condominiums purchased by parents for their school-age children. If the financial calculations come out in their favor, why not?

Helping the Kids to Buy a Home

You can help friends with the purchase of a home, and you can help your own parents to buy. But let's take the illustration of parents lending a hand (not to mention a few dollars) to the kids, the most common form of financial assistance parents are likely to make to the younger generation these days when it comes to expensive loans and gifts.

Your daughter, Jane, and her husband, Hal, need help. Maybe they can afford the downpayment on a home, but not the $1000 monthly mortgage payments. Or perhaps it's just the reverse. Their incomes are adequate to carry a mortgage, but the downpayment remains elusive. Sure, they could keep setting aside a little each payday until they have that magical figure. But is that practical? Home prices are rising at about 5 percent a year, a great deal more in some neighborhoods. And mortgage interest rates are almost always fluctuating, sometimes rising steeply. Jane and Hal may never be able to save enough to catch up. They can apply for private mortgage insurance (more about that on page 314) to assist with a downpayment, or they can come to Mom and Dad for help. Perhaps, if their financial situation is relatively stable (and their marriage, too!), the loan or gift from the folks that allows them to buy now makes more sense. We're assuming, of course, that Mom and Dad can afford that gesture without decimating their own savings.

Let's consider some plans that could work for all of you.

First, however, if you want to *give* Jane and Hal the gift of a downpayment, you should make sure that they know—and you are certain in your own minds, too—that this is indeed a gift and you are not expecting repayment. Similarly, if it is a loan and you are expecting repayment, spell that out. Terrible misunderstandings and hurt feelings can arise over the years from words left unsaid when it comes to loans versus gifts. If no one delicately skirts the issue, and someone comes right out and *says* what's what, the definition of gift or loan cannot be murky.

Remember, also, that you can give up to $10,000 a year ($20,000 if your spouse goes in on the gift with you) to a child without paying any gift tax. That's on a per-person basis. If you and your spouse want to give Jane and Hal each $20,000 you can, and that makes $40,000 toward the price of a home. Not a bad downpayment (too much to put down, probably).

If you are making an interest-free loan, better check with your tax advisor before signing the check. The subject of interest-free loans

For Lenders and Borrowers To Consider

Lenders should make clear to recipients that this is indeed a loan and not a gift.

Borrowers shouldn't feel that just because it's family it's alright to skip rent or mortgage payments, or loan repayments—unless there's a very good reason.

Lenders should look into any loan or gift to assure themselves the best tax advantage, including deductions for bad loans.

Borrowers shouldn't take advantage of a relative's bounty by asking for more assistance than they need.

Lenders shouldn't attach strings to their gift or loan: "If you go back to school . . . ," "If you buy in Hightone Heights . . . ," etc.

(or those carrying below-market interest rates) has been under review for some time now, with a number of questions remaining unresolved. Don't anticipate tax benefits before looking into *today's* standing on the subject.

Finally, in this preface, another point to give serious thought to if you are considering a very large loan is the kids' marriage. Sadly, with today's high divorce rate, it could be wiser, and safer for you, to offer them a mortgage rather than a loan. The loan could be harder to prove and recoup in the event of a split, while the mortgage is a very definite lien and can be foreclosed. There's always some way you can salvage your investment if it's a mortgage.

How to help Jane and Hal with a mortgage? You have several options, one of which is particularly good for all involved. Talk to your tax advisor, of course, to personalize these suggestions to your own financial and family situation. Note, too, before we get into *first* mortgages, that lenders usually prohibit parents from providing a *second* mortgage to their children. In fact, the first mortgage may contain a provision against secondary financing by anyone else, including relatives.

Now to your choices:

1. You can *co-sign* for their mortgage, which will not cost you any money (unless they default), but which may help them qualify for a

loan they otherwise could not secure. If you do co-sign, however, consider your own position. Do they need a co-signer because of bad credit? Will they be able to keep up mortgage payments (the lender will weigh this aspect, too, but you *know* your child and what's going on in his or her life). Think of yourself and *your* plans. If you wanted to borrow a sizable chunk of money some day soon, you could well be rejected for a loan because of your obligation toward your child's mortgage, even though he or she has made all payments with no problem. If you quit your claim of ownership, the lender could reinforce the mortgage's due-on-sale clause. The kids would then have to reapply for a loan on their own, if they could not find another co-signer. They would probably be able to secure a new loan, but the interest rate may be higher.

The FHA will insure mortgages with relatives as co-signers, or co-bondsmen, which means you are guaranteeing the mortgage, but not the title. The Veterans Administration, on the other hand, will probably not allow you to co-sign.

2. Jane and Hal make the downpayment and buy the house, but you put up enough money in advance of the purchase so that they can *buy-down* the mortgage interest rate, making the deal sweeter for them. The couple secures the usual mortgage available at the time, with an interest rate of perhaps 14 percent. But the monthly payments for the first year are based at a much lower 10 percent, then rise gradually to that 14 percent mark in the fifth year of the loan. By depositing a specified amount of money with the lender, you are allowing that institution to offer the lower rate to the kids, since your deposit supplements your child's monthly payments.

3. *Equity sharing* may be the best arrangement of all. It does not make the gifted ones feel beholden, and at the same time offers the donor excellent benefits. This is a fairly new buying concept for the small homeowner, although it has been in practice with builders and other pros. For your purposes it would work like this: You and your spouse and Jane and Hal buy a home together, but not in equal shares. Perhaps you will pay 90 percent of the cost, Jane and Hal 10 percent. Mortgage payments are made in that ratio. The couple will then pay you "rent" for living in your share of the home. The partner that puts up most of the money is the "investor"; the other party, the one needing the financial assistance, is the "buyer." An agreement between the two spells out who will handle maintenance and similar divisions of labor, time, and expense, right down to who has the right to vote in the condominium or cooperative association. This is all negotiable; whatever suits all of you is fine.

All buyers share in the benefits of ownership, proportionate to their share in the property. You as the parent and "investor" will get the biggest break, of course, since your financial investment is higher. Too, you will have a depreciation allowance for the portion of the property your child is "renting" from you.

Shared equity can be arranged between perfect strangers, too—the investor, for example, who is looking for just such a spot to watch his money earn sizable tax benefits.

The beauty of shared equity within the family is that it does not make the child feel quite so indebted as an outright loan or gift would. And from the investor's view it is, in all likelihood, going to be a wise investment (considering the location of the home and other points that enter into a solid housing buy). When the house or condo is sold, perhaps after a specified period of time, you will first get back your initial investment in the property, and then you and your child will split the proceeds from the sale, again, proportionate to your investment. Your child's rent money coming in each month will help defray *your* carrying costs. And you won't have to worry about finding and screening tenants! Tough situations some landlords face, such as what to do when a tenant defaults in rent payments, probably will not apply here, since in all likelihood you will be willing to see this particular tenant through a temporary rough spell.

Just a few points of caution for all concerned:

1. The party who is putting up most of the money should be sure he or she will be able to continue making that contribution. After all, if you stop, the "tenant" may lose his or her home if he or she cannot find another investor.

2. Since this is "family," you don't have to look at the agreement with too wary an eye, but remember that some contracts can give all the benefits to the investor and few to the homebuyer. Is this how you want your arrangement to work? Naturally, you will seek the advice of a skilled attorney to guide you through this purchase. Since parent and child are involved, you can even use the same lawyer, an impossible position if you were an unrelated investor and buyer.

3. Don't push the buyer—your child—into a house too expensive for him or her or otherwise inappropriate. "Go ahead. It's all right, I'm paying for it" won't wash. Let them choose the property best suited to their lifestyles and checkbooks.

Let's take another instance of helping out a relative who is not your child or partner, or who perhaps is a friend. Maybe it's Marge, your sister-in-law and an elderly widow who rents in a building that is being converted to condominiums. Marge can't afford to buy her unit, yet she hates the thought of leaving the home where she has lived in comfort for so many years. There are no protections in her state for the elderly caught in a condominium or cooperative conversion.

You can purchase the apartment for her, supply the downpayment, and assume the mortgage. You become the owner and Marge pays you rent. She's assured a home for life and you have the tax advantages of ownership, plus the rent she will pay, plus depreciation for an income-producing property (you must be sure in renting to relatives, however, to charge a fair market rent). If Marge ever decides to move you may realize a nice profit from the sale. This strategy won't help a family member become a homeowner, but it can work out well for the relative or friend who doesn't mind renting and may even prefer to do so. Their main concern is remaining in their home. Or perhaps you can help them to find a new home, which you would buy, one where they would not have to worry about conversions and bad service and other unpleasantries of renting, since their landlord would be you.

A Few Words About Estate Planning

This is a large and potentially complicated area of financial concern that includes, of course, other assets and situations besides real property. If you want to be smart about seeing that your money will go eventually to the person(s) you desire, and with the most favorable consequences to yourself or your estate, you will first see to having a will drawn up. During a visit to an attorney skilled in estate law you can also talk about any trusts you would like establish, either now or in that estate.

Bring with you to that meeting everything that pertains to what you own and what you plan for your estate: names, addresses, and ages of all members of your family and of anyone else for whom you want to make some provision. As for the real estate aspect of your assets, take along all deeds to property. If you have a home in more than one state tell the attorney.

Tell the attorney everything—your assets, your plans for the immediate future, your wishes for how your assets are to be apportioned after your death or perhaps through trusts right now. Talk, too, about problems, financial or otherwise, with those you plan to include in your will or make some other provision for. The attorney can make suggestions about lifetime annuities in those persons' names, the wisdom (and tax benefits and savings from probate) of transferring title to property now to your children, and the like. Laws governing taxation in certain estate situations, and with trusts, can vary widely from one community to another, and are changing all the time. You need to talk to someone whose knowledge is up to the minute.

Books have been written on the subject of estate planning. Indeed, we suggest you buy one or two to become acquainted with all your options on that subject before you visit an attorney. They cover the topic in far more depth than we can in these few pages. There are some common questions on the subject, however. Here are a few of them, along with some suggestions for their resolution:

Question: How much money can I leave in my estate without forcing my heirs to pay inheritance taxes?

Answer: Quite a bit; a lot more, in fact, than most of us will have to concern ourselves about. Everyone has a lifetime federal tax exclusion of $400,000 in 1985; $500,000 in 1986; and $600,000 in 1987 and the years after that—or at least until the law changes again. Remember, though, that several states require payment of state inheritance tax, and your estate will be required to pay those fees. You can check with your state tax office to see if such payments are due where you live.

Question: I see that my kids need money these days for their homes, their businesses, and *their* kids. What's wrong with giving them my money now instead of making them wait to inherit it after I die?

Answer: Make the kids cash gifts from time to time, by all means, and lend them money when they need a hand, but never give too much of your estate away. Always keep enough to support yourself and your spouse, and that does not mean just monthly incomes from pensions, Social Security, dividends, and the like. Keep a sizable chunk—if you are fortunate enough to have a chunk—of your other investments for yourself. What if you faced a major medical expense? And we won't even get into the nightmare of nursing home costs. What if the apartment you're now renting is about to become a condominium? Will you be able to buy if you've given most of your money away? Always, always, always hang on to enough to assure you a relatively worry-free retirement.

A final few words on this subject: Don't retire at 65 and give your children most of your assets at 65½ figuring, "Well, my life's over now, they might as well have it." There's many a retiree who sank into his easy chair at 65, contemplating the Last Roundup, and is still around at 85. The elderly are the fastest-growing segment of the population, and many, many of them enjoy those years in comparatively good health and financial shape. Consider long-range planning beyond your 60s. You're likely to be one of the growing number of Americans still perking along in their 80s. And you don't want to enter really old age broke, do you, having given your children title to your house and other assets in a fit of postretirement melancholia?

Question: What does the term "life estate" mean?

Answer: It means that the recipient of that largesse is allowed to stay in his or her home for a lifetime. Like Marge of a few pages back, they can be given a life estate by the buyer of their home if they cannot afford the purchase themselves. Individuals can request—and receive—life tenancy in a home they are donating to a historical or preservation society. Parents can, all other factors being equal, give their children title to their home, while asking a life estate for themselves.

There are life estates created by law—"dower rights," for example, which is the part of or interest in the real estate of a dead husband given by law to his widow during her lifetime. In some states the elderly (sometimes with income restrictions attached) are entitled to a life estate in their apartments when those buildings undergo a condominium or cooperative conversion.

A life tenant may pay rent, but does not have to concern him or herself with mortgage payments, real estate taxes, maintenance, or any other expenses that go along with running the property. He or she may have the right to the income derived from the property, however.

Another example of a life estate situation follows:

Question: I'm a widow living in my own home and planning to remarry. My future husband will move in with me. I'd like to leave the house to my children, but want to be sure that my husband can live there for the rest of his life. How can that be done?

Answer: You have a few choices here. You can have a prenuptial agreement drawn up where your husband-to-be waives any rights of inheritance to your home if you should die before he does. You would then will him a life estate in the house. You could also put the house into a trust, spelling out your wishes in the trust agreement. Finally, you might convey title to the house right now to your children, reserving a life estate in the home to both yourself and your prospective husband.

Question: Can I will my rent-controlled apartment to my son?

Answer: Not unless he has been living in the apartment with you, and it has been his principal residence for a reasonable length of time.

Question: What is a "Clifford Trust"?

Answer: This is a short-term plan for shifting income-producing assets (called principal) to a family member who is in a lower tax bracket than you are—perhaps your child, perhaps your parent. The trust must last at least ten years and one day. The beneficiary gets the income during that period and then the property reverts to the grantor—you. The income earned by the principal is taxable to the beneficiary, not the donor, and that's the advantage of the trust: the beneficiary's tax bracket is lower than the donor's. In considering the trust, remember that a lawyer skilled in estate planning will charge somewhere between $300 and just under $1000 to set up a Clifford Trust, so a somewhat substantial amount of money or other assets should be involved here. You should consider, too, that at the end of the ten years the principal reverts to you, of course, so you've really only given away the flow of income. If you are setting up the trust for your elderly parents, and they die before the ten-year period has expired, the trust reverts to you. If you die first, the trust continues to its expiration date and then becomes part of your estate.

Question: I'm divorced and my wife has custody of our twelve-year-old son. Can I put property in his and my name?

Answer: You can, but it may become confusing. By law minors cannot sell stock or real estate. If you put those assets in both your names, you'll find that you can't sell or trade without the consent of the child, and of course your twelve-year-old cannot give that consent. You might be able to get a court order, or you might consult your tax attorney about having a guardian appointed for the purpose of managing the transaction, but do you really need the hassle?

Question: My daughter, Sally, has always been a sensible girl, thrifty with money. I know she'll do well with her share of my estate. My son, Jake, is just the opposite. He'll go through it in no time. I'm thinking of leaving everything to Sally and letting her give Jake his share a little at a time. She'll keep an eye on my estate so that Jake doesn't squander his share. Would that work?

Answer: That's not such a good idea. It's unwise to give control of your estate to one child and can only make for bad feelings in the family after you've gone—hardly the legacy you would want. Let a lawyer advise you here. Perhaps a trustee can take care of meting out Jake's share so that Sally doesn't have to enter the picture. Far better for a stranger to tighten the purse strings than the lad's own sister.

You can see from the above examples of frequently asked estate questions how complicated this area of finance can be—and how emotions and family feelings can become embroiled with the dollars and deeds. No matter how little you believe you have to leave—and experts say we're all surprised at exactly how much we *are* worth—give this subject serious discussion and thought. And planning.

For More Information

You might contact your state's Attorney General's office for information about legislation concerning estate and gift taxes.

"Gift and Estate Taxes," IRS booklet #448, is available from your local IRS office.

39

Foreclosure:
What to Do If It Looms

The mortgage payment was due last Friday. Or three Fridays ago. Or, most damaging of all to your nervous system, two months ago. You are afraid to go to the mailbox. You jump when the phone rings, and your heart even skips when someone says "call for you" at the office.

It may not make you feel any better, but in bad times there are plenty of other homeowners in your shaky boat. In 1982, for instance, at the height of that recession, the highest number of home foreclosures occurred since the Great Depression of the 1930s. Even in relatively stable economic times a certain percentage—usually about 1 percent—of homeowners will fall behind in their mortgage payments and face foreclosure.

The reasons for being late in sending out that check vary, of course, and any one of them might apply to you at some time during the life of your mortgage: a job layoff; rapidly rising utility costs; high medical bills; a divorce; a weak real estate market that does not allow you to sell your home when you want; the inability to handle "creative financing" techniques; or difficulty in keeping up with second mortgage obligations.

You may be threatened with the loss of your home through failure to pay real estate taxes, in which case the house reverts to the local government (which may allow you to stay on as a tenant). You can also find yourself in trouble if you neglect to pay local water bills, and even home insurance premiums. The latter, however, while grounds for foreclosure, is rarely used.

Lenders do become nervous, though, when a mortgagor does any-

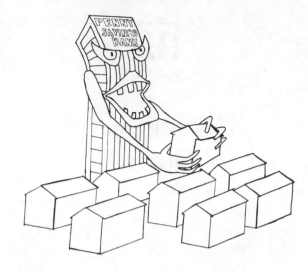

S. Zimmerman

thing to threaten the title or the value of his home. That is why many mortgage holders demand that homeowners pay real estate taxes along with their mortgage payments, with one check. That way the lender is sure that those obligations, at least, are being met.

If you're having trouble making a mortgage payment, it is vital that you *immediately call or visit the company that lent you the money to purchase your home*. In fact, calling before the payment you can't make is due is even better. Taking a head-in-the-sand approach to this serious problem will only worsen the situation, since the lender may well feel you are not interested in your plight. That officer will not know you are almost sick with worry. Your contacting the institution is an immediate signal to the lender that you are concerned and well-meaning about your debt—and that's quite a few points in your favor.

If you have mortgage insurance—private or government-issued—get in touch with that insurer, too. That could be the FHA, the VA, or any other appropriate government agency or any private insurance company. They are interested in helping you.

You should know that the lender may not inform you of special programs offered by insurers, which is why contacting them on your own is so important. The FHA, for example, has a plan for troubled borrowers who qualify whereby, among other options, you might be able to get your monthly payments reduced by one half or more. In dire cases, all payments can be suspended for up to three years. All of that money must be made up at some point, however, either by increasing the size of the monthly payments later or by extending the life of the loan. There are two principal ingredients for qualification for this program: Your problem must be a temporary one, such as an unexpected illness or the loss of a job, and you must have reasonable expectations of improving your situation within three years.

Private mortgage insurance companies are now beginning to offer help to troubled borrowers, too. The Mortgage Guaranty Insurance Corp. (MGIC), for example, will, in some instances and at the lender's request, lend the homeowner covered by its policy what he needs to make his monthly payment, provided those mortgage payments are already six months in arrears. The homeowner repays the amount when he or she gets back on the financial track, or sells the house. In the event of subsequent foreclosure, the sum MGIC has loaned is credited against the lender's claim under its insurance policy. By making this offer MGIC hopes to avoid having to pay some claims. But here, too, the program is only for solid folks who have run into a temporary difficulty, not for classic mortgage deadbeats.

Homebuilders are attempting to aid the buyer in danger of foreclosure, too, and this is another early 1980s development. Several of these companies, including U.S. Home Corporation, the nation's largest builder, are offering a mortgage insurance plan that pays principal, interest, tax, and hazard insurance payments for as long as one year after a homeowner loses his or her job involuntarily. The coverage of the policy runs for two years from the date of purchase.

If you have no insurance program, and you go straight to your lender, in almost every case you will be able to work out some kind of deal that will avert foreclosure, and that is because, for the most part, it is not in the lender's interest to foreclose. It's an expensive and time-consuming process for both parties, and lenders would rather see you through a bad time than take your home and try to sell it themselves in an uncertain market. (There are, however, some lenders who, eager to get single-digit loans off their books, will call in a loan when the homeowner is just a few days late with a payment. Some will wait a little longer, but will be just as eager to start the foreclosure process. Check your mortgage contract, and, if you hold a low-interest loan, be very careful about prompt payments. In some instances, instead of foreclosure you may be presented with refinancing at today's higher interest rate.)

When you visit your lending institution be open and honest in answering questions about the cause of your difficulty, your other regular expenses, and your family's current income. Caginess and outright lying, even feeling certain questions are not the lender's business, will get you nowhere here. Cooperation is the attitude called for. The lender may suggest that all mortgage payments be suspended for a certain period of time, with the delinquent payments added on when payments resume. (The penalty for late payments is generally about 5 percent of the amount due that month.) Or payments might be reduced for a while. Or your mortgage could be "reworked." Here you keep the same interest rate, but the balance due is spread over a longer period of time than the loan now calls for. All of these programs, and any other assistance, is known as "granting forbearance." You don't need a lawyer to negotiate a repayment schedule with the lender, but if you are engaged in actual foreclosure proceedings it is wise to retain counsel.

Taking Stock

When you've left the lender with some suggestions for solving your problem with delinquent payments, give serious thought to all your options—and you do have them. The first move to take, however, if you are married, is to tell your spouse about the delinquencies. Interestingly, lenders say foreclosure proceedings are commonly an alarming surprise to one spouse in a marriage, who had been sure his or her mate had been making regular payments! Often state laws mandate that each party in the marriage receive a separate notice of foreclosure, and that may be the first indication to a husband or wife that something is wrong. They are usually "joint tenants" on the mortgage. Persons who buy a home together as "tenants in common" will also in many cases receive individual notification of default and/or foreclosure proceedings.

Can you borrow the money to make up missed payments, from family or through a bank personal loan? Would it be wise to take out a second mortgage? Would you be able to make those payments along with existing first-mortgage bills? Remember, trying to keep current with both those loans is what got some homeowners in this fix in the first place.

You might also ask the mortgage holder if that institution provides financial counseling, which might help not just with your mortgage payments, but with your overall debt problem. Or you might ask if there is a local social service agency that can help. An outsider can frequently see through a financial predicament more easily than the folks involved. You might also check with your regional HUD office. That agency certifies individual financial counselors around the country. The address and telephone number of a HUD office near you can be found in Appendix A.

Private debt counseling is a field where charlatans prey on worried, sometimes frantic, individuals. But there are good offices and agencies that could help you get back on sound financial footing. One suggestion is the National Foundation for Consumer Credit. Members of NFCC, scattered around the country, provide free budgeting assistance, although you may have to pay a small fee if you need help in arranging payments and communicating with creditors—your mortgage lender, for example. If you send a stamped, self-addressed envelope to NFCC at 8701 Georgia Ave., Silver Spring, Md. 20910, they will send you a list of counseling services in your state.

Back to your immediate mortgage problem. If your money problems will be of long duration, the lender may suggest that you sell your house. By doing that you will be able to avoid foreclosure, keep whatever equity has built up in the property, and protect your credit report. This is a step that should not be taken in a hurry, however, and not before all other options have been exhausted.

Don't panic. Usually, a mortgage is "delinquent" when a payment is not made by the date it is due. It is in "default" when two or more payments are due but unpaid. Mortgage contracts usually allow for foreclosure proceedings to begin when a default exists, but most lenders are not that hasty (aside from those few mentioned earlier in this chapter).

In the case of FHA, VA, and some other government-supported loans, foreclosure cannot be started until the homeowner has missed three payments. Private lenders usually follow the same policy.

If you own your home under a trust deed, however, the procedure may vary, and can be speeded up so that the whole process is completed within ninety days after default.

If Foreclosure Proceedings Begin

Rules governing foreclosure proceedings vary from one state to another, although each state has very definite procedures attached to the process. It's a lengthy one that can take from three months to a year or more to conclude (except under the aforementioned trust deeds), and the homeowner's legal and court costs can run as high as 7 or 8 percent of the eventual sale price of the house. After the home, or the lien against it, has been sold, usually at a sheriff's auction, the homeowner is permitted to keep whatever amount of money is left—if there is any left—once the mortgage balance and foreclosure fees have been paid. The homeowner also has a certain

---

Late Payments and Condominiums

Fall behind in monthly condominium association payments and the association can decide to put a lien on your unit and threaten to foreclose. You should realize that failure to keep up with those payments is also a violation of your first-mortgage agreement, and that a foreclosure of the assessment lien could lead to a foreclosure of the mortgage itself, with the mortgagee joining in the suit. If that does happen, foreclosure would follow the route spelled out in the text of this chapter.

---

amount of time after the sale to redeem the property by paying off the loan and court costs (there is no redemption time under trust deeds).

Once it has begun, though, a lender in certain circumstances may give the homeowner a second chance to take care of the missed payments (plus any legal fees), and this avoids seeing foreclosure through to the end. With trust deeds, according to the laws of your state, if you can't come up with missed payments after ninety days, the property is advertised for sale for perhaps three weeks, during which time the house can be redeemed. But now the homeowner must pay off the entire mortgage, plus additional accrued costs. If he or she can't, the house is sold at the appointed time.

Sadly for the homeowner—as if all of this is not unhappy enough—it *is* possible that if the home is sold at auction, and the amount realized from the sale is not enough to satisfy the lender, that institution can sue for the shortfall. Say you owe $65,000 on your mortgage and the sale brings in $60,000. According to the rules of your state, you could be sued for the remaining $5000. The lender may be able to attach your personal assets to collect that loss. These so-called deficiency judgments against borrowers are becoming more difficult to obtain, however, and if it comes to foreclosure you can attempt to have your lawyer put a clause in any agreement with the lender stating that the property is the only security for the mortgage. With a trust deed, the beneficiary usually cannot file for a deficiency judgment.

One final point. Don't let the anxiety of this time drive you to those who will offer to solve your problem—for a fee. There are many get-rich schemes out there to bilk homeowners worried about their properties out of a few hundred dollars—while doing nothing to save them their houses. None of those individuals can do any more for you than your lawyer, the lender, and your insurer. Those people are genuinely interested in saving you your home.

Bankruptcy

Bankruptcy is a last-ditch measure for seeing that your house is not lost to foreclosure. Federal and state laws are tightening regulations for filing for bankruptcy because of what those concerned feel have been abuses of the practice by Americans too eager to rid themselves of debt obligations and start over. Bankruptcy should not be entered into lightly and never without the assistance of a lawyer. For most Americans it is a searing experience and it does not, as many assume, allow you to start over fresh. Credit may well be denied you after bankruptcy proceedings, and in any event that action will be a part of your credit record, usually for ten years.

In general you can expect to file under either Chapter 7 of the U.S. Bankruptcy Code, or Chapter 13, which is not truly bankruptcy, but rather a reorganization of your debt.

Under Chapter 7 you are absolved of all your debts and must sell almost all of your personal assets, presumably to pay off those creditors. Few people filing under Chapter 7 have that many assets, however. Among the possessions you can keep here is the equity in your principal residence—house, condo, or cooperative shares—up to around $10,000, a figure that varies from state to state.

Chapter 13 is different. If you qualify according to your income and your debts, with this action you will be allowed to pay off your debt obligations following a court-administered repayment schedule. You will be allowed to keep your home and other assets while the repayment is carried on. As it applies to your home, Chapter 13 will probably allow you to make current mortgage payments, while gradually paying off the past-due balance over a period of three years or so.

Once you've filed for Chapter 7 or Chapter 13, there is an automatic "stay" against creditors who may have already taken legal action against you. However, the bankruptcy judge can assign a part of your future earnings to pay off those past debts.

All of this is pretty grim, of course, but perhaps it can be avoided. Only about half of all foreclosure proceedings actually end up with the mortgagor losing his home. Your own situation may call for no more than a chat with your lender and a reassessment of your payment schedule. All it takes is that one important phone call or visit on your part.

For More Information

"Avoiding Mortgage Default" is a free booklet from HUD, available from your regional HUD office (address in Appendix A). Ask for booklet #426-PA (5).

Any number of free pamphlets are available from the National Foundation for Consumer Credit, 8701 Georgia Ave., Silver Spring, Md. 20910. Some titles: "The Emergency Problem: What to Do About It"; "Measuring and Using Credit Capacity"; and "Establishing Good Credit."

"Budgeting for the Family," a 14-page government-produced booklet, details steps in developing a budget, with charts for estimating income, planning family spending, and recording your expenses. Price: $2. Write to Consumer Information Center, Dept. G, Pueblo, Colo. 81009. Ask for Publication #185K.

"Credit: Use It to Your Advantage" is available from the Credit Union National Association. Write CUNA Supply Corp., P.O. Box 333, Madison, Wis. 53701. The cost of the 31-page booklet is $2.20. It describes types of loans available, protection for the borrower, and the like.

40

Housing Decisions as You or Your Parents Approach Retirement

Options abound here, and that can be both exhilarating and frightening. Freed from career considerations and child rearing, you can pick up and move 5000 miles away. Or stay put. Keep the old homestead or trade it for a smaller condo. Which is the better choice? What about maintaining a home on a diminished income? What happens if you should become unable to manage for yourself?

Fortunately retirement does not occur overnight. The years of planning and thought begin early for most of us—for some serious and careful planners as early as their forties. "Retirement" is a fluid term, too, which can take the edge off a harsh definition. While compulsory retirement may force you to leave the job you have held for the last thirty years, you may be staying on with that company in a consulting capacity, or as a part-time or seasonal employee. You may be retiring from that concern only to take a position with a different company, or to start your own business. Perhaps you're retiring but your spouse isn't, so life is not as flexible as the term "retiree" might suggest.

With everyone's life situation different—and that includes finances, family situations, health, and lifestyle expectations—there are no one, two, or three flatly laid-out guidelines for a successful retirement. No do this, avoid that, move here, sign there and you will be happy. The purpose of this chapter, therefore, is to give you a broad overview, as you approach gold-watch time, of your housing options—and there are many of them.

There are more than forty-eight million Americans, some 21 percent of the population, over 55 years old. The needs of these preretirement and retirement Americans are becoming more attention getting, simply by virtue of their growing numbers and corresponding importance to government and politicians. More and more innovative housing programs for seniors are turning up, some of them short-term pilots that disappear quickly, others with potential for long-range success. Every city of any size has special offices to assist the elderly that operate under a variety of titles such as The Aging Connection in Atlanta, or Cambridge Living Options for Elders (CLOE) in Cambridge, Mass., or just plain Office on Aging for that particular town or county. Any of those organizations can advise the retiree about his or her living situation and can direct him or her to agencies and offices that can be of further help.

There is another consideration in this chapter. Perhaps it is not you who will have to make housing decisions soon. It may be your elderly parent(s). Thanks to longer life spans it is not unusual to see a 60-year-old man worried about his 83-year-old mother and how she is managing on dwindling resources. This chapter will acquaint those of you in this position with housing options for the individual who is long retired and for the one who is incapacitated.

On a more optimistic note, bear these statistics in mind:

1. Only 5 percent of the nation's elderly reside in nursing homes or similar facilities.

2. Some 17 percent live with an adult child.

3. The overwhelming majority live independent lives, whether alone in houses or apartments or living with spouses or friends.

Many factors enter in the enjoyment of a successful retirement; indeed, books have been written on the subject (some of them are noted at the end of this chapter). A positive outlook is important, as are financial planning, potential work possibilities, maintaining health, and the like. All should be given respectful attention before the farewell luncheon and gift of matched luggage. When it comes to housing there are two prime considerations:

1. Plan early so that a family crisis does not force you into a living situation you would not have chosen and do not like.

2. Be familiar with all your options. Having choices, believe it or not, is one of the many factors that do contribute to enjoyable retirement years. Knowing what's going on in the area of housing for

seniors involves not only reading about choices but also keeping in regular contact with your state or local office on aging and your local senior citizen center and human resources agency.

We will almost guarantee that in reading this chapter you will come upon at least one style of housing for senior citizens, or one suggestion for helping a house bring in money for you, that you did not know about. All of those ideas can translate into much-needed dollars for the retiree, especially the one who is "house-rich, cash-poor"—living in a home with an attractive market value, but with a small, perhaps dangerously small, cash flow.

So. You're in your 50s or early 60s. When you retire your income is likely to drop, although perhaps it will not. You will have Social Security income and perhaps a company pension and additional monies from investments. Your greatest asset, no doubt, is likely to be your home. So let's start there, where you have spent so many years of your life, and see how that structure can help you earn a more comfortable retirement.

Finding Help in Keeping Your Home

Perhaps the most significant development in the senior citizen housing picture over the last few years has been the recognition that the elderly should not have to move out of their homes because they can no longer afford rising property taxes, fuel costs, or maintenance. If you'd like to stay in the home where you've lived so many years and raised a family, even though it's now too large for you, there are many programs and agencies that can help. All the following are worth looking into. (Of course this also applies if you are assisting an elderly relative or friend.)

• Every state offers a "homestead" exemption in the form of reduced property taxes for the elderly, usually those with incomes below a specified level.

• Your local utility may offer home energy assistance programs to senior citizens in the form of low-interest loans to make repairs and improvements. Also, some have emergency funds for those customers who cannot keep up with utility bills.

• Is your building likely to go condo or co-op and you do not want to buy? Some states protect those over 65 from having to purchase their units, and from having to move, too. They can stay on as renters, either for a specified period of time—say, five to ten years—or perhaps indefinitely.

• In apartments, renters over 65 years of age may be eligible for rent increase exemptions. Check with your local rent or housing office.

• Look into "deferred payment home improvement loans" at lending institutions. These programs are designed for older Americans, and loans allow for changes in homes (wheelchair accommodation, rental unit) that will allow owners to remain there.

• You can take in a roomer. There is no need to apply for permission or to check local zoning ordinances since it is only a room you are letting, not a full apartment with a kitchen. Expected income: $35 to $60 a week.

• You can look for a roommate—for companionship, safety, and help in carrying the expenses of the house. You can find a house sharer through your own devices, such as talking with friends,

---

Pause for Thought

If You Move	*On the Other Hand*	*Still . . .*
You are giving up a house that is too large for you, too difficult to maintain.	You may be trading it for a mortgage, one that is double or more the size of your old loan.	Many retirees pay cash for their retirement homes, money derived from the sale of existing homes. A good number of retirement homes—mobiles, for example—are less costly than traditional houses. If a mortgage is needed, it will be a small one.
You may feel better in a different climate.	Maybe the weather will be too warm or there will be too much snow, making for virtual isolation in the winter.	Periodic visits to the proposed retirement locale—not just in-season vacations—will ensure no unpleasant surprises when one has moved there bag and baggage after retirement.

If You Move	*On the Other Hand*	*Still . . .*
You will be making new friends in your new community.	You will be leaving the old ones behind, not to mention family members.	Families do move around these days. Who is to say your children will continue living in your hometown? Old friends can visit, and you can spend time at their place.
That new adult community will be "safer."	That self-containment can be sterile, too, with nothing for retirees to do except, as one Florida man put it, "sit on those damned benches and wait to die."	Don't move to any planned community if life with a homogeneous group does not appeal to you. There are usually plenty of activities for those not interested in more than occasional bench sitting.
A new move can be exciting, challenging.	Any move, even a happily anticipated one, is at least mildly upsetting.	Maybe we can all use a little positive excitement now and then. If moving far away disturbs you, make the change within your own town, or just a few communities away.

neighbors, church or synagogue members, and the local office on aging in your community. Or you can deal with a commercial room-mate placement agency if you live in a locale large enough to support those businesses. The agencies (and they are quite on the up and up) will find you a roommate for your home, and will also take someone who is looking for both a home and roommate and make the match there. The fee is around $35, and you are, of course, free to reject any prospective sharers the agencies suggest. Take all the time you need, but first decide whether you are looking simply for someone to share the expenses or for a friend. It's important to get that distinction understood up front.

Although most of their clients are young, single, professional people, roommate agencies are seeing a growing number of applicants who are single parents and retired persons. The latter matches may take a little longer than the more numerous young folks, but you can bet the agency will eventually come up with someone satisfactory. These concerns have always handled same-sex matches, but a growing number are now bringing together applicants of opposite sex.

There are other groups around the country interested in matching prospective home sharers. Sometimes it's bringing two people together in one house; sometimes it's organizing what has become known as "congregate housing" or "group homes" for retirees.

Usually this involves a group or charitable organization that purchases a house that is then shared by six or ten or twelve residents. Each has his or her own room and all share kitchen, living room, and other common facilities. Frequently a housekeeper is hired to keep the place in shape and do the cooking. Some programs offer financial assistance to the elderly; others charge the resident full market rent.

If sharing your home, or joining a congregate house (or creating one) appeals to you, you can contact the Shared Housing Resource Center Inc., 6344 Greene St., Philadelphia, Pa. 19144. If you send $1 they will send you a list of shared housing facilities in your area and more information about the concept.

A couple of points to note about a roommate situation. Sharing your own home could reduce the capital gains exemption you are allowed by the IRS in the event you sell, but you should know you can eliminate that problem by reverting the house to a non-income-producing property for one tax year before the sale. You might make some arrangement where your roommate would pay you a full year's rent in advance, putting that income into the tax year prior to your selling the house. Your house would then be income-free for the year of the sale. Also, by having a roommate you *could* lose some benefits from government programs if the amount of your assistance is based on total household income. New legislation is expected to remove that barrier, however. Do check with an attorney for the best procedure for you.

• How about dividing that too big house into two separate apartments, living in one and renting the other? This is an increasingly popular solution to the dilemma of the elderly person who wants to stay at home despite financial burdens. It has become so popular, in fact, that more and more communities that have "no apartments" restrictions are making exceptions only for those 62 years of age or older. Frequently the community offers a low-cost rehabilitation loan, too, for converting the place. Once the rent money starts coming in, it can go toward paying off the loan. Accessory apartments are an excellent, practical solution to an elderly person living alone in a ten-room house, and are worth investigating before deciding you *must* sell and move. Before seeking any type of loan for the conversion, however, be sure to check your local office on aging or regional HUD office to see if you qualify for a low-interest home improvement loan for the project, because of either your age or income.

• If you find you're likely to be one of those house-rich, cash-poor retirees, a couple of new plans have emerged over the last few years that tap into the equity of the homeowner—that potentially vast amount of money sitting there untouched—and provide him or her with an attractive monthly income. Remember these important caveats when considering them, however: (1) *they are not designed to make you money;* (2) *they do involve risk;* and (3) *they will reduce the size of your estate.*

The *reverse annuity mortgage* (RAM) is one of those plans. Let's say you own a home free and clear that is now worth $80,000 on the open market. That's $80,000 in equity that presumably you will not be able to use until you sell. But why wait till then, some lenders ask. Borrow on the house now, using it as collateral. (Their interests, let it be said, are not entirely altruistic. They have an eye on the huge $500 million-plus market that represents homes owned by the nation's elderly.)

So with a RAM the lending institution will allow you to borrow perhaps $64,000 (80 percent of market value) for ten years. The lender pays you several hundred dollars a month rather than your paying the lender. At the end of the ten-year term, your house is mortgaged for $64,000. If the mortgagor (you) dies before the maturity date, repayment usually comes from the settlement of the estate. If the mortgagor outlives the loan, the house can be sold to repay the debt, or be refinanced.

The RAM is not a mortgage as you are acquainted with the term. For one thing, you must already have paid up your existing mortgage, or have just a minimal balance due, to be considered for the loan.

This source of available cash should be tapped only after a great deal of studying and consultation. It has many still unresolved problems and can be a particularly poor choice if you are a *young* retiree. If you take out a RAM at 65, what happens when it falls due when you are 75 (the loans are usually offered at just ten or fifteen years)? Do you want to sign up for a regular mortgage at that time if you cannot repay in full then? Will you be able to renegotiate the RAM? Do you want to bother with all this when you are 75?

On the other hand, if you took out a ten-year RAM at 65 and you're still going strong at 75 and want to continue homeownership, you can probably tap your home for still more money. Property value appreciation is your hidden trump, especially if you have maintained your home carefully and neighborhood prices are generally upwardly mobile.

Even at a rate of appreciation of only 5 percent a year, your $80,000 property will be worth just under $125,000 at the end of your ten-year RAM. And what if the rate of appreciation approaches 9, 14, or even 20 percent a year, as it still does in some parts of the country? Your property could double or triple in value while you collect an income from it!

But let's take a conservative 5 percent annual appreciation rate. At the end of your RAM you will still have $61,000 equity in your home, which is now worth $125,000. You can sell and take your $61,000 after having received $64,000 in payments over the past ten years. Or, if you are determined to stay another five years or so, you can write another RAM. If the lender gives you an 80 percent loan on your equity, you will receive approximately $48,000 over the next five years. Those checks, however, will be larger, not smaller, than your previous RAM checks since the term of the loan is half as long. And if you're lucky, your property will keep right on appreciating.

Some of you may be gleefully filling scrap paper with figures after having read about RAMs. Others may be writing for cruise brochures. But still others, probably most others, will by now be hopelessly stuck in the mud of numbers. It does get murky when you start sounding mortgaging's deep waters, and most of us need a professional guide. So talk with a financial advisor (or two) about your complete financial and investment program for retirement before you sign up for a RAM or any of the other "creative" home-financing plans.

A variation on the ready-cash theme is the *sale-leaseback*, where you sell your home to an investor, who then rents it to you for as long as you live. The proceeds of the sale can be used for rent. This solution might interest you if you'd like to sell the house to your child, who would inherit anyway, allowing him or her the tax benefits of ownership now. The buyer takes on all property tax payments and all maintenance. You become a tenant, responsible for none of those bills. A downpayment to you provides you with a nice chunk of immediate income. If it's your child or other relative who becomes your landlord, bear in mind that the Treasury Department has declared that in order for the buyer to take advantage of tax benefits involved in this transaction, the rent paid by the seller must be no less than a fair-market figure. So Junior won't be able to charge you a token $100 a month to make things easier for you.

This program, too, is still in the early setting-up stages and it too requires a good deal of thought and discussion with your lawyer, the lending institution, and ombudsmen for the elderly.

For more information, you can write for the government pamphlet "Turning Home Equity into Income for Older Homeowners," available for $3 from the Consumer Information Center, Dept. 235L, Pueblo, Colo. 81009.

You can also contact the consumer watchdog group on the subject, the National Center for Home Equity Conversion, at 110 E. Main St., Room 1010, Madison, Wis. 53703, for printed material. A stamped, self-addressed envelope is requested.

Selling Your Home to Move . . . Where?

You may already know that if you or your spouse is 55 years of age or older and have owned and lived in your home any three consecutive years of the five years before you sell, you are entitled to a federal tax exemption on the first $125,000 profit from the sale. That exemption applies to principal residences only and can be used only once in a lifetime by either partner in a marriage. At this writing that restriction can cause problems, however. Let's say you're a woman of 50 and you and your husband, 56, decide to sell your home and retire to Florida. You are entitled to the $125,000 exemption, and you take it cheerfully. At age 58 your husband dies. A few years later you're now 56 and want to remarry. Your intended husband is 64 and lives in Florida, in a home he's owned for many years. If you both decide he'll sell that house, and the two of you will buy another one together, he will not be entitled to that tax exemption, *unless* he sells before you are married. Similarly, if you marry and you move into his house for two years and then the two of you decide you'd like to sell and move into something smaller, there, too, the exemption is forfeited because *you've* already taken it once. Legislation reconsidering the qualifications for this exemption is now being proposed, and no doubt the strong elderly lobby will contribute to its quick passage.

If You Want To Move To Another Part of the Country . . . Or the World

There are a number of books and guides that can help you decide on the wisdom of heading for warmer (or colder or just different) climes. These publications consider weather, cost of living, crime, health care, and other factors that could affect the quality of your life there, and your pocketbook.

Places Rated Retirement Guide by Richard Boyer and David Savageau. Rand McNally. 1984. $9.95.

Sunbelt Retirement by Peter Dickinson. E. P. Dutton. 1979. $14.95 cloth; $8.95 paper.

Travel and Retirement Edens Abroad by Peter Dickinson. E. P. Dutton. 1983. $12.95 paper.

Woodall's Florida and Southern States Retirement & Resort Communities Directory, 500 Hyacinth Pl., Highland Park, Ill. 60035. $7.00. Contains listings and photographs for Florida, North and South Carolina, Georgia, Mississippi, Alabama, Arkansas, Louisiana, and Texas.

The U. S. Bureau of Labor Statistics, Office of Information, Room 1539, GAO Building, 441 G St. N.W., Washington, D.C. 20212, publishes an annual budget estimate for retired couples for forty metropolitan and nonmetropolitan areas around the country. Taken into account are costs of housing, food, transportation, medical care, and the like. No charge.

If you are younger than 55 when you sell, then you must pay a tax on profit you realize from the sale. However, you can postpone the payment of that tax if you then reinvest the proceeds into another house of equal or greater value. You must do this twenty-four months before or after the sale of the original home.

To Rent or Buy?

Perhaps you are renting now and wonder if owning your own place, now that you are about to retire, is the wiser move. Or you might feel guilty in wishing you could sell your home and move into an apartment. Isn't rent just money down the drain, you wonder. There is a more complete discussion of the buy–rent issue in

Chapters 1 and 9. It should be mentioned here, however, that there is nothing intrinsically smarter in either decision these days. If you want and can afford a house, go ahead and buy. You should not expect the return for your investment, though, you may have earned pre-1979. Houses are more often purchased for shelter nowadays and are not appreciating in market value as rapidly as they did just prior to the 1980s. (This is subject to area and desirability, of course. Across the nation you will find annual housing increases ranging from an average of 5 percent to close to 25 percent in especially "hot" markets.) If you prefer renting and are prepared to cope with potentially dramatic rent rises if there is no rent control where you live, then go apartment shopping. Housing, as you will see from the diagram on page 652, is probably going to take over 30 percent of your retirement income. Whether you spend that money renting or owning is up to you to decide after much homework and fiddling around with numbers. Many, many retirees sell their older homes and pay cash for their new condos or mobiles. (Whether *that's* such a smart move will be considered further along in this chapter.)

Housing Options

From a large home to a smaller place is usually the theme here, with several choices as variations. All of the following options are for those who are still able to live independently, both in terms of general health and financial resources:

• *Sell and rent an apartment*. Use the proceeds from the home sale to pay the rent.

• *Condominiums and townhomes*. These are rapidly becoming *the* starter home for young people—and *the* housing choice for "empty nesters," too.

• *Cooperatives*. These are not as common as the condo, but here, too, you can have as small a space as you like, with minimal upkeep.

• *Mobile homes*. Although families and young single buyers are making inroads into the mobile home buyer profile, this housing style has always featured an overwhelming number of retirees. Attractive mobile home parks with congenial neighbors and a safe environment are a part of the reason. Another is the virtually maintenance-free living here: mobiles are usually paneled and carpeted throughout. Exteriors require no upkeep. There's a lengthier discussion of mobile homes in Chapter 24.

• *The single family home*. You can always purchase another house like the one you are leaving, only smaller. A two-family home would cut down even further on unused and unneeded rooms and would bring in a rental income besides, *if* you feel up to the role of landlord at this stage of your life.

• *Moving in with your children*. As mentioned above, nearly one in five retirees does just that. Perhaps in your case, since we are covering several generations here, you might move in with your *parent*.

• *Government-subsidized senior citizen housing*. These are buildings reserved strictly for those of retirement age and living within certain income limitations. Applicants must also be able to live independently as far as health considerations go. There are no medical services involved here. Besides ordinary apartment accouterments, you can expect to find such features as Braille elevator buttons in the buildings, emergency buzzers for assistance in each bedroom and bathroom, and usually a few apartments with widened doorways and appropriately positioned furnishings set aside for those confined to wheelchairs. Most of these complexes boast an active social program for residents.

If you qualify, you can expect to pay as rent the higher of 30 percent of adjusted income, 10 percent of gross income, or the portion of welfare assistance designated for housing costs.

Generally, you must be 62 years of age to qualify for senior citizen housing, and buildings almost always have lengthy waiting lists, perhaps of five years or more. Don't let that deter you, however. Apply anyway, and make application at as many of these complexes as you can. That's perfectly legal. Apply *before* you think you might like to move into senior citizen housing, so that you have a few years to make up your mind. You can apply before you want the housing, but you must wait until you are the minimum age for admittance. As mentioned, don't be too dismayed at the waiting list. Many times when there is a vacancy, names of waiting applicants are struck off rapidly. Some have found other housing, others have been admitted to other complexes.

For more information, contact your local housing authority.

• *The granny flat*. A fairly new housing concept that has come to these shores from Australia. It has the support of groups concerned about the elderly and, while far from commonplace at this writing, it does offer a housing alternative that's worthy of consideration.

The granny flat is a self-contained, single-story dwelling of about 500 square feet. Factory-made, it's designed for easy installation in a parent or child's backyard and it is meant strictly for an aged relative. Since only about fifty of the structures have been sold so far in this country, no special buying pattern has emerged, but zoning boards are expected to be favorable to the concept, provided the unit is sold and/or dismantled when no longer needed by the relative. The structure costs just under $20,000. So far it is being produced only by Coastal Colony Corporation in Lititz, Pa. (717) 665-6761, which manufactures a one-bedroom unit, complete with appliances and carpeting.

• *The adult community*. Finally, in considering housing options, a word about the adult community. You've no doubt seen at least one of them sprout up in your area over the last couple of decades. Perhaps you've visited friends who live in such a development. You may even have spent a few afternoons poking around yourself, visiting model homes and apartments. One of the more interesting aspects of these complexes, which are sometimes also called "retirement communities," is that you don't have to be retired to live there. Far from it. Age requirements are frequently as young as the mid-40s, and that just applies to at least one member of the household.

Adult communities are just that—strictly no children under 18 allowed on a permanent basis (although some cases now in the courts are testing that ban.) The developments offer residents attractive new homes, frequently of brand-new construction, plus security, the companionship of folks their own age and with their interests, and a cruise-ship variety of recreational activities. They often cost no more than a single-family home or condo in one's former neighborhood would. And who wouldn't want to live in a country club like that, muse many retirees.

This is an excellent concept, as the growing number of seniors moving into the developments would attest. A few points should be mentioned, however, before *you* sign a sales contract:

Be sure you really do want an age-segregated community. When it comes to day-in, day-out living, you may in fact prefer a more heterogeneous environment. And speaking of age, remember the "no children" clause in the deed is strictly enforced. What if one of your kids should lose a job, or become divorced, and want to come home for a while with his or her child? What if you are a single living in such a community and marry someone with children under 18? Would you have to move? Yes, in all likelihood, although a few couples having children while living in those communities are testing the "no kids" ban in the courts. Generally, children under 18—your own and guests of yours—are allowed to stay no longer than two weeks per year. Nonovernight visits, of course, are not restricted.

An attractive clubhouse, or community center, is an important feature of most adult communities. *Reprinted with permission of H. Hovnanian Companies.*

• *If the community in which you are interested is not near your present home, will you still be close enough to relatives and friends you want to keep in touch with?*

• *Keep in mind if you are coming from a private home that there will be a certain small shock at first in living in a "community."* Condos, townhomes, cooperatives, and mobile home parks all usually have some sort of owners' association, and very definite rules and regulations. Be sure you can live comfortably with those strictures, and allow yourself time to settle in. This isn't at all like just being a good neighbor was at your former home. You're all tied together a lot more closely here. A suggestion: Why not try to rent a home or apartment in one of those communities to see how you like it? Many owners travel from time to time and allow their units to be rented. Renting will give you an excellent look at the community, the activities, the complaints, and even the weather.

Finally, it should be pointed out that although the term "retirement community" is frequently used, it should not be confused with "continuing care community" or "lifecare community"—which are also sometimes referred to as "retirement" villages or communities. In the adult community discussed above, we are talking only about the purchase of a home. Continuing care facilities involve a cash "endowment" to the sponsor and usually medical care for the life of the resident. There's more about them later in this chapter.

For more information about adult communities in your area, and their locations, you can contact your state or local office on aging.

How to Pay for a Retirement Home

It's a whole new world of home financing out there, one far removed from the days when you purchased your existing home with perhaps a 7 percent mortgage running for twenty-five or thirty years. Maybe you now have no mortgage at all; indeed, celebrated a mortgage-burning party many years ago. You have not kept up at all—indeed why should you have?—with the growing and complicated maze of home-financing programs that have sprung up since 1979. If this sounds like your situation as you approach retirement, then welcome to the confusing world of "creative financing" for the late 1980s. There's a full discussion of mortgaging a home in Chapters 19 and 20. It should be pointed out here, however, that in a fixed-income situation such as retirement, some plans are going to be better than others.

Some 50 percent to 60 percent of Americans pay cash for their retirement homes, usually plunking down the proceeds from the sale of the home they are leaving. That can be a wise or a foolish move, and only you can figure which is the savviest way to go if you find yourself in the position of being able to pay outright for the home you select. In one way, it's a fine feeling to have no mortgage to worry about. On the other hand, if paying for a new home leaves you no money at all in the kitty for emergencies, that makes it not such a hot idea. Always hold back enough from the sale of a house to have some ready cash on hand, even if you have to take out a small mortgage. Also, the federal tax deduction you are allowed on the mortgage interest can reduce your annual federal income tax payments. In paying cash you forfeit that benefit.

Bear in mind, too, that real estate is not a liquid investment, so when you need cash in a hurry for any kind of unexpected crisis, you can't turn to your house (unless you have the sort of home equity loan where you have arranged for a line of credit before you actually need it so that the money is there when you do). So if all your other retirement savings are tied up in nonliquid investments, hold out some from a house sale to keep handy.

A mortgage also makes sense if you're not 100 percent certain you want, say, to move south and stay there the rest of your life. If you have no prepayment penalties on the loan, you can try living in the

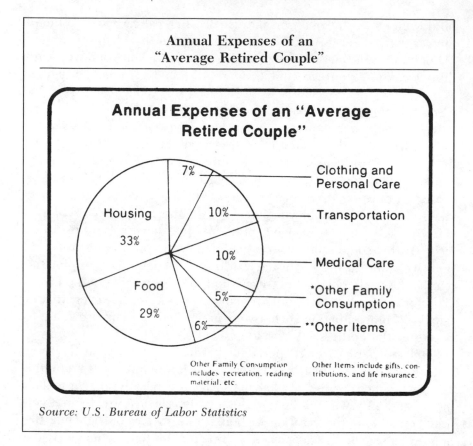

Annual Expenses of an "Average Retired Couple"

Source: U.S. Bureau of Labor Statistics

area you choose for a year or so, and then sell if it all doesn't turn out the way you had hoped. Your investment here is naturally much smaller and affords you the luxury of being able to cut your losses with a minimal financial penalty (points and closing costs).

When it comes to the style of mortgage, retirees probably do best with the fixed-rate loan, one that guarantees the same interest rate for twenty-five or thirty years. The new, adjustable plans with interest rates that fluctuate, frequently rising as interest rates in general move up, are not for those whose incomes do not rise.

If you are at the preretirement stage, perhaps in your 50s, there *is* one of the creative programs that could work well for you, and that's the growing equity mortgage (GEM). With this loan you make a good-size downpayment on your retirement house or condo. In the first three years of the GEM the monthly payments remain the same. After that they rise about 5 percent a year, with the additional money going to pay off the principal. With an increase of that size the house should be paid off in less than fifteen years, so you will own your home free and clear when you retire. It is presumed that folks in their 50s can afford the rising payments since they are at the peak of their earnings and child-rearing costs presumably have diminished. That's what makes the GEM a good buy at that time.

If it has been many years since you have had to concern yourself with mortgages, it's pretty important that you begin acquainting yourself with today's programs while you ponder housing choices. It's an entirely different world of home financing out there nowadays. Wait till you see!

The Life Care Facility, Home Health Care, and the Nursing Home

If you can no longer live alone, with medical problems that make it increasingly difficult for you to manage in your home—or if you have a parent in that situation—you might consider these choices.

The Continuing Care Community

These complexes are also called "life care facilities," and they are just that—for an entrance fee and regular monthly payments you are assured an apartment of any size you wish, meals, and a certain range of medical services and facilities for the rest of your life.

There are some 600 of these communities around the country, according to the American Association of Homes for the Aging, an association of nonprofit life care homes that is located in Washington, D.C. They aren't inexpensive. Single persons or couples must pay an entrance fee, also called an "endowment," that can range from $20,000 to well over $100,000. There is a monthly charge, similar to a maintenance fee or rent, that can run from around $250 to well over $500.

Life care complexes can be—indeed, usually are—among the most attractive of housing complexes. Many feature pools, golf courses, hotel-like lobbies with handsome furnishings, elegant dining rooms, beauty salons, and a range of shops on the premises. Residents are free to cook in their apartments or can take their meals in the communal dining room. Pets are usually allowed, and everyone can come and go as they please. This is not a hospital or nursing home, after all. To all appearances, in fact, the continuing care home resembles a first-class condominium community, but it is for the elderly only. The average age for admittance is 77, although it is possible to move in at 60 (hardly "elderly").

What makes this type of housing particularly distinctive, and what is contributing to its growing popularity, is the medical care that is available as long as the resident lives in the facility. The extent of doctor calls, physical and occupational therapy, drugs, and other medical benefits offered depends on the charge for admittance. Pay a lower up-front fee and medical services are likely to be extra, although almost always there is at least a staffed infirmary on the premises. If your endowment charge is high, substantial medical benefits are likely to be included. There is a portion of the entrance fee, high or low, and monthly maintenance charges that apply to medical care and are tax-deductible.

Life care is a fine concept, and the number of new communities is growing to meet a demand brought about by the rising population of the aged and the generally good services offered by continuing care. Still, some problems have surfaced over the last decade or so since the concept took off, and they can be sticklers.

One is that a few such homes are operated by charlatans. There aren't many, but if there is one group of people that brings out the bad guys in force, it's the elderly (another being the poor). A few life care operators (one of them a retired minister) have been under investigation by the Federal Trade Commission over the years for questionable business practices. Some continuing care complexes are just about to sink into insolvency. How would you like to put your life savings into one of those?

The second potential problem is the resident's own concern— what happens if you eventually run out of money, given inflationary increases in maintenance fees over the years? This can be handled in any number of ways. Most life care communities set aside emergency funds to subsidize such residents, but how long that underwriting lasts is a question you will certainly want answered in investigating a home.

When it comes to that investigation, here's what to look for, specifically:

1. Is the institution licensed? All nursing units must be licensed by the state, but only a few states require the *residential* part of retirement homes to be licensed.

2. Is it licensed as nonprofit or profit-making? Look cautiously at any homes run for profit, although they are certainly not all questionable operations. Nonprofit homes are usually affiliated with a religious denomination, although applicants of any faith—or no faith—are accepted. Do not assume, however, that that denomina-

tion's headquarters will bail out the home if it should fall into financial chaos.

3. Be sure to talk to the administrator of any home you are considering.

4. Ask for a copy of the contract and then have your lawyer go over it with you.

5. Be sure you know what services are included in the monthly maintenance fee and which are extra. Especially important is understanding how many, or how few, medical expenses will be included in the entrance price. Are you buying full care, limited care, or pay-as-you-go medical attention? (Medical care, not so incidentally, usually excludes—at least at no extra cost—dental care, podiatrists, hearing aids, and psychiatry.)

6. Ask for a copy of the home's most recent financial audit or its annual report.

7. Ask for a copy of the facility's rules to be sure you can live with them, literally.

8. Who is responsible for the home's debts (mortgage and the like), and how will you be protected against a possible bankruptcy of that institution, or any other severe financial problem?

9. How much do residents have to say about how the facility is run? Is there a residents' association? Are they involved in management decisions? Is there a newsletter for the complex that will give you an idea of what's going on?

10. What happens if you don't like the place you've chosen? Is there a trial period? What if you die shortly after moving in? What happens to your endowment? In most communities there is full repayment to the resident or his or her heirs within the first three months, and then there is a refund that depreciates about 2 percent or 3 percent a month for a specified period of time. After that, there is no refund.

11. Talk to residents. Have a meal in the dining room if you can.

12. Finally, if life care interests you, better plan ahead. You may be amazed to know that there are lengthy waiting lists for many communities, especially for the older, more desirable (translation: financially stable) complexes and those in locations where there is little competition. At the long-established Kendall–Crosslands, which is affiliated with the Quakers and consists of two facilities in the Delaware Valley in Pennsylvania, there are usually close to a thousand people on a waiting list, which means a wait of three to ten years, depending on the size of apartment sought. You can see that moving into a life care community cannot be a snap decision. If you

want to put money down on a unit you will move into in a few years, be sure that amount is deposited into a special escrow account for residents. You don't want any institution, especially one with a financially troubled management, to be dipping into your entrance fee.

For more information about life care communities you can send for:

"Continuing Care Homes: A Guidebook for Consumers," published by the American Association of Homes for the Aging (AAHA). It contains general information about this style of housing, including details about financing, administration, and the types of services offered. Write AAHA, Suite 770, 1070 Seventeenth St. N.W., Washington, D.C. 20036. Price: $2.00. Free brochure, "The Continuing Care Retirement Community" and the $13.95 book, "National Continuing Care Directory" are available from AARP (American Association of Retired Persons), 400 So. Edward St., Mt. Prospect, Ill. 60056. For the directory add $1.45 for postage. Both publications are a joint effort of AAHA and AARP.

Consumers Guide to Independent Living for Older Americans," a 24-page booklet to guide you in selecting a life care community, put out by the Life Care Society of America, Ferry & Iron Hill Rds., Doylestown, Pa. 18901. No charge.

A *Directory of Retirement Communities in the U.S.*, a listing of more than two thousand facilities nationwide of all types, not just continuing care homes. Price: $18.50, including postage. It is available from the National Housing Center, College of Architecture and Urban Planning, University of Michigan, Ann Arbor, Mich. 48109.

Home Health Care

For the elderly who would like to stay at home as long as possible, or who cannot afford the continuing care community, home health services can be considered. Because of the growing number of aged, this is an area of human services, both on the government and private levels, that has been expanding every year. It has enabled many seniors who would otherwise have to be hospitalized or confined to a nursing home to live with their families, or even alone.

All types of services are available here, from health care to shopping assistance. Fees vary, from about $15 an hour for a registered nurse to come to the home, to $6 per hour for a companion. You are entitled to unlimited services by a registered nurse reimbursable by Medicare as long as your doctor certifies the need and the agency that provides the nurse is approved by a specified government office. Other home services are also reimbursable by Medicare, but only in conjunction with professional nursing. This is a changing arena, however, as several private health insurance policies will now allow homemaking services and personal care even if no skilled nursing is involved.

How to find home health services? Your physician is the best source of information, but the director of social services at your local hospital can help, too. You might also direct any questions to the National Association of Area Agencies on Aging, 600 Maryland Ave. S.W., Suite 208, Washington, D.C. 20024; telephone (202) 484-7520.

The booklet "All About Home Health Care: A Consumers Guide" is available from the National HomeCaring Council, 235 Park Ave. South, New York, N.Y. 10003. Send a self-addressed business envelope. It will need two stamps.

Choosing a Nursing Home

When a parent or other loved one needs professional care that can no longer be provided at home, families usually look to the nursing home. All of the caveats listed in selecting a life care facility apply to nursing homes as well. They include in-person visits to check for an attractive, well-run, and *financially solvent* institution.

More than two thirds of the nation's 1.4 million nursing home residents receive some financial aid, either Medicaid or Medicare. Each state has its own requirements for eligibility to facilities in that state and to the availability of some form of government assistance. That can present a complicated picture even within a nursing home: the private patient versus the one receiving 100 percent government aid; the patient receiving medical treatment versus the one there only for "custodial care"; the one entering the home directly from a hospital versus the one coming in from home or another residence.

There is much investigative work to be done by families here, both in analyzing nursing homes and figuring out the family member's financial situation and ability to pay.

For more guidance and information on health care:

The National Council of Health Centers offers a free checklist to help evaluate a nursing home. Send a stamped, self-addressed envelope to NCHC at 2600 Virginia Ave. N.W., Suite 1100, Washington, D.C. 20037.

The National Citizens Coalition for Nursing Home Reform, a national consumer group, offers no printed material, but will be happy to answer any of your questions about nursing homes. The coalition is at 1309 L St. N.W., Washington, D.C. 20005, (202) 393-7979.

For More Information

The American Association of Retired Persons offers several free booklets that go along with a membership fee. That's $4 for one year's dues, $10 for three years'. Other benefits that go along with membership include a subscription to *Modern Maturity*, the bimonthly magazine of the AARP. The association is at 1909 K St. N.W., Washington, D. C. 20049. AARP can also answer inquiries about housing choices for older homeowners; life care communities, nursing homes, and day care centers for seniors. You must be at least 50 years old to join AARP, but you needn't be retired.

The National Council on Aging is at 600 Maryland Ave. S.W., West Wing 100, Washington, D. C. 20024.

"Housing as We Grow Older," five leaflets published by Cornell University. Price: $1.85 for all five. Write Cornell University Distribution Center, Seven Research Park, Ithaca, N.Y. 14850.

Your Personal Guide to Pre-Retirement Planning by the staff of Pilot Books. This is a workbook and contains checklists covering dozens of points to be considered in retirement planning—government benefits, legal and financial aspects of retirement; preparation and management of records; health and social factors. Price: $5. Write to Pilot Books, 103 Cooper St., Babylon, N.Y. 11702.

50 Plus magazine offers several guidebooks, including "Finding the Right Place for Your Retirement" and "Your Home and Your Retirement." Price: $3.15 each; New York state residents should add sales tax. Write *50 Plus* Guidebooks/Now, 850 Third Ave., New York, N.Y. 10022.

Planning Your Retirement Housing, by Michael Sumichrast, Ronald Shafer, and Marika Sumichrast. Published in conjunction with the American Association of Retired Persons. Available from AARP, 1909 K St. N.W., Washington, D.C. 20049. Price: $8.95.

"Protecting Older Americans Against Overpayment of Income Taxes" is available from: Special Committee on Aging, U.S. Senate, Dirksen Office Bldg., Rm. 6233, Washington, D.C. 20510.

"Turning Home Equity into Income for Older Americans," government publication #176M ($3), is available from Consumer Information Center, Pueblo, Colo. 81009.

"Estate and Gift Taxes," Internal Revenue booklet #448, available free from any IRS office.

41

Legal Strings: Zoning, Taxes, Eminent Domain, and the Deed

What would you think of if someone were to say "police power" to you? A hair-raising chase through city streets with sirens screaming and lights flashing? Detectives knocking at a door, revolvers drawn, a search warrant in hand? Uniformed crowd-control officers standing together elbow to elbow?

Yes, that's police power. But in legal terminology police power has a much broader meaning. So broad, in fact, that it directly affects every piece of real estate you own or use, even if yours is but a vine-covered cottage whose walkways have never been stepped upon by an officer of the law.

Police power is the right of a state to rule its citizens, including virtually all the powers that have not been turned over to the federal government. The state therefore can enact and enforce whatever laws are necessary to protect and enhance the public health, morals, safety, and general welfare. Think about that for a moment. It's a veritable panorama of power.

If we narrow the focus to real estate, a state's police power includes the right to tax real property, the right to regulate the use of land through zoning and building restrictions, and even (in extreme cases such as riot or war) the right to damage or destroy private property without payment when necessary for the public interest. (Seizure and condemnation of property with fair payment is not an aspect of police power but of *eminent domain*. More about that, however, later in this chapter.)

"But if police power gives the state government the right to regulate zoning, building, and taxation of real property," you ask, "Why do zoning, building codes, and real estate taxes differ from city to city within a single state?"

It's a good question, but the answer is quite simple. The state delegates these powers to municipal and county governments. The state court system, however, is available to hear cases where individuals feel that the laws of the municipal or county governments are either not just or not justly administered. The state also reserves the right to enact statewide legislation that will override local ordinances. (Condominium and co-operative apartment conversion rules and regulations are a good example of overriding statewide legislation.) Some municipal governments have added restrictions, regulations, and procedures to state laws, but none can negate them.

Considering the variety and complexity of real estate-related police powers, across the nation, from state to state, and from city to city, you're probably wondering if we can possibly say anything pertinent to your real estate interests in this chapter, or even in a volume if we had the time and space and you had the interest! And you may be surprised to hear us say, "Yes, we can!"

You see there is really less confusion, contradiction, and multiplicity than one would expect. Actually, the *concepts* of real property law are rather uniform throughout the country, and once you understand the concept (that is, once you understand what happens and why), you'll be able to ask the "right" questions of the "right" people in order to get the information or take the action necessary for your particular need. So read on. We'll keep as much legalese out of the writing as possible.

Zoning

The first zoning ordinance in this country was probably enacted in a colonial town, after a fire. Doubtless the townsfolk pointed the finger of blame at the business place of a local craftsman who needed an open hearth to pursue his trade. For the safety of the town, they relegated the new location for that man's business and all other "dangerous" businesses to one specified area on the outskirts of the town. Of course, the town then grew around the "dangerous business" area and more and more rules and regulations grew with it. Today, zoning laws and building codes in many counties, towns, and cities run to hundreds and hundreds of pages.

Zoning is generally divided into three main designations: industrial, commerical, and residential. But in many, in fact most areas, each of these has a number of subdivisions. Industry may be divided into "light," "heavy," or "research" zones. Residential zones may be very specific, such as "one-family houses on ½ acre," "not more than four living units to ¼ acre," "apartment buildings of no more than twelve stories," or "3000-square-foot or larger dwellings on 10 acres or more." The possible subdivisions and restrictions of zoning are almost as endless as human imagination can make them.

It is a general rule, however, that an area zoned for a given use can include lower-use buildings and land, but cannot include higher-use development. For example, let's assume we're talking about an area zoned for multifamily houses (no more than six separate living units on no less than ¼ acre). Within this zone you could build a single-family house on a lot of ¼ acre or larger, or you could build a two-family house on ¼ acre, or ten acres, but you could not build a convenience store, an auto-body repair shop, or an apartment building of twenty-four units.

Besides the use to be made of land and buildings in a given area, zoning law can also dictate the height of buildings, the materials used in their construction, the maximum and/or minimum square footage of floor space, the building's minimal distance from the street and side-and-rear property lines (called set-back lines), the placement and size of parking spaces, "green space," and on and on, even to the placement, size, and depth of waste disposal facilities and wells, if applicable.

These laws sometimes seem like so much superfluous red tape once an area is built upon and being used. But remember: if you buy a vacant lot upon which to build your dream house and then discover that you cannot comply with a zoning ordinance that requires a well and septic tank to be at least 300 feet apart, you may be stuck with an unbuildable lot. The laws seem superfluous because properties have been built in compliance with them; they are *not* superfluous to a property owner seeking to develop his or her land.

Nondisclosure of zoning restrictions is a valid reason for canceling a contract-to-purchase with full refund of your deposit monies. But you, the buyer, hold the ultimate responsibility of checking to see if the zoning requirements are consistent with your needs and plans. Zoning ordinances are a matter of public record; anyone can read through them and every buyer should check the restrictions on his or her intended purchase. Once you close on a property, it's yours. The fact that you didn't read through the zoning restrictions between the time you signed the contract and the closing is not a valid reason to rescind a consummated sale. Sometimes a title search will include a check on zoning restrictions, but don't count on it. Do it yourself.

Zoning Changes

Generally, zoning is established or changed by recommendation of a planning commission or planning board, which may be a group of professional planners, but is much more likely to be an appointed group of local citizens or a combination of appointed citizens and professional planners. Usually this group studies the projected growth of a community, its land-use problems, and other questions at hand and makes recommendations. Actual zoning *changes* are usually left to a vote of the town government. And before recommended changes are effected there are usually several open meetings at which members of the public may voice their opinions and concerns.

Zoning can be changed, however, "for the public good" without regard for the intended use of the landowners within a zone. For example, if you own 10 acres in Mudville upon which you decide to build townhouses, but the planning commission changes the zoning to single-family one-acre residential, you lose. You could take the case to court and try to prove that Mudville needs high-density, moderate-income housing. But the planners could point out that the town's sewerage treatment facilities are already overloaded and that poor drainage in the area rules out the possibility of using septic tanks for high-density housing. The planning board would probably win. If you wanted to develop the land, you'd have to build single-family houses (no more than ten of them) and you'd make a lot less money. Or you could wait until the town expanded its sewerage treatment plant.

All of which goes to illustrate some very good advice: *Don't buy land or plan to develop land you own unless you know not only the pulse beat but also the blood pressure of your local planning commission.* In other words, be aware of what is likely to happen in the near future.

Zoning can also be changed in areas of a community that are already at or near full development. Sometimes the change is gradual, over years. These areas of gradual change are sometimes called T zones, or transition zones. They are areas, for example, where commercial establishments are gradually being allowed to move into a residential area. Sometimes, however, a zoning change is simply assigned a date upon which it will take effect. This changeover

Many homeowners profit handsomely when a residential zone is changed to a T zone (Transition zone) and offices begin to displace private residences.

sometimes occurs when a town wishes to upgrade a rundown area, or change such an area into a shopping center or industrial park. For example, zoning may be changed from three-story multifamily dwellings to high-rise apartment buildings. This zoning change clears the way for developers to purchase the land and the rundown residences on it, clear them, and build new structures (sometimes with government help).

Many homeowners fear zoning changes, especially when T zones are used to allow commercial areas to expand. But many homeowners profit handsomely by selling their residential properties to a business needing a branch office or to a doctor or dentist or hairdresser needing a place to locate. Shopping-center and industrial-park developers have also been known to pay more than top dollar for houses that they plan to tear down and cover over with blacktop.

Sometimes zoning is changed after the fact, or in response to the obvious needs and usage of the public. In some areas of the country, for example, there were so many instances of property owners illegally converting their single-family houses to include rental units that the local government just conceded and changed the zoning to allow for such multifamily dwellings. Other towns have simply ignored the zoning law infringement and let the multifamily structures continue to exist in the single-family zoned areas.

Finally, zoning can be changed upon petition of a property owner

Some Sample Reasons for Getting a Variance
or Conditional Use Permit

You want to change your three-story townhouse from a one-family residence to three small apartments. The area is zoned for one-family dwellings.

You want to add on to your one-family house in a one-family zone an apartment with its own kitchen and bath for your mother-in-law. The addition will extend 2 feet beyond the front set-back line and have its own entranceway.

You want to build a fifty-unit rabbit hutch in your backyard but the zoning does not permit outbuildings or commercial enterprises.

The corner of your son's tree house will extend 9 inches into your neighbor's yard. Theoretically, you will need a building permit, a zoning variance, and an encroachment permit, maybe even a conditional use permit. All of which would surely cost more than the tree house. Some people would build the tree house without a permit (considering it an "insignificant construction") and, for fun, have the neighbor give the boy a very formal license to 9 inches of air rights.

You want to keep a horse. Local zoning law says one horse to three acres. You own 2.3 acres.

You are a hairdresser and you want to operate a salon in your basement. Or you wish to operate any professional office into which clients would come in a residential zone.

You want to add a three-story stone and glass contemporary addition to your Cape Cod house in a neighborhood of Cape Cods each on ¼ of an acre. Zoning limits the height of the buildings to two stories above the basement.

Your daughter wants to raise sheep as her 4-H project. Your half acre will be kept closely cropped, but isn't there something in the zoning law about sheep in a residential area?

You want to add a front porch and covered entrance stairway to your townhouse but the addition will bring the building right to the sidewalk. No one else in the neighborhood has built to the sidewalk.

You want to put in an in-ground pool. There's only one place to put it, and the pool's shallow end and the concrete walkway around it will extend 6 feet beyond the side set-back line and 6 feet into a water company easement that runs down the side of your lot. (You might get the variance for the pool, but remember if the water company pipe should break, you could one day find a backhoe quite legally digging up the shallow end of your pool!)

or community group. If you own a 90-acre tract, for example, and wish to sell 30 acres to a builder for the construction of a condominium retirement community, you may apply to the planning commission for a zoning change from farmland to high-density housing. Expect some objections, however. Virtually always, even when the most obviously beneficial changes are proposed, there are voices raised in objection. And there will certainly be delays.

Nonconforming Use

The enactment of a zoning law cannot force a property owner to move or to change an already established use of his property. If, for example, John Applewite has legally operated a roadside fruit and produce store in a certain location for three years (or any length of time) and a zoning law is then enacted making the area in which the store is located a ½-acre single-family residential zone, Applewite may continue to operate his business in its present building and location. The business and the building are termed a nonconforming use.

If Applewite decided to change the use of his building from a fruit stand to a movie theater, however, he would be in violation of the law since the theater did not predate the residential zoning.

Since it is an exception to the law, nonconforming use is rather strictly interpreted, usually with an eye to eventually eliminating it. In some areas, even repairs and maintenance to nonconforming use structures are limited to those that will not extend the useful life of the building. Usually the structure cannot be enlarged or the business significantly expanded in any way. In most cases, the business cannot even change owners. That is, the property cannot be sold as a business that does not conform to the zoning code, unless a variance is granted to the new owner. Sometimes the nonconforming use is even limited to a certain number of years. This number is most often determined by the estimated remaining useful life of the structure and is called "amortization of use."

How To Apply for a Variance or Conditional Use Permit

Talk with your town or county clerk. Ask about the local procedure. Is there a fee? Get an application form and read it, right there when you get it, to be sure you understand *everything*. If not, ask questions. Get the names of the members of the Board of Adjustment.

If possible meet informally with one, some, or all of the members of the Board of Adjustment. Ask if there should be any problems in getting a variance such as yours. The answer may be "none at all" and you can then rest a little easier. Or it may be a long list of "possibles," in which case you can start the research necessary to anticipate objections and answer them effectively at the hearing.

Talk with your neighbors. You want to "sound" for attitudes and objections. Be prepared to answer the questions and objections you hear or sense when your hearing comes up.

Gather all the supportive data that you will need. Architect's drawings, building plans, color slides, information on "perc test" results, a contour survey with probable drainage patterns indicated, well water tests and an opinion on the availability of water, the height of your building and its siting (will you block the sun from someone else?), an estimate of increased traffic flow due to your change in the use of your property—these are but a few suggestions. You should think through all the possibilities of what you might need to present your petition effectively. If you are unsure of yourself, get help from an architect, a member of the planning commission, or perhaps someone else in town who has a similar variance.

Fill out the application forms for all variances and permits you will need and pay application fees, if any. You can request that hearings for all your applications be heard at one meeting (if you need more than one, that is). Sometimes this works and sometimes you will have to appear several times, once for each permit that you are requesting.

Attend hearings well-dressed and well-prepared. Present your petition and its rationale clearly and as briefly but thoroughly as possible.

Answer all questions or objections. Again, briefly but thoroughly. Under no circumstances should you lose your temper. Shouting and fist-on-the-table pounding will lose supporters (and listeners).

Be prepared for time delays and postponements. They can go on for months.

If your variance or conditional use permit is approved, start work.

If it is denied, you can:
Make some changes and adjustments and apply again. And again, if you have the time, money, and perseverance. Sometimes you can wear down opposition by persistence.

File suit in the state court system if you think that you have a chance of proving that your petition is "reasonable" and that its denial is causing you a hardship. Get a lawyer at this point, a good one who knows local zoning and local officials.

The Variance and the Conditional Use Permit
Because each person in the population of a town is unique and sees the town through his or her own eyes, there are exceptions to almost every rule or law on the town's books. Zoning laws, however, are so often "adjusted" to individual needs that virtually every town that has a Planning Commission also has a Board of Adjustment (sometimes called the Zoning Board of Appeals).

Theoretically any potential violation or variation of the zoning law must be approved by the Board of Adjustment before the owner goes ahead with the intended improvement or "illegal" use. The property owner must apply for a *variance*.

In some states applications for the adjustment of zoning laws are further subdivided between a *variance* for tangible infringements (adding a second story in a one-story zone, for example) and a *conditional use permit* for exceptional use of a structure (as, for example, a psychiatrist's office in his home in a residential zone).

In some municipalities application for a variance is a simple procedure. You fill out the application and appear before the Board of Adjustment. In other areas, however, there is an application fee that can run between $500 and $2000 and sometimes a wait of several months for your appointment before the board.

Everywhere, however, there is a certain amount of politics involved in obtaining a variance. One member of the Board of Adjustment in a negative mood can cause delays of several months. And one or more negative members can sometimes sway others to vote "no" on your appeal. (Somehow it always seems to be easier to say "no" than to say "yes.")

And then there are your neighbors. In the majority of towns and counties across the country, whenever a property owner applies for a variance or a conditional use permit, registered letters are sent to all the other property owners in a designated area around his or her property to notify these neighbors of the date, time, and place of a public hearing on the application to the Board of Adjustment. Most often no one shows up, but a vociferous objection from a few neighbors can result in a refusal. (The application fee, if there is one, is usually not refundable even if the variance is refused.) If a property owner feels that his or her request for a variance has been unreasonably denied, he or she can appeal to the state judicial system. It would probably be wise to get a lawyer.

Architects, general contractors, and some savvy homeowners sometimes arrange informal meetings with members of the Board of Adjustment before applying for a variance in order to talk about the likelihood of its being approved and any potential stumbling blocks to that approval. These meetings may or may not be beneficial. They may not even be entirely accurate since an objection can be raised by a member of the community that no one anticipated. But the meetings can't hurt.

In contrast, there are those more willful (or perhaps foolhardy) property owners who go ahead with their remodelings or changes in the use of their buildings, ignoring the need for a variance. Sometimes they save themselves an application fee or fees, time, additional taxes, and trouble. And sometimes they don't. If someone, anyone, complains about the zoning violation, or if the building inspector or tax assessor happens to come along, local officials can get a court injunction to stop construction, even if stopping means that the property owner must cover newly cut holes in his outside walls with heavy plastic sheets! The delay can last for months and at worst the variance can be denied. In that event the person-who-went-ahead-and-did-it will have to put the property back to its original state, or at least to a state that conforms with the law.

PUDs

PUD stands for planned unit development, an idea that really took hold in the early 1970s as a solution to the problem of housing more people on less land while maintaining some "open space" or "green space." In a PUD, dwelling units are clustered and the open land is maintained for the use of the entire PUD community. Small shopping centers and some office space may be included in the PUD zoning, usually clustered conveniently in the center of the complex.

Today, most PUDs are condominium communities. Sometimes they are very large and include clusters of housing in different architectural styles and at different price levels. The condominium maintains the shared land and recreation facilities and sometimes even the roads.

Inclusionary Zoning

Inclusionary zoning is a child of the 1980s' housing crunch. With the price of new construction still rising and interest rates high, moderate-income Americans were being shut out of the new housing market. Until, that is, inclusionary zoning was tried in California, Maryland, New Jersey, and Oregon. In those states, and now in other areas too, planning commissions were persuading (or sometimes requiring) builders to include a proportionate number of low- and moderately-priced houses in their development plans. These houses would be sold at prices that were lower than comparable properties in the area.

Two questions pop into mind: How could the builders do that without losing money? And how did the planning commissions persuade them to accept the plan?

The persuasion was a kind of arm twisting. The planning commissions made the zoning changes that were necessary for approval of the development contingent upon the inclusion of the smaller houses. They also promised the builders that the necessary variances and permits would be processed quickly, thus saving the money that time delays eat up. The builders made up for the shortfall in profits on the smaller, sometimes below-cost houses by charging slightly more for the larger, more luxurious, and more profitable houses.

Building Codes

Building codes fall under the police power of a state to guard the health and welfare of its citizens. State governments do set some minimum statewide building code standards, such as elevator safety codes, but essentially the enactment of building codes and their enforcement are the province of the local governments.

Building codes can run to hundreds of pages and can cover practically everything. Consider this sample list:

• *Location on the lot*. Set-back lines beyond which the building cannot extend without a variance.

• *Construction*. The materials used, the manner in which they are put together, and even the licensing and supervision of the workers.

• *Chimneys*. Their composition, height, width, and structure.

• *Architectural design*. Not only style, but also the number of stories, size, span, height of ceilings, number of windows per room, number of exits, and on and on.

• *Occupancy*. The number of people per square foot of living space.

• *Fireproof construction*. Smoke alarms, sprinkler systems, barrier walls.

• *Plumbing*. Minimum standards for materials, venting, waste disposal (including septic tanks), sources of water and wells.

• *Electricity*. Kinds of wire, insulation, number of outlets per room, minimum service, fuse boxes, and circuit breakers.

• *Heating plant*. Minimum standards for efficiency and safety.

To a novice the building codes seem as formidable as reading through the *Encyclopedia Britannica*. But actually the codes add stability to the building process and are not nearly so intimidating to the people who use them. The codes, in fact, differ little from town to town throughout most areas of the country since most local governments have adopted, at least as a base, one of the four prevalent building codes now in use in the United States. These are:

In the West and some areas of the Midwest, the Uniform Building Code, developed by the International Conference of Building Officials.

In the South, the Southern Standard Building Code, developed by the Southern Building Code Congress.

In the East and North Central area, the Basic Building Code, developed by Building Officials and Code Administrators International.

In scattered other areas but not in the West, the National Building Code, developed by the American Insurance Association.

Also in use are a National Plumbing Code and a National Electrical Code that were developed by the National Fire Protection Association.

If you would like to know which building code is being used in your area, call your town building inspector or building inspection department and ask. If you want to know what the code specifies, go down to the office and read it; it's public information. Or arrange to have a copy of information on your specific question sent to you. If you have "why" and "how" questions on the code itself, you might try to contact the organization that created it. Your local reference librarian can get addresses and phone numbers for you.

Few people, however, have the patience to read building codes and, in fact, the local government employs building inspectors who should make it unnecessary for the lay person to be concerned with the codes. These inspectors inspect every building under construction at given checkpoints in the construction process. Even when a building is completed, it cannot be occupied until all inspections have also been completed satisfactorily and a certificate of occupancy (called a C-O) has been issued.

Public buildings and rental apartment buildings are also inspected periodically throughout their useful life, and code violations are noted for repairs. If between inspections, however, you believe that your rental apartment building or work place is in violation of the local building code, or if you are buying a new house and you think the builder did not meet the code requirements, you can file a complaint with your local building inspector and request an inspection of the property.

Private homes are usually not inspected after the first certificate of occupancy is issued unless a special request is made.

"So what about older homes?" you ask. "Say 60 or 70 years old, they couldn't possibly comply with the current-day codes. Are they safe? Are they ever inspected?"

Older homes that have not been remodeled are examples of nonconforming use; they may exist as they are until someone decides to alter them. Once a remodeling project is undertaken, however, whether it be a new kitchen or an addition, there is the very real possibility that local ordinances might require that the entire structure and all its working systems be brought up to code.

Do we need to add that you should check your local codes before starting a remodeling project if you own an older home? And you should talk to your building inspector about the codes before you buy a rundown house for restoration. Sometimes you can even get the building inspector to go through such a property with you and point out areas that will need repair or rebuilding in order to comply with the code. Without such knowledge, the house that you buy with an eye to fixing it up could cost you much more than you had thought.

Building inspectors are as much a part of the local government service staff as police officers or teachers, and their salaries are paid

How To Challenge Your Assessment

Your assessed valuation should be a fair expression of the relative value of your property in your community. But the possibility of error exists always and everywhere, and you do not have to sit quietly by and accept an assessment that you think too high or unfair. There are several steps you can take.

Checking Facts. If an on-site inspection is a part of the assessment process, go through the work sheet with the assessor before he or she leaves your property. Does the sheet indicate three *full* baths when in reality you have two and a half? Such small errors can mean higher taxes. You can also make an appointment to meet with the assessor in his or her office to check the facts on your property and to talk about how the assessment was determined. Correct errors and ask how the corrections will affect the assessment.

Comparing Properties and Assessments. Once a revaluation is complete, a tentative tax roll must be published and made available to the general public. Now you can compare your tax assessment with that of your neighbors and with other properties similar to yours in the town. You may contest an assessment that you feel is unequal, excessive, unlawful, or misclassified.

Contesting the Assessment. To contest your assessment go to the town clerk or the assessor's office and ask what forms must be filled out, by what date, and when you can appear before the assessment review board, if your community has one. Be sure that you understand everything on the forms that you fill out. If you have questions, ask them of the assessor's office staff or get the help of a local attorney. When you appear before the board, state your reasons for contesting the assessment clearly. Bring along all the supportive material and pertinent statistics that you have.

Going to Court. If your assessment review board turns you down or does not decrease your assessment to your satisfaction, or if your town does not have an assessment review board, you can go to court with your grievance. It is the burden of you, the property owner, however, to prove that the assessment is higher than it should be, so be prepared with adequate facts and figures. You may well want to have the help of an attorney.

Gathering Together. If a large number of property owners in a town feel that they have been assessed unfairly, it is sometimes a good idea to band together. You can consult with an attorney as a group and you might be able to arrange demonstrations or the like to attract media attention, which could put pressure on local officials.

from the same fund-raising effort: your local taxes. You guessed it! Taxes are next in our discussion of police power.

Property Taxes

Generally, local governments in this country get the major portion of their operating funds by taxing the real estate within their jurisdictions. Usually this is an *ad valorem tax*, that is, a tax according to valuation. However, determining value is often something of a knotty problem.

Until recently virtually all local governments in this country used periodic assessment to determine the value of property to be taxed. Then along came Proposition 13 in California, but let's save that for a little later.

In areas that currently use periodic assessment, professional assessors evaluate each piece of property and set an assessed valuation to it. These figures are then made public. Property owners are usually allowed to contest their assessments until a certain named date after the assessments are made public. Often adjustments are made, but after the named date the valuations are set. The town government then determines its mill rate. The mill rate and the assessed valuation, taken together, determine the amount of taxes each property owner will be required to pay.

A mill is one tenth of one cent and is the measure generally used to express the tax rate. A tax of one mill on a dollar is one tenth of one cent on a dollar. Thus if a town's tax rate was 43.5 mills and your property was assessed at $100,000 you would pay $4350 a year in taxes, figured as .0435 × $100,000 = $4350.

Revaluations for tax purposes are done periodically but the time interval differs from state to state or in some states from town to town, ranging from annual reassessments to periods of ten years or more. Tax rates can be based upon full-value assessment or they can be based upon a percentage of full value. In areas where revaluations are infrequent, most new construction is theoretically assessed in dollar value for the year of the last revaluation. The theory here is just, but the judgment not always so.

With the passage of Proposition 13 in California and its cousins in other states, property valuation for tax purposes became contingent upon the purchase price of a property when it changed hands. In many cases there were actually tax rollbacks. In some instances where purchase prices were inflated by creative financing, however, taxes went up disproportionately. These taxes were not based upon the fair market value of the property, contended buyers who were fighting their taxes in the court system. The buyers had knowingly paid a higher price for the property in order to get lower interest rates and beneficial financing terms. Tax valuation, however, is not tied to financing arrangements. Is the higher tax then fair? The decisions are varied and the court system is dotted with appeals. On those properties that do not sell in a given year, tax changes are tied to indices or stated percentages.

Taxation systems modeled on Proposition 13 are still in their infancy, but interest in them is high. Obviously there are many questions that still need to be tested and resolved. Whether this or some other method of determining fair taxation will replace the periodic revaluation by assessors remains to be seen.

Besides ad valorem property taxes, local governments can also tax for special improvements in a given area, sewers or sidewalks, for example. Such taxes are called assessments. They are usually made on a running-foot-of-frontage basis, not upon the value of the entire property. And usually you must pay your assessment even if you choose not to use the sewer line or the sidewalk or whatever the improvement is. After all, the improvement is for the good of the entire community. Unless you can prove otherwise, the government has the right to levy the tax.

Eminent Domain

The right of federal, state, or local government to acquire land needed for the public purpose is called eminent domain. The procedure by which the state acquires that land is called condemnation. The term *condemn*, however, has nothing to do with "being bad." A newly completed and decorated $250,000 house could be condemned by exactly the same procedure and for the same reason as a 45-year-old, vacant, six-family tenement building that has been neglected by its out-of-state landlord.

Two conditions are essential for a government to exercise legally its right of eminent domain and condemn a piece of property: (1) the land must be needed for a public purpose; and (2) the owner must be paid a fair price for it. *Public purpose* and *fair price* then are the two possible points of contention between a private citizen and a government that wishes to acquire his or her land.

Public Purpose

If you wish to contest a condemnation, you can ask the government to prove that your land is needed for a public purpose and that some other piece of land cannot reasonably be substituted. In questions of public purpose, much depends upon the nature of the use to which the government plans to put the land. A new school, for example, might reasonably be located somewhere else; an interstate highway, however, needs to go through your property, not around it.

Fair Price

Two or three appraisers are usually hired to make independent appraisals of a property in a condemnation proceeding. The property owner is then usually offered an average figure of the appraisals. Most often these offers are fair. You are not required, however, to accept the first offer that the government makes; you can negotiate. And most owners who negotiate do get a little more money. Negotiating, however, takes time, patience, perseverance, and sometimes nerves of steel.

While that time is passing, you have yet another effective tool at your disposal in a condemnation proceeding: group pressure. If many properties are being condemned, contact their owners and form a group. Negotiate as a group for better prices, more time, whatever it is you need. Attract media attention whenever possible to make your position known to the public. You probably won't get everything you ask for, but you will probably get something.

Going to Court

If you refuse to sell your condemned property, the government can (and usually will) take you to court, and months can then drag into years before the issue is resolved. Get a lawyer. You'll need professional advice (and you can be certain that "the other side" has an ample supply of it).

And remember, keep your property well maintained. Don't give in to the temptation to let its condition slip, thinking, "Oh, well, I'm going to end up losing it anyway!" In a condemnation, ultimately, the price you get for the property will be fair market value at the time of the sale. If the government wins its case, you'll get less if you've let it become run-down. You'll get more if property values in the area have appreciated over the year or more it has been tied up in court and you have kept the property in topnotch condition.

Partial Condemnations

Sometimes the government only takes a part of a piece of land, as, for example, when a road is made wider and the houses along it lose a part of their front yards. In such instances, the compensation must be fair market value for the land taken plus a payment for the depreciation in the property value as a result of the condemnation of the land.

Nongovernment Condemnations

Quasi-public companies such as electric, telephone, water, and railroads can also use the power of eminent domain to acquire land needed for the public good, and they, too, must pay a fair price for it. In fact, everything just said about government condemnation applies to public utility and transportation companies.

Many such companies, however, prefer to use easements rather than condemnation to acquire the use of land. An easement allows the company to cross or use a certain part of your land. They do not own it, but they are allowed to run power lines over it, bury pipe, and/or cross the land whenever necessary. They are even allowed to bring in heavy equipment and dig up your land in order to maintain their pipe, wire, or whatever.

Many properties have a 4- to 8-foot-wide utility easement running the entire road frontage. This easement is so common, in fact, that it is hardly noticed or mentioned at closings. Easements that cross through a property, however, usually lower its value somewhat.

Be particularly wary of easements if you are buying land upon which you plan to build. Be sure not to set the house on the easement. If you do, and it's a railroad easement, for example, the railroad might one day decide to lay its track right through your kitchen.

The Deed

Restrictions

There's a park in central Connecticut called Walnut Hill. From early spring to late in the fall, it is the scene of tennis matches, soccer games, baseball games, volley ball tournaments, and fly-ball fielding practices for many of the town's youth. Monday through Saturday, that is. On Sundays, no one is allowed to throw a ball in Walnut Hill Park.

Why? The park was deeded to the town upon the death of the owner of the land many years ago. That man wanted the townsfolk to enjoy the land as a place for recreation, which they do. But he also believed that Sunday was a day of rest and prayer and therefore he included in the deed a restriction that prohibited ball throwing on Sundays. The restriction is still enforced.

Few restrictions written into deeds are concerned with throwing balls, but there are many others just as strange. A restriction is a change in a deed that restricts or regulates the use of the real property to which the deed conveys title. When lawyers and local government officials work with deed restrictions, they usually couple them with covenants and conditions and talk about the CC&Rs (covenants, conditions, and restrictions). In fact, most people, even professional real estate dealers, think of all three as one and the same.

Actually there are slight differences. Covenants are promises: "The owner of this lot will keep his sidewalk clear of snow." Conditions are a little tougher: "If the owner of this lot cuts down the privet hedge along his property line, the land reverts back to the original owner (before the land was subdivided) or his heirs." They usually read that if you do this or don't do that, this or this will happen. Restrictions are restrictions: "No house will be built on this lot that is less than 2,000 square feet of living space."

CC&Rs of every imaginable type are written into deeds, most often when land or space is subdivided. Owners of condominiums, for example, are handed pages of CC&Rs before they even sign a contract to buy. CC&Rs are "rules" in addition to zoning laws and building codes, but they cannot override or negate the effect of the laws. For example, set-back lines according to zoning law may be 50 feet from the road, but the CC&Rs of a given housing development may dictate that all houses must be at least 100 feet from the road.

Usually violations of CC&Rs are brought to court only by a neighbor in the same area whose deed contains the same CC&Rs. Courts will enforce them unless they are illegal, such as those that limit the possession of the property to a specified race; or unreasonable, such as a restriction that prohibits planting roses; or unenforceable, such as a residential restriction in an area whose zoning has changed over the years from residential to commercial.

Some CC&Rs are limited in time. They may be written for twenty, fifty, or any given number of years or they may run for the life of the seller of the land or even the term of ownership of a named buyer. Many CC&Rs, however, are permanent restrictions on the use of the property. When they are written without time restrictions, they are said to "run with the land" or sometimes to "run with the deed," and they are binding upon every buyer of the property no matter how many times it changes hands.

Easements

Besides CC&Rs there are other possible legal strings that pass with the land. Easements are probably most common, and they can be a benefit or a burden to the property. Usually when a property is subdivided both beneficial and burdensome easements run with all the subdivided pieces of property. But this is beginning to sound like a legal text. Perhaps an example would clear it up.

Meet Susie Sandpiper, who owns a large piece of land with ocean frontage on Hilton Head Island. As the community grows, more roads are needed and the local government condemns a strip of land that bisects Susie's property in order to extend a road for "the public good." Ms. Sandpiper is paid a fair amount for the land area of the road and an additional amount for the diminished value of her property.

Susie Sandpiper and her family before her have been in real estate for many years, however. She knows that once the road is finished, her ocean-front land will be very valuable indeed. The land on the other side of the road will, of course, have less value. Or will it? Watch Susie go.

After the road is in use, Ms. Sandpiper aproaches the Planning Commission with a proposal to subdivide her land into two lots, one on each side of the road. A reasonable request, certainly. And quickly granted.

Then with an eye to maximum profit, Susie writes an easement into the deeds for both pieces of property. The owners, whoever they may be, of the ocean-front parcel must allow the owners, whoever they may be, of the road-front parcel to cross on a 10-foot wide strip of land from the road to the beach and to use the beach up to a line 50 feet beyond the normal high-tide water line.

This easement is a burden to the ocean-front property and a benefit to the road-front property, and it "runs with the deed." Ms. Sandpiper profits because the easement increases the value of her road-front property. It does not proportionately lower the value of her ocean-front piece, however, since "ocean front" is so desirable a feature that it substantially negates the burden of the easement, especially while the road-front lot remains undeveloped.

Susie Sandpiper sells the ocean-front piece to a private estate. Five years later, she sells the road-front property to a development company who builds a high-rise time-share condominium on the land.

What happens to the value of the ocean-front estate? You guessed it. The owner of each and every week of the time-share apartments has the right of way to the beach that was established by the easement in the deed. After a year or so, the owners of the estate sell their land to another time-share developer. Meanwhile Susie Sandpiper has moved to California.

Easements Not Written in the Deed

Not every right of way is deeded, nor is every one permanent. Sometimes a simple path through a property becomes a right of way through customary usage. If, for example, school children "cut through" your property on the way to school year after year until a path becomes worn in the grass and a hole is created in the hedges and you never stop them, every house in your neighborhood may eventually have a legal right of way through your land to the school. How long does this have to go on before it becomes "legal"? It depends upon the statutes of your state. It might be five years, it might be twenty.

But what can you do if you want to allow the children to cross your property but you do not want to establish a legal right of way? You can reduce the easement to writing, granting the right of way across your property to neighborhood children for as long as you own the property. The right to cross your property then ends with its sale. The easement does not "run with the deed," and the new owner can decide if he or she wants the children or not.

Or, if you don't want to bother with legal paperwork, you can ritually close the path for one full school day (twenty-four hours) a year. The closing of the path reestablishes your ownership and interrupts the passage of time (which must be continuous) toward the statutory requirement. You might put up boards or a barrier of boxes across the path or the hole in the hedges. Have someone take a picture of you standing alongside, just to be extra safe. You can explain to the children that they can come back tomorrow.

Will such action hold up in court? Absolutely. It's exactly the way that Rockefeller Center keeps possession of certain New York City streets that run through it. The center closes the private road portion of the street for a period of time each year, thus reestablishing ownership. Did you think the giant Christmas tree in the street was wholly an act of good will?

A Few More Legal Bits and Pieces

Acre: An acre is 43,560 square feet. However, a rectangular lot 200 feet by 200 feet is commonly referred to as a builder's acre.

Air Rights: The ownership of the right to use the air space over a piece of property. You can sell your air rights.

Ground Rights: In theory, the property you own extends down to the core of the earth. If someone discovers oil or gold or something else valuable under your house, you can sell the rights to mine it while still keeping title to your property.

Riparian Rights: The right to use water that runs through or along the border of your land, including boating rights if the "stream" is large enough. In most states, you cannot divert this water, nor can you use it in such a way that your use affects the use of others downstream.

Littoral Rights: Rights pertaining to property that borders upon a large body of water such as an ocean, sound, gulf, or one of the Great Lakes. Your rights, of course, are subject to government regulation.

Adverse Possession: A means of obtaining title to a piece of property by occupying it continuously for the statutory period against the will of the owner.

Tax Roll: A list of property owners in the town with the assessed valuation of each piece of property publicly printed.

Certiorari: The court proceeding to review a challenged assessed valuation.

Easement: A right of way.

Encroachment: A building, part of a building, or an obstruction that extends upon (trespasses upon) the property of another person or the city, state, or federal government (such as a building that overhangs a sidewalk).

Encumbrance: A claim, lien, or liability on a property. An encumbrance is *not* a building; rather, it is a legal judgment, unpaid taxes, or even a right of way.

Encroachments

Let's say you have a neighbor who is building a dog pen for his Saint Bernard on what he thinks is the back corner of his lot. When the pen is finished, however, he discovers that it actually extends 10 feet into your land. But you don't really mind. You never use that back corner anyway, and besides, you like Tinker Bell.

The dog pen and the dog house in it (which is situated partly on your land) is an encroachment on your property. If you let Tinker Bell or one of her cousins live there for the entire time prescribed by the statutory limitations of your state, she (and her owner) will have the legal right to keep a dog pen on your land. It may even become her owner's land!

In some parts of the country you can get an "encroachment permit" from the Board of Adjustment that will limit the dog pen's use and prevent the structure from becoming a permanent installation on that piece of land. If this kind of permit is not used in your area and you are worried about the encroachment, you and your neighbor can sign a statement licensing the land for Tinker Bell's use. The license need not pass with title to the property. If you sell your land, the new owner can decide whether or not he likes Tinker Bell.

And if you don't like Tinker Bell, and never did, you can insist that your neighbor remove the dog pen from your property when you first discover that it actually is on your property. The longer you let it stay there, the harder it will be to get rid of it.

For More Information

From the League of Women Voters (1730 M Street, N.W., Washington, D.C. 20036) the following three publications are available: "Know Your Community"; "The Politics of Change: Goals, Conflict and Power in the Community"; and "Anatomy of a Hearing."

From the National Trust for Historic Preservation (1785 Massachusetts Av. N.W., Washington, D.C. 20036) may be obtained: "Working with Local Government."

From the American Planning Association (1313 East 60th St., Chicago, Ill. 60637) may be obtained: "The Citizen's Guide to Zoning" (242 pages, $14.95).

From your local Internal Revenue Service office is available: "Zoning Condemnation of Private Property for Public Use," IRS publication #549 (free).

PART IV

Money–Making
Real Estate

42

What Every Investor
Should Know

Love and marriage,
A horse and carriage,
They go together like
. . . land and money.

OK, it's not exactly poetry, but you get the gist, right? Owning
property, "real" estate (the land and the buildings attached to it)
has, for centuries, been regarded as a means of acquiring wealth and
as a measurement of wealth acquired. In this country in particular,
hardly a great fortune has been accumulated that did not include
real estate investment.

But if real estate is the most reliably lucrative of all investments, it
is also the most complex. It is controlled, regulated, and taxed at
virtually every level of government in one way or another. Its investment unit is huge, both financially and physically. There are no
"penny stocks" in this field; even a one-week ownership of a time-
share apartment costs several thousand dollars. Nor does real estate
investment offer the equivalent of a Tiffany vase or a Persian rug,
something you can hold in your hands and/or store away for safe-
keeping. Even the smallest apartment is bigger than you are and
cries out for care (and use).

The complexity of choosing the "right" real estate investment is
increased by the absolute uniqueness of every piece of real property, since no other property occupies exactly that same space. And
this complexity is heightened still further by the complexity of the
act of changing ownership. No simple sales slip here! Real estate

---

Some Investment Possibilities for the Beginner

Multifamily houses, usually two to six families. You might consider living in one of the units.

Single-family houses to rent or to fix up and sell.

Old houses to remodel. Can you convert a rambling Victorian into three apartments? Check to see if you can get historic structure designation. See Chapter 35.

Small apartment buildings, under ten units.

Commercial property, the building in town that houses a bookstore, a doctor's office, a beauty parlor, a restaurant, etc.

Mixed commercial and residential property, perhaps a convenience store downstairs and a rental unit or two upstairs.

A local condominium apartment to rent. Check the restrictions in the deed and bylaws before you buy.

Rental-pool vacation condominiums. See Chapter 48.

Real estate syndicates. More information in Chapter 48.

Land or acreage to be subdivided. Be careful here, however, since this investment usually produces no income and has no tax benefits. See Chapter 44.

---

investment is tangled in legal and financial strings that are being held, pulled, and twisted at any given moment by a number of involved and uninvolved persons.

Hardly an arena for neophytes, amateurs, and dilettantes, yet thousands of people dabble in the field, some very successfully. Should you? It depends. Some people seem quite suited to the stresses and demands of real estate investment; others are not. If you are interested in testing your own mettle, you should train for your first investment.

"How?" you ask. "I've been playing Monopoly for years but it doesn't seem to help!"

No, the real game is too big to be learned at home. Oh, it starts in the home, to be sure, with reading. First, some basic material in books and other publications; then, on to the newspapers advertising properties for sale. But you can't even complete the basic training of real estate in your easy chair. You must get out into the marketplace. Talk with real estate agents and inspect properties that are for sale. Even if you can't possibly afford to invest at a given moment, act as though you can. Collect income and expense figures, work out the financing, ask yourself, "Would this be a good investment if I could afford it?"

In this way you will gather knowledge and skill that no book can give you. And you may even be pleasantly surprised at how willing people are to help you get started as an investor, even to the point of making a property affordable. But that's your adventure. Right now, let's get back to what this book can give you, which is some very indispensable knowledge.

To begin, let's say right up front that you can make a fortune by investing in real estate, and you can also lose your shirt. Or worse yet, take on a hair shirt, maybe even a bed of nails! We urge you therefore to start small and locally, in a neighborhood, section of town, or town that you know very well. After your "training runs" with agents, you should proceed with caution. To do that:

1. *Go slowly*. Let your money earn interest until you find a really good real estate investment.

2. *Never invest in real estate under financial pressure, time pressure, or emotional stress*. It's too hard to remedy a mistake.

3. *Read*. No one has all the knowledge. Choose real estate writers with different credentials and backgrounds. A New York City lawyer specializing in co-op conversions will give you different insights from an Arizona real estate broker, and a professor of real estate at the University of Miami will have something else to say.

4. *Think*. Take what you read and hear and apply it to your own unique investment situation.

5. *Calculate*. Work out figures, real and hypothetical, to test the worth of an investment to you.

6. *Look*. And look, and look. The more properties you walk through, climb through, even crawl through, the more sense of value you will have in your area.

7. *Ask questions*. Of real estate agents, bankers, tenants, other investors, town officials, cab drivers, anyone who'll talk with you. You never know when someone will toss a pearl of wisdom.

8. *Listen*. Don't be so quick to expound upon your theories. Listen to the ideas of others even if you think they are whistling in the wind. Much of investment savvy is discarding what doesn't ap-

ply and accumulating and piecing together the bits and scraps that
do.

9. *Weigh every property against others*. How can you know if a
deal is as good as the agent says it is if you haven't compared it to
another property?

10. *Negotiate*. There's not a deal anywhere that can't be sweet-
ened, at least a little.

And, most important of all:

11. *Understand the nature of your investment vehicle*. Investing
in apartment buildings is different from investing in commercial
office buildings, or the corner store, or land for potential subdivision, or a vacation resort. Before you jump in, try to find out what
the specific problems of your investment in your area of the country
are.

Many people consider their home as an investment and feel that
having successfully bought it, they are well prepared for the investment marketplace. Actually home buying and selling is a good intro-
ductory course to real estate investment, but it's a long way from a
robe and hood with "entrepreneur" embroidered along the edges.
You can use some of what you learned in your homebuying experience, but some ideas and attitudes you will have to discard.

As in homebuying, location is the most important factor in investment real estate. In homebuying, however, it's important that you
"love" the location and the house at least a little. In investment real
estate love has no place. Appreciation (financial, not aesthetic) and
rate of return, cash flow, and tax benefits have no basis in feelings.
And financing, maintenance, and management create more headaches than heartaches.

But enough generalizations! Let's take this bright investment
orange and peel it. Now we can look at the sections.

Appreciation

Why invest? To make money, of course, and one way to make
money on real estate investments is simply to watch as the value of
your property goes up. To appreciate in value, however, your investment must be desirable (something people want) and the demand for it in your area must be greater, at least by a little, than the
supply.

A piece of land zoned for five residential building lots but located adjacent to the town's sewerage treatment plant is not desirable and therefore not a good investment—no matter how cheaply the owner will sell it and no matter how great the demand for new single family houses in the area. (This land might be a good investment if you could buy it cheaply and then get it rezoned for another use, but that's another book.) Usually, desirability is a pretty obvious factor, however, and such undesirable properties as the neighbor of the sewerage treatment plant are rarely the downfall of the first-time investor. Overly abundant properties are.

This is how it happens. There is a shortage somewhere that heightens demand, condos in south Florida or rental apartments in the major cities of Texas, for example. Builders respond to the shortage by building and investors by investing. Suddenly a lot of people are making a lot of money and word gets out: *People are making money on apartment buildings in Xanadu!*

What happens? Builders rush to build more apartment buildings and investors jump on the bandwagon with their money in hand thinking: *Property values can only go up here!*

Surprise! When there are more apartments (or anything else) than people who want them, the value of the apartment buildings goes down. Thus small demand = small appreciation.

Except, sometimes (there are always excepts and sometimes in this business) an investment seems to appreciate on the wings of inflation. If inflation nationwide is at 10 percent and your building is appreciating at 10 percent a year, you are staying even, but you are not really increasing your investment base.

Much has been written about real estate as a hedge against inflation, and in homebuying the principle is a valid one. If your home appreciates at the same rate as inflation, it keeps you even in the housing marketplace while you enjoy its shelter. In investment real estate, however, the goal is not to stay even but to make more money. One should not buy investment real estate, therefore, just to hedge against inflation; and when calculating the past and prospective appreciation of a piece of property, the investor should take inflation into account.

Security

Everyone wants to make money, no one wants to lose money. (Were truer words ever written?) Fear of loss therefore causes a fair proportion of real estate deals to fall apart before they close. Justifiably? Sometimes.

Carefully selected real estate is one of the most secure investments available to the general public today. But "carefully selected" is the key phrase here. It is possible to lose money in real estate, especially:

- If you miscalculate future demand for your property.
- If you face a must-sell situation and time is a factor.
- If other properties surrounding yours become rundown.
- If you miscalculate the income-to-operating expense ratio.
- If economic reversals (either nationwide or local) negatively affect property values in your area.
- If governmental controls (rent control, for example, or environmental regulations) lessen the investment appeal of your property.

"Secure?" you say. "Sounds rather risky to me."

Yes, there is risk, but some risk is inherent in every investment. There are, however, some still safer places for your money. Bank accounts and bonds, for example, but you probably won't make as much on your money as you would with a good real estate investment choice.

Knowledge is the safety net in real estate investment, and you should use it to increase the security of your invested dollars. Know what you are choosing and why you are choosing it. To repeat: each real estate investment property should be carefully selected.

Historically, the performance of real estate as an investment has earned it highest regard as one of the most secure of the world's money-making ventures. Each piece of real estate is unique, tangible, immovable, and, in terms of the land, indestructible under all but the most extraordinary circumstances (pieces of the coast falling into the ocean, for example.) Lenders therefore have something real, safe, and lasting to hang their loans onto when real estate is mortgaged. This security has prompted larger loans in proportion to the value of the property (called loan-to-value ratio) than in most other lending situations. So you are siding with the bankers when you choose real property as a "secure" investment.

The Problem of Liquidity

If you can really make big bucks in real estate without a great deal of risk, why isn't everybody in the game? First, because it takes a certain kind of personality, a good deal of knowledge, some motivation, and usually a fair amount of money to get started. And second, because the investment has a drawback called time. Time on two levels. Managing real estate investments takes up time from your workweek (more about this later in this chapter), and selling real estate in order to get your investment money and profit out requires the passage of time, sometimes a lot of it.

Investment pros call it liquidity: the ability to convert your investment back to cash quickly and easily. It's an important investment feature. Real estate, however, is generally considered an illiquid investment. You may not be able to sell it when you want to or even when you need to. Under the best of circumstances in the best of times, selling a piece of investment real estate can take many months. Most experts, therefore, advise against putting into real estate money that you might need upon short notice to buy bread for your table or braces for your child's teeth.

There is, however, a school of thought that says, "Nonsense!" to such advice. These experts maintain that every piece of real estate is a liquid investment at a price. In other words, if you are willing to sell cheaply enough you can find an immediate buyer, often for cash. This is true, but remember, at a price. And that price is usually far below market value.

True liquidity is the ability to sell an investment not only quickly but also at or very near its market value. (Stocks are a liquid, if volatile, investment.) This kind of liquidity is just not realistically a feature of investment real estate.

Yes, you'll see the fast-deal millionaire featured in the newspaper saying, "I sold my property for a $50,000 profit after owning it for only twenty-seven days!" Read the article with interest but bear in mind that the article is being featured because the event is not ordinary. If you put your real estate investment property up for sale at or near its market value, you will find a buyer. But it may take six months, or a year.

Financing Investment Property

One of the most attractive aspects of real estate investing is the opportunity to use someone else's money to buy *your* investment property. Loan-to-value ratios are very high on income-producing properties. Second and third mortgages, seller financing, balloons, construction financing, and other "creative" arrangements are also common. In fact, with a little creativity, knowledge, and daring you sometimes can buy investment real estate without using a penny of your own money.

Nonrecourse Financing

For your safety and sanity try to mortgage your investment property with nonrecourse financing. A nonrecourse loan limits the liability of the borrower. In the event of default on the loan, the lender may foreclose and acquire the mortgaged property, nothing more. The borrower's other assets, such as his home, stocks, cash reserves on deposit, and other investment properties, cannot be affected by the foreclosure.

A nonrecourse arrangement can be made with most types of financing. One method is simply to omit the borrower's promissory note, which is usually an adjunct to the mortgage agreement. Another is to include a specific clause in that note releasing the borrower from any personal liability beyond the mortgaged property.

Some regulated lenders are prohibited from writing nonrecourse provisions, but the prohibition rarely stops a lender and borrower who mutually want to make a deal. Often a dummy corporation is formed as the borrower. This corporation executes the promissory note and becomes personally liable in the event of default. But liable for what? The corporation has no assets beyond the property that has been mortgaged. The net effect is the same as a nonrecourse loan to an individual.

One word of caution, however. Writing special loan provisions is not a do-it-yourself project. We've included this information so that you'll know what to ask for. Ask also for the advice of a good attorney.

Leverage

Leverage is a favorite word among amateur investors, but unfortunately its implications are not always clearly understood. The confusion stems from the glorious days of single-digit interest rates.

With low interest-rate financing, high inflation, and spiraling property values, the idea of leverage was to put down as little of your own money as possible and carry as large a mortgage as possible. In this way you would use borrowed money to increase your profit. Let's look at some numbers.

If you bought a $100,000 property with $10,000 of your money down and then sold it two years later for $130,000, you would have a gross profit of $30,000. (For the sake of round numbers we'll illustrate without taking into account expenses or equity build-up.) Thus in two years your $10,000 investment brought you an additional

---

Considerations Before You Buy Investment Real Estate

Location: Still the most important factor in potential appreciation.

Financing: Look for the best deal. Tap the seller as a resource.

Cash Flow: How much income does the property produce? What are the annual operating expenses? How much will it cost you to carry the financing?

Vacancy Rate: What if a portion of your property does not produce the expected income several months in a row? Can you handle the financial stress?

Time Interval of Ownership: How long before you foresee selling for a profit? Can you afford to hold the property for five years (just in case times turn bad and you have to ride out an economic slump)?

Time Required for Management: How much of your time are you willing to devote to your real estate investment?

Taxes: Will the investment bring you any special tax benefits?

$30,000. You now have $40,000 cash! Four hundred percent of what you had two years ago. What a great return on your money!

Yes, but not quite accurate. If you are talking about the return on your $10,000 investment you must also consider how much the borrowing of $90,000 cost you. At 8 percent a year in the good old days straight interest would cost you $14,400. That interest, however, is tax-deductible so its real cost would be dependent upon your tax bracket. Let's assume that you're one of the lucky ones in the 50 percent group. In that case borrowing $90,000 for two years really cost you approximately $7200, which means you really made $22,800 with your $10,000 investment. Still, a great return on your money and an excellent illustration of the positive benefits of leverage.

But, leverage can be negative.

In a time when mortgage interest rates are high and property values are increasing at a moderate rate, you can actually pay more for the use of borrowed money than you make in accumulated appreciation. Let's look at some numbers again.

The same $100,000 property with the same $10,000 of your money down, but now the interest rate is 14 percent and the property appreciates at approximately 5 percent per year. In two years, therefore, you sell for, let's say, $110,500. Meanwhile, you have paid out $25,200 in interest on your $90,000 loan. Even taking into account the interest payment deduction on your taxes, you've really spent $12,600 to carry the loan while your $10,000 investment brought you in $10,500. Thus, if you consider the cost of carrying the loan, your investment did not more than double. In fact, you are now short $2100! This is negative leverage.

Of course there are other important factors that we have omitted in this illustration (other tax benefits, income from the property, deductible expense, etc.). The point to be made, however, is that the maximum mortgage and minimum downpayment theory of leverage may not work in every economy.

Seller Financing

Seller financing is much more common in investment real estate than in homebuying, and often the rates and terms are far superior to anything you could possibly arrange through a commercial lender. Even when you choose to use a commercial lender for the first mortgage, secondary financing can often be arranged from the seller. Be sure to ask about it early in your negotiations.

Favorable Federal Tax Treatment

The tax laws of the United States encourage and sometimes even support the real estate investor. In fact, when all the benefits and allowances are considered, it's really no wonder that real estate is so large a part of the investment portfolios of the wealthy. But there's space, opportunity, and benefits for us "average Americans," too; we need only step forward and act.

"Easier said than done!" you say. And this time you are right— well, partly right. It is not difficult to find a real estate investment opportunity, but understanding the tax benefits (and regulations) and taking advantage of them is something of another story. Federal tax laws concerning real estate are complex and they seem, at least, to be everchanging.

In this section we can give but a nod to the highlights, what you absolutely must know before you even consider investing. Before you sign on a dotted line somewhere you should also check the IRS list of free tax-information publications for the latest booklets pertaining to your particular type of investment vehicle. Read them and then, if possible, talk with a tax advisor.

Deductible Expenses

At this writing, interest on money borrowed to buy real estate is deductible on federal income tax returns, thus effectively lowering the cost of the borrowing. Local real estate taxes are also deductible. And perhaps most important, repair, operating, and maintenance costs are deductible against the gross income from the property. The deductible maintenance and repair expenses, however, often add to the value of a property since good appearance and operating systems raise value. Thus your deductible outlay is often an investment in future return when you sell.

Capital Gains Tax

Profits from the sale of investment or business real estate are generally taxed as long-term capital gains, which means that you pay taxes on only 40 percent of the profit. If you should suffer a loss on a property, however, the full amount of the loss is deductible against ordinary income.

Depreciation Allowances

Federal depreciation guidelines have been largely responsible for the tax shelter concept that so many Americans have sought and used to their financial advantage. The methods of calculating depreciation, however, are many, multifaceted, and complex, and you'll need professional help in doing at least your first few returns. The federal government is also doing some financial sword-rattling about cutting depreciation benefits rather drastically. Time will tell, but it is unlikely that all depreciation deductions will be eliminated.

For tax purposes, the federal government recognizes that no building lasts forever. Upon purchase of an investment property, therefore, a buyer must anticipate according to governmental guidelines the expected useful life of the building. Each year thereafter during the buyer's ownership, a certain portion of the value (purchase price) of the building can be taken as a tax deduction against income. The actual portion taken in a given year is dependent upon the expected useful life and the depreciation method you and your tax advisor select. In other words, your investment property suffers a paper loss each year.

Because well-maintained buildings last much longer than the "useful life" prescribed by the government and often actually increase in value, the depreciation deduction is usually a deduction that represents neither a real loss of value nor a cash outlay. Yet it reduces the taxes the owner of the property must pay—thus the concept of "tax shelter."

Theoretically, such depreciation deductions will be compensated for when the property is sold since the profit is calculated from the depreciated base at the time of the sale, unless . . . Read on.

Tax-free Exchanges

Federal tax law allows investment real estate to be exchanged for "like-kind" real estate without paying any tax on the profit you have made at the time of the exchange. "Like kind" is rather broadly interpreted by the government although there are very specific guidelines. The exchange of an office building for an apartment house, for example, is an exchange of like-kind real estate; they are both income-producing properties. Under this concept, even undeveloped land in North Dakota held as an investment can be exchanged for a convenience store in Louisiana since both are owned fee simple for the purpose of making a profit.

This deferment of tax payment on the profits of investment or business property can go on as long as a person continues to exchange properties. Think of it as an interest-free loan from your Uncle Sam. He is letting you use money that you should have paid over to him to buy larger, better, or more real estate for yourself. Nice man.

But exchanging investment or business property is rarely as simple a procedure as "you give me your wigwam and I'll give you my lean-to." Often one or both parties exchange cash and sometimes other pieces of real estate or items of value in the deal. These extras are called boot. Cars, trucks, construction equipment, vacation homes, Russian lynx coats, old wine—boot can be anything. And when boot is involved, the IRS men get out their notepads and sneer a special little sneer, for they can be sure that someone owes something to the government on the deal.

Our advice: if you are getting into exchanges, hire the best financial advisor you can find. In fact, try to find an exchange specialist.

Rehabilitation

If you are willing to take on the task of modernizing an older building, you can get another kind of help from your Uncle Sam in the form of investment tax credits. As of this writing the age and percentage limitations are for:

• nonresidential structures between thirty and thirty-nine years old—a 15 percent investment credit

• nonresidential structures of forty or more—a 20-percent investment credit

• certified historic structures (see Chapter 35) that are either residential or nonresidential—a 25 percent investment credit (note, however, that residential structures must be income-producing to qualify for the credit)

As usual, we must caution you to check further before going out to buy an old warehouse that you plan to convert to a theater. There are a number of government guidelines here that must be taken into consideration. (To give just one example: the percentage of the original external walls that must remain standing!) And you'll need a tax accountant to help you combine your allowable tax credit with all of your allowable depreciation deductions.

Cash Flow

If you join their community, you'll certainly hear your fellow investors talk intensely of cash flow. When they do so they are talking about real money, not paper gains or losses.

A positive cash flow is the spendable money left over from gross income after making mortgage payments, and paying all operating expenses and property taxes. If you have a negative cash flow, it means that you must put additional cash into the investment property to meet these expenses. Negative cash flow, however, does not necessarily deter an investor from buying a property. Federal tax benefits and potential appreciation may well make the property a desirable investment despite its negative cash flow.

Time for Investment Management

Real estate investment requires a commitment of your time, but how *much* time is closely related to the type of investment vehicle that you choose. Raw land, for example, requires little beyond finding it, financing it, and closing. (Unless you get into subdividing, of course; then you may find yourself with a twenty-hour-a-week part-time job.) Owning and living in a three-family house demands a different time commitment from owning a 50-unit office building, and both are different from converting an old factory into condominiums.

Before you choose a real estate investment, decide how much of your time you wish to spend upon it and then investigate the time demands of the various investments you are considering. Or find out how much professional management of the property will cost; it's a legitimate, tax-deductible operating expense.

Expanding Your Investment Base

There's pretty general agreement on how to make money in investment real estate: buy below market, sell profitably after at least six months (in order to qualify for long-term capital gains tax treatment) and buy something else, also at a below-market price. That formula certainly leaves you with lots of options in the "something else" category. As we see it the secret of success can be a little more finely delineated with the advice: broaden your base before you expand upward or into different types of investments.

If you make a big profit on your first two-family house, for example, don't run off to buy a 30-unit apartment building. You could find yourself financially strapped by mortgage payments and operating expenses and pressured by unfamiliar demands upon your time and judgment. And you will still be committed to one investment property; in other words, all your eggs will still be in one basket.

Instead, buy or exchange for two other small two-family houses and at the appropriate time sell each of these and buy three or four more. Now you are becoming a specialist with expert knowledge and you are building the base of your investment pyramid. At the right time you might decide to sell two or more of your properties or exchange them for a different or larger property. By that time, you'll know what you are doing and why.

Bonne chance! Though you probably won't need it.

For More Information

Real Estate Investor's Deskbook by Alvin Arnold (Warren, Gorham & Lamont publishers) is an excellent general real estate investment guidebook. It is comprehensive, accurate, clear, and readable. It is also well worth its $64 price tag. Annual supplements are available at approximately $35.

Other books available include:

The Intelligent Investor's Guide to Real Estate by David W. Walters, *et al.* (John Wiley & Sons, Inc.) $19.95.

The Smart Investor's Guide to Real Estate by Robert Bruss (Crown) $13.95.

Real Estate Accounting and Mathematics Handbook by Robert J. Wiley (John Wiley & Sons, Inc.) $39.95.

The Real Estate Investor and the Federal Income Tax by Gaylon E. Greer (John Wiley & Sons, Inc.) $33.95.

The Real Estate Book by Robert L. Nessen (Little, Brown and Co.) $12.95.

43

So You Want to Be a Landlord

"Landlord" is a word that does not arouse much sympathy these days. More often it brings on the boos and hisses. Still, the public relations angle aside, you may be considering taking on the job of investment property owner. Should you go ahead with that first rental? *Is* this a profitable business? Will it be especially aggravating? Just what is involved here, anyway?

Landlord covers a wide range of property ownership, from Mrs. O'Leary who rents out the basement apartment in her small frame home to the group that owns the Empire State Building and rents commercial space in that tower. You're no doubt at the Mrs. O'Leary end of the spectrum—for now, at least—and interested in getting a foothold in residential real estate. You would like to rent your vacation home, or perhaps create an apartment in your permanent residence. Maybe you're considering buying a house or two to rent, or even a small apartment building.

If you've been thinking along those lines, congratulations. You're on the right track in trying to increase your investment portfolio. Becoming a landlord can be profitable. But there are a lot of qualifiers that go along with the potential for success. There is money to be made *if* you know the market in your area; *if* you have the time and interest to devote to maintaining your properties; *if* you study all the ins and outs of being a successful landlord, from advertising for tenants to keeping your buildings in repair without going broke; and, of course, *if* you have the money to invest, with some left over to keep your buildings in good working order.

Landlording is a "hands on" investment, not like, say, purchasing bank certificates or even joining a real estate syndicate, where your check is the only involvement that is needed. You're going to have

Do You Have What it Takes To Be a Landlord?

Can you survive financially if you have a vacant apartment for a month or two?

Do you have the time—and inclination—to see that hallways are clean, snow removed, lightbulbs replaced, and other chores completed promptly in your properties?

Can you handle tenants calling you at 2 A.M. on a January morning to say that the heating system has conked out?

Can you deal with city officials—building inspectors, rent-control board, and the like?

Are you well-organized? Sloppy recordkeeping and owning investment properties do not go together.

Can you handle the myriad small decisions you will be forced to make—should you allow pets in your buildings; what about the installation of a washer and dryer; can the tenant wallpaper if he chooses?

Tenants are vocal these days. Can you cope with a united tenant association that is striking your building?

Will you be up to the ticklish side of landlording, such as getting rid of problem tenants, handling the tenants who want to get out their leases?

to get your hands dirty as a landlord, literally and figuratively. You will have to cope not only with the dollars and cents of purchasing, maintaining, and repairing buildings, but also with the emotions of people looking for a place to live, moving into a property you own, and perhaps abusing that residence.

Take a look at the box above, "Do You Have What It Takes to Be a Landlord?"

Think you're up to it?

As a neophyte you will need plenty of guidance. These few pages will not allow for detailed explanations of how to keep records and whether to offer tenants a lease and what kind of door locks make for the best security. The purpose of this chapter is to give you a broad overview of what's involved in landlording. At the end of the chapter you should be saying either "Whew. That's not for me. I haven't the time or the interest. I'll find an easier way to invest my money." or "Sounds good. I think I can take it on and make it work well for me."

Also at the end of this chapter you will find a listing of several excellent books that *will* cover all the myriad details involved in being a successful landlord. And there are dozens of them!

There are two other sources that can be of help to you as you start this investment career. The first is your state office of landlord–tenant affairs, or whatever name it goes by where you live. That agency will have plenty of printed material to acquaint you with the rights and responsibilities of landlords—and of tenants, too. The office can also answer any question peculiar to where you live. Rent-control laws, security-deposit rulings, and eviction procedures all differ from one community to the next, so no one book can help *you* in particular. Your answers will have to come from local agencies.

The second source of information will be a building owners' association. If there is one in your locale, or your state, by all means join it. These fellow landlords can provide a wealth of information for the beginner, and with these groups you will also be tuned into the status of proposed new legislation affecting landlords. Another bonus of joining a property owners' group is that often those organizations will be able to secure a credit screening for you of prospective tenants. Sometimes credit-checking agencies will not report to a lone landlord.

The Good News

1. Fewer people can afford to buy a house in these days of still-high interest rates and housing prices, so the rental market is good. Rents are expected to outpace inflation in most parts of the country over the next few years. That's *most* of the country. There are pockets here and there—Houston is one example—where there has been an overbuilding of rental units. That could work against you as a beginning, small landlord.

2. The tax benefits of being a landlord are excellent. As the owner of real property you can, of course, deduct from your federal income tax mortgage interest and real estate taxes. But other expenses are also deductible: fire and liability insurance premiums; the cost of finding tenants (advertising); expenses of traveling to and from your property a reasonable number of times to make repairs; the cost of

those repairs and of ordinary maintenance; any cash losses you sustain in renting your property. And then there is depreciation. The Economic Recovery Tax Act of 1981 shortened what had been a thirty-to-forty-year period for depreciating residential real property to fifteen years. There is a movement afoot at this writing to return to the old thirty to forty-year depreciation schedules, but not to eliminate the concept of depreciation entirely. As of the 1984 tax year, you can depreciate your property in two ways. You can elect to deduct depreciation in fifteen equal installments, or take bigger deductions in the early years and smaller ones in the later years. Your accountant can help you choose the depreciation schedule for you and advise you on the latest tax changes.

3. You have purchased, it is hoped, a building that will appreciate in value, bringing you a profit when you sell.

The Bad News

1. Speaking of the above-mentioned profit, that isn't likely to be as great as it would have been in the late 1970s. Real estate in most sections of the country is now appreciating at an annual rate of 5 percent, although there are certainly exceptions where that rise is 15, even 25 percent. Still, 5 percent is a pretty far cry from the annual 8 to 15 percent we experienced in those seemingly get-rich days of the 1970s.

2. If rent control is in existence in your community, that may put a lid on how much money you will have coming in from the landlord venture, particularly if you purchase a multifamily dwelling (definitions vary on how many units such structures cover, ranging from three or more to six or more). Similarly, if there is a vacancy decontrol law that limits the amount you can raise the rent between tenants, that also holds down profits. Restrictions on rent increases after you make substantial repairs or renovation on your building? That's bad, too. In fact, purchasing any multifamily dwelling in an area with rent-control laws *can* be downright foolish. In some communities the owner-occupied building of three units or less is exempt from rent-control laws, but that is not uniformly the case.

3. Tenants can be a problem: selecting good ones, getting rid of bad ones, and cleverly handling those who organize to fight you. Tenants are vocal these days, and landlords must be prepared to justify their actions—or their inaction—to the satisfaction of those groups.

4. The time involved in landlording can become consuming, tak-

ing hours away from your full-time job and your family life, not to mention leisure time. The buildings *must* be maintained. Repairs *must* be made. Phone calls *must* be returned. Records *must* be kept. Being a landlord, as you will see, is indeed a job, not a hobby and not an invisible, paper investment. It is a part-time job that may, as you acquire more properties, grow to a full-time career. Perhaps that's what you are aiming for. Until that happy day, however, you will have to juggle too much work with too few hours in which to accomplish it all.

5. Because of high interest rates and the high purchase price of many homes these days you may experience a negative cash flow from your property—that is, you will be out of pocket for expenses attached to running the house after you have used the rent money to pay mortgage, taxes, fuel, etc. Having a positive cash flow is not the most important factor in landlording, and as the years pass and your rents rise the gap should be closed. But if you do buy high you should expect to have to put in some of your own money to cover all expenses attached to the house(s) you are renting. If you bought your property during single-digit interest days and are just now considering renting it, that's a different story. The woes are with the folks who bought at 14 percent and are looking for $400 rents to cover all their carrying costs.

On balance, if you have an attractive, not necessarily luxurious, property in a good neighborhood in a community where apartments are always in demand, if there is no rent control, and if you are conscientious about maintaining your property, it's hard to lose being a landlord. The hard times come in only if you are starting out in an already saturated market and must periodically face long stretches of vacancies. If you're buying a property just to make money from the rents, with no involvement or fixing up on your part, you can also expect to fail at the venture. Besides the questionable ethics involved in such a proposition, landlords in those situations will attract the worst sort of tenants who will contribute even further to the deterioration of the property. So the slumlord is helped along in seeing his building slip into ruin.

No one can, from a distance, tell you which buildings make good investments in your community. Talk to real estate agents, read the classified advertisements to see what rents apartments on different streets are commanding. And, of course, talk to as many landlords as you can, particularly those on the level at which you would like to buy—single-family home, small apartment building.

Where the Money to Buy Will Come From

There's an old saying, "You can't win with scared money." When it comes to real estate, that axiom is frequently tossed aside. Some investors will put their last dime on a real estate property. That can be just fine—indeed, it is how some fortunes are made—if you have nerves of steel and can cope with having virtually zilch in savings for a year or two or three until your property starts paying. Remember that real estate is not a liquid investment. It may be easier to quickly sell a single-family rental house than a 10-unit apartment building, but both of them will probably take at least three months from the oral agreement to the closing. So if you need a fast $20,000 for a family emergency, or even for one of your properties, be sure you know where you can get that money. A loan from relatives? A second mortgage?

Most novice investors use the equity in their principal homes to buy a second property, the one they plan to rent. If this is the path you want to take, beware of extracting too much money for the downpayment. Leverage is a very important word in investment real estate, and you should use as much leverage as is profitable. Leverage means controlling the most property with the least investment of your own money. That is how realty empires are built.

Why put $40,000 down on a $90,000 building if you only need a downpayment of $20,000? Use the other $20,000 to buy another building, or keep it in the kitty for renovations or repairs. If you have two houses instead of one, you can, if the need becomes drastic, sell one and still have the other. Be aware, however, that in these days of high interest rates, leverage can be negative. (See pages 692–694.)

You can try for seller financing in any rental house you buy, too. That can mean a lower downpayment and a lower rate of interest. Seller financing doesn't always work in a brisk seller's market, but if you look around long enough you can usually find a building owner open to negotiation. Banks and other lending institutions won't be.

Leasing with an option to purchase is another financing plan that can ease you gradually and less expensively into ownership. Here, too, however, you may find properties available only in a weak seller's market.

One increasingly popular style of buying rental properties is through forming a partnership. Know any friends or relatives or co-workers who would like to join with you in buying? There are many styles of partnerships. In some everyone puts up the same amount of money, but you may be able to form one where you make no capital investment at all, but will instead find, purchase, and rehabilitate the property. The others will be silent partners, putting up the entire cash investment. Any variation on that agreement can be worked out, as long as all parties agree. Syndicates are more complex than partnerships and are for more experienced investors. There's more about them in Chapter 48.

One of the reasons partnerships are so popular these days is that they lower the amount of dollar investment required for larger properties such as apartment buildings. But there is also the psychological benefit of sharing the risk. This can be an ideal venture for the neophyte investor. Sure, you share the profits, but sharing the aggravations and potential grief isn't such a bad idea either. The partnership usually agrees to hold the property for five or seven years and then sell, splitting the profits. There is a legal document involved, of course, setting forth, among other provisions, what happens if someone wants to get out of the agreement early, how much money should be put into fixing up the property, and the like.

So you have a few thousand dollars to spend. Where can you put that money? Let's first take a look at an almost-guaranteed good investment.

Converting Your Own Home into Apartments

It is not difficult to understand why more and more Americans are converting part of their homes into fully equipped apartments that they rent either legally or in defiance of local zoning ordinances. There are attractive tax advantages to owning an income-producing property, but, perhaps more urgently, higher property taxes, rising fuel costs, still-high unemployment, and today's double-digit mortgage rates are making many houses too expensive to carry. Recognize your own home here?

Social changes enter into the picture, too. Why should the elderly, today's thinking goes, be forced financially to leave a cherished home when they could rent part of that space for additional, needed income?

Then there are the grown children returning home unable to find work; married kids coming back with a divorce decree and a few children of their own; elderly parents moving in with their children; and young married couples living with "the folks" until they can swing $800-a-month mortgage payments. All need someplace, anyplace to hang their hats.

The formal title for these newly created units is "accessory apartments." They can be situated anywhere in the house—attic, basement, entire separate floor—but they must contain a kitchen of their own, separate from the owner's, to qualify as a full apartment. Homes containing two units are sometimes called "mother-in-law" or "mother–daughter" houses, which implies that one apartment is occupied by a parent, but that is not always the case.

On the national level accessory apartments have been approved by numerous planning associations, housing groups, municipalities—including the U.S. Conference of Mayors—and organizations for the elderly. All consider the conversions an idea whose time is way overdue.

The units can work well because the landlord lives in the structure and has close observation of the tenant. On the other hand, the tenant knows who owns the building and can just walk upstairs to talk to the landlord. There is close interaction between the two.

The U.S. Census Bureau estimates that nationally there are about 250,000 new conversions each year, both legal and underground. In many if not most communities, legal conversions are first approved for the elderly, either allowing those folks to convert their homes, or permitting a homeowner of any age to do the conversion, but taking in as a tenant only a retired member of the community.

As you might expect, new conversions are not always popular with neighbors. Mention a two-family house neighborhood to the average suburbanite and usually the response is negative. Traditionally, townspeople (unless and until they want to convert their own homes) complain that the units mean lower property values, parking problems, and a more transient population. Local officials concur, and add to the list stress on existing services such as parking, water, and the like. But let's not forget extra taxes the units would bring in.

Still, when it comes to illegal accessories, local authorities concede that it is difficult to find those units. Sometimes there is a check when a house is sold and changes hands, but in general inspectors and other local officials have no business poking around in private homes unless a specific complaint has been lodged. The overwhelming response to illegal or unregistered apartments has been to ignore them. Among the reasons:

• If no one complains, why do anything?

• There may be just one inspector for a community, and that individual has his or her hands full with regular assignments.

• Who wants to force homeowners to make expensive repairs or installations to bring otherwise quite adequate apartments up to code standards?

- Who wants to have to evict illegal tenants on some technicality?
- The extra units help ease that community's housing crunch.
- Happy homeowners and tenants make happy voters.

That's the situation vis-à-vis legal and illegal accessory apartments, and how the numbers of both are growing. If you are willing, even eager, to go ahead with a conversion and will take the legal route, following appropriate channels in your community, here are the steps you will follow:

1. Contact your appropriate municipal agency. Are accessory apartments allowed in your town, in accordance with existing zoning regulations? Are they allowed only to bring an aged parent into the home? If no apartments are allowed, you may want to seek a zoning variance. To do that you would make application to the zoning board, setting forth what you would like to do with your house and perhaps even showing plans. Read Chapter 41 on zoning.

2. Once you receive approval for the apartment, you can go ahead and think about the conversion process (although, no doubt, plans have been running through your mind since you began considering an apartment). Perhaps the division of your house is obvious. Let's say you have a large converted basement, with a powder room and wet bar. The powder room can be expanded to a full bath and the area around the wet bar can become a small pullman kitchen. *Voilà!* You have an apartment. Other divisions of a house are not so simple. Broadly speaking, a conversion where you will have to install a full bath and kitchen will cost $10,000 to $15,000.

Changing the outside appearance of your house is another consideration. Perhaps permission to create an accessory apartment hinges on your maintaining the existing exterior so that the house does not look like a two-family dwelling. If you are allowed to make changes, how to do so while retaining the character and attractiveness of the house should be a prime consideration. A local contractor may have some ideas, or you may prefer to call in an architect.

3. When you start the conversion process you will have to adhere to local building codes, which will be no problem when you deal with licensed contractors, plumbers, electricians, etc. Converting a private home into a two-family residence brings no special safety problems, as long as the construction work meets local standards. But switching to a three-family house is an important move that brings even more responsibility to the landlord. In most communities, structures of three or more living units are considered multiple dwellings and are subject to stringent regulations, one of which is

periodic visits by local housing inspectors. Such a house may require a fire escape. It will almost certainly require smoke detectors of a style called for by the state or municipality. An inspector will visit the house every two or three years or so and will hand down to you a list of any "violations" he or she finds. Some of them may be minor—a wobbly railing, too dim a light in the hallway—but others may require a sizable outlay of cash on your part. Don't fix them and you'll be fined. In a few communities some of the worst landlords are hauled into housing court and not only fined heavily but also deposited in jail for a brief spell.

It pays to consider this when you are contemplating dividing your house. Going from one to two units, no problem. From four to five units, again no problem. But in the area of switching from two to three units (or whatever the crossover line is in your locale) you are playing in an entirely different ballgame. You may have just four living units in your house, but you will be considered a multiple-dwelling landlord just like Mr. Bigbucks on the other side of town with his 400-unit Majestic Arms.

Whatever you decide, it could be the smartest move you ever made to convert some of that unused space in your own home into income-producing rental units. Headaches? Sure, from time to time, but it's a nice feeling the first of the month when that rent check or two comes rolling in.

Leasing a Single-Family Home or Condominium

Perhaps your idea of landlording involves the purchase and leasing of a single-family home. Or a condo unit. That's a good idea, isn't it? Any real estate purchase is likely to be a good one . . . isn't it?

If you're debating between the house and the condominium you'd probably be wiser to focus your attention on the house. This is a generalization, but buying condominium units for investment these days is not likely to be as profitable an investment as it was in the late 1970s, when prices were reasonably low and interest rates were, too. Today, it's a different story for investment condos. Prices are generally high, and—even more significant, of course—so are interest rates. Some areas are glutted with condo complexes, which may present a problem when you try to rent your unit. That saturation may also affect resale prices when you decide to sell. Your asking price may be more or less tied to going prices in the complex, too.

You and not the tenant will be paying the monthly maintenance

Renting the Vacation Home

Will you handle the renting yourself, or engage a real estate agent?

Will the tenant take care of maintenance chores, such as lawn mowing, or will you engage an outside individual or service for those jobs?

What about the off-season? Who will keep an eye on your property if you live too far to make regular checks on the place?

Will you take an inventory of furnishings and appliances you are leaving in the house? Perhaps photographing each room would be easier.

Have you checked your homeowner's insurance policy to see if there is a mention of tenants and their rights and responsibilities?

Are you familiar with IRS rulings about the renting aspect of vacation homes?

If you are in a resort condominium or cooperative, what will the owners' association or co-op board have to say about tenants?

Will rent include payment of utility bills? What about telephone service?

Are you prepared to contribute a few niceties to the business of renting—perhaps paying for beach passes or lift tickets, leaving behind brochures for tenants on nearby tourist attractions, restaurants, and the like?

fee, and that is a figure that is almost always escalating, sometimes going up too quickly for you to pass the rise on to your tenant. Your mortgage, real estate taxes, and other charges for the unit, plus the maintenance fee may well be more than the rent you will pull in, providing you with a negative cash flow.

You may also need owners' association approval of tenants or subtenants, which can be a nuisance (this naturally applies to co-ops as well as condos).

Finally, refinancing can be difficult in complexes with too many tenants.

Still, buying condos is popular, or at least has been so until interest rates headed skyward. According to the Condominium Associations Institute, a national network of professionals working in the condo field, some one third of all condo units around the country are owned by outside investors. If you do decide to invest in condominiums and join this group, be sure you know your local market and the economic situation as it stands today.

You may, after doing some homework, find that the single-family home will make a better investment for a beginning landlord. Here, too, important choices must be made to buy the best investment property. Not every house in every location is going to bring in top rental dollars.

The three important points in buying single-family houses are:

1. *Location*. There's that word again. It doesn't have to be the flossiest neighborhood for your purposes, just one that is not on the decline. Also, look for a house within reasonable driving distance of your own home. Long-distance landlording doesn't work well.

2. *Condition of the house*. Again, you do not have to buy the local showplace. Indeed, it can be the most rundown place on the block (but not the best house on a rundown block!). Envision it with good mechanical systems and some cosmetic beautifying that will make it rentable. Probably the most important point to keep in mind when shopping is that *you are not going to live in this house*. Don't turn a good prospect aside because you don't like the exterior siding, the kitchen, or whatever. Don't buy too much of a "handyman's special" either, unless you can do almost all of the repair work yourself. Otherwise your rental monies will be going to pay off improvement loans and contractors.

3. *Financing*. You want the best deal possible because houses cost money these days, a point you may have noticed. You want the lowest, simplest mortgage (FHA? VA?) and the least expensive closing costs. This is not your own home; every expense here you want pared to the bone.

There are some advantages to owning one or several single-family houses instead of an apartment building of six units or more. With the houses you are sometimes not subject to rent control. You can sell one of them reasonably quickly if you need fast cash without demolishing your entire portfolio. Tenant turnover is somehow not as great in a house as it is in an apartment building.

If you own ten houses with a total of 15 dwelling units, you could be better off than the owner of a 15-unit apartment building. The reason? The value of both your properties aside, he, as the owner of a multifamily dwelling, is subject to many, many more rules and regulations than you are. If all of your houses, for example, have three units or less, you probably will not have to pay interest on security deposits. There is the aforementioned exemption from rent control, admittedly not always the case. You have no inspections by building inspectors. And house renters are not likely to form a tenant union, whereas those in the 15-unit building may very well band together.

On the negative side of owning a house or houses is the upkeep of house, yard, garage, sidewalk, etc. Lots of property there. Usually a deal is made with tenants for them to maintain the property, but you are still the owner and are still likely to visit the place from time to time to see what's wrong. If the tenants are unwilling or unable to do so, it will probably be you who does the clipping and mowing and raking and shoveling.

Rents can sometimes be a problem with a house. Interestingly, there are communities where a 6-room apartment will command more in rent than a full-size 8-room house and yard. There may be a ceiling on how much you can expect for your rental house, no matter how lordly the structure and grounds. It's hard to make generalizations in this vast country, but a small, 4-room frame house in Peapatch might bring $300 a month in rent, while a 10-room house in a New York suburb may command $3000 a month. The important point for you as landlord is to be sure the number crunching for your rental houses works out. If you bought the house at a high price, and at a high rate of interest, will the rent cover most, if not all, of the expenses? If there is too wide a gap, you might consider converting that dwelling into a two-family house. If you can get no more than, say, $800 a month for a single-family house where you are, perhaps two full apartments would each bring in $500 a month, giving you an extra $200 a month cash flow. Zoning laws permitting, converting to a two-family house may well be the better deal. Single-family homes are considered to be easier to sell than two-family ones, but the difference between the two is not really that pronounced.

Buying an Occupied Apartment

This is an investment rather new to the realty marketplace. Let's say ABC Condo Sponsor has been converting the 200-unit Empire

Arms into a condominium. But the Arms is in a community that is under rent control, and a certain percentage of the tenants there who do not want to buy are protected by its regulations. The Empire Arms is also in a state that has protection for senior citizens or those on fixed incomes who are caught in a conversion and do not want to purchase their units. Those folks may stay in their apartments either for a set period of perhaps five or seven years, or even as long as they like. So ABC Condo Sponsor has 35 units in the Empire Arms that cannot be converted to condominiums. But the sponsor quite naturally wants to get out of the project the way he would in any conversion, turning it all over to the new unit owners. What to do? Increasingly he will sell those 35 apartments to individual buyers, either one by one or in packages of three or five or whatever figure is decided upon.

Who would want to purchase an occupied apartment? There are apparently plenty of investment-hungry buyers out there. Most of them are in the 50 percent tax bracket, looking for an immediate tax shelter and, of course, a chance to capitalize on appreciating property values. Buyers here pretty much have to be in high tax brackets. Otherwise the holding period will be too long for them to recoup their money.

The price offered to these investors is usually higher than the insider tenant's price, but lower than the outside market price, so it's a good deal cost-wise. The sponsor usually requires only a low downpayment—sometimes as low as 5 percent—and can probably arrange attractive financing. The tax benefits here are the same as for any form of investment real estate, including depreciation deductions.

This can be a very good deal for investors but there are—naturally—a few caveats:

• Investors often do not realize when they are buying an occupied apartment that *they* are the landlord. The tenant living in the unit you purchased is entitled to services that any landlord must provide. Not the owners' association, the landlord.

• Many investors will make the residing tenant an offer to vacate. Sometimes they are successful, sometimes not. If the tenant in the unit you buy is 28 years old, you're in luck. He or she is not likely to be living in that apartment too long. But what if the tenant is 67 years old, and living under that rent-control and/or senior citizen protection?

• Rents are likely to be low in these units. Can you carry them in light of the mortgage, tax, and maintenance fees *you* are responsible for? Remember, 80-year-old Mr. Jones in the apartment you buy

---

When You Need a Professional Manager

This is a personal decision on your part. If you own four houses in town, and find your full-time job and family responsibilities are not allowing you to spend the time needed to maintain and repair those properties, you might seek outside help. That doesn't have to be fancy or expensive. Perhaps a neighbor or someone else in town can be employed, either with a small monthly retainer or on a pay-as-you-go basis for jobs as they arise—snow shoveling, for example.

Apartment buildings of around eight units or more generally require professional management. You can hire an on- or off-premises superintendent to handle maintenance and repairs, and perhaps even tenant selection. Or you can call in an outside property manager, one who is employed by a large or small professional management company. Fees here usually run 6 percent to 10 percent of the rent (more for single-family houses), and duties include tenant selection and screening, record keeping, and whatever other services the company offers. You can find professional property managers by checking the Yellow Pages under "Real Estate." Ask for references, of course, and be sure you know all services the company or individual will provide. (Will they handle evictions for you? Secure estimates for repairs and follow through with those jobs? What about income tax services?)

---

may be paying $250 a month in rent, while your monthly maintenance charge goes from $300 in 1985 to $350 in 1986, etc.

On the whole, though, if you realize the responsibilities such a purchase entails, and if you can afford to carry the unit for a few years—or better yet, make the present tenant an offer he or she cannot refuse—you stand to make a nice bit of change from purchasing an occupied condo or co-op. Of course, never forget that the location of the building and its condition also enter into that equation.

Buying a Small Apartment Building

This is not an investment for the true novice. Potential problems with building inspectors, problem tenants, high maintenance costs, always-rising fuel bills, and rent-control boards abound. There are many sad tales of very conscientious landlords spending a year or three years or five on their properties, and then walking away from them, in effect, abandoning them to the city in which they are located. The landlord's investment is gone and he leaves with the pejorative "slumlord" flung after him. That is not to say there are not truly sleazy property owners who milk their buildings dry, taking what money they can from them and then abandoning them. What we are talking about here are the righteous folks who thought they saw in an 8- or 10-unit apartment house a way to financial security, yes, perhaps even riches.

If you would like to invest in a small apartment building you should own your own home or at least one other investment property, so the apartment building comes as the next step to someone who is already familiar with real estate ownership. You will know how owning property works. You will know your way around city hall. You've been to a few meetings of the city council and have a sense of how those ladies and gentlemen feel toward property owners. You know the local building inspector, at least by reputation. You are familiar with the rent laws in your community. You know how much fuel oil costs these days, what plasterers charge,

Some investors start with the small (under ten units) apartment buildings, but this is not for the true novice investor. *Reprinted with permission of Caroline Carlson.*

the cost of room air conditioners. You know what you will be able to charge for apartments, how much of an increase you can expect if you do substantial rehabilitation to the building, how much you can raise the rent between tenants. You know the going purchase price of buildings in which you are interested. And, of course, you know your own financial situation. Perhaps because this is such a big investment you will take in a few partners on the purchase.

There are those who would say that the neophyte's buying any small apartment building in a community with rent-control strictures is a recipe for disaster. You might want to bear this in mind if you are seriously considering the purchase of an apartment house. Know why so many rental landlords have been converting their buildings to condominiums and cooperatives? Sure, there's more profit in the conversion, but these property owners are also eager, very eager, to rid themselves of the rent-control headache— of rising maintenance costs and vocal tenants, too, but principally to get out of what they see as the rent-control trap. In what other segment of business or the economy, they ask, is there a lid put on the amount of money you can make? Only landlording. Where else can your expenses go up and up and up, while your income must stay static, or rise only slightly, coming nowhere near to closing the gap?

Still game to try, or living in a community where rent-control laws have not yet made an appearance?

Scouting the proper building will probably take a good deal of time and legwork. Obviously, a neat and well-maintained eight-unit building in an attractive part of town will carry a higher price tag and be less negotiable than an eight-unit building in a marginal section of town (obvious slums should not even be considered). But "marginal" is a word open to interpretation. The neighborhood may be on the decline, or it may be experiencing a renaissance. If it's the former, keep on walking, or driving. If the latter—and only you, with your ear to the ground in your own community, will know which is which— better grab it now. You'll have yourself a plum of an investment. Too often, however, the novice sees an apartment building with a reasonably low sale price and rubs his hands with glee at the thought of all those units for so little an investment. Let's see, a 10-unit building. That's ten units at $400 a month and that equals an annual rent roll of $48,000. Not bad. Ah, but is what you see what you're getting? Perhaps some of those rents are $250 a month. There may be some tenants five months behind in the rent. The present owner may be facing capital improvements to the building, and that's one of the reasons he's selling. Vandalism may be rife. Maintenance and fuel costs may have risen 18 percent over the last year, while rents went up only 4 percent, thanks to rent controls.

What *are* annual expenses for the building you are considering? Be sure to verify each item presented to you by the real estate broker or building owner. Bear in mind, too, your tax bill may jump substantially if your municipality reassesses the property based on its sale price, and/or on the improvements you will make.

Buying the small apartment building is a little like purchasing a used car, in that there is much that is *not* said during the transaction. For instance, you may not be allowed to examine the books of the property in which you are interested. What you might do, however, is specify in the purchase contract that "this offer is subject to the buyer's satisfactory inspection and approval of the seller's last two years' federal income tax returns for this property." That will tell you how the rent roll and expenses shape up. The owner is not likely to underestimate the latter or overestimate the former. It's also a good idea to drive around that complex frequently at night. The seller may say the building is fully occupied, but if you see the same units dark every night you will know differently. Of course, you should also have an engineer inspect any place you are planning to buy.

Buying a small apartment building with the thought of converting it to a condo or co-op is done frequently these days. Many buyers just do not want the hassle of being rental landlords, and conversion is certainly more profitable. If you decide to follow this road, first check with your state attorney general's office to see how conversions are handled in your state, if there are any rulings at all. Will you have to allow senior citizens, for example, to stay on as renters if they do not choose to buy? How will that affect your purchase plan if you are looking at a 15-unit garden complex just about filled with retirees? Check state rulings well before signing any contract to buy.

All of the above negatives are not to suggest that the small apartment building will not be a good investment. Some certainly will be. But far too often the reasonably attractive multifamily dwelling hides a multitude of problems, problems that the current landlord is wearily coping with and eager to pass along to a successor. Don't let that poor optimistic soul be you. Do plenty of homework before you commit $1 of your money and it won't be.

For More Information

"Dealing with Renters: A Guide for Absentee Owners and Associations," available from the Community Associations Institute Research Foundation. (CAI is a national group representing those involved in condominiums.) Write to CAI, 3000 South Eads St., Arlington, Va. 22202. Price: $7.00, plus $2.50 for shipping and handling.

Living with Tenants: How to Happily Share Your House with Renters for Profit and Security, by Doreen Bierbrier; available from the Housing Connection, Box 5536, Arlington, Va. 22205. Price: $7, including postage.

Landlording: A Handymanual for Scrupulous Landlords and Landladies Who Do It Themselves, by Leigh Robinson. Write Express, P.O. Box 1373, Richmond, Calif. 94802. Price: $15, plus $1 for shipping and handling.

Good News for Landlords and Tenants, Jeanies Classics, P.O. Box 4303, Dept. K., Rockford, Ill. 61110. Price: $9.95.

44

Is Land Investment Profitable?
Is It an Investment at All?

There is something about the opportunity to buy land that makes many otherwise intelligent people seem to lose their smarts. This is bound to make money, they reason. I'll hold it a while and then one day a developer will offer me thousands, maybe millions for it. Or I'll subdivide and sell each lot for thousands more than I paid. After all, as the old saying goes, "God stopped making land many years ago, but he didn't stop making people." So all land is valuable, right?

W-r-o-n-g. There is land that is barren and rocky, land regularly hit by flash floods and miles and miles of desert broiling under the sun. These aren't valuable, and unfortunately too often uninformed buyers are, sight unseen, paying out hard-earned dollars for them.

"Investing in land" is probably an inappropriate expression. "Speculating in land" is more accurate. Buying a home is an investment. Buying a rental apartment building, if properly chosen, is an investment, with a degree of speculation. Buying land is speculation. When the gamble percentage of the purchase overtakes the reasonably safe and sound percentage, then you're speculating. And buying land is very much of a gamble. This is a field riddled with deception and fraud (one of the biggest being that all land is valuable). Most land does not rise in value simply because there is no demand for it. This country has vast open spaces, but plenty of that acreage is not going to be used in the foreseeable future. So if you buy something in that vein you will be holding on to it for a long time because no other buyer will want it.

719

Cardinal Sins

Buying land sight unseen.

Thinking of a land purchase as an "investment." It is more accurately "speculation," offering none of the security inherent in the word investment.

Vacant land produces no income, yet you will have to pay property taxes on it every year, plus interest if you have financed the purchase. Your downpayment becomes money that is doing nothing for you. If you have paid cash, you will be losing interest on that money if you had invested it elsewhere. If you decide to sell, the broker's commission here is usually around a high 10 percent, which is sometimes negotiable and sometimes not. So that land had better grow in market value for you at a faster rate than the national cost of living index and the cost of housing in that area. Otherwise, you would have been better off putting your money into a high-yielding savings certificate or some other form of real estate investment.

Also, although there are tax deductions allowed with other forms of real estate ownership, there is none with raw land, because it is considered to have a limitless economic life. If you do sell that land for less than you paid one day, however, you are entitled to a loss for income tax purposes. For specifics it's best to talk to your accountant here so that you don't make a wrong move and instead incur a liability.

All of this is not to say that some land purchases aren't wise ones. A little sliver of downtown can one day return you triple, or more, on your investment—if wisely chosen. A lake-front parcel with nothing working against it, such as environmental controls that will prevent construction on the plot, should bring you a profit. A huge chunk in the country near a rising industrial park may attract a condo or single-family home developer who will pay you a huge chunk.

But how can you tell good land from bad? Which parcel will take off and which will sit there, with only a few empty beer cans tossed its way, year after year after year? Ah, of course, that's where the risk and speculation come in. Still, there are ways of lessening that gamble by judicious studying of the market.

Should You Buy Land at All?

Something funny happens to many Americans after they purchase their first home. Maybe it's happened to you. Your eyes become trained to pick up the real estate advertisements in your newspapers. You now notice "For Sale" signs tacked onto office buildings or to trees in wooded areas just outside town. A world of real estate opportunities you did not know existed has opened to you with the purchase of that home. You want to buy more, to own more. And here's where the problem comes in: Land can be far less expensive to buy than a house or other residential property, or perhaps less than any other form of real estate investment. If you can't afford a house in Happy Acres, you can afford $4000 for a lot there. You can't buy the Empire State Building, but you can put up $700 for a thin wedge of space in Brooklyn that New York City is selling for nonpayment of taxes. This is where the beginner becomes hooked. For a relatively small investment he or she can sit back and say to co-workers and house guests and relatives and neighbors, "I have a piece of property in . . . ," or ". . . my lot in New Mexico." It sounds so *rich*, so diversified, so knowledgeable, so cool.

Perhaps as you read on and consider some of the horror stories and experiences of burned buyers of land, that particular dream will be seen as impractical. For now, it is assumed that if you are thinking of buying land you are in a financial position to do so. Real estate is not liquid, and land especially. You can almost count on it being difficult to sell just when you want at the price you want, so if you need a quick cash fix you'll probably have to look elsewhere.

Still determined? Let's look at how you can wisely spend some of those dollars earmarked "buying land."

Uncle Sam Doesn't Give It Away

"BUY CHEAP GOVERNMENT LAND," "FREE GOVERNMENT LAND," scream the advertisements, and indeed, who should be a better party to do business with than the good old U.S. of A.? Unfortunately, the advertisements are misleading. The government is no longer in the business of giving away land or even selling it inexpensively. The days of homesteading are over. The government is in the business of trying to make money, just like you. Oh, there might be a free parcel once in a blue moon in the outreaches of Alaska, six hundred miles from the nearest community of any size, but that's it.

What land the government *does* sell these days is principally in the American West. The tracts are relatively small—usually 40 to 100 acres, but sometimes larger and sometimes smaller. Many of those parcels are in barren country, with difficult access. Land suitable for farming is rare, so there goes your vision of a simple, happy life plowing the North 40. Most land is suitable only for grazing or mineral exploration.

The land is sold at auctions and somewhat fewer than a hundred of them are held annually across the nation. Prices—and this is an especially important aspect of these purchases—*are at or even a little higher than market value*. Not cheap! No bargains! You can submit a bid by mail, but if you want it to be competitive you will have to attend the auction in person or send a representative. A certified check or money order for a deposit or the total amount, whichever is required, must accompany a sealed bid.

For more information about buying government land, including periodic listings of what is available for sale, contact the Bureau of Land Management, U.S. Department of the Interior, Washington, D.C. 20240. The bureau has branch offices in Anchorage, Alaska; Boise, Idaho; Billings, Montana; Cheyenne, Wyoming; Denver, Colorado; Phoenix, Arizona; Portland, Oregon; Reno, Nevada; Sacramento, California; Salt Lake City, Utah; and Santa Fe, New Mexico.

Deal only with this agency. Far too many gullible buyers plunk down dollars for services and publications that are meaningless.

A final point: The type of government land we're talking about here is not to be confused with "federal surplus lands," which were once used by the government but which are no longer needed. The most attractive surplus land parcels—recreational lands, islands—are usually offered first to state and local agencies. If none of them is interested—and these days they too have to pay and are offered nothing free as they had been in the past—then the general public has a shot. If you want to see what is available here, contact the Regional Commissioner of the General Services Administration, Public Buildings Service, at a regional office in Atlanta; Boston; Chicago; Denver; Fort Worth or Houston; Kansas City, Mo.; Los Angeles; New York City; San Francisco; Seattle; or Washington, D.C.

Where To Buy

The best land purchase if you are a novice is within twenty-five miles of your home. There you will know the communities, the zoning ordinances, the population (its growth, income range, and the like), and the politics.

S. Zimmerman

The most important factor in buying land at a decent price is to be ahead of the crowd in anticipating where growth will occur. Naturally, you will be able to judge that better in your own backyard. You will read and hear about the latest construction news and plans. When everyone in the state has heard that land development has begun, you are already too late to buy at a reasonable price. The land is "hot." A good example: Atlantic City, New Jersey, where nothing was happening at all until approval was given for casino gambling. Then, pow! Think you can find any bargain lots there now?

Buy land that has the most potential uses. Usually little can be done with off-the-beaten-path swampland unless you are holding out for pie-in-the-sky landfill. But land along a busy highway, which can be sold to a fast-food chain, gas station, motel, or other commercial enterprise, can be a good buy. Land around a proposed shopping center or industrial park, if you hear word of it before the masses do, is good, too. Watch the zoning ordinances where you are looking. If you want eventually to build a home on that site, that's one reason for purchasing; otherwise, land zoned for offices and stores has the best investment potential. Then come apartment buildings, industrial buildings, one-family homes, and farmland.

What will grow on this land, if that is your interest? Do you plan to hold raw land for a long-term investment, or do you want improved land? Can you establish a tree farm and sell Christmas trees once a year to help pay taxes until you're ready to sell? Can you sell firewood from trees that you clear? Do you have mining rights? You may not strike oil, but how about shale, or gravel, or sand? Can you remove it and sell it? What about a granite quarry? Can you allow people to camp on your land for a fee? Can you rent the use of your land to a hunt club for pheasant hunting or deer hunting? Field trials for dogs? Horseback riding? What do zoning laws in that community say about any of those enterprises?

Some buyers purchase land auctioned by local authorities for the owner's nonpayment of taxes. If you try this, ask yourself these questions (after seeing the land, of course). Why did the owner abandon this land? Did he really not have that tax money or someone to pay that outstanding amount for him? Or is there something about the land itself that made it not worth holding? Perhaps it is too hilly or rocky to allow for construction of a house. Or too small. Or there is no water in the area. Since these properties are generally sold at auction, you can call the county tax collector and ask when the next one will be held. When the list of properties to be auctioned is printed, you will be sent one. You may have to visit the county assessor's or tax collector's office to learn the assessed value of the property, and if there are any liens on it. For the latter, you may have to call at the buildings department. You will have to do all the homework on these parcels yourself; there is no broker.

Land buying in general is an area where the more people you talk to the more you will learn—and the more rumors you will pick up. Some of them you can profit by. When you get down to business, you will need a lawyer to go over every aspect of your purchase; a tax specialist who is probably already handling your financial affairs; and a professional appraiser. The latter can give you the background of the land in which you are interested and its current market value. And, of course, it can't hurt to keep in close touch with a knowledgeable real estate broker.

Some specific points to consider in purchasing land fairly close to where you live now:

1. *Environmental concerns.* If you are buying land you hope to build on one day—or even if not, for that matter—it will pay to keep an eye on what your state environmental agency is planning to buy for "land bank" or other purposes and where it will be putting a

moratorium on development. A growing number of communities are attempting to slow overall growth and lower speculation, too. No matter what is suggested in the way of development, they do not want it. Land banks are becoming more common. All of this could affect the resale of the acreage you buy, or your building plans for it.

2. *Water*. This can be a major problem. Getting water—and getting rid of it. Some individual lots, but not tracts of land, are bought subject to being able to get adequate water supply from a well. Where your area has city water, that's not a problem. If you are buying an individual lot you can make the purchase subject to adequate well water.

More common than purchase contracts that are subject to the availability of well water are contracts that are subject to a water percolation test. A "perc test," as it is often called, is a means of testing the soil to discover its absorbent qualities for drainage and septic tank purposes. A hole is dug, usually with a backhoe, and water is poured in. How fast it disappears into the earth is recorded. Sometimes the test is repeated several times during different kinds of weather.

Good drainage makes housing development on a property easier and less expensive. Poor drainage usually increases building costs since extra steps must be taken to assure foundations that will not settle unevenly and basements that will be dry. In areas where septic tanks are necessary for waste water disposal, poor drainage can make homebuilding impossible unless a community sewer system is installed. Generally speaking, the better the drainage, the more expensive the land and, of course, the reverse.

If you are buying a large tract, your individual buyers for the lots may make their purchase conditional on the availability of water. Bear in mind, too, that water on a property can change in the course of a year. A trickling brook can become a roaring river in spring, a scenic pond a dried-up, mosquito-breeding mudhole in the middle of summer.

3. *Terrain*. What may seem like a bargain (a parcel at $1000 an acre) may not be such a buy after all if most of the land is cliff or swamp. How much buildable land is there? How much *good* buildable land? Some cliffsides are all right for construction, but only at great expense. And the cost of draining a swamp or diverting a river can be virtually out of sight. Also to be considered: the cost of putting in a road over difficult terrain. The solution here may be to obtain a U.S. Geological Survey map of the area in which you are interested. That office publishes a collection of maps called the Na-

tional Topographic Map Series. For more information about these maps (the index to all of them is free; there is a small charge for the maps), contact: *for areas west of the Mississippi River*, Geological Survey, Distribution Section, Federal Center, Denver, Colo. 80225; *for areas east of the Mississippi River*, Geological Survey, Distribution Center, Washington, D.C. 20242; and *for maps of Alaska*, Geological Survey, 520 Illinois St., Fairbanks, Alaska 99701.

It's important to walk the property! Note what the weather has been like before evaluating standing water. Talk to local well-digging companies about the probability of finding water. Ask septic tank companies what they usually find under the ground in the area. That does not guarantee what will be found under the land *you're* considering, but it will give you a likely idea of what's there.

4. *Whether or not you will be landlocked.* The selling of landlocked lots is illegal in many states. Small plots in the middle of nowhere that can be reached only by helicopter can't be marketed anymore. A road must be provided for access.

5. *Shape of the parcel, road frontage.* The more road frontage on an already completed thoroughfare, the more valuable the piece of land. When it comes to the layout of the parcel, bear in mind that land is valuable usually to the degree that it can be subdivided. If zoning laws require 3-acre building lots, and you are sold 8 acres, you have only two lots. If you own a huge chunk of land, but only 100 feet (wide enough for a road) fronts on an already established road, your cost to subdivide will be proportionate to how much road you have to put in to establish buildable lots. The more expense required to develop the land, the cheaper your purchase price should be.

6. *Financing.* Many, many sales of land are cash only. The most common means of financing a sale is by the seller holding a short-term mortgage. Balloon loans are a possibility. In some economic situations and real estate markets you may also be able to buy land on time through the installment land-purchase contract, where you agree to pay the seller the purchase price in installments over a period of time. Title does not pass to you until you have made all payments, or at least a considerable number of them. A variation on this theme is the phased installment purchase contract, whereby you agree to buy from the seller separate parcels of land in successive transactions over what could be many years. That takes the financial sting away from making such a major purchase at one time.

Raising Cash From Your Land

While you are waiting for a buyer, or waiting for your land to appreciate, you can put that acreage to work earning money for you. How about planting crops? Raising and selling Christmas trees? A horse farm (zoning permitted)? Pony rides for area kids?

Another suggestion is placing a mortgage on the land, if you can. Ask a lender how much you can borrow. What would be the interest rate? The length of the loan?

For small purchases, lenders also offer personal loans. Downpayments for any of these land sales vary widely, but are generally in the 10 to 30 percent range.

7. *Release clauses.* If you buy a large piece of land with a house on it, and if you secure a bank mortgage and plan later to subdivide that land and sell the lots you have broken off, then you must be sure to have a release clause in your mortgage. The clause gives you the right to sell off parts of the mortgaged property. You will usually have to pay off a portion of the mortgage equal to the relative value of the parcel you are selling.

8. *Demographics.* Also if you plan to subdivide and sell, take a look at socioeconomic profiles of the area. Is it growing? What about new industry? The economic level of new people moving in? Is the town desirable? Can you get a look at a master plan, if one exists, to see what the community hopes and plans for itself?

9. *Survey.* This is often inaccurate for large tracts, and expensive, too. For subdivisions, land must be surveyed and prospective lot lines and road areas indicated on a plat plan, in order to secure preliminary subdivision approval. One means of making money here, however, is to buy a large tract, have the survey done, have professional surveyors draw a plat plan, get town approval for a subdivision, and then sell to a builder. Many developers look for such pieces since they allow them to start building immediately without having to wait for approvals from planning boards and environmentalists and anyone else with thoughts on the subject.

10. *Self-developing.* Another point in the area of subdividing, planning the subdivision community, and building and selling the houses is an extremely expensive and complicated procedure and

very definitely not for amateurs. What we're talking about here are road bonds, sidewalks, utilities, building permits, subcontractors, wind, rain, hail, and a few other disturbances and many high-priced expenditures. If you don't know what you're doing—and how many novices really do?—you can go broke just trying to figure out the next step to take.

11. *Planning boards.* This is a group of ladies and gentlemen found in just about every community who are likely to protect you as a resident from unwanted development and an invasion by outsiders. But if you are an investor or speculator or want to get a commercial foothold in the community, these good folks may present a totally different picture. They can often be inflexible and ignorant of your field, and almost always they will be conservative in their thinking. They want to keep Little Acorn just the way it is right now. Better yet, the way it was twenty five years ago. If any changes *are* to be made, they will argue only for the highest and best use, which may cancel out your plans to erect Pizza City down there on Main Street. Bear in mind that you will be grappling with these people for a few months, or even a few years. Planning-board approval is needed for virtually all commercial construction of any size and any residential development. Brace yourself.

Buying Resort Land

You say you don't want to buy 50 acres one county away, you want only 1 or 2 acres one thousand miles away in Cactus County. A nice plot of land in sunshine country where one day you may just build yourself a nice little retirement place. Or who knows, the land may become so valuable that by the time you're nearing 65 you could sell it for three times, maybe ten times, what you've paid. Anyway, it's pretty hot country out there—in more ways than one. You certainly can't go wrong plunking down $700 or $4000 or so for a slice of God's green earth, can you?

Yup, pardner, you sure can.

The number of free chicken dinners, with developers offering guests what is frequently turkey land, has diminished somewhat in the last several years because of tighter restrictions and regulations by the federal and state governments. Land purchasing in resort areas, however, is still an area an investor should regard with extreme caution, especially from an armchair hundreds, or thousands, of miles from the site.

Lots are being offered for vacation purposes not only in the sunshine meccas we are all familiar with, but also in northern regions near pine trees, lakes, rivers, or manmade recreational facilities designed to lure the buyer. Unprincipled developers look especially to eastern urbanites who, they feel (and sometimes they are right) look at any vacant land, probably because they see so little of it, as an outstanding investment opportunity and a chance to buy some of the country's few remaining open acres. So if you're a city slicker, watch out for fast-talking salespeople. They've got your number!

The interstate land sale industry is usually defined as comprising those companies engaged in selling subdivided land where the homes and other improvements on the site can be built and made at the expense of the buyer. You must seek out the best companies here. They may not be the ones that do the heaviest advertising, although lots of ads to get a project off the ground, or during a tight-money slump, should not in itself be considered suspicious.

The Office of Interstate Land Sales Registration, the federal agency that regulates those transactions, has received as many as five thousand letters a year from people complaining of being swindled. Some one thousand land development companies have been singled out by that agency over the last decade or so for noncompliance with the Interstate Land Sales Full Disclosure Act when investigative teams went out to search for violations. These violations can take several forms, including failure to meet deadlines for completion of facilities pledged in the offering statement, and fabricated accounts of lot sales transmitted by radio to the salesperson who is driving the prospective buyer around the site. In one instance, lot sales were suspended when the developer was accused by HUD of failure to disclose certain information to the prospective buyers, such as the fact that the subdivision "is in the immediate area of the Teddybear Lake Bombing Range"!

If you want to purchase land in a resort area, whether for long-term speculation or to build there eventually for yourself, consider these points:

1. On-site inspection of the property is a must. If you see it, you may not buy it. No matter that a hustling salesperson guarantees you your money back in six months if you are not pleased, no matter how little the downpayment is, *do not buy this land sight unseen*. Spend the cash for a plane ride if you have to, and consider that a

good investment against future financial loss and extreme aggravation and frustration.

2. Before buying, check the developer's references. Reputable firms offering fifty or more unimproved lots must furnish you with a set of government-required disclosure documents. If you do not receive those documents at least forty-eight hours before you sign for the land, you can cancel the contract by notifying the seller by midnight of the third business day after you do receive them.

3. Check with the Office of Interstate Land Sales Registration, under the Department of Housing and Urban Development, to see if any complaints have been filed against the outfit you are considering. You can ask them any other questions you have about buying property out of state, too. Their number in Washington is (202) 755-5860.

4. Be sure you will be offered clear title to the property.

5. When you make your on-site inspection, do so in the worst season in that area. Go to Arizona in August. "It's hot as hell here then," said one resident. "It's up to around 115 degrees during the day and cools off to 100 at night." The speaker is a retiree who is now heading back north after sweltering through a southwestern summer that came as an extremely unpleasant surprise to him. The temperature in Palm Springs, California, can hit 120°+ in the summer, and you'll have to put a cloth over an exterior door or car handle before you can touch it. But Palm Springs is chic and so the land there is valuable. Is the community you are considering equally smart—or just hot in the climate sense? New towns that land hustlers are selling have probably not "arrived" yet, and indeed may never do so.

6. Do not take proposed amenities for granted. If the developer promises shopping centers, golf courses, pools—well, he's under no obligation to provide them unless they are written into the contract—with a date for completion, too, unless you want to hear him repeatedly droning "next year" every time he's approached about them.

7. Bear in mind that if you are building a house on your lot, that does not mean your neighbors will, too. Yours may be the only home in a sea of vacant land, some of it already purchased, but with other lots still up for sale.

8. Can the land be used as a homesite? What kind of permit must be obtained? Are there water and sewer hookups? What about access roads? Is your lot large enough, according to local zoning laws, for construction of a home?

Also, if you plan to build, consider where the financing for that house is to come from before you buy the land. Say you own a lot with water, electricity, and fire hydrants, but no paved roads. A bank may turn you down for a mortgage just on the basis of the roads. A lender may also reject you if you are an amateur planning to build your own home. He'd rather offer money to a professional builder, or to you if you are buying an existing house. If you shop around, you may find a willing lender, but how much easier to buy land where you know that when you want to build a house there, you *can* build a house there.

9. Sometimes a lot sale is made dozens of miles from the subdivision headquarters. "But Mr. Smith, this lot is in the middle of no place. It's so far away from anything that I wouldn't even want to be buried here." That was the cry of an eastern businesswoman who had finally viewed the Florida property for which she had been paying over eight years. Remember that the attractive development with clubhouse, pool, and perhaps ten or so model homes is the sales tool for a project that could encompass three or four hundred homes. Your lot could be far, far away from the activity.

10. Take the time to go home and think about your decision to buy. Don't be taken in by sales tactics that give the impression that there is only one lot left and if you don't buy it within the next fifteen minutes, thirty-two other would-be buyers will take it right out of your hand. Remember those fraudulent radio transmissions? Have your lawyer back home look over all the printed material. Do not engage a lawyer two blocks from the subdivision. Too many people in those communities are in the pocket of the developer.

11. If the salesperson shows you that land prices in the development have risen over the last few years, it may be that the company itself is raising the prices, so the rise may have nothing to do with demand.

12. Once you decide to buy you will usually not, unless you pay in full, get title to the land or a mortgage. Instead, you sign a contract under which you agree to pay x dollars down and so much a month for as many as ten years. Interest rates vary widely. You do not get the right to build on your lot until you have made all the payments.

13. What will happen if you default on those payments? Be sure you understand how the company deals with payments and defaults. Most agreements give companies the right to take back the land and keep the money you have paid in. Sometimes you get back less than half the amount of the payments you've made. This is to absorb

some of the developer's costs in advertising and parceling the land. It is better to expect very little in the way of a refund.

14. If you already own subdivided land that you now want to sell, be wary of companies offering to do that for you for a fee of several hundred dollars in advance. Reputable developers offer sale programs, but they follow the usual practice of commissions paid after the sale is made. You should never have to pay anything in advance.

If you feel you have been taken in a land deal, you have some recourse. You can try to get your money back through your own efforts with a lawyer, or you can write a government agency for assistance. You will certainly not be the first buyer they have aided! You can contact: (1) the Office of Interstate Land Sales Registration, the federal agency that polices installment land sales, at Room 4108, 451 7th St. S.W., Washington, D.C. 20411, or (2) the Federal Trade Commission, 6th St. and Pennsylvania Ave. N.W., Washington, D.C. 20580, stating your grievance and why you feel your money should be refunded.

That's for a deal where you consider yourself an injured party. As stated a few pages back, you can stop payments on an installment sale to get out of buying property, although you will probably lose what you have paid in. If, on land you fully own, you want to stop paying real estate taxes and, in effect, abandon the property, in about two years the county will put the tract up for sale. If the sale brings more money than you owe, you get the balance. If your land is part of a community where you must pay association dues, the association might sue you for those unpaid dues, but that's unlikely to happen—too expensive.

All of the foregoing make quite a laundry list of "watch out for's" and "beware of's," but land-sale fraud is still occurring despite tightening regulation. Land buying is not really for the novice and is not in the forefront of good real estate investment. But if you do want to buy, educate yourself and then proceed with caution to avoid ending up with a patch of ugly scrub, and not the potentially profitable acreage you are counting on.

For More Information

"Buying Lots from Developers," Publication #169M, is a 20-page U.S. government booklet available from: Consumer Information Center, Dept. K, Pueblo, Colo. 81009. Price: $2.50. A 14-page U.S. government booklet, "Can I Really Get Free or Cheap Public

Land?" Publication #170M, is also available ($2.25) from the Consumer Information Center. (But the answer is "no"!)

"Before Buying Land . . . Get the Facts" is available, free, from: Office of Neighborhoods, Voluntary Associations and Consumer Protection, Office of Interstate Land Sales, HUD, 451 7th St. S.W., Rm. 4108, Washington, D.C. 20410.

45

Farms For Profit... And Fun

Ahhhhh . . . the country life! Clean air. Roosters crowing at 5:30
A.M. The chance to run barefoot through the cow pasture. The smell
of newly cut hay. The squeal of piglets. Who hasn't wished for it, at
least sometimes, while battling the 5:30 P.M. rush?

But owning a farm, have you actually thought of that? The life
of a farmer is not for everyone, but farm ownership may be right
for more people than you would suspect. Yes, perhaps even you.
As the end of the twentieth century approaches the purchase of a
farm is not motivated only by the business of farming but also by
investment interests, or as a vacation home, or as a family venture in self-sustaining independence. Let's look at some of the
what-to-buy and whether-or-not-to-buy considerations for each
type of ownership.

Is Farming Your Business?

Anyone can be a farmer. People are doing it successfully even
though they can neither read nor write, and people are doing it
successfully even though Ph.D.'s hang on the walls of their kitchens.
The choice of this vocation has more to do with temperament than
education, but experience helps. In fact, we can't imagine anyone
going out to buy a farm and farm equipment who hadn't done the
work of a farmer for a year or two. Yet some people do it, and some
even succeed.

Where to Get the Money to Buy a Farm

You probably won't be able to get your hands on a single penny until
you have actually found the farm you want to buy, but it helps to know

U.S. Department of Agriculture.

where to look for the money before you sit down to sign the contract. The following are the most common sources of farm financing.

• *Commercial and savings banks.* These institutions offer first mortgages, occasionally seconds. Most loan agreements are self-liquidating (they will be paid off at the end of their term), and most first mortgages are written for between 70 and 75 percent of the appraised value of the property. Interest rates are comparable to other business financing. Unlike most home mortgages, however, the payments on the loans need not be monthly. Payment schedules are usually arranged according to the needs and the cash flow of the specific type of farming being financed. Sometimes payments are made only once a year, when the harvest is in.

Try to get nonrecourse financing (see Chapter 42 of this section) whether you use a commercial lender or any other source.

• *Seller financing.* According to the U.S. Department of Agriculture an estimated 35 percent of real estate farm borrowing is financed by private individuals or groups not under federal regulation. Most often this is the seller of the farm. In fact, it is possible to buy a farm with nothing down. The most common method is a first mortgage to a commercial lender and a second, for the remainder of the purchase price (or most of it), to the seller. Get a lawyer to help you write the seller-financing agreement. And remember, nonrecourse!

• *Life insurance companies.* Many of the larger life insurance companies write mortgages for farm real estate, though they are usually interested in financing amounts in excess of $100,000. Interest rates are competitive with other sources. The term of most loans is twenty-five to thirty years, although you can occasionally find a company willing to write a forty-year loan.

• *Large businesses that depend upon farm produce.* Where does the company that sells tomato soup get the tomatoes? Some corporations whose product depends upon the productivity of farms will finance the purchase of land by a private individual to produce the crops they need. Take note of the most popular labels in your supermarket. The mortgage agreement, however, should not be substantially different from the one you would get from a bank.

• *Farmers Home Administration (FmHA).* This government agency both guarantees loans from institutional lenders and makes them directly. It is not easy for a first-time farmer to get this kind of government loan, however, since the FmHA considers itself a "lender of last resort." This means you should go to them only if you can't get financing elsewhere. Their loans are written for a forty-year term, and interest rates are comparable to other sources—unless you can qualify as a "limited-resource" farmer on the basis of low income, in which case you might just be able to get a loan at a special low rate. FmHA loan applications are made at county FmHA offices; check your phone book.

• *Farm Credit System.* This group of lenders is the country's largest supplier of farm credit. They are chartered and supervised by the federal Farm Credit Administration but no government money or guarantees are involved. The system is owned and controlled by its users (farmers and their cooperatives such as the federal land banks and production credit associations). A federal land bank can make farm ownership loans for up to forty-year terms. It requires a borrower to buy stock in the bank equal in value to 5 percent of the loan, however. There is an office in most rural county seats.

• *Small Business Administration.* Borrowers who cannot get a farm purchase loan elsewhere can try the SBA. The farm, however, must qualify as a small business (which means a top limit on annual income). For more details write to Small Business Administration, 1441 L St., N.W., Washington, D.C. 20416; or call (202) 653-6832.

The Art of Farm Finding

There are essentially two ways to get into farming: (1) find a farm and buy it, and (2) find some open land and create a farm. The first way is easier and less risky. The second may or may not be cheaper depending upon how good a deal you make on the land and how lucky and skilled you are in converting dirt to farmland. There are particular things to watch out for in each farm-acquiring method; in fact, enough of them to write a book. The best we can do for you here, however, is to list the most important and most common.

If you buy a working farm, consider the following:

1. *Location.* Do you want to live and work there? Do you have good access to your markets?
2. *Financial success.* Get financial statements for the past five years if possible. Is the farm making money? Do you think it can make more money? Why? How?
3. *Condition.* Of the buildings? Of the soil? Of the equipment?
4. *Water and energy sources.* Will they be adequate for the kind of farming *you* want to do?
5. *Availability of financing.* Good financing can make the difference between success and failure.

If you buy open land, consider:

1. *Location and access.* Same considerations as for a working farm.
2. *Topography.* Is the contour of the land suitable to farming? *Your* kind of farming? You can get topographical maps of the land from your regional office of the U.S. Geological Survey. (Office addresses are listed on page 726.)
3. *Soil.* The Soil Conservation Service (SCS) of the U.S. Department of Agriculture makes and publishes soil surveys including maps of agricultural areas. They also offer cost-sharing programs and technical assistance.
4. *Climate.* What farm products will survive in your climate? Your County Extension Service can supply you with climate maps, rainfall and frost information.
5. *Acquiring water and energy.* Is it available? What will it cost to get it? To use it? Talk with well drillers, utility companies, other farmers in the area.

Some Farm Products

Crops
alsike seed
alfalfa
other hays
herbs
vegetables
  corn
  peppers
  tomatoes
  carrots
  lettuce
  potatoes, etc.
berries
  strawberries
  blueberries, etc.
melons
pumpkins and squash
tree fruits
  apples
  peaches
  plums
  oranges, etc.
grapes
oats
wheat
barley
flax
nuts
maple syrup
shrubs and other
  landscape plants
flowers
Christmas trees
honey

Livestock
cattle
dairy cows
sheep
hogs
goats
chickens
ducks
geese
turkeys
pheasants
other game birds
eggs
rabbits
fish
mink
puppies
horses

6. *Drainage.* As important as getting the water. The Soil Conservation Service can help.

7. *Cost of necessary improvements.* Roads and buildings, and don't forget fences. Do you have or can you get this money? Don't forget to add in the cost of financing.

8. *Choice of farm products.* All of the above factors can influence or limit your choices but there does seem to be an endless number. The box on page 738 lists a few suggestions. Bear in mind, however, that if no other farmer in your area is producing a particular product, there might just be a reason.

9. *Availability of farm labor.* This is another make-or-break success factor.

Property Taxes and the Farmer

Farmers simply can't afford to pay taxes on their land as though every acre were bringing in the revenues of a five-story apartment building. Recognizing this, most states have passed some form of tax-relief legislation for farmers. Laws vary across the nation and even from county to county, but the most common types of programs are zoning for farming, deferred taxation, and specialized farm assessment.

In states where farm zoning is used, the designated lands must be used for farming. As such they are given special tax protection.

Deferred taxation is a form of rollback tax. Farmland is given special tax treatment as long as it is being used as farmland. Upon sale or conversion to another use, however, a tax must be paid upon the savings accumulated over the years. In some states the deferred taxation for farmland is automatic; in others the farmer must apply for it to state or local government.

In states that use a specialized farm assessment, the tax on farmland is computed differently from the tax on other land. Usually some projection of the productivity of the land is used as the basis for taxation. In other words, taxation is based upon land value according to how much income the land produces. No rollback tax applies under this form of tax relief, but the assessment changes if the farmland is converted to another use; a condominium community, for example.

Farms as Investment Real Estate

Why would anyone want to invest in a farm? To make money, of course. But with a farm investment that can be a tricky accomplishment. Consider the following.

Income

Is anything more uncontrollable than the weather? Yet farm products often depend upon it. Is anything more volatile than food prices and feed prices? Yet farm income is related to the cost of operation versus the price at the marketplace. Is anything more unpredictable than the world economy? Yet farm income is often related to exports, which are related to international everything (war, peace, diplomacy, good will, the value of the dollar, foreign debt, trade agreements, the Olympics, you get the idea . . .).

Most experts agree that the current return on farm investments runs about 6 to 8 percent a year. You can do better in money market funds with no headaches and high security.

Tax Shelter

Farms offer little tax shelter in comparison to other investment real estate; apartment buildings or shopping centers, for example. Why? Primarily because the land cannot be depreciated and your primary farm investment is in the land.

Personal Use

Yes, some investors buy a farm for personal use, a weekend retreat, vacation home, or even as a primary residence, although they have no intention of working the farm. The farm as a business is leased or managed while the owner enjoys the benefits of country living and realizes a modest profit (it is hoped). More about this mode of investment as we move through this chapter.

Appreciation

The most important motivator for most farm investors is the hope of future gain through the sale of the land. Between the mid-1950s and 1982 prices of farmland across the nation climbed. Farms were a good investment, sometimes a great investment, especially when the land could be subdivided and sold for housing lots or commercial development.

But the upward spiral came to a halt in 1982/83, especially in the Corn Belt. Some parts of the country and some individual farms are still moving upward in value today, but the investor needs to be more wary. Location has become even more important a factor in investment success. But don't discount farm investment. The investor who picks a farm on a spot that in five years or so will become desirable—as the site for single-family homes, a condominium community, or, even better, a shopping center—will raise his glass and toast, "To farms!"

During the time a farm is held as an investment, however, it must be operated, unless the investor is willing to carry a heavy debt and expense load without income. Few investors have the time, inclination, or skills to take on the responsibility of operating their investment. As a result, leasing and professional farm management become factors to consider in the investment decision. There are three most commonly used lease arrangements. Farm manager employment is worked out between the manager and the investor but there are some generally accepted standards.

The Share Lease

Under this type of an agreement an investment farmer participates in the farm operation, financially at least but often in the decision making also. The investor provides the farm, pays the property taxes, and pays half of all expenses. The working farmer provides the labor, often the equipment, and pays the other half of the expenses. They split the profits. Usually share leases are renegotiated on a year-to-year basis.

The Cash Lease

When a cash lease is used the working farmer quite literally rents the farm. The investor pays the usual expenses of a landlord: property taxes, insurance, and upkeep on the buildings. The working farmer makes his or her own decisions about how to use the land and improvements. The investor's income from the farm is thus fixed by the amount of the rent for the term of the lease. The working farmer may make a lot or a little from his or her labors depending upon the success of the farming and the prices the produce of the farm gets at the marketplace.

The Standing Rent Lease

Under this agreement the investor is not paid in cash but in crops or livestock, usually a fixed quantity rather than a percentage of the total produce of the year. The investor still takes on no responsibility for the farm operation and has no say in decision making. The return on his or her investment for the year, however, will vary depending upon the year's market price for the produce grown or raised on the farm.

The Farm Manager

Rather than lease their farms, some investors hire a farm manager. Usually this person's pay is a percentage of the investor's net income from the farm (10 percent is common). Housing is also often provided for the farm manager. In return for his or her salary, the manager takes on the responsibility of making the farm work, including procuring and supervising labor and "keeping the books."

If you are still reading and still considering a farm as your investment vehicle, remember that everything we said about choosing a farm to work as your business applies to your choice of an investment farm. In fact you must be even more careful in your choosing since someone else will be working your land. If they can't "make a go of it" you may find yourself carrying a heavy debt load with little or no income and little tax relief. And farms are much harder to sell than houses.

Vacation Farms

What can you do on a farm?

Walk. Talk. Picnic. Sleep. Eat and drink. Grow roses. Fish. Ice skate. Cross-country ski. Ski-mobile and hay ride. Ride horses. Hunt. Chase butterflies. Read (uninterrupted). Bird watch at 5 A.M. Not answer the phone. Count stars on a summer night. Jog. Cuddle on the porch swing. Practice your tuba. Entertain friends. Raise Saint Bernards.

Think about it. If you convert a corner of a barn or other outbuilding to a comfortable apartment or perhaps build yourself a little kit house (see Chapter 23), you can have a vacation home with acres of land to enjoy.

And think a little more. If you have leased your farm to a working farmer or have a resident farm manager, your little vacation hideaway can require minimum maintenance time from you. There are no "industry guidelines" for vacation cabins on working farms, but investors and working farmers have little trouble working out maintenance agreements.

So the farm vacation home can be virtually work-free. And guess what. Virtually cost-free, too. If your investment farm brings you a cash return, even of only 6 percent a year, while the land gradually appreciates in value, even at the rate of inflation, and you get to escape to your own place two or three weekends a month and a week or two in the summer, what's it really worth to you?

Now take your thinking still one step further. . . . Farm vacations are becoming more and more popular as the nation's hotel and motel rates approach $100 a night. Well, what if you built two or

---

Have You Thought About . . .

Smells: Farms are famous for them. But not everyone finds all farm smells pleasant.

Flies, bees, ticks, and other insects: All are abundant in the country.

Dust: It can come in great clouds.

Ragweed: This and other delightful allergy-causing plants are also abundant in the country.

Neighbors: No coffee klatsches in the country. Will you mind not seeing anyone but your own family for several days running?

Driving: What if going to the dentist means a seventy-minute drive each way? If you hate driving, you may want to reconsider city life.

Entertainment: Oh, there's the TV of course. But your choice of a movie may be limited to what's playing at the only theater within driving distance, and eating out will be limited by the relatively small number of nearby restaurants to choose from.

Bookkeeping: Farming is a business and it requires paperwork. You won't be able to spend all of your time out-of-doors, even if you want to.

---

three cottages on a corner of the farmland? Or sited two or three manufactured homes? Or established a camping area for travelers to park their motor homes? Could you make an arrangement to split the profits with the working farmer and his family in return for maintenance of your farm vacation business? And once you have a business, could you justify a swimming pool? Maybe one tennis court?

"You are dreaming!" you say.

Well . . . yes. And no. This is a dream that can materialize. Of course it helps if your farm is located within easy driving distance of a popular vacation area or a major city. But there are vacation guides in every bookstore that feature farm accommodations and there are vacationers that seek them out. The local chamber of commerce nearest your farm and often even a county or state tourism office may offer a listing of farm accommodations to the public. You can get listed. You can make a modest income.

Consider a Rent-Your-Own-Farmland Business

Some farm investors near suburbs and cities have successfully supported their appreciating land investment by dividing their farmable acreage into garden-sized plots that "city folk" rent in order to grow their own vegetables.

But remember, *all at the same time*, to:

1. Weigh the choice of your farm purchase as though you were a working farmer planning to make a living by farming that farm. If you don't have good farmland, in fact, a "good farm," you will have difficulty finding a working farmer who is willing to lease your farm much less care for your vacation retreat.

2. Weigh the choice of your farm as though its chief value were its investment potential. Will you be able to show a profit at least two years out of five consecutive years? (IRS tax rules establish this guideline to differentiate hobby farming from farming for profit. That differentiation may be very important when you file your income tax return.) Will the land appreciate in value?

3. Weigh the choice of your farm as though it were only a vacation place. Is this a place you would like to return to often? Is it within reasonable driving distance of your work-a-day residence?

4. Choose your working farmer or farm manager carefully. New people every year can throw a wet blanket on the nicest vacation spot.

Five Acres and Independence

In the absolute middle of the Great Depression—1935—M. G. Kains wrote a book called *Five Acres and Independence* that promised to teach its readers how to become self-sustaining. The book is still being sold today (Dover Books), and it seems to be the inspiration for real estate advertisements for "mini-farms" and in some areas the development of mini-farm communities.

Can it work? Can you really produce enough meat, vegetables, and dairy products to cut those seemingly endless trips to the supermarket down to an occasional foray for flour, sugar, cinnamon and spice, shaving cream, and maybe a can or two of pork and beans in case you don't have time to fix dinner one night?

Yes. But. And this is a big but: are you and your family willing to do the work and spend the time it takes?

"Oh, I'll collect the eggs!" says 7-year-old Janie. And she does for eleven days. Then it becomes a chore and a source of nagging and fighting between her and her mother.

Raising crops and livestock requires a commitment of time; some crops and some livestock more time than others. Your family can indeed come close to self-sustaining independence on five acres, but not if both parents work at other jobs and the children are so involved in "extracurricular" activities that the family rarely eats a weekday meal together.

There are several books available on self-reliant living besides *Five Acres and Independence*, including the very fine *The Manual of Practical Homesteading*, by John Vivian (Rodale Press). We suggest you do some reading before you buy a mini-farm and suddenly find yourself uncomfortable, neither gardener nor farmer.

For More Information

The U.S. government through the Department of Agriculture and other agencies offers a wealth of information and technical assistance. A good place to start your reading is "Getting Started in Farming on a Small Scale," Agriculture Information Bulletin #451. Price: $3.25. It contains a listing of other available publications. Write to Office of Governmental and Public Affairs, U.S. Dept. of Agriculture, Washington, D.C. 20250.

Also from the U.S. Department of Agriculture is a booklet more specific to your purpose: "Assistance Available from the Soil Conservation Service," Bulletin #345. It is free. Write to U.S. Dept. of Agriculture, Soil Conservation Service, P.O. Box 2890, Washington, D.C. 20250.

On the subject of financing, three booklets may be of help: "Rural Housing Site Loans," "Economic Emergency Loans," and "Farm Ownership Loans." All are available from your local Department of Agriculture; or you may write to U.S. Dept. of Agriculture, 14th and Independence Ave. S.W., Rm. 4121 South, Washington, D.C. 20250.

The United Farm Agency, a real estate firm, offers a free guide to farmhouses for sale across the nation, as well as regional catalogs for Western, Central, and Eastern sections of the country. Write to United Farm Agency, 612 W. 47th St., Kansas City, Mo. 64112.

The Internal Revenue Service offers free help in the form of its "Farmer's Tax Guide," Publication #225.

Rural America is a national organization of people from rural areas and small towns. They are committed to keeping rural Americans up to date on all topics of interest concerning life away from America's cities. An individual membership in this grassroots-oriented advocacy organization is $20 and includes a subscription to their bimonthly magazine *Ruralamerica*. The magazine subscription, alone, is $10. For a free sample copy, write to Rural America, 1302 18th St. N.W., Suite 302, Washington, D.C. 20036.

The most comprehensive book on the subject is *Farmland Buying Strategies*, by Merrill Oster, Jerry Carlson, and Elizabeth Curry, John S. Wiley & Sons. Price: $27.95.

46

Buying, Fixing Up, and Selling Rundown Houses— Still Profitable in the 1980s?

In the 1970s the scenario went something like this: You bought a rundown single-family home for a song, put in a few thousand dollars for repairs, and sold the now-sparkling jewel for a substantial profit. Then you bought another house, and another. Sometimes you sold the houses after rehabilitation, sometimes you held on to them and rented them. In no time at all you were rich, rich, rich.

But that was the 1970s, the seemingly golden days of single-digit interest rates and affordable house prices. Home improvement loans were reasonable then, too, and government grant and loan programs accessible. Buyers could snap up your improved houses because mortgage money was readily available and at terms within more budgets than today.

So now the question: Can you still play the buy, fix up, sell, and make a fortune tune in today's market?

Well, yes and no and how's that for a straight answer? This time around you must approach the investment like the proverbial two porcupines making love: v-e-r-y carefully. It's not an automatic success story anymore, but for the canny beginner the profits are still there.

This is not a get-rich-quick scheme, however, regardless of what you may read or see on television. Get in for the wrong reasons and, with a few other factors working against you, you can go broke. The land mines are everywhere.

Are you the "type" for this type of real estate investment? Let's see:

• Can you adopt an investor's attitude about these properties, seeing them as houses, not homes? If you are going to take this investment route you must not be slowed down or sidetracked by considering only houses *you like,* homes where you would like to live. This business requires a whole different mind set than buying your own homes entailed. Here you may buy ugly houses, houses that do not appeal to you in the least—but houses that will sell.

• Can you afford the investment? There is more about the financial aspects of this avocation later, but for now we'll say that it does take some money, no matter how inexpensive the property or how great the financing. You'll need a cushion in your own savings to protect you against misfortunes that can happen to any investor, as well as a few extra dollars to cope with any of life's emergencies unrelated to the house.

• Are you prepared to do most of the rehabilitation yourself? If you call in professionals, you are narrowing your profit margin to the point where you may lose money when you resell the finished house. Of course it's important to understand that you may have to call in licensed plumbers and electricians to satisfy local building codes. Figure those costs in with your estimate of how much renovation will cost.

• Will you know when to stop renovating? Doing most of the work yourself is important, but you must not let yourself get so caught up in sprucing the place up that you don't know when to stop and at what point you are losing money. No house is ever finished, you know. Have any of the ones where you have lived ever been 100 percent "done"?

• Do you have time to spend working on the house? Is your full-time job too demanding to allow you regularly scheduled renovating time? Will your family be behind you in this venture? Some investors remain in their own home as they buy investment properties, while others move into the houses on which they are working. If you choose the latter strategy, does the family know what it is letting itself in for, moving into a house that needs much work and then, just when it's finished, moving on to the next dilapidated property? Do you, for that matter?

• Are you prepared to do plenty of homework before purchasing your first investment property? That means scouting the neighborhood looking at houses for sale, talking to real estate people, touching base with folks in the neighborhood you are considering, studying the economic climate of the community, doing cost analyses of purchase price, cost of renovation, likely resale price, carrying

See what a little elbow grease can do. *Reprinted with permission of Caroline Carlson.*

charges until you sell, and the like. If you plan to rent you should look into rent laws in that community and every other aspect of becoming a landlord.

• Finally, keep in the front of your mind that the principle behind this investment is "Buy low, fix up"—not minimally, but not going overboard, either—and "Sell as high as you can. And do it all quickly." Rapid turnover of properties is important. Dally in fixing up the house and you are carrying mortgage payments and all the other expenses that go with homeownership, month after month.

That money is going out, with nothing coming in. Speed is essential here.

You can see from the above that just because you have done a fine job in fixing up your own home, that talent will not necessarily make you a superb rehabilitation strategist. This is a business calling for a peculiar alchemy of putting a little of the human touch into the properties you upgrade, while keeping a cold eye on the bottom line. Think you're up to it? "Sure," you say, pounding the kitchen table for emphasis. Good. Now the answers to a few more questions.

Where to Buy

Here we come to those three superimportant real estate words again: location, location, location. A rundown house in a rundown community spells Disaster City for your investment money; a rundown house in a good neighborhood spells a likely win. You have three points to keep in mind when scouting where to buy. First, you want the lowest price, where rapid appreciation is likely to take place. Second, you want most or all of your investment properties to be within the same geographic area. You don't need a Victorian house twenty miles north of your home, a second house in your own hometown, and the third property fifteen miles to the east. Stick to the same town, or at least an adjoining community, unless you are considering vacation areas, which is discussed later.

The third consideration is which town? Which neighborhood? This is where you can lose the ball game, or become an extremely successful entrepreneur. We'll take the easiest decisions first:

• Any town on an ocean (or a resort lakefront community) is likely to be a successful investment. They aren't making any more ocean and those properties will be of enduring, and growing, value. The same goes for houses in choice ski resorts, near popular golf courses or other major recreational attractions. But very near, not 8 miles away.

• You can't miss if you buy in a college town either, where there is always a demand for housing. Or in a company town (if the company is a secure one). There, too, the demand for homes may continually exceed the supply. Choose near an army installation and again you're likely to hit the bull's eye.

• If you buy within a block or two of a grammar school or playground your house(s) will be in demand.

• Where you live now may have an upcoming area designated as "hot," a growing community with new people moving in and spruc-

---

For Those Considering Vacation-Home Properties

Is this structure really habitable, or is it a "shack"?

What's the water like—is it a mud hole or can it truly be considered a lake?

Does it snow more than three days a year here, enough so that I can genuinely promote the place as a ski house?

How's the plumbing? What keeps the pipes from freezing in the winter?

How about the fresh-water supply?

How is the resale market? Will I be competing with a professional marketing concern? That can happen if, say, you buy a cottage near a planned community of three hundred homes and try to rent your house while that sales office and its crack team is renting and selling several hundred of theirs.

What are zoning laws like? Can I improve my property by expanding it? Can I create apartments within the house? Can I turn the garage into a rental?

Who's going to look after the house in the off-season? Can I find a manager in this community to keep an eye on it for me?

---

ing up old houses. Or perhaps the whole town is hot and in demand. If you buy here, before prices go sky-high, you'll be pocketing dollars. Because you live in or near the town you will know just when that spot has caught on and can step in before outside investors and speculators force prices up. New revival neighborhoods of old cities, for example, seeing an influx of Yuppies (young urban professionals), are prime candidates for this investment. The Park Slope section of Brooklyn, the Otterbein section of Baltimore, and Society Hill in Philadelphia are a few of the more notable examples of that phenomenon. There are few, if any, bargains there now, but oh, if you had bought ten years or so ago you'd certainly be sitting pretty now.

Those are the simpler choices when it comes to location. The more difficult ones are the average city or suburban neighborhood. The point to remember here, of course, is that you are buying an old house, one that needs work. So we'll eliminate neighborhoods with new ranch or split-level houses. They will be priced too high if they are in attractive suburban enclaves, and since they are usually in fairly good shape there will be virtually no difference between the price you pay and what you will be asking when you sell. If the neighborhood is very good, you may not even be able to get that much of a bargain when you buy the house.

What would work well for you in the suburbs would be towns *not* in the orbit of an urban center, the ones that are not posh bedroom communities for city commuters. If you had access to your county Board of Realtors' printout of home sale prices for the year in all of the towns in the county, you would probably do well to invest in the bottom half of that listing, depending, of course, on just what could be wrong with some of those lower-priced towns. If there's a plan for a nuclear power plant that has kept prices low in Pumpkin Creek, you will know to avoid buying in Pumpkin Creek. But if Hardworking-town has low sales prices only because its residents have lower incomes, and the houses are well-kept (aside from the rundown ones you are looking for), there's nothing wrong with investing in that town if the numbers can be made to work out for you.

Cities can be particularly confusing for investors just starting out. The problem here is that cities, always changing as they are, give hazy messages about which neighborhoods are on the way up and which are sliding down. Naturally you'll run from the latter.

How to tell which is which? If you live in or near the city, you will know from reading real estate stories in local papers where the rehabilitation action is these days. Talk with real estate agents, even drive around the town. Look for newly spruced-up houses among those that aren't so hot. Talk to those owners. Is there an influx of new people buying homes there and fixing them up? Some clues to revival: hanging plants in windows, pots of flowers on the stoop or windowboxes, shutters, exteriors painted in interesting color combinations. Go on house tours, too, to get an inside look at what's going on in neighborhoods.

Older, ethnic neighborhoods that seem to stay the same year after year are another consideration. These homes are always in demand because the young people tend to stay in the neighborhood after they marry, continuing the demand for housing. The houses may be quite prosaic, even somewhat unattractive, but they are well-maintained and their prices continue to rise. They sell quickly, too. One potential problem here, however, is that you may find few fixer uppers. With little to be done on houses for sale, there's no profit for you. Your best bet might be to buy a single-family house and convert it to two or more rental units. Your rents would create a positive cash flow and, of course, you would have the likely appreciation of the property working for you. But expect no big profit from investing in these neighborhoods. You'd do better a few blocks down, buying into the enclave just starting a renaissance.

If you're interested in country fixer uppers, remember that distances can be great once you get beyond the last suburban boundary. Driving to and from the investment house can be a problem, lengthening the time it will take you to fix it up and resell. And time is money.

Vacation homes are another potential investment. Crowded resorts may be your best choice, offering a variety of properties in need of rehabilitation. Depending on the style of house you may be wise to create two or three rental units within it. Rentals are always in demand in recreational areas. If you hold on to the house(s) and rent, you'll have that income to defray your carrying costs. If you sell, the buyer will likely appreciate apartments, too.

There is more than location to consider, of course. Here are some commandments for buying investment property that cover those other aspects of the purchase, and include location too.

1. Look near your principal residence (unless you are buying vacation houses in resort communities, and then give serious thought to how you are going to rehab those properties from your home base).

2. Pick the worst house in the best neighborhood, but bear in mind the neighborhood may be so good that even an absolute horror will be priced too high both for your budget and for you to make an acceptable profit.

3. Avoid houses of new construction. Usually there isn't enough upgrading needed to bring you a wide enough profit margin. Concentrate on the oldies.

4. Investigate zoning restrictions before you buy. Can you create apartments out of that house? Can a business or retail establishment be put into the ground floor? Can additions be put on?

5. Look for the house that has been on the market for a long time. That shows there's something wrong with the property. Perhaps it's overpriced, but maybe there's just too much work needed to attract buyers. That's fine with you, of course. Bargain well over these homes, offering 20 to 25 percent below the asking price. The owner may be desperate at this point. However . . .

6. *Beware of* the house with a poor layout or traffic pattern. *That* may be why that home has been on the market for months, and that's a condition almost impossible to remedy unless a simple knocking down of a wall or two can be managed. Going through one bedroom to get to the next, for example, is bad, and most buyers spot a poor layout immediately. Steer clear of these homes.

7. Have the house inspected. It is vitally important that you know what repairs are going to cost.

8. Before buying any fixer upper, ask the real estate agent selling the property to give you a market analysis of the block or neighborhood. All that is is a listing of sales prices of nearby homes sold recently. She or he can obtain that information readily enough from computer printouts, and it will give you an excellent idea not only of what you should be paying, but what you can expect to sell the house for when you have finished rehabbing. You will also see that if estimates for repairs are high, you may realize no profit. Buy that house and you may be stuck with that dreadful albatross—a house overpriced for its neighborhood.

9. Do plenty of mental calculations as you go through fixer uppers. What work can you do yourself? What jobs will you have to farm out to professionals? Can you go around the place with the engineer or house inspection person and let them give you an idea of prices?

10. You *must* know where to spend money, where to skimp, and what to skip altogether. Good mechanicals are essential to a house you want to sell at a profit. Buyers look for modern kitchens, but beware of creating the most lavish kitchen in the neighborhood—a $20,000 number in a $60,000 house is disproportionate. A second bath is a wise installation. Solar anything is an uncertain value at this time, whether built in the North or South. Leave it alone. If you're planning rehabilitation of very high priced houses you may want to consider such crowd pleasers as beam ceilings, A-one kitchen appliances, ceramic tile, perhaps wall-to-wall carpeting. If a house is dark and that has been scaring away buyers and keeping the price low, you in your wisdom may see that installing a skylight or two will turn the place into a delightful sun-splashed haven. All of this takes time and studying—to know what's hot right now and what's not, what's a standard good home improvement ploy and what's a waste of your money and installation time.

11. (More commandments here than for life in general, aren't there? See how serious this form of investment can be?) Look to government auctions for properties at reduced prices. Check in with

---

The Fixer Upper You Buy

Profitable	*Unprofitable*
Needs paint	Wet basement
Dirty	Structurally unsound—buckling,
Worn floor covering	uneven settling or severe cracks (hairline cracks can be expected
Outdated kitchen	in elderly structures)
Ancient bathroom fixtures	Inadequate plumbing
Broken windows	Serious termite problem
Termites (early stages)	Thermopane windows with
Broken downspouts and gutters	broken seals (they must be replaced)
Poor or nonexistent landscaping	Restrictive zoning that may force
No "charm"	you to keep an eighteen-room behemoth a single-family home

---

your regional HUD office to see about sales of homes taken through foreclosure, and investigate city and county auctions for houses taken for nonpayment of taxes, water bills, and other liens. Sometimes you can pick up a bargain at these auctions, and sometimes the community sponsoring the sale will offer attractive financing. But you should know that many of the houses go for far more than the lowest bid acceptable, many are virtual shells requiring many times the purchase price to make them habitable, and the good financing may be available only for owner-occupiers. You will see these houses advertised in local papers a few times a year. You can phone local governmental agencies to see when the next sale is coming up.

12. Consider a joint venture. If all of this is beginning to make you wilt, take in a friend or two on the investment. Usually one of you will act as the general contractor, the others as silent partners. There's more about this "passive" style of investing in Chapter 48.

Two Terms to Become Acquainted With

One is *rent control* and the other is *gentrification*.

If you are planning to hold onto your houses and rent them, be sure you know if there are rent-control strictures in that community.

Do those laws apply to dwellings of three units or less? Will the house you buy be delivered vacant? How much can you raise rents then? Are there restrictions on how much you can charge tenants in the new rents even though you are doing a major rehabilitation? What is considered a "major" rehabilitation? Once new tenants are in, how much can you raise their rents each year?

Working in a rent-controlled community isn't the greatest way to spend your investment dollar, and, indeed, we have advised skipping becoming a landlord in towns where rent control is in force, but you can come out all right with this proposition, since you are dealing in houses and not apartment buildings. Just know your rights and be aware of just how the debit–credit equation will work for you.

We've mentioned earlier that many old city neighborhoods have seen a resurgence of popularity as new people move in, upgrading houses and commercial districts. One effect of that renaissance has been higher housing prices and escalating rents that frequently force out long-time residents. You should know if you buy into one of these communities—and they can be the very best of investments— you may be excoriated as one taking advantage of the poor and elderly, and may be held up to civic groups and others as an ex- ample of all that is going wrong with that neighborhood. There is as yet no solution to the gentrification problem. Just be aware that you may be in for a helping of unpleasant PR, depending on what stage the renaissance is in. Buy in the beginning and you can go about your business quietly. It's at the point where the neighborhood is garnering much publicity and outside speculators are moving in that you can expect tomatoes tossed by irate tenant groups. Figuratively speaking, of course. If you're lucky.

The Importance of "Charm"

No, not you—the house(s) you buy. Let's say there are two homes for sale on Elm Street. One is your standard 1930s front- porch, wood-frame house, neat and well-kept, but rather sterile. The other is another 1930s oldie, but look at the difference! Attrac- tive hedges are planted around the front porch and on the steps are pots of colorful geraniums. Inside, the place is distinctive: handsome mantel in the living room (there is no working fireplace behind it, it's just for show and "detail"); an interesting wood rail- ing separating the kitchen from the dining area; a stained-glass window in the bathroom. The walls are all painted white to please universal tastes, but one small room, designated the den, has been "papered" with a handsome paisley fabric. Matching tieback curtains hang at the windows. There's extra fabric available for the buyer who may want to carry that theme further with toss pillows or sofa cushions.

Both of these houses will sell because they are sound structures and are in a community where homes are in demand. But which is likely to sell faster, and perhaps at a higher price? Right. But sure, you say, the renovator had to spend a lot of money improving that house. Not really. If you are going to enter the rehabbing business in a serious way—and how else, with that investment of time and money?—you'd be wise to start collecting materials and odds and ends to "charm up" the houses you buy. That's what the professionals do. These can be inexpensive flea market finds or items, such as fabric purchased on sale. Look around demolition sites. Peer into dumpsters, where other houses are being emptied. Keep an eye on the trash collection in your own neighborhood. Anything distinctive—french doors, old brick, mantels, shutters, glass door knobs, planters, bathtubs—can be incorporated with little effort and practically no cost when you are fixing up a house. And those touches *do* make a difference. Most fixer-upper specialists have basements, toolsheds, or, eventually, a warehouse full of "stuff." It all goes somewhere, sometime—and makes more money for those foresighted investors.

The Economics of the Business

Now we get down to the numbers. The all-important bottom line. How do you pay for these houses? How do you buy the first one?

You want to buy the most you can for the least investment of your own money (leverage) when you buy a home for yourself, but in purchasing investment houses that strategy becomes even more important. This is a business. You are not likely to hold on to these houses ten, twenty, or thirty years. Again, you must train your mind to think "profit" and get away from expensive and time-consuming steps toward purchases you may have made with your own homes (having too many people take a look at houses you are considering, taking the advice of those more inexperienced than you, paying more than you should because you like the house, or some feature of it, etc.). *Pay as little down* as possible. You can borrow this sum from traditional sources—relatives, insurance policies, and the like; but many new investors opt for second mortgages or home equity loans on their principal residence.

If It's Such a Good Deal,
Why Hasn't Someone Snapped It Up?

How long has this property been on the market? Why?

How many hours will be required to fix the place up?

How much will supplies cost?

What will outside professionals (electricians, roofers, plumbers, etc.) cost?

How much financing can I get?

Will I need a zoning variance for my plans?

How will improvements affect the taxes on the property?

What is the local economic climate like?

How long do I plan to hold this property before selling it? Will I live in it during rehab? Will I rent it when it's finished instead of selling?

How much am I likely to make from a sale? How soon and how certain is that sale and profit likely to be?

What's all this about starting a house-fixing investment career by buying with nothing down? That is a possible ploy—for about two in one hundred neophytes. Let's say you've found a dilapidated house you can purchase for $50,000. You've put together some cost estimates and tell a lender it will cost you another $50,000 to fix up the place. It will sell, you figure, for $150,000. You secure an appraisal for the house in its "as is" state and another for its "renovated" condition. The lender you approach says, yes, he will give you a $100,000 construction loan, allowing you to pay outright for the house. The fixing-up money he will release in stages as work progresses. You will notice that no money has left your pocket. You buy the house and start the rehabbing, keeping an eye on the calendar. The bank has given you six months to complete the job (although usually that time can be extended a bit). Then you must pay back the loan, either by selling the house or securing a traditional mortgage. Before the house is finished, you may look for a buyer. You have now spent $20,000 on the renovation. Your asking price is $150,000. A buyer comes along and says "$150,000 is too high, but I'll give you $140,000." You have spent $50,000 to buy the house, $20,000 in rehabbing, and you figure the place will take another $30,000 before the job is finished. That makes your investment, and the amount you owe the lender, $100,000. If you sell at $140,000 you will realize a $40,000 profit. Not being greedy, you decide to accept the offer. That's not bad, either, considering you haven't spent one cent of your own money, and have made $40,000 not in years but in months.

This is a legitimate way of buying, but we can't caution too strongly that it is not as simple as it reads. It is not for beginners, unless they have a friendly banker who can guide them through the process, or a partner better schooled in nerve-wracking financing. And nerve-wracking it is. We have presented a beautifully laid out scenario here, but life, as you may have noticed, doesn't always proceed so smoothly. Let's look at what can go wrong with the house you have bought for nothing:

• Maybe you won't find a buyer before the construction loan runs out. Will you be prepared to take out a mortgage for that house?

• Maybe the house is in a company town—and the company closes down, putting thirty-five other houses on the market.

• Maybe you run into trouble with subcontractors, or with supplies. Perhaps there's a lumber strike out West and there you sit waiting for delivery of the top floor.

• Maybe there's a family emergency, and you must drop your rehab plans to tend to that situation.

See how that financing is for those with the style of riverboat gamblers?

There are more traditional loans, of course, and you would be wise when buying any old house(s) to check with your regional HUD office to see about any buying or rehabilitation money that might be available for the block you have chosen. Good buys can also come from FHA- and VA-backed assumable mortgages, or from sellers' mortgages that, admittedly, may not always be available in upbeat markets.

Beware of negative leverage. When interest rates are high and the rate of appreciation is low, you can get into trouble with fixer uppers. A small downpayment and a large mortgage can saddle you with high carrying costs until you can resell the house; and, depending on the state of the economy, that may be a while. The appreciation of the property may not be enough to cover the debt you incur. There are ways of getting an unprofitable property off the books in bad times—offering the buyer a mortgage or a lease-purchase option, for example—but remember there *is* the chance you will be stuck with carrying costs far longer than you would like, costs that will narrow the profit margin when you sell, perhaps to the point of that profit disappearing altogether.

Selling the House

You should start looking for a buyer when your fixer upper is about 40 percent finished. Make as many cosmetic improvements as you can and have it looking as good as possible so that househunters can visualize the finished product. Never wait until the last nail is hammered into place. It may take months to find a buyer, and better that that process should proceed while you are still working on the house.

You and the IRS

As the owner of a house you are entitled, of course, to federal income tax deductions on mortgage interest and real estate taxes. If you rent the houses you fix up, you become eligible for investors' deductions of depreciation and maintenance and repair bills.

The IRS sees a line between those buying property for investment and those who are "dealers." If you are considered a dealer, your real estate profits will be taxed as ordinary income. But if you are an investor, you will be taxed at the more favorable capital gains rates when you sell. There's a fine line—and a regularly changing one—between the two but, in general, your reasons for buying the property and the length of time you hold it make the determination. Dealers buy for a fast resale, investors hold their properties longer. Check with your accountant or your regional IRS office to see which category describes your buying activities.

There is more to buying fix-up properties than space permits us to talk about here. Some books that delve more deeply into that investment are listed at the end of this chapter, and there are several chapters in this book that can also help. We've mentioned a few earlier, but you might also read the chapters on negotiating for the best deal on a house, buying old, possibly historic, houses, and how the government can help you buy. All of that reading is part of your homework, of course, to prepare you for what could become an extremely lucrative *full-time* career one day. Go for it!

For More Information

How We Made a Million Dollars Recycling Great Old Houses, by Sam and Mary Weir, Contemporary Books, Inc., 1979. Price: $12.95.

House Recycling: The Best Real Estate Opportunity for the 80s, by Mary Weir, Contemporary Books, Inc., 1982. Price: $11.95.

How to Buy and Fix Up an Old House: A Step-by-step Course on How to Find and Buy an Old House, How to Pay for It and How to Plan, Estimate and Contract the Renovation (10.95) and *Professional Cost Estimating for Residential Remodeling, Renovation, Rehabilitation and Repair* ($18.75) are both available from Home Tech Publications, 5161 River Rd., Bethesda, Md. 20816. No charge for handling.

Landlording: A Handymanual for Scrupulous Landlords and Landladies Who Do It Themselves, by Leigh Robinson (Express Publishing Co., P.O. Box 1373, Richmond, Calif. 94802); third edition, 1980. Price: $15.00, plus $1 for postage and handling.

How I Turned $1,000 into $3,000,000 in Real Estate in My Spare Time, by William Nickerson, Simon & Schuster, revised edition, 1980. Price: $16.95.

47

Housing Your Business

What's Your Business?

☐ Barber ☐ Butcher ☐ Baker ☐ Candy Maker ☐ Doctor
☐ Dentist ☐ Lawyer ☐ Tax Accountant ☐ Toy Maker
☐ Wine Seller ☐ Literary Agent ☐ Realtor ☐ Artist
☐ Cosmetologist ☐ Clown ☐ Hose Clamp Manufacturer
☐ Sausage Stuffer ☐ Butler ☐ Bondsman ☐ Baby Sitter
☐ Restaurateur ☐ Tutor ☐ Tailor ☐ Typist ☐ Tympanist
☐ None of the Above

Whatever it is, it needs a home. Even the Internal Revenue Service recognizes that a business needs an address, a place to be, as it were, and allows deductions for the costs involved in housing it. But those costs are only one of the essential factors to be considered in choosing a home for your business. Where and how that business is housed can mean the difference between success and failure.

Location

If location is the most important factor in real estate, it is seven times seven the most important factor in commercial real estate. What is the right location for one kind of business, however, may be all wrong for another. You must know the needs of your particular trade and then evaluate each of the following points in terms of those needs.

Access

Ask yourself, "How can the public get to my business?" For some businesses, proximity to major thoroughfares is absolutely essential. Other businesses, those without high public contact, can be located in a dusty, fifth-floor loft without elevator service as long as the telephone facilities are excellent.

Barriers, natural and social, are also a factor to be considered. A steep road or driveway, a narrow bridge, a "tough" neighborhood can all turn away customers or clients, and even delivery trucks.

And think about giving directions. Not many people are really good at finding "new" places. If you must explain more than two or three turns, you will lose some customers or clients before they even find you.

Parking

Even in our largest cities, those served by subways and other highly refined mass transit systems, parking is an essential consideration of American business, virtually *every* American business. Even if yours is the kind of business in which you will see only one client or customer at a time, you must still consider where that person will park, and, in fact, where the person who comes next will park, too. Even the smallest business, therefore, must consider two parking spaces, not to mention where you will park.

Owners of professional offices must consider not only waiting-room space, but parking space for everyone in that waiting room. Manufacturers must consider space for deliveries and pickups and space for employee parking. Retail store owners who do not want to lose customers to the competition must have adequate parking available for a lazy afternoon in July and for the pre-Christmas shopping frenzy.

Services

Those things so many of us take for granted in our homes, electricity, water, sewerage disposal, heat, police and fire protection, cannot be taken for granted in locating a business. If there is no water line to a beautiful historic house that would be perfect for a gourmet restaurant, for example, can you open the restaurant? Would a well support the draw of filling water glasses, cooking, and dishwashing? Could a septic tank adequately handle the waste water?

If you have your heart set on building your widget manufacturing plant in a rural setting, can you get electric power adequate to run the machinery and support the air-conditioning system? And what will your annual insurance bill be for that widget plant if the town has an all-volunteer fire department and no municipal water supply? Do you think the insurance company will give you a break if you tell them about the pumper and the fact that Woonuski Pond is just three quarters of a mile down the road?

But what if you don't want to manufacture widgets in the country? What you had in mind was a discount diamond mart and you know just the abandoned building where you could locate at minimum cost. Are you aware that the town's police force had recently been cut by 20 percent due to lack of funds? Why was the building abandoned anyway?

Sounds and Smells

Because they are invisible and intangible, sounds and smells are factors often overlooked when locating a business, but they are real and an important consideration. If you don't believe this, imagine a psychologist's office located directly above a video-game parlor; a diet and exercise salon next door to a Chinese fast-food restaurant; Porch 'n Patio's "outdoor showroom" within a half-mile of the sewerage treatment plant on a day in August; an investment counselor's office located near the commuter railroad tracks.

Municipal Character

Will your tannery be welcomed in Flowerville? Does the town and the surrounding area have an adequate labor pool for your business? How about zoning regulations? Can you work within them or get a variance? Does the town allow signs? Sunday business? Will the mail service be adequate? Is there a place where your employees and clients can go to lunch?

Competition

How many businesses like yours already exist in a given area? Los Angeles may be able to support seven theatrical agents in a two-block area, but could Bangor? Does the town or area of town really need another grocery store, restaurant, theater, shoe repair shop, pharmacy, word-processing studio, or photographer? Get some statistics on your town, then take a ride through the area you were considering. Are there really enough people for your business?

The Shopping Center

If you choose to locate your business in a shopping center, your concerns about access, parking, and services will be eliminated; the developer has already made adequate provisions in most cases. But you must still judge the likelihood that the character of the area will support your particular business. You must also evaluate competition. And finally, you must choose your location within the shopping center most carefully. A gourmet cheese shop, for example, will want to be highly visible to the largest possible number of people in order to attract as many impulse buyers as possible. On the other hand, customers will walk to the far corner of the second floor for a custom furrier.

Physical Space

If your business is writing, you need but a cozy room and a typewriter. No one will judge the worth of your work by the place in which you do it. Unfortunately, however, that statement cannot be made about most other professions.

Space is essential to both retail sales and manufacturing. Space and "decor" are essential to most service businesses. It follows quite naturally then that most commercial property transactions (both sales and leases) are rooted in the question of square footage. And of course the essential question is, "How much do you need?"

When housing your business, think not only of what you need today but also of what you might need two years from now. If at all possible, it is best not to move your business just because it is growing. Can you expand to include another floor? Can you add to main-floor space by taking over the lease of another business? By adding on to the building? On the other hand, what will you do with extra space if you discover at some point that you do not need it? Can you subdivide? Sublet?

Few commercial properties are "just right" for a new tenant or new owner. Can you go beyond redecorating to remodeling? If you are leasing, how much of the renovation will be paid for by the landlord? Can you take down walls, put up partitions? Opening up space by eliminating walls, or creating privacy by putting them up, can make the difference between a work area conducive to your business and one that undermines it. And don't forget: light; heat; air conditioning; ventilation; rest rooms; closets; storage space; structural soundness (Will the building's floor support the machines you plan to bring in?); ingress and egress; traffic flow within the building; security; elevators; maintenance; and orientation (are you going to get morning sun, afternoon sun, north light, or no sun?).

It is difficult to judge interior space when you stand alone in the center of an empty room. If you have any doubts about a place, try a mock-up. Get some cardboard boxes and pile them up where you expect to have desks, or display cases, or whatever. Then invite a number of your friends to help you get the feel of your prospective place by coming with you to an inspection of the property and standing about among the dummy boxes doing what people do in your business. Does it feel comfortable? Empty? Too crowded?

If you are still unsure, visit a competitor who has approximately the same square footage of business area that you are considering. How well do equipment, merchandise, and people fit together? How can you improve on his manner of doing business?

Should You Buy?

One of the strongest motivators for buying one's *home* is favorable tax treatment. Owners can deduct a large part of their cost of housing (interest and property taxes) against their incomes on federal tax returns. Renters usually have no such recourse. As far as the IRS is concerned, all the money they spend on housing could just as well have been spent on vacations in the Carribean. As a result, homeownership is more appealing than renting to most Americans.

That is not the case with housing a business, however, where the cost of renting space *is* tax-deductible. Renting and buying, therefore, compete more nearly as equals for the business owner's choice. In fact, the choice you make will depend primarily upon your particular needs. Let's look at some plus and minus points.

Reasons to Buy
No one factor should unduly influence your decision as to where to locate your business, but everything else being equal, any one of these could tip the balance to the side of buying:

• *Security*. If you "own the place," you won't be asked to move out on a given date. Also, your rent won't go up unexpectedly or unexpectedly high (although your mortgage payments on an ARM might rise and your property taxes could go up). And not incidentally, you will be accumulating equity in your property as you operate your business.

• *Control*. You can decide whether to paint or panel. You can install wall-to-wall carpeting at will, or have the old windows replaced by one huge "picture" window. You can remodel, renovate, or add on (if you can get a building permit and zoning variance, that is). Or you can subdivide the space you own and rent the part not needed by your business.

• *Depreciation*. This is a tax benefit of ownership, especially in the early years. If you plan to stay in business well into a second decade, however, depreciation will eventually be worth less to you.

Reasons Not to Buy

Now for the other side of the coin. And some of these points make renting look very good indeed:

• *Downpayment required*. Buying property ties up cash that could be invested in the business.

• *Maintenance*. You, the owner, are responsible for fixing the leaky roof, pumping out the flooded basement, snow removal from the parking area, and keeping the exterior painted. And don't forget lawn mowing, sidewalk sweeping, interior decoration, vacuum cleaning, floor waxing, and "What did you say happened to the water pipes in the basement!" If you must pay someone for these maintenance chores, the added expenditures may bring your housing payments close to those of a rental. If you do the chores yourself, they could demand almost as much time as the business itself.

• *Mobility*. Usually it's harder and takes longer to sell a commercial property than to sell a house. And like a house, the sale of a business property is affected positively and negatively by the economic climate of the nation and of the local area. If you choose to buy, therefore, a mistake in the choice of location can prove very costly indeed (or sometimes very profitable). In either case, you probably won't be able to move until you sell.

• *Available stock*. Sometimes, especially in major cities, the best places to do business are rentals. There simply are no properties for sale that suit your needs. If you find this to be the case, don't waste a minute crying over your lost purchase. Choose the best place from among the rental properties available. If your heart is set upon ownership, sign the shortest lease possible and include a provision that allows you to assign or sublet. Start your business, and in your "spare time," keep an eye out for a place of your own.

The Commercial Condominium

Somewhere between buying and renting comes the commercial condominium. Ownership of such a unit features many of the advantages of ownership of a detached building. Your monthly payment won't go up (although your maintenance fee probably will), you won't be asked to leave, you can build equity, and you can depreciate the property. Control, however, is limited to your interior space.

On the other hand, maintenance is not a concern for the individual unit owner and shared space can be an advantage. In some commercial condos, shared space extends to the use of conference rooms, a luncheon area or restaurant, and even secretarial and receptionist pools.

When commercial condominiums began to take hold in the 1970s many developers foresaw a huge demand. That demand has not materialized, due partly at least to the economic instability of the early 1980s. The number of commercial condos is growing steadily, however, and some experts still see shopping center condos and manufacturing condos as well as office building condos as major factors in the landscape of the coming decade.

A Primer on Commercial Leases

The world of commercial leasing is an intricate maze. There are more ifs, wherefores, and contingencies than most property buyers could ever imagine. In fact, we recommend that you do *not* sign such a lease until after you talk with your attorney. To sharpen the focus of that talk, you may want to consider the following points:

• *Flat rental lease.* A flat rental lease names a periodic (usually monthly) rental payment that is fixed for the entire term of the lease.

• *Graded lease or graduated lease.* The tenant agrees to a fixed rental amount at the inception of the lease but there are provisions for graduated increases or decreases at specific points during the term.

• *Rent escalation.* Many commercial leases provide for rent escalation during their term. Theoretically, this escalation provides coverage against increased operating expenses to the owner of the property. Sometimes, however, rent increases can exceed expenses, especially when rent escalation is tied to an index unrelated to the business of the tenant, such as the Consumer Price Index. Some rent escalation clauses are tied to utility costs and/or local taxes. Generally, you will find no governmental rent controls on commercial leases.

• *Net lease.* The tenant pays rent and all operating expenses for the property.

• *Net net lease*. The tenant pays rent, all operating expenses, and all insurance premiums.

• *Net net net lease (triple net lease)*. The tenant pays rent, all operating expenses, insurance premiums, and property taxes.

• *Percentage lease*. The total rent paid by the tenant is a percentage of the total amount of business done by that tenant. "Total amount of business" may be gross sales, gross receipts, gross income, or any other mutually agreeable delineation. The term "net profits," however, is likely to cause discord since legitimate deductions before the "net" are often a matter of opinion.

• *Ground lease*. A ground lease covers the use of land alone, usually land without improvements. Often the tenant constructs his or her own building. Most ground leases are long-term; ninety-nine years is common. A valid ground lease can sometimes be used as a "downpayment" for construction financing. With such security, a business owner may be able to finance 100 percent of the cost of his or her building.

• *Landlord fix-up*. Some landlords agree to remodel to suit the tenant. In this case, the lease should define exactly what is to be done with as many product names and quality standards specified as possible.

• *Nondisturbance clause*. This clause guarantees the tenant possession of the premises for the entire term of the lease even if the ownership of the building changes.

• *The right to sublease*. If you sublease the whole or part of your space, you collect the rents from the subtenant and continue to pay the landlord the amount of rent agreed upon in your lease, which might be more or less than the amount you collect from the sublet. The right to sublet protects the tenant who comes upon hard times. If the landlord insists that a sublet be subject to his approval, include a clause in the lease stating that his approval cannot be unreasonably withheld.

• *The right to assign the lease*. In an assignment situation, the tenant finds another tenant to take his or her place. That new tenant is bound by the stipulations of the original lease. The right to assign can be a safety net in the event you decide to move or close your business.

• *Renewal options*. If you plan to stay in a given location, the right to renew your lease should be written into it.

• *Arbitration of disputes*. Some disagreement is almost inevitable. It's a good idea to name an arbitrator when there is no dispute, that is, when the lease is signed.

Buying or Leasing Through a Real Estate Agent

Commissions on commercial property sales are higher than those on residential property. Ten percent is most common. Sellers agree to pay this commission on their listing agreements, but when it comes down to the nitty-gritty, who pays the commission often becomes a negotiating point.

Some business owners prefer to use a "buyer's agent," that is, a real estate agent working exclusively for the buyer. Payment of this agent's commission can be arranged in any way that is mutually agreeable. It can also be a point of negotiation between the buyer and the seller.

Relatively few commercial properties are listed in multiple-listing service books. Most smart business owners not using a buyer's agent make contacts in several different real estate offices. To eliminate unnecessary phone calls, prepare a flyer describing your needs and listing those properties that you have already seen. It is sometimes helpful to include a few words as to why each of the "have seen" properties was rejected.

If possible choose as your agent a commercial specialist. Most residential agents are not qualified to handle the intricacies of a commercial lease or sale.

• *Business closure clause*. If your business closes and you cannot find a subtenant or an assignee, you are still bound by your lease. Try to have a minimum rent written into your lease in the event of closure. The low figure will motivate the building owner to find another tenant.

Housing Your Business in Your Home

In your basement, the garage, a spare bedroom . . . Why not? There's no cheaper rent anywhere, nor more security and control. Uncle Sam even allows tax deductions for the portion of the operating expenses of your home equal to the amount of space devoted exclusively to business use. Now there's a little break!

Also, just think. There is: no commuting cost; no need to dress for

---

How to Survive Working at Home

Don't answer the phone. Or have an answering machine answer it and return only business calls during business hours.

Close the door to your work area when you are working. In fact, you might consider hanging a sign on the door. In bright red letters:

AT BUSINESS
DO NOT ENTER

Locate your work area as far from the refrigerator as possible.

Establish how many hours a day you intend to work. Then don't work during off-hours and don't take off during work hours.

Disconnect the television set.

When you feel lonely, down, unappreciated, and underpaid, take a job with a temporary employment agency for a few days. Your home business will look better for it. And if it doesn't, maybe you shouldn't be in that home business after all!

---

success; no need to hire baby-sitters when you're working late; no need to send out for coffee; no need to "be there" between 9 and 5.

There certainly are advantages to a home-based business, but before you run off to hang out your shingle, consider:

- *Zoning.* Will the code in your area allow your home-based business? Can you get a variance?
- *Customers/clients.* Do you have an appropriate place to meet them? Will they be able to *find* your home address (which is also your business address) easily?
- *Space.* Do you have adequate storage space? Adequate working space? Parking space?
- *Distractions.* Is your business compatible with the "normal noise" of a residential neighborhood: children laughing, crying, screaming; dogs barking; the smells and clatter of pots and whirr of the food processor from the kitchen; someone talking on the phone; the TV playing; Tommy practicing his trumpet; eight-year-old Marcie knocking at your door to invite you to tea with her friends.

• *Motivation and discipline.* It's so very easy *not* to work at home. Can you resist the temptation to do anything *but* what you should be doing?

For More Information

From the Small Business Administration (P.O. Box 15434, Fort Worth, Tex. 76119) are available the following: "Store Location: Little Things Mean a Lot," Management Aids booklet #2.024 (free); "Factors in Considering a Shopping Center Location," Management Aids booklet #2.017; and "Women's Handbook, How the SBA Can Help You Go into Business," Management Aids booklet #5 (free). SBA publication #115A contains a list of free publications. SBA publication #115B contains a list of for-sale publications. The Small Business Administration has management-counseling programs. Check in your phone book under U.S. Government, SBA, for the address and phone number of your regional office.

From your local office of the Internal Revenue Service are available: IRS booklet #587, "Business Use of Your Home" (free) and IRS booklet #334, "Tax Guide for Small Business" (free).

Your local chamber of commerce in a city of more than 125,000 usually has a division devoted primarily to assisting budding owner-managers in finding suitable locations for their businesses. This is a free service that surprisingly few people take advantage of.

Many trade organizations have literature available for newcomers to the field. For a list of national trade organizations and their addresses consult the reference librarian in your local library.

48

Group Investing

Paul and Pamela Average make go-carts. It's their business. They own a small factory employing thirty-six people, and the little cars sell well in area stores. In fact, Paul and Pamela are making more money than they need. It's time to invest some of it.

"Why not get into bigger cars?" says Paul.

And why not indeed! They buy several hundred shares of General Motors stock. It's the American way.

Until the past two decades, however, the small real estate investor with a little extra money was pretty much limited to a "little" property. No matter how much you wanted to get into "something bigger," you could not easily buy the equivalent of a few hundred shares of General Motors in a real estate enterprise such as a shopping center, luxury resort, or 900-unit apartment complex. There was no easy way "in" for the average investor with an average amount of cash. And if by chance such an investor did get together enough money to get in on one of these deals, he or she soon discovered that the investment was essentially illiquid (there was no easy way out).

"But why?" you ask. "Why can't you buy a few hundred shares of stock in the Heaven's Gate Shopping Center?"

Theoretically, you can, but in reality there are relatively few real estate investment corporations.

Again, why? It comes down to United States tax law. Uncle Sam favors real estate ownership and has granted it special tax benefits the likes of which no other investment can boast. Everyone investing in real estate wants the benefits. When a corporation owns the real estate, however, these tax benefits do not pass on to the owners of the corporate stock (with the exception of cooperative apartments

773

held for personal residence and Subchapter S corporations). We've talked about co-ops in Chapters 11 and 16; there will be more about Subchapter S in just a bit.

The formation of real estate investment corporations, therefore, was avoided when possible, and until recently real estate was primarily a local investment. Big real estate investment required big bucks. Then popularity smiled upon the REITs (real estate investment trusts) in the early 1970s and the syndicates in the late 1970s. She's flirting with joint ventures in the 1980s. As a result, "little-guy" investors can now get into big properties and often with little risk or responsibility.

Does that sound too good to be true? Well, it isn't quite as good as it sounds in a sentence. There are drawbacks and expenses, but there are benefits, beautiful benefits. Let's look at the various group investment options and see how they compare.

Corporations

Perhaps the greatest disadvantage of using corporate ownership of real estate investment is double taxation. The corporation pays taxes on its profits and then passes the remaining profit monies on to its shareholders in the form of dividends, which are taxed again.

Losses, however, are not passed on to the shareholders. Now this may sound reassuring on paper, but in real estate investment it is detrimental. The greatest portion of the tax-shelter aspect of real estate derives from the fact that the *loss* generated by depreciation is tax-deductible. Since this loss is often not real (the building is actually appreciating in value and the loss on the tax return represents not a single dollar from your pocket), every real estate investor cherishes the depreciation "losses" that lower his taxable income. If you own real estate through a corporation, however, the corporation can deduct the depreciation losses against its income, but you cannot.

Corporations are also subject to various state and local taxes. These, however, are deductible against the income of the corporation.

If you can live with the double taxation and the elimination of tax-shelter benefits (most people can't), there are some advantages to corporate ownership of real estate:

1. *Anonymity*. The corporation is the "artificial person" up front. No one need know who the stockholders are.

2. *Freedom from liability*. The stockholders are not responsible for the debts or the acts of the corporation. The stockholders also cannot be sued, although the corporation can.

3. *Liquidity*. Shares can be sold much more easily than land and buildings.

4. *Freedom from responsibility*. Stockholders are not responsible for the management of the company simply because they own stock. Even in the smallest company, you need to have a title, like vice-president of something, in order to be responsible for anything.

Subchapter S Corporations

There is one form of corporation that combines the advantages of individual or partnership ownership of real estate with the advantages of corporate ownership. And it's legal. Formed under Subchapter S of the Internal Revenue Code, Subchapter S corporations have some advantages of both corporations and partnerships:

Corporation advantages:
Insulate shareholders from personal liability for corporate debts or acts. Allow ownership to be transferred by the sale of shares, and are thus relatively liquid investments.

Partnership advantages:
Are not taxed as independent tax entities, thus eliminating double taxation. Can pass losses on to shareholders, thus capturing depreciation benefits.

Do the Subchapter S corporation's benefits sound a little too generous even for the bounty of your favorite uncle? There is a restriction. Subchapter S corporations are intended for small businesses, with under 35 shareholders. The tax benefits of the real estate that it owns, however, *are* passed on to you. If you are offered a Subchapter S investment, be sure to consult with a tax expert in the field before investing your money.

Partnerships

A partnership might be:
• two couples buying a tract of land to subdivide and sell as building lots
• a mother, father, and three children ages 15, 13, and 7 who own equal portions of a small apartment house
• seven guys from the office buying a farm to hunt the land (and for potential appreciation)

Family Partnerships

It's perfectly legal in most states for a three-year-old to be a partner in a real estate investment, and the tax benefits are not child-sized. By creating a family partnership, a family can shift income from an investment property to family members in a lower tax bracket. This will of course mean a lower overall tax payment each year. The parent, or the appointed guardian of the child's trust, however, may not use the income for any purpose other than the interest of the child.

On a long-term basis, appreciation of the investment property could create a considerable profit. Wouldn't you like that four-family house you bought and renovated to pay your child's college costs? It's not a far-fetched dream. See your attorney or tax advisor about how to establish and maintain a family partnership in your state.

• your Uncle Joe, who is remodeling an old school into condominium office units and who invited thirteen relatives to join in the venture by contributing some cash

• forty-nine investors who accepted the opportunity (for a contribution of $20,000 each) to buy, remodel, and convert to a cooperative a city skyscraper

• two grandmothers buying an investment condominium for their first grandchild's christening (they plan to sell upon her graduation from high school)

• seven hundred investors in the purchase of Isla del Amor Resort Hotel

A partnership can be as few as two people or as many as it takes. Partners can be equal or unequal, general or limited. A handshake agreement between friends can be a partnership; the largest nationwide syndicates are still partnerships.

Obviously this form of real estate ownership needs a little more explanation. Let's look at the characteristic features of a partnership.

General and Limited Partners

There are two ways to be a part of a partnership: as a general partner or as a limited partner. General partners have personal liability for all the debts of the partnership and usually make the decisions and carry on the business of the partnership. The death, retirement, withdrawal, or insanity of a general partner usually means the dissolution of the partnership.

Limited partners are just that, limited. Their liability is limited to the amount of their investment. They may not participate in the management of the partnership business. Often they cannot transfer their investment in the partnership to another party without the consent of the general partner(s). They cannot continue the partnership if a general partner withdraws.

A partnership can be composed of only general partners; most small investment groups are. No partnership, however, can be composed entirely of limited partners; someone must be the general partner and be personally liable for the debts and affairs of the partnership.

Taxation and the Partnership

If, in the eyes of the IRS, a corporation is an "artificial person" (a responsible, taxpaying artificial person), then a partnership must be a kind of ghost. Generally the IRS works as though the partnership were a transparent entity, one that does not really exist. This "spirit" pays no taxes, thus eliminating the double taxation drawback of the corporation.

Partnership gains or losses are computed, however, even though they are not reported whole. Instead, each partner assumes and reports his or her portion of both ordinary income or loss and capital gains or losses. Depreciation is a legal deduction, as are management fees and interest payments made on the partnership debt.

The big advantage of real estate loss and depreciation deductions is that the government allows investors to make deductions beyond their at-risk investment. Just as an example, let's say that you put $10,000 down on a one million-dollar building. You are allowed to take depreciation on your share of the $1,000,000 value of the building, not just your $10,000 investment in it.

Interdependence of the Partners

In a general partnership, any one of the partners may commit the partnership to an obligation and the other partners must assume liability for the commitment. This rule applies as long as the act of the partner is related to the business of the partnership. For example, if your partner decides to buy a 42-foot yacht as an adjunct to your ocean-front development project, you would probably be responsible for payments on the yacht. If, however, he buys a 42-foot yacht to be berthed in Monterey Bay and your partnership tract of development land is in Iowa, you probably will not be responsible for the yacht.

Some Things To Think About Before You Put Your Money Into a Real Estate Limited Partnership

Who is the general partner? An individual? A group? A corporation? How long have they been in the business of real estate syndicates? What's their record of successes? Failures?

How much of your investment dollar is the general partner getting for his or her fee the day you sign up? This is money you'll never see again, money that is not being invested (although these fees *are* deductible on your federal income tax return). The usual fee is somewhere in the vicinity of 15 percent. If it's over 20 percent, ask, "Why?" and "For what service?"

How long does the syndicate plan to hold a given property? Your tax benefits diminish with each passing year. If the investment needs ten years or more for inflation and appreciation to catch up with a generously high initial purchase price, are you really making a good investment? Remember the general partner is probably being paid as his or her "compensation" a percentage of the purchase price! To check on the property value, try to get some comparison figures on the value of similar properties. Examining the offerings of other limited partnerships might help here.

Are your tax write-offs approaching three or four times your annual dollars invested? If so, prepare yourself for an IRS audit. And remember, the IRS can disallow inflated or unrealistic deductions. Could you afford to pay additional taxes and penalties?

How is the property financed? If interest payments are deferred, you can deduct the amount of interest accrued as an expense while not actually paying a penny. Nice? Not really. The deferred interest begins to collect interest of its own, all of which is usually added to the principal to be repaid at some future date. What if the property has not appreciated enough to repay its debt when the time to sell finally arrives? Would you be willing, or could you afford to actually pay in money in order to sell? Also, new tax laws are clamping down on deferred interest arrangements.

Can you afford the annual cash flow? You may have stars in your eyes about the tax deductions you are being promised, but can you put the required cash in each year?

Is the syndicate buying property for more than the asking price for that property? Don't laugh. It happens a lot. In return for the favor of spreading payment of the purchase price over three, five, or more years or for below-market financing or special terms, the purchase price is inflated. You are actually paying for the use of money in the purchase price, which is not necessarily bad in itself, but it will certainly cut into your profits when the property is sold. Also, new federal tax laws now discourage this type of financing arrangement by requiring sellers of high-priced property who carry financing at below-market rates to pay federal income taxes as though they were being paid interest at or near the market rate.

Possibility of Breakup

In a corporation, the major stockholders can all sell their stock and the corporation goes on. A general partnership is both more finite and more fragile. It can end on a specified date or at the end of a specified project. Unless there is a written agreement to the contrary, it can end upon the decision of any one of the partners. It ends when all the partners agree that it ends. It also ends when a partner breaks the agreement of partnership seriously enough to merit expulsion. It ends upon the death, retirement, or insanity of a partner. If there are other partners who wish to continue the undertaking, a new partnership must be formed.

A limited partnership functions as something of a blend between a general partnership and a corporation. Limited partners may withdraw and new ones may be added while the partnership goes on. If the general partner withdraws, however, the partnership is dissolved.

Limited Transferability of the Investment Interest

It's much harder to transfer your interest in a partnership than in a corporation. In a small general partnership, your working partners may not want to work with the successor you choose and therefore refuse to enter into a partnership with that successor. In which case you have only three options: stay in the partnership, withdraw from it or sell out to your partners, or find another (acceptable) successor.

In a large syndicate, the limited partners are often obliged to get the permission of the general partner before transferring their interest to another person. Some syndicates offer buy-back arrangements for limited partners who wish to withdraw, but you can bet that the money being offered on the buy-back is a long way from top dollar.

Syndicates

Legally a syndicate is any group of people who organize themselves in order to conduct specific business activities. In the real estate world, however, the term has become synonymous with investment groups. These groups are virtually always structured as limited partnerships, but the intricacies of these partnerships can often compare well with the stonework of a medieval cathedral.

Limited Partnership Structure

The general partner or partners of a syndicate find the properties, make the decisions, and manage the investments. The limited partners put up the cash necessary to purchase. Sometimes the general partner is a corporation, which complicates things in terms of taxes and the SEC, but the government has an abundance of printed "guidelines."

Federal and State Regulators

The sale of securities (and limited partnership interests are considered securities) is regulated by both the federal government and each state government. The Securities and Exchange Commission (SEC) is the federal enforcement arm. Each state also has its own securities commission, and the rules differ from state to state.

Generally, the laws regulate the method by which the syndicate can offer and sell the limited partnership interests. Laws also forbid fraudulent, deceptive, or manipulative sales techniques. State and federal laws, however, do not in any way guarantee the quality of an investment offering. You can pay too much for a "bad" investment even when the offering complies with every letter of the law. Evaluation of an investment rests with you.

Public Offerings

In terms of real estate syndicates, a public offering is the offering of limited-partnership-interest investment shares that has been registered with the SEC (if interstate) and/or appropriate state commissions. It may be advertised, in compliance with state and federal rules, of course, and it may be offered for sale to anyone in the general public.

Many public offerings are large multiproperty investments (the real estate equivalent of a mutual fund), and some are in fact sponsored by large Wall Street brokerage firms. Investment units sell at low prices (as real estate goes), sometimes four or five thousand dollars a share.

Private Offerings

Under certain conditions, syndicates are exempt from registration with the SEC and sometimes even with state securities commissions. Among the essentials to qualifying as a private offering are:

- no advertising of the offering to the public
- no public dissemination of information about the offering
- a limit on the number of possible investors (thirty is common)
- sale only to investors who have adequate investment knowledge to understand the offering
- sale only to investors who can afford the financial risk of the limited partnership (there are often minimum annual income requirements)

Most private offerings sell at much higher price-per-unit figures than public offerings: $25,000 a unit is pretty much a lower limit, $150,000 a unit is not uncommon. Most are also one-property offerings, say, a huge resort hotel or a high-rise office building. Whether they are more or less risky than public multiproperty offerings is entirely dependent upon which syndicates you compare.

The Specified Property Syndicate

Many syndicates name the properties or property to be acquired in their printed offerings. The investor therefore knows exactly what he or she will "own a share of" and can work out projections about operating expenses, property taxes, vacancy rates, cash flow, and potential appreciation. Or examine the professional projections of the syndicate and make comparisons with other offerings. The majority of specified property syndicates are also private offerings.

Unspecified Property Syndicates

So-called blind-pool syndicates collect the money first and then buy the properties necessary to achieve the promised return to the investor. Advocates of this type of investing point to the ability of the general partner to act quickly on desirable properties as a major plus. They also claim cash on hand helps in negotiating a better purchase price and therefore favors a better return.

Unspecified property syndicates are almost always multiproperty operations, and advocates contend further that the diversification reduces the risk of loss. Nevertheless, putting your money into a pool for you-know-not-what requires considerable faith in the general partner. Many states have stricter regulations for unspecified property syndicates. The majority of these blind-pool syndicates are public offerings.

The Group of Friends

Group investing doesn't have to be tangled with federal and state regulations or slickly printed "offerings." People have been doing it for years, around the kitchen table. Any group of friends or family can join together to buy property, and they don't need to register with any state or federal agency to do so. It is a good idea, however, to put some things down on paper at the outset of the venture. You might also want to talk with a real estate lawyer, although extensive legal paperwork is not usually necessary.

Consider making some written notes and/or agreements about the following questions:

1. Is the property well located?
2. Why is it a good group investment?
3. Is the cash flow positive or negative?
4. What are the investment goals of the members of the group?
5. How long do you plan to own the property?
6. What portion of the property will each investor own?
7. Who will make the decisions? If the majority rules, does each investor have one vote or is the number of votes allocated according to the amount of investment interest?
8. Does anyone or everyone have veto power? On all subjects, or just certain ones, such as "Shall we sell at this price?"
9. Who will supervise maintenance work?
10. Who will collect rents? Pay property taxes? Make mortgage payments?
11. Who will do the bookkeeping?
12. What will the group do if one member wants to withdraw from the investment before the agreed-upon time of sale?
13. What will be done with the investment interest if one of the

investors dies? Will his or her heir have a say in investment management or merely a right to a fair share of the profits?

Real Estate Investment Trusts (REITs)

Investing in REITs is investing in real estate *one step removed*. You don't buy or sell real property, you buy or sell shares of stock in a company (it may be organized as a corporation or as a trust) that primarily holds real estate or real estate securities. And you trade your shares just as you would trade General Motors, through a stock broker.

Real estate investment trusts were first authorized in 1960 by an amendment to the IRS Code. After a climb to popularity, they went through some rough waters in the recession of 1974/75 when nine folded completely and many more floundered and cut their dividends. REITs are making a comeback in the 1980s, but many investors are still wary.

There are three kinds of REITs:

1. *Equity REITs*, whose funds are invested primarily in income-producing properties.
2. *Mortgage REITs*, whose funds are lent to developers and buyers and produce income by collecting interest.
3. *Hybrid REITs*, which combine both of the above types of investments.

The cost of purchase for all three kinds is relatively low. You can usually buy one hundred shares of stock for around $3000. Not a penny stock, but not expensive either.

Owning REIT stocks will feel a lot like owning any other type of corporate stock. They are a liquid investment, and the value of the shares can go up or down with the market or against its trend. They pay dividends, most making respectable returns of 8 to 12 percent. The REIT investor's liability is limited to his or her invested money. And REITs are regulated by the SEC and state securities commissions.

But REITs also have some distinguishing features. Unlike corporations, they do not carry a double tax. The REIT can pass gains directly to its shareholders without paying a corporate tax upon them. Equity REITs can also use depreciation deductions to shelter some of its shareholders' taxable income, but the REITs cannot pass losses directly through to the investors as a limited partnership can. REITs, therefore, have less appeal as a tax shelter.

This lack of shelter opportunity is probably the chief reason that

---

Some Things To Think About Before Putting Money Into a Real Estate Investment Trust (REIT)

How long has the REIT been in existence? Did it survive the 1974/75 crunch? (If it did, it's a plus.)

How much is being paid in advisory fees? Advisors or managers are paid a percentage of the total assets of the REIT or a percentage of the income and gains realized during the year. (Sometimes they are paid by a combination of the two methods.) There are no federal or state limitations on these percentages, however. The advisor may have actually created the REIT and is now getting rich by advising it.

What exactly does the REIT own? You may want to choose a mortgage REIT if you think interest rates are going up. On the other hand, an equity REIT with large holdings in apartment buildings may be your choice if you think housing demand is about to increase dramatically.

Are the REIT's assets undervalued? (A plus if your answer is yes.) Values often stay on the books at acquisition cost rather than present-day appraisal. If some of the holdings have been there a while, quietly appreciating, the REIT may be worth a good deal more than its "book value" indicates.

What is the past record of cash disbursements to share owners? A good indication of how well the REIT is being managed.

---

most investors generally prefer limited partnerships to REITs. Other disadvantages are:

• a restriction to 95 percent passive investment income such as interest, rents, dividends, and gain from the sale of stock (this is really a limitation on growth potential)

• the requirement that at least 95 percent of its taxable income be distributed as dividends to its shareholders (this provision guarantees the best possible return on the investment dollar but limits growth; the remaining 5 percent of income and all cash flow gained by depreciation deductions *can* be used for growth, however)

• the restriction that REIT trustees cannot actively participate in the business of buying and selling real estate (this restriction necessitates the hiring of advisory or managerial personnel who must do all buying and selling).

Among the advantages of REITs are:
- liquidity
- income—return on the investment
- limited liability
- diversification of investments—which insulates against loss
- no time demand or decision making on the part of the investor

Rental Pool Condominiums

How would you like to own a vacation home with a pool, tennis courts, ski facilities, a gourmet restaurant within walking distance of your door, a health club complete with masseur, perhaps some boating or horseback riding, even a golf course? And how would you like to own that "little place" with absolutely no maintenance responsibilities, in fact, with a full-time caretaking staff? And how would you like to deduct on your federal income tax return not only property taxes and interest paid on the mortgage to your place, but all the benefits (maintenance costs and depreciation allowances) of a piece of investment real estate? And how would you like a little income from the place, too?

"And how!" you say. "Where is this piece of Paradise?"

Actually there are many of them. They are located in major resort areas across the country, and their number is growing with the growth of discretionary income and leisure time. This dream "little vacation home" is called a rental pool condominium. It's a rather creative blending of individual ownership and group investing. And the IRS regards it as an investment property, not a vacation home.

You buy your resort condominium apartment and own it just as you would any other condo. Its offering, however, must be registered with the SEC and the state securities commission since it is a property sold with the opportunity and promise of economic benefits. That opportunity is the rental pool, which may be mandatory or optional.

In a rental pool arrangement, the unit owners in the condominium make their units available for rental just as though the condominium were a hotel. All the members of the pool share in the cost of the rental operation, which is often managed under contract with a major hotel chain such as Hilton or Marriott. Net profits from the rental pool are divided at the end of the year and each member receives his or her pro rata share. In most pools, it does not matter what the vacancy rate of your particular apartment was during a given year, you share in the profits according to your share of ownership in the condominium.

"Sounds great," you say. "But how do *I* get a vacation out of this?"

Most rental pools allow the owner of the unit the use of his or her apartment for up to twenty-eight days (four weeks) a year, during which time the unit is out of the rental pool. Other plans allow the owner unlimited use of the apartment at 75 percent or so of the ordinary rental rate, with the apartment remaining in the pool for the full year.

And in some glorious plans there are even exchange programs. The rental pool of the Camelback Inn in Scottsdale, Arizona, is managed by Marriott. An owner of a condominium unit at Camelback may vacation there for twenty-eight days at a fee of under $20 a day as of this writing; or, for the same fee, the owner can vacation at any other Marriott property, anywhere!

"Wow! And this is all still eligible for investment tax treatment?"

Yes. The owner can use his or her vacation unit for fourteen days a year, or 10 percent of the total rental time (whichever is greater) and still retain all the tax benefits of an investment property.

"The catch?" you say. "There must be a catch somewhere."

Well, yes, a minor consideration. Most such resort units are relatively expensive (many in the hundreds of thousands of dollars range). If you pay cash for the condominium unit, you will probably receive a rather good return on your money. However, if you finance your purchase with a mortgage, interest on your debt may wipe out any positive cash flow from the investment. Then you must consider tax shelter, possible appreciation of the property, and the joy of vacationing as factors against the annual cost of ownership.

Joint Ventures

A joint venture is a partnership. Usually there are at least two general partners in a joint venture, a lending partner who supplies the money and a borrowing partner who supplies the planning, vision, management, equipment, manpower, and work. For the borrowing partner, a joint venture is a means to get into a real estate project with *no money down*. For the lending partner, it is an investment with the possibility of excellent return and the requirement of only minimal time or work.

There are almost limitless possibilities as to the projects around which a joint venture can be structured, and that structuring can be done in an almost limitless number of ways. For the sake of both clarity and brevity, we'll talk only of the most common arrangement here.

Who Is the Lending Partner?

Anyone can actually be the lending partner in a joint venture, anyone with money, that is. Most common sources are: commercial banks, savings and loan associations, savings banks, insurance companies, real estate syndicates, pension funds, investor groups, and wealthy relatives.

Who Is the Borrowing Partner?

Usually the borrowing partner is a person with some experience in real estate development. A lender is unlikely to invest with someone with a dream and no track record. Besides a good track record, a nice liquid net worth and a community reputation for integrity won't hurt. But there are no rules. If you can envision a great project and need only money, go for it. You may or may not find a lending partner, but even if you don't, think of all the experience you've gained and the people you've met. The next time will surely be easier.

The Partnership

Any arrangement that is agreeable to both parties is possible. Usually, in a joint venture, the lender supplies all the money needed for the project; that's 100 percent financing. In return, the lender gets half (or more) interest in the project. That half ownership means half of everything: half the cash flow, half the tax benefits, half the profit when the property is sold.

The joint venture is a way to go if you have some expertise and big dreams, but limited available funds. Or if you have plenty of money, but little expertise, time, or desire to get your hands into the actual building project. It's high-involvement investment, however, whether you are the borrower *or* the lender.

If you ride out storms and setbacks pretty well and have no history of high blood pressure, this form of group investment may be just right for you. If you'd like to count sheep in the night rather than dollar signs, however, you might want to explore another investment vehicle.

For More Information

For information on group ownership of real estate investments, as well as the names of people working in the field in your area, write to Real Estate Securities and Syndication Institute, 430 N. Michigan Ave., Chicago, Ill. 60611.

For names of Realtors who, for a fee, will discuss and evaluate your investment interests with you, write to American Society of Real Estate Counselors, 430 N. Michigan Ave., Chicago, Ill. 60611.

For tables that will enable you to determine your rate of return on an investment, write to Financial Publishing Company, 82 Brookline Ave., Boston, Mass. 02215.

A publisher that has a huge list of real estate investment books is John Wiley & Sons, Inc.; write to the company at Somerset, N.J. 08873. Most of the books are sold by mail; also, you may ask for a free current catalog. Among Wiley titles currently in print is: *Real Estate Limited Partnerships*, by Theodore S. Lynn and Harry F. Goldberg. Price: $55.

A specialized real estate investment publisher which offers a wide selection of books, magazines, newsletters, and working guides is Warren, Gorham, & Lamont, 210 South St., Boston, Mass. 02111. Write for a list of publications.

A firm that publishes a newsletter with a rating system for REITs is Audit Investment Research, 230 Park Ave., New York, N.Y. 10017.

49

Real Estate as Your Livelihood

Reginald d'Argent graduated from Vassar with high honors in psychobiology. At 22 he had a job in a major city, in fact, you could call it a promising career, but no place to live. There was not an apartment to be found (that he could afford) even by doubling up. Bunking at the "Y," he spent evenings and weekends apartment hunting until one day he noticed a "For Sale" sign on a four-family house that was not exactly dilapidated, but certainly rundown.

One of the units was vacant, the price was low. Reggie appealed to his family for help.

"What are you doing thinking about buying a rundown place like that!" they said. "Concentrate on your career! Find a nice girl. Get married."

Reggie was having a hard time concentrating on his career or anything else while sleeping in a too-narrow top bunk. Now he spent his free time going from lender to lender, visiting "his" house, and talking (with the real estate agent, with the three tenants, with the owner, and with the credit union of his company). A lender, the broker, and the seller put together a no-money-down, fix-up-the-place package, and Reggie moved in.

Now he spent his free time reading about home repair and remodeling and of course "fixing up." He was surprised to discover that he liked this. He even had a talent for it.

Two years later, Reggie sold his four-family house for double what he paid for it and bought two others, not quite so badly in need of tender loving care. And three years after that he sold those two and bought a ten-unit apartment building and a lovely three-story brownstone. His mother now talked with her friends more about his real estate dealings than his career in psychobiology.

Reggie had just settled into his brownstone, mortgaged up to his eyelids, as it were, when he came upon the bargain of the century. A partly occupied sixty-unit apartment building in need of repair, but located on the very edge of an area undergoing renaissance and revitalization. All he could see were dollar signs and he had not a penny to spare!

Reggie went to his family again. He needed $40,000 in downpayment money, so he talked with them about a partnership in that magical building. There would be ten owners, he proposed, each ownership share costing $5000. He sold one such share to each of nine relatives, thus raising the downpayment he needed plus the money for closing costs and incidentals. He kept one ownership unit for himself, earning it, he reasoned, by his efforts in locating the property and putting together the partnership. After borrowing a little more money from the credit union at work for fix-up costs, and doing some of the work himself, the building was soon 100 percent occupied and the rents were paying all operating expenses including debt service and a management salary to Reggie.

Everything was going great when a broker friend called to tell Reggie about a rather large building on the other side of town, for sale and ripe for conversion to condominiums. The broker had three people interested in putting in ten or fifteen thousand, but no one to "run the show."

Reggie bought a six-month option on the property and began studying securities law, limited partnerships, and financing. He hired a lawyer. He talked with his family and friends. Two uncles, a maiden aunt, a second cousin, and the cousin's brother-in-law volunteered $10,000 each to "get in on the deal." The three from the broker and just two more investors and Reggie would have the $100,000 down he needed. Reggie's boss volunteered, as did one of the girls he was dating.

Reginald d'Argent quit his job and became, you guessed it, a real estate syndicator.

This story is pure fiction, of course, yet it is the true story of so many real estate professionals. "Big bucks" real estate seems to be a career that people stumble into. They come from every conceivable ethnic and educational background: a lawyer might become a condominium converter, a high school dropout might become a residential land developer, an "unskilled" immigrant might get into apartment-building management, a sociologist into shopping center development and leasing, an English teacher into residential sales.

Real estate is a multifaceted, many-leveled field with lots of money to be made for the not-too-faint-of-heart. Its market encompasses every person, for every person uses its product. Its projected time of ongoing use in our society is unlimited. And potential earnings? Well, let's just say the range is very wide. No wonder the field stimulates the dreams of virtually everyone at some time or another.

As we close this book, let's take a brief look at some of the many possibilities for making a living in real estate.

Residential Land Development

You will need imagination, perseverance, and tact in this career. Sometimes, but not always, money.

Well, you need some money for incidentals like surveys and plat plans, but surprisingly you can often buy land with little or no money down if you can get the seller to carry a purchase money mortgage. Occasionally you can also get joint-venture financing: you do the work, someone else puts up the needed money, for which he or she gets a share in the profits.

Imagination or vision is the really important personal characteristic for success in this type of endeavor. Can you walk over acres of woods, fields, and maybe even a "bit" of a swamp and imagine a community of homes with the swamp as, well, a lake? Can you evaluate the potential growth of the community in which the land is located, its future appeal as a place to live? What price range of homes would sell best here? And from that, how big should the lots be?

What if a piece of land that interested you and was well within your affordability range turned out to be landlocked? The only access to it was a walkover right of way. Would you buy an option on the land, and then try to purchase a piece of property between it and a main road? And if you were able to get your land and a 200-foot-wide lot between it and the road, would you be able to get your subdivision approved? Did you have the foresight to check zoning regulations? What are the chances of a variance? Re-zoning?

Here's where the perseverance and tact part come in. Planning board approval can take months. You will have to answer such questions as: How will the roads be laid out? What about utilities and street sewers? How about waste disposal for the individual homes? Septic tanks: Is the drainage adequate? Municipal sewer hook-up: Can the town's sewage treatment system handle the additional load? A package sewer treatment plant: Will the planning board approve it?

Once you have your subdivision approved, you will face another decision. Should you sell the lots to individuals and allow them to secure their own builders? Do you want a say in how large the houses will be? Architectural style? Have you considered deed restrictions? Most land developers have found the process of selling building lots without a builder exceedingly slow. Most members of the general public are intimidated by the thought of "building their own place," or even securing their own builder.

OK, maybe you should sell to a builder. A good option. Many builders are on the lookout for tracts of land that already have subdivision approval. You may well take your profit on this sale and run (to the bank).

But if you are a little more adventurous, patient, and/or greedy, you might want to team up with a builder. You keep the money from the sale of the building lots, of course, but you and the builder arrange a mutually agreeable split on the profits from the house construction.

If you choose to become a residential land developer, or think you might want to try it, we suggest you start out small: a few acres with good road frontage will do fine. Work through the process of subdividing this small piece, even if you subdivide the one lot into two. You will get the feel of the business as you work on the project evenings and weekends. You will get to know zoning and planning board members and procedures. And your initial financial risk will be relatively small. If you are successful and if land development becomes your full-time job, your working hours and your income will be irregular. But you will have no "boss" but yourself and you can take the winter off to ski in Switzerland if you like.

Remember, however, that once you start actively buying and subdividing land and selling individual lots or "improved" parcels, your income from this endeavor may be taxed by the federal government as ordinary income, not as capital gain. Think of it as a part of the price you'll pay for that Swiss vacation.

Condominium or Cooperative Conversion

The mix of many factors contributed to the conversion craze of the late 1970s. Among them are:

• *Demand*. The high demand for starter homes by baby boomers coupled with high prices made apartment ownership look more and more attractive.

• *Image*. The concept of shared-space ownership became generally accepted nationally. Owning a condo was "in."

• *Inflation*. Higher fuel, energy, maintenance, and property tax costs were not always reflected proportionately in higher rents. The rate of return on the investment property therefore diminished.

• *Rent-control laws*.

• *Federal property tax-depreciation guidelines*. Because the early years of building ownership provided the best shelter, many owners wanted to turn over their investments. There was a far greater demand for individual units than for whole apartment buildings, however.

• *Profit*. There was more money to be made selling individual units than selling buildings.

The conversion craze subsided with the economic problems of the early 1980s, but it is showing signs of revitalization now. The fact of the matter is that the desire and demand for homeownership in this country is very high and that there are simply not enough new units being built in most areas of the country. In other words, the outlook for the sale of converted apartments in economically sound areas looks very good. And if the federal government rolls back depreciation schedules to the old 30- or 40-year guidelines, as is being suggested, you will probably see even more conversion, since rental-building ownership will become less profitable and less appealing as its tax shelter value diminishes.

Hmmmmmmm. . . . Maybe you could make your fortune by buying apartment buildings (cheap) and turning them into condominiums or co-operatives? Let's see . . . $300,000 for that ten-unit building. Comparable apartments are selling for $55,000 each. Ten times $55,000 is $550,000. Wow! A quarter of a million dollars profit!

Not quite. And besides it's not easy to do a conversion and sell the units. In fact, the figures in this example may not be profitable at all!

First, federal income taxes. If you convert a building and sell the units, you lose your favorable capital gains tax treatment. The number of units you are selling plus the fact that you must promote the sale of the units is enough to convince the government that you are a "dealer" in real estate. Your income from the sale of the apartments therefore is "ordinary income." Furthermore, if you promote the sale of the units as an "investment," you may also be subject to federal Securities and Exchange Commission regulation, or at least the regulation of your state securities commission.

Some apartment building owners who wish to convert are able to retain their capital gains tax treatment by "selling" the building to a corporation (even though they may own the corporation). The problem here is that the profits from the sale of the units are subject to the corporate double tax. So expense item number one: you will need the services of a good tax accounting firm.

Next problem: state conversion legislation. In most states you can't just convert a building, you must proceed through state-designated channels. In fact, in some states with strict legislation and high conversion rates like New York, it may take you eighteen months or more just to get state approval of your conversion plan. Will income from rents be adequate during this waiting time? Plus: you now need a specialized lawyer. Have you calculated that fee in your estimated profits?

OK, let's assume that you have conversion approval and you are now ready to sell the units. How much are they worth? Are you qualified to estimate their value? Will anyone believe you if you do? Do you need the services of a real estate appraiser? How about the shared-space element? Every prospective buyer is going to want to know what kind of shape the building is in. How much will an inspection and report by a professional engineering firm cost you?

You have a fair market price for the units, the building has been inspected, and you have ninety copies of the printed report; you're ready to go! To start, you offer the apartments to the tenants at what you think is a bargain price . . . 20 percent off fair market value. Only two of the ten buy. Now you must market the other eight units. Do you really have the time to act as your own sales agent? Can you act effectively? Few, very few, owners can answer "yes" to those two questions. Therefore, another expense: real estate commissions. And maybe some small change for marketing and promotion, too.

Finally, have you thought about tenant protection legislation? Many states protect the elderly and disabled from eviction. A variety of state laws also provide for tenants' notification and protection periods from three months to five years! And some areas have governmental rent controls that provide virtually lifetime protection for tenants in noneviction plan conversions.

Can you afford to continue as the "owner" of those protected apartments, collecting rents, maintaining the interiors, and paying condominium or cooperative maintenance fees? Or would you choose to sell the protected units as "occupied apartments"? Which means of course that they will sell for much less money since the new owners cannot move in. Or are you ready to spend thousands of dollars to "buy out" protected tenants?

If your state has no protection legislation for tenants, will you be able to evict 79-year-old Mr. Boneface and his two cats? Or how about 27-year-old Ms. Lieberdich who always pays the rent on time but is raising four children and working two jobs?

Can you turn off your emotional responses to the cries of your tenants? Your emotional responses to their unreasonable demands? Do you have the patience and perseverance to go through, step by step including forward-two-back-one, your state's conversion procedures? And most important, do you have the savvy necessary to choose a building that will prove to be a financially successful conversion? This is not a career to be embarked upon with a spirit of abandon.

Creating and Selling Time-Share Vacation Apartments

"Time-share" is the vacation watchword of the 1980s. New resorts are being built and many older ones are being converted to this ownership form. The problems are in many ways similar to condominium and cooperative apartment conversion, with a few added risks. Among them:

• Your promotion and marketing costs will be one of your major expenses.

• State time-share legislation is growing almost as fast as the time-share industry. Can you keep abreast of and comply with laws in your state?

• Many vacation places are seasonal. Time-share units in prime time may sell quickly, those in other times of the year may not sell at all. What will you do with the unsold units?

• Do you plan to run the company that does the maintenance work? It's best that you know something about hotel management if you do.

• How can you protect yourself against a glutted market (too many conversions in one area) during the time you are selling your properties?

Newsprint is full of stories of shady time-share deals, many of which have prompted government investigation. Can you avoid being associated with these nefarious characters? Can you, in fact, offer a good time-share vacation investment to your buyers that is *at the same time* profitable to you? There are some who say that people with too much conscience should stay out of this field.

Property Management

"Property manager"—what does that mean, anyway? A lot of things. The term is applied to the person who heads the company that manages 240 high-rise buildings. It's applied to the person who supervises the workings of a shopping center. It's applied to the couple who, for a rent-free apartment and a small salary, vacuums the hallways, sweeps the walks, and fixes leaky pipes.

Property managers can lease space, collect rents, handle the assignment of repairs (or do them), buy supplies, hire maintenance personnel, keep the books, pay property taxes, and often even settle tenant–tenant or tenant–owner disputes. An even temper, tact, perseverance, attention to detail, resourcefulness, and fairness are the cardinal virtues of the career. All of which are called upon in the course of managing virtually every kind of property, including apartment houses, rented single-family or multifamily houses, condominiums and cooperatives, office buildings, government-sponsored housing, time-share resorts, senior citizens' housing, shopping centers, and industrial parks. Managers are paid either a flat fee or a percentage of the rent roll.

You don't need any special education or credentials to get started in the field. In fact, taking the job of a property manager might just be a means of getting a rent-free apartment at first. It can grow into much more. Sometimes a property management career starts in managing the four-family house you bought as an investment. You discover that you're not only good at the job but that you also like it. Why not manage the houses of a few friends while you're at it, for a reasonable fee. Next thing you know, you own your own business, a business that you started with virtually *no* at-risk capital!

There are two private sector professional credentials in this field. CPM (Certified Property Manager) is the designation of the Institute of Real Estate Management, a trade organization affiliated with the National Association of Realtors. To earn a CPM designation you must attain certain levels of experience and education. For information on current requirements write: Institute of Real Estate Management, 430 North Michigan Ave., Chicago, Ill. 60611.

The National Apartment Association (NAA) is a trade organization of owners, builders, developers, managers, and management companies of multifamily housing units. It bestows the designation CAM (Certified Apartment Manager) upon members who complete its educational program. For information on the requirements and the career write: National Apartment Association, 1825 K St. N.W., Suite 604, Washington, D.C. 20006.

The federal government, through the nonprofit National Center for Housing Management, also has two professional designations: CHM (Certified Housing Manager) and PASH (Professional Administrator Senior Housing). For free information on certification requirements and training programs write: National Center for Housing Management, 1133 Fifteenth St. N.W., Washington, D.C. 20005.

Syndication

Besides real estate, race horses, antique collections, paintings, movies, Broadway shows, even yachts and airplanes are being syndicated. The term simply means that some kind of group ownership has been created. There is no mystery, no magic fortune. A real estate syndicator, sometimes called a sponsor, is one who gathers together a group of investors each of whom contributes a portion of the money necessary to buy a real estate investment. The syndicate may be organized as a simple joint ownership, a limited partnership, a corporation, or even a partnership one or more of whose members are corporations.

At this time, the limited-partnership organization is by far the most popular and, in fact, is enjoying almost explosive growth. To real estate people it seems as though everyone's brother or cousin-in-law is starting a syndicate. But it's really not so easy.

You can go along "syndicating" among family and friends as Reggie d'Argent did without much trouble, but as soon as you begin to gather strangers into your investment enterprises you walk a fine line with the government. When does your friendly group venture become an offer of securities?

To become a professional syndicator you are required to register with the federal Securities and Exchange Commission (SEC) and with the securities commission of your state. Your investment offerings must also be registered with the SEC and/or state commissions. And you must abide by their regulations. If your business grows, every salesperson who works for you will also have to register.

Syndicating is a big-bucks business. A successful syndicator may well drive a Mercedes, own a house with an indoor swimming pool, and walk a borzoi or two. But the requirements for success are stiff. The work is nerve-racking, time-consuming, and volatile. Hundreds of thousands of dollars can hinge on a few words. You must not only find good investments but also convince people to entrust their money to you in order to buy the properties you find. You need a track record of success and an unblemished reputation in the community. You also need a veritable mountain of self-assurance, especially when and if "times are tough" and your investors start asking you about disappointing returns on their money. A cool, rational head is essential for the many times you'll be negotiating, and poise, enthusiasm, and knowledge for the many times you'll find yourself speaking before a group and fielding questions. Freedom from time constraints and schedules will also help. Your day may not start until ten or eleven, but it may well go until midnight two or three days a week. And money. You will need money for an office (elegance counts), a staff, entertainment, lawyers, accountants, and promotional materials. Most important, you will need an unfailing drive to get up each morning and go, go, go. You must self-motivate and you must motivate others.

"I can do all that!" you say. "But tell me about the nuts and bolts. How do I actually start a syndicate. What are the problems? The shortcuts?"

It would take another book! If you are really serious, however, you could join a large securities firm that handles public or private syndicates. Working there for a year or two will not only teach you a great deal but forge invaluable contacts at the same time. Or you could arrange to attend one of the many syndication conferences that are given in hotels and conference centers in major cities across the country by a number of educational institutions. The cost of these seminars if relatively high, $400 to $600 for two or three days, *not* including accommodations or food. But if you go, you will hear experts speak and often you will have the opportunity to join small "workshops" where your individual questions will be answered. Some of the most active and prestigious institutions running such conferences are listed below. A letter to any of them will enter your name on their mailing list and thus secure notification of upcoming conferences.

Laventhol & Horwath, 919 Third Ave., New York, N.Y. 10022 (a nationwide accounting firm with offices in thirty-seven cities, so you might also check your phone book).

Northwest Center for Professional Education, 13555 Bel-Red Rd., Bellevue, Wash. 98009.

The Real Estate Institute, New York University, 11 W. 42nd St., New York, N.Y. 10036.

Practicing Law Institute, 810 Seventh Ave., New York, N.Y. 10019.

Wharton School of Business, University of Pennsylvania, Dietrich Hall, Philadelphia, Pa. 19104.

Real Estate Securities and Syndication Institute (RESSI), 430 North Michigan Ave., Chicago, Ill. 60611 (a group associated with the National Association of Realtors).

You might also contact colleges and universities in your state. Many now offer courses in real estate syndication and other enterprises in which you can enroll without matriculating as a full-time student.

Commercial and Industrial Development and Leasing

This is *the* field for a juggler. Instead of bowling pins, however, *this* juggler must keep in the air: location hunting, negotiating, financing, zoning-board problems, construction problems, and prospective tenants as large as K Mart and as small as Bea's Better Bras. It is not a field for the inexperienced in real estate matters or for the timid.

Success in commercial and industrial real estate development requires a good deal of aggressiveness and a minimum of emotion. Personality tendencies toward self-criticism, indecisiveness, and impulsiveness are serious drawbacks. It portends well, however, if your fourth-grade teacher said you had "stick-to-it-iveness" or your high school football coach called you a stubborn mule, or worse.

When commercial or industrial development and leasing is mentioned, most people think of giant shopping centers featuring a Neiman-Marcus or a Macy's or industrial parks like the Research Triangle in the Raleigh-Durham area. But these are multimillion dollar projects and no place for an aspiring beginner to start. "Commercial development" might be a vacant corner lot in your town upon which you build a convenience store that you subsequently lease to 7 Eleven. "Industrial development" might be a huge, old, abandoned factory building that you buy for almost nothing, renovate, and then subdivide into seven small "job shops." Remember a "shopping center" can be seventy stores or seven, an "office building" can be a black-glass monolith or a renovated Victorian mansion.

Office condominium conversion is a kind of "subspecialty" in the field of commercial development. The acceptance and development of office condominiums, however, is not spreading as rapidly as expected, and if they are not accepted in your area, it is probably not a good idea to try to break new ground when you yourself are still getting established. Check out the market situation carefully before you charge this particular windmill.

If you are interested in a little serious study before committing your time, money, and reputation to a commercial development project, the educational institutions listed under *Syndication* (page 799) (with the exception of RESSI) also sponsor conferences and seminars on commercial leasing and development. In addition, you may wish to check with trade and professional organizations for published material. Write to: International Council of Shopping Centers, 445 Park Ave., New York, N.Y. 10022; or Society of Industrial Realtors, 925 15th St. N.W., Washington, D.C. 20005.

Advising a REIT

Since the trustees of a real estate investment trust are not allowed to participate actively in the management or trading of real estate, they generally employ an "advisor" to handle the day-to-day business of the trust. Or that's the way it appears on paper.

In reality, experienced and ambitious real estate people or companies often *form* the REIT and then have themselves appointed as its advisor. The money is good for those who are good at the job. This is another field, however, that is not for the beginner.

Sales

In every state in the United States you must be licensed in order to sell real estate. Each state, however, has two kinds of real estate license: the broker's license and the salesperson's license. Only the broker can really act as an agent in buying or selling property. The salesperson must work under the sponsorship and supervision of a broker with whom he or she must usually split earnings. And it's harder to get a broker's license than a salesperson's license.

Every state requires that an applicant take a licensing exam, but the exams and the education requirements that precede them are different from state to state. Some states have virtually no education requirements (not even a high school diploma), others require a certain number of classroom hours studying the state's real estate laws, and still others require college credits. (Texas, in fact, requires thirty-six semester hours, the equivalent of a major in real estate!) Besides education requirements, most states also require that experience as a licensed salesperson precede the broker's license. These "apprenticeship" requirements range from one year to five.

I have: an aggressive go-get-it attitude
assertiveness
a demeanor that inspires confidence
competitiveness
self-motivation
self-reliance
self-confidence
an active rather than passive response to situations
risk-taking ability and inclination
creativity
decisiveness
energy
tact
perseverance
gregariousness
a good reputation in the community

Many people, especially women in mid-life, enter real estate sales because they have an interest in their communities or in residential housing. Statistics show, however, that most of them drop out within the first year. Why? Usually because the work is not what they expected. The job of a real estate agent is a sales job. Even though the product is not something you can carry from door to door, and even though the job carries a professional image, success in the field requires selling and all the personality traits of a *sales*person.

Check those qualities in the above boxed list that you think you have. (If you plan a career in real estate sales, you should be checking most of them.)

The job of a real estate sales agent is an unstructured one and its time demands are unpredictable, often including a good deal of weekend and evening work. Income is almost always predicated upon successful selling, and commissions run to peaks and valleys during the course of even the best year. Hard economic times can be financially devastating, good times can be exhausting although lucrative. Few sales agents ever make the 50 percent tax bracket, however.

You can get more information about the career and its requirements in your state by writing to your state real estate commission (addresses are listed in Appendix B.). Or you can stop by the office of your local Board of Realtors.

Appraisal

To be an appraiser you need experience. All the "book learning" in the library can not replace the skill and knowledge gained by going out into your local marketplace, inspecting properties, and checking sales prices against asking prices. It's no wonder, therefore, that many appraisers come from the ranks of real estate sales agents.

Even after years of experience, however, appraisal remains an art. There is no formula, no procedure that can be used to render an exact and always correct valuation because the fair market value is a sale price, that is, the highest price a ready, willing, and able buyer will pay and the lowest price a ready, willing, and able seller will accept. The appraiser renders an educated, experienced opinion as to that fair market value when there is in fact no buyer on the horizon. From this it is easy to determine the most essential personality trait of the appraiser: faith in your own ability.

Sometimes, notably in the job of bank appraiser, the appraiser is called upon more to verify that the purchase price of a property is at or near fair market value than to estimate that value. This work requires not only faith in your ability but also the courage to stand up and speak your opinion if that opinion differs from what is expected (the price named in the purchase contract).

The job of the appraiser is less competitive and pressured and more structured and stable than that of a sales agent. Sometimes it is salaried, sometimes it is based upon a fee, but it is never based upon a commission. Appraisers very rarely work weekends or evenings, but like real estate agents they have "busy" seasons and "slow" seasons. Many real estate brokers are also appraisers, collecting their appraisal fees as a source of extra income; but it is not necessary to be a broker to be an appraiser.

For more information on the career, its qualifications, and training programs you should write to one or more of its professional organizations: Society of Real Estate Appraisers, 7 S. Dearborn, Chicago, Ill. 60603; American Institute of Real Estate Appraisers, 430 N. Michigan Ave., Chicago, Ill. 60611; and National Association of Real Estate Appraisers, 853 Broadway, New York, N.Y. 10003.

Entrepreneur

Are you the kind of dreamer who builds empires? Would you like to do it all? Have it all? Do you want to own companies that own companies? Acreage? Shopping centers? Office buildings? Half-a-dozen vacation homes? Too many apartment houses to count? A horse farm or two? And maybe at the same time you'd like to be the general partner in a syndicate or two?

It's possible. Be aware, however, that your business will consume most of your waking hours (and maybe some of your sleeping hours, too).

You don't mind, you say. You just want to get started on getting rich.

OK, go out and find yourself a multifamily house in a neighborhood you know very well. It's as good a place to start as any.

For More Information

There are many books available on careers in real estate. Check *Books in Print* at your library and the card catalogue at your state university or a nearby college. We have also already listed many at the conclusions of other chapters in this section. The following is a selection of additional titles:

The Arnold Encyclopedia of Real Estate, by Alvin L. Arnold and Jack Kusnet (Warren, Gorham & Lamont), is a comprehensive reference book that everyone interested in real estate as a career should own. Updated supplements are published annually.

Questions and Answers on Real Estate, by Robert W. Semenow (Prentice-Hall), has helped a generation of real estate people prepare for licensing examinations. Be sure to get the latest edition.

Guide to Examinations and Careers in Real Estate, published by Reston Publishing Co., Reston, VA 22090, is a compilation of useful material from the National Association of Real Estate License Law Officials (NARELLO).

Construction Lending, by Joseph Tockarshewsky, (American Bankers Association, 1120 Connecticut Ave. N.W., Washington, D.C., 20036), is an invaluable aid to everyone embarking upon a career in land development or building rehabilitation.

Condominium Development Guide: Procedures, Analysis, Forms, by Keith B. Romney (Warren, Gorham & Lamont), is a comprehensive guide well described by its title. Annual updated cumulative supplements are issued.

How to Profit From Condominium Conversions, by Paul Bullock (Enterprise) is a basic guide.

Not necessarily for women only are:

A Woman's Guide to New Careers in Real Estate, by Ruth Rejnis (Contemporary Books).

The Woman's Guide to Selling Residential Real Estate Successfully, by Carolyn Janik (Dodd, Mead).

APPENDIX A

Directory of HUD Area Offices

Region I

Boston Regional Office
Room 800, John F. Kennedy
Federal Building
Boston, Massachusetts 02203-0801
(617) 223-4066
and
Bulfinch Building, 15 New
Chardon Street
Boston, Massachusetts 02114
(617) 223-4111

FIELD OFFICES

Bangor Office
U.S. Federal and Post Office
Building
202 Harlow Street
Bangor, Maine 04401
(207) 947-8410

Burlington Office
110 Main Street
Fairchild Square
Burlington, Vermont 05402
(802) 951-6274

Hartford Office
One Hartford Square West
Hartford, Connecticut 06104
(203) 722-3638

Manchester Office
Norris Cotton Federal Building
275 Chestnut Street
Manchester, New Hampshire
03101
(603) 666-7681

Providence Office
330 John O. Pastore Federal
Building
and U.S. Post Office—Kennedy
Plaza
Providence, Rhode Island 02903
(401) 528-5351

Region II

New York Regional Office
26 Federal Plaza
New York, New York 10278
(212) 264-8068

Albany Office
Leo W. O'Brien Federal Building
North Pearl Street and Clinton
Avenue
Albany, New York 12207
(518) 472-3567

Buffalo Office
Mezzanine, Statler Building
107 Delaware Avenue
Buffalo, New York 14202
(716) 846-5733

Camden Office
The Parkade Building, 519 Federal
Street
Camden, New Jersey 08103
(609) 757-5081

Caribbean Office
Federico Degetau Federal Building
U.S. Courthouse, Room 428
Carlos E. Chardon Avenue
Hato Rey, Puerto Rico 00918
(809) 753-4201

Newark Office
Military Park Building
60 Park Place
Newark, New Jersey 07102
(201) 645-3010

Region III

Philadelphia Regional Office
Curtis Building, 6th and Walnut
Streets
Philadelphia, Pennsylvania 19106
(215) 597-2560

Baltimore Office
The Equitable Building
3rd Floor, 10 North Calvert Street
Baltimore, Maryland 21202
(301) 962-2121

Charleston Office
Kanawha Valley Building
Capitol and Lee Streets
Charleston, West Virginia 25301
(304) 347-7036

Pittsburgh Office
Fort Pitt Commons
445 Fort Pitt Boulevard
Pittsburgh, Pennsylvania 15219
(412) 644-2802

Richmond Office
701 East Franklin Street
Richmond, Virginia 23219
(804) 771-2721

Washington, D.C. Office
Universal North Building
1875 Connecticut Avenue, NW
Washington, D.C. 20009
(202) 673-5837

Wilmington Office
IBM Building
800 Delaware Avenue, Suite 101
Wilmington, Delaware 19801
(302) 573-6300

Region IV

Atlanta Regional Office
Richard B. Russell Federal
Building
75 Spring Street, SW
Atlanta, Georgia 30303
(404) 221-5136

FIELD OFFICES

Birmingham Office
Daniel Building
15 South 20th Street
Birmingham, Alabama 35233
(205) 254-1630

Columbia Office
Strom Thurmond Federal Building
1835-45 Assembly Street
Columbia, South Carolina 29201
(803) 765-5592

Coral Gables Office
Gables 1 Tower
1320 South Dixie Highway
Coral Gables, Florida 33146
(305) 662-4510

Greensboro Office
415 North Edgeworth Street
Greensboro, North Carolina 27401
(919) 378-5363

Jackson Office
Federal Building, Suite 1016
100 West Capital Street
Jackson, Mississippi 39269
(601) 960-4702

Jacksonville Office
325 West Adams Street
Jacksonville, Florida 32202
(904) 791-2626

Knoxville Office
One Northshore Building
1111 Northshore Drive
Knoxville, Tennessee 37919
(615) 558-1384

Louisville Office
539 Fourth Avenue
Post Office Box 1044
Louisville, Kentucky 40201
(502) 582-5251

Memphis Office
100 North Main Street, 28th Floor
Memphis, Tennessee 38103
(901) 521-3367

Nashville Office
1 Commerce Place, Suite 1600
Nashville, Tennessee 37239
(615) 251-5213

Orlando Office
Federal Office Building
80 North Hughey
Orlando, Florida 32801
(305) 420-6441

Tampa Office
700 Twiggs Street
Post Office Box 2097
Tampa, Florida 33601
(813) 228-2501

Region V

Chicago Regional Office
300 South Wacker Drive
Chicago, Illinois 60606
(312) 353-5680
and
547 West Jackson Blvd.
Chicago, Illinois 60606
(312) 353-7660

FIELD OFFICES

Cincinnati Office
Federal Office Building, Room 9002
550 Main Street
Cincinnati, Ohio 45202
(513) 684-2884

Cleveland Office
777 Rockwell Avenue, 2nd Floor
Cleveland, Ohio 44114
(216) 522-4065

Columbus Office
200 North High Street
Columbus, Ohio 43215
(614) 469-7345

Detroit Office
Patrick V. McNamara Federal Building
477 Michigan Avenue
Detroit, Michigan 48226
(313) 226-7900

Flint Office
Genesee Bank Building
352 South Saginaw Street, Room 200
Flint, Michigan 48502
(313) 234-5621 Ext. 352

Grand Rapids Office
2922 Fuller Avenue, NE
Grand Rapids, Michigan 49505
(616) 456-2225

Indianapolis Office
151 North Delaware Street
Indianapolis, Indiana 46204
(317) 269-6303

Milwaukee Office
Henry S. Reuss Federal Plaza
310 West Wisconsin Avenue
Suite 1380
Milwaukee, Wisconsin 53203
(414) 291-1493

Minneapolis-St. Paul Office
220 Second Street, South
Minneapolis, Minnesota 55401
(612) 349-3002

Springfield Office
524 South Second Street, Room 600
Springfield, Illinois 62701
(217) 492-4276

Region VI

Fort Worth Regional Office
221 W. Lancaster
Post Office Box 2905
Fort Worth, Texas 76113
(817) 870-5401

FIELD OFFICES

Albuquerque Office
625 Truman Street, NE
Albuquerque, New Mexico 87110
(505) 766-3251

Dallas Office
1403 Slocum Street
Post Office Box 10050
Dallas, Texas 75207
(214) 767-8293

Houston Office
2 Greenway Plaza East, Suite 200
Houston, Texas 77046
(713) 954-6821

Little Rock Office
Savers Building
320 West Capitol, Suite 700
Little Rock, Arkansas 72201
(501) 378-5401

Lubbock Office
Federal Office Building
1205 Texas Avenue
Lubbock, Texas 79401
(806) 743-7265

New Orleans Office
1661 Canal Street
New Orleans, Louisiana 70112
(504) 569-2301

Oklahoma City Office
Murrah Federal Building
200 N.W. 5th Street
Oklahoma City, Oklahoma 73102
(405) 231-4891

San Antonio Office
Washington Square
800 Dolorosa, Post Office Box 9163
San Antonio, Texas 78285
(512) 229-6800

Shreveport Office
New Federal Building
500 Fannin Street
Shreveport, Louisiana 71101
(318) 226-5385

Tulsa Office
Robert S. Kerr Building
440 South Houston Avenue, Room 200
Tulsa, Oklahoma 74127
(918) 581-7435

Region VII

Kansas City Regional Office
Professional Building
1103 Grand Avenue
Kansas City, Missouri 64106
(816) 374-2661

FIELD OFFICES

Des Moines Office
Federal Building
210 Walnut Street, Room 259
Des Moines, Iowa 50309
(515) 284-4512

Omaha Office
Braiker/Brandeis Building
210 South 16th Street
Omaha, Nebraska 68102
(402) 221-3703

St. Louis Office
210 North Tucker Boulevard
St. Louis, Missouri 63101
(314) 425-4761

Topeka Office
444 S.E. Quincy Street, Room 297
Topeka, Kansas 66683
(913) 295-2683

Region VIII

Denver Regional Office
Executive Tower Building
1405 Curtis Street
Denver, Colorado 80202
(303) 837-4513

Casper Office
4225 Federal Office Building
P.O. Box 580
100 East B Street
Casper, Wyoming 82601
(307) 261-5252

Fargo Office
Federal Building, P.O. Box 2483
653 2nd Avenue North
Fargo, North Dakota 58102
(701) 237-577-5136

Helena Office
Federal Office Building Drawer
1009
301 S. Park, Room 340
Helena, Montana 59626
(406) 449-5205

Salt Lake City Office
125 South State Street
Salt Lake City, Utah 84138
(801) 524-5237

Sioux Falls Office
119 Federal Building, U.S.
Courthouse
400 South Phillips Avenue
Sioux Falls, South Dakota 57102
(605) 336-2980

Region IX

San Francisco Regional Office
Phillip Burton Federal Building
and U.S. Courthouse
450 Golden Gate Avenue
Post Office Box 36003
San Francisco, California 94102
(415) 556-4752

Indian Programs Office, Region IX
Arizona Bank Building
101 North First Avenue, Suite
1800
Post Office Box 13468
Phoenix, Arizona 85002
(602) 261-6671

Fresno Office
1315 Van Ness Street, Suite 200
Fresno, California 93721
(209) 487-5036

Honolulu Office
300 Ala Moana Boulevard, P.O.
Box 50007
Honolulu, Hawaii 96813
(808) 546-2136

Las Vegas Office
720 S. 7th Street, Suite 221
Las Vegas, Nevada 89101
(702) 385-6525

Los Angeles Office
2500 Wilshire Boulevard
Los Angeles, California 90057
(213) 688-5973

Phoenix Office
Arizona Bank Building
101 North First Avenue, Suite
1800
Post Office Box 13468
Phoenix, Arizona 85002
(602) 261-4434

Reno Office
1050 Bible Way
Post Office Box 4700
Reno, Nevada 89505
(702) 784-5356

Sacramento Office
545 Downtown Plaza Suite 250
Post Office Box 1978
Sacramento, California 95809
(916) 440-3471

San Diego Office
Federal Office Building
880 Front Street
San Diego, California 92188
(619) 293-5310

Santa Ana Office
34 Civic Center Plaza, Box 12850
Santa Ana, California 92712
(714) 836-2451

Tucson Office
Arizona Bank Building
33 North Stone Avenue, Suite 1450
Tucson, Arizona 85701
(602) 629-6237

Region X

Seattle Regional Office
Arcade Plaza Building
1321 Second Avenue
Seattle, Washington 98101
(206) 442-5414

FIELD OFFICES

Anchorage Office
701 "C" Street, Box 64
Anchorage, Alaska 99513
(907) 271-4170

Boise Office
Federal Building - U.S.
Courthouse
P.O. Box 042
550 West Fort Street
Boise, Idaho 83724
(208) 334-1990

Portland Office
520 Southwest Sixth Avenue
Portland, Oregon 97204
(503) 221-2561

Spokane Office
West 920 Riverside Avenue
Spokane, Washington 99201
(509) 456-4571

APPENDIX B

Directory of State
Real Estate Commissions

ALABAMA

Real Estate Commission
State Capitol
750 Washington Ave.
Montgomery, Ala. 36130

ALASKA

Department of Commerce &
Economic Development
Real Estate Commission
142 E. Third Ave.
Anchorage, Alaska 99501

ARIZONA

Department of Real Estate
1645 W. Jefferson
Phoenix, Ariz. 85007

ARKANSAS

Real Estate Commission
#1 Riverfront Pl., Suite 660
North Little Rock, Ark. 72114

CALIFORNIA

Real Estate Commission
P.O. Box 160009
Sacramento, Calif. 95816

COLORADO

Real Estate Commission
110 State Services Bldg.
1525 Sherman St.
Denver, Colo. 80203

CONNECTICUT

Real Estate Commission
90 Washington St.
Hartford, Conn. 06115

DELAWARE

Real Estate Commission
Box 1401, Margaret O'Neill Bldg.
Dover, Del. 19901

DISTRICT OF COLUMBIA

Real Estate Commission
Room 109
614 "H" St. N.W.
Washington, D.C. 20001

FLORIDA

Real Estate Commission
Department of Professional &
Occupational Regulation
400 W. Robinson St.
Orlando, Fla. 32801

GEORGIA

Real Estate Commission
40 Pryor St. S.W.
Atlanta, Ga. 30303

HAWAII

Department of Regulatory Agencies
Real Estate Commission
P.O. Box 3469
Honolulu, Hawaii 96801

IDAHO

Real Estate Commission
State Capitol Bldg.
Boise, Idaho 83720

ILLINOIS

Real Estate Commission
Department of Registration &
Education
55 E. Jackson Blvd., 17th Fl.
Chicago, Ill. 60604

INDIANA

Real Estate Commission
1022 State Office Bldg.
100 N. Senate Ave.
Indianapolis, Ind. 46204

IOWA

Real Estate Commission
Executive Hills
1223 E. Court
Des Moines, Iowa 50319

KANSAS

Real Estate Commission
535 Kansas Ave.
Rm. 1212
Topeka, Kans. 66603

KENTUCKY

Real Estate Commission
100 E. Liberty St.
Suite 204
Louisville, Ky. 40202

LOUISIANA

Real Estate Commission
P.O. Box 14785
Capitol Station
Baton Rouge, La. 70808

MAINE

Department of Business Regulation
Real Estate Commission
State House—Station #35
Augusta, Maine 04333

MARYLAND

Real Estate Commission
One S. Calvert St.
Rm. 600
Baltimore, Md. 21202

MASSACHUSETTS

Board of Registration of Real Estate
Brokers and Salesmen
100 Cambridge St.
Boston, Mass. 02202

MICHIGAN

Deputy Real Estate Commissioner
Department of Licensing &
Regulation
P.O. Box 30018
Lansing, Mich. 48909

MINNESOTA

Real Estate Director
Real Estate Commission
500 Metro Square Bldg.
St. Paul, Minn. 55101

MISSISSIPPI

Real Estate Commission
754 N. President St.
Jackson, Miss. 39202

MISSOURI

Missouri Real Estate Commission
P.O. Box 1339
Jefferson City, Mo. 65102

MONTANA

Board of Real Estate
42½ N. Main, LaLonde Bldg.
Helena, Mont. 59601

NEBRASKA

Real Estate Commission
301 Centennial Mall S.
Lincoln, Nebr. 68509

NEVADA

Real Estate Division
Department of Commerce
201 S. Fall St.
Carson City, Nev. 89710

NEW HAMPSHIRE

New Hampshire Real Estate
Commission
3 Capitol St.
Concord, N.H. 03301

NEW JERSEY

New Jersey Real Estate
Commission
201 E. State St.
Trenton, N.J. 08625

NEW MEXICO

New Mexico Real Estate
Commission
Suite 608
600 Second St. N.W.
Albuquerque, N.M. 87102

NEW YORK

Department of State
Real Estate Licensing Office
270 Broadway
New York, N.Y. 10007

NORTH CAROLINA

Real Estate Commission
1200 Navaho Dr.
P.O. Box 17100
Raleigh, N.C. 27619

NORTH DAKOTA

Real Estate Commission
410 E. Thayer Ave.
P.O. Box 727
Bismarck, N.D. 58502

OHIO

Department of Commerce
Division of Real Estate
180 E. Broad St., 14th Fl.
Columbus, Ohio 43215

OKLAHOMA

Oklahoma Real Estate Commission
4040 N. Lincoln Blvd.
Suite 100
Oklahoma City, Okla. 73105

OREGON

Real Estate Commission
158 12th St. N.E.
Salem, Oreg. 97310

PENNSYLVANIA

Real Estate Commission
P.O. Box 2649
Rm. 611, Transportation & Safety
Bldg.
Commonwealth Ave. & Forster St.
Harrisburg, Pa. 17120

RHODE ISLAND

Real Estate Division
100 N. Main St.
Providence, R.I. 02903

SOUTH CAROLINA

Real Estate Commission
2221 Divine St., Suite 530
Columbia, S.C. 29205

SOUTH DAKOTA

Real Estate Commission
P.O. Box 490
Pierre, S.D. 57501

TENNESSEE

Real Estate Commission
556 Capitol Hill Bldg.
Nashville, Tenn. 37219

TEXAS

Texas Real Estate Commission
P.O. Box 12188, Capitol Station
Austin, Tex. 78711

UTAH

Real Estate Division
330 E. Fourth S.
Salt Lake City, Utah 84111

VERMONT

Executive Secretary
Vermont Real Estate Commission
7 E. State St.
Montpelier, Vt. 05602

VIRGINIA

Real Estate Commission
2 S. 9th St.
Richmond, Va. 23219

WASHINGTON

Real Estate Division
P.O. Box 247
Olympia, Wash. 98504

WEST VIRGINIA

Real Estate Commission
1033 Quarrier St., Suite 400
Charleston, W.V. 25301

WISCONSIN

Real Estate Commission
Rm. 281
1400 E. Washington
Madison, Wis. 53702

WYOMING

Director of Real Estate
Supreme Court Bldg.
Cheyenne, Wyo. 82002

APPENDIX C

U.S. Government Printing Office Bookstores

Many of the government publications recommended in this book can be purchased at U.S. government bookstores. Addresses are:

ATLANTA

Rm. 100, FB
275 Peachtree St. N.E.
Atlanta, Ga. 30303
(404) 221-6947

BIRMINGHAM

9220-B Parkway E.
Roebuck Shopping City
Birmingham, Ala. 35206
(205) 254-1056

BOSTON

Rm. G25, John F. Kennedy FB
Sudbury St.
Boston, Mass. 02203
(617) 223-6071

CHICAGO

Rm. 1463, 14th Fl.
Everett McKinley Dirksen Bldg.
219 S. Dearborn St.
Chicago, Ill. 60604
(312) 353-5133

CLEVELAND

First Fl., FOB
1240 E. Ninth St.
Cleveland, Ohio 44199
(216) 522-4922

COLUMBUS

Rm. 207, FB
200 N. Eighth St.
Columbus, Ohio 43215
(614) 469-6956

DALLAS

Rm. 1050, FB
1100 Commerce St.
Dallas, Tex. 75242
(214) 767-8076

DENVER

Rm. 117, FB
1961 Stout St.
Denver, Colo. 80294
(303) 844-3964

DETROIT

Patrick V. McNamara FB
Suite 160
477 Michigan Ave.
Detroit, Mich. 48226
(313) 226-7816

HOUSTON

45 College Center
9319 Gulf Freeway
Houston, Tex. 77017
(713) 226-5453

JACKSONVILLE

Rm. 158, FB
400 W. Bay St.
P.O. Box 35089
Jacksonville, Fla. 32202
(904) 791-3801

KANSAS CITY

Rm. 144, FOB
601 E. 12th St.
Kansas City, Mo. 64106
(816) 374-2160

LOS ANGELES

ARCO Plaza, C-Level
505 S. Flower St.
Los Angeles, Calif. 90071
(213) 688-5841

MILWAUKEE

Rm. 190, FB
517 E. Wisconsin Ave.
Milwaukee, Wis. 53202
(414) 291-1304

NEW YORK

Rm. 110
26 Federal Plaza
New York, N.Y. 10278
(212) 264-3825

PHILADELPHIA

Rm. 1214, FOB
600 Arch St.
Philadelphia, Pa. 19106
(215) 597-0677

PITTSBURGH

Rm. 118, FOB
1000 Liberty Ave.
Pittsburgh, Pa. 15222
(412) 644-2721

PUEBLO

Majestic Bldg.
720 N. Main St.
Pueblo, Colo. 81003
(303) 544-3142

SAN FRANCISCO

Rm. 1023, FOB
450 Golden Gate Ave.
San Francisco, Calif. 94102
(415) 556-0643

SEATTLE

Rm. 194, FOB
915 Second Ave.
Seattle, Wash. 98174
(206) 442-4270

FB = Federal Building
FOB = Federal Office Building

WASHINGTON, D.C., AND VICINITY

Government Printing Office
710 N. Capitol St.
Washington, D.C. 20402
(202) 275-2091

Glossary

Abandoned building. A structure, frequently a multifamily dwelling, that has been given up by a landlord who considers his or her investment lost and has no intention of reclaiming the property.

Absolute fee simple. The unqualified ownership of real property. Title that contains no stipulations or restrictions. This is the best title available, but in reality it is rare in today's world of governmental restrictions and utility easements. The term *fee*, or *fee simple*, is often used more loosely to mean ownership of property that is yours to use and/or sell at your discretion.

Absentee ownership. Property that the owner does not use or personally occupy.

Abstract of title. A synopsis of the history of a title, indicating all changes in ownership and including liens, mortgages, charges, encumbrances, encroachments, or any other matter that might affect the title.

Access. The means of approaching a property.

Access right. The right of an owner to enter and leave his or her property.

Acceleration clause. A stipulation in a mortgage agreement that allows the lender to demand full payment of the loan immediately if any scheduled payment is not made by a given time.

Acre. A measure of land. One acre equals 43,560 square feet, or 208.71 feet on each side. A "builder's acre" is generally 200 × 200 feet.

Addendum. Something added. In real estate contracts, a page added to the contract. It should be initialed by all parties concerned.

Agreement of sale. A written agreement by which a buyer agrees to buy and a seller agrees to sell a certain piece of property under the terms and conditions stated therein.

Air rights. The title, vested in the owner of a parcel of land, to the use of the air space above the land. Frequently granted for the space above railroad tracks, highways, etc. Perhaps the most notable use of air rights is Madison Square Garden, which was constructed over Pennsylvania Station in New York.

Amenities. Features of a property that make it more attractive to buyer or renter: pool, clubhouse, tennis courts and the like.

Amortization. Prorated repayment of a debt. Most mortgages are being amortized every month that you make a payment to the lender.

Apartment, garden. A unit with the entrance on the ground floor and the use by the tenant of a back or front yard. Can also refer to a two-story apartment complex, usually in a suburban locale.

Apartment, railroad. Indigenous to older buildings, these units are laid out so that one room follows another, railroad-car style, and you must pass through room A to reach room B.

Apportionment. The costs and expenses that are prorated between the buyer and seller at the closing. These may include taxes, maintenance fees, special assessments, and even oil in a storage tank. Also known as adjustments.

Appreciation. The increase in the value of real estate due to inflation and other economic factors.

Appraisal. Procedure employed by a disinterested professional to estimate the value of a piece of property.

Appurtenances. Whatever is annexed to land or used with it that will pass to the buyer with conveyance of title; e.g., a garage, a gatehouse.

As is. A term used in a contract to mean that the buyer is buying what he sees as he sees it. There is no representation as to quality and no promise of repair or fix-up.

Assessed valuation. An evaluation of property by an agency of the government for taxation purposes.

Assessment. Tax or charge levied on property by a taxing authority to pay for improvements such as sidewalks, streets, and sewers.

Assumption (of mortgage). Buyer taking over seller's old mortgage at the interest rate and terms of the original mortgage.

Binder. A lay term that is usually taken to mean a signed agreement to purchase accompanied by earnest money that is subject to contracts being drawn at a later date. A binder may or may not be legally enforceable.

Block-busting. The unlawful practice employed by some realty people of increasing the sale of houses in a neighborhood by circulating rumors that a number of minority buyers are moving in and will lower existing property values. The block-buster's objective is to see sale prices drop substantially in the ensuing panic selling. The broker then sells the houses at inflated prices to minority families. Block-busting can lead to the loss of the culpable salespersons' and brokers' licenses.

Bona fide. In good faith, without deceit or deception.

Buffer zone. An area that separates two or more types of land use from each other.

Builder's warranty. A written statement by a builder assuring that a dwelling was completed in conformity with a stipulated set of standards. The purpose is to protect the purchaser from latent defects.

Building codes. State or locally adopted regulations, enforceable by police powers, that control the design, construction, repair, quality of building materials, use and occupancy of any structure under its jurisdiction.

Cancellation clause. Any stipulation in a contract that allows a buyer or seller to cancel the contract if a certain specified condition or situation occurs.

Capital appreciation. The increase in market value for a property beyond the price you paid for it.

Capital gain. The portion of your taxable profit realized on the sale of real estate that is *not* taxed at your ordinary income-tax rate.

Cash flow. The dollar income generated by a rental property after all expenses are met. Negative cash flow occurs when expenses generated by a property exceed its income.

Caveat emptor. A Latin phrase meaning "Let the buyer beware." Legally, however, in virtually no state is the law of caveat emptor still in effect.

Certificate of occupancy. Known as a "C-O" or "C of O," this is an official authorization to occupy premises, the builder or rehabilitator having complied with local zoning ordinances and building codes.

Certified check. Payment that is guaranteed by the bank upon which it is drawn. A certified check for the balance of the downpayment is usually required at the closing.

Chattel. Items of personal property, such as furniture, appliances, lighting fixtures that are not permanently affixed to the property being sold.

Closing. The meeting of all concerned parties in order to transfer title to a property.

Closing costs. Expenses over and above the price of the property that must be paid before title is transferred. Also known as *settlement costs*.

Closing statement. A written account of all expenses, adjustments, and disbursements involved in a real estate transaction.

Cloud on the title. A defect in the title that may affect the owner's ability to market his or her property. This might be a lien, a claim, or a judgment.

Cohabitation. Legal term for two persons of the opposite sex living together.

Collateral. Security pledged for the repayment of a loan.

Commission. Payment given by the seller of a property to a real estate agent for his or her services. Usually paid at the closing.

Common facilities. Areas in a condominium, cooperative, mobile home park, apartment building or private home association shared by all residents: hallways, grounds, laundry room, parking facilities, swimming pool, or golf course, for example.

Condominium. Housing style where the buyers own their apartment units outright, plus an undivided share in the common areas of the community.

Consideration. Anything of value, but usually a sum of money. A contract must have a consideration in order to be binding.

Contingency. A provision in a contract that keeps it from becoming binding until certain activities are accomplished. A satisfactory inspection report might be a contingency.

Contract. An agreement between two parties. To be valid, a real estate contract must be dated; must be in writing; and must include a consideration, a description of the property, the place and date of delivery of the deed, and all terms and conditions that were mutually agreed upon. It must also be executed (signed) by all concerned parties.

Convey. To transfer property from one person to another.

Conveyance. The document by which title is transferred. A deed is a conveyance.

Cooperative. A housing style where buyers purchase shares in the corporation that owns the building. The number of shares varies according to the size of the apartment unit being bought or its purchase price. Tenant-shareholders have a proprietary lease that gives them the right to their units.

Deed. A written instrument that conveys title to real property.

Default. A breach of contract or failure to meet an obligation. Nonpayment of a mortgage beyond a certain number of payments is considered a default.

Density. Number of dwellings and commercial units per acre of land. Can also refer to people; e.g., ten persons per acre.

Depreciation. Gradual loss on paper in market value of real estate, especially because of age, obsolescence, wear and tear, or economic conditions.

Discount. See *points*.

Dower rights. The interest a wife has in real estate owned by her husband at his death. The less common *courtesy rights* refer to those a husband has in his wife's estate after her death.

Downpayment. Your initial cash investment in purchasing real estate, usually a percentage of the sale price.

Duplex. A two-family house, or an apartment unit that takes up two floors.

Duress. The use of force or unlawful coercion.

Dwellings, multiple. Buildings consisting of three or more living units having common access. In some communities that number is five or more units.

Earnest money. Sum of money that accompanies a signed offer to purchase as evidence of good faith. It is almost always a personal check, certified check, or money order rather than cash.

Easement. A right of way or access. The right of one party to cross or use for some specified purpose the property of another. Water, sewage, and utility suppliers frequently hold an easement across private property.

Eminent domain. The right by which a government may acquire private property for public use without the consent of the owner, but upon payment of reasonable compensation.

Encroachment. A building or part of a building that extends beyond its boundary and therefore intrudes upon the property of another party.

Encumbrance. A right or restriction on a property that reduces its value. This might be a claim, lien, liability, or zoning restriction. The report of the title search usually shows all encumbrances.

Equity. The value an owner has in a piece of property exclusive of its mortgage and other liens. For example, if the market value of a house is $70,000 and the owner has paid off $5000 of a $35,000 mortgage, the owner has $40,000 equity.

Escrow. Money or documents held by a third party until specific conditions of an agreement or contract are fulfilled.

Escrow account. A trust into which escrow monies are deposited and from which they are disbursed. Both lawyers and real estate brokers maintain escrow accounts.

Et al. Abbreviation of *et alia*, meaning "and others." This term is often used in a contract concerning a piece of property that is owned jointly by several people.

Et ux. Abbreviation for *et uxor*, meaning "and wife." It is preferable that the woman be named.

Eviction. The legal expulsion of a person from a property. Several specific breaches of a contract (lease) can be a reason for an eviction.

Exclusionary zoning. Abuse of zoning to exclude low-income groups from desirable residential areas. Many court cases against suburban communities have come up in the last several years charging that zoning laws are creating economic and racial segregation and ruling that exclusionary practices are illegal.

Exclusive agent. A real estate broker with the sole right to sell a property within a specified period of time. The property becomes an "exclusive listing." See Chapter 26 for more detailed explanation.

Execute. To perform what is required to give validity to a legal document, usually to sign it.

Exurbia. Semirural area just beyond the suburbs.

Fee simple. See *absolute fee simple*.

FmHA. Farmers Home Administration, an agency of the U.S. Department of Agriculture that insures and sometimes gives home loans in rural communities.

FHA. Federal Housing Authority, an agency created within HUD (see below) that insures mortgages on residential property, with downpayment requirements usually lower than the prevailing ones.

Fiduciary. A person acting in a position of trust.

Fixtures. Items of personal property that have been permanently attached to the real property and are therefore included in the transfer of real estate. The kitchen sink is a fixture.

Foreclosure. Legal proceedings instigated by a lender to deprive a person of ownership rights when mortgage payments have not been kept up.

Gentrification. Process whereby private or government-sponsored development in certain neighborhoods results in the displacement of low- or moderate-income families by those in higher income categories.

Government-assisted housing. New or rehabilitated apartment projects leased to low- or moderate-income families or individuals and assisted financially by local, state, or federal governments.

G. I. loan. See *VA loan*.

Grace period. An allowed reasonable length of time to meet a commitment after the specified date of that commitment. For example, most lending institutions allow a two-week grace period after the due date of the mortgage payment before a late fee is imposed.

Ground lease. A lease of land alone, usually for a long term (ninety-nine years), upon which the tenant constructs a building.

Groupers. A number of persons, usually single, who band together to rent an apartment or house. Groupers are most often found in resort areas and college towns, and their presence has in recent years led to zoning ordinances in some communities prohibiting the use of houses by unrelated persons. And some of *those* ordinances have been challenged by the groupers with varying degrees of success.

Hand money. See *earnest money.*

Historic structures. Buildings of historical or architectural significance, perhaps landmarks, so designated by federal, state, or local historical commissions. Investors can earn generous tax benefits by buying and rehabilitating historic structures.

Holdout. A property owner who refuses to sell, thus preventing the assemblage of a site by a developer.

Housing authority. A public body empowered to provide and manage housing, especially for low-income groups and the elderly. Housing authorities aim to clear slums, issue bonds, and in general carry out the public housing program of a city. All depend on federal subsidies, although some also operate with state or municipal funds.

Housing code. Local regulations setting forth minimum conditions under which dwellings are considered fit for human habitation. It guards against unsanitary or unsafe conditions and overcrowding.

HUD. U.S. Department of Housing and Urban Development, from which almost all of the federal government's housing programs flow.

"In rem" foreclosure. Legal action to take property ownership from a person who has not paid taxes for a specified period of time. The city or local taxing authority then becomes owner of the property and frequently disposes of it by auction.

Industrial park. An area ranging from a few hundred to several thousand acres zoned for industrial use, usually with common services for tenants. Many are low-rise office or light industrial buildings in suburban or exurban parklike settings.

Infrastructure. The basic equipment, utilities, installations, and services necessary to run a city. Includes roads, railways, sewers, bridges, and, on the larger scale, the nation's military installations.

Inspection. The act of physically observing and testing a piece of property.

Installment payment. The periodic payment (usually every month) of interest and principal on a mortgage or other loan.

Installment sales contract. A sales contract for property in which the buyer receives possession of the property but does not take title to it until he or she makes regular installment payments to the seller and fulfills other specified obligations. Also called a "land contract."

Instrument. Any written legal document.

Interest. A fee paid for the use of money.

Intestate. Refers to any person who dies leaving no will, or a will that is found to be defective.

Joint tenancy. Property ownership by two or more persons with an undivided interest. If one owner dies, the property automatically passes to the others. (With right of survivorship.)

Judgment. A decree of a court that states that one person is indebted to another and specifies the amount of the debt.

Land bank. Accumulation or stockpiling of vacant land by municipalities or others for future use not yet determined.

Land lease. See *ground lease*.

Land, raw. Land available for building but lacking utilities or improvements such as electricity, roads, water.

Land use plan. Official formulation by a community of how it will use its land in future years: for residential, commercial, industrial, and institutional purposes.

Lease. A contract that allows one party the possession of a piece of property for a specified period of time in return for a consideration (usually rent) paid to the owner of the property.

Lease/purchase option. Opportunity to purchase a piece of property by renting for a specified period, usually one year, with the provision that you may choose to buy after or during the leasing period at a predetermined sale price.

Lessee. The tenant; someone who rents under a lease.

Lessor. The landlord; someone who rents to another party through a lease.

Leverage. The effective use of money to buy property by using the smallest amount of one's own capital that is permitted and borrowing as much as possible in order to obtain the maximum percentage of return on the original investment.

Lien. A debt on a property; a mortgage, back taxes, or other claim.

Liquidity. The speed at which an investment can be converted to cash. For example, there is little liquidity in a house, but shares of stock can ordinarily be sold quickly for cash.

Lis pendens. Notice of a suit pending.

Listing. A contract or agreement for employing a real estate agent to sell a piece of property. Also a piece of property that is for sale.

Loan-to-value ratio. The relationship of a mortgage loan to the appraised value of a piece of property. Often expressed to the buyer in terms of how much the lender will lend—for example, 75-percent financing.

Loft building. Structure of more than one story that was built for storage, manufacturing, or some other commercial use.

Low-balling. Practice employed by some builders of underestimating maintenance and carrying charges in a new condominium or cooperative project to make the development more attractive to buyers. The builder absorbs those extra costs himself, but then when the community is completed and control is passed to the residents, they are hit with more realistic higher monthly maintenance costs. Also means an unrealistically low first bid to purchase a piece of property.

Manufactured housing. Homes that are built in a factory, then shipped to the building site where the components are assembled. Nowadays refers more narrowly to mobile homes.

Market value. Generally accepted as the highest price that a ready, willing, and able buyer will pay and the lowest price a ready, willing, and able seller will accept for the property in question.

Marketable title. A title that is free from clouds and encumbrances.

Maturity date. The date on which principal and interest on a mortgage or other loan must be paid in full.

Meeting of the minds. Mutual agreement of two parties who are ready to enter into a contract.

Mill. Equal to one-tenth of one cent. A mill is the unit of measure for calculating property tax rates.

Model apartment or home. A completed and often decorated living unit that a builder promises to duplicate at a given price in another location.

Mortgage. A legal document that creates a lien upon a piece of property. Descriptions of today's many mortgage styles can be found in Chapter 19.

Mortgagee. The party or institution that lends the money.

Mortgagor. The party or person that borrows the money, giving a lien on the property as security for the loan.

Mortgage company or *mortgage banker*. A financial intermediary that offers mortgages to borrowers, and then resells them to various lending institutions, government agencies, or private investors.

Multiple listing. An agreement that allows real estate brokers to distribute information on the properties that they have listed for sale to other members of a local real estate organization in order to provide the widest possible marketing of those properties. Commissions are split by mutual agreement between the listing broker and the selling broker.

Multiple Listing Service (MLS). The office that supervises the printing and distribution of listings shared by members of the local Board of Realtors.

Net lease. In commercial properties a long-term lease whereby the tenant agrees to pay a certain fixed, usually low, rent and also agrees to pay some or all operating expenses, including real estate taxes, insurance, utilities, and the cost of maintenance.

Notary public. A person licensed by the state to authenticate documents and certain transactions.

Offer. A proposal, oral or written, to buy a piece of property at a specified price.

Offering plan. See *prospectus*.

Operating expenses. All costs incurred in keeping a property in usable and rentable condition. Operating expenses do not include mortgage payments or interest.

Option. The exclusive right to purchase or lease a property at a stipulated price or rent within a specified period of time.

Origination fee. A charge by the lender for granting the mortgage.

Percolation test. Means of testing soil to discover its absorbent qualities for drainage and septic tank purposes.

Percentage lease. Whereby landlords collect from retail stores either a flat rent or a percentage of the business's gross sales, whichever is larger.

Planned Unit Development (PUD). Residential complex of mixed housing types. Offers greater design flexibility than traditional developments. PUDs permit clustering of homes, sometimes not allowed under standard zoning ordinances, utilization of open space, and a project harmonious with the natural topography.

Plat book. Planning volume that shows location, size, and name(s) of owner(s) of every piece of land within a specific development, or for an entire neighborhood or town.

Points. Sometimes called *discount*. A fee that a lending institution charges for granting a mortgage. One point is one percent of the face value of the loan.

Power of attorney. Instrument in writing that gives one person the right to act as agent for another in signing papers, deeds, etc.

Premises. The land and everything attached to it; the property in question.

Prepayment. Paying back of a loan before it has reached its maturity date.

Principal. The amount of money borrowed; the amount of money still owed.

Probate. Establishes officially the authenticity of the will of a deceased person.

Proprietary lease. The legal agreement that allows you to use your apartment in a cooperative purchase.

Prospectus. A document, also known as an *offering plan*, offered by condominium and cooperative sponsors, detailing ownership of the development, location, prices and layouts of the units, procedures to purchase, and numerous aspects of how the project will be sold and run.

Public hearing. A meeting, open to everyone, that is required by law before land may be acquired for a project that needs public funding, and frequently for other proposals by a municipality. Provides an opportunity for private citizens and community organizations to present their views on the proposal.

Real estate investment trust (REIT). An entity that allows a very large number of investors to participate in the purchase of real estate, but as passive investors. The investors do not buy directly. Instead, they purchase shares in the REIT that owns the real estate investment. REITs are relatively inexpensive—shares can be had for as little as $10 each.

Real property. Land and buildings and anything permanently attached to them.

Real estate broker. Man or woman who has passed state broker's test and represents others in realty transactions. Anyone having his or her own office must be a broker.

Real estate salesperson. Man or woman who has passed a state examination for that position, and must work under the supervision of a broker.

Real estate taxes. Levies on land and buildings charged to owners by local governing agencies. Those charges, sometimes known as *property taxes*, are a primary source of local government revenues.

Realtor. A real estate broker who is a member of the National Association of Realtors, a professional group. Not every broker is a Realtor (a word, incidentally, that is a registered trademark and always capitalized).

Recreation lease. A legal agreement that allows condominium buyers to use that complex's pool, tennis courts, and other amenities. The owner of those facilities is usually the developer, and there is often a charge for that use. It is preferable that the condominium own its recreational facilities.

Red herring. Preliminary offering plan submitted by the sponsor of a condo or co-op conversion to tenants while the plan is awaiting approval by the appropriate state agency. The sponsor is not allowed to sell apartments from the "red herring," but must wait until the formal prospectus is approved. The term is most commonly used in New York City.

Redlining. Alleged practice of some lending institutions involving their refusal to make loans on properties they deem to be bad risks. The same applies to some insurance companies offering policies.

Refinance. To pay off one loan by taking out another on the same property.

Rent control. Regulation by local government agency of rental charges, usually according to set formulas for increase.

Report of title. Document required before title insurance can be issued. It states the name of the owner, a legal description of the property, and the status of taxes, liens, and anything else that might affect the marketability of the title.

Reserve fund (general operating). Monies from a condo or co-op community that are accumulated on a monthly basis to provide a cushion of capital to be used when and if a need arises.

Reserve fund (replacement). Monies from a condo or co-op community that are set in escrow to replace or repair common elements, such as roofs or elevators, at some future date.

Restriction. A limitation to control the use of a piece of property.

Right of survivorship. Granted to two joint owners who purchase under that buying style. Stipulates that one gets full rights and becomes sole owner of the property on the death of the other. Right of survivorship is the basic difference between buying property as joint tenants and as tenants in common.

Riparian rights. The right of a property owner whose land abuts a body of water to swim in that water, build a wharf, etc.

Scatter-site housing. Multifamily dwellings dispersed in small numbers throughout a middle-income community by a local housing authority to achieve economic and/or racial integration.

Second mortgage. A lien on a property that is subordinate to a first mortgage. In the event of default, the second mortgage is repaid after the first. Also called a *junior mortgage,* and in some circumstances a *home equity loan.*

Security deposit. Amount of money, usually a month to two months' rent, paid by a tenant to the landlord in advance of moving into an apartment. The money is held against possible damage to the apartment, default in rent, etc., but should be returned to the tenant when he or she leaves the premises in satisfactory order.

Semidetached. One structure containing two dwelling units separated vertically by a common wall.

Settlement costs. See *closing costs.*

Specific performance. A court order that compels a party to carry out the terms of an executed (signed) contract.

Sponsor. The individual or corporation that wants to convert a rental complex into a condominium or cooperative.

Square foot. Used to measure buildings in realty transactions. For example, if a two-story home has dimensions of 30 feet by 30 feet, the area is 900 square feet on each floor, for a total of 1,800 square feet.

Squatter. One who occupies another's property illegally.

Statutory tenant. One whose lease has expired, but who remains on the premises and is still protected by its provisions.

Subletting. A leasing of property by one tenant from another tenant, the one who holds the lease.

Subsidized housing. See *government-assisted housing.*

Survey. An exact measurement of the size and boundaries of a piece of land by civil engineers or surveyors.

Syndicate. An entity, usually a limited partnership, that is established for the purpose of making an investment.

Tax credit. An allowed deduction that can be subtracted from your income tax. If you are entitled to a $2000 credit, let's say, and your income tax would otherwise be $8000, the credit would reduce that tax due to $6000.

Tax shelter. A realty investment that produces income-tax deductions.

Tenancy in common. Style of ownership in which two or more persons purchase a property jointly, but with no right of survivorship. They are free to will their share to anyone they choose, a principal difference between that form of ownership and joint tenancy.

Time is of the essence. Phrase used in a contract to indicate that specific dates are essential to the contract and that the contract terms must be performed on those dates. Most often used in regard to closing dates.

Title. Actual ownership; the right of possession; evidence of ownership.

Title insurance. An insurance policy that protects against any losses incurred because of defective title.

Title search. A professional examination of public records to determine the chain of ownership of a particular piece of property and to note any liens, mortgages, encumbrances easements, restrictions, or other factors that might affect the title.

Townhouse. A two- or three-story city house of some architectural or historical distinction, or a living unit operating under the condominium or townhouse form of ownership.

Trust deed. An instrument used in place of a mortgage in certain states; a third-party trustee, not the lender, holds the title to the property until the loan is paid out or defaulted.

Urban homesteading. Government program that offers, sometimes through a lottery system, inner-city houses to qualified buyers at nominal prices, with certain conditions attached to the sale (rehabilitation) before title passes to that buyer.

Urban renewal. Renovation or restoration of a section of a city—demolishing slums, rehabilitating housing, upgrading the commercial center, all to provide more and better services and amenities to residents and workers.

Useful life. The period of time over which a commercial property can be depreciated for federal income-tax purposes. Also known as *economic life*.

Usury. Charging a higher rate of interest on a loan than is legally allowed.

Vacancy rate. Ratio between the number of vacant apartment units and the total number of units, either in one specified building or in an entire city. When the vacancy rate falls below 3 to 5 percent, that usually means a housing crisis for would-be tenants. The figure is difficult to determine, however, because some units are considered no longer habitable and vacancies checked with utilities and telephone companies fluctuate.

Valuation. Estimated or determined value.

Variance. An exception to a zoning ordinance granted to meet certain specified needs.

VA loan. Veterans Administration-backed mortgage. The VA, a federal agency, operates a loan guarantee program for honorably discharged veterans and widows of veterans who died of a service-related injury. Mortgages call for low or no downpayment. Sometimes referred to as *GI loan*.

Void. Canceled; not legally enforceable.

Waiver. Renunciation, disclaiming, or surrender of some claim, right, or prerogative.

Write-off. Depreciation or amortization an owner takes on a commercial property.

Yield. The annual percentage rate of return on an investment in real estate.

Zoning. Procedure that classifies real property for a number of different uses: residential, commercial, industrial, etc. in accordance with a land-use plan. Ordinances are enforced by a governing body or locality.

Index